**Ordnance Survey**

C000141311

STREE

West Kent

Contents

III Key to map symbols
IV-V Key to map pages
VI Administrative and post code boundaries
1 Street maps
190 Town plans of Ashford and Canterbury
191 Town plans of Dover and Folkestone
192 Index of hospitals, railway stations, schools, shopping centres, street names and universities
238 Town and village index

PHILIP'S

First edition published 1994
First colour edition published 1997
Reprinted in 1999, 2000 by

George Philip Ltd, a division of
Octopus Publishing Group Ltd
2-4 Heron Quays, London E14 4JP

ISBN 0-540-07369-5 (pocket)

To the best of the Publishers' knowledge, the information in this
atlas was correct at the time of going to press. No responsibility
can be accepted for any errors or their consequences.

The representation in this atlas of a road, track or path is no
evidence of the existence of a right of way.

**The mapping between pages 1 and 191 (inclusive) in this
atlas is derived from Ordnance Survey® OSCAR® and
Land-Line® data and Landranger® mapping.**

Ordnance Survey, OSCAR, Land-line and Landranger are
registered trade marks of Ordnance Survey, the national
mapping agency of Great Britain.

Printed and bound in Spain by Cayfosa

Digital Data

The exceptionally high-quality mapping
found in this book is available as
digital data in TIFF format, which is
easily convertible to other bit-mapped
(raster) image formats.

The index is also available in digital
form as a standard database table.
It contains all the details found in the
printed index together with the
National Grid reference for the map
square in which each entry is named
and feature codes for places of
interest in eight categories such as
education and health.

For further information and to discuss
your requirements, please contact
Philip's on 020 7531 8440 or
george.philip@philips-maps.co.uk

22a	**Motorway** (with junction number)
	Primary routes (dual carriageway and single)
	A roads (dual carriageway and single)
	B roads (dual carriageway and single)
	Minor through road (dual carriageway and single)
	Minor roads
	Roads under construction
	Railways
	Tramway, miniature railway
	Rural track, private road or narrow road in urban area
	Gate or obstruction to traffic (restrictions may not apply at all times or to all vehicles)
	All paths, bridleways, byway open to all traffic, road used as a public path
	The representation in this atlas of a road, track or path is no evidence of the existence of a right of way
29 / 130	**Adjoining page indicators**
Leeds Castle	**Non-Roman antiquity**
ROMAN FORT	**Roman antiquity**

Acad	**Academy**	Mon	**Monument**
Cemy	**Cemetery**	Mus	**Museum**
C Ctr	**Civic Centre**	Obsy	**Observatory**
CH	**Club House**	Pal	**Royal Palace**
Coll	**College**	PH	**Public House**
Ex H	**Exhibition Hall**	Resr	**Reservoir**
Ind Est	**Industrial Estate**	Ret Pk	**Retail Park**
Inst	**Institute**	Sch	**School**
Ct	**Law Court**	Sh Ctr	**Shopping Centre**
L Ctr	**Leisure Centre**	Sta	**Station**
LC	**Level Crossing**	TH	**Town Hall/House**
Liby	**Library**	Trad Est	**Trading Estate**
Mkt	**Market**	Univ	**University**
Meml	**Memorial**	YH	**Youth Hostel**

⇌	**British Rail station**
D	**Docklands Light Railway station**
🚂	**Private railway station**
●	**Bus, coach station**
◆	**Ambulance station**
◆	**Coastguard station**
◆	**Fire station**
◆	**Police station**
✚	**Casualty entrance to hospital**
+	**Church, place of worship**
H	**Hospital**
i	**Information centre**
P	**Parking**
PO	**Post Office**
West Kent College	**Important buildings, schools, colleges, universities and hospitals**
	County boundaries
River Medway	**Water name**
	Stream
	River or canal (minor and major)
	Water
	Tidal water
	Woods
	Houses

The dark grey border on the inside edge of some pages indicates that the mapping does not continue onto the adjacent page

■ The small numbers around the edges of the maps identify the 1 kilometre National Grid lines

The scale of the maps is 3.92 cm to 1 km (2½ inches to 1 mile)

0	¼	½	¾	1 mile
0	250m	500m	750m	1 Kilometre

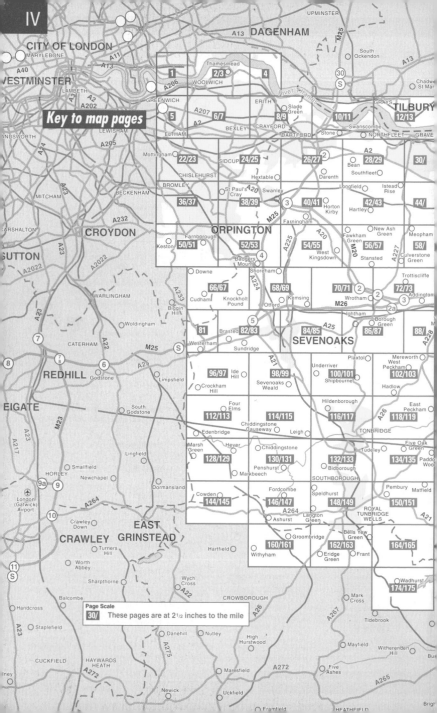

IV

Key to map pages

Page Scale
30/ These pages are at 2½ inches to the mile

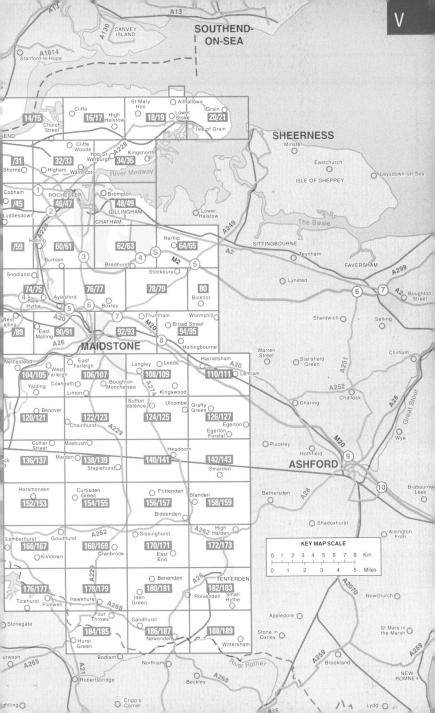

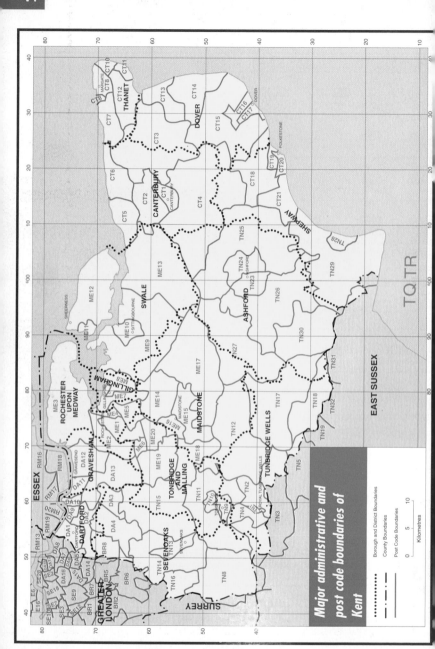

Major administrative and post code boundaries of Kent

· · · · · · · Borough and District Boundaries

─ · ─ · ─ County Boundaries

───────── Post Code Boundaries

0   5   10
Kilometres

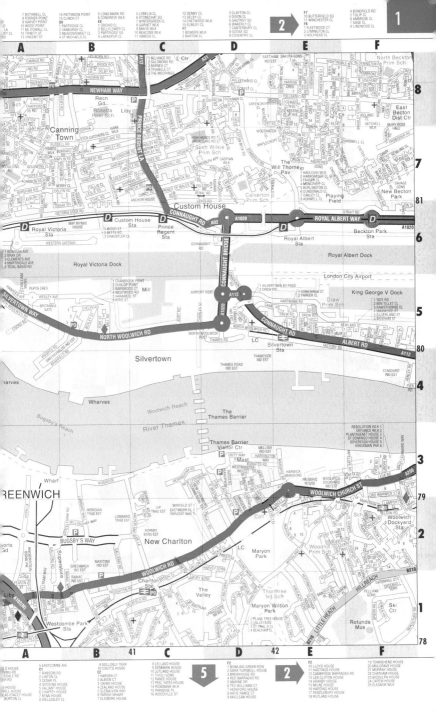

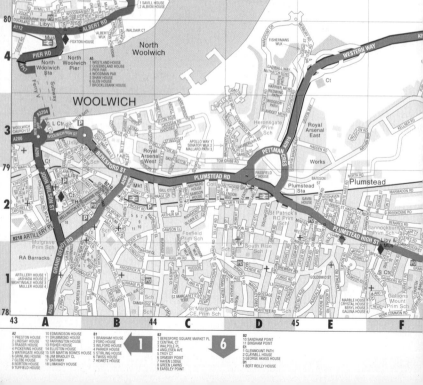

A B C D E F

Creekmouth

Sewage
Works

Barking
Horse Barrier
End

8

ALPINE
BSNS CTR
EASTBURY
RD
RODING RD

ALPINE WAY
THE
LONDON
IND PK
Beckton
Beckton
Sta

WINSOR TERR
STONEWALL

WOOLWICH MANOR WAY

ROYAL DOCKS RD

A1020

7

Works

Jetty

Winsor
Prim
Sch

WEYMOUTH CL

81

SAMGA WAY

FOUNDER CL
Gallions
Reach
Sta

Mast

Margaret or
Tripcock Ness

D ROYAL ALBERT RD
A1020 ROYAL ALBERT
WAY
Cyprus

6

Cyprus Sta

GALLIONS RD

1 ARTISAN CL
2 WEAVER CL
3 COLLIER CL

River Thames

Gallions Reach

Royal Albert
Dock

WOOLWICH MANOR WAY

A117

Albert
Basin

Newham Coll
of FE (Royal
Docks)
Campus

London City
Airport

King George V
Dock

Custom
House

5

Storey Prim
Sch

1 SAVILL HOUSE
2 ALBION CL

80
A112 Liby
Mus

ALBERT RD

WALDAIR CT

North
Woolwich

4 PIER RD FOXTON HOUSE

North
Woolwich
Sta

North
Woolwich Pier

A5
1 WESTLAND HOUSE
2 QUEENSLAND HOUSE
3 PIER PAR
4 WOODMAN PAR
5 SHAW HOUSE
6 GLEN HOUSE
7 BROCKLEBANK HOUSE

FISHERMANS
WLK

WESTERN WAY

Ferry V
Subway

WOOLWICH

A206

Royal Arsenal
East

Royal Arsenal
West

Heronsgate
Prim
Sch

PETTMAN CRES

3
WOOLWICH
CHURCH ST

A206
A205

L Ctr
WOOLWICH NEW RD

P

A1204

Uni

APOLLO WAY 1
SENATOR WLK 2
MALLARD PATH 3

Works

Plumstead

79
A205 St Mary's

JOHN WILSON ST

Liby

P

BERESFORD ST

A206

PLUMSTEAD RD

Mkt

Plumstead
Sta

NORTH RD

Plumstead

2 ARTILLERY PL

B210 ARTILLERY PL

P

Foxfield
Prim Sch

St Patrick's
RC Prim
Sch

South Rise
Sch

St Patrick's
RC Prim
Sch

PLUMSTEAD HIGH ST Liby &
Mus

Bannockburn
Prim Sch

1

RA Barracks

Mulgrave
Prim
Sch

GRAND DEPOT RD

ARTILLERY HOUSE 1
JASHADA HOUSE 2
NIGHTINGALE HOUSE 3
MULLER HOUSE 4

FREDERICK PL

P

St Margaret's
Sch

St Margaret's
CE Prim Sch

MARBLE HOUSE 1
CRYSTAL HOUSE 2
BERYL HOUSE 3
GALENA HOUSE 4

Gallions
Mount
Prim Sch

78
43 A B 44 C D 45 E F

1

6

A B C D E F

8

MANOR WAY
BSNS CTR

FAIRVIEW
IND EST

BLACKWATER
CL

ALBRIGHT
IND EST

LORIMAR
BSNS CTR

DENVER
IND EST

LC

Beam River

FRESTA DRV

FROG LA

MARSH WAY

ORWELL
CL

STAR
BSNS CTR

MARLOW WAY

BARE LANE WAY

MOUNT RD

FERRY LA

SALAMONS WAY

Car Compounds

Jetty

Jetty

Jetty

Hornchurch
Shoot

Rainham Marshes

7

Halfway Reach

Frog
Island

81

Old Man's
Head

6

Jetty

River Thames

Erith Reach

Works

COLDHARBOUR LA

Works

Wharf

Chys

5

Jenningtree
Point

Jetty

Common Watercourse

BELVEDERE
IND EST

Wharf

Silt Lagoon

80

A2016 EASTERN WAY

PICARDY MANORWAY

CLAYTONVILLE
TERR

CHERRYTREE MANORWAY

FISHER'S WAY

ANDERSON WAY

4

Works

HAILEY RD

B328

ST THOMAS
RD

Works

Sports
Gd

Pier

Jetty

Wennin
Marsh

YARNTON WAY

WATERFIELD

Mill

Pier

3

SUTHERLAND RD

RAILWAY RD

STATION RD N

PICARDY MANORWAY

B253

ELBOURNE
TRAD EST

KEATS RD

BELVEDERE LINK
BSNS PK

CHURCH MANORWAY

VIKING WAY

Pier

Jetty

GILBERT RD

B213

Liby

DYLAN RD

PICARDY ST

Belvedere
Sta

NETHEWODE
CT

B213

B219 LOWER RD

Belvedere
Cty Prim
Jun Sch

THORNTON

METHUEN

B219

1 CORINTHIAN RD
2 ST FRANCIS RD

COLDHARBOUR
MANORWAY

Coldharbo
Point

79

PO

PALMIRA RD

COLMBROOK RD

UPPER ABBEY

B253

HALL ROBIN TER

PICARDY RD

HALL ROBIN RD

GALLEON

Erith Rands

2

UPPER
SHERIDAN

COWPER RD

KELVIN

FRANTILE

CALVERT

Picardy Sch
(Beeches Site)

Frank's Park

Bexley
Coll

PEMBROKE
CL

PARK
GDNS

NORDENFELDT
RD

1 CARRACK HOUSE
2 SALTFORD CL
3 BOSWORTH HOUSE
4 BEXLEY RD

Landing
Stage

Belvedere

Trinity Sch
Belvedere

David
Coffer
Ct

HILLSIDE

SYCAMOR
CT

Liby
& Mus

TH

Pie

ERITH RD

Bexley
Coll

PARKSIDE
LODGE

PO

B252

PO

Wharf

1

A206 WOOLWICH RD

Liby

PO

Court
Lodge

NEWNHAM
LODGE

ROBERTS RD

HOLLY

FILSTON RD

DE LUCI
RD

EUROPA
TRAD EST

Erith
Sta

A2016

Wharf

STONE

P

FLAXMAN

Sch

CHAPMAN RD

Lessness
Heath

STILE

FRASER RD

A206

78

49

A B 50 C D 51 E F

3 8

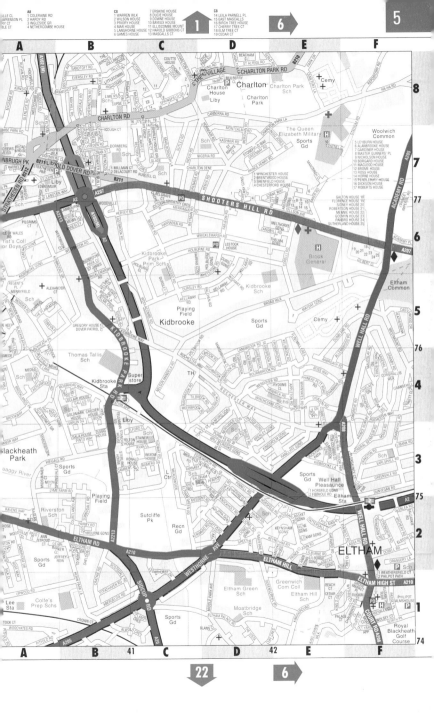

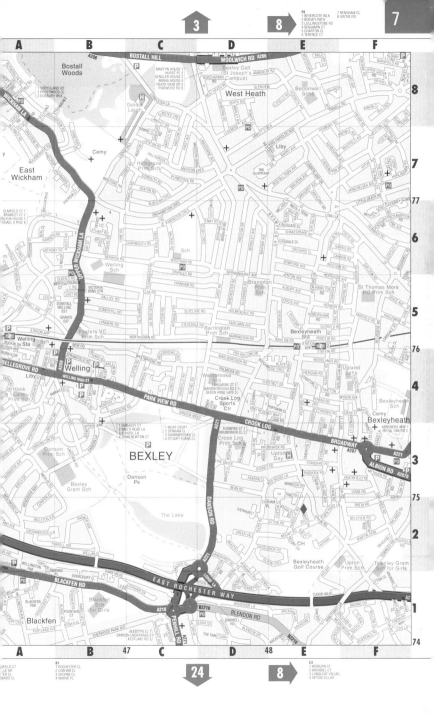

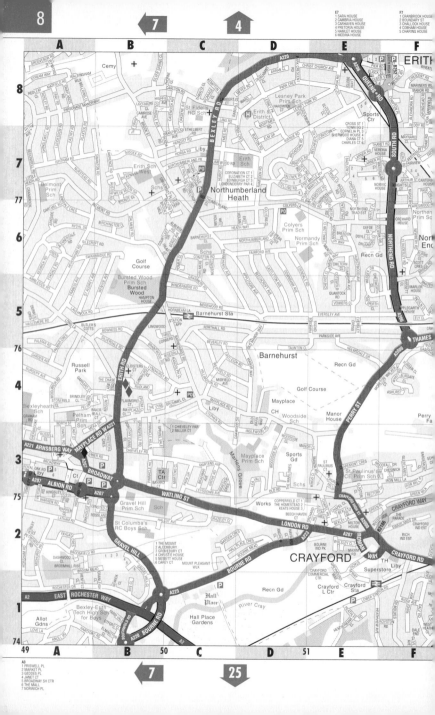

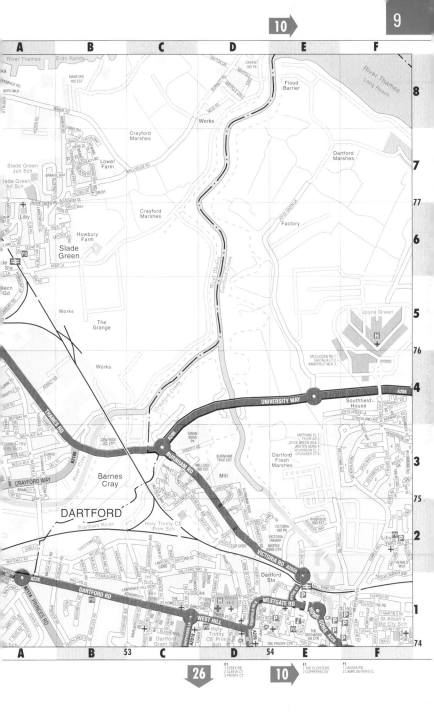

A B C D E F

55 A B 56 C D 57 E F

8

7

77

6

5

76

4

3

75

2

1

74

Purfleet

A1090 LONDON ROAD PURFLEET

Paper Mills

HUTSON TERR

STONEHOUSE LA

QUARRY WAY

TUNNEL EST

WATERGLADE IND PARK

LINDEN CL

DARRAH COTTS

STONEHOUSE CNR

LONDON ROAD WEST THURROCK

OLIVER CL

Wks

LC

LC

Purfleet Thames Terminal

Wks

Jetties

River Thames
Long Reach

Dartford Tunnel

Jetties

Sewage Works

Chy

Littlebrook Power Sta

Tanks

Queen Elizabeth 2 Bridge

CANTERBURY WAY

Stone Marshes

Pontoon

Littlebrook Nature Park

A3
1 WILKINSON CL
2 CHAUCER WAY
3 MACMILLAN GDNS
4 NIGHTINGALE GR
5 PEPYS CL
6 NORWOOD CT
7 RIVER VIEW

CLIPPER BVD

Freightliner Terminal

Cemy

A206

UNIVERSITY WAY

CROSSWAYS BVD A206

Tolls

ANCHOR BVD

UPPER RD

Marsh St

Temple Hill

Crossways

ST MARY S RD

CHARLES ST

Stone Crossing Halt

LC

BELL LA

Stone

St Anselm's RC Prim Sch

B1
1 DONNINGTON CT
2 HARDWICK CRES
3 DENNY CT
4 BEESTON CT
5 BROUGHAM CT
6 PEVERIL CT
7 DUNSTER CT

8 CALSHOT CT
9 LYDFORD CT
10 LONGTOWN CT
11 PICKERING CT
12 BARNARD CT
13 TATTERSHALL CT
14 CARRISBROOKE CT
15 BOWES CT
16 NORHAM CT
17 MIDDLEHAM CT
18 PRUDHOE CT
19 BRIDGE CT

COTTON LA

ORCHARD TERR

ELIZABETH ST

Lads of the Village (PH)

LOWER CHURCH HILL
UPPER CHURCH HILL

JACKSON CL 1
SUTHERLAND CL 2
RICHARDSON CL 3

GRIFFIN WLK

SWALLOW

UNICORN WLK
BISHOP'S CT

A2
1 KNIGHTS MANOR WAY
2 REDWOOD CT
3 BEECH CT
4 CHURCHILL PK
5 ASPEN CT

Archery House

Rifle & Pistol Ranges

TA Ctr

Horns Cross

Milestone Sch

Univ Stone House

Stone Lodge Farm Park

LONDON RD

HEDGE PLACE RD

Bow Arrow

New Town

BOW ARROW LA

Recn Gd

A226

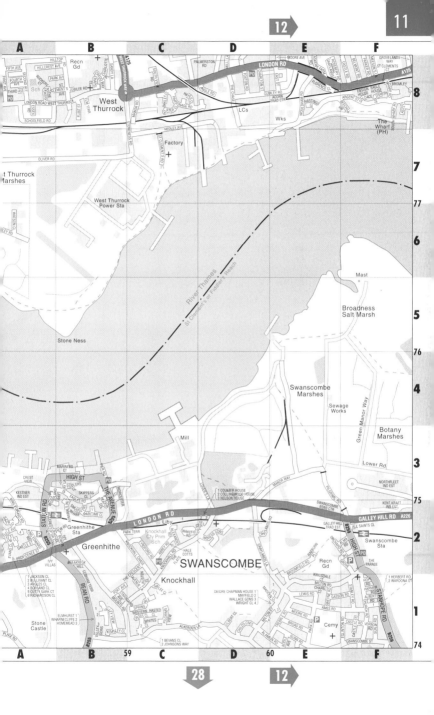

11

GRAYS

Tilbury
Marshes

Little
Thurrock
Marshes

Hypermarket

Warehouses

River Thames

Tilbury
Docks

Tilbury
Ness

NORTHFLEET

Rosherville

Sports
Gd

11
29

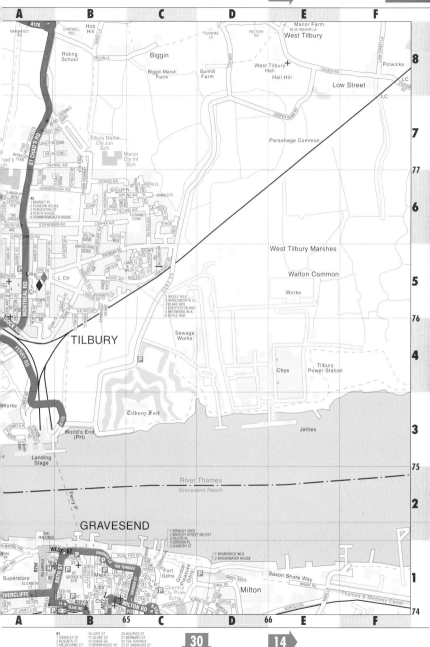

A126

MARSHFOOT RD

CHADWELL HILL

Hob Hill

Riding School

Biggin

Biggin Marsh Farm

Gunhill Farm

TURNPIKE LA

RECTORY RD

West Tilbury

Manor Farm
BLUE ANCHOR LA

West Tilbury Hall

Hall Hill

Low Street

Polwicks

CHURCH RD

LOW STREET LA

LC

LC

ST CHADS RD

Tilbury Manor Cty Jun Sch

Manor Cty Inf Sch

Parsonage Common

COOPER SHAW RD

LANGBURY GDNS

CENTRAL AVE

SOUTH VIEW AVE

CHRISTCHURCH RD

MONTREAL RD

DOCK RD

FERRY RD

LOWER RD

Works

West Tilbury Marshes

Walton Common

Works

A5
1 MARKET PL
2 DUNEDIN HOUSE
3 PREVENTON CT
4 PERTH HOUSE
5 COMMONWEALTH HOUSE

1 WOOLF WLK
2 WORDSWORTH CL
3 BLAKE WAY
4 CHESTERTON WAY
5 BROWNING WLK
6 DOYLE WAY

Liby

L Ctr

L Ctr

Crown Ct

THE BEECHES

TILBURY

Sewage Works

P

Tilbury Fort

Chys

Tilbury Power Station

World's End (PH)

Landing Stage

Jetties

Ferry P

ELIZABETH

River Thames
Gravesend Reach

75

Works

GRAVESEND

THE MALTINGS

WEST ST

BATH ST

St George's Ctr

Superstore

OVERCLIFFE

ST JAMES'S RD

NEW RD

CLIVE RD

Liby

Royal Pier Rd

THE TERRACE

Fort Gdns

Gordon Pleasure Gdns

Chantry Cty Prim Schs

1 BERKLEY CRES
2 BENTLEY STREET IND EST
3 PILOTS PL
4 GORDON PL
5 CHANTRY CT

1 BRUNSWICK WLK
2 BROADWATER HOUSE

Canal Basin

CANAL RD

Saxon Shore Way

WHARF RD

Milton

NORFOLK RD

Thames & Medway Canal

B1
1 CRAWLEY CT
2 REGENTS CT
3 MELBOURNE CT
4 TOWN PIER
5 BULL YD
6 HORN YD
7 NEW SWAN YD
8 MARKET ALLEY
9 CHURCH ALLEY
10 JURY ST
11 GLOBE YD
12 CHASE SQ
13 BREWHOUSE YD
14 BARRACK ROW
15 GARRICK ST
16 ANGLESEA PL
17 ANGLESEA CTR
18 RAILWAY PL
19 MANOR RD
20 WILFRED ST
21 BERNARD ST
22 THE TERRACE
23 ST ANDREWS CT
24 CROSS ST

8

7

77

6

5

76

4

3

75

2

1

74

A B C D E F

8

Ind Est

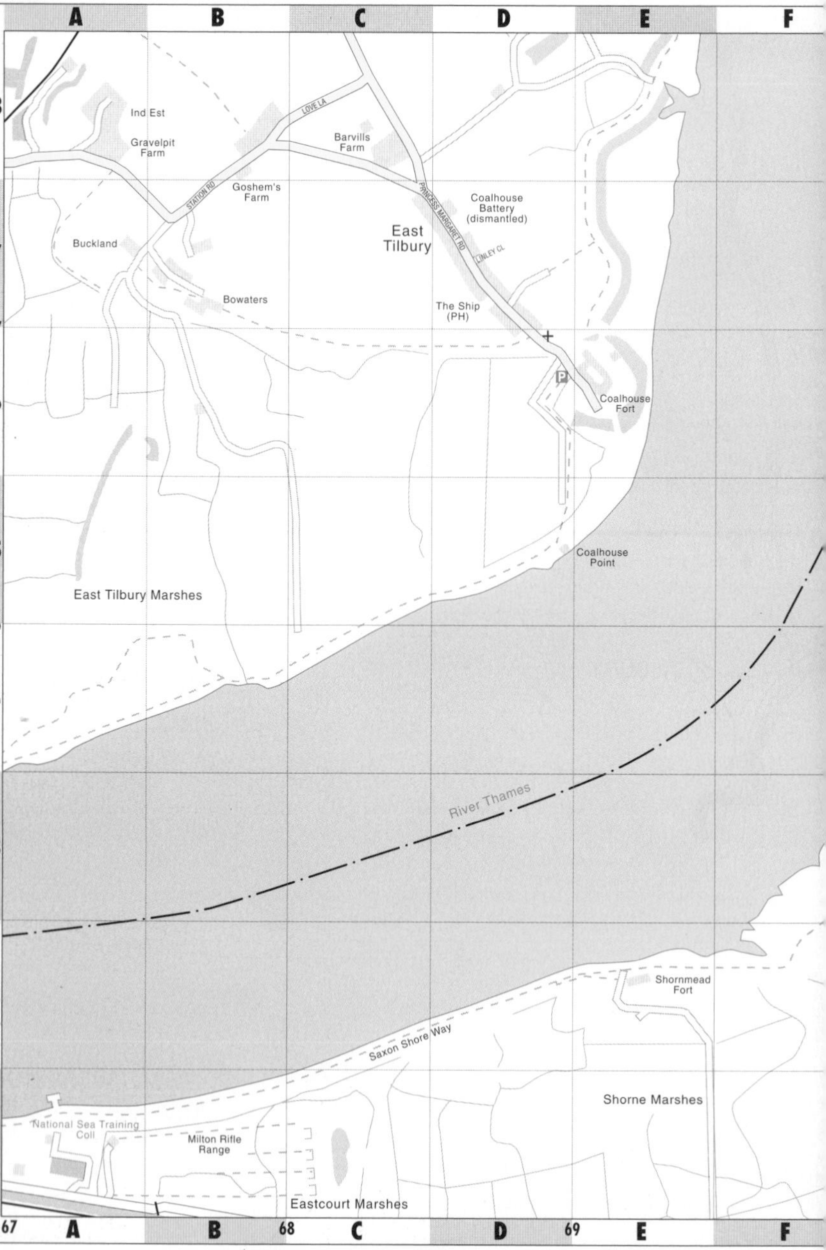

Gravelpit
Farm

LOWER LA

Barvills
Farm

Goshem's
Farm

East
Tilbury

PRINCESS MARGARET RD

Coalhouse
Battery
(dismantled)

7

Buckland

LINLEY CL

Bowaters

The Ship
(PH)

77

+

P

6

Coalhouse
Fort

P

Coalhouse
Point

5

East Tilbury Marshes

76

4

River Thames

3

75

Shornmead
Fort

2

Saxon Shore Way

Shorne Marshes

National Sea Training
Coll

Milton Rifle
Range

1

Eastcourt Marshes

74

67   A   B   68   C   D   69   E   F

River Thames
The Lower Hope

A **B** **C** **D** **E** **F**

8

COASTGUARD COTTS

Pier

Boatrick House

7

77

Cliffe Creek

Cliffe Fort (dis)

Saxon Shore Way

Jetties

6

Higham Creek

Conveyor

Depot

5

76

Royal Albert (PH)

4

CONCRETE COTTS

Quarries (dis)

SALT LA

Wks

West Court

LC

3

Higham Marshes

75

Higham Common

Barrow Hill

2

Beckley Hill

Oakleigh

1

Higham or Church Street

CHURCH ST

74

A **B** 71 **C** **D** 72 **E** **F**

15

8

7

77

6

Ryestreet
Common

Farthing Wall

Ham Wall

PICKLES WAY

MEAD WALL

Allen's
Hill

THAMES
TERR

CHURCH
CL

MEDWAY RD

WHARF LA

REED ST

ST HELENS RD

COMMON WALL

P

Buttway La

MISKIN COTTS

ROOKERY CRES

COMMON LA

Rye Street
Farm

Manor
Farm

SWINGATE AVE

WADLANDS RD

Saxon Shore Way

West
Street

QUICKRELLS
AVE

RECERY RD

Cliffe

5

West Street
Farm

St Helens
CE Prim Sch

Mars

CHURCH ST

TURNER ST

MILLCROFT RD

Cooling
Castle
Farm

76

NEW
RD

NORWOOD CL

MORNING
CROSS COTTS

COOLING RD

Cooling Rd

Cooling

Hoo
and

4

HIGHAM RD

BUCKLAND RD

SALT LA

Berry Court
Farm

Mour
Pleasa

Redbarn

STATION RD

Newlands
Farm

WELLAM RD

Gattons
Farm

Cooling Court
Farm

3

75

RECTORY RD

Alma
House

Buckland
Farm

The Rectory

SOUTH BANK

2

The
Grange

TOWN RD

B2000

Cooling
Street

New Barn
Farm

Bell
Farm

Spendiff
Farm

PERRY HILL

COOLING RD

Perry Hill
Farm

1

Mortimers
Farm

Rough
Shaw

74

73 A   B   74   C   D   75   E   F

A   B   C   D   E   F

8

Cooling
Marshes

Old Sea Wall

Decoy Fleet

The Mean

Swigshole

Buckland
Marshes

Buckland Fleet

7

Decoy
Farm

77

Whalebone
Marshes

6

Masts

Eastborough
Farm

Saxon Shore Way

Northward Hill

Decoy Hill Rd

5

Bromhey
Farm

SPARING RD

Northward Hill
Nature Reserve

Clinchstreet
Farm

Childs
Farm

76

Eastborough
Bungalow

Buckhole
Farm

MARSH CRES

THAMES AVE

NEWLANDS AVE

LONG HILL RD

WILLOWWARD DR

4

SPARELL HILL

BUCKHOLE FARM RD

HARRISON DR

HELSTON RD

GOODWORTH DR

HIGH MEADOW DR

High
Halstow

Dalham
Farm

High Halstow
Cty Prim Sch

THE STREET

3

COOLING RD

ROUGE LA

✝ PH

ST MARGARET'S
CT

PO

LC

WYBOURNES LA

HILL GRN
CL

CHRISTMAS LA

Wybournes
Farm

75

2

Lodge Hill
Wood

Wybornes
Wood

Ducks
Court

Solomon's
Farm

RATCLIFFE HIGHWAY

A228

1

74

A   B   77   C   D   78   E   F

A B C D E F

8

7

77

6 Ramsgreen

Coombe House

May Land

Moat Farm

St Mary Hoo

Ross Farm

Noreland Cottage

HOOPERS LA

MOAT FARM RD

COOMBE FARM LA

HALL RD

5 Newlands Farm

RATCLIFFE HIGHWAY

ST MARY'S

76

Walnut Tree Farm

Bell Wood

4 OLD LA

Saxon Shore Way

Fenn Street

Fenn Bell Inn (PH)

Maimaynes Hall Farm

BELLWOOD LA

Jackson's Corner

Turkey Hall Farm

MALMAYNES HALL RD

THE STREET

3 Fenn Farm

Fisher's Wood

New Barn Farm

75 CHRISTMAS LA

RATCLIFFE HIGHWAY

Parbrook Cott

2 Tudor Farm

GORSES ST

LOWER CHASE LA

Sharnal Street

A228

STOKE RD

1 Cold Arbour

North Street

North Street Farm

74

Tunbridge Hill

79 A B 80 C D 81 E F

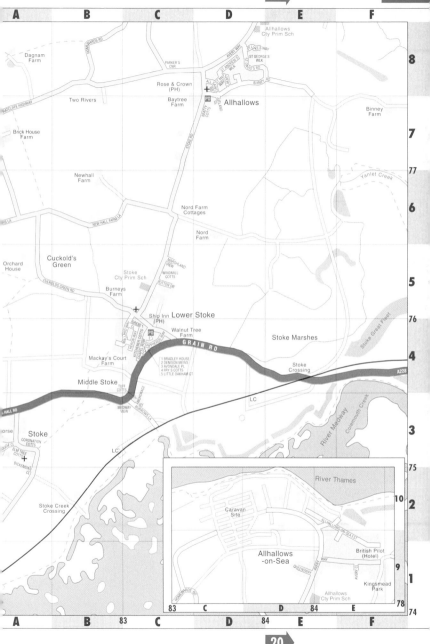

A   B   C   D   E   F

8

Allhallows
Cty Prim Sch

Dagnam
Farm

HOWARDS RD

PARKER'S
CNR.

ST JAMES'S WAY

ST ANDREW'S WK

ST GEORGE'S
WLK

ST JAMES'S RD

Rose & Crown
(PH)

Baytree
Farm

Two Rivers

RATCLIFFE HIGHWAY

PO

Allhallows

BINNEY RD

Binney
Farm

7

Brick House
Farm

STOKE RD

77

Newhall
Farm

Yanlet Creek

IRS LA

NEW HALL FARM LA

6

Nord Farm
Cottages

Orchard
House

Cuckold's
Green

CUCKOLDS GREEN RD

Nord
Farm

MARSHLAND
VIEW

WINDMILL
COTTS

Stoke
Cty Prim Sch

SUTTON DR

5

Burneys
Farm

Ship Inn
(PH)

Lower Stoke

PO

Walnut Tree
Farm

76

Stoke Marshes

Stoke Great Fleet

Mackay's Court
Farm

GRAIN RD

1 BRADLEY HOUSE
2 DENISON MEWS
3 AVONDALE PL
4 FRY'S COTTS
5 LITTLE OAKHAM CT

Stoke
Crossing

A228

4

Middle Stoke

TUFF
COTTS

HALL RD

MEDWAY
VIEW

BURDOCK LA

LC

River Medway

Colemouth Creek

3

orse

Stoke

CORONATION
COTTS

ELM TREE
COTTS

DICKENHAM
CO

LC

75

Stoke Creek
Crossing

River Thames

Caravan
Site

10

2

Allhallows
-on-Sea

ALLHALLOWS-ON-SEA EST

AVERY WAY

QUEENSWAY

British Pilot
(Hotel)

9

Kingsmead
Park

HOMEWARDS RD

Allhallows
Cty Prim Sch

1

78

83   C   D   84   E   74

A   B   83   C   D   84   E   F

19

	A	B	C	D	E	F

8

DANGER AREA

Yantlet Creek

Allhallows
Marshes

Bucks
Pounds

7

Wharf

Grain
Marsh

77

PEAT WAY

6

Old Counter Wall

Perry's
Farm

ISLE OF GRAIN

Newlands

5

76

Home
Farm

Ppg Sta

4

LC

Wallend

A228

Kent Oil Refinery

3

A228

B2001

LC

G R A I N   R D

75

Colemouth Creek

2

River Medway

1

Elphinstone
Point

74

19

A B C D E F

8

Grain Spit

River Thames

The Flats

7

77

Works

P B2001

Grain

+

St James'
CE (VA) Sch

6

ecourt
arm

WEST LA

CAMBELL RD

HIGH ST

PH

PO

EDINBURGH RD

CORINTHIAN
CT

Whitehouse
Farm

SHELLDRAKE CL

SMITHFIELD RD

PORT VICTORIA RD

RAIN RD

+

+

5

76

Grain
Tower

Smithfield
Marshes

4

Garrison
Point

Grain Power
Station

Chy

LB
Sta

GARRISON RD

SLIPWAY RD

BOATHOUSE
RD

ANCHOR LA

Docks

SHEERNESS WHARF

SHEERNESS

3

Jetty

SHEERNESS
HARBOUR EST

GREAT BASIN RD

75

2

House Fleet

River Medway

Piers

Cockleshell
Hard

Jetty

Horseshoe
Point

The
Lappel

1

74

A B 89 C D 90 E F

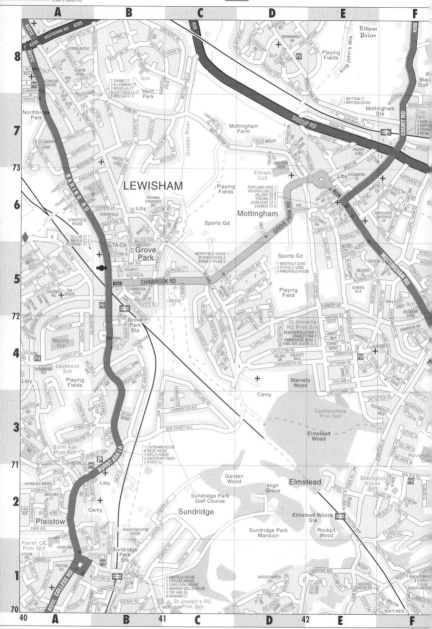

A8
1 WILDWOOD CL
2 ST MILDREDS RD
3 SWALLOW CT
4 HONEYSUCKLE CT
5 VENTURE CT
6 WAITE DAVIES RD

7 CHERITON CT
8 ASKHAM LODGE
9 SYON LODGE

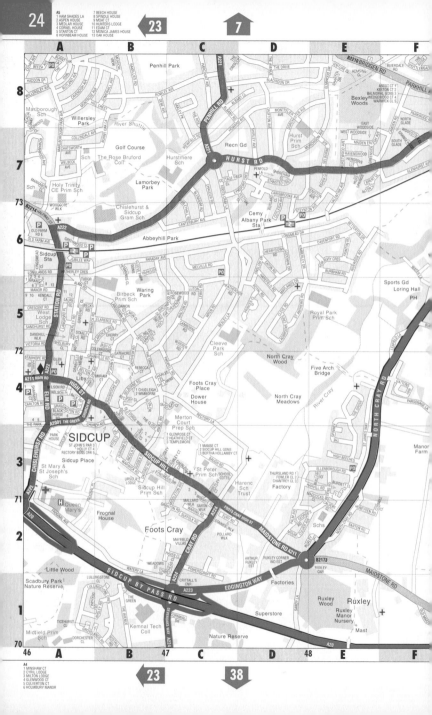

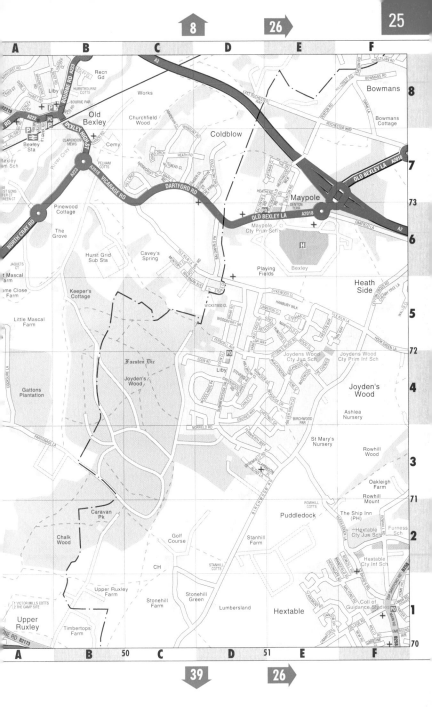

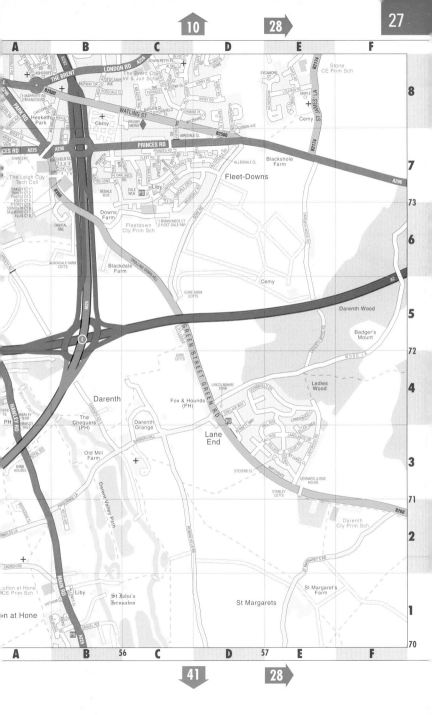

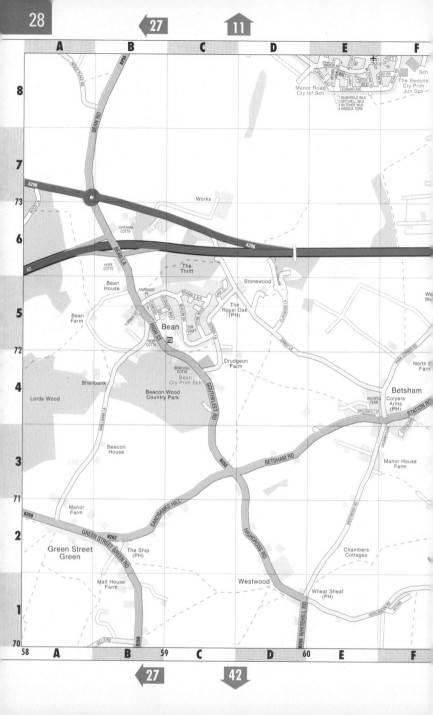

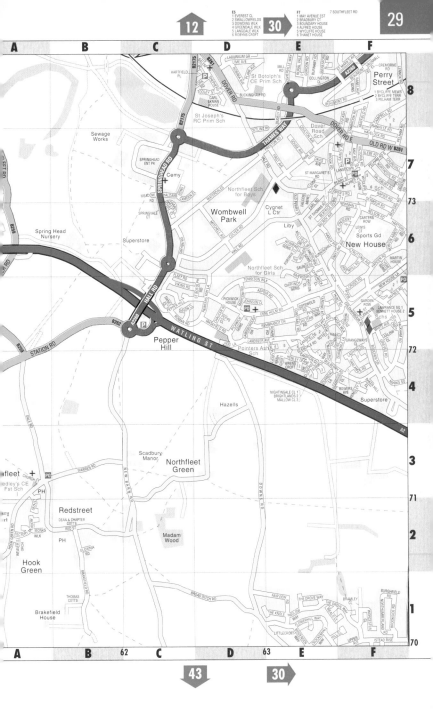

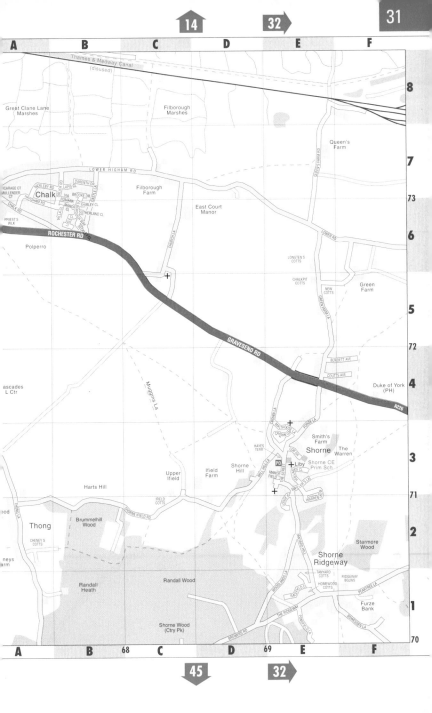

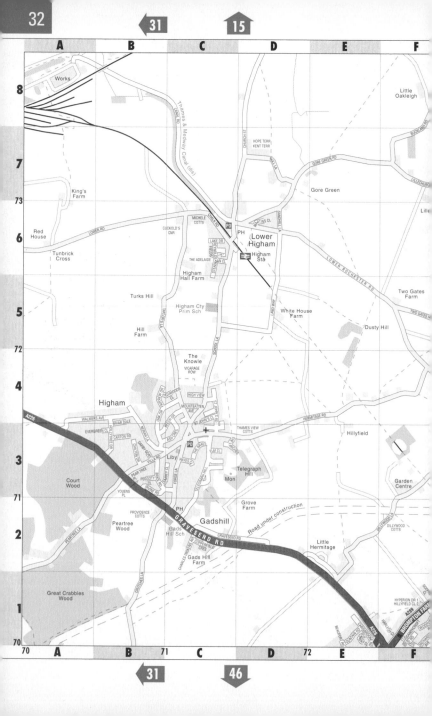

A B C D E F

8

Berry Court Wood

MERRY BOYS RD
WENTWORTH DR
WENBURY DR
MELTOR AVE
LINGDENE CL

Tile Barn Farm

DOOLING COMM

Cliffe Woods Mid Sch
Cliffe Woods Cty Prim Fst Sch

MORTIMERS AVE
LADYCLOSE AVE

Hill

WOODSIDE
TENNYSON AVE

Ratley Hills Wood

Great Chattenden Wood

Lodge Hill Camp

7

Cliffe Woods

ASHWOOD CL

Bingham Roughs

73

TOWN RD

NORTH TERR

Ash Wood

Round Top Wood

6

Stone Horse Wood

CENTRAL TERR

WYLIE HOUSE 1
HENDRY HOUSE 2
BUTTON HOUSE 3
STEWART HOUSE 4
ELMWOOD RD
HILL LA

Lee Green

Haven Street Wood

SWINTON AVE

Nursery

KIRBY RD

5

Sandy Hill

The Mount

Chattenden Barracks
Royal Sch of Military Engineering

SUTTON SIMMONDS RD

Mockbeggar Farm

Islingham Farm

KITCHENER RD

TUDOR DR PH

CHATTENDEN TERR

72

Chattenden Cty Sch

OLD SCHOOL RD

Noke Street

BUNTERS HILL RD

WOODFIELD WAY

DOVER ELMS RD

MAIN RD A228

4

Bunters Farm

LEE GREEN RD

BEACON HILL RD

BALLS COTTS

Chattenden

e Horse
(H)

FOUR ELMS HILL

Beacon Hill

Beacon

SPRINGDALE COTTS

Blacklands Farm

HIGHAM RD

UPPER RD

Works

3

one
ouse
rm

LOWER ROCHESTER RD

Sale Street Farm

Wainscott

HOO RD A289

A228

71

Brickhouse Farm

Road under construction

Wainscott Cty Prim Sch

ge

STONEHORSE LA

B2000

HOLLYWOOD LA

WAINSCOTT WLK

PO

2

BROMPTON FARM RD

LINDSEY DR

HOLLYWOOD DR

PH

Upnor Castle

P PO

Temple Sch

PH

ADMIRALTY RD

CLIFFE RD B2000

Sch

A228

PO

P

RICHMOND CL

1

1 WALMER HOUSE
2 DOVER HOUSE
3 HEVER HOUSE
4 TONBRIDGE HOUSE
5 CHILHAM HOUSE
6 LEEDS HOUSE
7 MEREWORTH HOUSE
8 SCOTNEY HOUSE

Sewage Works

Upper Upnor

KING ARTHUR'S DR

MURRAY RD

Tower Hill

70

A B C D E F

White Hall
Farm House

Beluncle
Farm

BELUNCLE
VILLAS

er's
arm

STORE RD

STORE RD

URDEE
OTTS

JACOB'S LA

SCHOOL RD

RYDER RD

ACORN PL

BUCK RD

JETTY RD

MAIN RD

SAXMAS RD

Works

Kingsnorth

Abbots
Court

Saxon Shore Way

Sewage
Works

Damhead Creek

Power
Station

Jetty

Hoo Flats

River Medway

Long Reach

Middle Creek

Darnet Ness

Darnet
Fort

Bishop Saltings

Pinup Reach

South Yantlet Creek

Hoo Fort

Folly Point

Gillingham Reach

Nor Marsh

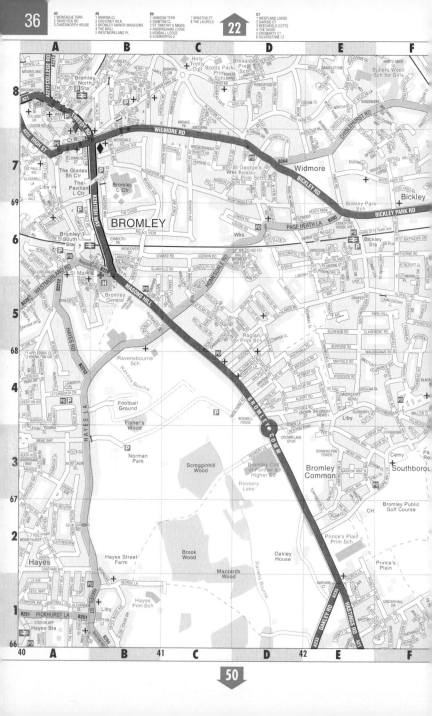

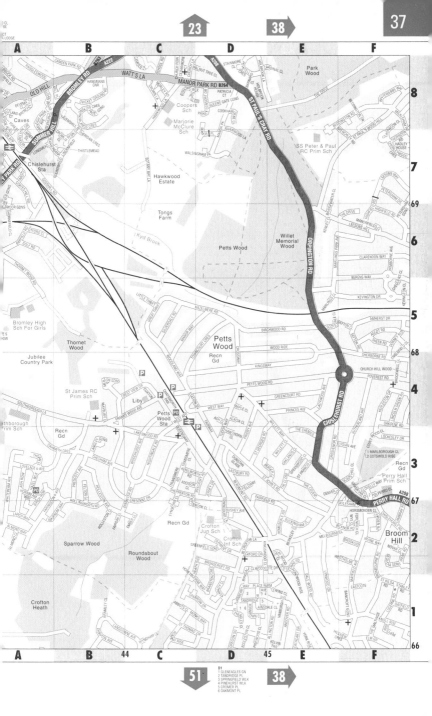

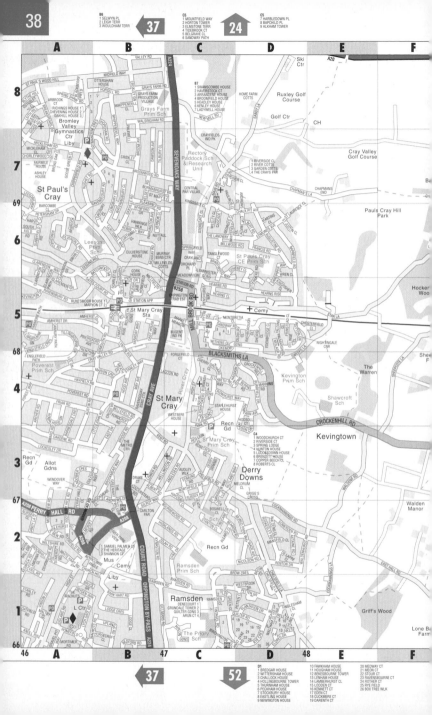

37

24

B6
1 SELWYN PL
2 LEIGH TERR
3 WOULDHAM TERR

C5
1 MOUNTFIELD WAY
2 HORTON TOWER
3 ELMSTONE TERR
4 TIDEBROOK CT
5 BELGRAVE CT
6 SANDWAY PATH

C5
7 HARBLEDOWN PL
8 BAPCHILD PL
9 ALKHAM TOWER

B7
1 SWANSCOMBE HOUSE
2 HAVERSTOCK CT
3 AMARANTHE HOUSE
4 BROOMFIELD HOUSE
5 HEADLEY HOUSE
6 KEMLEY HOUSE
7 LADYWELL HOUSE

C7
1 RIVERSIDE CL
2 RIVER COTTS
3 GARDEN COTTS
3 THE CRAYS CRAY

C4
1 WOODCHURCH CT
2 RIVERSIDE CT
3 SPRING LODGE
4 HUNTON HOUSE
5 LUDDESDOWN HOUSE
6 BRENZETT HOUSE
7 COPPER BEECH CL
8 ROBERTS CL

Ski Ctr

A20

Ruxley Golf Course

Golf Ctr

Home Farm Cotts

CH

Cray Valley Golf Course

Pauls Cray Hill Park

Hocker Woo

St Paul's Wood Hill

Bromley Valley Gymnastics Ctr Liby

St Paul's Cray

Leesons Prim Sch

St Pauls Cray CE Prim Sch

St Mary Cray Sta

Cemy

St Mary Cray

Poverest Prim Sch

The Warren

Shee F

Blacksmiths La

Kevington Prim Sch

Shawcroft Sch

Crockenhill Rd

Kevingtown

St Mary Cray Prim Sch

Derry Downs

Walden Manor

Recn Gd

Allot Gdns

The Metro Ctr

Griff's Wood

Lone Ba Farm

Ramsden Prim Sch

Mus

Cemy

Liby

L Ctr

Ramsden

The Priory Sch

D1
1 BREDGAR HOUSE
2 WITTERSHAM HOUSE
3 CHALLOCK HOUSE
4 HOLLINGBOURNE TOWER
5 THURNHAM HOUSE
6 PECKHAM HOUSE
7 STOCKBURY HOUSE
8 EASTLING HOUSE
9 NEWINGTON HOUSE

10 FAWKHAM HOUSE
11 HOUGHAM HOUSE
12 BEKESBOURNE TOWER
13 LENHAM HOUSE
14 LAMBERHURST CL
15 LODDEN CT
16 KENNETT CT
17 EDEN CT
18 CUCKMERE CT
19 DARENTH CT

20 MEDWAY CT
21 MEON CT
22 STOUR CT
23 RAVENSBOURNE CT
24 ROTHER CT
25 RYE FIELD
26 BOX TREE WLK

46   A   47   B   C   47   D   48   E   F

8
7
69
6
68
5
4
67
3
2
66
1

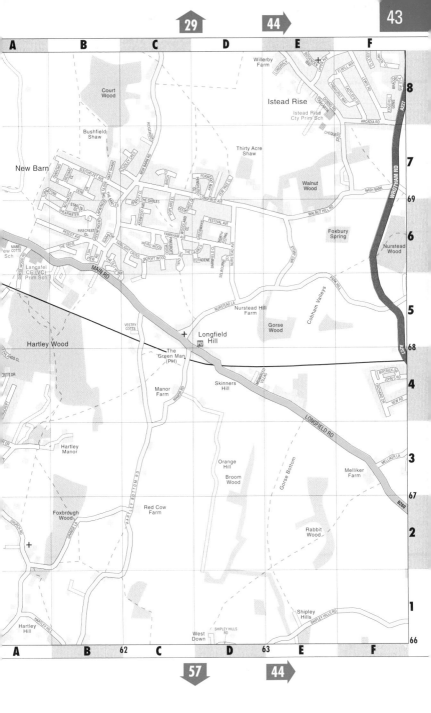

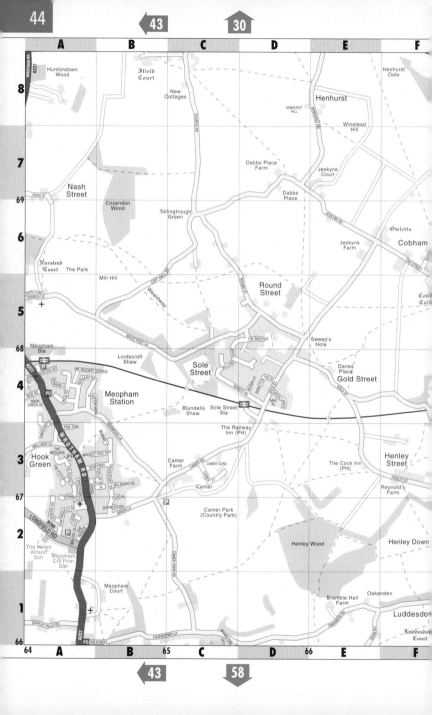

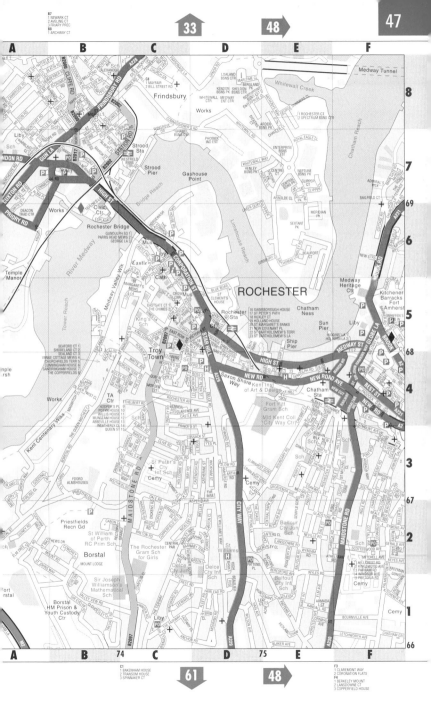

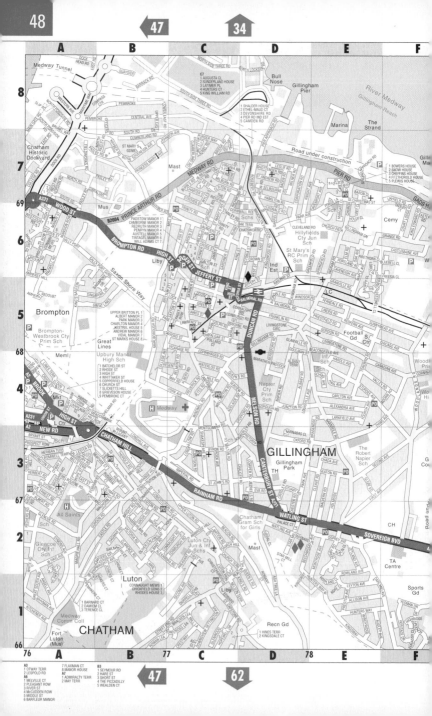

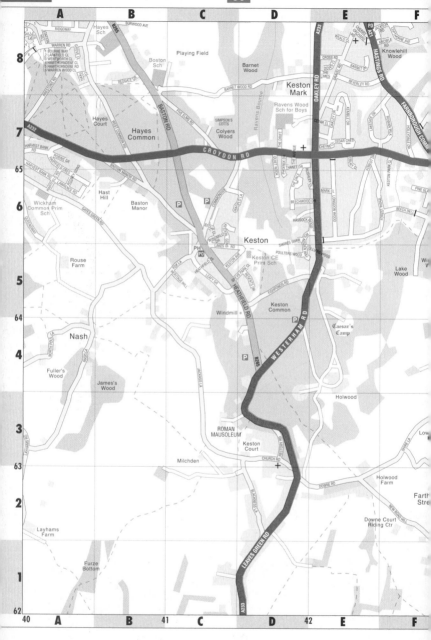

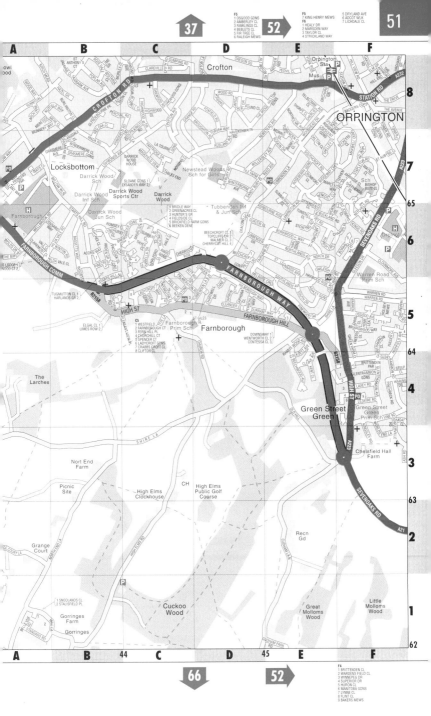

37

F5
1 OSGOOD GDNS
2 AMBERLEY CL
3 RAWLINGS CL
4 BEBLETS CL
5 FIR TREE CL
6 RALEIGH MEWS

52

F5
7 KING HENRY MEWS
F6
1 HEALY DR
2 MARSDEN WAY
3 TAYLOR CL
4 STRICKLAND WAY

5 DRYLAND AVE
6 ADCOT WLK
7 LICHDALE CL

51

Crofton

Orpington
Sta.
Mus

ORPINGTON

Locksbottom

Darrick Wood
Sch
Darrick Wood
Inf Sch
Darrick Wood
Sports Ctr
Darrick
Wood
Darrick Wood
Jun Sch

Newstead Woods
Sch for Girls

Farnborough

F
1 BRIDLE WAY
2 GREENACRES CL
3 HUNTER'S GR
4 FIELDSIDE CL
5 BRICKFIELD FARM GDNS
6 BEEKEN DENE

Tubbenden Inf
& Jun Sch

BEECHCROFT CL 1
TOPCLIFFE DR 2
WALMER CL 3
CHERRYCROFT CL 4

Sch
Bishop
Justus

Warren Road
Prim Sch

FARNBOROUGH WAY

HIGH ST

C5
1 WESTFIELD
2 FARNBOROUGH CT
3 FERN HILL PL
4 CHURCHILL CT
5 SPENCER CT
6 LADYCROFT GDNS
7 CRABBS CROFT CL
8 CLIFTON CL

Farnborough
Prim Sch

ST GILES
CL

Farnborough

FARNBOROUGH HILL

DOWNSWAY 1
WENTWORTH CL 2
CONTESSA CL 3

ELGAL CL 1
LIMES ROW 2

The
Larches

Green Street
Green

Green Street
Green
Prim Sch

Chelsfield Hall
Farm

Nort End
Farm

Picnic
Site

High Elms
Clockhouse

CH

High Elms
Public Golf
Course

SHIRE LA

SEVENOAKS RD
A21

Grange
Court

Recn
Gd

1 SNODLANDS CL
2 STALISFIELD PL

Gorringes
Farm

Gorringes

Cuckoo
Wood

Great
Molloms
Wood

Little
Molloms
Wood

66

52

F4
1 BRITTENDEN CL
2 WARDENS FIELD CL
3 WINNEPEG DR
4 SUPERIOR DR
5 HURON CL
6 MANITOBA GDNS
7 LYNNE CL
8 FLINT CL
9 BAKERS MEWS

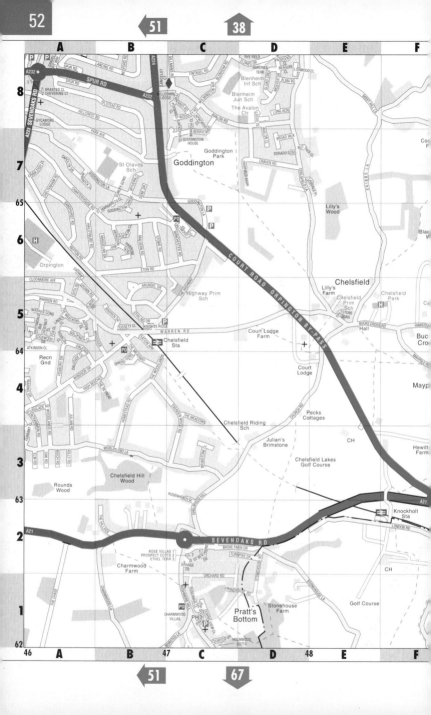

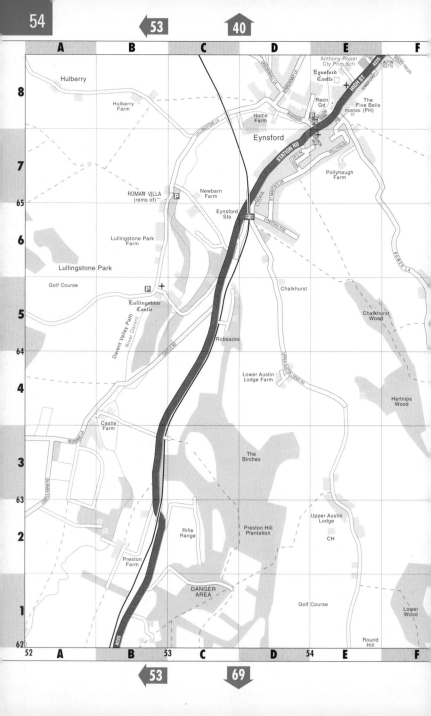

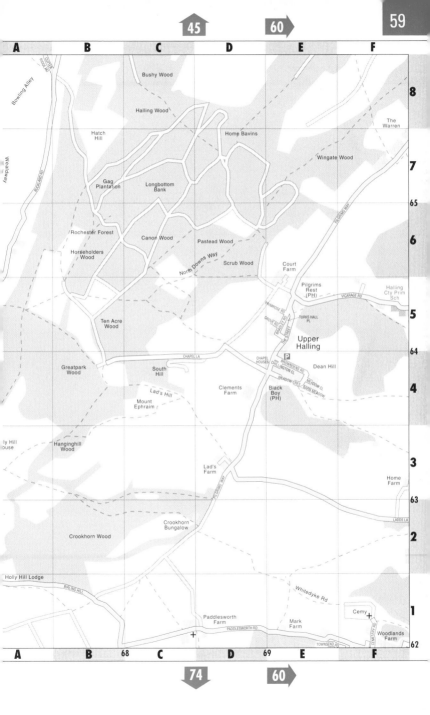

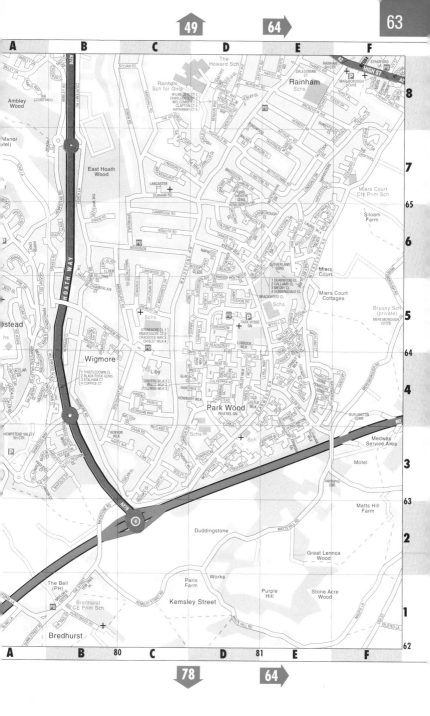

A B C D E F

1 SHELDEN DR
2 LONGFORD CL
3 LONGFORD CT
4 THE OLD ORCH

BLACKTHORNE RD
PEARTREE COTTS
HIGH ST
MOOR ST
WINCHESTER
GLOUCESTER
SUDBURY
HEREFORD
OAST LA
HAZELDENE
CHESTNUTFIELD
ST PARK
WESTMINSTER
A2
P

Westmoor Farm
WAKELEYS COTTS
Moor Street
Orchard Cottage
MERESBROUGH RD
SOUTH BUSH LA
DANE LA

Moor Street
LONDON RD
Orchard House
Culvers Hill
Hurst Hill
Kaine Farm
Gore House
B
Hartlip Hill
HARTLIP HILL

FOURACRE COTTS

Lower Dane
DANE LA
MUNN S LA
OAK C
PARADISE COTTS
Paradise Farm

MERESBROUGH LA
Titus Farm
Meresborough
Yaugher
Place Farm
Hartlip Place
HARTLIP LA
PLACE LA
Hartlip Endowed CE Prim Sch
Hartlip
HOLLOW LA
LOWER HARTLIP RD
Rose & Crown (PH)
Lower Hartlip

Oak Barn
The Parsonage
Sweepstakes Farm
OLD HOUSE RD
Oldhouse Farm Cotts
Nunfield Farm

M2
MUNN LA
YAUGHER LA
WARREN LA
Nunfield House

Yaugher Woods
Queendown Warren
Potters Wood
Queen Down Warren
Warren Cottage
Cowstead

MAGPIE LA
Holly House Farm
CHADLEY RD
Cowstead Wood
BULL LA
GREEN LA

Water Works
Yelsted
YELSTED LA
Yelsted Farm
Yelsted Court Farm
Hill Green
HILL GREEN RD
Walnut Tree Cottage
Nettlestead

WALNUT TREE RD

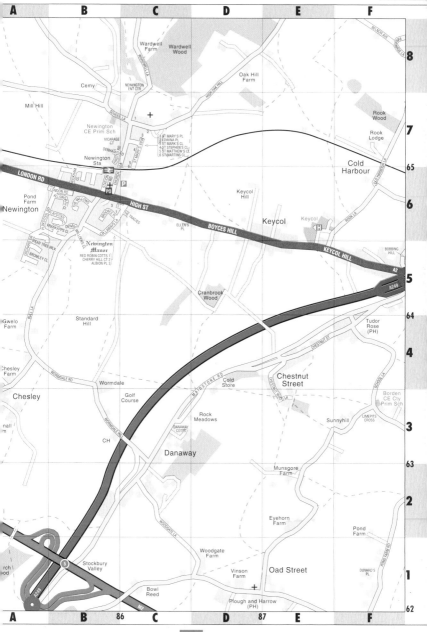

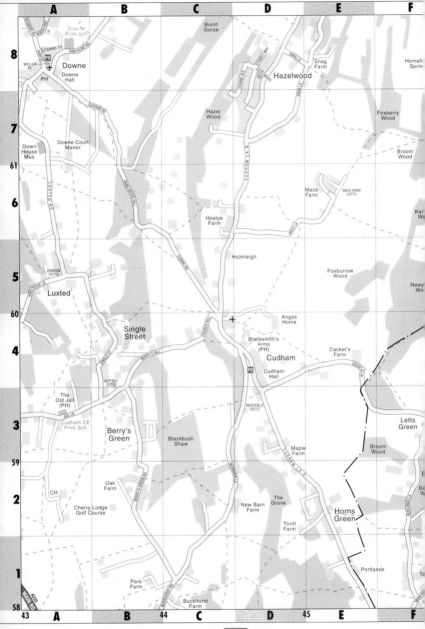

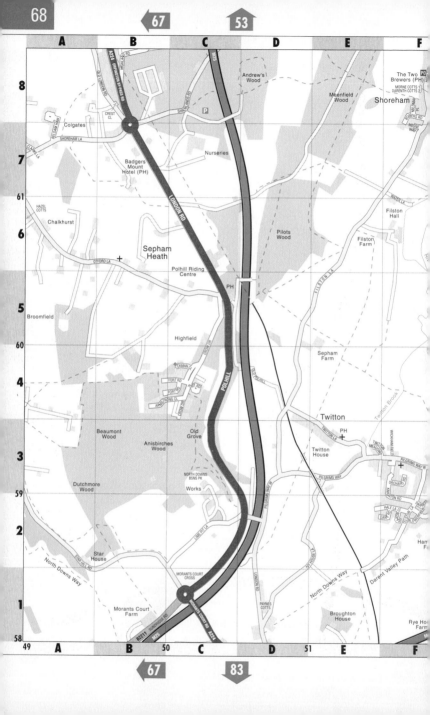

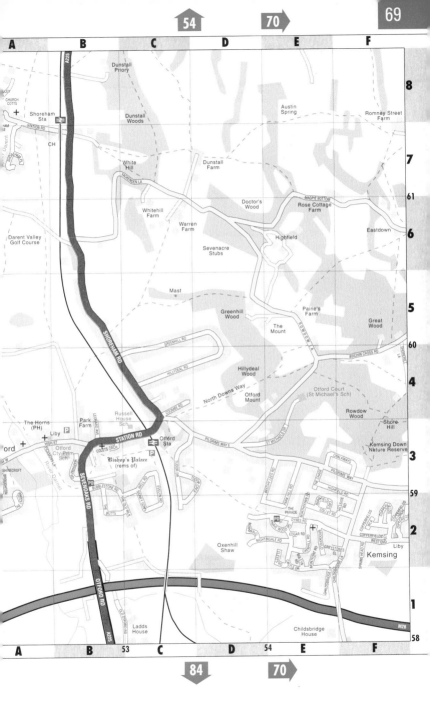

A B C D E F

8

Broom
Wood

Little East Hill
Farm

Knatts
Valley

KNATTS VALLEY RD

EAST HILL RD

SCHOOL LA

The
Fox & Hounds
(PH)

Leize
Wood

Pecken
Wood

Water Wood

HOLLYWOOD
MANOR

7

Romney
Street

Knockmill

Knockmill
Wood

ST CLERE HILL RD

61

Littlehurst
Farm

Mast

Porter's
Farm

Goodbury
Farm

Woodlands Manor
Golf Course

6

MAGPIE BOTTOM

CLARKES GREEN RD

Fernbank
Farm

Woodlands

CH

TINKER POT LA

Drane
Farm

BIRCHIN CROSS RD

GOODBURY RD

HILLS RD

WHITE DYKE

5

Beech Lees
Wood

Rising
Sun
(PH)

Summeryards
Wood

60

Shorehill
Farm

Fab's
Wood

Ashdown Farm
Bungalow

Cotman's
Ash

COTMAN'S ASH LA

OLD TERRY'S

4

North Downs Way

Kester

Otford
Manor

3

PILGRIMS WAY

St Clere

59

PILGRIMS WAY
COTTS

ORCHARD WAY

THE LANEWAY

WEST END

Kemsing
Cty Prim
Sch

PH

YH

P

MARY
BURROWS
GDNS

HIGH ST

HEAVERHAM RD

2

Crowdleham

Heaverham

Lower
St Clere

Dynes
Farm

PO

Chequers Inn
(PH)

1

RUSHYMEAD

OLD BAZES CL

THE FRED WAY

Hill's
Wood

Bushy
Wood

Broughton

ST EDITH'S RD

St Edith's
Farmhouse

FAIRFIELD

WATER LA

58

M26

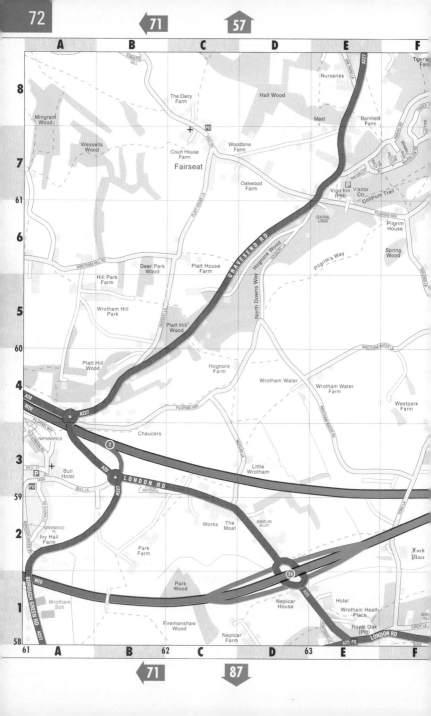

A   B   C   D   E   F

Whitehorse Wood

Vigo Cty Prim Sch
ASH
KEYS
THE CHURCH
Liby
PO
Vigo Village

Great Wood

Trosley Ctry Pk

Coldrum Trail

North Downs Way

Coney Lodge Farm

PILGRIMS WAY

Park Farm

FINGLESHAM LA

COLDRUM LA

Trosley Court

Trottiscliffe

Coldrum Trail

CHURCH LA

Ryarsh Wood

CHAPEL LA

Cleggett's Farm

PO
HOLMES CT

Trottiscliffe CE Prim Sch
NORTH DOWNS TERR

Ryarsh

Orchard House

BIRLING RD

THE STREET
OLD SCHOOL LA

Wealdway

Woodgate

WOODGATE RD

Little Woodgate

Works

Leney's Cottages

LAST STREET N

M20

3

Addington
THE CHESTNUTS
PO
MILLHOUSE LA

PARK RD

CHURCHFIELD

THE CLOSE

EAST ST

FLOWERED...

East Street

The Roughetts

Golf Course

CHURCH RD

ROUGHETTS...

Westfields Farm

59

ST VINCENTS LA

Addington Park

THE LINKS

WEST MALLING IND PK

St Vincents

CH

Golf Course

A20

Wrotham Heath

Shaw Hill

LONDON RD

Aldon

Church RD

Stubberdown Wood

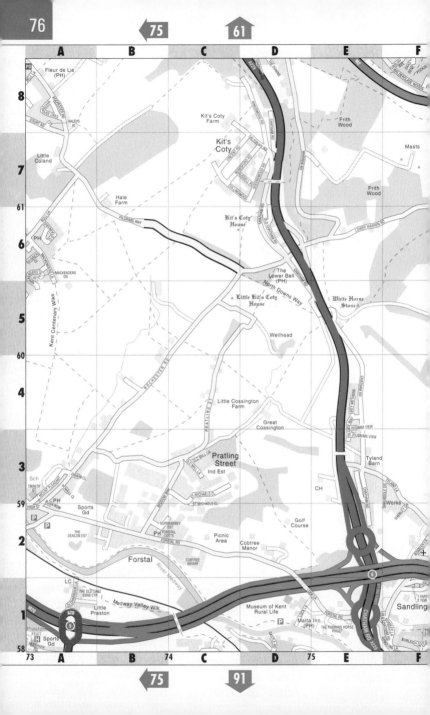

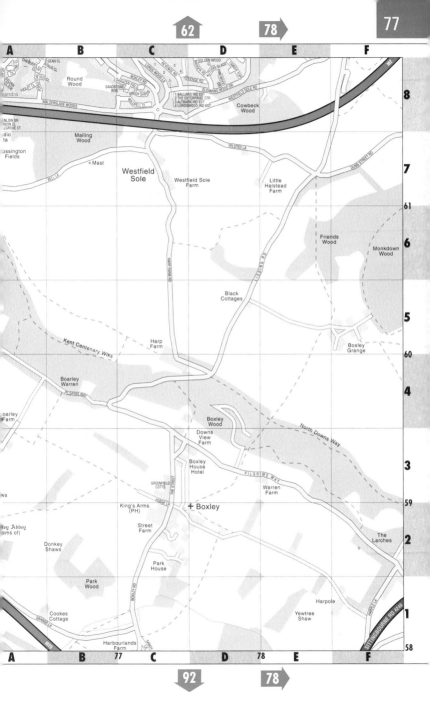

A   B   C   D   E   F

8

Dunn
Street

Bennetts
Cotts

Manor
Farm

Magpie
Farm

Little
Magpie
Farm

Cockhill
Farm

7

Arran Bank
Farm

Bredhurst
Hurst

Oak
Farm

Scragged
Oak

Cockhill
Wood

61

Monkdown
Wood

Scragged Oak
Farm

Lower Cox
Street

Barngarth
Farm

Beaux Aires
Wood

FOX RD

6

SCRAGGED OAK RD

Court
Farm

Newlands
Wood

5

Pollyfields
Farm

COURT LA

Challenge
Farm

Sewage
Works

60

Depot

4

Eight Acre
Wood

High Noon
Farm

PENFOLD LA

Stockings
Wood

Murrain
Wood

3

Amber
Wood

Mount
House

Kent
County Show
Ground

Beacon

Forsters

Highland
Garage

Resrs

Scragged Oak
Caravan Pk

BROAD LA

Murrain
Place

59

Penny Spring
Farm

Mast

Friningham
Manor

2

The
Lynch

DETLING HILL

Gorse Tor
Farm

CASTLE HILL

North Downs Way

A249 SITTINGBOURNE RD

East
Court

Detling

1

Detling
CE Prim Sch

PH

PO

PILGRIMS WAY

ST MARTINS CLOSE

Thurnham
Castle

Civiley
Wood

58

79   A   80   B   C   D   81   E   F

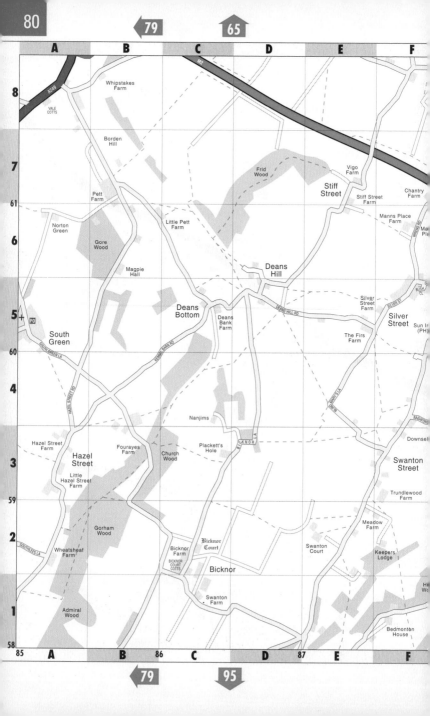

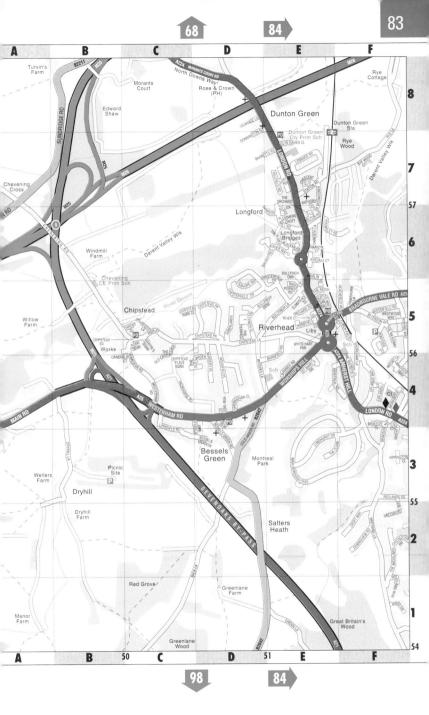

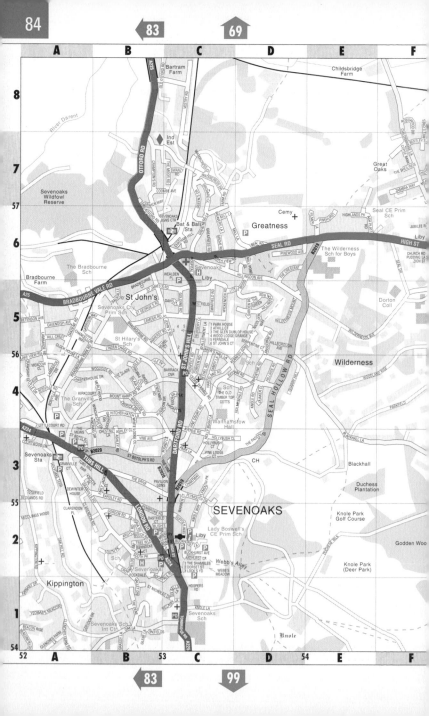

70

86

A   **B**   **C**   **D**   **E**   **F**

Noah's Ark

Penfield

Cockney's Wood

CHAUCER IND PK

Kemsing Sta

HONEYPOT LA

GREEN HILLS RD

NOAH'S ARK

CHURCH ST

Tanners Cross

WATERY LA

Stonepitts

8

7

57

eal

Fullers Hill Farm

Broomsleigh

Chart Farm

6

Oldbury Hill

MAIDSTONE RD

GROVE RD

The Grove

CACKET RD

PILGRIM RD

Larchwood Farm

Styants Bottom

STYANTS BOTTOM RD

Oldbury Wood

5

56

Idernesse olf Course

Chance Wood

PARK HILL

Seal Chart

Redhill Wood

Styants Wood

P

SEVENOAKS RD

A25

4

CH

Hanger Wood

Frankfield House

Crown Point Inn (PH)

Hall Place

Buck's Head (PH)

FOX LA

Godden Green

The Padwell (PH)

STONE STREET RD

CHURCH RD

Seal,St Lawrence CE Prim Sch

Fish Ponds Wood

Raspit Hill

3

55

Great Roger's Wood

Stone Street

Rose & Crown (PH)

2

Stake Farm

Lord's Spring Wood

Diantshatch Wood

PINES LA

Sevenoaks Prep Sch

Rambles Wood

Lower Bitchet

Bitchet Green

1

54

A   **B**   56   **C**   **D**   57   **E**   **F**

100

86

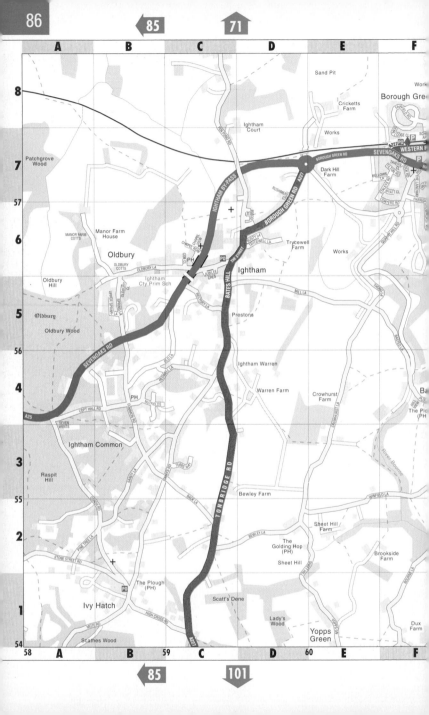

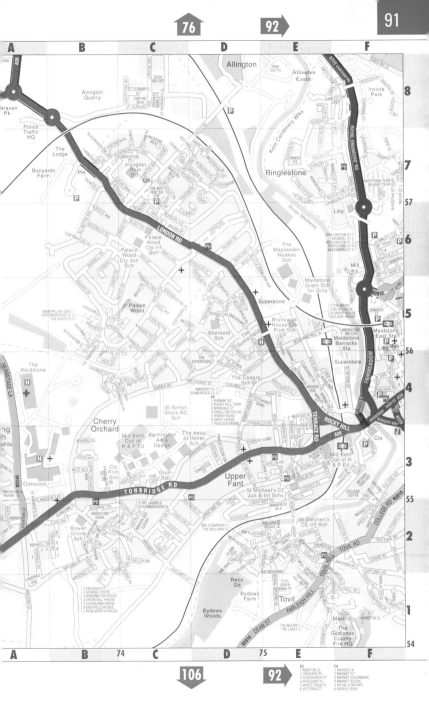

Allington

Allington Quarry

Allington Castle

Invicta Park

Police Traffic HQ

Caravan Pk

The Lodge

Bunyards Farm

PH

Kent Centenary Wlks

Ringlestone

Allington Prim Sch

Liby

The Mid Kent Sch

River Medway

Liby

LONDON RD

Palace Wood Cty Inf Sch

Palace Wood Cty Jun Sch

The Maplesden Noakes Sch

Drillington St 1
Arundel St 2
Wellington St 3
Thirlstone Ct 4
Alexandra St 5

Mill

Palace Wood

Superstore

1 The Mews
2 Ruth House
3 Garrot House
4 Claire House

Maidstone Gram Sch for Girls

Staceys

The Somerfield

Shernold Sch

Brunswick House Cty Prim Sch

Maidstone Barracks Sta

Maidstone East Sta

Liby Mus

The Maidstone

H

The Cedars Sch

Amherst Cl 1
Somerfield Cl 2
1 Burnam Sq
2 Rocky Hill Terr
3 Birkdale Ct
4 Swallow House
5 Robin House
6 Swift House
7 Peacock Mews

Superstore

The Sovereigns

The Spires

Cherry Orchard

St Simon Stock RC Sch

Mid Kent Coll of H & F Ed

Kent Inst of Art & Design

The Astor of Hever Sch

ROCKY HILL

Mid Kent Coll of H & F Ed

Oakwood

Cty Prim Sch

Gram Sch

Upper Fant

Pembury Gdns

Cts

College Cotts

Bower Grove Sch

TONBRIDGE RD

1 The Laurels
2 Farnborough Cl

St Michael's CE Jun & Inf Schs

St Stephen's CE Inf Sch

1 The Stampers 1
2 The Spillway 2

Millers Wharf

Recn Gd

Bydews Farm

Tovil

St Andrew's RD

The Meadows

TOVIL HILL

TOVIL RD

Bydews Woods

Bydews Farm

The Quern 1
The Laxey 2

FARLEIGH HILL

DEAN ST

Mast

The Godlands County Fire HQ

E3
1 NEWTON CL
2 ORCHARD PL
3 OLDCHURCH CT
4 RYECOURT CL
5 WHITE ROCK PL
6 VICTORIA CT

F4
1 HAVOCK LA
2 MARKET ST
3 MARKET COLONNADE
4 MARKET BLDGS
5 ROYAL STAR ARC
6 MIDDLE ROW

92

A5
1 MANDEVILLE CT
2 CRUNDALE
3 WALMER CT
4 PRIORY GATE
5 STARNES CT
6 LAMBARD HOUSE
7 WINCHESTER PL
8 LOWER BOKLEY RD
A6
1 TELFORD HOUSE
2 WALSHAM HOUSE
3 WALSINGHAM HOUSE

← 91

A7
1 ADEN TERR
2 BARBADOS TERR
3 CANADA TERR
4 NORWAY TERR
5 MALTA TERR
6 LIBYA TERR

↑ 77

A7
7 KENYA TERR
8 HONDURAS TERR

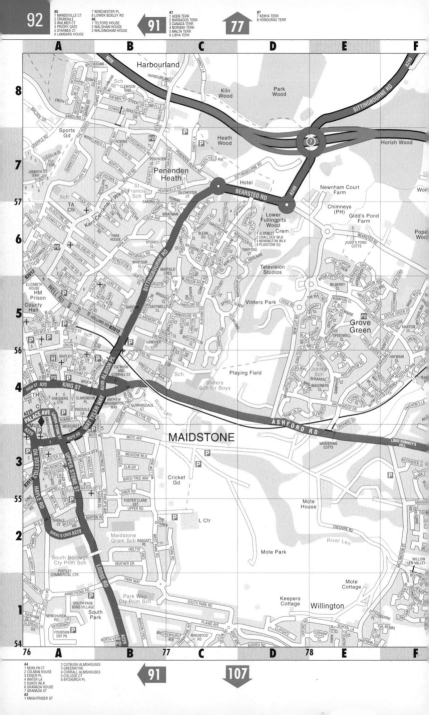

A4
1 NEWLYN CT
2 COLMAN HOUSE
3 EDGER PL
4 WATER LA
5 DUKES WLK
6 GRANADA HOUSE
7 GRANADA ST
A3
1 KNIGHTRIDER ST
2 CUTBUSH ALMSHOUSES
3 GREENHITHE
4 CORRALL ALMSHOUSES
5 COLLEGE CT
6 BYCHURCH PL

← 91   107

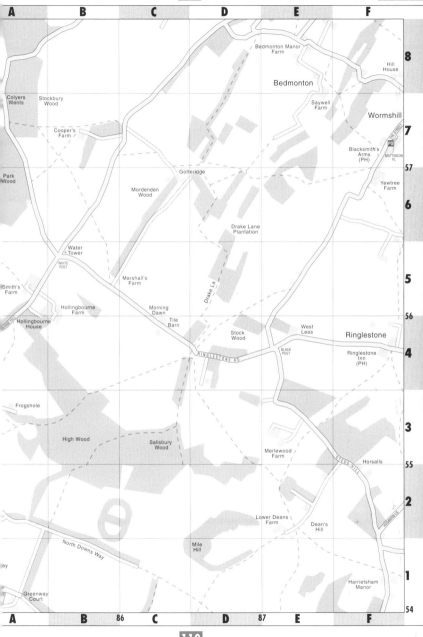

A B C D E F

8 Bedmonton Manor Farm

Hill House

Bedmonton

Colyers Wents

Stockbury Wood

Saywell Farm

Wormshill 7

Cooper's Farm

PO

Blacksmith's Arms (PH)

MATTINSON PL

THE STREET

57

Park Wood

Gotteridge

Mordenden Wood

Yewtree Farm

6

Drake Lane Plantation

Water Tower

WHITE POST

Marshall's Farm

5

Smith's Farm

Drake La

Hollingbourne Farm

Morning Dawn

Tile Barn

Stock Wood

West Leas

56

Hollingbourne House

Ringlestone 4

RINGLESTONE RD

BLACK POST

Ringlestone Inn (PH)

Frogshole

High Wood

Salisbury Wood

3

Merlewood Farm

Horsalls

STLOE HILL

55

2

Lower Deans Farm

Dean's Hill

Mile Hill

North Downs Way

1

Harrietsham Manor

Greenway Court

54

A B 86 C D 87 E F

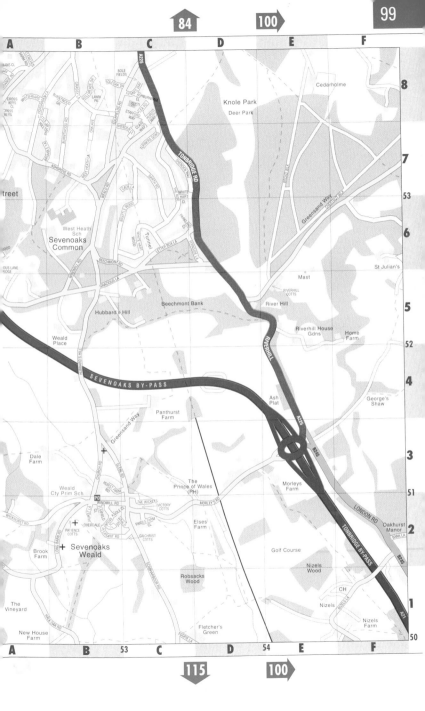

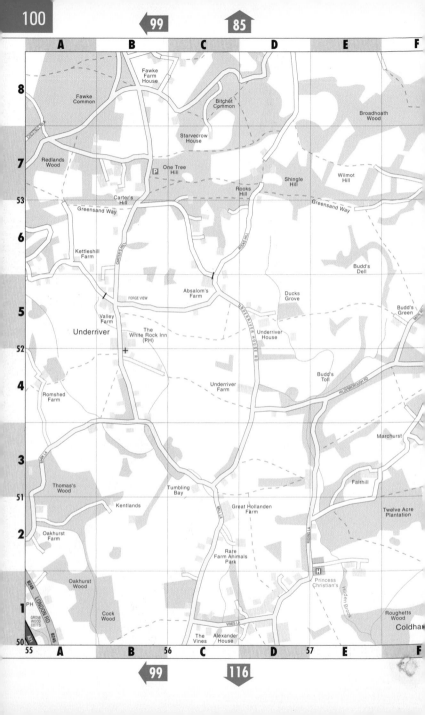

A B C D E F

8

Fawke
Farm
House

Fawke
Common

Bitchet
Common

Broadhoath
Wood

7

Starvecrow
House

Redlands
Wood

One Tree
Hill

Shingle
Hill

Wilmot
Hill

53

Carter's
Hill

Rooks
Hill

Greensand Way

Greensand Way

6

Kettleshill
Farm

Budd's
Dell

Absalom's
Farm

Ducks
Grove

Budd's
Green

5

FORGE VIEW

Valley
Farm

The White Rock Inn
(PH)

Underriver
House

Underriver

52

Budd's
Toll

4

Romshed
Farm

Underriver
Farm

Marchurst

3

Thomas's
Wood

Fairhill

51

Tumbling
Bay

Kentlands

Great Hollanden
Farm

Twelve Acre
Plantation

2

Oakhurst
Farm

Rare
Farm Animals
Park

Princess
Christian's

Roughetts
Wood

1

Oakhurst
Wood

Cock
Wood

Coldha

PH

GROVE
WOOD
COTTS

LONDON RD

Hilden Brook

50

The
Vines

Alexander
House

VINES LA

55 A B 56 C D 57 E F

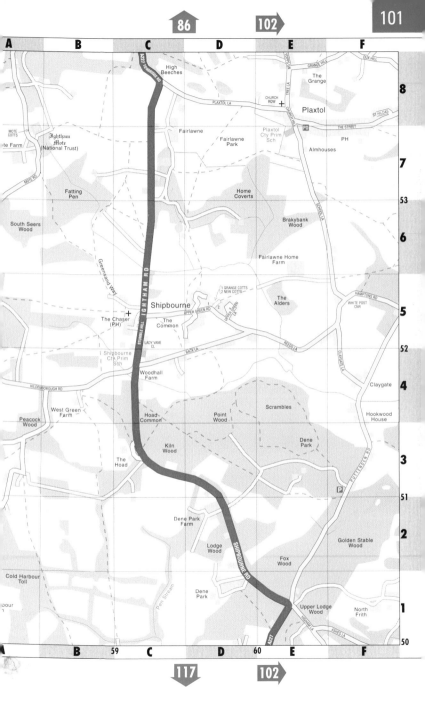

A | **B** | **C** | **D** | **E** | **F**

A227 TONBRIDGE RD

High Beeches

MOTE COTTS

Mote Farm

Ightham Mote (National Trust)

MOTE RD

Fatting Pen

South Seers Wood

Greensand Way

IGHTHAM RD

STUMBLE HILL

The Chaser (PH)

Shipbourne

The Common

Lady Vane Cl

Shipbourne Cty Prim Sch

HILDENBOROUGH RD

West Green Farm

Peacock Wood

Hoad Common

Kiln Wood

The Hoad

Dene Park Farm

Lodge Wood

Cold Harbour Toll

Pen Stream

Dene Park

SHIPBOURNE RD

Fox Wood

A227

Fairlawne

Fairlawne Park

Home Coverts

PLAXTOL LA

CHURCH ROW

THREE LA

GRANGE HILL

DUX HILL

The Grange

Plaxtol

CHURCH HILL

Plaxtol Cty Prim Sch

ST HILLAS

THE STREET

PO

PH

Almhouses

SCHOOL LA

Brakybank Wood

Fairlawne Home Farm

1 GRANGE COTTS
2 NEW COTTS

UPPER GREEN RD

UPPER GREEN LA

The Alders

HAMPTONS RD

WHITE POST CNR

White Post Cnr

REEDS LA

BACK LA

Woodhall Farm

CLAYGATE LA

Claygate

Scrambles

Point Wood

Hookwood House

Dene Park

P

POTTERY LA

P

Golden Stable Wood

Upper Lodge Wood

North Frith

HIGH LA

ASHES LA

A | **B** | 59 | **C** | **D** | 60 | **E** | **F**

8 | 53 | 7 | 6 | 5 | 52 | 4 | 3 | 51 | 2 | 1 | 50

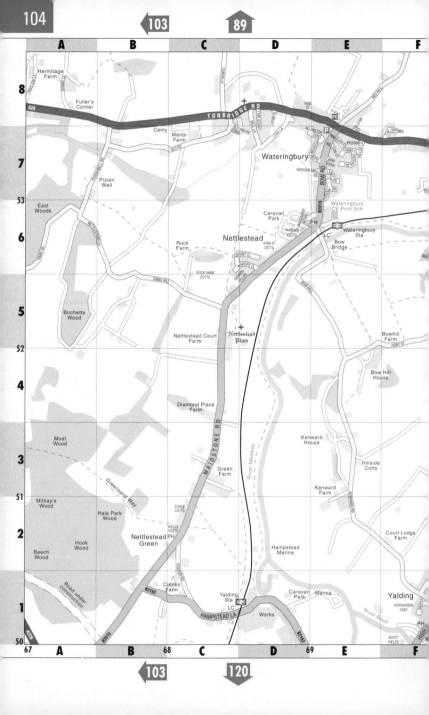

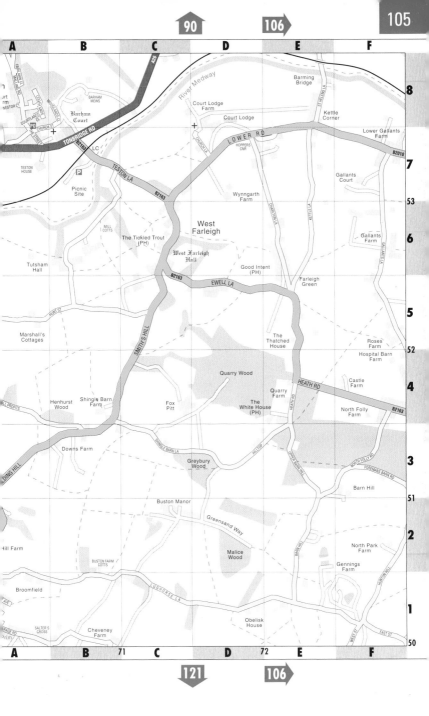

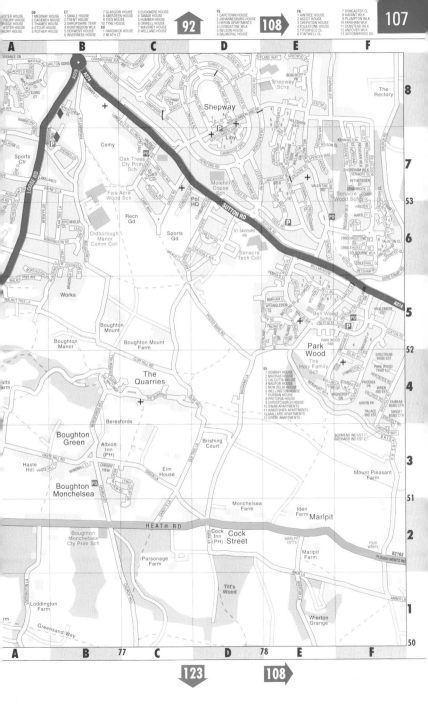

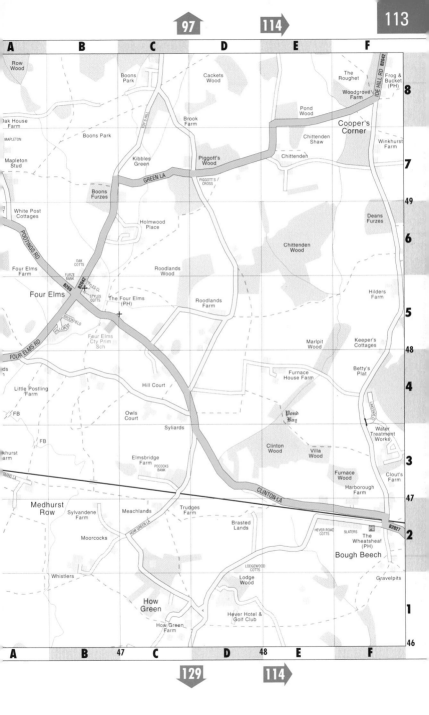

8

7

49

6

48

4

3

47

2

1

46

A   B   C   D   E   F

Faulkners Hill Farm

Bushes Wood

Bushes Plantation

Winkhurst Green

Nature Reserve

Bushes Farm

Nature Centre

Bore Place

Deans Wood

Field Trail

Sharp's Place

Batfold Wood

Kilnhouse Farm

The Old Forge

Little Sidcup

Hale Farm

Bough Beech Resr

Bushy Wood

Damper's Wood

Hickens

Brownings Cottage

Brownings Farm

CH

Mountjoy Farm

HALE OAK RD

Polebrook Farm

Cole's Farm

Breeches Wood

Birdfield Plantation

Waterlake

The Horseshoes

Camp Hill

Waterlake Cottage

Somerden

Chiddingstone Causeway

CHEQUERS HILL COTTS THE GLEBE

Jessop's Farm

Baldocks

B2027

Trad Est

PO

River Eden

Ppg Sta

Chested Farm

Beckett's Farm

Penshur Sta

Mill Farm

Chested

Sandhole

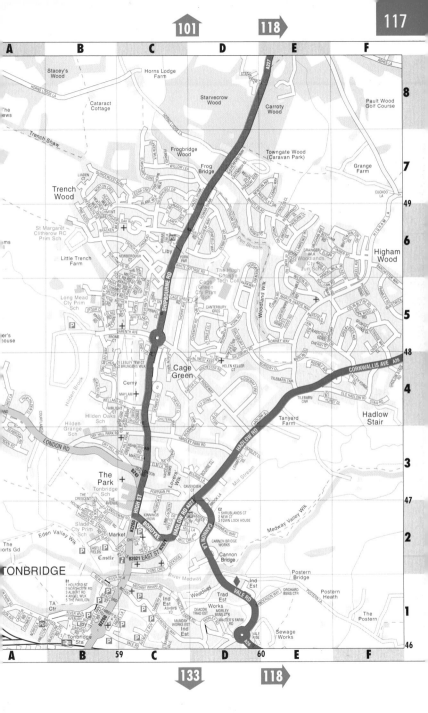

8

Three Squirrels (PH)

Pittswood

Nursery

PITTSWOOD COTTS

The Poult House

Pitt's Wood

Rhoden Farm

The Rose Revived (PH)

The Hermitage

Bourne Grange Farm

Hadlow Coll of Agriculture & Horticulture

Nursery

Faulkners Farm

High St

PH

Hadlow Castle

CAXTON LA

Prim Sch
Liby

ALMA

COURT LANE PL

THE TICKSTAL

COURT LA

HAILSTONE CL 1
POUND HOUSE 2
THE SQUARE 3
THE BROADWAY 4
CASTLE TERR 5
LITTLEFIELD 6
KENWARD CT 7

7

TONBRIDGE RD

Faulkners

Cuckoo Farm

CUCKOO LA

49

Parker's Green

Sewage Works

Bourneside Farm

River Bourne

6

Applegarth Farm

The Carpenters Arms (PH)

Honeycroft Farm

THREE ELM LA

Easterfield Farm

Titheward

PH

HADLOW RD

5

Hadlow Place House

Hadlow Place Farm

BELL ROW

G
G

Goldhill House

48

A26

Little Fish Hall

Fish Hall

Hadlow Place Farmhouse

Goldhill Farm

4

Hartlake Cottages

Hartlake Barn

Medway Valley Wlk

Mill Stream

3

Wealdway

River Medway

Hartlake Bridge

Ottershaw

HARTLAKE RD

47

2

Hammer Dyke

1

Postern Park

Wenhams Farm

Latter's Farm

Sherenden Farm

Tudeley Hale

SHERENDEN RD

Upper Postern Oast

Hale Farm

The Hartlake (PH)

46

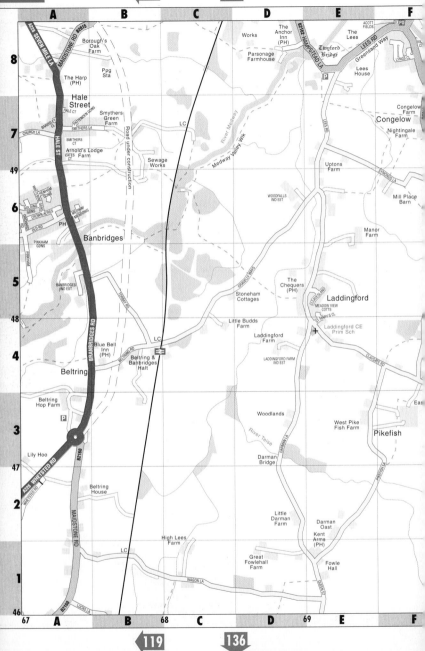

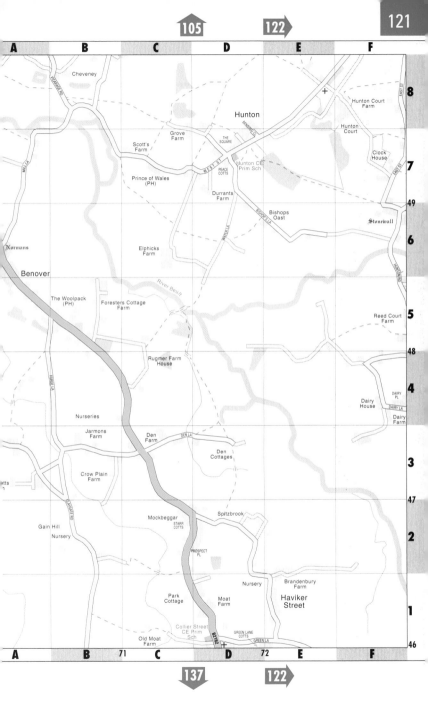

A B C D E F

8

Cheveney

Hunton

Hunton Court Farm

Hunton Court

Grove Farm

THE SQUARE

Scott's Farm

Clock House

7

WEST ST

PEACE COTTS

Hunton CE Prim Sch

Prince of Wales (PH)

Durrants Farm

49

Bishops Oast

Stonewall

Normans

WATER LA

BRIDGE LA

Elphicks Farm

6

Benover

River Beult

The Woolpack (PH)

Foresters Cottage Farm

Reed Court Farm

5

Rugmer Farm House

48

DAIRY PL

Nurseries

Dairy House

DAIRY LA

4

Dairy Farm

Jarmons Farm

Den Farm

DEN LA

Den Cottages

Crow Plain Farm

3

Spitzbrook

47

Mockbeggar

STARR COTTS

Gain Hill Nursery

PROSPECT PL

Nursery

Brandenbury Farm

2

Haviker Street

Park Cottage

Moat Farm

1

Collier Street CE Prim Sch

GREEN LANE COTTS

GREEN LA

Old Moat Farm

46

A B 71 C D 72 E F

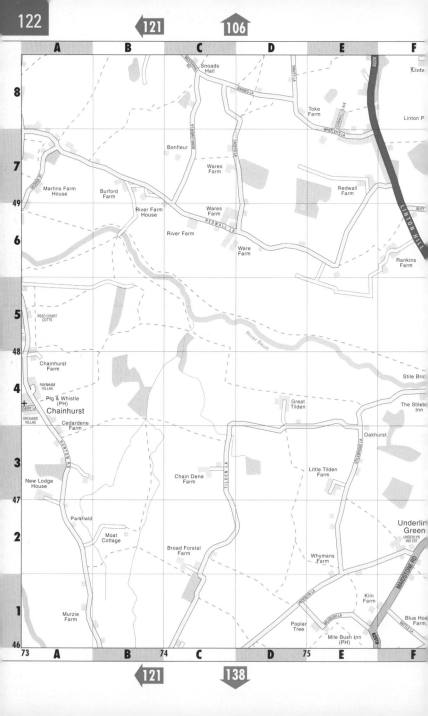

Snoads
Hall

Linto

Toke
Farm

Linton P

Bonfleur

Wares
Farm

Redwall
Farm

Martins Farm
House

Burford
Farm

River Farm
House

Wares
Farm

REDWALL LA

River Farm

Ware
Farm

Rankins
Farm

REED COURT
COTTS

River Beult

Chainhurst
Farm

Stile Bric

RAYNHAM
VILLAS

Pig & Whistle
(PH)

Chainhurst

The Stileb
Inn

Great
Tilden

DAIRY LA

ORCHARD
VILLAS

Cedardene
Farm

Oakhurst

New Lodge
House

Chain Dene
Farm

Little Tilden
Farm

TILDEN LA

Parkfield

Underlin
Green

UNDERLYN
IND EST

Moat
Cottage

Broad Forstal
Farm

Whymans
Farm

MAIDSTONE RD

Kiln
Farm

Murzie
Farm

Blue Hou
Farm

Poplar
Tree

Mile Bush Inn
(PH)

123
108

	A	B	C	D	E	F

8
Ambercourt
Ladds Court Farm
Chart Hill
Underhill Jun Sch
Court Farmhouse
Greensand Way
Sports Gd
Haven Farm
NORTH ST
Sports Gd
Sutton Valence Cty Prim Sch
Sutton Valence Sch

7
Heronden
CHART HILL RD
Parkhouse Farm
CHART RD
SCHOOL LA
Liby
HIGH ST
BROAD ST
LOWER RD
THE PLATT
TUMBLERS HILL
G

49
RECTORY LA
Rectory Farm
Coombe Farm
Sutton Valence
Stallance

6
LUCKS LA
Noons Farm
Place Wood
SOUTH LA
CHURCH RD
THE HARBOUR

5
LAMB'S CROSS
Brookside
Spark's Hall
Sewage Works
The Harbour
HENIKER LA
HEADCORN RD

48
White House Farm
GREEN LA
Brook House

4
Moat Farm
Lake Farm
Gladwish Farm
Thornhill Farm

3
Devil's Den
Sutton Gate Farm
Lake Farm
Golden Acres Farm

47
Ashurst Court
Lower Farm

2
BABYLON LA
Parkenden
NEW BARN RD
Moa

1
Dunbury Farm
Viney Farm
Richmond Farm
Farthing Green
Greenways Farm
South Point Farm
Moater Man
Moatenden Farm

46
Babylon Farm

79	A	B	80	C	D	81	E	F

123
140

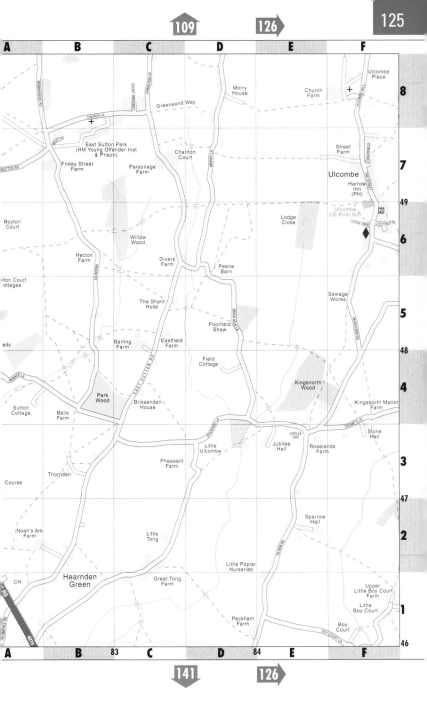

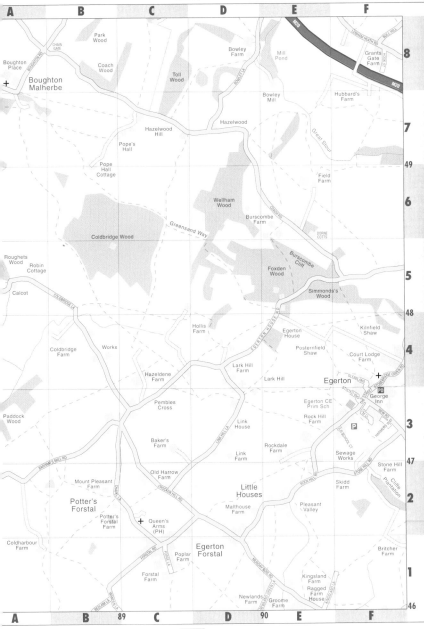

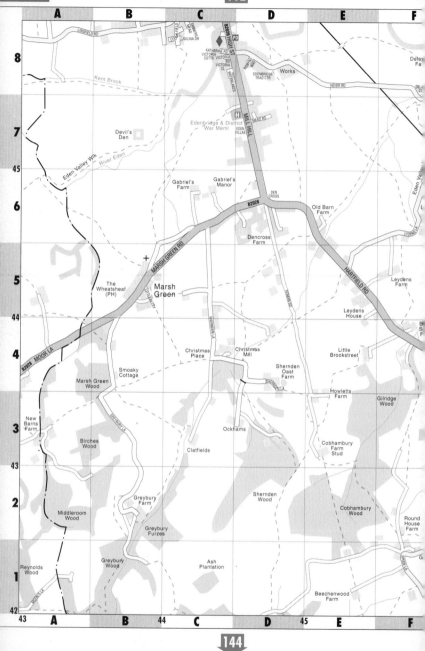

A **B** **C** **D** **E** **F**

8

7

45

6

5

44

4

3

43

2

1

42

43 **A** **B** 44 **C** **D** 45 **E** **F**

LINGFIELD RD

Kent Brook

Devil's
Den

Eden Valley Wlk

River Eden

KATHERINE RD
VICTORIA
COTTS
RED
VICTORIA
VICTORIA

EDENBRIDGE
TRAD CTR

Works

HEVER RD

Delay
Fa

DEL

Edenbridge & District
War Meml

MILL HILL
MEAD RD
EDEN
VILLAS

H

Gabriel's
Farm

Gabriel's
Manor

DEN
CROSS

B2028

Old Barn
Farm

Eden Valley

LYONS LA

MARSH GREEN RD

Marsh
Green

Dencross
Farm

The Wheatsheaf
(PH)

COTTAGE LA

HARTFIELD RD

Leydens
Farm

Leydens
House

B2028

MOOR LA

Smoaky
Cottage

Marsh Green
Wood

Christmas
Place

Christmas
Mill

TOWAN RD

Shernden
Oast
Farm

SHERNDEN LA

Little
Brookstreet

B
S F

New
Barns
Farm

OXENEY LA

SHERNDEN LA

Howletts
Farm

Gilridge
Wood

Birches
Wood

Ockhams

Clatfields

Cobhambury
Farm
Stud

Middleroom
Wood

Greybury
Farm

Greybury
Furzes

Shernden
Wood

Cobhambury
Wood

Round
House
Farm

Reynolds
Wood

MOON LA

Greybury
Wood

Ash
Plantation

Beechenwood
Farm

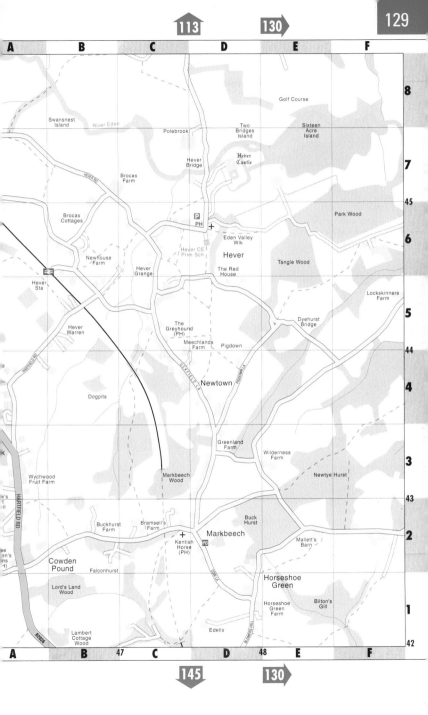

129
114

	A	B	C	D	E	F

8

River Eden

Mill Shaw

Somerden Green

7

Gilwyns

Chiddingstone

Larkin's Farm

Hampkins Hill

Vexour Bridge

Vexour

River Eden

Castle Inn (PH)

Chiddingstone CE Prim Sch

45

Chiddingstone Castle

6

THRESHER FIELD

Moor Wood

Hill Hoath

Chantlers

BOURNE ROW

Hill Hoath Farm

Eden Valley Wlk

Weller's Town

SOUTH ROW

Mounters

5

The Slips

Gillridge

Double Cottag

44

Sliders

Stock Wood

Robins Land

Lew Cross Cotts

Wat Stock

4

Trugger's Gill

Salmans Farm

River Eden

Trugger's Farm

The Rock Inn (PH)

Yewtree Wood

Russell's Wood

Harden Cottage

3

Hoath Corner

Puckden Wood

43

Harden Farmhouse

Penshurst Vinyard

2

Chiddingstone Hoath

Oakenden Farm

Oakenden

Vine Cottage

Hoath House

Stonewall Wood

Courtlands Wood

LONDON RD

South Park Wood

The Rangers

Brookers Farm House

Stonewall Park

1

Bottle House (PH)

BOTTLE HOUSE COTTS

42

| 49 | A | | B | 50 | C | | D | 51 | E | | F |

129
146

A B C D E F

8

The Round House

Lilley Farm

B2017 TUDELEY LA

Somerhill Mews and Stud

7 Tudeley

Bank Farm

SHEPHERDS RD

HARTLAKE RD

The Toll

Park Farm

The Carpenters (PH)

45 MILLERS COTTS

Brampton Bank

Tatlingb

FIVE OAK GREEN RD

George & Dragon (PH)

Shepherds Cottage

6 Crockhurst Street

Halfmoon Wood

ALDERS RD

Burgess Rough

Old Furze Field

Rushpit Wood

The Plants

C

5 Boys Wood

Knowles Bank

44 Bouncers Bank

Amhurst Bank

High Weald WLK

4 Brakeybank Wood

DISLINGBURY RD

Dislingbury Farm

CASTLE HILL

A21

Potter's Wood

Kenward

Amhurst Hill Farm

AMHURST BANK RD

3 Well Wood

Kent Coll

Hawkwell Farm

PEMBURY HALL RD

43 Pembury Hall

MAIDSTO

Litt Hawk Far

PEMBURY RD

2 Pembury Walks

PEMBURY WLK

Alder Stream

OLD CHURCH RD

REDWINGS LA

MAIDSTONE RD

HAWKWELL COTTS

Colebrooke

Yew Tree Farm

Rowley Hill

1 A21

Downingbury

Pippin

STONE CT (OLD CHURCH)

ELMHURST LA

STONE COURT LA

Stone Court Farm

42 CAMBRIDGE RD

A228

GAMBLE WAY

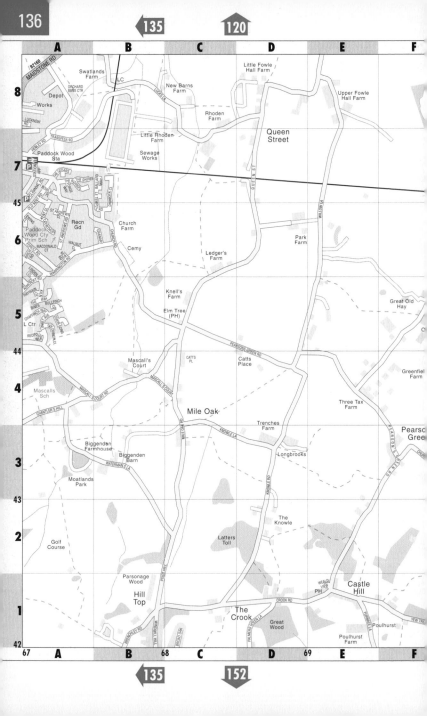

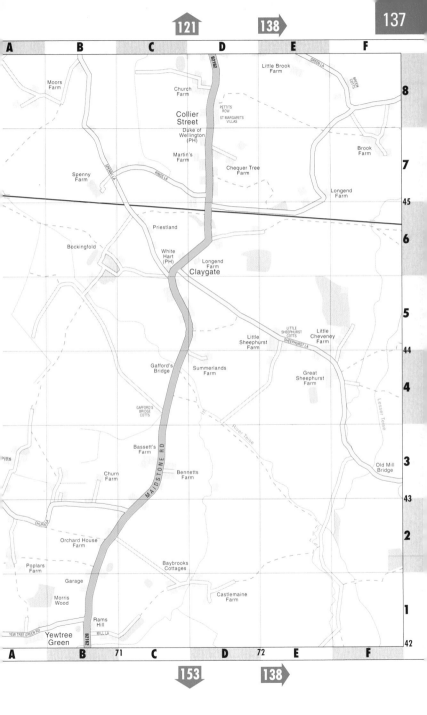

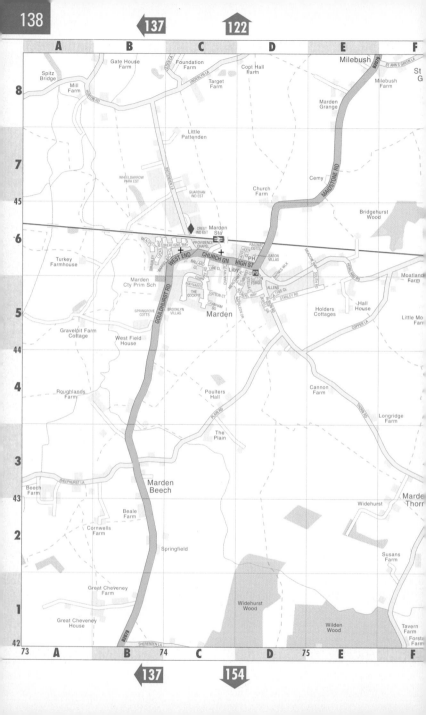

123
140

A B C D E F

8

Little Crew Den

Allingham
Farm

Sundridge
Nurseries

Sweetlands
Farm

MAIDSTONE RD A229

Clapper
Farm

7

Newhaven
Farm

Wanshurst
Green

45

Springfield
Cottage

Abbotsleigh

Knowles
Hill

6

Overbridge
Farm

Duckhurst
Farm

Sewage
Works

NEWTOWN
COTTS

Staplehurst
Sta

LINDRIDGE LA

Mountain
Farmhouse

HONEYCREST
IND PK

PH

Fisher's
Farm

Lindridge

Limekiln
Farm

Works

STATION RD

5

Fouracre

44

Baldwins
Farm

Hen &
Duckhurst
Farm

1 BENDEN CL
2 WEAVERS CL
3 KNOWLES WLK

4

Staplehurst

MARIAN SQ

Great Pagehurst
Farm

Aydhurst
Farm

BOWER WLK

Staplehurst
Cty Prim
Sch
Liby

Little
Pagehurst

3

The Wild Duck
(PH)

CHAPEL LA

HIGH ST

Dourne
Farm

PAGEHURST RD

KIRKMAN CT

43

2

CRANBROOK RD A229

FRITTENDEN RD

The
Laurels

Clarkes
Farm

Brattle
Farm Mus

Henhurst
Farm

The
Quarter

Iden Park

1

FIVE OAK LA

Saynden
Farm

Ely Court

Gooseberry
Wood

42

A B 77 C D 78 E F

155
140

139
124

A   **B**   **C**   **D**   **E**   **F**

8

Forge Farm

Bardingley

New Barn Farm

Four Oaks Wood

Hawkenbury

New Barn Wood

Four Oaks

PLUMTREE RD

Sweetlands Couchman Green

7

Leighbridge Farm

POST OAK RD

NEW BARN RD

Newstead Farm

Hawkenbury Farm

45

The Hare & Hounds (PH)

Boarden Farm

Little Hawkenbury

6

HAWKENBURY RD

Hawkenbury Bridge

Turley Farm

Kelsham Farm

5

River Beult

Slaney Place

44

Cottons Farm

Spills Hill Farm

Place Farm

Works

WOODS RD

4

Sunny Mead

Chickenden Farm

Crab Tree Farm

Oak Tree Farm

CRADDOCKS LA

Spilsill Farm

3

Spilsill Court

Bailey Farm

Little Craddock

43

Exhurst Manor

2

FRITTENDEN RD

Folly Farm

Nursery

Sinkhurst Green

Applet Farm Hous.

Pullen Barn

PARK WOOD LA

Staplehurst Manor

1

Park Wood

Broadlake

STAPLEHURST RD

Sandhurst Bridge Farm

Maplehurst Farm

MILL LA

The Twins

Sandhurst Bridge

42

SANDHURST CROSS

79   **A**   **B**   80   **C**   **D**   81   **E**   **F**

139
156

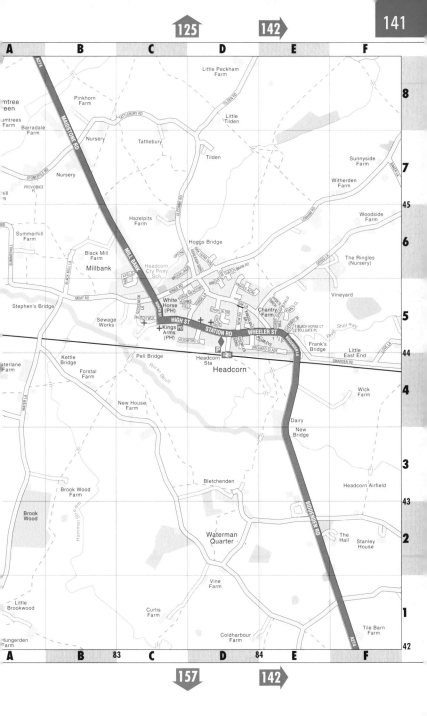

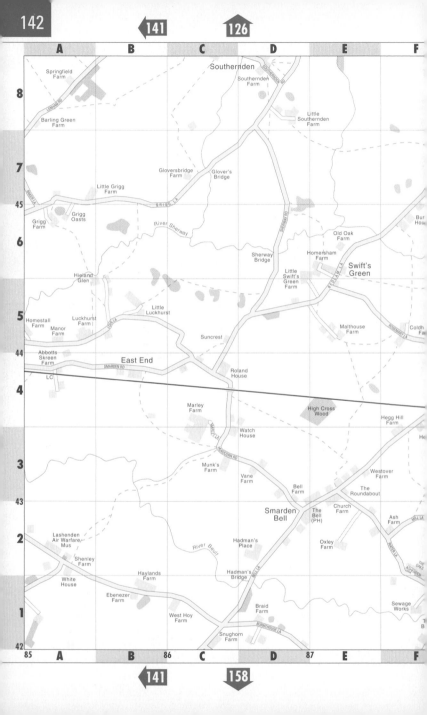

ark Hill
Farm

Box
Farm

Newland
Green

MUNDAY BOIS
COTTS

Oak's
Farm

8

Heronsdale

Wanden
Farm

Acorn
Wood

Shaw
Farm

Munday
Bois

Appleby
Farm

Little
Mundy
Bois Farm

Weeks
Farm

gsden
Farm

Wanden

Little
Wanden

Wheeler
Wood

Woodland
Farm

Alfred
Wood

Rose &
Crown
(PH)

7

45

Stace
Wood

Frith
Wood

Frith
Farm

6

Clover
Farm

usins
arm

School
Wood

Kite
Farm

Park
Farm

The
Quarter

Oaklands

Roughland
Wood

Dering Wood

Giles
Farm

5

44

Roughlands

Berry
Court

4

Dering
Lodge

Mount
Pleasant
Farm

Ash
Plantation

Mainey
Wood

Woodside
Farm

3

aw House
Farm

Little
Biddenden
Green Farm

Tilden
Field
Hassock

Tolhurst
Farm

Maltman's
Hill

43

Baker's
Bridge

Dering
Farm

PLUCKLEY RD

Biddenden
Green

Round
Wood

Little
Wood

Mainey
Wood

Mainey
Wood

Snapmill

2

Smarden
Cty Prim
Sch

HASLEWOOD CL

Smarden

Gain
Bridge

Romden

River Beult

Romden
Bridge

Dadson
Farm

1

Vesper Hawk
Farm

Romden
Castle

The
Gorse

Tuesnoad
Farm

42

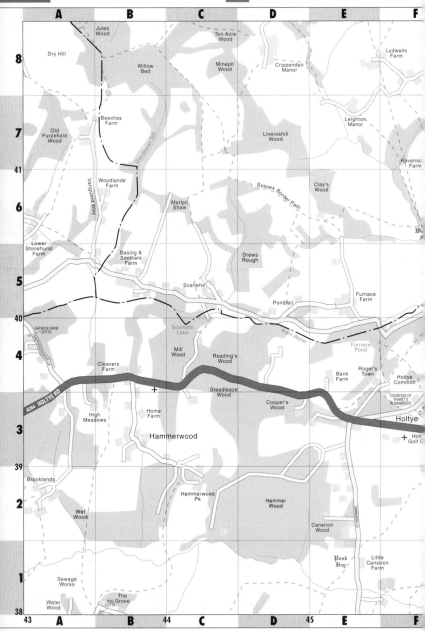

8
7
41
6
5
40
4
39
2
1
38

A B C D E F

Jules Wood
Dry Hill
Ten Acre Wood
Willow Bed
Minepit Wood
Crippenden Manor
Ludwells Farm
Beeches Farm
Old Furzefield Wood
Liveroxhill Wood
Leighton Manor
Ravensc Farm
Gouldhurst Gill
Woodlands Farm
Sussex Border Path
Clay's Wood
Vanguard Way
Marlpit Shaw
Lower Stonehurst Farm
Basing & Smithers Farm
Drews Rough
Scarletts
Furnace Farm
GATWICK FARM COTTS
Pondtail
Kent Water
Scarletts Lake
Furnace Pond
Mill Wood
Reading's Wood
Bank Farm
Roger's Town
Holtye Common
Cleavers Farm
A264 HOLTYE RD
Steadleaze Wood
Cooper's Wood
COUNTESS OF THANET'S ALMSHOUSES
High Meadows
Home Farm
Holtye
Hammerwood
Holt Golf C
Brooklands
Hammerwood Pk
Hammer Wood
Cansiron Wood
Wet Wood
Cansiron La
Pond Bay
Little Cansiron Farm
Sewage Works
The Grove COTTS
Water Wood

43 A B 44 C D 45 E F

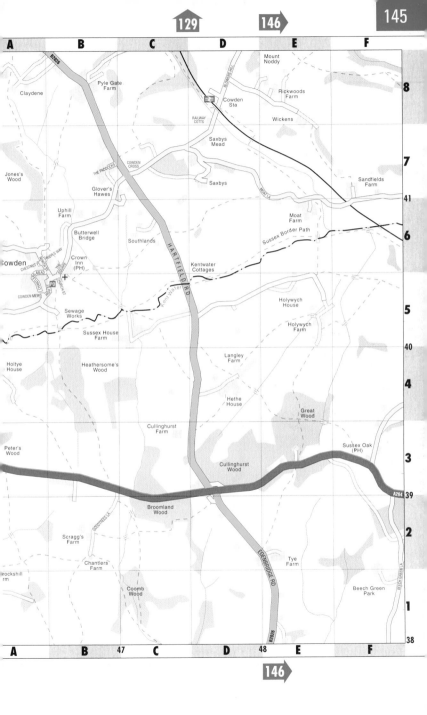

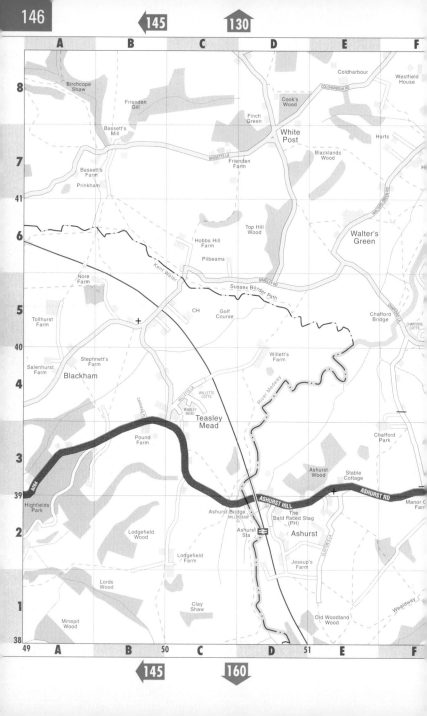

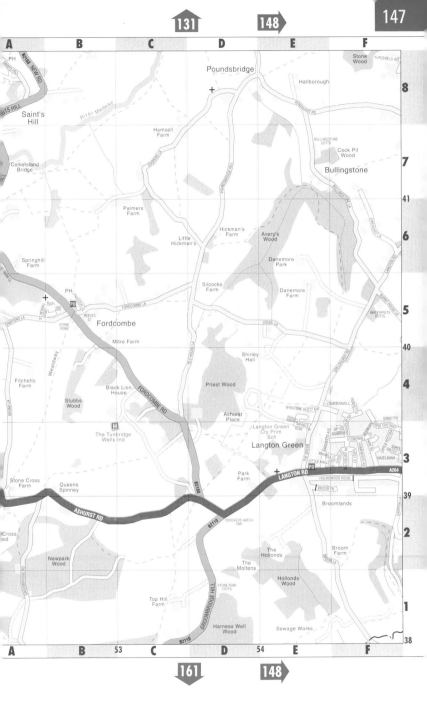

Matfield

Widmore Farm

Nature Reserve

8

The Wheelwrights Arms (PH)

Tutty's Farm

Goshen Farm

Three Towns Farm

Court Farm

Grove Cottage Farm

The Hopbine (PH)

7

Hayes View Farm

Friars Coach House

41

Lodge Farm

Porter's Wood

PORTERS WOOD

Petteridge

MAIDSTONE RD

HUMPHREYS

6

Kings Toll Farm

Matfield Grange

Egypt Farm

Kings Toll Farm

Becketts

Kingsmead

CRYALS CT

Cryals Farm

Beckett's Grove Farm

SOIPURST WOOD

CRYALS RD

Old Cryals

5

Kipping's Cross Farm

Kingsmead Farm

40

Kipping's Cross

Bassetts Farm

COUNCIL COTTS

Blue Boys Inn (PH)

Beechy Wood

4

Key's Green

Marlpit Wood

Hanger Wood

3

Old Farm

39

Swan Farm

Brookland Wood

2

Great Sandhurst Wood

Little Dunks Farm

The Grange

Lindridge Place Farm

Three Horseshoe Farm

Lamberhurst Quarter

1

Little Sandhurst Wood

Little Grange

Lindridge Lodge Farm

A21

38

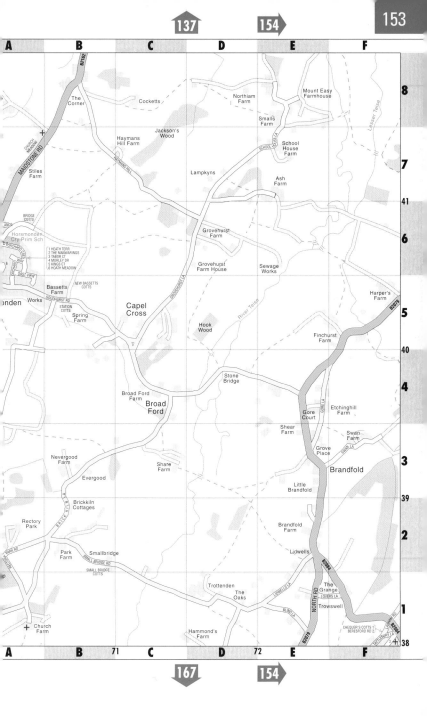

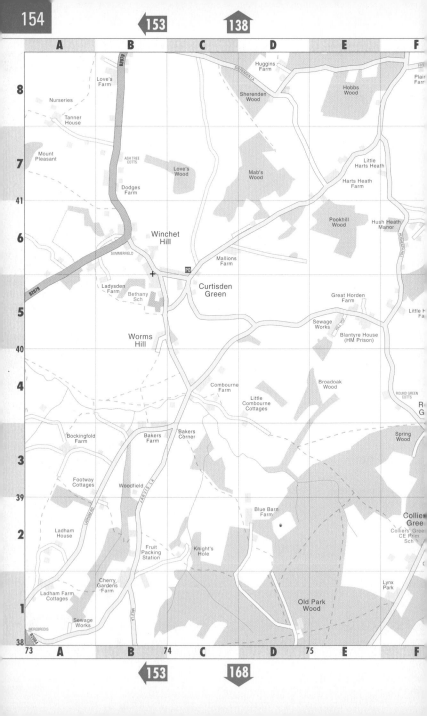

A **B** **C** **D** **E** **F**

8

Love's Farm

Nurseries

Tanner House

Huggins Farm

Sherenden Wood

Hobbs Wood

Plain Farm

7

Mount Pleasant

ASH TREE COTTS

Love's Wood

Dodges Farm

Mab's Wood

Little Harts Heath

Harts Heath Farm

41

6

Winchet Hill

SUMMERFIELD

Mallions Farm

Pookhill Wood

Hush Heath Manor

Ladysden Farm

Bethany Sch

Curtisden Green

Great Horden Farm

5

Worms Hill

Sewage Works

Blantyre House (HM Prison)

Little H Fa

40

4

Combourne Farm

Little Combourne Cottages

Broadoak Wood

ROUND GREEN COTTS

R G

3

Bockingfold Farm

Bakers Farm

Bakers Corner

Spring Wood

39

Footway Cottages

Woodfield

Blue Barn Farm

Collie Gree

2

Ladham House

Fruit Packing Station

Knight's Hole

Colliers' Green CE Prim Sch

Lynx Park

1

Ladham Farm Cottages

Cherry Gardens Farm

Old Park Wood

Sewage Works

MEREBREDIS

38

73 **A** **B** **74** **C** **D** **75** **E** **F**

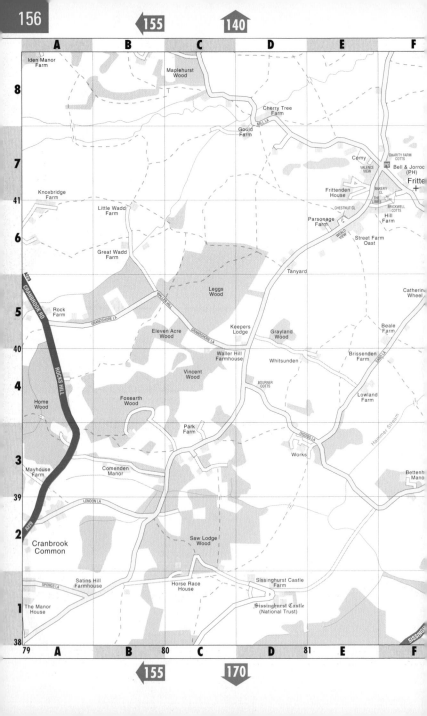

A B C D E F

River Beult

Haffenden
Quarter

Sandhurst
Farm

Blinks
Farm

High
Brooms

Buckman Green
Farm

BIDDENDEN RD

Old Man's
Acre

Romden
Wood

Wissenden
Lodge Farm

Wissenden
House
Farm

Sunnyside
Farm

Wissenden

Tyde Brook
Farm

Bliberry
Wood

Hamden Grange
Farm

Langley

New Langley
Farm

BETHERSDEN RD

Faggs
Mount

Cook
Wood

Odiam
Farm

Tearnden
Farm

Park
Wood

New Langley
Farm

Long's
Corner

Pierson House
Farm

Honeyfield
Wood

Old House
Farm

Gate's
Farm

Potkiln
Farm

Potteries
Farm

DADGET LA

Further
Quarter

Dent's
Farm

GRISBY LA

GRISBY LA

Brickhouse
Farm

Ledger
Farm

Brunger
Farm

Marlands
Farm

Bridge
Farm

Middle
Quarter

Beale's
Farm

CRIPPLE HILL

Ramstile
Farm

8
7
41
6
5
40
4
3
39
2
1
38

89 90

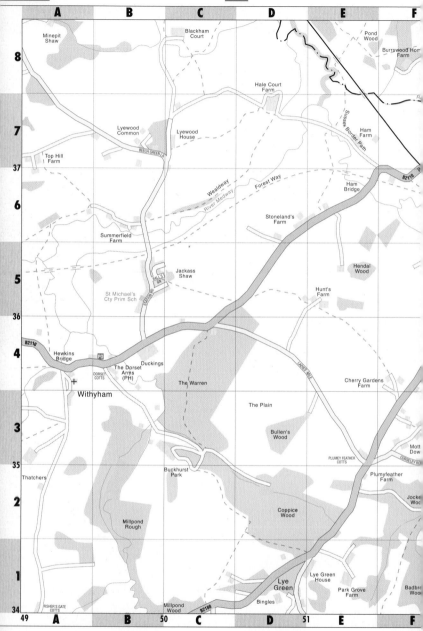

Adam's Well
Crossing

Ramslye
Wood

Ramslye
Farm

EASTLANDS CL

ERIDGE RD A26

Sch

Strawberry
Hill

BROADWATER
CT

BROADWATER DOWN

Broadwater
Down

Ruffet
Wood

The
Firs

Broadwater
Forest

Strawberry Hill
Farm

Spratsbrook
Farm

Hargate
Forest

Broadwater
Lodge

Sprat's Brook

Firtree
Plantation

The
Warren

The
Roundabouts

BUNNY LA

Kennels

Bohemia

Eridge
Rocks

The Nevill
Crest & Gun
(PH)

WARREN FARM LA

Eridge
Park

Eridge
Park

Warren
Farm

Eridge
Green

Crown
House

A26

Mill
Wood

Steel
Bridge

Keepers
Cottages

Steel Bridge
Farm

Forge
Wood

Eridge
Old Park

Bushy
Wood

Great Robbins
Shaw

Bushy
Shaw

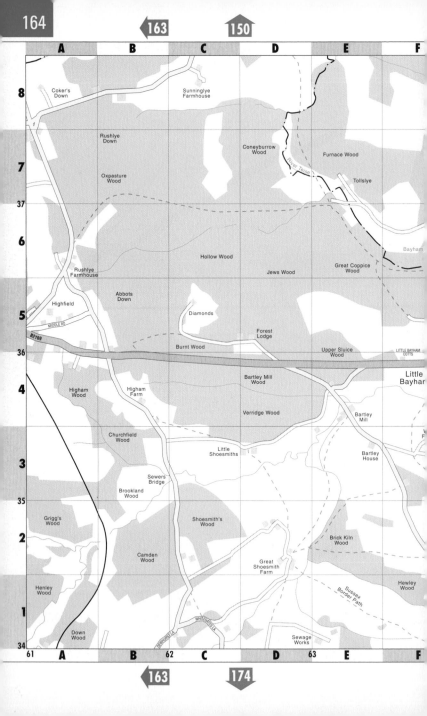

8
A21
Windmill Farm
Hayden Wood
Stunts Wood

Parsonage Wood
A262
The Horizon Farm
Pittsgate Farm
East Wood
LAMBERHURST RD
A21/A21

7
Grantham Hall Farm
Forstal Farm

37
Crooked Wood

6
The Priory Farm
B2162
CHURCH RD
The Priory
CH
MOUNT PLEASANT LA
SCHOOL HILL
PERSIMMON LA
Court Lodge
Fir
Lamberhurst CE Prim Sch
MANOR COTTS
Lamberhurst
Lamberhurst Golf Course

BREWER ST
THE BROADWAY
George & Dragon Inn
River Teise
Foxbury Wood
Little Scotney Farm

5
PO
Chequers Inn
P
Pierce Barn
B2100
HIGH ST
CASTLE LA

36
TOWN HILL
Broadham Wood

4
Ridge Farm
SLADE HILL
Down Farmhouse
SPRAY HILL
Invicta House
PH
B2169 FURNACE LA
FURNACE AVE
Spray Hill Farm
Scotney Castle
River Bewl

3
PROSPECT COTTS
THE SLADE
B2169
The Down
P
Scotney Castle (rems of)
Kilndown Wood

Slade Farm

35
Whiskett's Farm

BEECH LANE

2
B2100
Sweet Bourne
Bewl Bridge
Wiskett's Wood
Bewl Bridge Farm
Bewlbridge

1
Kiln
Poultry
Water Treatment Works
Nursery Farm
A21

34
A21

A   B   C   D   E   F

8

WEALDON VIEW 1
CHURCHILLS ROPEWALK 2
WEAVERS COTTS 3
THE PLAIN 4
CLAY COTTS 5
BALCOMBE COTTS 6

CRANBROOK RD
A262

Crowbourne
Farm

NORTH RD
B2079

CHURCH RD

Star & Eagle
Hotel

Goudhurst & Kilndown CE
Prim Sch

Goudhurst

HIGH ST

CLAYHILL

Bell Farm
Barn

PO

BALCOMBES HILL

Maypole
Farm

MAYPOLE LA

Fruit Packing
Station

River Teise

Little
Meadow

STATION RD

Goudhurst
Hotel

Thatchers
Hall

HIGH RIDGE
MARY DAY'S
BANFIELD
LOVERS RISE
CULPEP

Sewage
Works

BEDGEBURY RD

Whitestocks
Farm

7

37

Riseden

Paine's
Farm
House

Risebridge
Farm

PEASLEY LA

Pattenden
Farm

Whitestocks
Lands

Smugley
Farm

6

Gatehouse
Farm

Trillinghurst
Farm House

Beresford
Lodge

5

Gatehouse

Lillesden
Wood

Marlingate
Farm

Forge
Farm

36

4

Crouch's
Wood

Twyssenden
Farm

Twyssenden
Manor

Larchfield

3

35

ROGERS ROUGH RD

Park
Wood

BEDGEBURY
CROSS

LADY OAK LA

Great
Lake

Bedgebury
Sch

Bedgebury
Park

2

Shearnfold
Wood

B2079

Home
Farm

Lady's
Lake

1

34

A   B   71   C   72   D   E   F

167
154

	A	B	C	D	E	F

8

Chequers Inn (PH)

A262

CRANBROOK RD

Frog's Hole

MILE LA

Iden Green

Paynetts Oast Farm

Lime Tree Farm

Iden Green Farm

Four Wents

Trigg's Farm

The Peacock Inn (PH)

B2085

Flish

7

Gill Wood

Glassenbury Park

37

6

Glassenbury House

Glassenbury

Wenman Cottage

Little Glassenbury

Saffrons

Beech Hill

Angl

5

Windmill House

36

Mast

WT Station

Angley Farm

4

Wet Wood

Blackbush Wood

Hug H

3

Furnace Wood

35

Furnace Farm

2

Pond Bay

Bull Farm

Three Chimneys Bank

RAILWAY COTTS

Hartley

1

Iron Latch

Hall Wood Farm

34

73	A	B	74	C	D	75	E	F

167
178

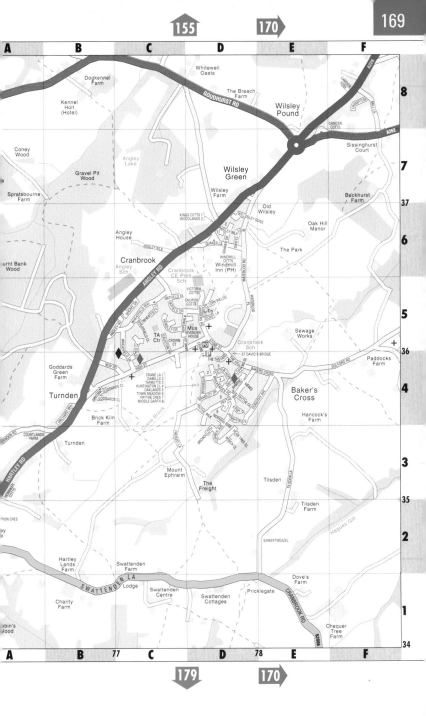

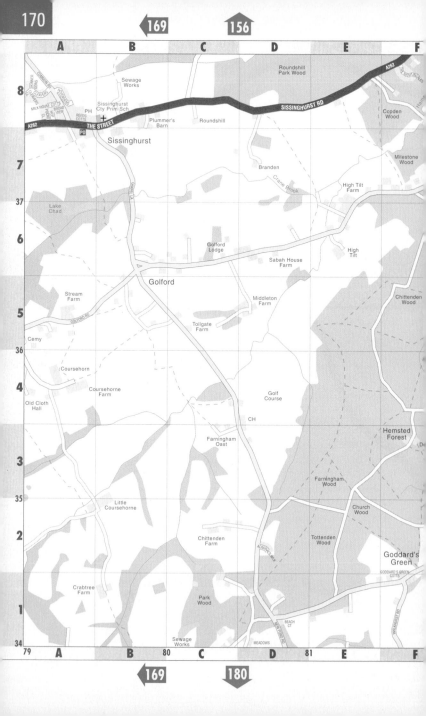

Goose Green

Castweazel
Farm

Castweazel
Manor

Low
Poles

Birchley
House

Roger's
Wood

Caravan
Park

Kennels

Medhurst

Rogley
Wood

Park
Farm

Elmstone
Farm

Bargate
Farm

Fosten Green
Nurseries

Birch
Wood

Clapper
Hill

ROGLEY HILL

CRANBROOK RD

Fosten
Green

Rogley
Farm

Birchwood
Farm House

Castleton's
Oak
(PH)

Causton
Wood

Summer
Hill

Little
Whatmans

Pedlars
Farm

BENENDEN RD

GRIBBLE BRIDGE LA

Little
Mockbeggar

MOCKBEGGAR LA

Halden
Wood

Trump
Farm

The
Brogues

THEDENIA RD

Brogues
Wood

Timber
Wood

East
End

Bishopsden
Farm

Benenden

FRON HOLE LA

Cleveland
Farm

Bexhill
Farm

Bishopsdale
Farm

Uppergate
Wood

GREEN LA

HALDEN LA

edhouse
Farm

Pympne Manor
Farm

Backtilt
Wood

Beston
Farm

Tinker
Wood

Pump
Wood

TOPHALL FARM LA

A B 83 C D 84 E F

8 7 37 6 5 36 4 3 35 2 1 34

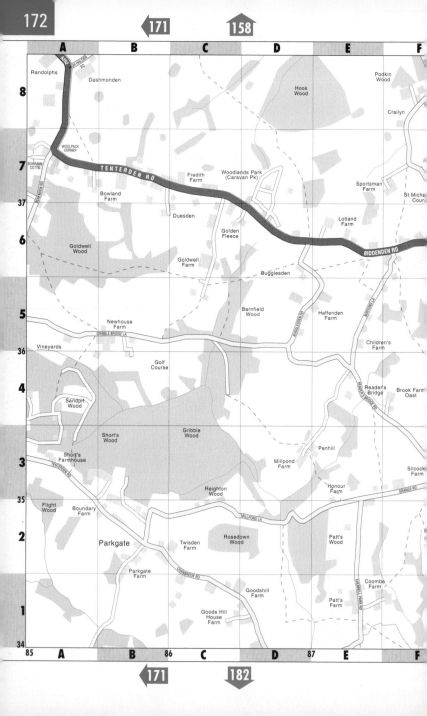

171
158

A **B** **C** **D** **E** **F**

8

Randolphs

Dashmonden

Hook Wood

Podkin Wood

Crailyn

7

WOOLPACK CORNER

BOWMAN COTTS

TENTERDEN RD

Fredith Farm

Woodlands Park (Caravan Pk)

Sportsman Farm

St Micha Cour.

Bowland Farm

37

Duesden

Golden Fleece

Lotland Farm

6

Goldwell Wood

Goldwell Farm

Bugglesden

BIDDENDEN RD

5

Newhouse Farm

Barnfield Wood

Haffenden Farm

GRIBBLE BRIDGE LA

36

Vineyards

Children's Farm

Golf Course

4

Sandpit Wood

Reader's Bridge

Brook Farm Oast

Short's Wood

Gribble Wood

Penhill

3

Short's Farmhouse

TENTERDEN RD

Millpond Farm

Honour Farm

Silcock Farm

GRANGE RD

35

Flight Wood

Boundary Farm

Reighton Wood

MILLPOND LA

2

Parkgate

Twisden Farm

Rosedown Wood

Patt's Wood

1

Parkgate Farm

CRANBROOK RD

Goodshill Farm

Coombe Farm

Patt's Farm

Goods Hill House Farm

34

85 **A** **B** 86 **C** **D** 87 **E** **F**

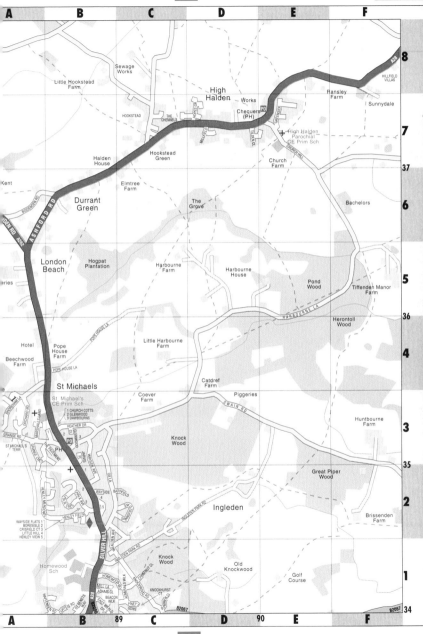

164

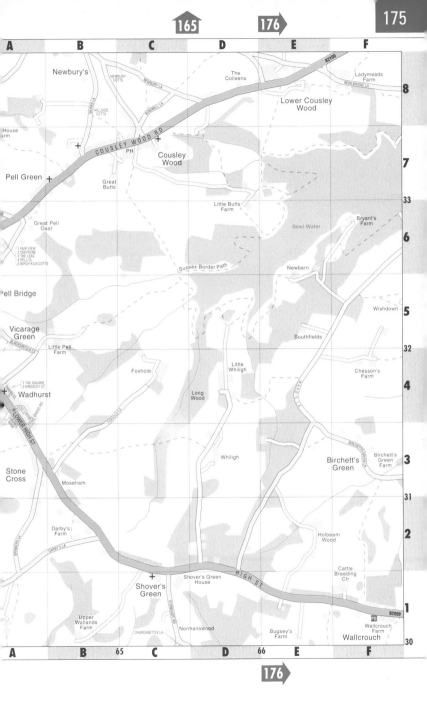

A B C D E F

Newbury's

NEWBURY COTTS

NEWBURY LA

WINDMILL LA

HILLSIDE COTTS

BUNDS LA

The Colleens

B2100

Lower Cousley Wood

Ladymeads Farm

BEWLBRIDGE LA

8

House Farm

COUSLEY WOOD RD

PH

Cousley Wood

7

Pell Green

Great Butts

33

Little Butts Farm

Bewl Water

Bryant's Farm

Great Pell Oast

1 FAIR VIEW
2 DEEPDENE
3 THE LEAS
4 PELL CL
5 BIRCH KILN COTTS

Sussex Border Path

Newbarn

6

ell Bridge

Wishdown

5

Vicarage Green

BLACKSMITH'S LA

Little Pell Farm

Southfields

32

Foxhole

Little Whiligh

Chesson's Farm

4

1 THE SQUARE
2 KINGSLEY CT

Wadhurst

FOROES LA

Long Wood

B2099

LOWER HIGH ST

Whiligh

Birchett's Green

BIRCHETTS GREEN LA

Birchett's Green Farm

3

Stone Cross

Moseham

31

Darby's Farm

Holbeam Wood

2

BRINKERS LA

DARBY'S LA

Shover's Green House

HIGH ST

Cattle Breeding Ctr

Shover's Green

STONEGATE RD

PO

B2099

1

Upper Wallands Farm

CHURCHSETTLE LA

Normanswood

Bugsey's Farm

Wallcrouch Farm

Wallcrouch

30

A B 65 C D 66 E F

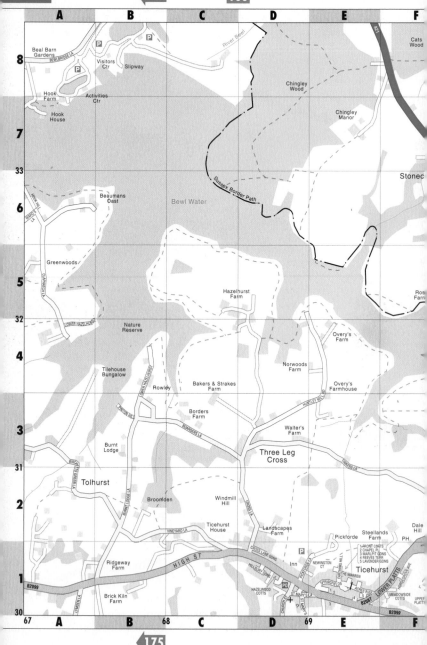

8 Beal Barn Gardens Cats Wood

BEWL BRIDGE LA

P P

Visitors Ctr Slipway

P

Hook Farm Activities Ctr

Hook House

River Bewl

Chingley Wood

Chingley Manor

7

33 Stonec

INNOX HILL

Beaumans Oast

Bewl Water

Sussex Border Path

6

CLAPHOUSE LA

Greenwoods

Hazelhurst Farm

Ros Farn

5

32 LOWER HAZELHOUSE

Nature Reserve

Overy's Farm

4 Tilehouse Bungalow Rowley

LOWER FAULKNERS

Bakers & Strakes Farm

Norwoods Farm

Overy's Farmhouse

HUNTLEY MILL RD

PANTON HILL

Borders Farm

BORDERS LA

Walter's Farm

3 Burnt Lodge

Three Leg Cross

FINCHES LA

31 BIRCHETTS GREEN LA

Tolhurst

BURNT LODGE LA

Broomden

Windmill Hill

CROSS LA

2

VINEYARD LA

Ticehurst House

Landscapes Farm

Pickforde

Steellands Farm

Dale Hill

PH

P

HIGH ST

Ridgeway Farm

CROSS LANE GDNS

HILLBURY GDNS

Inn

NEWINGTON CT

EARTHEN HILL'S

1 FRONT COTTS
2 CHAPEL PL
3 MARLPIT GDNS
4 REEVES TERR
5 LAVENDER GDNS

THE WARREN

Ticehurst

MEADOWSIDE COTTS

UPPER PLATT

1 B2099

Brick Kiln Farm

HAZELWOOD COTTS

CHURCH LA

ST MARY'S LA

PO

SPRINGFIELD

1 2 3

ST MARY'S

ACRES RISE

LOWER PLATTS

PRIESTLEY DR

B2087

30 B2099

B2099

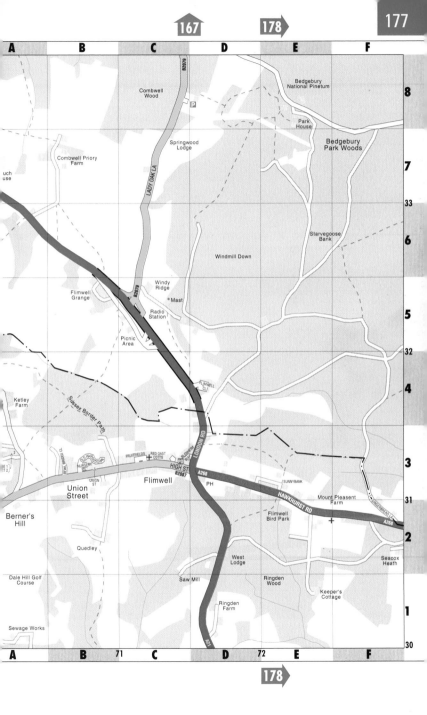

8 Brick Kiln Cottages
   Sugarloaf Hill
   Hedgingford Wood
   WHITELIMES
   Louisa Lodge
   Foresters Cottage
   Tubslak
   Badger's Oak
   Frith Wood
   Osborne's
   HAWKHURST

7 PARK LA

33 Louisa Lake
   Trenley Farm
   Yewtree Farm

6 Frith Farm
   LIMES GR
   STATION COTTS

5 Tanyard Farm
   Gill's Green
   Gill's Green Farm

32 Siseley Farm
   WELLINGTON
   Wellington Arms (PH)

4 SOPER'S LA
   SLIP MILL RD
   Trewint Farm
   Soper's Lane Farm

3 Slip Mill
   SYDNEY TERR 1
   CASTLE TERR 2
   SANDROOK VILLAS 3
   Golf Course
   Little Pix Hall Farm
   LIGHTFOOT GN
   SPRINGFIE
   RD ES

31 Lightfoot Green
   Elm Hill Farm
   Lightfoot Green
   High Street
   CH

2 A268
   Hawkhurst Cottage H
   PHILPOT'S CROSS
   HIGH ST
   Elm Hill House
   IDDENDEN COTTS
   Marlborough House Sch
   Seacox Poultry Farm
   F3
   1 EDEN CT
   2 DAINTONS COTTS
   3 OAK TERR
   4 NORMAN VILLAS
   5 ARMITAGE PL
   6 SCHOOL TERR
   7 WESTERN AVE
   8 HIGHGATE CT
   9 NORTHGROVE RD
   10 CRANE HOUSE GDNS
   11 CRANE HOUSE
   12 POST OFFICE RD

1 Delmonden Manor
   DELMONDEN RD
   Hurstwood Cottage
   Hensill House
   Cocksh

30 Sussex Border Path

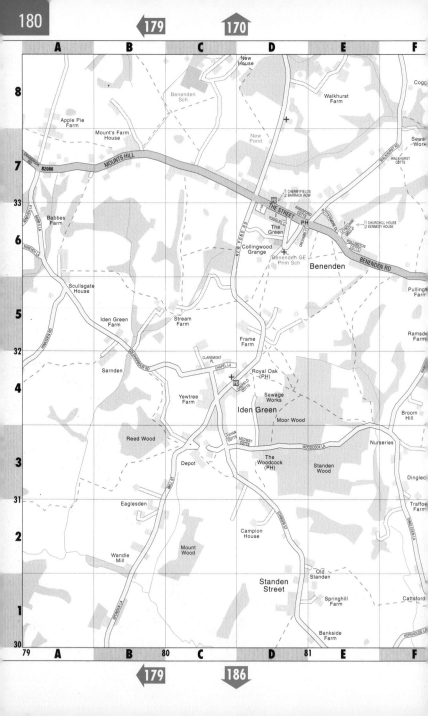

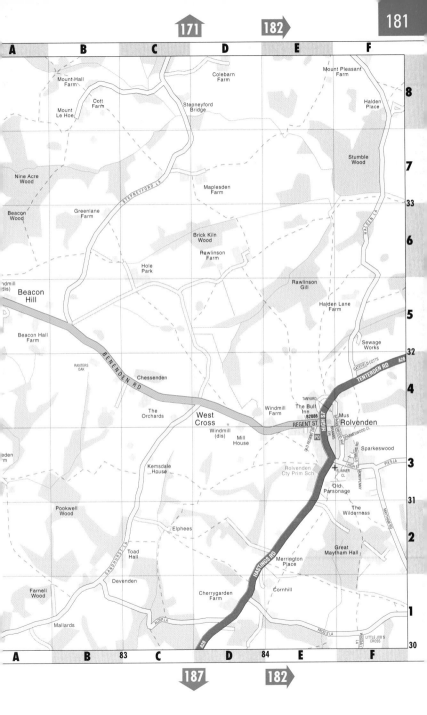

171
182

8
7
33
6
5
32
4
3
31
2
1
30

A B C D E F

Mount Pleasant Farm
Mount Hall Farm
Colebarn Farm
Halden Place
Cott Farm
Mount Le Hoe
Stepneyford Bridge

Stumble Wood

Nine Acre Wood
STEPNEYFORD LA
Maplesden Farm

Greenlane Farm
Beacon Wood

HALDEN LA
Brick Kiln Wood

Rawlinson Farm

Hole Park
indmill (dis)
Beacon Hill
Rawlinson Gill

Halden Lane Farm

Beacon Hall Farm
Sewage Works

RANTERS OAK
BENENDEN RD
Chessenden
GATEFIELD COTTS A28
TENTERDEN RD

The Orchards
West Cross
Windmill Farm
TANYARD
The Bull Inn
B2086
REGENT ST
Mus Rolvenden
HIGH ST
SHERWOOD CL

Windmill (dis)
Mill House
OLD REGENT ST
PO
SPARKES WOOD AVE
Sparkeswood

Kemsdale House
Rolvenden Cty Prim Sch
HIGH ST
SUMNER CL
MONYPENNY
Old Parsonage
PIX'S LA

Pookwell Wood
The Wilderness
MAYTHAM RD

SANDHURST LA
Elphees
Great Maytham Hall

Toad Hall
HASTINGS RD
Merrington Place

Devenden
Cornhill
den m

Farnell Wood
Cherrygarden Farm
FROG'S LA
LITTLE JOB'S CROSS
WALNALL

Mallards
A DUR LA
A28
83 84

187
182

181
172

A B C D E F
8
7
33
6
5
32
4
3
31
2
1
30
85 86 87
CRANBROOK RD
Little Halden Place
GOODS HILL
CHENNELL PARK RD
Chennell Park
Watermill Farm
CRANBROOK RD
LC
New Barn Farm
Ruffets
HURST CL
LAWN CL
WESTWELL HOUSE
ROLVENDEN RD
Ashbourne Mill
WESTFIELD PARKS
OLD TANN
PLUMMER LA
LC
Rolvenden Sta
West View
H
He
Old Halden
Cold Harbour
PLUMMER LA
ROLVENDEN HILL
Sewage Works
Plummer Farm
Kent & East Sussex Rlwy
Osborn Farm
Folly Farm
PUDDINGCAKE LA
Plummer Wood
Strood
Puddingcake Farmhouse
A28
TENTERDEN RD
Winton Farm
Sparkes Gill
Newmill Channel
Heronden
Lower Woolwich
Gazedown Wood
Morghew Farm
MOUNTS LA
PIX'S LA
Upper Woolwich
Kingsgate
Winser Farm
Rolvenden Layne
MAYTHAM RD
OAKFIELD
FRENSHAM RD
FROG'S LA
PH
WINSER RD
Friezingham Farm
MAYTHAM BGLWS
Frensham Manor
THORNDEN LA

181
188

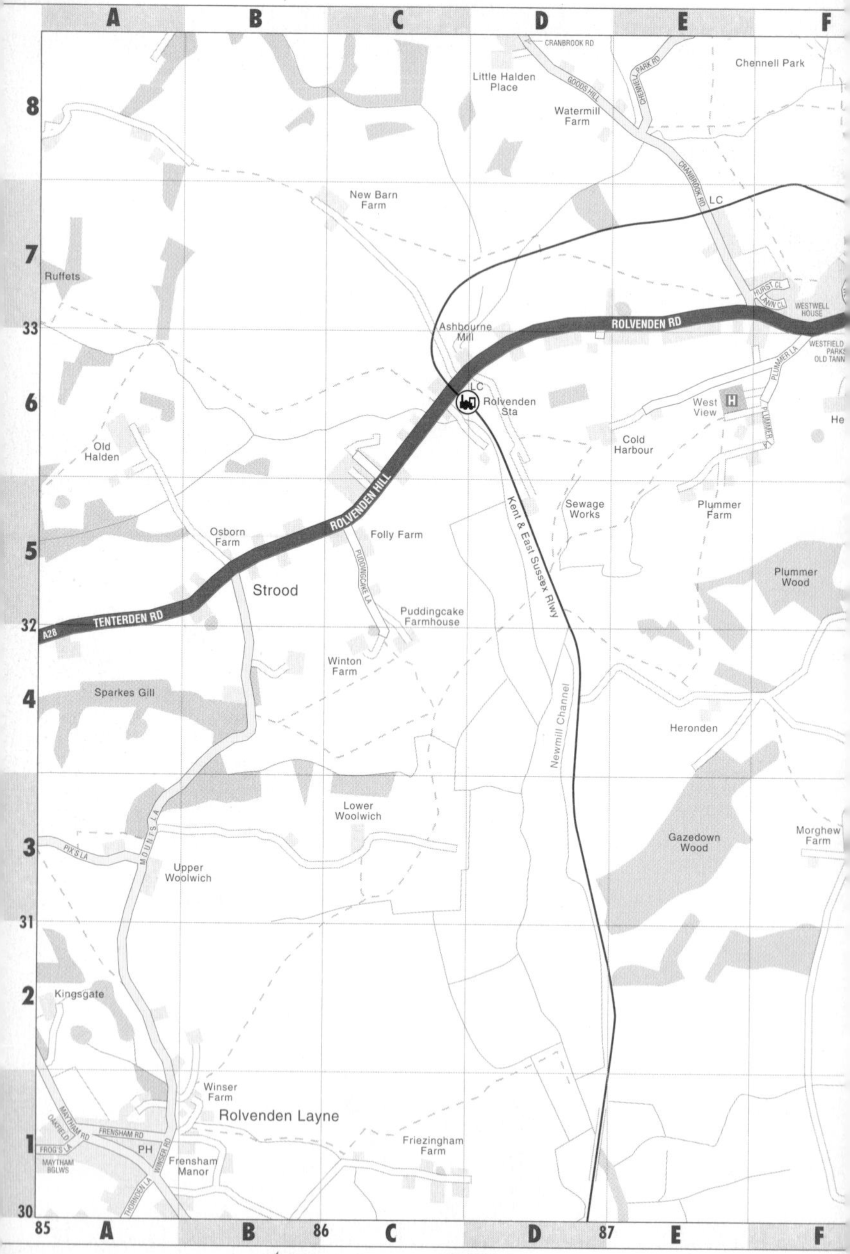

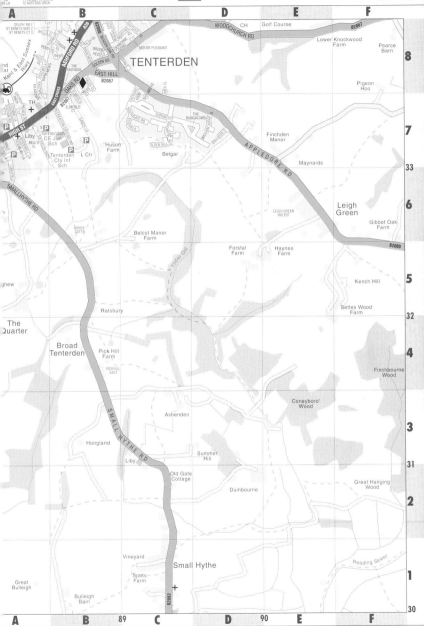

178

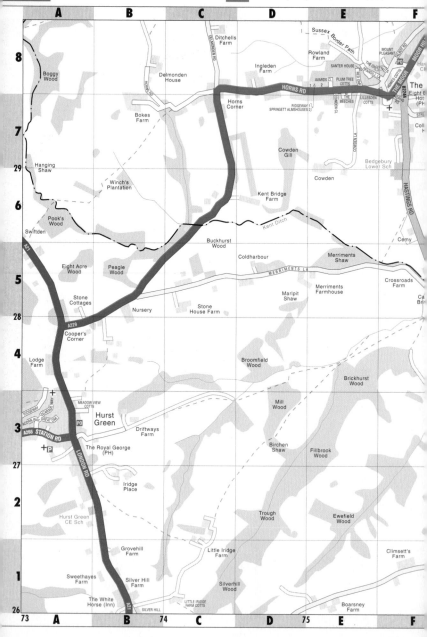

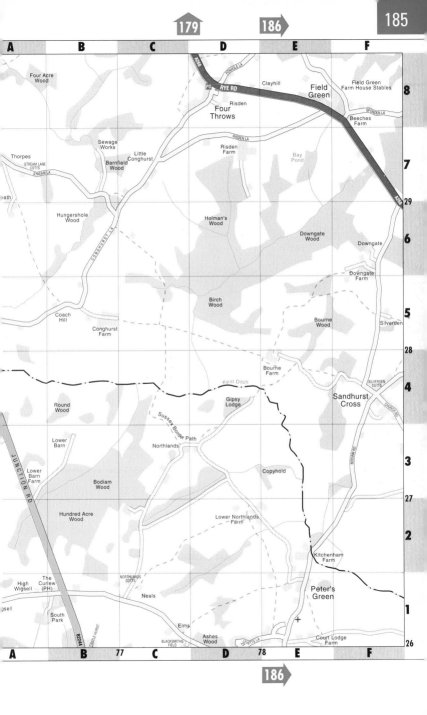

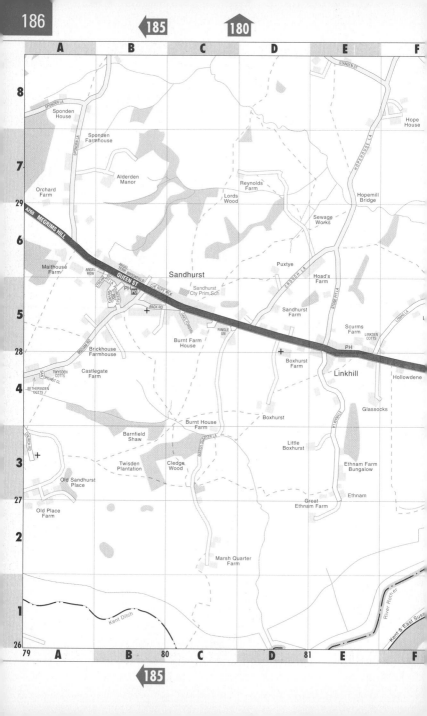

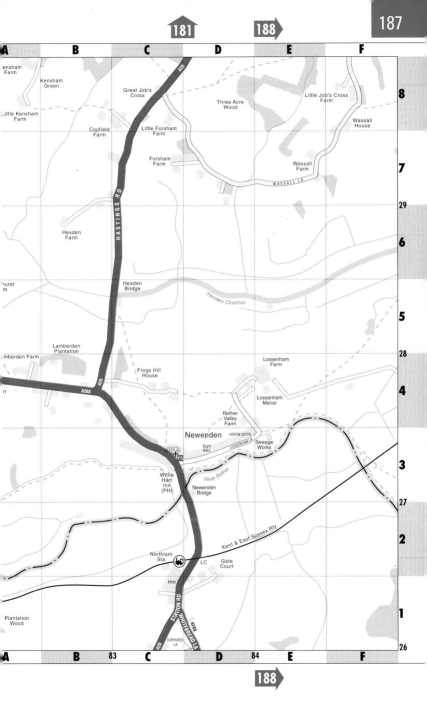

	A	B	C	D	E	F

THORNDEN CT

THORNDEN LA

Thornden Farmhouse

Sewage Works

Lowden Farm

Hillgate Farm

Britcher's

MAYTHAM RD

8

7

29

Lambsland Farm

Ingles

6

Tench Pit

LC

Wittersham Road Sta

Castle Toll

Kent & East Sussex Rly

Maytham Farm

5

28

Pumping Station

Hexden Channel

WITTERSHAM RD

Potman's Heath

Spurban Farm

4

Maytham Wharf

New Barn Farmhouse

Bush Wall

River Rother

3

27

Methersham Farm

Wet Level

2

Brickhurst Wood

Newmill Channel

Reading Sewer

Potman's Heath Channel

Maytham Sewer

Wittersham Sewer

Otter Channel

1

Methersham Wood

26

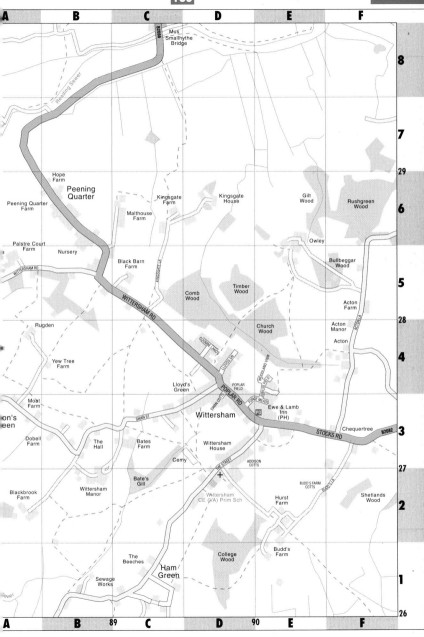

Mus Smallhythe Bridge

B2082

Reading Sewer

8

7

29

Hope Farm

Peening Quarter

Kingsgate Farm

Kingsgate House

Gilt Wood

Rushgreen Wood

Peening Quarter Farm

Malthouse Farm

6

Palstre Court Farm

Nursery

Black Barn Farm

KINGSGATE LA

Owley

Bullbeggar Wood

WITTERSHAM RD

WITTERSHAM RD

Comb Wood

Timber Wood

Acton Farm

5

28

Rugden

COOMBE LANDS

LLOYDS LN

Church Wood

Acton Manor

Acton

KNOCK LA

Yew Tree Farm

Lloyd's Green

POPLAR FIELD

WOODLAND VIEW

4

Moat Farm

SWAN COTTS

POPLAR RD

FORGE MEADS

JUBILEE FIELD

Ewe & Lamb Inn (PH)

on's
een

SWAN ST

Wittersham

PO

Dobell Farm

The Hall

Bates Farm

Wittersham House

STOCKS RD

Chequertree

B2082

3

Blackbrook Farm

Wittersham Manor

Cemy

ADDISON COTTS

BUDD'S FARM COTTS

BUDD'S LA

Shetlands Wood

27

Bate's Gill

OXE STREET

Wittersham CE (WA) Prim Sch

Hurst Farm

2

The Beeches

College Wood

Budd's Farm

Ham Green

Sewage Works

1

26

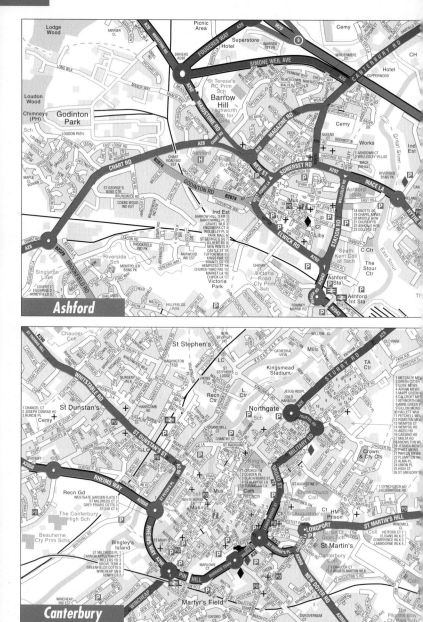

Ashford

Canterbury

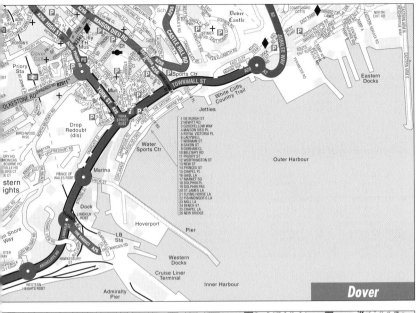

Dover

1 DE BURGH ST
2 HEWITT RD
3 GOODFELLOW WAY
4 MAISON DIEU PL
5 ROYAL VICTORIA PL
6 LADYWELL
7 NORMAN ST
8 SAXON ST
9 DURHAM CL
10 MILITARY RD
11 PRIORY ST
12 WORTHINGTON ST
13 NEW ST
14 PRINCES ST
15 CHAPEL PL
16 GAOL LA
17 MARKET SQ
18 DOLPHIN PL
19 DOLPHIN PAS
20 ST JAMES LA
21 FLYING HORSE LA
22 FISHMONGER'S LA
23 MILL LA
24 BENCH ST
25 CHAPEL LA
26 NEW BRIDGE

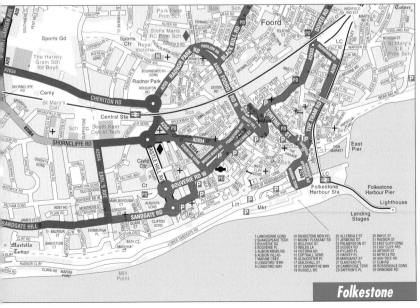

Folkestone

1 LANGHORNE GDNS
2 SHAKESPEARE TERR
3 BOUVERIE SQ
4 BOUVERIE PL
5 ALBION MEWS RD
6 ALBION VILLAS
7 MARINE CRES
8 LONGFORD TERR
9 LONGFORD WAY
10 BRADSTONE NEW RD
11 MOUNT PLEASANT RD
12 BELLEVUE ST
13 INGLES LA
14 VICTORIA GR
15 COPTHALL GDNS
16 GLOUCESTER PL
17 GUILDHALL ST
18 ST EANSWYTHE WAY
19 RUSSELL RD
20 ALLENDALE ST
21 JESMOND ST
22 PALMERSTON ST
23 SUSSEX RD
24 RYLAND PL
25 HARVEY PL
26 MARGARET ST
27 ELMSTEAD PL
28 CAMBRIDGE TERR
29 SAFFRON'S PL
30 BAYLE ST
31 RADNOR ST
32 EAST CLIFF GDNS
33 EAST CLIFF PAS
34 ARTHUR ST
35 MYRTLE RD
36 ASH TREE RD
37 ELM RD
38 ROSSENDALE GDNS
39 ORMONDE RD

Street names are listed alphabetically and show the locality, the Postcode District, the page number and a reference to the square in which the name falls on the map page

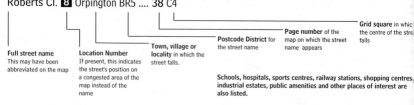

Roberts Cl. **8** Orpington BR5 .... 38 C4

Full street name
This may have been abbreviated on the map

Location Number
If present, this indicates the street's position on a congested area of the map instead of the name

Town, village or locality in which the street falls.

Postcode District for the street name

Page number of the map on which the street name appears

Grid square in whic the centre of the stre falls

Schools, hospitals, sports centres, railway stations, shopping centres, industrial estates, public amenities and other places of interest are also listed.

Abbreviations used in the index

App	Approach	Cl	Close	Espl	Esplanade	Orch	Orchard	Sq	Square
Arc	Arcade	Comm	Common	Est	Estate	Par	Parade	Strs	Stairs
Ave	Avenue	Cnr	Corner	Gdns	Gardens	Pk	Park	Stps	Steps
Bvd	Boulevard	Cotts	Cottages	Gn	Green	Pas	Passage	St	Street, Saint
Bldgs	Buildings	Ct	Court	Gr	Grove	Pl	Place	Terr	Terrace
Bsns Pk	Business Park	Ctyd	Courtyard	Hts	Heights	Prec	Precinct	Trad Est	Trading Estate
Bsns Ctr	Business Centre	Cres	Crescent	Ind Est	Industrial Estate	Prom	Promenade	Wlk	Walk
Bglws	Bungalows	Dr	Drive	Intc	Interchange	Ret Pk	Retail Park	W	West
Cswy	Causeway	Dro	Drove	Junc	Junction	Rd	Road	Yd	Yard
Ctr	Centre	E	East	La	Lane	Rdbt	Roundabout		
Cir	Circus	Emb	Embankment	N	North	S	South		

20/20 Ind Est. ME16 .... 91 C8
Abbess Cl. **1** E6 .... 1 E8
Abbeville House. ME1 .... 47 C4
Abbey Court Sch. ME2 .... 46 E8
Abbey Cres. DA17 .... 4 A2
Abbey Gate Cotts. ME20 .... 76 F2
Abbey Gr. SE2 .... 3 B2
Abbey Pl. DA1 .... 9 D2
Abbey Prim Sch. SE2 .... 3 C3
Abbey Rd. Bexley DA6 & DA7 .. 7 E3
Abbey Rd. Erith DA17 .... 3 E3
Abbey Rd. Gillingham ME8 .. 49 A2
Abbey Rd. Gravesend DA12 . 30 E7
Abbey Rd. Rochester ME2 ... 46 F8
Abbey Rd. Swanscombe DA9 11 C2
Abbey Terr. SE2 .... 3 C2
Abbey Wood Rd.
   Kings Hill ME19 .... 89 A5
Abbey Wood Rd.
   Woolwich SE2 .... 3 C2
Abbey Wood Sch. SE2 .... 3 A3
Abbey Wood Sta. SE2 .... 3 C3
Abbeyhill Rd. DA15 .... 24 C6
Abbotts Cl. BR5 .... 37 C1
Abbots Court Rd. ME3 .... 34 F5
Aberdeen House. **8**
   ME15 .... 107 E7
Aberford Gdns. SE18 .... 5 E6
Abergeldie Rd. SE12 .... 5 B1
Abery St. SE18 .... 2 E2
Abigail Cres. ME5 .... 62 A1
Abingdon Rd. ME16 .... 90 F2
Abingdon Way. BR6 .... 52 B6
Abinger Cl. BR1 .... 36 C6
Abinger Dr. ME5 .... 62 D2
Absalom Ct. ME8 .... 49 C2
Acacia Cl. BR5 .... 37 D4
Acacia Rd. Dartford DA1 .... 26 D7
Acacia Rd. Stone DA9 .... 10 E1
Acacia Way. DA15 .... 23 F7
Acacia Wlk. BR8 .... 39 D7
Academy Dr. ME7 .... 48 F1
Academy Pl. SE18 .... 6 A6

Academy Rd. SE18 .... 5 F7
Acer Ave. TN2 .... 163 C8
Achilles Rd. ME5 .... 62 C2
Acland Cl. SE18 .... 6 D7
Acorn Cl. Chislehurst BR7 ... 23 C3
Acorn Cl.
   Five Oak Green TN12 .... 135 B7
Acorn Gr. ME20 .... 90 D8
Acorn Ind Pk. DA1 .... 9 A2
Acorn Pl. ME15 .... 107 E6
Acorn Rd. ME7 .... 48 F4
Acorn Trad Ctr. RM16 .... 11 E8
Acorn Way.
   Hurst Green TN19 .... 184 A3
Acorn Way. Orpington BR6 . 51 B6
Acorns The. TN27 .... 142 F1
Acott Fields. ME18 .... 120 F8
Acre Cl. ME4 .... 47 E1
Acres Rise. TN5 .... 176 E1
Acton La. TN30 .... 189 F4
Acton Pl. ME18 .... 105 A1
Acworth House. **1** SE18 .... 6 B8
Acworth Pl. DA1 .... 9 C1
Adam Cl. ME17 .... 106 D3
Adams Cl. TN30 .... 173 B1
Adams Sq. DA6 .... 7 E4
Adamson Rd. E16 .... 1 A7
Adbert Dr. ME15 .... 106 B4
Adcot Wlk. **6** BR6 .... 51 F6
Adderley Gdns. SE9 .... 23 A4
Addington La. ME19 .... 73 B4
Addison Cl.
   East Malling ME19 .... 74 F1
Addison Cl. Orpington BR5 .. 37 C3
Addison Cotts. TN30 .... 189 D3
Addison Dr. SE12 .... 5 B2
Addison Rd. BR2 .... 36 C4
Addlestead Rd. TN12 .... 119 E6
Adelaide Cl.
   Chislehurst BR7 .... 23 B3
Adelaide Rd.
   Gillingham ME7 .... 48 C4
Adelaide Rd. Tilbury RM18 .. 12 F5
Adelaide The. ME3 .... 32 C6
Aden Terr. **1** ME14 .... 92 A7
Adisham Dr. ME14 .... 91 B7
Admaston Rd. SE18 .... 6 C8
Admers Way. DA13 .... 73 B8
Admiral Moore Dr. **3** ME20 75 F1
Admiral Seymour Rd. SE9 .... 5 F3
Admiral's Wlk. ME4 .... 47 F7
Admirals Wlk.
   Chatham ME5 .... 62 B3

Admirals Wlk.
   Goddard's Green TN17 .... 170 D2
Admirals Wlk.
   Swanscombe DA9 .... 11 B2
Admirals Wlk.
   Tenterden TN30 .... 173 C1
Admiralty Rd. ME2 .... 33 F1
Admiralty Terr. **1**
   Gillingham ME4 .... 48 A7
Admiralty Terr.
   Upper Upton ME2 .... 33 F1
Afghan Rd. ME4 .... 47 E4
Agate Cl. E16 .... 1 D7
Agaton Rd. SE9 & SE12 ...... 23 C6
Agnes Cl. E6 .... 2 A6
Ainsdale Cl. BR6 .... 37 D1
Aintree Cl. DA12 .... 30 B5
Aintree House. **1** ME15 .. 107 F6
Aintree Rd. ME5 .... 62 C3
Airedale Cl. DA2 .... 27 C7
Airport Rdbt. E16 .... 1 D5
Aisher Rd. SE28 .... 3 C6
Aisher Way. TN13 .... 83 E6
Ajax Rd. ME1 .... 61 C8
Akehurst La. TN15 .... 84 C7
Alabama St. SE18 .... 6 E7
Alamein Ave. ME5 .... 61 F7
Alamein Gdns. DA2 .... 27 D8
Alamein Rd. DA10 .... 11 D1
Alan Cl. DA1 .... 9 C3
Alanbrooke. DA12 .... 30 C8
Alanbrooke House. SE18 ...... 5 E7
Alanthus Cl. SE12 .... 5 A1
Alban Cres. DA4 .... 41 A1
Albany Cl. Sidcup DA5 .... 24 D8
Albany Cl. Tonbridge TN9 .. 133 D7
Albany Hill. TN2 .... 149 C5
Albany Park Sta. DA14 .... 24 D6
Albany Rd. Chatham ME4 .... 48 B2
Albany Rd. Chislehurst BR7 .. 23 B3
Albany Rd. Erith DA17 .... 7 F8
Albany Rd. Gillingham ME7 .. 48 D4
Albany Rd. Rochester ME1 .. 47 C4
Albany Rd. Sidcup DA5 .... 24 C8
Albany St. ME14 .... 92 B5
Albany Terr. Chatham ME4 .. 47 E4
Albany Terr. Gillingham ME7 48 D4
Albatross Ave. ME2 .... 46 C6
Albatross St. SE18 .... 6 E7
Albemarle Rd. ME5 .... 62 C2
Albert Cotts. TN1 .... 149 B4

Albert Murry Cl. **4** DA12 ... 30 C8
Albert Pl. ME2 .... 47 B7
Albert Rd. Bromley BR2 ...... 36 D4
Albert Rd. Chatham ME4 ..... 48 A3
Albert Rd. Chislehurst SE9 .. 22 E5
Albert Rd. Erith DA17 .... 3 F1
Albert Rd. Gillingham ME7 .. 48 C4
Albert Rd. Newham E16 .... 1 F5
Albert Rd.
   Orpington,Chelsfield BR6 .. 52 A5
Albert Rd.
   Orpington,St Mary Cray BR5 38 B3
Albert Rd. Rochester ME1 ... 47 C3
Albert Rd. Sidcup DA5 .... 25 B8
Albert Rd.
   Swanscombe DA10 .... 11 F1
Albert Rd. **3**
   Tonbridge TN9 .... 117 B1
Albert Rd. Wilmington DA2 .. 26 C5
Albert St. Maidstone ME14 .. 91 F6
Albert St.
   Royal Tunbridge Wells TN1 149 B4
Albert Wlk. E16 .... 2 B4
Alberta Rd. DA7 .... 8 C6
Albion Cl. **2** SE7 .... 1 E2
Albion House. E16 .... 2 B5
Albion Pl. Maidstone ME14 .. 92 B4
Albion Pl. Newington SE9 ... 65 B6
Albion Rd. Bexley DA6 .... 8 A3
Albion Rd. Chatham ME5 ..... 62 B2
Albion Rd. Gravesend DA12 . 30 C8
Albion Rd. Marden TN12 ... 138 D5
Albion Rd. Royal Tunbridge Wells
   TN1 .... 149 C5
Albion Terr. DA12 .... 13 D1
Albion Way. TN8 .... 112 C4
Albright Ind Est. RM13 .... 4 F8
Albury Ave. DA7 .... 7 E5
Albury Cl. ME5 .... 62 D2
Albyfield. BR1 .... 36 F6
Alchins Cotts. ME17 .... 106 E2
Alconbury. DA6 .... 8 B2
Aldeburgh St. SE18 .... 1 A1
Alder Cl. TN2 .... 133 D1
Alder La. TN17 .... 181 C1
Alder Rd. DA14 .... 23 F5
Alder Way. BR8 .... 39 D7
Aldermary Rd. BR1 .... 36 A8
Aldermay Rd. DA8 .... 9 A7
Alders Cotts. TN11 .... 135 A5
Alders Meadow. TN9 .... 116 F2
Alders Rd. TN11 & TN12 ... 134 E6
Alders The. ME18 .... 103 D7

Aldersgrove Ave.
   SE12 & SE9 .... 22 **
Aldershot Rd. ME5 .... 62 **
Alderwood Prim Sch. SE9 ..... 6 **
Alderwood Rd. SE9 .... 6 **
Aldington Cl. ME5 .... 62 **
Aldington La. ME14 .... 93 **
Aldington Rd.
   Greenwich SE18 .... 1 [
Aldington Rd.
   Maidstone ME14 .... 92 **
Aldon Cl. ME14 .... 92 **
Aldon Ct. ME14 .... 92 (
Aldon La. ME19 .... 88 (
Aldwick Cl. BR7 .... 23 **
Alen Sq. TN12 .... 139 **
Alers Rd. DA6 .... 7 [
Alestan Beck Rd. E16 .... 1 [
Alexander Cl. Hayes BR2 .... 36 **
Alexander Cl. Sidcup DA15 .... 6 **
Alexander Ct. Greenwich SE3 .. 5 [
Alexander Ct.
   Rochester ME2 .... 47 [
Alexander McLeod Inf Sch.
   SE2 .... 3 [
Alexander McLeod Jun Sch.
   SE2 .... 3 **
Alexander Rd. Bexley DA16 .. 7 [
Alexander Rd.
   Chislehurst BR7 .... 23 [
Alexander Rd.
   Swanscombe DA9 .... 11 (
Alexandra Ave. ME7 .... 48 **
Alexandra Cl. BR8 .... 39 **
Alexandra Glen. ME5 .... 62 **
Alexandra Hospl The. ME5 .. 77 **
Alexandra Rd.
   Chatham ME4 .... 48 [
Alexandra Rd. Erith DA8 .... 8 **
Alexandra Rd.
   Gravesend DA12 .... 30 [
Alexandra Rd. Tilbury RM18 12 **
Alexandra Rd.
   Tonbridge TN9 .... 133 [
Alexandra St.
   Maidstone ME14 .... 91 **
Alexandra St. Newham E16 .. 1 **
Alfan La. DA2 .... 25 [
Alford House. **6** SE18 .... 6 **
Alford Rd. DA8 .... 4 **
Alfred Cl. ME4 .... 48 [
Alfred House. **4** DA11 ...... 29 **
Alfred Pl. DA11 .... 29 **

red Rd. Erith DA17 ...... 3 F1
red Rd. Gravesend DA11 .. 26 F4
red Rd. Hawley DA2 ...... 26 F4
red St. RM17 .... 12 C8
icia Thompson Cl. SE12 .. 22 C6
cia House. DA16 .... 7 B6
ori Cl. E6 .... 2 A7
erden La. DA9 & DA10 .... 11 C1
kham Rd. ME14 .... 92 C5
kham Tower. 9 BR5 ...... 38 C5
Saints' CE Prim Sch.
hatham ME4 .... 48 A3
Saints CE Prim Sch.
hatham ME15 .... 92 A3
Saints Cl. DA10 .... 11 C1
Saints Hospl. ME4 .... 48 A2
Saints Rd.
allhallows ME3 .... 19 D8
Saints Rd.
lawkhurst TN18 .... 179 A1
Saints' Rd.
orthfleet DA11 .... 29 F7
Saints Rd.
oyal Tunbridge Wells TN4 149 B6
Saints Rise. TN4 .... 149 A6
an Cl. TN4 .... 148 C4
andale Pl. BR6 .... 52 D7
andale Rd. TN2 .... 149 D7
ard Cl. BR5 .... 38 C2
en Cl. ME5 .... 62 C6
en St. ME4 .... 92 B5
endale Cl. DA2 .... 27 C7
ens. TN12 .... 138 D5
ens La. TN15 .... 102 A7
enswood Rd. SE9 .... 5 F5
hallows Cty Prim Sch.
ME3 .... 19 D8
hallows Rd. 1 E7
hallows-on-Sea Est.
ME3 .... 19 E10
iance Rd. Newham E16 .... 1 C8
iance Rd. Woolwich SE18 .. 7 A7
iance Way. TN12 .... 135 F6
ington Cl.
onbridge TN10 .... 118 A8
ington Gdns. ME18 ..... 104 E7
ington Prim Sch. ME16 .. 91 C7
ington Rd.
illingham ME8 .... 49 A3
ington Rd. Orpington BR6 37 E1
ington Rd.
Paddock Wood TN12 .... 135 F7
ington Way. ME16 ...... 91 B6
ison Ave. ME7 .... 48 E1
nutt Mill Cl. ME15 ...... 91 C2
ma Pl. Hadlow TN11 .... 118 E8
ma Pl. Rochester ME2 ... 47 A7
ma Rd. Eccles ME20 .... 75 F6
ma Rd. New Town ME19 .. 89 A8
ma Rd.
Orpington BR5 & BR6 .... 52 D8
ma Rd. Sidcup DA14 .... 24 A5
mon Pl. ME1 .... 47 C2
mon Cl. BR2 .... 37 A2
mond Dr. BR8 .... 39 D7
mond Gr. ME7 .... 63 A4
mond Rd. DA2 .... 27 C8
mond Way. BR2 .... 37 A2
monds The. ME14 ...... 93 A4
ms Row. TN16 .... 82 B3
mshouses. TN18 .... 179 A2
wick Rd. Eltham SE12 ... 22 B8
wick Rd. Newham E16 ... 1 C7
onso House. 3 DA17 .... 4 A1
oha Cl. ME3 .... 35 D7
pine Bsns Ctr. E6 ...... 2 A8
pine Copse. 2 BR1 ..... 37 A7
pine Way. E6 .... 2 A8
sike Rd. DA18 .... 3 E3
tash Way. SE9 .... 23 A6
tbarn Ind Est. ME5 ..... 77 C8
ton Cl. DA5 .... 24 E7
ton Cotts. DA4 .... 54 E8
verstone Gdns. SE9 .... 23 C7
wold Cres. SE12 .... 5 C1
nanda Cl. ME5 .... 61 F3
nar Ct. SE18 .... 2 F1
nardeep Ct. SE18 ...... 2 F1
mbassador Gdns. E6 .... 1 F8
mber La. ME17 .... 108 A1
mber Way. ME17 ...... 108 B1
mberleaze Dr. TN2 .... 150 D6
mberley Cl. 2
Orpington BR6 .... 51 F5
mberley Cl.
Tronbridge TN9 .... 133 A8

Amberley Ct.
Royal Tunbridge Wells TN4 149 C8
Amberley Ct. Sidcup DA14 .. 24 C3
Amberley Rd. SE2 .... 7 D8
Amblecote Cl. SE12 .... 22 B5
Amblecote Meadow. SE12 .. 22 B5
Amblecote Rd. SE12 .... 22 B5
Ambleside Rd. DA7 .... 8 A6
Ambley Gn. ME7 .... 63 A8
Ambley Rd. ME7 .... 63 B8
Ambrook Rd. DA17 .... 4 A3
Ambrose Cl. Crayford DA1 .. 9 A3
Ambrose Cl. 6 Newham E6 .. 1 F8
Ambrose Cl. Orpington BR6 . 51 F7
Ambrose Hill. ME4 & ME5 ... 48 C2
Amels Hill. ME9 .... 79 F8
Ames Ave. ME14 .... 93 A4
Amesbury Rd. ME1 .... 61 E6
Amethyst Ave. ME5 ...... 61 E6
Amherst Cl.
Maidstone ME16 .... 91 D4
Amherst Cl. Orpington BR5 .. 38 A5
Amherst City Jun Sch.
TN13 .... 83 E4
Amherst Dr. BR5 .... 38 A5
Amherst Hill. Chatham ME4 . 48 A6
Amherst Hill.
Sevenoaks TN13 .... 83 F4
Amherst Rd. Rochester ME1 47 D3
Amherst Rd. Royal Tunbridge Wells
TN4 .... 149 A5
Amherst Rd.
Sevenoaks TN13 .... 83 E4
Amherst Redoubt. ME4 .... 48 A5
Amhurst Bank Rd.
TN11 & TN2 .... 134 F4
Amhurst Wlk. SE28 .... 3 A5
Amies House. ME15 ...... 106 F3
Ampleforth Rd. SE2 ...... 3 C4
Amsbury Rd. ME17 ...... 106 B2
Amshurst Villas. ME15 ... 106 A4
Ancaster St. SE18 .... 6 D2
Anchor and Hope La. SE7 .. 1 C2
Anchor Bvd. DA9 .... 10 D3
Anchor House. DA16 ...... 1 C7
Anchor La. ME12 .... 21 F3
Anchor Rd. ME1 .... 47 C1
Anchorage Cl. SE18 ...... 19 C3
Ancona Rd. SE18 .... 2 C5
Andace Pk. BR1 .... 36 C8
Anderson Way. DA17 ..... 4 B4
Andorra Ct. BR1 .... 36 C8
Andover Ave. E16 .... 1 C8
Andover Rd. BR6 .... 51 F8
Andover Wlk. 12 ME15 ... 107 F6
Andrew Broughton Way.
ME14 .... 92 B4
Andrew Cl. DA1 .... 27 B8
Andrew Manor. ME7 ..... 48 C6
Andrew House. TN4 ..... 149 C8
Andrew Wells House. BR1 .. 22 B1
Andrewes Gdns. E6 ...... 1 E8
Andrews Cl.Royal Tunbridge Wells
TN2 .... 149 D5
Andrews Cl.
St Paul's Cray BR5 ...... 38 C6
Andringham Lodge. 4
BR1 .... 36 B8
Andwell Cl. SE2 .... 3 B6
Anerley Cl. ME16 .... 91 D7
Angel La. TN9 .... 117 B1
Angel Row. TN18 .... 186 B5
Angel Terr. TN18 .... 186 B6
Angel Wlk. 4 TN9 .... 117 B1
Angelica Dr. E6 .... 2 A8
Angerstein Bsns Pk. SE10 .. 1 A2
Angle Rd. RM16 .... 11 D8
Anglesea Ave. 4 SE18 ... 2 B2
Anglesea Ctr. 17 DA11 ... 13 B1
Anglesea Pl. 18 DA11 .... 13 B1
Anglesea Rd. Orpington BR5 38 C3
Anglesea Rd. Woolwich SE18 2 B2
Anglesey Ave. ME15 ..... 107 A7
Anglesey Cl. ME5 .... 62 A6
Anglesey Gdns. SE18 .... 2 C3
Angley Cl. TN12 .... 153 A5
Angley Rd. TN17 .... 169 C6
Angley Sch. TN17 .... 169 C5
Angley Wlk.
Cranbrook TN17 .... 169 C6

Annex The. BR8 .... 40 B6
Annie Rd. ME6 .... 74 F6
Ansell Ave. ME4 .... 48 A1
Anson Cl. ME5 .... 62 C6
Anson Rd. ME18 & ME19 .. 88 E2
Anstridge Rd. SE9 ...... 6 D1
Antelope Rd. SE18 ...... 1 F3
Anthony Cl. TN13 .... 83 E7
Anthony Rd. DA16 ...... 7 A6
Anthony Roper Cty Prim Sch.
DA4 .... 54 E8
Antonios La. BR8 .... 40 A8
Antonys Way. ME2 ...... 47 E8
Aperfield Rd. DA8 ...... 8 F8
Apollo Ave. BR1 .... 36 B8
Apollo House. ME5 ...... 62 A6
Apollo Way. SE18 .... 2 C3
Apple Cl. ME6 .... 75 A6
Apple Ct. TN12 .... 135 F6
Apple Tree Cl. ME16 .... 90 F7
Apple Tree La. ME1 & TN2 149 D8
Appleby Cl. ME1 .... 61 D7
Appleby Rd. E16 .... 1 A7
Appledore Ave. DA7 .... 8 D5
Appledore Cl. BR2 ...... 36 A4
Appledore Cres. DA15 ... 23 F5
Appledore Cl. ME16 ..... 91 C7
Appledore Rd.
Gillingham ME8 .... 49 A3
Appledore Rd.
Tenterden TN30 .... 183 E7
Applegarth Dr. DA1 ..... 26 F6
Applegarth House. DA8 .. 8 F5
Applegarth Rd. SE28 .... 3 C6
Appleshaw Cl. DA11 .... 30 A3
Appleton Rd. SE9 .... 5 F2
Appletons. TN11 .... 118 E8
Appold St. DA8 .... 8 F7
Approach The. BR6 ..... 51 F8
April Cl. BR6 .... 51 F5
Apsledene. DA12 .... 30 D2
Apsley St. TN4 .... 148 D4
Aragon Cl. BR2 .... 36 F1
Arbroath Rd. SE9 .... 5 E6
Arbrook Cl. BR5 .... 38 A8
Arbrook Ct. BR5 .... 38 A8
Arbuthnot La. DA5 ...... 7 E1
Arcade The. 2 SE9 ...... 6 A1
Arcadia Rd. DA13 .... 43 F8
Arcadian Ave. DA5 ...... 7 E1
Arcadian Cl. DA5 .... 7 E1
Arcadian Rd. DA5 ...... 7 E1
Archer Rd. Chatham ME5 .. 62 B8
Archer Rd. Orpington BR5 .. 38 A4
Archer Way. BR8 .... 40 A7
Archery Cl. ME4 .... 33 B7
Archery House Hospl. DA2 . 10 B1
Archery Rd. SE9 .... 5 F2
Archway Ct. 1 ME4 ..... 47 B8
Arden Bsns Pk. ME2 .... 47 E8
Arden Cty Jun Sch. ME7 .. 48 D6
Arden Gr. BR6 .... 51 B6
Arden Rd. ME7 .... 48 C6
Ardenlee Dr. ME14 ..... 92 B5
Arethusa Rd. ME16 ..... 61 C8
Argall House. 3 DA18 ... 3 E3
Argent St. RM17 .... 11 E8
Argles Cl. DA9 .... 11 A2
Argyle Cl. ME2 .... 47 B8
Argyle Rd. Newham E16 ... 1 B7
Argyle Rd.
Royal Tunbridge Wells TN4 133 A2
Argyle Rd. Sevenoaks TN13 . 84 B2
Argyll Rd. SE18 .... 2 C3
Ariel Cl. DA12 .... 30 F4
Ariel Ct. DA17 .... 4 A1
Arkwright Rd. RM18 .... 13 A5
Arlington Cl. DA15 ..... 23 E8
Arlott Cl. ME14 .... 91 F6
Armada Ct. ME4 .... 47 F3
Armada Way. Chatham ME4 47 F3
Armada Way. Newham E6 .. 2 C7
Armitage Pl. 8 TN18 ... 178 F2
Armoury Dr. DA12 ...... 30 D8
Armstrong Cl. Bromley BR1 . 36 E6
Armstrong Cl. Newham E6 . 1 F7
Armstrong Cl.
Shepham Heath TN14 .... 68 B4
Armstrong Rd. ME15 .... 92 A1
Armytage Cl. ME3 ...... 34 E4
Arne Cl. TN10 .... 117 E6
Arne Gr. BR6 .... 51 F7
Arnhem Dr. ME5 .... 61 F3
Arnold Ave. DA13 ...... 58 B8
Arnold Pl. RM18 .... 13 C6
Arnold Rd. DA12 .... 30 D6
Arnolde Cl. ME2 .... 46 F8
Arnolds La. DA2 & DA4 .. 27 A2
Arnott Cl. SE28 .... 3 C5
Arnsberg Way. DA7 .... 8 A3
Arnside Rd. DA7 .... 8 A6

Arran Cl. DA8 .... 8 D8
Arran Gn. ME2 .... 46 C7
Arran Rd. ME15 .... 107 A6
Arrandene House. 3 BR5 . 38 B7
Arras House. SE2 ...... 7 D8
Arsenal Rd. SE9 .... 5 F4
Artemis Cl. DA12 ...... 30 E8
Arthur Gr. SE18 .... 2 C2
Arthur Rd. Gillingham ME8 4 C1
Arthur Rd. Rochester ME1 .. 47 D3
Arthur Ruxley Est. DA14 .. 24 D2
Arthur St. Erith DA8 .... 8 F7
Arthur St. Gravesend DA11 . 30 A8
Arthur St. Grays RM17 ... 12 C8
Arthur Toft House. 6
RM17 .... 12 B8
Artillery House SE18 .... 2 A1
Artillery Pl. SE18 ...... 2 A1
Artillery Row. DA12 .... 30 C8
Artington Cl. BR6 ...... 51 C6
Artisan Cl. E16 .... 2 B6
Arun Ct. BR5 .... 38 C1
Arundel Cl. Chatham ME5 .. 62 D1
Arundel Cl. Sidcup DA5 ... 7 E1
Arundel Cl. Tonbridge TN9 133 A8
Arundel Cl. 2 DA2 ..... 27 C8
Arundel Dr. BR6 .... 52 B5
Arundel Rd. Dartford DA1 .. 9 C3
Arundel Rd. Royal Tunbridge Wells
TN1 .... 149 B2
Arundel St. ME14 ...... 91 F6
Ascot Cl.
Borough Green TN15 .... 87 B7
Ascot Cl. Chatham ME5 .. 62 C2
Ascot Cl. DA5 .... 24 F8
Ascot House. 2 ME15 ... 107 F6
Ascot Rd. Gravesend DA12 . 30 F5
Ascot Rd. Orpington BR5 .. 37 F5
Ash Cl. Aylesford ME20 .. 75 F4
Ash Cl. Chatham ME5 .... 48 C1
Ash Cl. Edenbridge TN8 .. 112 B1
Ash Cl. Gillingham ME8 .. 49 B3
Ash Cl. Orpington BR5 .. 37 D4
Ash Cl. Royal Tunbridge Wells
TN2 .... 163 D7
Ash Cl. Sidcup DA14 .... 24 B5
Ash Cl. Swanley BR8 .... 39 D7
Ash Cres. ME3 .... 32 C3
Ash Cl. SE12 .... 22 A8
Ash Gr. Lewisham SE12 .. 22 A7
Ash Gr. Maidstone ME16 .. 91 C3
Ash Keys. DA13 .... 73 B8
Ash La. TN15 .... 56 D2
Ash Platt Rd. TN15 .... 84 E6
Ash Rd. Ash TN15 ..... 56 D6
Ash Rd. Dartford DA1 ... 26 D7
Ash Rd. Gravesend DA12 .. 30 C4
Ash Rd. Hartley DA3 .... 42 F3
Ash Rd. Hawley DA2 .... 26 F4
Ash Rd. Orpington BR6 .. 51 F3
Ash Rd. Rochester ME2 .. 46 F6
Ash Rd. Westerham TN16 .. 81 E2
Ash Row. BR2 .... 37 A3
Ash Tree Cl. TN15 ..... 55 E4
Ash Tree Cotts. TN12 ... 154 B7
Ash Tree Dr. TN15 ..... 55 E4
Ash Tree La. ME5 ...... 48 D1
Ashbank Cotts. ME17 ... 109 B7
Ashbee Cl. ME6 .... 75 A7
Ashbourne Ave. DA7 .... 7 E2
Ashbourne Rise. BR6 ... 51 E6
Ashburn Ct. ME1 ...... 22 A1
Ashburnham Cl. TN13 ... 99 C8
Ashburnham Rd. Erith DA21 .. 4 C2
Ashburnham Rd.
Maidstone ME16 .... 91 D3
Ashburnham Rd.
Tonbridge TN10 .... 117 C3
Ashburton Rd. E16 ..... 1 A7
Ashby Cl. ME2 .... 60 A4
Ashbys Yd. TN9 .... 117 C1
Ashcombe Dr. TN6 ...... 112 B4
Ashcroft Ave. DA15 .... 7 A1
Ashcroft Cres. DA15 .... 7 A1
Ashcroft Ct. Dartford DA1 . 27 A8
Ashcroft Ct. 5 Eltham SE9 . 6 A1
Ashcroft Rd. TN12 ..... 136 A5
Ashdale Rd. SE12 ...... 22 B7
Ashden Wlk. TN10 ...... 117 D7
Ashdown Cl. Coldblow DA5 . 25 C8
Ashdown Cl.
Maidstone ME16 .... 91 D3
Ashdown Cl. Royal Tunbridge Wells
TN4 .... 148 F4
Ashden. E6 .... 2 A8
Ashden Dr. DA1 .... 9 A1
Ashen Grove Rd. DA4 ... 55 B1
Ashenden. TN27 .... 142 F2
Ashenden Cl. ME2 ...... 33 C2
Ashenden Wlk. TN2 .... 149 E8

Ashes La. TN11 .... 118 E6
Ashfield La. BR7 .... 23 C1
Ashfield Pl. BR7 .... 23 D1
Ashford Dr. ME17 ..... 109 D3
Ashford Green
TN26 & TN30 .... 173 A6
Ashford Rd.
Harrietsham ME17 ..... 110 C6
Ashford Rd. Maidstone,
Grove Green ME14 & ME15 92 D4
Ashford Rd.
Maidstone,Silver Hill ME14 . 93 D3
Ashford Rd.
Tenterden TN30 .... 183 B8
Ashgrove Rd. TN13 ..... 99 B7
Ashlar Pl. SE18 .... 2 B2
Ashleigh Cl. DA13 ..... 57 F1
Ashleigh Gdns. TN27 ... 141 D6
Ashley Cl. TN13 .... 84 B3
Ashley Gdns. Orpington BR6 51 E5
Ashley Gdns. Rusthall TN4 148 C5
Ashley House. BR5 ..... 38 B7
Ashley Park Cl. TN4 .... 148 C5
Ashley Pk. TN4 .... 148 C5
Ashley Rd.
Hildenborough TN11 .... 116 E5
Ashley Rd. Sevenoaks TN13 . 84 B3
Ashmead Cl. ME5 ...... 62 C3
Ashmead Gate. BR1 .... 36 C8
Ashmore Gn. DA18 ..... 6 C7
Ashridge Cres. SE18 ... 6 C7
Ashridge House. DA14 ... 23 F4
Ashton Way. ME19 ..... 89 C6
Ashtree Cl. BR6 .... 51 B6
Ashurst Cl. DA1 .... 8 F4
Ashurst Hill. TN3 ...... 146 D2
Ashurst Rd.
Maidstone ME14 .... 92 C5
Ashurst Sta.
Stone Cross TN3 ...... 147 B2
Ashurst Sta. TN3 ...... 146 D2
Ashwater Rd. SE12 ..... 22 A7
Ashwell Cl. 8 E6 ...... 1 E7
Ashwood Cl. ME3 ...... 33 C7
Ashwood Pl. DA2 ...... 28 B5
Askern Cl. DA6 .... 7 D3
Askews Farm Rd. ME14 .. 11 E8
Askham Lodge. 8 SE12 .. 22 A8
Aspdin Rd. DA11 ...... 29 E5
Aspen Cl. Orpington BR6 .. 52 A5
Aspen Cl. Swanley BR8 .. 39 D8
Aspen Copse. BR1 ..... 36 F7
Aspen Ct. DA1 .... 10 A2
Aspen Gn. DA18 .... 3 F3
Aspen House. 2 DA15 ... 24 A5
Aspen Way. 2
Chatham ME5 .... 61 E4
Aspen Way. Royal Tunbridge Wells
TN2 .... 133 C1
Aspian Dr. ME17 ...... 106 D3
Asquith Rd. ME8 ...... 63 C3
Association Wlk. ME1 .. 61 C7
Aster Rd. ME3 .... 34 E3
Astley. RM17 .... 11 F8
Astley St. ME14 .... 92 A4
Aston Cl. Chatham ME5 .. 62 A2
Aston Cl. Sidcup DA14 .. 24 A5
Astor Cl. E16 .... 1 C7
Astor of Hever Sch The.
Astor Rd. TN15 .... 55 E4
Astra Dr. DA12 .... 30 F3
Atcost Rd. IG11 .... 3 A8
Athelstan Gn. ME17 .... 94 C2
Athelstan Rd. ME4 ..... 47 F2
Athill Ct. TN13 .... 84 C5
Athol Rd. DA8 .... 4 C1
Atkinson Cl. BR6 ...... 52 A5
Atkinson Rd. E16 ...... 1 C8
Atlantic Cl. ME1 ...... 47 D3
Atlas Gdns. SE7 .... 1 C1
Atlanta Ct. ME1 .... 9 F4
Atterbury Cl. TN16 .... 81 D1
Attlee Dr. DA1 .... 10 A2
Attlee Rd. SE28 .... 3 B6
Attwaters La. TN18 .... 179 C6
Atwater Ct. ME17 ...... 111 D5
Auckland Cl. ME4 ...... 13 A5
Auckland La. TN11 ..... 149 C5
Auden Rd. ME20 .... 75 A3
Audley Ave. Gillingham ME7 48 E1
Audley Ave. Tonbridge TN9 116 F2
Audley Cl. ME5 .... 61 E4
Audley Rise. TN9 ...... 116 F1
Audley Wlk. BR5 .... 38 C2
Audrey Sturley Ct. TN4 .. 148 D4
Augusta Cl. 1 ME7 .... 48 C7

Augustine Rd.
Gravesend DA12 .... 30 C8
Augustine Rd.
St Paul's Cray BR5 .... 38 D6
Austell Manor. ME7 .... 48 C6
Austen Cl. Swanscombe DA9 .. 11 C1
Austen Cl. Tilbury RM18 .... 13 C5
Austen Cl. Woolwich SE28 ...... 3 B5
Austen Gdns. 9 F3
Austen Rd. DA8 .... 8 B7
Austen Way. ME20 .... 74 F4
Austens Orch. ME12 TN30 ..... 183 A7
Austin Ave. BR1 & BR2 .... 36 E4
Austin Cl. ME5 & ME7 .... 48 E2
Austin Rd. Gravesend DA11 .... 29 F7
Austin Rd. Orpington BR5 ..... 38 A4
Austral CI. DA15 .... 23 F5
Autumn Glade. ME14 .... 77 D8
Avalon CI. BR6 .... 52 D7
Avalon Ctr. The. BR6 .... 52 D8
Avalon Gdns. BR5 .... 38 C1
Avalon Rd. BR5 .... 52 C6
Avard Gdns. BR6 .... 51 C6
Avards CI. TN18 .... 184 E8
Avebury Ave. TN9 .... 117 B1
Avebury Rd. BR6 .... 51 D7
Aveling CI. ME3 .... 34 D6
Aveling CI. 2 ME2 .... 47 B7
Avenons Rd. 3 E16 .... 1 A8
Avenue La. DA9 .... 11 C1
Avenue Le Puy. TN9 .... 117 C1
Avenue Rd. Bexley DA7 & DA6 7 E4
Avenue Rd. Erith DA8 .... 8 D7
Avenue Rd. Erith DA8 .... 8 E8
Avenue Rd. Sevenoaks TN13 84 C3
Avenue The. Aylesford ME20 75 E1
Avenue The.
  Borough Green TN15 .... 87 A8
Avenue The. Bromley BR1 ..... 36 D6
Avenue The.
  Gravesend DA11 .... 30 A8
Avenue The. Hill Park TN16 . 81 A4
Avenue The.
  Keston Mark BR2 .... 50 E8
Avenue The. Orpington BR6 . 51 F8
Avenue The. Sidcup DA5 ..... 24 D8
Avenue The.
  St Paul's Cray BR5 .... 24 B1
Avenue The.
  Swanscombe DA9 .... 11 B2
Avenue The.
  Tonbridge TN9 .... 117 B2
Averenches Rd. ME14 .... 92 F5
Avery Cl.
  Allhallows-on-Sea ME3 ..... 19 E9
Avery CI. Maidstone ME15 .... 91 F1
Avery Hill Rd. SE9 .... 23 D7
Avery La. ME15 .... 108 D6
Avery Way. ME3 .... 19 D8
Aviemore Gdns. ME14 .... 92 F4
Avington CI. ME15 .... 91 F1
Avocet Mews. SE28 .... 2 D3
Avocet Wlk. ME5 .... 62 D2
Avon CI. Gravesend DA12 ..... 30 D6
Avon CI. Tonbridge TN10 .... 117 C5
Avon St. TN1 .... 149 C2
Avondale Mews. BR1 .... 22 A2
Avondale PI. ME3 .... 19 C4
Avondale Rd. Bexley DA16 .... 7 C5
Avondale Rd. Bromley BR1 .. 22 A2
Avondale Rd.
  Chislehurst SE9 .... 22 E6
Avondale Rd.
  Gillingham ME7 .... 48 D5
Avonmouth Rd. DA1 .... 9 D2
Awliscombe Rd. DA16 .... 6 F5
Axford CI. ME8 .... 64 A8
Axminster Cres. DA16 .... 7 C6
Axtaine Rd. BR5 .... 38 D2
Axtane. DA13 .... 28 F1
Axtane CI. DA4 .... 41 C8
Axton Chase Sch. DA3 .... 42 F6
Aycliffe CI. BR1 .... 36 F5
Ayelands. DA3 .... 56 E8
Ayelands La. DA3 .... 56 E8
Aylesbury Rd. BR2 .... 36 A6
Aylesford Cres. ME8 .... 49 B4
Aylesford Cty Prim Sch.
  ME20 .... 75 D1
Aylesford Sch. ME20 .... 75 D1
Aylesford Sta. ME20 .... 75 E2
Aylesham Rd. BR6 .... 37 F2
Ay.nscombe Angle. BR6 .... 38 A2
Azalea Dr. BR8 .... 39 E5

Babb's La. TN17 .... 180 A6
Babbacombe Rd. BR1 .... 22 B1
Babington House Sch. BR7 . 22 F2

Babylon La. ME17 & TN12 . 124 B1
Back La. Godden Green TN15 85 A2
Back La. Goudhurst TN17 ... 167 E8
Back La. Horsmonden TN12 153 A6
Back La.
  Ightham Common TN15 .. 86 C2
Back La. Marlpit ME17 .... 107 E1
Back La.
  Sevenoaks TN13 & TN14 .. 63 A2
Back La. Shipbourne TN11 . 101 D4
Back La. Sidcup DA5 .... 25 B8
Back Rd. Sandhurst TN18 .. 186 B5
Back St. ME17 .... 108 E6
Backfields. ME1 .... 47 B3
Baden Powell House. 11
  DA17 .... 4 A3
Baden Powell Rd. TN13 ...... 83 E5
Baden Rd. ME7 .... 48 D7
Bader Cres. ME5 .... 62 A7
Badger Rd. ME5 .... 62 C1
Badgers Copse. BR6 .... 51 F8
Badgers Croft. SE9 .... 23 A5
Badgers Rd. TN14 .... 53 B1
Badgers Rise. TN14 .... 53 A1
Badlow CI. DA8 .... 8 E7
Badsell Park Farm. TN12 .. 135 E2
Badsell Rd. TN12 .... 135 D6
Baffin CI. ME4 .... 47 F2
Bailey Dr. ME7 .... 49 A1
Bakenham House. 1 ME1 .. 47 C1
Baker Beall CI. BR7 .... 8 B4
Baker Hill CI. DA11 .... 29 F4
Baker La. Headcorn TN27 .. 141 F7
Baker La.
  Sutton Valence ME17 ..... 124 F7
Baker Rd. SE18 .... 5 E6
Baker St. Burham ME1 .... 60 F1
Baker St. Rochester ME1 .... 47 C3
Baker's Wlk. ME1 .... 47 C6
Bakers Ave. TN15 .... 55 E3
Bakers Cross. TN17 .... 169 E4
Bakers Mews. 9 ME6 .... 51 F4
Bakery CI. TN17 .... 156 E7
Balcaskie Rd. ME15 .... 175 A6
Balcaskie Rd. SE9 .... 5 F2
Balchen Rd. SE3 .... 5 D5
Balcombe CI. DA6 .... 7 D3
Balcombe Cotts. TN17 .... 167 E8
Balcombes Hill. TN17 .... 167 E8
Balder Rise. SE12 .... 22 B6
Baldock Rd. TN5 .... 174 E4
Baldwin's Pk. DA5 .... 25 D6
Baldwyn's Rd. DA5 .... 25 D6
Balfour Cty Inf Sch. ME4 ... 47 E1
Balfour Cty Jun Sch. ME4 .. 47 E2
Balfour Rd. Bromley BR2 .... 36 D4
Balfour Rd. Chatham ME4 ... 47 E2
Balgowan St. SE18 .... 2 F2
Ball's Gn. TN7 .... 160 B5
Ballamore Rd. BR1 .... 22 A5
Ballard Bsns Pk. ME2 .... 46 F5
Ballard CI. TN12 .... 138 C6
Ballard Ind Est. ME5 .... 77 C8
Ballard Way. TN12 .... 136 B7
Ballens Rd. ME5 .... 62 C3
Balliol Rd. DA16 .... 7 B5
Balls Cotts. ME3 .... 33 F4
Balmer CI. ME8 .... 63 D7
Balmoral Ct. SE12 .... 22 B4
Balmoral Gdns. DA5 .... 24 F8
Balmoral House. 6 ME5 . 107 F5
Balmoral Rd.
  Gillingham ME7 .... 48 D5
Balmoral Rd.
  Sutton at Hone DA4 .... 27 B1
Balmoral Trad Est. E6 .... 2 F8
Baltic Rd. TN9 .... 133 B7
Baltimore Rd. ME4 .... 47 F1
Banbridges Ind Est. TN12 120 A5
Banbury Villas. DA13 .... 28 F1
Banchory Rd. SE3 .... 5 B7
Banckside. DA3 .... 42 E5
Bancroft Gdns. BR6 .... 37 F1
Bancroft Rd. TN15 .... 71 F3
Bandfield Wlk. DA1 .... 9 F4
Bangor Rd. ME2 .... 46 D6
Bank Cotts. ME17 .... 47 E3
Bank Houses. DA2 .... 27 A3
Bank La. TN11 & TN15 ...... 100 A3
Bank St. Chatham ME4 .... 48 B3
Bank St. Cranbrook TN17 ... 169 C5
Bank St. Gravesend DA11 ... 13 B1
Bank St.
  Maidstone ME14 & ME15 .. 92 A4
Bank St. Sevenoaks TN13 .. 84 C2
Bank St. Tonbridge TN9 .... 117 C2
Bankfield Way. TN12 .... 167 E7
Bankfields. TN27 .... 141 C5
Banks La. DA6 .... 7 F3

Banks Rd. ME2 .... 47 C8
Bankside. Chatham ME5 ..... 48 B4
Bankside. Northfleet DA11 ... 12 C1
Bankside. Sevenoaks TN13 .. 83 C6
Bankside.
  Sparrow's Green TN5 .... 174 E5
Bankside CI. DA2 .... 25 D4
Banky Meadow. ME16 .... 90 F3
Banner Farm Rd. TN2 .... 149 B2
Banning St. ME2 .... 47 B7
Bannister Gdns. BR5 .... 38 C1
Bannister Rd. ME14 .... 92 A7
Bannockburn Prim Sch.
  SE18 .... 2 F2
Bannockburn Rd. SE18 .... 2 F2
Banwell Rd. DA5 .... 7 D1
Bapchild Pl. 8 BR5 .... 38 C5
Barbados Terr. 2 ME14 ..... 92 A7
Barberry Ave. ME5 .... 61 E5
Barcham CI. ME15 .... 106 F5
Barchester Way. TN10 .... 117 F6
Barclay Ave. TN10 .... 118 A5
Barcombe CI. BR5 & BR7 ... 38 A6
Bardell Terr. ME1 .... 47 D5
Barden CI. ME14 .... 92 B5
Barden Park Rd. TN9 .... 117 A1
Barden Rd. Printstile TN3 .. 131 C7
Barden Rd. Tonbridge TN9 117 B1
Barden St. SE18 .... 6 E7
Bardsley CI. TN12 .... 120 A7
Barfield. DA4 .... 41 B8
Barfield Rd. BR1 & BR7 ...... 22 C1
Barfleur Manor. 6 ME4 ..... 48 A6
Barfreston CI. ME15 .... 91 F2
Bargate CI. SE18 .... 2 F1
Barge House Rd. E16 .... 2 B4
Bargrove Rd. ME14 .... 92 C5
Barham CI. Chislehurst BR7 . 23 B3
Barham CI. Gravesend DA12 30 F7
Barham CI. Keston Mark BR2 36 E1
Barham CI.
  Park Wood ME15 .... 107 C5
Barham CI. ME2 .... 36 E1
Barham Mews. ME16 .... 105 B8
Barham Rd. Chislehurst BR7 23 B3
Barham Rd. Dartford DA1 ... 27 B8
Barham's Mill Rd. TN27 ... 127 B3
Baring CI. SE12 .... 22 A6
Baring Prim Sch. SE12 .... 22 A6
Baring Rd. SE12 .... 22 A6
Bark Hart Rd. BR6 .... 38 B1
Barker Rd. ME14 .... 91 F3
Barking Rd. E16 .... 1 A8
Barkis CI. ME1 .... 61 D7
Barley Fields. ME1 .... 92 D4
Barleycorn. ME19 .... 74 E1
Barleycorn Dr. ME8 .... 63 E6
Barleymow CI. ME5 .... 62 C7
Barling CI. ME5 .... 61 D1
Barlow CI. ME8 .... 63 E5
Barlow Way. RM13 & RM9 .. 4 E8
Barming Cty Prim Sch.
  ME16 .... 90 F2
Barming Rd. ME19 .... 89 F2
Barming Sta. ME16 .... 90 F6
Barn End Ctr. DA2 .... 26 C5
Barn End La. DA2 .... 26 C5
Barn End La. DA2 .... 26 C4
Barn Hill. ME15 .... 105 E2
Barn Meadow. ME2 .... 59 E4
Barnaby Terr. ME1 .... 47 D2
Barnard CI. Chislehurst BR7 . 37 D8
Barnard CI. Woolwich SE18 .. 2 A3
Barnard Ct. Chatham ME4 .. 48 A2
Barnard Ct. 10
  Dartford DA2 .... 10 B1
Barncroft CI. ME14 .... 92 F4
Barncroft Dr. ME7 .... 62 F4
Barned Ct. ME16 .... 90 F7
Barnehurst Ave. DA7 & DA8 .. 8 C6
Barnehurst CI. DA8 .... 8 C6
Barnehurst Inf Sch. DA8 .... 8 C6
Barnehurst Jun Sch. DA8 .. 8 C6
Barnehurst Rd. DA7 .... 8 C5
Barnehurst Sta. DA7 .... 8 B5
Barnes Cray Prim Sch. DA1 .. 9 A3
Barnes Cray Rd. DA1 .... 9 A3
Barnes CI. E16 .... 1 C8
Barnes La. ME17 .... 122 D8
Barnes Wlk. TN12 .... 138 D6
Barnesdale Cres. BR5 .... 38 A4
Barnet Dr. BR2 .... 50 E8
Barnet Wood Rd. BR2 .... 50 C8
Barnett CI. DA8 .... 8 F5
Barnetts CI. TN2 & TN4 ... 133 C1
Barnetts Rd. TN11 .... 116 A2
Barnetts Way. TN4 .... 133 C1
Barney CI. SE7 .... 1 C1
Barnfield. Chatham ME5 .... 62 A8
Barnfield.
  Royal Tunbridge Wells TN2 162 F7

Barnfield.
  St Michaels TN30 .... 173 C2
Barnfield CI. Crockenhill
  BR8 .... 39 C2
Barnfield CI. New Barn DA3 . 43 D6
Barnfield CI. Stone DA9 ..... 10 F1
Barnfield Cres. TN14 .... 69 E2
Barnfield Gdns. SE18 .... 6 B8
Barnfield Rd. Erith DA17 ...... 7 F8
Barnfield Rd.
  Sevenoaks TN13 .... 83 E4
Barnfield Rd.
  St Paul's Cray BR5 .... 38 D6
Barnhill Ave. BR2 .... 36 A4
Barnhurst Rd. ME14 .... 92 A8
Barnsole Cty Inf Sch. ME7 . 48 E4
Barnsole Cty Jun Sch. ME7 . 48 E4
Barnsole Rd. ME7 .... 48 E3
Barnwell Rd. DA1 .... 9 F4
Barnwood CI. ME1 .... 61 B8
Barnwood CI. E16 .... 1 B5
Baron CI. Gillingham ME7 ... 48 C7
Baron CI. Maidstone ME14 ... 92 F5
Barons Ct. TN4 .... 149 A5
Barr Rd. DA12 .... 30 F6
Barrack Cnr. TN13 .... 84 C4
Barrack Rd. ME4 .... 48 B8
Barrack Row.
  Berenden TN17 .... 180 D6
Barrack Row. 14
  Gravesend DA11 .... 13 B1
Barrel Arch CI. TN12 .... 138 C6
Barretts Green Cotts. 5
  TN18 .... 179 A2
Barretts Rd.
  Hawkhurst TN18 .... 179 A2
Barretts Rd.
  Sevenoaks TN13 .... 83 E2
Barrie Dr. 7 ME20 .... 74 F4
Barrier Rd. ME4 .... 47 F5
Barrington CI. ME5 .... 61 C5
Barrington Prim Sch. ... 7 D5
Barrington Rd. DA16 .... 7 D5
Barrington Villas. SE18 .... 6 A6
Barrow La. TN3 .... 147 F1
Barrowfields. ME5 .... 62 D1
Barry Ave. DA7 .... 7 E3
Barry CI. BR6 .... 51 E7
Barry Rd. E6 .... 1 E7
Barth Rd. SE18 .... 2 E2
Bartholomew Way. BR8 ..... 39 E6
Bartlett CI. ME5 .... 62 C1
Bartlett Rd.
  Gravesend DA11 .... 30 A7
Bartlett Rd.
  Westerham TN16 .... 81 C1
Bartley Mill. TN3 .... 164 E4
Barton CI. Bexley DA6 .... 7 E2
Barton CI. 2 Newham E6 .... 1 F7
Barton CI. Yalding ME18 .... 104 F1
Barton Cotts. TN11 .... 102 A6
Barton Rd. Maidstone ME15 . 92 A2
Barton Rd. Rochester ME2 .. 47 A7
Barton Rd. Sidcup DA14 .... 24 E2
Barton Rd.
  Sutton at Hone DA4 .... 41 B8
Basden Cotts. 2 TN18 ... 179 A2
Baseing CI. E6 .... 2 A6
Bashford Barn La. ME9 ...... 80 F8
Basi CI. ME2 .... 33 C1
Basildon Rd. SE2 .... 3 A1
Basilon Rd. DA7 .... 7 E5
Basing CI. ME15 .... 92 B3
Basing Dr. DA5 .... 7 F1
Basket Gdns. SE9 .... 5 E2
Basmere CI. ME14 .... 92 C6
Bassant Rd. SE18 .... 6 F8
Bassett's Forge. TN5 .... 174 E5
Bassetts CI. BR6 .... 51 B6
Bassetts La. TN11 & TN6 .. 146 C7
Bassetts Way. BR6 .... 51 B6
Basted La. Basted TN15 .... 86 F5
Basted La. Crouch TN15 .... 87 B4
Bastion Rd. SE18 & SE2 ...... 3 A1
Baston Manor Rd.
  BR2 & BR4 .... 50 B6
Baston Rd. BR2 .... 50 B7
Bat & Ball Sta. TN14 .... 84 C6
Batchelor St. ME4 .... 48 A4
Batchelors. TN2 .... 150 E8
Batchwood Gn. BR5 .... 38 B6
Bates CI. ME20 .... 75 A3
Bates Hill. TN15 .... 86 C5
Bateson St. SE18 .... 2 E2
Bath Hard. ME1 .... 47 D5
Bath Rd. DA1 .... 26 B8
Bath St. DA11 .... 13 B1
Baths Rd. BR1 & BR2 .... 36 D5
Bathurst CI. TN12 .... 139 E4
Bathurst Rd. TN12 .... 139 E3

Bathway. 17 SE18 2
Batt's Rd. DA12 & DA13 45
Batten CI. E6 ....
Battery Rd. SE28 ....
Battle La. TN12 139
Battle Rd. DA8 & DA17 4
Battle St. DA2 4
Battlefields. TN1 7
Battlesmere Rd. ME3 .... 3:
Baugh Rd. DA14 2
Baxter Rd. E16 ....
Bay CI. ME3 3
Bay Manor La. RM16 1
Bay The. DA13 ....
Bayard Ct. DA7 ....
Bayeux House. 10 SE7 ....
Bayfield Rd. SE9 ....
Bayhall Rd. TN2 149
Bayham Abbey (rems of).
  TN3 .... 16!
Bayham Ct. TN5 174
Bayham Rd. Royal Tunbridge We
  TN2 & TN3 .... 16:
Bayham Rd.
  Sevenoaks TN13 84
Bayley's Hill. TN14 .... 9i
Bayliss Ave. SE28 3
Bayly Rd. DA1 .... 1(
Bayne CI. E6 ....
Bayswater Dr. ME8 .... 6:
Baytree CI. Bromley BR1 ... 3(
Baytree CI. Sidcup DA15 ... 2:
Baywell. ME19 & ME20 74
Bazes Shaw. DA3 .... 5(
Beach Ct. Eltham SE9 ....
Beach Ct.
  Goddard's Green TN17 ... 170
Beacham CI. SE7 ....
Beacon CI. ME8 .... 6:
Beacon Dr. DA2 .... 2(
Beacon Hill. ME5 .... 4(
Beacon Hill La. ME3 .... 3:
Beacon Oak Rd. TN30 .... 18:
Beacon Rd. Chatham ME5 ... 4(
Beacon Rd. Erith DA8 ....
Beacon Rd. Lenham ME17 .. 11:
Beacon Rise. TN13 .... 8/
Beacon Wlk. TN30 .... 17:
Beacon Wood Cty Pk. DA2 . 2(
Beaconfields. TN13 .... 2/
Beacons The. ME17 .... 10(
Beacons Wlk. 10 E6 ....
Beaconsfield Ave. ME7 ...... 4i
Beaconsfield CI. SE3 .... !
Beaconsfield Par. SE3 .... 2/
Beaconsfield Rd.
  Bromley BR1 .... 3(
Beaconsfield Rd.
  Chatham ME4 .... 4'
Beaconsfield Rd.
  Chislehurst SE9 .... 2/
Beaconsfield Rd.
  Greenwich SE3 .... !
Beaconsfield Rd.
  Maidstone ME15 91
Beaconsfield Rd.
  Maypole DA5 .... 2!
Beadon Rd. BR2 .... 3(
Beagles CI. BR5 .... 5:
Beagles Wood Rd. TN2 ... 15(
Beal CI. DA16 ....
Beamish Rd. BR5 .... 3i
Beams The. ME15 92
Bean Cty Prim Sch. DA2 ... 2i
Bean Hill Cotts. DA2 .... 2i
Bean La. DA2 .... 2i
Bean Rd. Bexley DA6 7
Bean Rd. Swanscombe DA2 . 2i
Beanshaw. BR7 & SE9 .... 2:
Bearsted CI. ME8 49
Bearsted Green Bsns Ctr.
  ME14 93
Bearsted Rd. ME14 92
Bearsted & Thurnham Sta.
  ME14 .... 9:
Beaton CI. DA9 .... 1:
Beatrice Gdns. DA11 29
Beatty Ave. ME7 .... 4i
Beatty Cotts. ME3 19
Beatty Rd. ME1 ....
Beaufighter Rd. ME19 .... 8i
Beaufort. E6 ....
Beaufort Ct. ME2 .... 4'
Beaufort Rd. ME2 .... 4(
Beaufort Wlk. ME15 .... 10i
Beaulieu Hill. ME10 .... 11.
Beaulieu Rise. ME1 ....
Beaulieu Wlk. ME16 .... 9!
Beaumanor Gdns. SE9 .... 2:
Beaumont Dr. DA11 .... 2!

...umont Rd.
...idstone ME16 .... 91 B2
...lamont Rd.
...rthfleet DA11 .... 29 E8
...oington BR5 & BR6 .... 37 D3
...worth Rd. ME15 .... 107 E8
...berbank Rd. SE9 .... 23 D7
...pers Lodge. DA14 .... 23 F3
...yerwood Rd. BR7 .... 23 E2
...erwood Sch for Girls.
...7 .... 23 E2
...pington Rd. SE18 .... 2 E2
...ets Cl. 4 BR6 .... 51 F5
...kenham Dr. ME16 .... 91 D7
...kenham La. BR1 & BR2 .. 36 A7
...kets Cl. TN27 .... 141 D5
...kets Field. TN11 .... 131 A3
...kett Cl. DA17 .... 3 F3
...ketts Cl. BR6 .... 51 F7
...kton Cl. BR5 & BR6 ...... 37 D2
...oley Cl. DA12 .... 31 B6
...oley Mews. ME5 .... 61 F5
...kman Cl. TN14 .... 68 C4
...ks Rd. DA14 .... 24 A5
...ksbourne Cl. ME14 ...... 92 A8
...kton Park Sta. Cl. 1 F6
...kton Rd. Cl. 1 A8
...kton Sch. E16 .... 1 D8
...ston Sta. E6 .... 2 A8
...on Pl. DA8 .... 8 C6
...ale Wlk. DA1 .... 27 B7
...pington Gn. BR5 .... 37 F8
...wood Rd. BR5 .... 37 F8
...dow Way. ME20 .... 76 B3
...ens Rd. DA14 .... 24 E3
...ord Ave. ME8 .... 49 D1
...ord Pl. ME16 .... 91 A4
...ford Rd. Dartford DA1 .. 27 A8
...ford Rd. Northfleet DA11 29 F6
...ord Rd. Orpington BR6 .. 38 B1
...ord Rd.
...yal Tunbridge Wells TN4 133 A1
...ord Rd. Sidcup DA15 .... 23 E5
...ord Sq. DA3 .... 42 E6
...ord Terr. 9 TN1 ...... 149 A2
...gebury Cl.
...atham ME1 .... 61 D8
...gebury Cl.
...idstone ME14 .... 92 C6
...gebury Cross. TN17 .... 167 D2
...gebury Lower Sch.
...18 .... 184 F7
...gebury National Pinetum.
...17 .... 177 E8
...gebury Rd. Eltham SE9 .. 5 D3
...gebury Rd.
...udhurst TN17 .... 167 E7
...gebury Rd. TN17 ...... 167 E1
...vere Rd. BR1 .... 22 A5
...am La. TN27 .... 142 E6
...onwell Jun Sch. DA17 .... 7 E8
...onwell Prim Inf Sch. DA7 7 F6
...onwell Rd. Bexley DA7 .. 7 F6
...onwell Rd.
...th DA7 & DA17 .... 7 E8
...well Rd. DA17 .... 4 A1
...win Cl. ME1 .... 61 D7
...g Rd. E16 .... 1 B8
...ch Ave. Sidcup DA15 .... 24 A8
...th Ave. Swanley BR8 .... 39 F5
...h Copse. BR1 .... 36 F7
...ch Ct. DA1 .... 10 A1
...ch Dell. BR2 & BR6 ...... 50 F6
...ch Dr. ME16 .... 91 C5
...ch Gr. ME3 .... 32 C4
...ch Green La.
...ackham TN7 .... 145 F1
...ch Green La.
...thyham TN7 .... 160 B7
...ch Haven Ct. DA1 .... 8 D2
...ch House. 7 DA15 ...... 24 A5
...ch Hurst. TN2 .... 150 D7
...ch La. TN12 .... 151 C4
...ch Rd. Dartford DA1 .... 26 D7
...ch Rd.
...ast Malling ME19 .... 89 F7
...ch Rd.
...erne Pound ME18 .... 88 D2
...ch Rd.
...oo St Werburgh ME3 .... 34 E3
...ch Rd. Newenden TN18 187 C3
...ch Rd. Orpington BR6 .. 52 A3
...ch Rd. Rochester ME2 .. 46 F6
...ch Rd. Sevenoaks TN13 .. 84 B2
...ch St. TN1 .... 149 B4
...ch Wlk. DA1 .... 9 A3
...cham Rd. TN10 .... 117 C6
...chcroft. BR7 .... 23 A1
...chcroft Ave. DA7 .... 8 D5
...chcroft Cl. BR6 .... 51 D6

Beechcroft Rd. BR6 .... 51 D6
Beechen Bank Rd. ME5 .... 62 A1
Beechenlea La. BR8 .... 40 B6
Beeches Cl. BR1 .... 22 A2
Beeches The.
Aylesford ME20 .... 75 E1
Beeches The. Chatham ME5 . 62 A4
Beeches The.
Royal Tunbridge Wells
TN2 .... 149 D5
Beeches The.
Sole Street DA12 .... 44 D5
Beeches The.
The Moor TN18 .... 184 E7
Beeches The. Tilbury RM18 . 13 B5
Beechfield Cotts. 3 BR1 .. 36 C7
Beechfield Rd.
Bromley BR1 .... 36 C7
Beechfield Rd. Erith DA8 .. 8 E7
Beechhill Rd. SE9 .... 6 A2
Beechill Dr. RM17 .... 11 F8
Beechin Wood La. TN15 .. 87 D5
Beeching Rd. ME5 .... 62 B3
Beechings Gn. ME8 .... 49 C3
Beechings Way. ME8 ...... 49 C3
Beechlands Cl. DA3 .... 43 A4
Beechmont Rd. TN13 ...... 99 B6
Beechmont Rise. TN10 .. 117 B6
Beechmore Dr. ME5 .... 62 A2
Beechway. DA5 .... 7 F8
Beechwood Ave.
Chatham ME5 .... 48 D2
Beechwood Ave.
Orpington BR6 .... 51 E4
Beechwood Cres. DA7 .... 7 E4
Beechwood Dr. Keston BR2 . 50 D6
Beechwood Dr.
Vigo Village DA13 .... 58 A1
Beechwood Gdns. DA13 .. 58 A1
Beechwood Mews. TN2 .. 149 E4
Beechwood Rd. ME16 ...... 90 F3
Beechwood Rise. BR7 ...... 23 B3
Beechwood Sch (Sacred Heart).
TN2 .... 149 E4
Beechy Lees Rd. TN14 .. 69 E3
Beeken Dene. BR6 .... 51 C6
Beesfield La. DA4 .... 41 A1
Beeston Ct. DA1 .... 10 B1
Begbie Rd. SE3 .... 5 C6
Beggars La. TN16 .... 81 E3
Begonia Ave. ME8 .... 49 C2
Beke Rd. ME8 .... 63 D4
Bekesbourne Tower. 12
BR5 .... 38 D1
Beldam Haw. TN14 .... 68 A8
Belfield Rd. TN2 .... 150 D6
Belford Gr. SE18 .... 2 A2
Belgrave Cl. 5 BR5 .... 38 C5
Belgrave Ct. SE7 .... 5 C7
Belgrave Rd. TN1 .... 149 B4
Belgrave St. ME20 .... 75 F6
Belgrove. 5 TN1 .... 149 A2
Bell Cl. DA9 .... 10 F2
Bell Cres. ME1 .... 75 F8
Bell Gdns. BR5 .... 38 C4
Bell House. SE3 .... 3 D1
Bell La. Burham ME1 ...... 75 F8
Bell La. Larkfield ME20 .. 75 B2
Bell La. Lashenden TN27 .. 158 B8
Bell La. Maidstone ME14 . 93 A5
Bell La. Newham E16 ...... 1 A5
Bell La. Staplehurst TN12 . 139 E3
Bell La. Westfield Sole ME14 77 B7
Bell Rd. ME15 .... 107 E5
Bell Row. TN11 .... 118 F5
Bell Water Gate. SE18 .... 2 A3
Bell Way. ME17 .... 109 E2
Bell Wood City Inf Sch.
ME15 .... 107 E5
Bell Wood City Jun Sch.
ME15 .... 107 E5
Bell's Cl. TN30 .... 183 A7
Bell's La. ME3 .... 34 E6
Belle Vue Rd. BR6 .... 51 A1
Bellefield Rd. BR5 .... 38 B4
Bellegrave Par. DA16 .... 6 F4
Bellegrove Cl. DA16 ...... 6 E5
Bellegrove Rd. DA16 ...... 6 E5
Bellevue Rd. DA6 .... 7 F2
Bellflower Cl. 2 E6 .... 1 E8
Bellgrove Ct. ME5 .... 77 A8
Bellman Ave. DA12 ...... 30 E7
Bellmeadow. ME15 ...... 107 E6
Bellows La. TN15 .... 86 F7
Bellring Cl. DA17 .... 8 A8
Bells Farm La.
TN11 & TN12 .... 119 C8
Bells Farm Rd. TN12 .... 103 D1
Bells La. 7 TN30 .... 183 A7
Bellwood Dr. ME3 .... 18 C3
Belmont Ave. DA16 .... 6 E4

Belmont Cl. ME16 .... 90 F2
Belmont La. BR7 .... 23 C3
Belmont Par. BR7 .... 23 C3
Belmont Prim Sch. DA7 .. 8 A7
Belmont Rd.
Chislehurst BR7 .... 23 B3
Belmont Rd. Erith DA8 .... 8 B6
Belmont Rd. Gillingham ME7 48 C4
Belmont Rd. Grays RM17 .. 11 F8
Belnor Ave. ME9 .... 65 F8
Belson Rd. SE18 .... 1 F2
Beltana Dr. DA12 .... 30 E4
Belton Rd. DA14 .... 24 C4
Beltring & Banbridges Halt.
TN12 .... 120 B4
Beltring Hop Farm. TN12 . 120 A3
Beltring Rd. Beltring TN12 120 B4
Beltring Rd. Royal Tunbridge Wells
TN4 .... 149 A6
Beltwood Rd. DA17 .... 4 C2
Beluncle Villas. ME3 ...... 35 C7
Belvedere Cl. DA12 .... 30 C7
Belvedere Cl. DA17 .... 3 F3
Belvedere Cty Prim Jun Sch.
DA17 .... 4 B3
Belvedere Ind Est. DA17 .. 4 D5
Belvedere Link Bsns Pk.
DA17 .... 4 B3
Belvedere Rd. Bexley DA7 . 7 F5
Belvedere Rd. Erith SE28 . 3 D5
Belvedere Sta. DA17 ...... 4 B3
Belvoir Cl. SE9 .... 22 E5
Ben Tillet Cl. E16 .... 1 F5
Benares Rd. SE18 & SE2 . 2 F2
Benden Cl. TN12 .... 139 F4
Bendmore Ave. SE2 ...... 3 A2
Bendon Way. ME8 .... 63 D8
Benedict Cl. 9 Erith DA17 . 3 E3
Benedict Cl. Halling ME2 .. 60 B4
Benedict Cl. Orpington BR6 . 51 C7
Benenden Ce Prim Sch.
TN17 .... 180 D6
Benenden Gn. BR2 .... 36 A4
Benenden Hospl. TN17 .. 171 C3
Benenden Manor. ME8 .. 49 B3
Benenden Rd.
Benenden TN17 .... 181 B4
Benenden Rd. Fosten Green
TN17 & TN27 .... 171 F5
Benenden Rd.
Rochester ME2 .... 33 C1
Benenden Sch. TN17 .... 180 C8
Benenenden Rd. TN27 .. 172 A7
Benhall Mill Rd.
TN2 & TN3 .... 163 D8
Benjamin Ct. 4 DA17 .... 7 F8
Benn House. 7 SE7 ...... 1 C1
Bennett Cl. DA16 .... 7 A5
Bennett House. DA11 .... 29 F5
Bennett Memorial Diocesan Sch.
TN4 .... 148 E6
Bennett Way. DA2 .... 27 D3
Bennetts Ave. TN15 ...... 71 C7
Bennetts Copse. BR7 .... 22 E2
Bennetts Cotts. ME7 ...... 78 A8
Bennetts Mews. 11
TN30 .... 183 A7
Benover Rd. ME18 .... 120 F7
Benson Rd. RM17 .... 12 C8
Bensted Cl. ME15 .... 121 D7
Bentfield Gdns. SE9 ...... 22 D5
Bentham Hill. TN3 & TN4 . 132 D1
Bentham Rd. SE28 .... 3 B5
Bentley Cl. Aylesford ME20 . 75 F2
Bentley Cl. Chatham ME5 . 62 D2
Bentley Cl. New Barn DA3 . 43 C7
Bentley St. DA11 .... 13 C1
Bentley Street Ind Est.
DA11 .... 13 C1
Bentley's Meadow. TN15 . 84 F7
Bentlif Cl. ME16 .... 91 D5
Berber Rd. ME2 .... 47 B8
Bercta Rd. SE9 .... 23 C6
Berengrave La. ME8 ...... 49 F2
Berens Ct. DA14 .... 23 F4
Berens Rd. BR5 .... 38 D4
Berens Way. BR5 & BR7 . 37 F6
Beresford Ave. ME4 ...... 47 E2
Beresford Cl. TN17 ...... 166 F2
Beresford Dr. BR1 .... 36 E6
Beresford Rd.
Gillingham ME7 .... 48 D4
Beresford Rd.
Goudhurst TN12 .... 153 F1
Beresford Rd.
Kit's Coty ME20 .... 76 D7
Beresford Rd.
Northfleet DA11 .... 29 E8
Beresford Square Market Pl. 1
SE18 .... 2 B2
Beresford St. SE18 .... 2 B3

Beresfords Hill. ME17 .... 107 B4
Berger Cl. BR5 .... 37 E3
Bergland Pk. ME2 .... 47 D8
Bering Wlk. E16 .... 1 D7
Berkeley Ave. DA16 ...... 6 E3
Berkeley Cl. Chatham ME1 . 61 D8
Berkeley Cl.
Orpington BR5 & BR6 .. 37 E2
Berkeley Cl. Pembury TN2 . 150 E7
Berkeley Cres. DA1 ...... 26 F7
Berkeley Ct. 8 BR8 ...... 39 E6
Berkeley Mount. 1 ME4 . 47 F4
Berkeley Rd.
Gravesend DA11 .... 13 B1
Berkeley Rd. 7 Royal Tunbridge
Wells TN1 .... 149 A2
Berkeley Terr. ME18 ...... 13 A7
Berkhampstead Rd. 8
DA17 .... 4 A1
Berkhurst Cl. DA11 ...... 13 C1
Berkshire Cl. ME5 .... 62 C8
Bermuda Rd. RM18 ...... 13 A5
Bernal Cl. SE28 .... 3 D6
Bernard Ashley Dr. SE7 .. 1 B1
Bernard St. 21 DA11 .... 13 B1
Bernersmede. SE3 .... 5 A4
Berry Rd. ME3 .... 34 E3
Berry's Green Rd. TN16 .. 66 B2
Berry's Hill. TN14 & TN16 . 66 B4
Berryfield Cl. BR1 .... 36 E7
Berryhill. SE9 .... 6 B3
Berryhill Gdns. SE9 ...... 6 B3
Berrylands. Hartley DA3 . 43 A3
Berrylands. Orpington BR6 . 52 C7
Bert Reilly House. 1 SE18 . 2 D1
Bertha Hollamby Ct. DA14 . 24 C3
Bertrand Way. SE28 ...... 3 C6
Bertrey Cotts. TN16 ...... 66 B3
Berwick Cres. DA15 ...... 6 E1
Berwick Rd. Bexley DA16 . 7 B6
Berwick Rd. Newham E16 . 1 C7
Berwick Way. TN14 ...... 84 B7
Berwyn Gr. ME15 .... 107 A6
Beryl Ave. E6 .... 1 E8
Beryl House. SE18 .... 2 F1
Besant Ct. 15 SE28 ...... 3 B6
Bessels Green Rd. TN13 .. 83 D3
Bessels Meadow. TN13 .. 83 D3
Bessels Way. TN13 ...... 83 D4
Bessie Lansbury Cl. E6 .. 2 A7
Best St. ME4 .... 47 F4
Betenson Ave. TN13 ...... 83 F5
Bethany Sch. TN17 ...... 154 B5
Bethel Rd. Bexley DA16 .. 7 C4
Bethel Rd. Sevenoaks TN13 . 84 C4
Betherinden Cotts. TN18 . 186 A4
Bethersden Ct. ME15 .... 107 F7
Bethersden Rd.
TN27 & TN26 .... 159 C5
Bethersden Rd.
Gillingham ME8 .... 49 B3
Betony Gdns. ME14 ...... 92 F5
Betsham Rd. Betsham DA13 28 D3
Betsham Rd. Erith DA8 .. 8 F7
Betsham Rd.
Maidstone ME15 .... 107 F6
Betsham Rd.
Swanscombe DA10 ...... 28 E8
Betterton Dr. DA14 ...... 24 E6
Bettescombe Rd. ME8 .... 63 E7
Betts Rd. E16 .... 1 B6
Beulah Rd. TN1 .... 149 C4
Beult Meadow. TN27 .... 143 A1
Beult Rd. DA1 .... 9 A3
Bevan Pl. BR8 .... 39 F5
Bevan Rd. SE2 .... 3 B1
Bevans Cl. DA9 .... 11 C1
Bevercote Wlk. 1 DA17 . 7 F8
Beveridge Ct. 1 SE28 .... 3 B6
Beverley Ave. DA15 ...... 23 F8
Beverley Cl. ME8 .... 63 E8
Beverley Cres. TN9 ...... 132 F7
Beverley Rd. Bexley DA7 . 8 C5
Beverley Rd.
Keston Mark BR2 .... 50 E8
Beverley Rd.
Maidstone ME16 .... 90 F2
Bevile House. RM17 ...... 12 B7
Bevis Cl. DA2 .... 27 C8
Bewl Bridge Cl. TN5 .... 177 B3
Bewl Water. TN5 .... 176 C6
Bewlbridge La.
Bewlbridge TN3 & TN5 . 166 B1
Bewlbridge La.
Lower Cousley Wood TN5 . 175 F8
Bewley La. TN15 .... 86 D2
Bexley Cl. DA1 .... 8 E2
Bexley Coll. Erith DA17 .. 4 B1
Bexley Coll. Erith DA17 .. 4 C2
Bexley Coll
(St Joseph's Campus). SE2 7 D8

Bexley Gram Sch. DA16 .. 7 B3
Bexley High St. DA5 ...... 25 B7
Bexley Hospl. DA5 .... 25 E6
Bexley La. Crayford DA1 .. 8 E2
Bexley La. Sidcup DA14 .. 24 C5
Bexley Rd. Eltham SE9 .. 6 C2
Bexley Rd. Erith DA8 ...... 4 F1
Bexley Rd. Erith,
Northumberland Heath DA8 . 8 C8
Bexley Sta. DA14 .... 24 C4
Bexley-Erith Tech
High Sch for Boys. DA5 .. 8 B1
Bexleyheath Golf Course.
DA6 .... 7 E2
Bexleyheath Sch. DA7 .... 7 F4
Bexleyheath Sta. DA7 .... 7 F5
Bexon La. ME9 .... 80 F5
Bickley Cres. ME1 .... 36 E5
Bickley Park Rd. BR1 & BR7 . 36 F6
Bickley Park Sch. BR1 .... 36 E6
Bickley Rd. Bromley BR1 . 36 F7
Bickley Rd. 4
Tonbridge TN9 .... 133 B8
Bickley Sta. BR1 .... 36 E6
Bickmore Way. TN4 ...... 132 D3
Bicknor Court Cotts. ME9 . 80 C2
Bicknor La. ME9 .... 80 B8
Bicknor Rd. Orpington BR6 . 37 F2
Bicknor Rd.
Park Wood ME15 .... 107 F4
Bidborough CE Prim Sch.
TN4 .... 132 D3
Bidborough Ridge. TN4 .. 132 E4
Biddenden Cl. ME15 ...... 92 F3
Biddenden La. TN27 .... 141 E5
Biddenden Rd.
Durrant Green TN26 .... 173 A6
Biddenden Rd.
Headcorn TN27 .... 141 E2
Biddenden Rd. London Beach
TN26 & TN27 .... 172 E6
Biddenden Rd.
Tylden TN27 .... 158 F8
Biddenden Way. Eltham SE9 23 A4
Biddenden Way.
Istead Rise DA13 .... 29 E1
Biddulph House. 23 SE18 . 1 F2
Bideford Rd. DA16 .... 7 B7
Biggin La. RM17 .... 13 B8
Bignell Rd. SE18 .... 2 B1
Bilberry Cl. ME14 .... 92 E5
Bill Hamling Cl. SE9 ...... 22 F6
Bill Street Rd. ME2 ...... 33 C1
Billet Hill. TN15 .... 56 C6
Billings. DA3 .... 42 F3
Bilsby Gr. SE9 .... 22 D4
Bilsington Cl. ME5 ...... 62 B5
Bilton Rd. DA8 .... 9 A8
Binbury La. ME14 .... 79 A5
Bines The. TN12 .... 136 A5
Bingham Point. 11 SE28 . 2 B2
Bingham Rd. ME2 .... 33 C1
Bingley Cl. ME6 .... 74 F8
Bingley Rd. Chatham ME1 . 47 E4
Bingley Rd. Newham E16 . 1 C7
Binland Gr. ME5 .... 61 D5
Binnacle Rd. ME1 .... 61 C8
Binney Rd. ME3 .... 19 D8
Binsey Wlk. 1 SE2 ...... 3 C4
Birbeck Prim Sch. DA14 . 24 B5
Birbetts Rd. SE9 .... 22 F6
Birch Cl. Eynsford DA4 .. 54 D7
Birch Cl.
Hildenborough TN11 .... 116 D4
Birch Cl. Matfield TN12 .. 135 D1
Birch Cl. New Barn DA3 .. 43 C7
Birch Cl. Royal Tunbridge Wells
TN1 .... 149 B8
Birch Cl. Sevenoaks TN13 . 84 B4
Birch Cres. ME20 .... 90 D8
Birch Ct. ME5 .... 62 D1
Birch Gr. Bexley DA16 .... 7 A3
Birch Gr. Gillingham ME7 . 63 A5
Birch Kiln Cotts. TN5 .... 175 A6
Birch Mead. BR2 & BR6 .. 51 A8
Birch Pl. DA9 .... 10 E1
Birch Rd.
Hoo St Werburgh ME3 .. 34 E3
Birch Rd.
Paddock Wood TN12 .. 136 A6
Birch Row. BR2 .... 37 A3
Birch Tree House. 18 SE7 . 5 C8
Birch Tree Way. ME15 .. 92 B3
Birch Way. TN1 & TN2 .. 149 D7
Birchden Cotts. TN3 .... 161 C6
Birchdene Dr. SE28 ...... 3 A5
Birches The. Greenwich SE7 . 5 B8
Birches The. Orpington BR6 . 51 A6

Birches The. Swanley BR8 ...... 39 E7
Birches The.
Tonbridge TN9 .... 133 B7
Birchetts Ave. TN3 .... 147 E3
Birchetts Green La. TN5 .... 176 A2
Birchfield Cl. ME15 .... 107 B6
Birchfields. ME5 .... 62 A3
Birchin Cross Rd.
TN15 & TN14 .... 70 A5
Birchington Cl. Bexley DA7 ... 8 B6
Birchington Cl.
Maidstone ME14 .... 92 C5
Birchington Cl.
Orpington BR5 .... 38 C1
Bircholt Rd. ME15 .... 107 F4
Birchway. TN15 .... 55 F2
Birchwood Ave.
Bidborough TN4 .... 132 E3
Birchwood Ave.
Sidcup DA14 .... 24 C5
Birchwood Cty Prim Sch.
BR8 .... 39 D8
Birchwood Dr. DA2 .... 25 E4
Birchwood La. TN14 .... 67 F4
Birchwood Par. DA2 .... 25 E4
Birchwood Park Ave. BR8 ... 39 F6
Birchwood Rd.
Joyden's Wood DA2 .... 25 D3
Birchwood Rd.
Maidstone ME16 .... 91 C5
Birchwood Rd.
Orpington BR5 .... 37 E5
Birchwood Terr. BR8 .... 39 C8
Bird House La. BR6 .... 66 A5
Bird in Hand St. TN3 ...... 161 B8
Bird La. TN5 .... 174 E2
Bird-in-Hand La. BR1 .... 36 D7
Birdbrook Rd. SE3 & SE9 .... 5 C4
Birdham Cl. BR1 .... 36 E4
Birkbeck Rd. DA14 .... 24 A5
Birkdale. TN4 .... 149 B6
Birkdale Cl. BR6 .... 37 D2
Birkdale Cl. ME15 .... 91 E4
Birkdale Rd. SE2 .... 3 A2
Birken Rd. TN1 & TN2 .... 149 D6
Birkhall Cl. ME5 .... 62 A5
Birling Ave. Gillingham ME8 . 49 E1
Birling Ave.
Maidstone ME14 .... 93 A4
Birling Cl. ME14 .... 93 A4
Birling Dr. TN2 .... 149 A1
Birling Hill. DA13 & ME6 .... 59 B1
Birling Park Ave. TN2 ...... 163 B8
Birling Pk. ME19 .... 74 C5
Birling Rd. Erith DA8 .... 8 E7
Birling Rd. Leybourne ME19 . 74 C3
Birling Rd. Royal Tunbridge Wells
TN2 .... 163 B8
Birling Rd. Ryarsh ME19 .... 74 A5
Birling Rd. Snodland ME6 .. 74 F7
Birling Rd. Snodland ME6 .. 74 F8
Birnam Sq. 1 ME16 .... 91 E4
Birtrick Dr. DA13 .... 43 F4
Bishop Butt Cl. BR6 .... 51 F7
Bishop John Robinson
CE Prim Sch. SE28 .... 3 C6
Bishop's Down. TN4 .... 148 F3
Bishop's Down Cty Prim Sch.
TN4 .... 148 F3
Bishop's Down Park Rd.
TN4 .... 148 F4
Bishop's Down Rd. TN4 ... 148 F3
Bishop's La. ME15 .... 121 D6
Bishopbourne Gn. ME8 ..... 49 B4
Bishops Ave. BR1 .... 36 C6
Bishops Cl.
Nettlestead ME18 .... 104 D6
Bishops Cl. Royal Tunbridge Wells
TN4 .... 148 F3
Bishops Ct. Stone DA9 ...... 10 F2
Bishops Gn. BR1 .... 36 C8
Bishops Mews. TN9 .... 133 C8
Bishops Oak Ride. TN10 .. 117 C6
Bishops Way. ME15 .... 91 F4
Bishops Wlk.
Chislehurst BR7 .... 37 C8
Bishops Wlk. Rochester ME1 47 C5
Bishopsbourne House. BR1 22 B1
Black Eagle Cl. TN16 .... 81 C5
Black Horse Cl. TN27 ...... 141 E5
Black Horse Mews. TN15 .... 87 A7
Black Horse Rd. DA14 .... 24 A4
Black Mill La. TN27 .... 141 B6
Black Post. ME17 .... 95 E4
Black Rock Gdns. ME7 ...... 63 B4
Blackberry Field. BR5 .... 38 A8
Blackbrook La. BR1 & BR2 ... 37 A5

Blackdale Farm Cotts. DA1 . 27 B6
Blackfen Par. DA16 .... 7 A1
Blackfen Rd. DA15 .... 7 B1
Blackfen Sch for Girls. DA15 . 7 B1
Blackhall La. TN15 .... 84 E3
Blackheath Bluecoat CE Sec Sch.
SE3 .... 5 B7
Blackheath High Sch. SE3 .... 5 A7
Blackheath High Sch GPDST
(Jun Dept). SE3 .... 5 A5
Blackheath Pk. SE3 .... 5 A5
Blackhurst La. TN2 .... 149 F6
Blacklands.
East Malling ME19 .... 89 F8
Blacklands. Mill Street ME19 89 F7
Blacklands Cty Jun Sch.
ME19 .... 89 F7
Blacklands Dr. ME19 .... 89 F8
Blackman Cl. ME3 .... 34 D7
Blackman's La. TN11 .... 118 D6
Blackmans Cl. DA1 .... 26 C7
Blackmanstone Way. ME16 91 B7
Blackmead. TN13 .... 83 E6
Blackness La. BR2 .... 50 D2
Blacksmith Dr. ME14 .... 92 D5
Blacksmith's La. TN5 ...... 174 E4
Blacksmiths Field. TN32 .. 185 C1
Blacksmiths La. BR5 .... 38 C4
Blacksole La. TN15 .... 71 F3
Blacksole Rd. TN15 .... 71 F3
Blackthorn Ave.
Chatham ME5 .... 62 A3
Blackthorn Ave.
Royal Tunbridge Wells
TN2 & TN4 .... 133 C1
Blackthorn Cl. TN15 .... 55 F2
Blackthorn Dr. ME20 .... 75 B2
Blackthorn Gr. DA7 .... 7 E4
Blackthorne Rd. ME8 .... 64 B8
Blackwater Cl. RM13 .... 4 E8
Bladindon Dr. DA5 .... 24 D8
Blair Cl. DA15 .... 6 F2
Blair Dr. TN13 .... 84 B4
Blake Cl. DA16 .... 6 E6
Blake Dr. 3 ME20 .... 74 F4
Blake Gdns. DA1 .... 9 F3
Blake Way. Royal Tunbridge Wells
TN1 .... 149 D7
Blake Way. Tilbury RM18 .... 13 C5
Blakemore Way. DA17 .... 3 E3
Blakeney Cl. ME14 .... 93 B4
Blaker Ave. ME1 .... 47 E1
Blaker Ct. SE7 .... 5 D3
Blanchard Cl. SE9 .... 22 E5
Bland St. SE9 .... 5 D3
Blanmerle Rd. SE9 .... 23 B7
Blann Cl. SE9 .... 5 D1
Blatchford Cl. ME19 .... 74 F1
Blaxland Rd. TN11 .... 149 B1
Bleak Hill La. SE18 .... 6 F8
Bleakwood Rd. ME5 .... 61 F4
Blean Rd. ME8 .... 49 C2
Blean Sq. ME14 .... 92 C6
Bleddyn Cl. DA15 .... 7 C1
Bledlow Cl. SE28 .... 3 C3
Blendon Dr. DA5 .... 7 D1
Blendon Rd.
Maidstone ME14 .... 92 C5
Blendon Rd. Sidcup DA5 ...... 7 D1
Blendon Terr. SE18 .... 6 B8
Blenheim Ave. ME1 & ME4 .. 47 E2
Blenheim Cl. Dartford DA1 ... 9 C1
Blenheim Cl.
Maidstone ME14 .... 92 F3
Blenheim Cl.
Meopham DA13 .... 58 B8
Blenheim Cl. DA15 .... 23 D5
Blenheim Dr. DA16 .... 6 F6
Blenheim Gr. DA12 .... 30 C8
Blenheim Inf Sch. BR6 ...... 52 C8
Blenheim Jun Sch. BR6 ..... 52 C8
Blenheim Rd.
Bromley BR1 & BR2 .... 36 E5
Blenheim Rd. Dartford DA1 ... 9 C1
Blenheim Rd.
Orpington BR5 & BR6 ..... 52 C8
Blenheim Rd. Sidcup DA15 . 24 C7
Blenheim Way. TN5 .... 177 C3
Bletchington Ct. 3 DA17 .... 4 A2
Blewbury House. 3 SE2 ...... 3 C4
Bligh Cty Prim Inf Sch The.
ME2 .... 46 C7
Bligh Rd. DA11 .... 13 A1
Bligh Way. ME2 .... 46 D6
Bligh's Rd. TN13 .... 84 B2
Blind La. Bredhurst ME7 .... 63 A1
Blind La. Goudhurst TN17 . 153 E1
Blind La. Lidsing ME7 .... 62 E6
Blind Mary's La. ME9 .... 80 E4
Bliss Way. TN10 .... 117 E5
Blithdale Rd. SE2 .... 3 A2

Blockhouse Rd. 5 RM17 .... 12 C8
Blockmakers Ct. ME4 .... 48 B1
Bloomfield Rd.
Bromley BR2 .... 36 D4
Bloomfield Rd.
Woolwich SE18 .... 2 B1
Bloomfield Terr. TN16 ...... 81 C2
Bloors La. Gillingham ME8 .. 49 D1
Bloors La. Gillingham ME8 .. 49 D1
Bloors Wharf Rd. ME7 ...... 49 F4
Blowers Grove Wood. ME7 . 63 B3
Blowers Hill. Cowden TN8 . 145 D8
Blowers Hill.
Speldhurst TN3 .... 148 B8
Bloxam Gdns. SE9 .... 5 C2
Blue Anchor La. RM18 ...... 13 E8
Blue Boar La. ME1 .... 47 D5
Blue Chalet Ind Pk. TN15 ... 55 D4
Bluebell Cl. Gillingham ME7 . 48 F6
Bluebell Cl. Orpington BR6 . 51 C8
Blueberry La. TN14 .... 67 C4
Bluecoat La. TN17 .... 167 C6
Bluett St. ME14 .... 92 A5
Blunden La. ME18 .... 105 A1
Blunts Rd. SE9 .... 6 A2
Blyth Rd. SE28 .... 3 B5
Blythe Hill. BR5 .... 38 A8
Blythe Rd. ME15 .... 92 B4
Boakes Meadow. TN14 ...... 68 F8
Boarders La. TN5 .... 176 C3
Boarley Ct. ME14 .... 76 F1
Boarley La. ME14 .... 76 F2
Boathouse Rd. ME12 .... 21 F3
Bobbing Hill. ME9 .... 65 F5
Bocking Cl. TN5 .... 174 E4
Bockingford La. ME15 ..... 106 F8
Bodiam Cl. ME8 .... 49 C3
Bodiam Rd. TN18 & TN32 . 185 F3
Bodle Ave. DA10 .... 11 E1
Bodsham Cres. ME15 .... 93 B3
Boevey Path. 2 SE2 .... 7 F8
Bognor Rd. DA16 .... 7 D6
Boley Hill. ME1 .... 47 C6
Boleyn Rd. TN14 .... 69 E2
Boleyn Way. DA10 .... 28 E8
Bolner Cl. ME5 .... 61 F2
Bombay House. 1 ME15 ... 107 E5
Bombers La. TN16 .... 81 D7
Bonar Pl. BR7 .... 22 E1
Bonaventure Ct. DA12 ...... 30 F4
Bond Cl. TN14 .... 67 D4
Bond Rd. ME8 .... 63 E5
Bond St. RM17 .... 12 C8
Bondfield Rd.
East Malling ME19 .... 89 F8
Bondfield Rd. 4 Newham E6 1 F8
Boneashe La. TN15 .... 87 D6
Boneta Rd. SE18 .... 1 F3
Bonflower La. ME17 .... 122 C7
Bonney Way. BR8 .... 39 E6
Bonnington Gn. ME8 .... 49 C3
Bonnington Rd. ME14 ...... 92 C6
Bonnington Tower. BR2 .... 36 E3
Booth Cl. SE28 .... 3 B6
Booth Rd. ME4 .... 47 F2
Bootham Cl. ME2 .... 46 D5
Borden CE Cty Prim Sch.
ME9 .... 65 F3
Bordyke. TN9 .... 117 C7
Boreham Ave. E16 .... 1 A7
Boresisle. TN30 .... 173 B2
Borgard House. SE18 .... 1 F7
Borgard Rd. SE18 .... 1 F7
Borkwood Pk. BR6 .... 51 F6
Borkwood Way. BR6 .... 51 E6
Borland Cl. DA9 .... 11 A2
Borough Green Prim Sch.
TN15 .... 87 A7
Borough Green Rd.
Borough Green TN15 .... 86 E7
Borough Green Rd.
Ightham TN15 .... 86 D6
Borough Green Rd.
Wrotham TN15 .... 72 A1
Borough Green Rd.
Wrotham TN15 .... 72 A1
Borough Green & Wrotham Sta.
TN15 .... 87 A7
Borough Rd. ME7 .... 48 D4
Borstal HM Prison & Youth
Custody Ctr. ME1 .... 47 B1
Borstal Manor Cty Jun Sch.
ME1 .... 46 F2
Borstal Rd. ME1 .... 47 A3
Borstal St. ME1 .... 47 A2
Bostall Hill. SE2 .... 3 B1
Bostall La. SE2 .... 3 B1
Bostall Manorway. SE2 .... 3 C2
Bostall Park Ave. DA7 .... 7 E7
Bostall Rd. BR5 .... 24 B1

Boston Gdns. ME8 .... 49 C1
Boston Rd. ME5 .... 62 C2
Boston Sch. BR2 .... 50 B8
Bosville Ave. TN13 .... 84 A4
Bosville Dr. TN13 .... 84 A4
Bosville Rd. TN13 .... 84 A4
Boswell Cl. BR5 .... 38 C3
Boswell House. DA8 .... 36 D4
Bosworth House. DA8 .... 4 E1
Botany. TN9 .... 117 C1
Botany Bay La. BR7 .... 37 C7
Botha Rd. E13 .... 1 C8
Bothwell Cl. 7 E16 .... 1 A8
Botsom La. TN15 .... 55 D4
Bott Rd. DA2 .... 26 F4
Bottle House Cotts. TN11 . 130 F1
Bottlescrew Hill. ME17 .... 107 B4
Boucher Dr. DA11 .... 29 F4
Boughton Cl. ME8 .... 49 B3
Boughton La. ME15 .... 107 B6
Boughton Monchelsea
Cty Prim Sch. ME17 ...... 107 B2
Boughton Par. ME15 .... 107 A7
Boughton Place Cotts.
ME17 .... 127 A8
Boughton Rd.
Boughton Malherbe ME17 111 B2
Boughton Rd. Woolwich SE28 2 E3
Boultwood Rd. E6 .... 1 F7
Boundary House. 3 DA1 .... 29 F7
Boundary Rd.
Chatham ME1 & ME4 ...... 47 E3
Boundary Rd.
Royal Tunbridge Wells
TN2 .... 149 D1
Boundary Rd. Sidcup DA15 . 6 E2
Boundary St. 2 DA8 .... 8 F7
Boundary The. TN3 & TN4 148 B3
Bounds Cross. TN27 .... 157 F7
Bounds Oak Way. TN4 ..... 132 E3
Bounds The. ME20 .... 75 E1
Bourdillon Ct. SE9 .... 22 E6
Bournbrook Rd. SE3 & SE9 .. 5 D4
Bourne Cl. TN9 .... 117 D3
Bourne Ent Ctr. TN15 .... 87 A7
Bourne Grange La. TN11 .. 118 D8
Bourne Ind Pk. DA1 .... 9 A2
Bourne La. Silver Hill TN32 184 F1
Bourne La. Tonbridge TN9 . 117 D3
Bourne La.
Yopps Green TN15 .... 86 F1
Bourne Mead. DA5 .... 8 D2
Bourne Par. DA5 .... 25 B8
Bourne Pk. TN11 .... 118 F5
Bourne Place Sch. TN11 .. 116 A7
Bourne Rd. Bexley DA1 & DA5 8 D2
Bourne Rd. Bromley BR2 .... 36 D5
Bourne Rd. Gravesend DA12 30 F5
Bourne Rd. Sidcup DA5 ...... 25 B8
Bourne Row. TN8 .... 130 D6
Bourne Vale. Hayes BR2 ... 36 A2
Bourne Vale.
Plaxtol Spoute TN15 .... 102 A8
Bourne Way. Hayes BR2 .... 50 B2
Bourne Way. Swanley BR8 .. 39 C6
Bourner Cotts. TN17 .... 156 D4
Bourneside Terr. ME17 ...... 94 D2
Bournewood Cl. ME15 .... 92 F1
Bournewood Rd.
Bexley SE18 & SE2 .... 7 A7
Bournewood Rd.
Orpington BR5 .... 38 C2
Bournville Ave. ME4 .... 47 F1
Bow Arrow La. DA2 .... 10 B1
Bow Hill. ME18 .... 104 D5
Bow Rd. ME18 .... 104 E7
Bow Terr. ME18 .... 104 E7
Bowater Pl. SE3 .... 5 B7
Bowater Rd. SE18 .... 1 D3
Bowen Rd. TN4 .... 148 B4
Bower Cl. ME16 .... 91 E3
Bower Gr. ME5 .... 62 C1
Bower Grove Sch. ME16 ..... 91 B2
Bower La. Eynsford DA4 ..... 54 F6
Bower La. Maidstone ME16 . 91 E3
Bower Mount Rd. ME16 .... 91 D4
Bower Pl. ME16 .... 91 E3
Bower Rd. BR8 .... 26 A2
Bower St. ME16 .... 91 E4
Bower Terr. ME16 .... 91 E3
Bower Wlk. TN12 .... 139 E3
Bowers Ave. DA11 .... 29 F4
Bowers House. ME7 .... 48 E7
Bowers Rd. TN14 .... 68 F8
Bowers Wlk. 1 E6 .... 1 F7
Bowes Cl. DA15 .... 7 B1
Bowes Rd. ME2 .... 47 B8
Bowes Wood. DA2 .... 56 F7
Bowesden La.
Shorne Ridgeway DA12 .... 31 F1

Bowesden La.
Shorne Ridgeway ME2 4
Bowford Ave. DA7 ....
Bowley La. ME17 12
Bowling Green Row. 1
SE18 ....
Bowls Pl. TN12 13
Bowman Ave. E16 ....
Bowman Cl. ME5 ....
Bowman Cotts. TN27 17
Bowmans Rd. DA1 ....
Bowmead. SE9 ....
Bown Cl. RM18 ....
Bowness Rd. DA7 ....
Bowyer Cl. E6 ....
Boxwell Rd. TN14 ....
Box Tree Wlk. 26 BR5 3
Boxgrove Prim Sch. SE2 ....
Boxgrove Rd. SE2 ....
Boxley Cl. ME14 ....
Boxley Cotts. DA4 ....
Boxley Rd. Chatham ME5 ...
Boxley Rd. Maidstone ME14 . 9
Boxley St. E16 ....
Boxmend Ind Est. ME15 ... 10
Boxshall House. 7 SE18 .....
Boy Court La. TN27 12
Boyard Rd. SE18 ....
Boyces Hill. ME9 ....
Boyle House. 12 DA17 ....
Boyne Pk. TN4 14
Boyton Court Rd. ME17 ... 12
Brabourne Ave. ME8 ....
Brabourne Cres. DA7 ....
Bracken Cl. Newham E6 ......
Bracken Cl. Royal Tunbridge W
TN2 ....
Bracken Hill. ME5 ....
Bracken Lea. ME5 ....
Bracken Rd. ME2 14
Bracken Wlk. TN10 11
Brackendene. DA2 & DA5 ...
Brackens The. BR6 ....
Brackley Cl. ME14 ....
Brackwood Cl. ME8 ....
Bracondale Ave. DA13 ....
Bracondale Rd. SE2 ....
Bradbourne Ct. TN13 ....
Bradbourne La. ME19 ....
Bradbourne Park Rd. TN13 .
Bradbourne Rd.
Grays RM17 ....
Bradbourne Rd.
Sevenoaks TN13 & TN14 8
Bradbourne Rd. Sidcup DA5
Bradbourne Sch The. TN14 .
Bradbourne Vale Rd.
TN13 & TN14 8
Bradbury Ct. 3
Greenwich SE3 ....
Bradbury Ct. 2
Northfleet DA11 ....
Braddick Cl. ME15 10
Bradenham Ave. DA16 ....
Bradfield Rd. E16 ....
Bradfields Ave. ME5 ....
Bradfields Ave W. ME5 ....
Bradfields Sch. ME5 ....
Bradford Cl. BR2 ....
Bradford St. TN9 11
Bradley House. ME3 ....
Bradley Rd.
Upper Halling ME2 5
Bradley Rd.
White Post TN3 14
Bradley Stone Rd. E6 ....
Bradymead. E6 ....
Braemar Ave. DA7 ....
Braemar Gdns. DA15 2
Braes The. ME3 ....
Braeside Ave. TN13 ....
Braeside Cl. TN13 ....
Braeside Cres. DA7 ....
Braesyde Cl. DA17 ....
Brake Ave. ME5 ....
Brakefield Rd. DA13 ....
Bramble Ave. DA2 ....
Bramble Bank. DA13 ....
Bramble Cl.
Hilden Park TN11 11
Bramble Cl.
Maidstone ME16 ....
Bramble Croft. DA8 ....
Bramble La. TN13 ....
Bramble Reed La. TN12 15
Bramble Wlk. TN1 14
Bramblebury Rd. SE18 ....
Brambledown.
Chatham ME5 ....
Brambledown. Hartley DA3 .
Bramblefield Cl. DA3 ....

bletree Cotts. ME1 ...... 46 E2
bletree Cres. ME1 ...... 46 F2
dean Gdns. SE12 ...... 22 A7
dean Gdns. SE12 ...... 22 A7
hope La. SE7 ...... 5 B8
ey Cl. Gillingham ME8 . 64 B8
ey Cl.
al Rise DA13 ...... 29 F1
ey Cl. Orpington BR6 ... 37 B1
ey Cl. Swanley BR8 ..... 39 E5
ey Cres. ME15 ...... 92 F3
ey Ct. Bexley DA5 ...... 7 B6
ey Ct. Marden TN12 .. 138 B6
ey Dr. TN17 ...... 169 D4
ey Gdns.
heath ME17 ...... 106 C3
ey Gdns.
dock Wood TN12 ... 135 E7
ey Pl. DA1 ...... 9 A3
ey Rd.
Peckham TN12 ...... 119 F6
ey Rd. Snodland ME6 .. 75 A8
ey Rise. ME2 ...... 46 E8
eys. TN27 ...... 141 D5
pton Prim Sch. DA16 ... 7 F7
shot Ave. SE3 & SE7 .... 5 B8
shott Cl. ME16 ...... 91 C6
aridges Rd. TN12 .... 120 B4
lon Rd. DA1 ...... 27 A8
ton St. DA11 ...... 30 B8
dreth Rd. E6 ...... 1 F7
ds Hatch Circuit. DA3 .. 55 F6
ds Hatch Cotts. TN15 ... 56 A6
ds Hatch Rd. TN15 ..... 56 A7
aam House. 1 SE18 .... 2 B1
as Dr. TN12 ...... 181 E3
ell Cl. BR8 ...... 39 C3
gore Cl. ME8 ...... 63 D7
ton Cres. BR5 ...... 37 D1
stone Cl. ME16 ...... 10 B8
ingham Cl. TN9 ..... 132 F7
con Rd. DA9 ...... 10 F1
wood Ave. DA8 ...... 8 C7
wood Rd. DA7 ...... 8 A4
wood Way. BR5 ...... 38 C6
nose Rd. ME7 ...... 48 E4
ar Dr. ME20 ...... 90 D8
ed Cl. Bexley DA6 ...... 7 D2
ed Cl. Orpington BR6 .. 52 A8
ed Ct. Brasted TN14 ... 82 D2
ed Ct. Rochester ME2 .. 33 A1
ed Hill. TN14 ...... 82 A7
ed Hill Rd.
4 & TN16 ...... 82 C5
ed La. TN14 ...... 67 A1
ed Rd. Oxted DA8 ...... 8 E7
ed Rd.
kneck Hill DA7 ...... 8 A4
terham TN16 ...... 81 E1
e Farm Mus. TN12 ... 139 D1
e Wood. TN13 ...... 99 C6
dton Ave. DA15 ...... 23 F7
Dr. E16 ...... 1 A6
Gdns. ME15 ...... 106 F5
vood Rd. SE9 ...... 6 D3
ch La. ME9 ...... 64 F8
h Rd. RM16 ...... 10 F8
adod Rd. DA9 ...... 11 B2
kspears Dr. BR5 ...... 38 A8
side Prep Sch. BR1 .. 36 D8
onmead. BR1 ...... 36 C7
n Ct. 7 SE9 ...... 6 A1
ar Cl. ME14 ...... 92 C5
ar House. 1 BR5 ... 38 D1
ar Rd. ME8 ...... 49 B4
hurst CE Prim Sch.
...... 63 B1
hurst Rd.
ngham ME8 ...... 63 B4
ngham ME8 ...... 63 C5
lton Ave. TN4 ...... 132 F1
ner Cl. BR8 ...... 40 A5
hley Ave. DA11 ...... 30 B3
hley Cl. Chatham ME1 . 47 D2
hley Cl.
lelshurst BR7 ...... 37 A8
hley Cl. Hayes BR2 .... 36 A4
hley & Matfield CE
) Prim Sch. TN12 .... 152 A8
hley Rd.
ngham ME8 ...... 49 B2
hley Rd.
smonden. TN12 ..... 152 F6
hley Rd.
dstone ME15 ...... 91 F2
hley Rd.
field TN12 ...... 151 F8
hley Rd.
Paul's Cray BR5 ..... 37 F7
da Terr. DA10 ...... 28 E8

Brendon Ave. ME5 ...... 62 A3
Brendon Cl. Erith DA8 ..... 8 E6
Brendon Cl. Royal Tunbridge Wells
TN2 ...... 149 D5
Brendon Rd. BR7 ...... 23 D6
Brenley Gdns. SE9 ...... 5 D3
Brennan Rd. RM18 ...... 13 B5
Brent Cl. Chatham ME5 ... 61 E5
Brent Cl. Dartford DA2 .... 10 B1
Brent Cl. Sidcup DA5 ..... 24 E7
Brent Cty Prim Inf Sch The.
DA2 ...... 27 C8
Brent Cty Prim Jun Sch The.
DA2 ...... 27 C8
Brent La. DA1 ...... 27 A7
Brent Rd. Newham E16 ..... 1 A8
Brent Rd. Woolwich SE18 .... 6 B7
Brent The.
Dartford DA1 & DA2 .... 27 B8
Brent The. Tonbridge TN10 117 C6
Brent Way. DA2 ...... 10 B1
Brentfield Rd. DA1 ...... 27 B8
Brentlands Dr. DA1 ...... 27 A7
Brentor Ct. TN2 ...... 149 D6
Brentwood Cl. SE9 ...... 23 C7
Brentwood House. SE18 ..... 5 D7
Brenzett Cl. ME5 ...... 62 B5
Brenzett House. 6 BR5 .. 38 C4
Bretland Rd. TN4 ...... 148 D4
Breton Rd. ME1 ...... 47 C2
Brett Wlk. ME8 ...... 63 D4
Brett Wlk. ME8 ...... 33 B7
Brewer St.
Lamberhurst TN3 ...... 166 A5
Brewer St. Maidstone ME14 . 92 A5
Brewers Field. DA2 ...... 26 C4
Brewers La. TN13 ...... 84 C2
Brewery Rd.
Keston Mark ME2 ...... 36 E1
Brewery Rd. Woolwich SE18 . 2 D1
Brewhouse Rd. 3 SE18 ..... 1 F2
Brewhouse Yd. 1 DA11 ... 13 B1
Brian Cres. TN4 ...... 149 B8
Brian Ct. Larkfield ME20 .... 75 A2

Brimstone Cl. BR6 ...... 52 C3
Brimstone Hill. DA13 ..... 58 D8
Brindle Gate. DA15 ...... 23 E7
Brindle Way. ME5 ...... 62 C1
Brindle's Field. TN9 ..... 133 A7
Brinklow Cl. DA7 ...... 8 A4
Brindley Way. BR1 ...... 22 B3
Brinkburn Cl. SE3 ...... 3 A2
Brinkers La. TN5 ...... 175 A2
Brinklow Cres. SE18 ..... 6 B7
Brionne Gdns. TN9 ..... 133 D8
Brisbane House. RM18 .... 12 F6
Brisbane Rd. ME4 ...... 48 A3
Briset Prim Sch. SE9 ..... 5 D3
Briset Rd. SE9 ...... 5 D3
Brishing Cl. ME15 ...... 107 E5
Brishing La. ME17 ...... 107 D4
Brishing Rd. ME15 & ME17 107 F3
Brisley's Row. ME1 ...... 60 F1
Brissenden Cl. ME2 ...... 34 A3
Bristol Cl. ME2 ...... 46 D5
Bristol Rd. DA12 ...... 30 D5
Bristow Rd. DA7 ...... 7 E6
Britannia Bsns Pk. ME20 ... 90 E7
Britannia Cl. ME2 ...... 60 A4
Britannia Dr. DA12 ...... 30 F3
Britannia Gate. E16 ...... 1 A5
Brittain Cl. SE9 ...... 22 E7
Brittain House. SE9 ...... 22 E7
Brittains La. TN13 ...... 83 F2
Britten Cl. TN10 ...... 117 F6
Brittenden Cl. 1 BR6 ..... 51 F4
Brittenden Parade. BR6 .... 51 F4
Britton St. ME7 ...... 48 B5
Brixham Rd. DA16 ...... 7 D6
Brixham St. E16 ...... 2 A5
Broad Bridge Cl. SE3 ...... 5 A7
Broad Ditch Rd. DA13 .... 29 D1
Broad Gr. TN2 ...... 149 A1
Broad La. Heath Side DA2 .. 26 B4
Broad La. Stone Cross TN3 147 A4
Broad Lawn. SE9 ...... 23 A7
Broad Oak. Brenchley TN12 152 C8
Broad Oak.
Groombridge TN3 ...... 161 C6
Broad Oak Cl.
Brenchley TN12 ...... 152 C8
Broad Oak Cl.
Royal Tunbridge Wells
TN2 ...... 148 F1
Broad Oak Cl.
St Paul's Cray BR5 ...... 38 A7
Broad Rd. DA10 ...... 11 E1
Broad St. ME17 ...... 124 E7
Broad View. TN17 ...... 170 A8
Broad Wlk.
Eltham SE18 & SE3 & SE9 ..... 5 E5
Broad Wlk.
Greenwich SE18 & SE3 & SE9 5 E5
Broad Wlk. Orpington BR6 .. 52 D7
Broad Wlk. Sevenoaks TN15 99 F7
Broadcloth. TN17 ...... 169 D3
Broadcroft. TN2 ...... 162 F8
Broadcroft Rd. BR5 ...... 37 D2
Broadcroft. TN2 ...... 162 F8
Broadacre La. ME14 ...... 78 B2
Broadfield Rd. ME15 .... 107 A8
Broadheath Dr. BR7 ...... 22 F3
Broadhoath. TN15 ...... 85 E1
Broadlands Dr. ME5 ...... 62 B4
Broadlands Rd. BR1 ...... 22 B4
Broadmead. TN2 ...... 162 F8
Broadmead Ave. TN2 .... 162 F8
Broadoak. ME9 ...... 74 E2
Broadoak Ave. ME15 .... 107 A8
Broadoak Cl. DA2 & DA4 .. 27 A2
Broadoak Rd. DA8 ...... 8 D7
Broadview. DA13 ...... 57 F6
Broadview Ave. ME8 ...... 63 E8
Broadwater Ct. TN2 ..... 162 E8
Broadwater Down. TN2 .. 162 F8
Broadwater Down Cty Prim Sch.
TN2 ...... 162 F8
Broadwater Gdns. BR6 .... 51 C6
Broadwater House. DA12 ... 13 D1
Broadwater La.
Royal Tunbridge Wells
TN2 & TN4 ...... 148 F1
Broadwater La.
Royal Tunbridge Wells TN2 162 F8
Broadwater Rd.
Well Street ME19 ...... 89 D6
Broadwater Rd.
Woolwich SE18 ...... 2 D3
Broadwater Rise. TN2 .... 148 F1
Broadway. Bexley DA6 ...... 7 F3
Broadway. Bexley DA6 & DA7 8 A3
Broadway. Crockenhill BR8 .. 39 C3
Broadway. Gillingham ME8 .. 49 A3

Broadway. Grays RM17 ..... 12 C8
Broadway. Maidstone ME16 . 91 F4
Broadway. Tilbury RM18 .... 12 F5
Broadway Sh Ctr. 5 DA6 ... 8 A3
Broadway The.
Hadlow TN11 ...... 118 E8
Broadway The.
Lamberhurst TN3 ..... 166 B5
Broadwood. DA11 ...... 30 B3
Broadwood Rd. ME3 ...... 34 A4
Brock Rd. E13 ...... 1 B8
Brockenhurst Ave. ME15 .. 92 C1
Brockenhurst Cl. ME8 ..... 63 F5
Brocklebank House. 7 E16 .. 2 A5
Brocklebank Rd. SE7 ...... 1 B2
Brockway. TN15 ...... 87 A7
Brockwell Cl. BR5 ...... 37 F4
Brodrick Gr. SE2 ...... 3 B3
Brogden Cres. ME17 .... 108 F7
Broke Farm Dr. BR6 ...... 52 C2
Brokes Way. TN4 ...... 149 B8
Brome House. SE18 ...... 5 E6
Brome Rd. SE9 ...... 5 F4
Bromhedge. SE9 ...... 22 F5
Bromholm Rd. SE2 ...... 3 B3
Bromley. RM17 ...... 11 F8
Bromley Cl. Chatham ME5 .. 62 B4
Bromley Cl. Newington ME9 . 65 A5
Bromley Coll of Further
& Higher Ed. BR2 ...... 36 D3
Bromley Comm. BR2 ...... 36 D3
Bromley General Hospl.
BR1 ...... 36 B5
Bromley High Sch for Girls.
BR1 ...... 37 A5
Bromley Ind Est. BR1 .... 36 D6
Bromley La. BR7 ...... 23 D1
Bromley Manor Mansions. 3
BR1 ...... 36 A6
Bromley North Sta. BR1 .... 36 A8
Bromley Public Golf Course.
BR2 ...... 36 E2
Bromley Rd. BR7 ...... 37 B8
Bromley South Sta. BR2 .... 36 A6
Bromley Valley Gymnastics Ctr.
BR5 ...... 38 C6
Brompton Dr. DA8 ...... 9 B7
Brompton Farm Rd. ME2 .. 33 A2
Brompton Hill. ME4 ...... 47 F6
Brompton La. ME7 ...... 47 A8
Brompton Rd. ME7 ...... 48 B6
Brompton-Westbrook
Cty Prim Sch. ME7 ...... 48 A5
Bronington Cl. ME5 ...... 62 A5
Bronte Cl. Erith DA8 ...... 8 B7
Bronte Cl. Lunsford ME20 .. 74 F3
Bronte Cl. Tilbury RM18 ... 13 C5
Bronte Cl. DA1 ...... 9 F3
Bronte Sch. DA12 ...... 30 C7
Brontes Rd. DA12 ...... 30 C7
Brook. ME4 ...... 48 A4
Brook Cotts.
Collier Street TN12 .... 137 F8
Brook Cotts.
Dean Street TN12 ...... 106 C7
Brook Ct. 10 TN8 ...... 112 D3
Brook General Hospl. SE18 ... 5 E6
Brook Hill Cl. SE18 ...... 2 B1
Brook La. Bexley DA5 ...... 7 D2
Brook La. Bromley BR1 .... 22 A2
Brook La. Greenwich SE3 ... 5 B5
Brook La.
Plaxtol Spoute TN15 .... 102 A8
Brook La. Snodland ME6 .... 75 A6
Brook La. Tonbridge TN9 .. 117 D2
Brook Rd. Lunsford ME20 .. 74 F4
Brook Rd. Northfleet DA11 .. 29 E7
Brook Rd. Royal Tunbridge Wells
TN1 ...... 149 D7
Brook Rd. Swanley BR8 .... 39 D7
Brook St. Erith DA8 ...... 8 B7
Brook St. Snodland ME6 .... 75 B8
Brook St. Tonbridge TN9 ... 133 A8
Brook Vale. DA8 ...... 8 B6
Brookbank. ME14 ...... 92 A8
Brookdale Rd. DA5 ...... 7 E1
Brookdene Rd. SE18 & SE2 .... 2 F2
Brooke Dr. DA12 ...... 31 B7
Brookend Rd. DA15 ...... 23 E7
Brookes Pl. ME9 ...... 65 B6
Brookfield. Four Elms TN8 . 113 B5
Brookfield. Kemsing TN14 .. 69 E2
Brookfield.
Sandhurst TN18 ...... 186 B5
Brookfield Ave. ME20 ..... 75 A4
Brookfields. TN11 ...... 102 E1
Brookhill Rd. SE18 ...... 2 B1
Brookhurst Gdns. TN4 .... 132 E3
Brooklands. Dartford DA1 ... 26 E7
Brooklands.
Headcorn TN27 ...... 141 C6

Brooklands. Royal Tunbridge Wells
TN1 ...... 149 D7
Brooklands Ave. DA15 .... 23 D6
Brooklands Farm Cl. TN3 . 147 A6
Brooklands Pk. SE3 ...... 5 A4
Brooklands Prim Sch. SE3 ... 5 A4
Brooklands Rd. ME20 ..... 75 A4
Brooklyn Paddock. ME7 .... 48 D6
Brooklyn Rd. BR2 ...... 36 D4
Brooklyn Villas. TN12 ... 138 C5
Brookmead. TN11 ...... 116 E4
Brookmead Ave.
BR1 & BR2 ...... 36 F4
Brookmead Cl. BR6 ...... 38 B2
Brookmead Rd. ME3 ...... 33 B7
Brookmead Way.
BR5 & BR6 ...... 38 B3
Brookes Cl. Eltham SE9 .... 23 A6
Brooks Cl.
Staplehurst TN12 ...... 139 E4
Brooks Pl. ME14 ...... 92 A4
Brookside.
Cranbrook TN17 ...... 169 D4
Brookside.
Hoo St Werburgh ME3 .... 34 E5
Brookside. Orpington BR6 .. 37 F2
Brookside Rd. DA13 ...... 29 F1
Brookway. SE3 ...... 5 A4
Broom Ave. BR5 ...... 38 B7
Broom Cl. BR2 ...... 36 E3
Broom Hill Rd. ME2 ...... 46 F8
Broom La. TN3 ...... 147 E2
Broom Mead. DA6 ...... 8 A2
Broom Pk. TN3 ...... 147 E3
Bromcroft Rd. ME8 ...... 49 F2
Broomfield House. 4 BR5 . 38 B7
Broomfield Rd. Bexley DA6 .. 8 A2
Broomfield Rd.
Broomfield ME17 ...... 109 D4
Broomfield Rd.
Sevenoaks TN13 ...... 83 F5
Broomfield Rd.
Swanscombe DA10 ...... 11 E2
Broomfields. DA3 ...... 42 E4
Broomhill Bank Sch. TN3 . 148 C6
Broomhill Park Rd. TN4 ... 148 F8
Broomhill Rd. Dartford DA1 ... 9 B7
Broomhill Rd.
Orpington BR6 ...... 38 A2
Broomhill Rd.
Royal Tunbridge Wells
TN3 ...... 148 D7
Broomhill Rise. DA6 ...... 8 A2
Broomhills. DA13 ...... 28 E4
Broomleigh. BR1 ...... 36 A8
Broomscroft Cotts. ME18 .. 89 C1
Broomshaw Rd. ME16 ..... 90 F3
Broomwood Rd. BR5 ...... 38 B7
Brougham Ct. 2 DA2 ..... 10 B1
Broughton Rd.
Orpington BR6 ...... 51 D8
Broughton Rd. Otford TN14 . 69 A3
Brow Cl. BR5 ...... 38 D2
Brow Cres. BR5 ...... 38 D2
Brown Rd. DA12 ...... 30 E7
Brown St. ME8 ...... 49 F1
Browndens Rd. ME2 ...... 59 E4
Brownelow Copse. ME5 .... 62 B1
Browning Cl. ME5 ...... 62 A4
Browning Cl.
Lunsford ME20 ...... 74 F4
Browning Rd. DA1 ...... 9 F3
Browning Wlk. RM18 .... 13 C5
Brownings. TN8 ...... 112 C4
Brownspring Dr. SE9 ..... 23 B5
Broxbourne Rd. BR6 ...... 37 F2
Bruce Cl. DA16 ...... 7 B6
Bruce Ct. DA15 ...... 23 F4
Bruce Gr. BR6 ...... 38 A1
Bruces Wharf Rd. RM17 .... 12 A8
Brucks The. ME18 ...... 104 E7
Brummel Cl. DA7 ...... 8 C4
Brunel Cl. RM18 ...... 13 B4
Brunel Way. ME4 ...... 48 A7
Brungers Wlk. TN10 .... 117 B5
Brunswick Cl. DA6 ...... 7 D3
Brunswick House Cty Prim Sch.
ME16 ...... 91 E5
Brunswick Rd. DA6 ...... 7 E3
Brunswick St. ME15 ...... 92 A3
Brunswick St E. ME15 .... 92 A3
Brunswick Terr. TN1 ..... 149 A2
Brunswick Wlk. 1 DA12 ... 30 B8
Brushwood Lodge. 1 DA17 . 4 A2
Bruton Cl. BR7 ...... 22 F1
Bryanston Rd. RM18 ...... 13 C5
Bryant Cl. ME18 ...... 104 D6

Bryant Rd. ME2 .... 47 A7
Bryant St. ME4 .... 48 A3
Bryony Sch (private). ME8 .. 63 F5
Bubblestone Rd. TN14 .... 69 B3
Buckden Cl. SE12 .... 5 A4
Buckham Thorns Rd. TN16 . 81 C1
Buckhole Farm Rd. ME23 .... 17 C4
Buckhurst Ave. TN15 .... 84 C2
Buckhurst La.
  Rockrobin TN5 .... 174 A6
Buckhurst La.
  Sevenoaks TN13 & TN15 .. 84 C2
Buckhurst Rd. TN16 .... 81 B7
Buckingham Ave. ME17 ...... 37 E2
Buckingham Dr. BR7 .... 23 C3
Buckingham Rd.
  Gillingham ME7 .... 48 D5
Buckingham Rd.
  Northfleet DA11 .... 29 D8
Buckingham Rd.
  Royal Tunbridge Wells
  TN1 .... 149 B2
Buckingham Row. ME15 .... 107 E7
Buckland Cl. ME5 .... 62 A2
Buckland Hill. ME16 .... 91 E5
Buckland La. ME16 .... 91 D6
Buckland Pl. ME16 .... 91 E4
Buckland Rd.
  Cliffe Woods ME3 .... 33 A8
Buckland Rd.
  Lower Luddesdown DA13 . 59 A7
Buckland Rd.
  Maidstone ME16 .... 91 E4
Buckland Rd. Orpington BR6 51 E6
Buckler Gdns. SE9 .... 22 F5
Bucklers Cl. TN2 .... 149 C3
Bucklers Cl. SE2 .... 3 D2
Buckley Cl. DA1 .... 8 F5
Buckmore Park (Scout Camp).
  ME5 .... 61 C3
Bucks Cross Rd.
  Chelsfield BR6 .... 52 E5
Bucks Cross Rd.
  Northfleet DA11 .... 29 F5
Buckthorn House. DA15 ..... 23 F5
Buckwheat Ct. SE2 .... 3 D3
Budd's Farm Cotts. TN30 .. 189 F2
Budd's La. TN30 .... 189 F2
Budgin's Hill. BR6 & TN14 .. 67 C8
Budleigh Cres. DA16 .... 7 C6
Bugglesden Rd. TN27 .... 172 D5
Bugsby's Way. SE10 & SE7 ... 1 A2
Bull Alley. DA16 .... 7 B4
Bull Fields. ME6 .... 75 A8
Bull Hill. ME17 .... 127 F8
Bull La. Chislehurst BR7 .... 23 D1
Bull La. Eccles ME20 .... 75 F5
Bull La. Lower Higham ME3 . 32 D7
Bull La. Stockbury ME9 .... 64 E2
Bull La. Wrotham TN15 .... 72 A3
Bull Lane Cotts. TN13 .... 165 C4
Bull Orch. ME16 .... 90 F1
Bull Rd. ME19 .... 74 C5
Bull Yd. [5] DA11 .... 13 B1
Bullbanks Rd. DA17 .... 4 C3
Bulldog Rd. ME5 .... 62 B2
Bullen La. TN12 .... 119 E7
Buller Rd. ME4 .... 47 F2
Bullers Cl. DA14 .... 24 E3
Bullers Wood Dr. BR7 .... 22 F1
Bullers Wood Sch for Girls.
  BR7 .... 36 F8
Bullfinch Cl.
  Paddock Wood TN12 ..... 136 A5
Bullfinch Cl.
  Sevenoaks TN13 .... 83 D5
Bullfinch Cnr. TN13 .... 83 E5
Bullfinch Dene. TN13 .... 83 D5
Bullfinch La. TN13 .... 83 E5
Bullingstone Cotts. TN3 ... 147 E7
Bullingstone La. TN3 .... 147 F7
Bullion Cl. TN12 .... 135 F6
Bullivant Cl. DA9 .... 11 A2
Bulls Pl. TN2 .... 150 D6
Bulrush Cl. ME5 .... 61 F3
Bumbles Cl. ME1 .... 61 D7
Bungalows The. TN30 .... 183 D7
Bunker's Hill. Erith DA17 ..... 4 A2
Bunker's Hill. Ridley TN15 .. 57 B4
Bunkers Hill. DA14 .... 24 F5
Bunny La. TN3 .... 162 E5
Bunters Hill Rd. ME3 .... 33 B4
Bunton St. SE18 .... 2 A3
Burberry La. ME17 .... 109 B5
Burch Rd. ME17 .... 12 F1
Burcharbro Rd. SE2 .... 7 D8
Burdett Ave. DA12 .... 31 F4
Burdett Cl. DA14 .... 24 E3
Burdett Rd. TN4 .... 148 B4
Burford Rd. BR1 .... 36 E5
Burgate Cl. DA1 .... 8 F4
Burgess Hall Dr. ME17 ..... 108 F6
Burgess Rd. ME2 .... 47 B7
Burgess Row. [8] TN30 ...... 183 A7
Burghclere Dr. ME16 .... 91 B2
Burghfield Rd. DA13 .... 29 F1
Burgoyne Ct. ME14 .... 91 F7
Burham CE Prim Sch. ME1 . 75 F8
Burham Rd. ME1 .... 60 E8
Burial Ground La. ME15 ..... 91 E1
Burleigh Ave. DA15 .... 6 F2
Burleigh Cl. ME2 .... 46 E8
Burleigh Dr. ME14 .... 76 F1
Burley Rd. E16 .... 1 C8
Burlings La. TN14 .... 66 F2
Burlington Cl. [5] Newham E6 1 E7
Burlington Cl.
  Orpington BR6 .... 51 B8
Burlington Gdns. ME8 .... 63 E4
Burlington Lodge. BR7 .... 22 F1
Burma Way. ME5 .... 61 F6
Burman. Cl. DA2 .... 27 C8
Burmarsh Cl. ME5 .... 62 B5
Burn's Rd. ME7 .... 48 C7
Burnaby Rd. DA11 .... 12 E1
Burnell Ave. DA16 .... 7 A5
Burnett Rd. DA8 .... 9 D8
Burnham Cres. DA1 .... 9 F3
Burnham Rd. Dartford DA1 ... 9 F3
Burnham Rd. Sidcup DA14 .. 24 E6
Burnham Terr. DA1 .... 9 D2
Burnham Trad Est. DA1 .... 9 D3
Burnham Wlk. ME8 .... 63 E3
Burns Ave. DA15 .... 7 B1
Burns Cl. Bexley DA16 .... 6 F6
Burns Cl. Erith DA8 .... 8 F6
Burns Cres. TN9 .... 133 E7
Burnt Ash Hill. SE12 .... 22 A7
Burnt Ash La. BR1 & SE12 .. 22 B3
Burnt Ash Prim Sch. BR1 ... 22 A3
Burnt House Cl. ME2 .... 33 C2
Burnt House La.
  Dartford DA1 .... 26 F5
Burnt House La.
  Hawley DA2 .... 26 F4
Burnt House La.
  Speldhurst TN3 .... 148 A5
Burnt Lodge La. TN5 .... 176 B2
Burnt Oak Jun Mix Sch.
  DA15 .... 24 A7
Burnt Oak La. Sidcup DA15 ... 7 A1
Burnt Oak La. Sidcup DA15 . 24 B7
Burnt Oak Terr. ME7 .... 48 B6
Burntash Rd. ME20 .... 90 F8
Burnthouse La. TN27 .... 142 D1
Burntwood Gr. TN13 .... 99 B8
Burntwood Rd. TN13 .... 99 B7
Burr Bank Terr. DA1 .... 26 C4
Burr. Cl. DA7 .... 7 F4
Burrage Gr. SE18 .... 2 C2
Burrage Pl. SE18 .... 2 B1
Burrage Rd. SE18 .... 2 C1
Burrard Rd. E16 .... 1 B7
Burrfield Dr. BR5 .... 38 D4
Burrows La. ME3 .... 19 C3
Burrswood Villas. TN3 ..... 161 B7
Bursdon Cl. DA15 .... 23 F6
Burslem Rd. TN2 .... 149 E7
Bursted Wood Prim Sch.
  DA7 .... 8 B5
Burston Rd. ME17 .... 106 B2
Burt Rd. E16 .... 1 C5
Burwash Ct. BR5 .... 38 C4
Burwash Rd. SE18 .... 2 D1
Burwood Ave. BR2 .... 50 B8
Busbridge Rd. Loose ME15 106 E6
Busbridge Rd.
  Snodland ME6 .... 74 E7
Bush Cl. ME9 .... 80 F5
Bush Rd. Cuxton ME2 .... 46 B2
Bush Rd.
  East Peckham TN12 .... 119 E8
Bush Row. ME20 .... 76 A3
Bushell Way. BR7 .... 23 A3
Bushey Ave. BR5 .... 37 D2
Bushey House. SE12 .... 22 C5
Bushey Lees. DA15 .... 6 F1
Bushfield Wlk. DA10 .... 28 E8
Bushmeadow Rd. ME8 .... 49 F2
Bushmoor Cres. SE18 .... 6 B6
Bushy Gill. TN3 .... 148 A3
Bushy Gr. ME17 .... 109 D2
Buston Farm Cotts. ME18 105 D2
Busty La. TN15 .... 86 D6
Butcher La. TN12 .... 139 E3
Butcher Wlk. DA10 .... 28 E8
Butcher's La. ME19 .... 88 D1
Butchers La. TN15 .... 56 D8
Butchers Rd. E16 .... 1 A7
Butler House. [9] RM17 .... 12 B8
Butler's Cotts. DA7 .... 8 A5
Butler's Pl. DA3 .... 56 E7
Butt Green La. ME17 .... 123 A7
Butt Law Cl. ME3 .... 34 E5
Butterfield Sq. [10] E6 .... 1 F7
Butterfly Ave. DA1 .... 26 F6
Butterfly La. SE9 .... 6 B1
Buttermere Cl. ME7 .... 49 A5
Buttermere Rd. BR5 .... 38 D5
Buttmarsh Cl. SE18 .... 2 B1
Button Dr. ME3 .... 19 C5
Button House. ME3 .... 33 F6
Button La. ME15 .... 93 B2
Button St. BR8 .... 40 C5
Butts The. ME14 .... 69 B2
Buttway La. ME3 .... 16 A6
Buxton Cl. Chatham ME5 .... 62 C1
Buxton Cl.
  Maidstone ME15 .... 107 A8
Buxton Rd. DA8 .... 8 D7
Buzzard Creek Ind Est. IG11 . 3 A8
Bychurch Pl. [6] ME15 .... 92 A3
Bycliffe Mews. DA11 .... 29 F8
Bycliffe Terr. DA11 .... 29 F8
Byland Cl. SE2 .... 3 B3
Byng Rd. TN4 .... 148 F5
Bynon Ave. DA7 .... 7 F4
Byrneside. TN11 .... 116 E4
Byron Cl. SE28 .... 3 C5
Byron Cty Prim Sch. ME7 ... 48 C3
Byron Dr. DA8 .... 8 B7
Byron Gdns. RM18 .... 13 C6
Byron Rd. Dartford DA1 ...... 10 B3
Byron Rd. Gillingham ME7 .. 48 C3
Byron Rd. Maidstone ME14 .. 92 B7

Cabbage Stalk La. TN4 ...... 148 E2
Cacket's La. TN14 .... 66 E4
Cade La. TN13 .... 99 C7
Cadlocks Hill. TN14 .... 52 F1
Cadnam Cl. ME2 .... 46 E8
Cadogan Ave. DA2 .... 27 D8
Cadogan Gdns. [6] TN1 .... 149 B4
Cadogan Rd. SE18 .... 2 C3
Cadwallon Rd. SE9 .... 23 C6
Caerleon Cl. DA14 .... 24 C3
Caernarvon Dr. ME5 .... 61 F1
Cage Green Cty Prim Sch.
  TN10 .... 117 D5
Cage Green Rd. TN10 .... 117 C5
Cage La. TN27 .... 142 F1
Cairns Cl. ME1 .... 9 D2
Caistor Rd. TN9 .... 117 A1
Caithness Gdns. DA15 .... 6 F1
Calais Cotts. DA3 .... 56 A8
Calcott Wlk. SE9 .... 22 D4
Calcutta House. [8] ME15 . 107 E5
Calcutta Rd. RM18 .... 13 A5
Calder Rd. ME14 .... 91 E7
Calderwood. DA12 .... 30 E2
Calderwood St. SE18 .... 2 A2
Caldew Ave. ME8 .... 49 C1
Caldy Rd. DA17 .... 4 B3
Caledonian Cl. ME8 .... 63 E8
Calehill Cl. ME14 .... 92 C6
Caley Rd. TN1 .... 149 D7
Calfstock La. DA4 .... 40 F5
Caling Croft. DA3 .... 42 E7
Caliph Cl. DA12 .... 30 F5
Callams Cl. ME8 .... 63 D6
Callaways La. ME9 .... 65 B6
Calshot Ct. [5] DA2 .... 10 B1
Calverley Ct. TN2 .... 149 C3
Calverley Park Cres. [1]
  TN1 & TN2 .... 149 B3
Calverley Park Gdns.
  TN1 & TN2 .... 149 B3
Calverley Pk. TN1 & TN2 .. 149 B3
Calverley Rd. TN1 & TN2 .. 149 B4
Calverley St. TN1 .... 149 A4
Calvert Cl. Erith DA17 .... 4 B2
Calvert Cl. Sidcup DA14 ..... 24 E2
Calverton Prim Sch. E16 ...... 1 D7
Calvin Cl. BR5 .... 38 D6
Calydon Rd. SE7 .... 1 B1
Cambert Way. SE9 .... 5 B3
Camberwell La. TN14 .... 99 F4
Camborne Manor. ME7 ...... 48 C6
Camborne Rd. Bexley DA16 ... 6 F5
Camborne Rd. Sidcup DA14 . 24 C5
Cambray Rd. BR6 .... 37 F2
Cambria Ave. ME1 .... 46 F2
Cambria Cl. DA15 .... 23 E7
Cambria Cres. DA12 .... 30 F4
Cambria House. [2] DA8 ...... 8 E7
Cambrian Gr. DA11 .... 30 A8
Cambrian Rd. TN4 .... 149 C7
Cambridge Ave. DA16 .... 6 F3
Cambridge Barracks Rd. [12]
  SE18 .... 1 F2
Cambridge Cres. ME15 .... 107 D7
Cambridge Dr. SE12 .... 5 A2
Cambridge Gdns. TN2 ...... 149 B2
Cambridge Gn. SE9 .... 23 B7
Cambridge House. [3]
  ME15 .... 107 D7
Cambridge Rd.
  Bromley BR1 .... 22 A1
Cambridge Rd.
  Gillingham ME8 .... 63 C6
Cambridge Rd.
  Rochester ME2 .... 47 A8
Cambridge Rd. Sidcup DA14 23 E4
Cambridge Row. SE18 .... 2 B1
Cambridge St. TN2 .... 149 C3
Cambridge Terr. ME4 .... 47 F4
Cambus Rd. E16 .... 1 A8
Camdale Rd. SE18 .... 6 F7
Camden Ave. TN2 .... 150 C6
Camden Cl. Chatham ME5 ... 62 B5
Camden Cl. Chislehurst BR7 37 D2
Camden Cl. Northfleet DA11 29 C7
Camden Cotts. TN17 .... 169 F8
Camden Gr. [1] Erith DA17 ... 4 A1
Camden Cl. Pembury TN2 .. 150 D6
Camden Ct. [2]
  Royal Tunbridge Wells TN1 149 B4
Camden Gr. BR7 .... 23 B2
Camden Hill. TN1 & TN2 .. 149 B3
Camden Park (Golf Course).
  BR7 .... 23 A1
Camden Park Rd. BR7 .... 23 A1
Camden Pk. TN2 .... 149 C2
Camden Rd. Gillingham ME7 48 D7
Camden Rd.
  Royal Tunbridge Wells TN1 149 B4
Camden Rd.
  Sevenoaks TN13 .... 84 B5
Camden Rd. Sidcup DA5 ..... 24 F8
Camden St. ME14 .... 92 A5
Camden Terr. TN17 .... 169 F8
Camden Way. BR7 .... 23 A1
Camel Rd. E16 .... 1 D5
Camellia Cl. ME8 .... 63 D7
Camelot Cl. SE18 .... 2 D6
Camer Gdns. DA13 .... 44 C3
Camer Park. DA13 .... 44 C3
Camer Park Rd. DA13 .... 44 C2
Camer Rd. DA13 .... 44 C3
Camer St. DA13 .... 44 C3
Cameron Cl. Chatham ME5 .. 62 B8
Cameron Cl.
  Joyden's Wood DA5 ...... 25 E5
Cameron Rd. BR2 .... 36 A4
Camerons. [4] TN18 .... 179 A2
Camomile Dr. ME14 .... 92 F5
Camp Hill. TN11 .... 115 A3
Camp Site The. BR8 .... 25 A1
Camp Way. ME15 .... 107 C6
Campbell Cl. SE18 .... 6 A6
Campbell Rd.
  Gravesend DA11 .... 29 F8
Campbell Rd.
  Maidstone ME15 .... 92 A3
Campbell Rd.
  Royal Tunbridge Wells TN4 149 B8
Campfield Rd. SE9 .... 22 D8
Campion Cl. Chatham ME5 .. 61 E3
Campion Cl. Newham E6 ...... 1 F6
Campion Cl.
  Northfleet DA11 .... 29 E4
Campion Cres. TN17 .... 169 A2
Campion Cl. [5] RM17 .... 12 D8
Campion Pl. SE28 .... 3 B5
Campleshon Rd. ME8 .... 63 D5
Campus Way. ME7 .... 63 A8
Camrose Ave. DA8 .... 8 B8
Camrose St. SE2 .... 3 A2
Canada Farm Rd. DA4 .... 42 A6
Canada Rd. DA8 .... 9 A5
Canada Terr. [3] ME14 ...... 92 A7
Canadian Ave. ME7 .... 48 F4
Canal Basin. DA12 .... 13 D1
Canal Rd. Gravesend DA12 . 13 D1
Canal Rd.
  Lower Higham ME3 ...... 32 C8
Canal Rd. Rochester ME2 .... 47 C7
Canal Road Ind Pk. [2]
  DA12 .... 20 D8
Canberra Rd. Erith DA7 ...... 7 D8
Canberra Rd. Greenwich SE7 5 D8
Canberra Sq. RM18 .... 13 A5
Canbury Path. BR5 .... 38 A5
Canning St. ME14 .... 92 A6
Cannock Sch. BR6 .... 52 F5
Cannon Bridge Works.
  TN9 .... 1...
Cannon La. TN9 .... 1...
Cannon Pl. SE7 ....
Cannon Rd. DA7 ....
Canon Cl. ME1 ....
Canon La. ME18 ....
Canon Rd. BR1 ....
Cansiron La. TN7 & TN8 ... 1...
Canterbury Ave.
  DA14 & DA15 ....
Canterbury Cl. Dartford DA1
Canterbury Cl. [7]
  Newham E6 ....
Canterbury Cres. TN10 ..... 1...
Canterbury House. Erith DA8
Canterbury House. [2]
  Maidstone ME15 .... 1...
Canterbury Rd.
  Gravesend DA12 ....
Canterbury Rd.
  Pembury TN2 .... 1...
Canterbury St. ME7 ....
Canterbury Way.
  RM16 & DA1 ....
Cantwell House. SE18 ....
Cantwell Rd. SE18 ....
Capel Cl. Gillingham ME8 ... (
Capel Cl. Keston Mark BR2 ..
Capel Cty Prim Sch. TN12 . 1...
Capel Pl. DA2 ....
Capelands. DA3 ....
Capell Cl. ME17 1
Capetown House. [1]
  ME15 .... 1...
Capstan Cl. DA9 ....
Capstan Ctr. RM17 ....
Capstone Farm Country Pk.
  ME7 ....
Capstone Rd.
  Chatham ME5 ....
Capstone Rd.
  Gillingham ME7 ....
Capstone Rd.
  Lewisham BR1 ....
Captain's Cl. ME17 ....
Captain's Wlk The. TN15 ....
Caraway Cl. E13 ....
Cardens Rd. ME3 ....
Cardiff St. SE18 ....
Cardinal Cl. Chislehurst BR7
Cardinal Cl. Tonbridge TN9 1...
Cardwell Prim Sch. SE18 .....
Cardwell Rd. SE18 ....
Carew House. [24] SE18 ......
Carey Ct. DA6 ....
Carhaven House. [3] DA8 ....
Caring La. ME15 ....
Caring Rd. ME15 ....
Carisbrooke Ave. DA5 ....
Carisbrooke Ct. [9] DA2 .....
Carisbrooke Dr. ME16 ....
Carisbrooke Rd.
  Bromley BR2 ....
Carisbrooke Rd.
  Rochester ME2 ....
Carl Ekman House. DA11 ....
Carleton Pl. DA4 ....
Carleton Rd. DA1 ....
Carlisle Cl. ME2 ....
Carlisle Rd. DA1 ....
Carlton Ave. Gillingham ME7
Carlton Ave. Stone DA9 ......
Carlton Cres. Chatham ME5 .
Carlton Cres.
  Royal Tunbridge Wells TN2 1...
Carlton Gdns. ME15 .... 1...
Carlton Gn. DA14 ....
Carlton Par. BR5 ....
Carlton Rd. Bexley DA16 ....
Carlton Rd. Erith DA8 ....
Carlton Rd.
  Royal Tunbridge W...
  TN2 .... 1...
Carlton Rd. Sidcup DA14 ....
Carlyle Ave. BR1 ....
Carlyle Rd. SE28 ....
Carman's Cl.
  ME15 & ME17 .... 1...
Carmelite Way. DA3 ....
Carnation Cl. ME19 & ME20 .
Carnation Cres. ME19 ....
Carnation Rd. ME2 ....
Carnation St. SE2 ....
Carnbrook Rd. SE3 ....
Carnecke Gdns. SE9 ....
Caroline Cres. ME16 ....
Carolyn Dr. BR6 ....
Carpeaux Cl. ME4 ....
Carpenters Cl. ME4 ....
Carpenters La.
  Hadlow TN11 .... 1...

...enters La.
plehurst TN12 ..... 139 C8
inus Cl. ME5 ..... 62 B1
Gr. SE18 ..... 1 E2
ack House. DA8 ..... 4 E1
age Mus. ME15 ..... 92 A3
ageway The. TN14 ..... 82 D3
ck Dr. TN13 ..... 84 B4
e House. ME16 ..... 91 E5
ers Pl. TN3 ..... 146 B3
ers Rd. TN17 ..... 169 D5
ll Way. DA17 ..... 3 D3
don Rd. DA1 ..... 10 A1
oll Gdns. ME20 ..... 74 F3
pnade Pl. SE18 ..... 2 C3
ington Gdns. DA1 ..... 26 D6
on Rd. E16 ..... 1 A8
ton Cl. SE12 & SE13 ..... 5 A2
ers Hill. TN15 ..... 100 B6
ers Hill La. DA3 ..... 57 F2
ers Row. DA11 ..... 29 F6
mel Rd. DA7 ..... 8 A6
on Cl. ME1 ..... 47 D2
on Rd. ME3 ..... 32 B3
ille Ave. TN4 ..... 132 F1
organ Way. ME8 ..... 63 C5
ers. BR5 ..... 38 C6
ades L Ctr. DA12 ..... 31 A4
ian Wlk. E16 ..... 1 D7
ilda Rd. SE2 ..... 3 A2
tine Cl. BR8 ..... 25 F1
lia Cl. DA1 ..... 9 F4
erbridge Rd. SE3 ..... 5 A4
ile Rd. SE18 ..... 2 A2
illion House. BR1 ..... 22 B1
le Ave. ME1 ..... 47 C4
le Dene. ME14 ..... 91 F6
le Dr. TN14 ..... 69 E2
e Farm Rd. TN14 ..... 54 A3
le Fields. TN9 ..... 117 B2
le Hill. Hartley DA3 ..... 42 E4
le Hill. Rochester ME1 ..... 47 C6
le Hill. Thurnham ME14 ..... 78 E5
le Hill. Tonbridge TN11 ..... 133 F5
le Hurst. TN32 ..... 185 B1
le La. DA12 ..... 31 B6
le Rd. Chatham ME4 ..... 48 B2
le Rd. Eynsford DA4 ..... 54 C5
le Rd. Grays RM17 ..... 11 F8
le Rd. Maidstone ME16 ..... 91 D7
le Rd. Royal Tunbridge Wells
4 ..... 149 A3
le Rd.
anscombe DA10 ..... 11 F1
le St. [2]
yal Tunbridge Wells,
unt Sion TN1 ..... 149 A2
le St. [5]
yal Tunbridge Wells,
thborough TN4 ..... 132 F2
le St. Stone DA9 ..... 11 A2
le St.
anscombe DA10 ..... 11 F1
le St. Tonbridge TN10 ..... 117 C2
le St. Upper Upton ME2 ..... 33 E1
le St. Wouldham ME1 ..... 60 C4
le Terr. Hadlow TN11 ..... 118 E8
le Terr.
wkhurst TN18 ..... 178 F3
le View Rd. ME2 ..... 47 A7
le Way. ME19 ..... 74 D2
le Wlk. TN5 ..... 174 E4
lecombe Prim Sch. SE9 ..... 22 E3
lecombe Rd. SE9 ..... 22 E4
lefields. DA13 ..... 43 F8
leford Ave. SE9 ..... 23 B7
lemaine Ave. ME7 ..... 48 F6
leton Ave. DA7 ..... 8 D5
leton Rd. SE12 & SE9 ..... 22 D4
lewood Day Hospl.
18 .....
lewood Dr. SE9 ..... 5 F5
es Ct. TN12 ..... 120 A7
ncart Dr. BR6 ..... 37 E1
herine Rd. ME3 ..... 91 A3
herine Pl. [7] TN1 ..... 149 B4
herin Cl. ME5 ..... 47 D3
kin Cl. ME5 ..... 61 F1
y Cl. ME19 ..... 90 A8
erick Rd. ME5 ..... 62 D2
istock Rd. SE9 ..... 22 F3
s Pl. TN12 ..... 136 C4
ston Rd. TN17 ..... 169 C5
le Hill. ME15 ..... 91 F1
ell Cres. DA1 ..... 10 B3
le Rd. Bexley DA16 ..... 6 F4
endish Ave. Erith DA8 ..... 8 C8
endish Ave.
lingham ME8 ..... 48 E6

Cavendish Ave.
Sevenoaks TN13 ..... 84 A5
Cavendish Ave.
Sidcup DA15 ..... 24 A8
Cavendish Cl. TN10 ..... 117 D7
Cavendish Ct. TN9 ..... 117 D3
Cavendish Dr. TN2 ..... 149 B1
Cavendish Rd. ME1 ..... 47 D3
Cavendish Sq. DA3 ..... 42 D6
Cavendish Way. ME15 ..... 93 B3
Caverley Rd. TN1 ..... 149 B4
Caversham Cl. ME8 ..... 49 F1
Caveside Cl. BR7 ..... 37 A8
Caxton Cl. Hartley DA3 ..... 42 F5
Caxton Cl. Tenterden TN30 ..... 182 F7
Caxton La. TN11 ..... 118 E8
Cayser Dr. ME17 ..... 109 E2
Cazenueve St. ME1 ..... 47 C5
Cecil Ave. Gillingham ME8 ..... 49 A2
Cecil Ave. Rochester ME2 ..... 47 B8
Cecil Rd. Gravesend DA11 ..... 29 F7
Cecil Rd. Rochester ME1 ..... 47 C3
Cecil Road Cty Prim Sch.
DA11 ..... 29 F7
Cecil Way. BR2 ..... 36 A1
Cedar Ave. Gravesend DA12 ..... 30 C4
Cedar Ave. Sidcup DA15 ..... 24 A8
Cedar Cl. Ditton ME20 ..... 90 D8
Cedar Cl. Keston Mark BR2 ..... 50 E7
Cedar Cl.
Meopham Station DA13 ..... 44 A3
Cedar Cl. Swanley BR8 ..... 39 C7
Cedar Copse. BR1 ..... 36 F7
Cedar Cres.
Keston Mark BR2 ..... 50 E7
Cedar Cres.
Tonbridge TN10 ..... 117 C7
Cedar Ct. Eltham SE9 ..... 5 E1
Cedar Ct. [10] Greenwich SE7 ..... 5 C8
Cedar Ct. Royal Tunbridge Wells
TN4 ..... 149 A5
Cedar Ct. [10]
Tenterden TN30 ..... 183 A7
Cedar Dr. Edenbridge TN8 ..... 112 B2
Cedar Dr. Maidstone ME16 ..... 90 E2
Cedar Dr.
Sutton at Hone DA4 ..... 41 B7
Cedar Gdns. ME20 ..... 79 E8
Cedar Gr. Gillingham ME7 ..... 63 A5
Cedar Gr. Sidcup DA5 ..... 7 D1
Cedar Lodge. TN4 ..... 148 F3
Cedar Mount. SE9 ..... 22 D7
Cedar Pl. [3] SE7 ..... 1 C1
Cedar Rd. Bromley BR1 ..... 36 C7
Cedar Rd. Dartford DA1 ..... 26 D7
Cedar Rd. Erith DA8 ..... 9 A6
Cedar Rd.
Hoo St Werburgh ME3 ..... 34 E3
Cedar Rd. Rochester ME2 ..... 46 F6
Cedar Ridge. TN2 ..... 149 D5
Cedar Terrace Rd. TN13 ..... 84 C4
Cedarhurst Dr. SE9 ..... 5 D3
Cedarmore Ct. BR7 ..... 37 C8
Cedars Sch The.
Maidstone ME16 ..... 91 D4
Cedars Sch The.
Rochester ME1 ..... 47 C4
Cedars The. TN12 ..... 135 F2
Cedarwood House. ME15 ..... 106 B6
Cedric Rd. SE9 ..... 23 C5
Celandine Dr. SE28 ..... 3 B5
Celestine Cl. ME5 ..... 61 F3
Cement Block Cotts. RM17 ..... 12 C8
Cement Industry Heritage Ctr.
DA11 ..... 12 B2
Cemetery La.
Hadlow TN11 ..... 103 A1
Cemetery La. Woolwich SE7 ..... 5 E8
Cemetery Rd. Halling ME2 ..... 60 A4
Cemetery Rd. Woolwich SE7 ..... 5 E8
Cemetery Rd. Woolwich SE2 ..... 7 B7
Centenary Ct. DA4 ..... 41 A2
Central Ave. Bexley DA16 ..... 7 A5
Central Ave. Gillingham ME4 ..... 48 B8
Central Ave.
Gravesend DA12 ..... 30 B5
Central Ave. Tilbury RM18 ..... 13 A6
Central Bsns Pk. ME2 ..... 47 E7
Central Ct. [3] SE28 ..... 2 B2
Central Lodge. TN15 ..... 72 E6
Central Par. ME1 ..... 47 D2
Central Par Villas. BR5 ..... 38 C7
Central Park Gdns. ME1 ..... 47 E2
Central Rd. Dartford DA1 ..... 9 E2
Central Rd.
New Hythe ME20 ..... 75 B4
Central Rd. Rochester ME2 ..... 47 A7
Central Sta. TN1 ..... 149 A3
Central Terr. ME3 ..... 33 F6
Central Way. SE28 ..... 3 B6
Centre 2000. ME16 ..... 91 C8

Centre Common Rd. BR7 ..... 23 C1
Centre Ct. ME2 ..... 47 E7
Centre Rd. DA3 ..... 56 F7
Centurian Way. DA18 ..... 4 A3
Centurion Cl. ME7 ..... 48 F1
Century Rd. ME8 ..... 63 D8
Ceres Rd. SE18 ..... 2 F2
Cerne Rd. DA12 ..... 30 E5
Cervia Way. DA12 ..... 30 F5
Chada Ave. ME7 ..... 48 E3
Chadd Dr. BR1 ..... 36 E6
Chadfields. RM18 ..... 13 A7
Chadwell Hill. RM17 ..... 13 A8
Chadwick Cl. DA11 ..... 29 E5
Chadwick Ct. [4] SE28 ..... 3 B5
Chadwick Way. SE28 ..... 3 D6
Chadwin Rd. E13 ..... 1 B8
Chaffey House. [6] SE7 ..... 1 C1
Chaffinch Cl. ME5 ..... 62 A7
Chaffinch Way. TN12 ..... 136 A5
Chafford Cotts. TN13 ..... 146 F5
Chafford La. TN3 ..... 146 F5
Chain Gate. TN27 ..... 127 A8
Chalcombe Rd. SE2 ..... 3 B3
Chalet Cl. DA2 ..... 25 D4
Chalfont Dr. ME8 ..... 63 D6
Chalice Way. DA9 ..... 10 F2
Chalk Ave. TN30 ..... 173 B2
Chalk Ct. RM17 ..... 12 A8
Chalk Pit Ave. BR5 ..... 38 D6
Chalk Pit Hill. ME4 ..... 48 A3
Chalk Rd. Chalk DA12 ..... 31 A6
Chalk Rd.
Lower Higham ME3 ..... 32 C6
Chalk Rd. Newham E13 ..... 1 C8
Chalkenden Ave. ME8 ..... 49 A2
Chalket La. TN2 ..... 150 C5
Chalkpit Cotts. DA12 ..... 31 E5
Chalkstone Cl. DA16 ..... 7 A4
Chalkways. TN14 ..... 69 F3
Chalky Bank. DA11 ..... 30 A3
Chalky Rd. ME9 ..... 79 C6
Challenge Cl. DA12 ..... 30 F4
Challenger Cl. TN12 ..... 135 F6
Challock House. [3] Erith DA8 ..... 8 F7
Challock House. [3]
Orpington BR5 ..... 38 D1
Challock Wlk. ME14 ..... 92 C6
Chamberlain Ave. ME16 ..... 91 C2
Chamberlain Cl. SE18 ..... 2 D3
Chamberlain Rd. ME4 ..... 63 B5
Chamberlain Rd. ME4 ..... 48 B2
Chancel Cl. TN15 ..... 55 E3
Chancellor House. TN4 ..... 148 F3
Chancellor Way. TN13 ..... 84 A5
Chancelot Rd. SE2 ..... 3 B2
Chancery Cl. DA1 ..... 27 A7
Chancery La. ME15 ..... 92 B3
Chancery La. SE18 ..... 2 D3
Chanctonbury Cl. SE9 ..... 23 B5
Chandler Ave. E16 ..... 1 A8
Chandler's Hill. DA13 ..... 58 C5
Chandler's Rd. DA13 ..... 58 C5
Chandlers Dr. DA8 ..... 4 E2
Chandos Rd. TN1 ..... 149 C5
Chantler's Hill. TN12 ..... 136 A4
Chantlers Mead. TN8 ..... 145 A5
Chantrey Cl. DA14 ..... 24 E3
Chantry Ave. DA3 ..... 42 E3
Chantry Ct. DA11 ..... 13 C1
Chantry Cty Prim Schs.
DA12 ..... 13 C1
Chantry La. BR2 ..... 36 D4
Chantry Pl. TN12 ..... 138 C6
Chantry Rd. TN12 ..... 138 C6
Chapel Alley Cotts. TN14 ..... 69 A8
Chapel Cl. Crayford DA1 ..... 8 E2
Chapel Cl. Ryarsh ME19 ..... 73 F5
Chapel Cl.
West Thurrock RM16 ..... 11 B8
Chapel Cotts. ME17 ..... 108 F5
Chapel Ct. DA10 ..... 11 E1
Chapel Farm Rd. SE9 ..... 22 F6
Chapel Field Cotts. DA4 ..... 41 B8
Chapel Hill. DA1 ..... 8 E2
Chapel Houses. ME2 ..... 59 E4
Chapel La.
Gillingham,Hempstead ME7 ..... 63 A4
Chapel La.
Gillingham,Lidsing ME7 ..... 63 A2
Chapel La.
Iden Green TN17 ..... 180 C4
Chapel La. Maidstone ME14 ..... 93 A5
Chapel La.
Potter's Forstal TN27 ..... 127 B2
Chapel La.
Sissinghurst TN17 ..... 170 B7
Chapel La.
Staplehurst TN12 ..... 139 F3
Chapel La.
Upper Halling ME2 ..... 59 C4

Chapel Pl. [8]
Royal Tunbridge Wells TN1 ..... 149 A2
Chapel Pl. Ticehurst TN5 ..... 176 E1
Chapel Rd. Bexley DA7 ..... 8 A3
Chapel Rd. Grain ME3 ..... 21 B5
Chapel Rd. Snodland ME6 ..... 75 A8
Chapel Rd.
Sutton Valence ME17 ..... 124 E7
Chapel Row. Ightham TN15 ..... 86 C6
Chapel Row.
Lower Stoke ME3 ..... 19 C4
Chapel St.
East Malling ME19 ..... 90 A6
Chapel St. Ryarsh ME19 ..... 73 F5
Chapel View. TN15 ..... 86 C6
Chapel Wlk. TN14 ..... 98 B5
Chapel Wood. DA3 ..... 56 E8
Chapel Wood Rd. DA3 ..... 56 E8
Chaplin Dr. TN27 ..... 141 D5
Chapman Ave. ME15 ..... 107 F8
Chapman Rd. DA17 ..... 4 B1
Chapman Way.
East Malling ME19 ..... 89 F8
Chapman Way.
Royal Tunbridge Wells TN4 ..... 149 C8
Chapman's Hill.
DA13 & TN15 ..... 57 E4
Chapman's La.
Hockenden BR8 ..... 39 A7
Chapman's La.
St Paul's Cray BR5 ..... 38 D7
Chapmans End. BR5 ..... 38 E7
Chapmans The. TN14 ..... 82 E3
Chapter Rd. ME2 ..... 46 F8
Chapter Sch. ME2 ..... 46 F8
Chardwell Cl. SE2 ..... 3 C1
Charford Rd. E16 ..... 1 A8
Charges St. ME7 ..... 51 F6
Charing House. [5] DA8 ..... 8 F7
Charing Rd. ME8 ..... 49 B3
Chariot Way. ME2 ..... 46 F7
Charity Farm Cotts. TN17 ..... 156 F7
Charlbury Cl. ME16 ..... 91 C3
Charldane Rd. SE9 ..... 23 B5
Charlecote Ct. ME8 ..... 63 D8
Charles Busby Ct. [2] ME20 ..... 75 F1
Charles Cl. Sidcup DA14 ..... 24 B4
Charles Cl. Snodland ME6 ..... 75 A8
Charles Ct. Erith DA8 ..... 8 E8
Charles Ct. Royal Tunbridge Wells
TN2 ..... 149 C3
Charles Dickens Ave. ME2 ..... 32 C2
Charles Dr. ME2 ..... 46 B2
Charles Grinling Wlk. SE18 ..... 2 A2
Charles Rd. TN14 ..... 53 B1
Charles St. Chatham ME4 ..... 47 E3
Charles St. Maidstone ME16 ..... 91 E3
Charles St. Newham E16 ..... 1 C5
Charles St. Rochester ME2 ..... 47 A7
Charles St. Royal Tunbridge Wells
TN4 ..... 149 A8
Charles St. Stone DA9 ..... 10 F2
Charlesfield. SE12 ..... 22 C5
Charlesford Ave. ME17 ..... 109 D3
Charlieville Rd. DA8 ..... 8 C7
Charlotte Cl. Bexley DA6 ..... 7 E2
Charlotte Cl. Chatham ME5 ..... 62 B6
Charlotte Dr. ME8 ..... 49 C1
Charlotte Park Ave. BR1 ..... 36 E6
Charlotte Pl. RM16 ..... 11 B8
Charlottes Cotts. TN11 ..... 115 F1
Charlton Church La. SE7 ..... 1 C1
Charlton Dene. SE7 ..... 5 D7
Charlton La.
Chartway Street ME17 ..... 125 C8
Charlton La. Greenwich SE7 ..... 1 D1
Charlton La.
West Farleigh ME15 ..... 105 E6
Charlton Manor. ME7 ..... 48 B5
Charlton Manor Prim Sch.
SE7 ..... 5 D7
Charlton Park La. SE7 ..... 5 E8
Charlton Park Rd. SE7 ..... 5 D8
Charlton Park Sch. SE7 ..... 5 E8
Charlton Rd. SE3 & SE7 ..... 5 B8
Charlton St. Grays RM16 ..... 11 D8
Charlton St.
Maidstone ME16 ..... 91 C2
Charlton's Way. TN4 ..... 148 E1
Charminster Rd.
SE12 & SE9 ..... 22 D4
Charmouth Rd. DA16 ..... 7 C6
Charnwood Cl. BR6 ..... 52 B1
Charnwood Villas. BR6 ..... 52 C1
Charne The. TN14 ..... 69 A2
Charnock. BR8 ..... 39 E5
Chart Cnr. ME17 ..... 108 B1
Chart Hills Golf Course.
TN27 ..... 158 A5

Chart La. TN16 ..... 97 B7
Chart Pl. ME8 ..... 63 C3
Chart Rd. ME17 ..... 124 C7
Chart View. TN15 ..... 70 B2
Charter Dr. DA5 ..... 24 E8
Charter St. Chatham ME4 ..... 47 F2
Charter St. Gillingham ME7 ..... 48 C7
Charterhouse Dr. TN13 ..... 84 A4
Charterhouse Rd. BR6 ..... 52 A6
Charton Cl. [5] DA17 ..... 7 F8
Chartway. TN13 & TN15 ..... 84 C3
Chartway St. ME17 ..... 109 C1
Chartwell Cl.
Rochester ME2 ..... 33 B1
Chartwell Cl. Sidcup BR7 ..... 23 D6
Chartwell Dr. BR6 ..... 51 D5
Chartwell (National Trust).
TN16 ..... 96 F4
Chase Sq. [2] DA11 ..... 13 B1
Chase The. Bexley DA7 ..... 8 B4
Chase The. Bromley BR1 ..... 36 B6
Chase The. Chatham ME1 ..... 47 D2
Chase The. Gillingham ME8 ..... 49 A2
Chase The. Kemsing TN14 ..... 69 E3
Chase The.
Pratt's Bottom BR6 & TN14 ..... 52 A1
Chase The.
Tonbridge TN10 ..... 117 C5
Chase The.
West Thurrock RM16 ..... 11 D8
Chastilian Rd. DA1 ..... 26 A8
Chatham Ave. BR2 ..... 36 A2
Chatham Gr. ME4 ..... 47 F2
Chatham Gram Sch for Boys.
ME4 ..... 61 F8
Chatham Gram Sch for Girls.
ME5 ..... 48 C2
Chatham Hill. ME4 ..... 48 B3
Chatham Hill Rd. TN14 ..... 84 C6
Chatham Historic Dockyard.
ME4 ..... 48 A7
Chatham House. [22] SE18 ..... 1 F2
Chatham Rd.
Chatham ME20 ..... 76 D8
Chatham Rd.
Kit's Coty ME20 ..... 76 D6
Chatham Rd.
Kit's Coty ME20 ..... 76 D7
Chatham Rd.
Maidstone ME14 ..... 76 E1
Chatham Rd. Sandling ME14 ..... 76 E3
Chatham Rd. Sandling ME14 ..... 76 E3
Chatham Ski Ctr. ME7 ..... 62 E6
Chatham South Sec Sch.
ME4 ..... 61 F8
Chatham St. SE18 ..... 2 B3
Chatham Sta. ME4 ..... 47 E4
Chatsworth Ave.
Bromley BR1 ..... 22 B4
Chatsworth Ave.
Sidcup DA15 ..... 24 A7
Chatsworth Dr. ME2 ..... 33 B1
Chatsworth House. [3] BR2 ..... 36 A1
Chatsworth Inf Sch. DA15 ..... 24 A7
Chatsworth Par. BR5 ..... 37 C4
Chatsworth Rd. Dartford DA1 ..... 9 D3
Chatsworth Rd.
Gillingham ME7 ..... 48 C6
Chattenden Barracks Royal Sch
of Military Engineering.
ME3 ..... 33 F5
Chattenden Ct. ME14 ..... 92 B6
Chattenden Cty Prim Sch.
ME3 ..... 33 F4
Chattenden La. ME3 ..... 33 F5
Chattenden Terr. ME3 ..... 33 F4
Chatterton Rd. BR2 ..... 36 C4
Chaucer Cl. Rochester ME2 ..... 47 E8
Chaucer Cl. Tilbury RM18 ..... 13 C5
Chaucer Gdns. TN9 ..... 132 F7
Chaucer Ind Pk. TN15 ..... 85 D8
Chaucer Pk. DA1 ..... 26 F8
Chaucer Rd. Bexley DA16 ..... 6 F6
Chaucer Rd. Gillingham ME7 ..... 48 D3
Chaucer Rd.
Northfleet DA11 ..... 29 D5
Chaucer Rd. Sidcup DA15 ..... 24 C7
Chaucer Way. ME19 ..... 75 A3
Chaundrye Cl. SE9 ..... 5 F1
Chauntler Cl. E16 ..... 1 B6
Chauncey Way. [2] DA1 ..... 10 A3
Chave Rd. DA1 ..... 26 E5
Cheeselands. TN27 ..... 157 F2
Cheffins House. ME7 ..... 48 E7
Chegwell Dr. ME5 ..... 62 B4
Chegworth La. ME17 ..... 110 A6
Chegworth Rd. ME17 ..... 109 F5
Chelmar Rd. ME7 ..... 48 B4

Chelmsford Cl. E6 .... 1 F7
Chelmsford Rd. ME2 .... 46 D6
Chelsfield Hill. BR6 .... 52 C2
Chelsfield La. Badgers Mount
 BR6 & TN14 .... 53 B2
Chelsfield La.
 Chelsfield BR5 & BR6 .... 52 D7
Chelsfield La.
 Orpington BR5 .... 38 D2
Chelsfield Lakes Golf Course.
 BR6 .... 52 E3
Chelsfield Park Hospl. BR6 . 52 F5
Chelsfield Prim Sch. BR6 ..... 52 E5
Chelsfield Rd. BR5 .... 38 C3
Chelsfield Sta. BR6 .... 52 E3
Chelster Ct. DA14 .... 23 F4
Chelsworth Dr. SE18 .... 6 D8
Cheltenham Cl.
 Gravesend DA12 .... 30 C3
Cheltenham Cl.
 Maidstone ME15 .... 107 F6
Cheltenham Rd. BR6 .... 52 A7
Cheney Cl. ME8 .... 63 D5
Cheney's Cotts. DA12 .... 31 A2
Chenies Cl. TN2 .... 163 A8
Chenies The.
 Joyden's Wood DA2 .... 25 E4
Chenies The.
 Orpington BR5 & BR6 .... 37 E3
Chennell Park Rd. TN30 ...... 172 E1
Chennells The. TN26 .... 173 C7
Chepstow House. 3
 ME15 .... 107 F6
Chequer's Cotts. TN17 .... 153 F1
Chequers Cl. Chatham ME5 .. 77 A8
Chequers Cl.
 Istead Rise DA13 .... 43 F7
Chequers Cl.
 St Paul's Cray BR5 .... 37 F5
Chequers Ctr. ME15 .... 92 A4
Chequers Hill Cotts. TN8 .. 114 A2
Chequers La. RM9 .... 3 F8
Cherbourg Cres. ME5 .... 61 F7
Cherbury Cl. SE28 .... 3 D7
Cheriton Ave. BR2 .... 36 A4
Cheriton Cl. 7 SE12 .... 22 A8
Cheriton Dr. SE18 .... 6 E8
Cheriton Rd. ME8 .... 63 D8
Cheriton Way. ME16 .... 91 C7
Cherries The. ME10 .... 63 F8
Cherry Ave. BR8 .... 39 D5
Cherry Ct. DA14 .... 24 B5
Cherry Gr. TN10 .... 117 E5
Cherry Hill Ct. ME9 .... 65 B6
Cherry Lodge Golf Course.
 TN16 .... 66 A2
Cherry Orch. Ditton ME10 .. 90 C8
Cherry Orch. Greenwich SE7 .. 5 C8
Cherry Orch.
 Tenterden TN30 .... 183 A6
Cherry Orch The. TN11 ...... 102 E1
Cherry Orchard Cl. BR5 .... 38 C4
Cherry Orchard Inf Sch. SE7 .. 5 C7
Cherry Orchard Rd. BR2 .... 50 E8
Cherry Orchard Way.
 ME16 .... 91 B3
Cherry Rd. ME3 .... 34 E3
Cherry Tree Cl. RM17 .... 12 C8
Cherry Tree Ct. 17 SE7 .... 5 C8
Cherry Tree Gr. DA4 .... 55 B1
Cherry Tree La. DA2 .... 25 F5
Cherry Tree Rd.
 Gillingham ME8 .... 63 F8
Cherry Tree Rd.
 Royal Tunbridge Wells TN2 148 E1
Cherry Trees. DA3 .... 42 F4
Cherry View. ME17 .... 107 B3
Cherry Wlk. BR2 .... 36 A1
Cherrycot Hill. BR6 .... 51 D6
Cherrycot Rise. BR6 .... 51 C6
Cherrydown Rd. DA14 .... 24 D6
Cherrywood Dr. DA11 .... 29 F5
Chervil Mews. SE28 .... 3 B5
Chervilles. ME16 .... 91 A2
Cherwell Cl. TN10 .... 117 B4
Chesfield Cl. TN11 .... 116 E5
Chesham Ave. BR2 & BR5 .... 37 B3
Chesham Dr. ME8 .... 63 E5
Cheshire Rd.
 Maidstone,Shepway ME15 107 E7
Cheshire Rd.
 Maidstone,Willington ME15 92 E2
Cheshunt Cl. DA13 .... 44 A3
Cheshunt Rd. DA17 .... 4 A1
Chessenden La. TN27 .... 143 A1
Chessington Ave. DA7 .... 7 E7

Chester Ave. TN2 .... 149 D2
Chester Cl. ME2 .... 46 D6
Chester Rd. Gillingham ME7 . 48 D2
Chester Rd. Sidcup DA15 .... 6 E2
Chesterfield Cl. BR5 .... 38 D5
Chesterfield Dr. Dartford DA1 9 B2
Chesterfield Dr.
 Sevenoaks TN13 .... 83 D5
Chesterfield Dr.
 Sevenoaks TN13 .... 83 E5
Chesterford House. SE18 ...... 5 F7
Chesterton Rd. 5 ME20 ...... 74 F4
Chesterton Way. RM18 .... 13 C5
Chestfield Cl. ME8 .... 49 E2
Chestnut Ave. Chatham ME5 61 F3
Chestnut Ave.
 Hill Park TN16 .... 81 A6
Chestnut Ave.
 Royal Tunbridge Wells
 TN4 .... 149 B8
Chestnut Ave.
 Staplehurst TN12 .... 139 F4
Chestnut Cl.
 Edenbridge TN8 .... 112 B2
Chestnut Cl.
 Frittenden TN17 .... 156 E6
Chestnut Cl. Kings Hill ME19 89 A2
Chestnut Cl.
 Northfleet DA11 .... 12 F1
Chestnut Cl. Orpington BR6 . 52 A5
Chestnut Cl. Royal Tunbridge Wells
 TN4 .... 149 B8
Chestnut Cl.
 Tenterden TN30 .... 173 C1
Chestnut Cl.
 Ulcombe ME17 .... 125 F6
Chestnut Dr. Bexley DA7 .... 7 E4
Chestnut Dr.
 Coxheath ME17 .... 106 B3
Chestnut Dr.
 Kingswood ME17 .... 109 D2
Chestnut Gr. DA2 .... 25 E4
Chestnut La.
 Matfield TN12 .... 135 D1
Chestnut La.
 Sevenoaks TN13 .... 84 B3
Chestnut La.
 Vigo Village DA13 .... 73 B8
Chestnut Pl. TN8 .... 145 A5
Chestnut Rd.
 Rochester ME2 .... 46 E6
Chestnut Rise. SE18 .... 2 E1
Chestnut St. ME9 .... 65 E4
Chestnut Wlk.
 Larkfield ME20 .... 75 B2
Chestnut Wlk.
 Sevenoaks TN15 .... 99 F6
Chestnut Wlk.
 Tonbridge TN9 .... 116 F2
Chestnut Wood La. ME9 ...... 65 E3
Chestnuts The.
 Addington ME19 .... 73 C3
Chestnuts The. 10
 Erith DA17 .... 4 A1
Chestnuts The.
 The Moor TN18 .... 184 F8
Chestnuts The.
 Woolwich SE18 .... 6 B6
Cheswick Cl. DA1 .... 8 F3
Chesworth Cl. DA8 .... 8 E5
Chetney Cl. ME2 .... 46 F8
Chetwood Wlk. 14 E6 .... 1 E8
Cheveney Wlk. 2 BR2 .... 36 A6
Chevening CE Prim Sch.
 TN13 .... 83 B5
Chevening Cl. ME5 .... 62 A5
Chevening Ct. BR6 .... 52 A8
Chevening House. BR5 .... 38 A8
Chevening La. TN14 .... 67 E3
Chevening Rd. 2
 Greenwich SE10 .... 1 A1
Chevening Rd.
 Sevenoaks TN13 & TN14 .. 83 B6
Chevenings The. DA14 .... 24 C5
Cheviot Cl. Erith DA7 .... 8 F4
Cheviot Cl. Tonbridge TN9 . 117 C4
Cheviot Gdns. ME15 .... 93 A1
Chevron Cl. E16 .... 1 A7
Chevron House. RM17 .... 12 B7
Cheyne Cl. BR2 .... 50 E4
Cheyne Wlk. Longfield DA3 . 42 D6
Cheyne Wlk.
 Meopham DA13 .... 58 A8
Chicago Ave. ME7 .... 48 F5
Chichester Cl.
 Gillingham ME8 .... 64 A8
Chichester Cl. Greenwich SE3 5 C6
Chichester Cl. Newham E6 .. 1 E7

Chichester Ct. 3 DA5 .... 25 A8
Chichester Dr. TN13 .... 83 F2
Chichester Rd. Stone DA9 .. 10 F1
Chichester Rd.
 Tonbridge TN9 .... 133 A8
Chichester Rise. DA12 .... 30 D4
Chickfield Gdns. ME5 .... 48 C2
Chicks La. ME17 .... 167 A2
Chiddingstone Ave. DA7 ...... 7 F7
Chiddingstone Castle.
 TN8 .... 130 D7
Chiddingstone CE Prim Sch.
 TN8 .... 130 C7
Chidley Cross Rd. TN12 ..... 119 E6
Chieftain Cl. ME7 .... 49 B1
Chieveley Dr. TN2 .... 149 D1
Chieveley Par. DA7 .... 8 B3
Chieveley Rd. DA7 .... 8 B3
Chiffinch Gdns. DA11 .... 29 E5
Childs Cres. DA10 .... 11 D1
Childs Way. TN15 .... 71 F3
Childsbridge La.
 TN14 & TN15 .... 84 F7
Childsbridge Way. TN15 ..... 84 F7
Childscroft Rd. ME8 .... 63 F5
Chilham Cl. Chatham ME4 ... 47 E3
Chilham Cl. Sidcup DA5 ...... 24 F8
Chilham House. ME2 .... 33 C1
Chilham Rd. Chislehurst BR7 22 E8
Chilham Rd. Gillingham ME8 49 A3
Chilham Rd.
 Maidstone ME16 .... 91 C7
Chilham Way. BR2 .... 36 A2
Chillington Cl. ME2 .... 59 E4
Chillington St. ME14 .... 91 F6
Chilliwack Rd. ME3 .... 33 F5
Chilston Cl. TN4 .... 149 A5
Chilston Rd. Lenham ME17 111 D5
Chilston Rd. Royal Tunbridge Wells
 TN4 .... 149 A5
Chiltern Cl. Erith DA7 .... 8 E6
Chiltern Cl. Maidstone ME15 92 F1
Chiltern Ct. 11 SE9 .... 6 A1
Chiltern Rd. DA11 .... 29 E5
Chiltern Rd. TN9 .... 117 C4
Chiltern Wlk. TN2 .... 149 D4
Chilton Cl. ME15 .... 49 E1
Chilton Dr. ME3 .... 32 B3
Chimes Dr. ME1 .... 47 C5
Chinbrook Cres. SE12 .... 22 B5
Chinbrook Rd. SE12 .... 22 B5
Chippendale Cl. ME5 .... 61 F1
Chippendale Dr. ME17 ...... 110 D6
Chipperfield Rd. BR5 .... 38 A7
Chipstead Cl. ME16 .... 91 D6
Chipstead La. TN13 .... 83 D5
Chipstead Park Cl. TN13 ..... 83 C5
Chipstead Pk. TN13 .... 83 D5
Chipstead Place Gdns.
 TN13 .... 83 D5
Chipstead Rd. Erith DA8 ...... 8 E7
Chipstead Rd.
 Gillingham ME8 .... 63 D4
Chipstead Sq. TN13 .... 83 C5
Chislehurst CE Prim Sch.
 BR7 .... 23 C1
Chislehurst Cl. ME15 .... 107 F6
Chislehurst High St. BR7 ..... 23 B2
Chislehurst Rd.
 Bromley BR1 & BR7 .... 36 E8
Chislehurst Rd.
 Orpington,Broom Hill BR6 .. 38 A2
Chislehurst Rd.
 Orpington,Petts Wood
 BR5 & BR6 & BR7 .... 37 E4
Chislehurst Rd.
 Sidcup DA14 .... 24 A3
Chislehurst & Sidcup Gram Sch.
 DA15 .... 24 B6
Chislehurst Sta. BR7 .... 37 A2
Chislet Wlk. ME8 .... 63 D5
Chiswell Sq. SE3 .... 5 B5
Chorleywood Cres. BR5 .... 38 A7
Christ Church Ave. Erith DA8 8 E8
Christ Church Ave. 1
 Royal Tunbridge Wells TN4 149 A2
Christ Church CE Sch. SE18 .. 6 A6
Christ Church Cres. 2
 DA12 .... 30 C8
Christ Church Rd. 3 DA12 .. 30 C8
Christ's Coll for Boys. SE9 .. 5 A6
Christchurch Ct. ME5 .... 48 C2
Christchurch House. 9
 ME15 .... 107 E5
Christchurch Rd.
 Dartford DA1 .... 9 C1
Christchurch Rd.
 Sidcup DA15 .... 23 F5
Christchurch Rd.
 Tilbury RM18 .... 13 A6

Christen Way.
 ME15 & ME17 .... 107 F3
Christian Fields Ave. DA12 .. 30 C4
Christie Cl. ME8 .... 62 B6
Christie Dr. 8 ME20 .... 74 F4
Christie House. DA6 .... 8 B2
Christies Ave. TN14 .... 53 B1
Christmas La. ME23 .... 17 F3
Christmas St. ME7 .... 48 E7
Christopher Cl. DA15 .... 6 F2
Chudleigh. DA14 .... 24 B4
Chulkhurst. TN27 .... 157 F1
Church Alley. 1 DA11 .... 13 B1
Church Ave. DA14 .... 24 B3
Church Cl. Brenchley TN12 152 C8
Church Cl. Cliffe ME3 .... 16 B6
Church Cotts.
 Mereworth ME18 .... 103 D8
Church Cotts.
 Cranbrook TN17 .... 169 D5
Church Cotts.
 Crockenhill BR8 .... 39 D2
Church Cotts.
 Shoreham TN14 .... 69 A8
Church Cotts.
 St Michaels TN30 .... 173 B3
Church Cres. ME17 .... 110 F6
Church Farm Cl.
 Crockenhill BR8 .... 39 D3
Church Farm Cl.
 Hoo St Werburgh ME3 ...... 34 E4
Church Field. Dartford DA1 .. 26 D8
Church Field.
 Edenbridge TN8 .... 112 D1
Church Field. Snodland ME6 60 B1
Church Field Cotts. TN15 ... 84 F7
Church Fields.
 New Town ME19 .... 89 B8
Church Fields.
 Sevenoaks TN13 .... 83 F5
Church Gn. Marden TN12 .. 138 C6
Church Gn. Rochester ME2 .. 47 C8
Church Gn.
 Staplehurst TN12 .... 139 E2
Church Hill.
 Boughton Monchelsea
 ME17 .... 123 B7
Church Hill. Chatham ME5 .. 48 C2
Church Hill. Crayford DA1 .... 8 E3
Church Hill. Cudham TN14 .. 66 C4
Church Hill. Dartford DA1 ... 26 D6
Church Hill.
 High Halden TN26 .... 173 E7
Church Hill. Leigh TN11 .... 115 F2
Church Hill. Orpington BR6 .. 38 A2
Church Hill. Plaxtol TN15 .. 101 E8
Church Hill. Stockbury ME9 .. 79 F7
Church Hill. Stone DA9 .... 10 E2
Church Hill. Woolwich SE18 .. 1 F3
Church Hill Wood. BR5 .... 37 F4
Church Hyde. SE18 .... 6 E8
Church La. Capel TN11 ...... 134 F6
Church La. Chalk DA12 .... 31 C6
Church La.
 Chartway Street ME17 .... 125 B8
Church La. Chatham ME4 .... 47 F6
Church La. Chislehurst BR7 .. 37 C8
Church La.
 East Peckham TN12 .... 119 F7
Church La. Frant TN3 .... 163 B4
Church La.
 Harrietsham ME17 .... 110 E6
Church La. Kemsing TN15 ... 70 B2
Church La. Keston Mark BR2 36 E1
Church La. Maidstone ME14 93 B4
Church La. Newington ME9 .. 65 B6
Church La. Stockbury ME9 .. 79 E8
Church La. Tonbridge TN9 .. 117 C2
Church La.
 Trottiscliffe ME19 .... 73 B5
Church La.
 West Farleigh ME15 .... 105 D7
Church Manor Way.
 SE18 & SE2 .... 3 A2
Church Meadow. TN12 ...... 153 A7
Church Mews. ME8 .... 63 F8
Church Path.
 Gillingham ME7 .... 48 C1
Church Path.
 Northfleet DA11 .... 12 C1
Church Path. Stone DA9 ...... 10 F1
Church Rd.
 Bexley, DA7 & DA6 .... 7 F4
Church Rd.
 Bexley,Welling DA16 .... 7 B5
Church Rd. Brasted TN16 .... 82 B2
Church Rd.
 Bromley BR1 & BR2 .... 36 A7
Church Rd.
 Chart Sutton ME17 .... 124 C8

Church Rd. Chelsfield BR6 ... 52 [
Church Rd. Crockenhill BR8 .39
Church Rd. Erith DA8 .... 8 [
Church Rd.
 Goudhurst TN17 167
Church Rd.
 Grafty Green ME17 126
Church Rd. Gravesend DA12 . 30
Church Rd.
 Harrietsham ME17 110
Church Rd. Hartley DA3 42
Church Rd. Henhurst DA13 .. 44
Church Rd.
 Hildenborough TN11 116
Church Rd. Hucking ME17 ... 79
Church Rd. Keston BR2 50
Church Rd.
 Lamberhurst TN3 166
Church Rd. Low Street RM18 13
Church Rd. Maidstone,Shepway
 ME15 107
Church Rd. Maidstone,Tovil
 ME15 91
Church Rd. Offham ME18 88
Church Rd. Orpington BR6 ... 51
Church Rd.
 Paddock Wood TN12 136
Church Rd. Royal Tunbridge Wells
 TN1 & TN4 149
Church Rd. Royal Tunbridge Wells
 Southborough TN4 132
Church Rd. Ryarsh ME19 74
Church Rd.
 Sandhurst Cross TN18 188
Church Rd. Seal TN15 8
Church Rd.
 Sevenoaks Weald TN14 99
Church Rd. Sidcup DA14 24
Church Rd. Stone DA9 10
Church Rd.
 Stone Street TN15 85
Church Rd. Sundridge TN14 . 82
Church Rd.
 Sutton at Hone DA4 26
Church Rd.
 Sutton at Hone DA4 27
Church Rd.
 Swanley Village BR8 40
Church Rd. Swanscombe DA10 11
Church Rd.
 Tenterden TN30 183
Church Rd. Tilbury RM18 12
Church Rd.
 West Kingsdown TN15 55
Church Rd.
 West Peckham ME18 103
Church Row.
 Chislehurst BR7 37
Church Row. Plaxtol TN15 . 10
Church Row.
 West Peckham ME18 103
Church Row Mews. BR7 23
Church Sq. ME17 111
Church St. Boughton Monchelsea
 ME17 107
Church St. Burham ME1 60
Church St. Chatham ME4 48
Church St. Cliffe ME3 16
Church St. Cowden TN8 145
Church St. Edenbridge TN8 112
Church St. Gillingham ME7 .. 48
Church St. Gravesend DA11 . 13
Church St. Grays RM17 12
Church St. Hadlow TN11 118
Church St.
 Hoo St Werburgh ME3 34
Church St. Looe ME15 106
Church St.
 Lower Higham ME3 32
Church St. Maidstone ME14 . 92
Church St.
 Maidstone,Tovil ME15 91
Church St. Newham E16 2
Church St. Rochester ME1 ... 47
Church St. Seal TN15 85
Church St. Shoreham TN14 .. 69
Church St. Southfleet DA13 . 29
Church St. Teston ME18 105
Church St. Ticehurst TN5 .. 176
Church St. Tonbridge TN9 .. 117
Church Terr. ME5 48
Church View.
 Biddenden TN27 157
Church View. Swanley BR8 .. 39
Church Wlk. Dartford DA1 ... 26
Church Wlk.
 East Malling ME19 90
Church Wlk. Eynsford DA4 .. 54
Church Wlk.
 Gravesend DA12 30

...ch Wlk.
...khurst TN18 .... 179 A1
...ndcorn TN27 .... 141 C5
...chbury Rd. SE9 .... 22 C8
...chfield Rd. ME19 .... 73 D3
...chfield Rd. DA16 .... 7 A4
...chfield Sch. SE2 .... 3 A2
...chfields Terr. ME1 .... 47 B4
...chill Ave. ME5 .... 62 A7
...chill CE Prim Sch.
...C6 .... 81 C2
...chill Cl. DA12 .... 27 B7
...chill Cotts. ME17 .... 108 F6
...chill Cl. 4 BR6 .... 51 C5
...chill Rd.
...henden TN17 .... 180 E6
...chill House.
...idstone ME16 .... 91 B2
...chill Pk. DA1 .... 10 A2
...chill Rd.
...vesend DA11 .... 29 F7
...chill Rd. Grays RM17 .... 12 D8
...chill Rd.
...ton Kirby DA4 .... 41 C5
...chill Rd. Newham E16 ... 1 C7
...chill Sq. ME19 .... 89 A3
...chill Way. BR1 .... 36 A7
...chills Ropewalk.
...7 .... 167 E8
...chsettle La. TN5 .... 175 C1
...chside. DA13 .... 73 A8
...chyard Cotts. TN3 .... 148 A8
...n La. TN12 .... 137 A2
...le Cl. ME8 .... 63 D4
...agton Cl. DA15 .... 23 F5
...a Wood. DA12 .... 30 E4
...erhill La. TN11 .... 115 C1
...erhill Wood. TN12 .... 135 C2
...abar Cl. ME5 .... 62 A1
...le The. RM18 .... 13 A6
...uit Rd. SE28 .... 3 A4
...ular Way. SE18 .... 6 A8
...s Cres. DA12 .... 30 E3
...Way. ME1 .... 47 D2
...Sq. RM18 .... 13 A5
...ket La. TN1 .... 149 A3
...ket La. ME16 .... 96 A8
...ne House. ME16 .... 91 C5
...don Cr. BR1 .... 22 A2
...don Rd. ME5 .... 62 D2
...ricarde Gdns. 1 TN1 149 A3
...ricarde Rd. 2 TN1 ... 149 A3
...hatch La. TN5 .... 176 A5
...per La. TN12 .... 139 D6
...on Ct. ME8 .... 63 D8
...Pl. SE18 .... 2 A2
...Ave. TN9 .... 116 F1
...e Cnr. SE9 .... 23 B8
...Ct. BR7 .... 36 F8
...e La. ME19 .... 89 E8
...e Way. Bexley DA7 .. 7 E6
...e Way. Sevenoaks
...3 .... 99 C8
...emont Cl. Newham E16 ... 2 A5
...emont Cl.
...ington BR6 .... 51 A6
...emont Cres. DA1 .... 8 E3
...emont Cty Prim Sch.
...2 .... 149 B2
...emont Gdns.
..., & TN2 .... 149 B2
...emont Pl. 1
...vesend DA11 .... 30 B8
...emont Pl.
...n Green TN17 .... 180 C4
...emont Rd. Bromley BR1 36 F5
...emont Rd.
...stable BR8 .... 25 E1
...emont Rd.
...dstone ME14 .... 92 B5
...emont Rd.
...val Tunbridge Wells
...149 B2
...emont St. E16 .... 2 A4
...emont Way. 1 ME4 ... 47 F3
...ence Ave.
...mley BR1 & BR2 .... 36 E5
...ence Ave.
...chester ME1 .... 47 C4
...ence Cres. DA4 .... 24 B5
...ence Cres. ME14 .... 92 E4
...ence Pl. DA11 .... 30 B7
...ence Rd. Bexley DA6 ... 7 E3
...ence Rd.
...mley BR1 & BR2 .... 36 E6
...ence Rd. Chatham ME4 .. 48 B2
...ence Rd.
...silehurst SE12 .... 22 E6
...ence Rd. 2
...rys RM17 .... 12 A8

Clarence Rd. Royal Tunbridge Wells
TN1 & TN4 .... 149 A3
Clarence Rd. Sidcup DA14 .. 24 B5
Clarence Row.
Gravesend DA11 .... 30 B8
Clarence Row.
Royal Tunbridge Wells
TN1 .... 149 A3
Clarendon Cl.
Maidstone ME14 .... 93 A4
Clarendon Cl.
St Paul's Cray BR5 .... 38 A6
Clarendon Gdns.
Dartford DA2 .... 27 D8
Clarendon Gdns.
Rochester ME2 .... 33 A1
Clarendon Gdns.
Royal Tunbridge Wells
TN2 .... 149 A1
Clarendon Gn. BR5 .... 38 A5
Clarendon Gr. BR5 .... 38 A5
Clarendon Mews. DA5 .... 25 B7
Clarendon Path. BR5 .... 38 A6
Clarendon Pl.
Joyden's Wood DA2 .... 25 E3
Clarendon Pl.
Maidstone ME14 .... 92 A4
Clarendon Pl.
Sevenoaks TN13 .... 84 A2
Clarendon Rd.
Gravesend DA11 .... 13 C1
Clarendon Rd.
Sevenoaks TN13 .... 84 A2
Clarendon Way.
Royal Tunbridge Wells
TN2 .... 149 A1
Clarendon Way.
St Paul's Cray BR5 & BR7 ... 37 F6
Clareville Rd. BR5 & BR6 .... 51 C8
Clarewood Dr. ME19 .... 89 E8
Claridge. TN4 .... 149 B6
Claridge Cl. ME7 .... 62 F4
Clark Cl. DA8 .... 9 A6
Clark Mews. ME20 .... 75 F1
Clarkborne Dr. RM17 .... 12 D8
Clarkes Green Rd. TN15 ... 70 B5
Clarks La. TN14 .... 67 F7
Claston Cl. DA1 .... 8 E3
Clavadel Rd. TN12 .... 136 A7
Clavell Cl. ME8 .... 63 E4
Clay Cotts. TN17 .... 167 E8
Clay Hill Rd. TN3 .... 165 D6
Clay Wood Cl. BR6 .... 37 E2
Claybridge Rd. SE12 .... 22 C4
Clayfarm Rd. SE9 .... 23 C6
Claygate. ME15 .... 92 D1
Claygate Cross. TN15 .... 87 A3
Claygate La. TN11 .... 101 F4
Claygate Rd. TN12 .... 121 B2
Clayhill. TN17 .... 167 D8
Clayhill Cres. SE12 & SE9 .. 22 D4
Claymill House. 2 SE18 ... 2 C1
Clayton Cl. 3 E6 .... 1 F7
Clayton Croft Rd. DA2 .... 26 A6
Clayton's La. TN3 .... 146 E2
Claytonville Terr. DA17 ..... 4 C4
Claywood La. DA13 & DA2 .. 28 D5
Clayworth Cl. DA15 .... 7 B1
Cleanthus Cl. SE18 .... 6 B6
Cleanthus Rd. SE18 .... 6 B6
Clearway. TN15 .... 73 A1
Clearways Bsns Est. TN15 .. 55 E3
Cleave Ave. BR6 .... 51 E4
Cleave Rd. ME7 .... 48 E3
Cleavers. TN17 .... 170 A8
Cleavers Cl. TN17 .... 170 A8
Cleavesland. ME18 .... 120 E5
Cleeve Ave. TN2 .... 149 D2
Cleeve Ct. 2 DA1 .... 9 D1
Cleeve Park Gdns. DA14 .... 24 B6
Cleeve Park Sch. DA14 ..... 24 C5
Clegg House. SE3 .... 5 B3
Clematis Ave. ME8 .... 63 B5
Clement Cl. ME16 .... 91 D5
Clement St. BR8 .... 26 E2
Clements Ave. E16 .... 1 A6
Clenches Farm La. TN13 .. 84 A1
Clenches Farm Rd. TN13 .. 84 A1
Clendon Way. SE18 .... 2 C2
Clerks Field. TN27 .... 141 D5
Clermont. ME7 .... 63 A4
Cleve Rd. DA14 .... 24 D5
Cleveland. TN2 .... 149 D4
Cleveland House.
Maidstone ME16 .... 91 B2
Cleveland House.
Northfleet DA11 .... 12 D1
Cleveland Rd. Bexley DA6 .. 6 F5
Cleveland Rd.
Gillingham ME7 .... 48 D6
Clevely Cl. SE7 .... 1 D2

Cleves Rd. TN14 .... 69 E2
Clewer House. 8 SE2 .... 3 D4
Clewson Rise. ME14 .... 92 B8
Cliff Hill. ME17 .... 107 D4
Cliff Hill Rd. ME17 .... 107 C4
Cliffe Rd. ME2 .... 33 A1
Cliffe Woods Cty Prim Fst Sch.
ME3 .... 33 C8
Cliffe Woods Mid Sch.
ME3 .... 33 C8
Clifford Ave. BR7 .... 22 F2
Clifton Cl. Maidstone ME14 .. 92 B5
Clifton Cl. 8 Orpington BR6 51 C5
Clifton Cl. Rochester ME2 .. 46 F7
Clifton Cotts. TN1 .... 149 D8
Clifton Gr. DA11 .... 30 B8
Clifton Marine Par. DA11 .. 12 F1
Clifton Pl. TN1 .... 149 B2
Clifton Rd. Bexley DA16 .... 7 C4
Clifton Rd. Gillingham ME7 .. 48 C7
Clifton Rd. Gravesend DA11 . 13 A1
Clifton Rd. Royal Tunbridge Wells
TN1 .... 149 C7
Clifton Rd. Sidcup DA14 ..... 23 E4
Cliftonville Ct. SE12 .... 22 A7
Clinch Cl. TN15 .... 1 A8
Clinch St. ME3 .... 18 A4
Clinton Ave. Bexley DA16 ... 7 A3
Clinton Ave. Rochester ME2 46 E8
Clinton Cl. ME17 .... 106 B3
Clinton La. TN8 .... 113 E3
Clipper Bvd. DA9 .... 10 E3
Clipper Bvd W. DA9 .... 10 D4
Clipper Cl. ME2 .... 47 E7
Clipper Cres. DA12 .... 30 F4
Clipper Ct. ME2 .... 47 E7
Clock House La. TN13 .... 84 A4
Clock Tower Mews. ME6 ... 60 A1
Clockhouse. TN2 .... 149 F6
Cloisterham Rd. ME1 .... 61 D7
Cloisters Ave. BR1 & BR2 ... 36 F4
Cloisters Ct. DA7 .... 8 B4
Cloisters The. 1
Dartford DA1 .... 9 E1
Cloisters The.
Lenham ME17 .... 111 C5
Cloonmore Ave. BR6 .... 51 F6
Close The. Addington ME19 . 73 C2
Close The. Birling ME19 ..... 74 B5
Close The.
Borough Green TN15 ..... 87 A8
Close The.
Bough Beech TN8 .... 114 A2
Close The.
Groombridge TN3 .... 161 C6
Close The. Ightham TN15 .. 86 D6
Close The. New Barn DA3 .. 43 B7
Close The. Orpington BR5 ... 37 E3
Close The. Rochester ME1 .. 47 C4
Close The. Sevenoaks TN13 . 83 E3
Close The. Sidcup DA14 ..... 24 B3
Close The. 1
Sidcup,Old Bexley DA5 ..... 25 A8
Close The. Wilmington DA2 .. 26 D5
Cloth Hall Gdns. TN27 .... 158 A2
Clothier House. SE7 .... 1 E1
Clothworkers Rd. SE18 ..... 6 D7
Cloudesley Cl. ME1 .... 47 B1
Cloudesley Rd. Bexley DA7 .. 7 C4
Cloudesley Rd. Erith DA8 ... 8 F6
Clovelly Rd. DA7 .... 7 E8
Clovelly Way. BR6 .... 37 F3
Clover Bank View. ME5 ..... 62 B6
Clover Rd. 11 RM17 .... 12 D8
Clover Rd. ME13 .... 34 E3
Clover St. ME4 .... 47 F4
Clover Wlk. 13 TN8 .... 112 D3
Cloverdale Gdns. DA15 ..... 6 F1
Clovers The. DA11 .... 29 E4
Club Gardens Rd. BR2 .... 36 A2
Clyde Rd. TN10 .... 117 C6
Clydesdale House. DA18 .... 3 E4
Clydon Cl. DA8 .... 8 E8
Coach Dr The. DA13 .... 72 E7
Coach & Horses Pas. 13
TN2 .... 149 A2
Coach Rd. Egerton TN27 .. 127 E6
Coach Rd.
Ightham Common TN15 .. 86 B2
Coalhouse Fort. RM18 ...... 14 E6
Coastguard Cotts.
Cliffe ME3 .... 15 C8
Coastguard Cotts.
Grain ME3 .... 21 B5
Coates Hill Rd. BR1 .... 37 A7
Cob Cl. TN15 .... 86 C6

Cob Dr. DA12 .... 31 E3
Cobb Cl. ME2 .... 46 D8
Cobbett Cl. ME19 .... 89 F8
Cobbett Rd. SE9 .... 5 E4
Cobbett's Ride. TN2 .... 148 F1
Cobblestones. ME7 .... 62 F5
Cobbs Cl.
Paddock Wood TN12 .... 135 F6
Cobbs Cl.
Wateringbury ME18 .... 104 E7
Cobden Cl. 9 SE28 .... 3 C5
Cobden Rd. Orpington BR6 . 51 D6
Cobden Rd.
Sevenoaks TN13 .... 84 C4
Cobdown Cl. ME20 .... 75 C2
Cobfield. ME17 .... 108 A1
Cobham Cl. Bromley BR2 ... 36 E2
Cobham Cl.
Maidstone ME16 .... 91 E4
Cobham Cl. Rochester ME2 . 46 E7
Cobham Cl. Sidcup DA16 ... 7 B1
Cobham Cty Prim Sch.
DA12 .... 45 A5
Cobham Hall. DA12 .... 45 C6
Cobham House. 4 DA8 .... 8 F7
Cobham Pl. DA6 .... 7 D2
Cobham St. DA11 .... 30 B8
Cobham Terr. DA9 .... 11 B1
Cobhambury Rd.
DA12 & DA13 .... 45 B4
Cobhams. TN3 .... 148 A8
Cobland Rd. SE12 .... 22 C4
Cobsdene. DA12 .... 30 D2
Cobtree Cl. ME5 .... 62 C8
Cobtree Rd. ME17 .... 106 C3
Cobtree Wharf. ME20 ...... 76 C2
Cockerhurst Rd. TN14 ...... 53 E2
Cockmannings La. BR5 ..... 38 E1
Cockmannings Rd. BR5 .... 38 D2
Cockmount La. TN5 .... 174 F5
Cockpit The. TN12 .... 138 C5
Cocksett Ave. BR6 .... 51 E4
Cocksure La. DA14 .... 25 A4
Codrington Cres. DA12 .... 30 D3
Codrington Gdns. DA12 .... 30 D3
Cogate Rd. TN12 .... 135 E6
Colchester Cl. ME5 .... 62 A7
Cold Arbor Rd. TN13 .... 83 D3
Cold Blow Cres. DA5 .... 25 D7
Cold Harbour La. ME9 ...... 65 F6
Coldblow La. ME14 .... 79 A2
Coldbridge La. TN27 ...... 127 B5
Coldharbour Crest. SE9 .... 23 A5
Coldharbour La.
Aylesford ME20 .... 76 A1
Coldharbour La.
Hildenborough TN11 ..... 116 E7
Coldharbour La.
Hucking ME14 .... 79 B1
Coldharbour La.
Rainham RM13 .... 4 F6
Coldharbour Rd.
Iden Green TN17 .... 180 B4
Coldharbour Rd.
Northfleet DA11 .... 29 F5
Coldharbour Rd.
White Post TN11 .... 146 E8
Coldharbour Sports Ctr.
SE9 .... 23 A6
Coldred Rd. ME15 .... 107 F4
Coldrum La. ME19 .... 73 C6
Cole Cl. SE28 .... 3 B5
Cole Terr. ME17 .... 111 C4
Colebrook Ind Est. TN2 ... 133 E1
Colebrook Rd. TN4 .... 149 C8
Colebrooke Cl. DA14 .... 24 B4
Colegate Dr. ME14 .... 93 C4
Coleman Rd. DA17 .... 4 A2
Colemans Heath. SE9 .... 23 B5
Colepits Wood Rd. SE9 .... 6 E2
Coleraine Rd. 1 SE3 .... 5 A8
Coleridge Cl. 4 ME20 ...... 74 F4
Coleridge Rd. Dartford
DA1 .... 10 B3
Coleridge Rd. Tilbury RM18 . 13 C5
Coleridge Way. BR6 .... 38 A3
Coles Cl. TN2 .... 149 C3
Coles La. TN16 .... 82 C4
Coleshall Cl. ME15 .... 107 F6
Colets Orch. TN14 .... 69 B8
Colewood Dr. ME2 .... 46 B8
Colfe's Prep Sch. SE12 .... 5 B1
Colin Blythe Rd. TN10 ..... 117 F5
Colin Chapman Way. DA3 .. 55 E6
Colin Cl. DA2 .... 10 B1
Coll of Guidance Studies.
BR8 .... 25 F1
College Ave.
Gillingham ME7 .... 48 B4
College Ave.
Maidstone ME15 .... 91 F3

College Ave.
Tonbridge TN9 .... 133 A7
College Cotts. ME16 .... 91 F3
College Ct. 5 ME15 .... 92 A3
College Dr. TN2 .... 149 D4
College Gn. BR1 .... 36 A8
College Rd. Bromley BR1 .... 22 A1
College Rd. Chatham ME4 .. 48 A7
College Rd. Hextable BR8 ... 25 F1
College Rd. Maidstone ME15 91 F2
College Rd.
New Hythe ME20 .... 75 B3
College Rd. Northfleet DA11 12 B2
College Vale. SE9 .... 22 D7
College Yd. ME1 .... 47 C6
Coller Cres. DA2 .... 27 E3
Collet Rd. TN14 .... 69 E2
Collet Wlk. ME8 .... 63 D4
Collier Cl. E16 .... 2 B6
Collier Street CE Prim Sch.
TN12 .... 121 D1
Colliers' Green CE Prim Sch.
TN17 .... 154 F2
Colliers Wood. ME2 .... 50 D5
Collindale Ave. Erith DA8 ... 8 B8
Collindale Ave. Sidcup DA15 24 A7
Collings Wlk. ME8 .... 63 D4
Collington Cl. DA11 .... 29 E8
Collington House. SE7 .... 5 B8
Collington Terr. ME15 ..... 107 E4
Collingwood House. DA9 .. 11 D2
Collingwood Ind Ctr.
ME17 .... 108 E2
Collingwood Rd. ME20 ..... 76 C7
Collis St. ME2 .... 47 A8
Collison Pl. TN30 .... 183 D7
Colman House. 2 ME14 .. 92 A4
Colman Rd. E16 .... 1 C8
Colne Rd. TN10 .... 117 B5
Colney Rd. DA1 .... 9 F1
Colonade The. 14 TN10 ... 179 A2
Colonel's Way. TN4 .... 133 A2
Coltness Cres. SE2 .... 3 B1
Colts Hill Pl. TN12 .... 135 B5
Coltsfoot Cl. RM17 .... 12 D8
Coltsfoot Dr. ME14 .... 92 F4
Coltstead. DA3 .... 56 E7
Columbia Wharf Rd. RM17 . 12 A8
Columbine Ave. E6 .... 1 E8
Columbine Cl.
East Malling ME19 .... 74 F1
Columbine Cl.
Rochester ME2 .... 46 E7
Columbine Rd.
East Malling ME19 .... 89 F8
Columbine Rd.
Rochester ME2 .... 46 E7
Columbus Sq. DA8 .... 8 F8
Colville Ct. SE9 .... 22 D7
Colyer Cl. SE9 .... 23 B6
Colyer Rd. DA11 .... 29 D6
Colyers Cl. DA8 .... 8 D6
Colyers La. DA8 .... 8 D6
Colyers Prim Sch. DA7 ..... 8 D6
Colyton Cl. DA16 .... 7 D6
Combe Bank Cotts. TN14 .. 82 D5
Combe Bank Sch. TN14 .... 82 E4
Combedale Rd. SE10 .... 1 A1
Combeside. SE18 .... 6 F7
Combwell Cres. SE2 .... 3 A3
Comfrey Ct. RM17 .... 12 D8
Command Rd. ME14 .... 91 F8
Commercial Pl. DA11 .... 13 C1
Commercial Rd.
Paddock Wood TN12 .... 135 F6
Commercial Rd.
Rochester ME2 .... 47 A7
Commercial Rd.
Royal Tunbridge Wells
TN1 .... 149 B5
Commercial Rd.
Tonbridge TN9 .... 133 C8
Commissioner's Rd. ME2 ... 47 C8
Commodore Rd. ME14 ...... 92 C5
Common La. Cliffe ME3 ..... 16 C6
Common La.
Heath Side DA2 .... 26 B5
Common Rd. Burham ME1 .. 61 B1
Common Rd.
Cliffe Woods ME3 .... 33 B6
Common Rd. Hadlow TN11 102 E2
Common Rd.
Ightham Common TN15 .. 86 B4
Common Rd.
Sissinghurst TN17 .... 170 A8
Common The. ME1 .... 47 C6
Common View. TN4 .... 148 C4

Common Wall. ME3 .... 16 D6
Commonside. BR2 .... 50 C6
Commonwealth House. 5
RM18 .... 13 A5
Commonwealth Way. SE2 .... 3 C1
Commority Rd. DA13 .... 73 B8
Com La. TN15 .... 87 E6
Compass Cl. ME1 .... 47 C1
Compass Ctr. ME4 .... 48 B8
Compasses Rd. TN11 .... 115 B2
Compasses The. TN11 .... 115 B2
Compton Cl. ME5 .... 62 D2
Compton Pl. DA8 .... 8 F8
Concord Ave. ME5 .... 61 E5

Concord Cl.
Paddock Wood TN12 ...... 135 C7
Concord Cl. Royal Tunbridge Wells
TN2 .... 149 C4
Concorde Dr. E6 .... 1 F8
Concrete Cotts. ME3 .... 15 E4
Condover Cres. SE18 .... 6 B7
Conduit Rd. SE18 .... 2 B1
Coneyburrow Rd. TN2 .... 149 E5
Conference Rd. SE2 .... 3 C2
Conghurst La. TN18 .... 185 B6
Congleton Gr. SE18 .... 2 C1
Congo Rd. SE18 .... 2 D1
Congress Rd. SE2 .... 3 C3
Congreve Rd. SE9 .... 5 F4
Congreve Wlk. 6 E16 .... 1 D8
Conifer Ave. DA3 .... 42 E3
Conifer Cl. BR6 .... 51 D6
Conifer Dr. Chatham ME5 ... 62 D1

Conifer Dr.
Culverstone Green DA13 ... 57 F2
Conifer Way. BR8 .... 39 C8
Coniscliffe Cl. BR7 .... 37 A8
Coniston Ave. Bexley DA16 .. 6 E4

Coniston Ave.
Royal Tunbridge Wells
TN4 .... 148 E5
Coniston Cl. Bexley DA7 .... 8 C4
Coniston Cl. Dartford DA1 ... 26 B7
Coniston Cl. Erith DA8 .... 8 C7
Coniston Cl. Gillingham ME7 .. 49 A6
Coniston Rd. DA7 .... 8 C6
Connaught Br. E16 .... 1 C6
Connaught Cl. ME15 .... 107 F4

Connaught Mews.
Chatham ME4 .... 48 C2
Connaught Mews.
Woolwich SE18 .... 2 A1

Connaught Rd.
Chatham ME4 .... 48 C2
Connaught Rd.
Gillingham ME7 .... 48 C5

Connaught Rd.
Newham,Custom House E16 . 1 C6
Connaught Rd.
Newham,Silvertown E16 ..... 1 D5
Connaught Rd.
Woolwich SE18 .... 2 B1
Connaught Way. TN4 .... 148 F5
Conquest Ind Est. ME2 .... 47 A6
Conrad Cl. ME8 .... 63 D4
Consort Cl. ME14 .... 92 B5

Constable Cl.
Northfleet DA11 .... 29 E5
Constable Cl.
Tonbridge TN10 .... 117 C5
Constance St. E16 .... 1 E5
Constitution Hill.
Chatham ME4 .... 48 B4
Constitution Hill.
Gravesend DA12 .... 30 C7
Constitution Hill.
Snodland ME6 .... 75 A8
Constitution Rd. ME4 .... 48 C2
Constitution Rise. SE18 .... 6 A6
Constitutional Hill Rd.
TN4 .... 132 F1
Consul Gdns. BR8 .... 26 A1
Contessa Cl. BR6 .... 51 E5
Convalescent La. TN17 ...... 155 F2
Convent Prep Sch. DA12 .... 30 C6
Conway Cl. ME2 .... 32 E1
Conway Gdns. RM17 .... 12 B7

Conway Inf & Jun Sch.
SE18 .... 2 E2
Conway Mews. ME7 .... 48 A6

Conway Rd.
Maidstone ME16 .... 91 C6
Conway Rd. Woolwich SE18 ... 2 B2
Conyerd Rd. TN15 .... 86 F6
Conyers Wlk. ME8 .... 63 D4
Cooden Cl. BR1 .... 22 B1
Cook Cl. ME5 .... 62 C6
Cook Sq. DA8 .... 8 F7

Cookham Dene Cl. BR7 .... 37 D8
Cookham Hill. ME1 .... 47 A2
Cookham Rd. BR8 .... 39 A8
Cookham Wood Rd. ME1 .... 61 B8
Cookhill Rd. SE2 .... 3 B3
Coolfin Rd. E16 .... 1 B7
Cooling Cl. ME14 .... 92 C6
Cooling Comm. ME3 .... 33 D8
Cooling Rd. Cliffe ME3 .... 16 C4
Cooling Rd. Cooling ME3 ..... 16 E4

Cooling Rd.
High Halstow ME23 .... 17 C3
Cooling Rd. Rochester ME2 . 33 B2
Cooling St. ME3 .... 16 D1
Coomb Field. TN8 .... 128 C8
Coombe Ave. TN14 .... 84 B7
Coombe Cl. Chatham ME5 .. 62 B3
Coombe Cl. Snodland ME6 .. 75 A7
Coombe Farm La. ME3 .... 18 E6
Coombe La. TN30 .... 183 A7
Coombe Lands. TN30 .... 189 D4
Coombe La. BR1 .... 36 E6
Coombe Lodge. SE7 .... 5 C8

Coombe Rd.
Gravesend DA12 .... 30 C6
Coombe Rd.
Hoo St Werburgh ME3 .... 34 E5

Coombe Rd.
Maidstone ME15 .... 91 F2
Coombe Rd. Otford TN14 .... 69 C4
Coombfield Dr. DA2 .... 27 D4
Cooper Cl. DA9 .... 10 F2
Cooper Ct. SE18 .... 6 B8
Cooper Rd. Chatham ME5 ... 62 B3
Cooper Rd. Snodland ME6 ... 74 F6
Cooper Shaw Rd. RM18 ..... 13 E7
Cooper's Rd. DA11 .... 29 F7
Coopers Cl. DA4 .... 41 D8
Coopers Cotts. DA2 .... 27 A4
Coopers La. Lewisham SE12 12 B6

Coopers La. Poundsbridge
TN11 & TN3 .... 147 C7
Coopers' Lane Prim Sch.
SE12 .... 22 B6
Coopers Sch. BR7 .... 37 C8
Coote Rd. DA7 .... 7 F6
Copenhagen Rd. ME7 .... 48 C4
Copley Dene. BR1 .... 36 D8
Coppards La. TN31 .... 187 D1

Copper Beech Cl.
Gravesend DA12 .... 30 D8
Copper Beech Cl. 7
Orpington BR5 .... 38 C4
Copper La. TN12 .... 138 E5
Copper Tree Ct. ME15 .... 107 A5
Copper Tree Wlk. ME15 ...... 62 C1
Copperfield Cl. Chalk DA12 . 31 A7
Copperfield Cl. Erith SE28 ... 3 C7
Copperfield Cres. ME2 .... 32 C2
Copperfield Ct. DA1 .... 26 B8
Copperfield Dr. ME17 .... 108 E4
Copperfield House. ME4 ..... 48 A4
Copperfield Rd. ME1 .... 47 C2
Copperfield Way. BR7 .... 23 C2
Copperfields. 2
Dartford DA1 .... 9 E1
Copperfields. Kemsing TN15 69 F2
Copperfields Cl. TN15 .... 69 F2
Copperfields Orch. TN15 .... 69 F2
Copperfields The. ME1 .... 47 B4
Copperfields Wlk. TN15 ...... 69 F2
Coppergate. ME7 .... 62 F5
Coppergate Cl. BR1 .... 36 B8
Copperhouse La. ME7 .... 49 B6
Copperhouse Rd. ME2 .... 46 C7
Coppice Cl. ME7 .... 63 B4
Coppice Rd. ME5 .... 62 C2

Coppice The.
Aylesford ME20 .... 75 E1
Coppice The.
Bitchet Green TN15 .... 85 D1
Coppice The.
Pembury TN2 .... 150 D7
Coppice The.
Vigo Village DA13 .... 73 B8
Coppice View. ME14 .... 92 E6
Copping's Rd. TN11 .... 115 C4
Copse Bank. TN15 .... 84 F7
Copse Cl. SE7 .... 5 B8
Copse Rd. TN11 .... 116 E4
Copse Side. DA3 .... 42 E6
Copse The. ME3 .... 34 E3
Copsehill. ME20 .... 74 E2
Copsewood Way. ME15 ...... 93 A3
Copt Hall. TN18 .... 187 D3

Copt Hall Rd.
Ightham Common TN15 ..... 86 A4
Copt Hall Rd.
Sole Street DA13 .... 44 B5
Coptefield Dr. DA17 .... 3 E3
Copthall Ave. TN18 .... 179 A1

Copthorne Ave. BR2 .... 50 F8
Coralline Wlk. 4 SE2 .... 3 C4
Corbyland Rd. DA15 .... 23 E7
Corbylands Rd. DA15 .... 23 D8
Cordelia Cres. ME1 .... 46 F2
Corelli Rd. SE18 & SE3 .... 5 E6
Corinthian Cl. ME1 .... 21 B5
Corinthian Manorway. DA8 .. 4 D2
Corinthian Rd. DA8 .... 4 D2
Cork House. BR5 .... 38 B6
Cork La. TN12 .... 155 D8
Cork St. ME20 .... 75 F6
Corkwell St. ME4 .... 47 E3
Cormorant Cl. ME2 .... 46 C7
Corn Mill Dr. BR6 .... 38 A2
Cornel House. 4 DA15 .... 24 A5
Cornelia Pl. DA8 .... 8 E8
Cornell Cl. DA14 .... 24 E2
Corner Farm Rd. TN12 ..... 139 E4
Corner Gn. SE3 .... 5 A5
Cornfield Way. TN10 .... 117 D6
Cornflower Cl. ME14 .... 92 E4
Cornford Cl. Hayes BR2 ...... 36 A4
Cornford Cl. Pembury TN2 150 B6
Cornford La. TN2 .... 150 B5
Cornford Pk. TN2 .... 150 C6
Cornforth Cl. TN12 .... 139 F4
Cornwall Ave. DA16 .... 6 F4
Cornwall Cl. ME15 .... 107 E7
Cornwall Cres. ME1 .... 60 D4
Cornwall Dr. BR5 .... 24 C1
Cornwall Rd. Dartford DA1 ... 9 F4

Cornwall Rd.
Gillingham ME7 .... 48 D6
Cornwall Rd. Rochester ME1 47 C3
Cornwallis Ave.
Chatham ME4 .... 47 E1
Cornwallis Ave.
Gillingham ME8 .... 49 A4
Cornwallis Ave.
Linton ME17 .... 122 E8
Cornwallis Ave.
Sidcup DA15 .... 23 D6
Cornwallis Ave.
Tonbridge TN10 .... 117 F4
Cornwallis Cl. DA8 .... 8 F8
Cornwallis Cotts. ME17 .... 106 E2
Cornwallis Rd.
Maidstone ME16 .... 91 D4
Cornwallis Rd.
Woolwich SE18 .... 2 B3
Cornwallis Sch The. ME15 106 F2
Cornwallis Wlk. SE9 .... 5 F4
Cornwell Ave. ME12 .... 30 C5
Corona Rd. SE12 .... 22 A8
Corona Terr. ME6 .... 74 F6
Coronation Cl. DA5 .... 7 E1
Coronation Cotts.
Berner's Hill TN5 .... 176 F2
Coronation Cotts.
Stoke ME3 .... 19 A3
Coronation Ct. DA8 .... 8 D7
Coronation Flats. 2 ME4 .... 47 F3
Coronation Rd.
Chatham ME5 .... 48 C2
Coronation Rd. Grain ME3 .. 21 B5
Corporation Rd. ME7 .... 48 D7
Corporation St. ME1 .... 47 C5
Corral Cl. ME5 .... 48 D2
Corrall Almshouses. 4
ME15 .... 92 A3
Corrance Gn. ME15 .... 107 A8
Correnden Rd. TN11 .... 117 A3
Corseley Rd. TN3 .... 161 B5
Cossack St. ME1 .... 47 D3
Cossington Rd. ME5 .... 62 B1
Costells Meadow. TN16 ...... 81 D1
Cot La. TN27 .... 158 B3
Cotleigh Ave. DA5 .... 24 D6
Cotman Way. TN12 .... 119 E6
Cotman's Ash La. TN15 ..... 70 D4
Cotmandene Cres. BR8 ...... 38 A7
Coton Rd. DA16 .... 7 A4
Cotswold Cl. DA7 .... 8 E5
Cotswold Gdns. ME15 .... 93 A2
Cotswold Rd. DA11 .... 29 E5
Cotswold Rise. BR6 .... 37 F3
Cottage Ave. BR2 .... 36 E1
Cottage Field Cl.
DA5 & DA14 .... 24 C7
Cottage Rd. ME4 .... 47 F6
Cottall Ave. ME4 .... 47 F2
Cottenham Cl. ME19 .... 89 F7
Cotton La. DA9 .... 10 D2
Coulman St. ME7 .... 48 D5
Coulter House. DA9 .... 11 C2
Coulters Cl. ME14 .... 92 D5
Coulton Ave. DA11 .... 29 E7
Council Ave. DA11 .... 12 C1
Council Cotts.
Coxheath ME15 .... 106 A4

Council Cotts.
Key's Green TN12 .... 151 C4
Council Houses. TN15 ...... 102 A8
Countess of Thanet's
Almshouses. TN8 .... 144 F3
County Gate. BR7 .... 23 C5
County Gr. ME19 .... 89 B8
County Rd. Maidstone ME14 92 A5
County Rd. Newham E6 .... 2 B8
Coupland Pl. SE18 .... 2 C1
Course The. SE9 .... 23 A5
Court Ave. DA17 .... 3 F1
Court Broomes. ME17 .... 125 C8
Court Cres. BR8 .... 39 E5
Court Dr. ME16 .... 91 D4
Court Farm Rd. SE9 .... 22 E5
Court La. Detling ME14 .... 78 C5
Court La. Hadlow TN11 ..... 119 B7
Court Lane Pl. TN11 .... 118 F8
Court Lodge. DA17 .... 4 A1
Court Lodge Cotts.
East Farleigh ME15 .... 106 A7
Court Lodge Cotts.
Horton Kirby DA4 .... 41 C6
Court Lodge Rd. ME7 .... 48 F6
Court Meadow.
Gillingham ME8 .... 49 B2
Court Meadow.
Wrotham TN15 .... 71 F3
Court Rd. Burham ME1 .... 75 E8
Court Rd. Eltham SE9 .... 22 F7
Court Rd. Lane End DA2 ..... 27 E3
Court Rd. Royal Tunbridge Wells
TN4 .... 148 F4
Court Road (Orpington By-Pass).
Chelsfield BR6 & TN14 ..... 52 D5
Court Road (Orpington By-Pass).
Orpington BR5 & BR6 .... 38 B2
Court St. BR1 .... 36 A7
Court Yd. SE9 .... 5 F1
Courtaulds Cl. SE28 .... 3 A5
Courtenay Rd. ME15 .... 91 F2
Courteney Rd. ME8 .... 63 B8
Courtenwell. TN3 .... 147 E4
Courtfield Ave. ME5 .... 62 B3
Courthope. TN12 .... 136 A6
Courthope Ave. TN5 .... 174 F4
Courtland Gr. SE28 .... 3 D6
Courtlands.
Hilden Park TN11 .... 117 A3
Courtlands. Teston ME18 ... 105 A8
Courtlands Ave. SE12 .... 5 B2
Courtlands Cl. ME18 .... 105 A8
Courtlands Farm. TN17 .... 169 A3
Courtleet Dr. DA7 .... 8 B6
Courtwood Dr. TN13 .... 84 A3
Courtyard Gdns. TN15 .... 71 F3
Courtyard The. ME7 .... 63 A8
Cousley Wood Rd. TN5 .... 175 C7
Couthurst Rd. SE3 .... 5 B7
Coutts Ave. DA12 .... 31 E4
Coutts House. SE7 .... 5 C8
Covelees Wall. SE9 .... 5 F4
Coventry Cl. 9 Newham E6 .. 1 F7
Coventry Cl. Rochester ME2 46 D6
Coventry Rd. TN10 .... 117 D5
Coverdale Ave. ME15 .... 107 D6
Coverdale Cl. ME5 .... 62 B7
Covert The. Chatham ME5 .. 62 B1
Covert The.
Orpington BR5 & BR6 .... 37 E3
Covert The.
Vigo Village DA13 .... 72 E7
Covet Wood Cl. BR5 .... 37 F3
Covey Hall Rd. ME6 .... 60 A1
Cow La. TN8 .... 129 D1
Cow Leaze. TN8 .... 2 A7
Cowan Cl. E6 .... 1 E8
Cowbeck Cl. ME8 .... 63 D6
Cowden Cl. TN18 .... 184 E8
Cowden Cl. TN8 .... 128 D8
Cowden Cross. TN8 .... 145 C7
Cowden La. TN18 .... 184 E7
Cowden Mews. TN8 .... 145 A5
Cowden Rd.
Maidstone ME14 .... 92 C5
Cowden Rd. Orpington BR6 .. 37 F2
Cowden Sta. TN8 .... 145 D8
Cowdrey Cl.
Maidstone ME16 .... 91 B2
Cowdrey Cl. Rochester ME1 . 47 B2
Cowdrey Ct. DA1 .... 26 B8
Cowen House. 4 SE28 .... 6 B8
Cowley Ave. DA9 .... 11 A2
Cowper Ave. RM18 .... 13 B6
Cowper Cl. Bexley DA16 .... 7 A2
Cowper Cl. Bromley BR2 .... 36 D5
Cowper Rd. Bromley BR2 ... 36 D5
Cowper Rd. Erith DA17 .... 4 A2
Cowper Rd. Gillingham ME7 48 D3
Cowstead Rd. ME9 .... 64 D2
Cox St. ME14 .... 78 E6

Cox's Cl. ME6 74
Coxheath Cty Prim Sch.
ME17 106
Coxmount Rd. SE7 5
Coxwell Rd. SE18 2
Cozenton Cl. ME8 4
Crabbs Croft Cl. 7 BR6 51
Crabtree Cl. ME8 & ME19 .. 89
Crabtree Manorway.
Erith DA17 ....
Crabtree Manorway.
Erith DA17 ....
Crabtree Rd. ME8 63
Craddock Way. ME8 63
Cradducks La. TN12 140
Cradles Rd. ME9 65
Cradley Rd. SE9 23
Cragie Wlk. ME8 64
Craigerne Rd. SE3 & SE7 5
Craigholm. SE18 6
Craigton Rd. SE9 5
Crampton's Rd. TN14 84
Cramptons. TN17 169
Cranborne Ave. ME15 92
Cranborne Ave. ME15 107
Cranbrook CE Prim Sch.
TN17 169
Cranbrook Cl.
Gillingham ME8 49
Cranbrook Cl. Hayes BR2 ... 36
Cranbrook Cl.
Maidstone ME15 107
Cranbrook House. 1 DA8 8
Cranbrook Point. E16 1
Cranbrook Rd.
Benenden TN17 179
Cranbrook Rd. Erith DA7 2
Cranbrook Rd. Fosten Green
TN27 & TN17 173
Cranbrook Rd.
Gill's Green TN18 178
Cranbrook Rd.
Goudhurst TN17 168
Cranbrook Rd. Knox Bridge
TN12 & TN17 155
Cranbrook Rd. Parkgate
TN27 & TN30 172
Cranbrook Rd.
Tenterden TN30 182
Cranbrook Sch. TN17 169
Crandalls. TN11 115
Crane House. 11 TN18 178
Crane House Gdns. 10
TN18 178
Crane La. Cranbrook TN17 169
Crane La. Cranbrook TN17 169
Cranford Cl. ME8 49
Cranford Rd. Dartford DA1 .. 26
Cranford Rd.
Tonbridge TN10 118
Cranham Sq. TN12 138
Cranleigh Cl. Bexley DA5 8
Cranleigh Cl. Orpington BR6 52
Cranleigh Dr. BR8 39
Cranleigh Gdns.
Chatham ME1 47
Cranleigh Gdns.
Maidstone ME16 91
Cranley Par. SE9 22
Cranley Rd. E13 1
Cranmer Ct. ME15 107
Cranmer Rd. TN13 83
Cranmore Rd. BR7 & SE9 ... 22
Cranwell Rd. TN4 148
Crathie Rd. SE12 5
Craven Rd. BR6 52
Crawfords. BR8 25
Crawley Ct. 1 DA11 13
Crawshay Cl. TN13 84
Cray Ave. BR5 38
Cray Cl. DA1 9
Cray Rd. Crockenhill BR8 39
Cray Rd. Erith DA17 8
Cray Rd. Sidcup DA14 24
Cray Valley Golf Course.
BR5 38
Cray Valley Rd. BR5 38
Craybrooke Rd. DA14 24
Crayburne. DA13 28
Craybury End. SE9 23
Craydene Rd. DA8 8
Crayfields Ind Pk. BR5 38
Crayford Cl. ME14 92
Crayford Commercial Ctr.
DA1 8
Crayford High St. DA1 8
Crayford Ind Est. DA1 8
Crayford L Ctr. DA1 8
Crayford Rd. DA1 8
Crayford Sta. DA1 8
Crayford Way. DA1 9

...ands. BR5 .... 38 C6
...ands La. DA10 .... 11 D2
...ands La. DA10 .... 11 D2
mill Sq. DA1 .... 8 F5
s Par The. BR5 .... 38 C7
 side Ind Est. DA1 .... 9 B3
horne. TN30 .... 183 B8
sey's Row. TN14 .... 97 E5
enhall Dr. BR2 .... 36 F1
ton Rd. E16 .... 1 A7
o Way. RM16 .... 11 B8
k The. DA11 .... 12 B2
horne Rd. DA11 .... 29 F8
don Pk. TN4 .... 149 A8
cent Ave. RM17 .... 12 D8
cent Cotts. TN13 .... 83 E7
cent Ct. **1** RM17 .... 12 D8
cent Gdns. BR8 .... 37 C3
cent Gdns. BR8 .... 39 C7
cent Rd. Bromley BR1 ..... 22 A1
cent Rd. Erith DA8 .... 8 F8
cent Rd.
cent
al Tunbridge Wells
& TN2 .... 149 B3
cent Rd. Sidcup DA15 ...... 23 F5
cent Rd. Woolwich SE18 . 2 B2
The. Bexley DA6 .... 24 C8
cent The.
borough TN4 .... 132 E4
cent The.
ough Green TN15 .... 87 A8
cent The.
ombridge TN3 .... 161 C7
cent The. Longfield DA3 42 E6
cent The.
idstone ME14 .... 91 F8
cent The.
rthfleet DA11 .... 29 F6
cent The.
venoaks TN13 .... 84 D6
cent The. Sidcup DA14 .. 23 F4
cent The.
ranscombe DA9 .... 11 C2
cent The.
nbridge TN9 .... 117 B3
cent Way.
atham ME5 .... 61 D5
cent Way.
pington ME4 .... 51 E5
sey Ct. ME4 .... 47 E4
singham Ct. **1** DA17 ..... 4 A3
Ave. RM17 .... 12 B7
t Cl. TN14 .... 68 B8
t Ind Est. TN12 .... 138 C6
t Rd. ME1 .... 47 C1
t View. DA1 .... 11 A3
t View. Dr. BR5 .... 37 C4
stway. ME5 .... 62 B8
e Hall Rd. DA11 .... 12 E1
on St. SE18 .... 2 A3
e Coeur Cl. ME14 .... 93 A5
et Ground Rd. BR7 .... 37 B8
keters Cl. Erith DA8 ...... 8 E8
keters Cl.
rrietsham ME17 .... 110 D6
keters Dr. DA13 .... 58 A7
ple Hill. TN26 .... 159 D1
ple St. ME15 .... 107 A7
ield Ct. TN30 .... 173 B2
mill La. ME14 .... 93 F4
mill Rd. ME14 .... 93 F3
pe Cl. ME8 .... 63 D4
pin Ct. ME17 .... 106 C3
oin Rd. ME2 .... 46 E8
all's Cnr. DA14 .... 24 C1
enden Bglws. ME15 .... 106 A4
enden Cotts. ME15 ...... 106 A4
enden Rd. TN12 .... 135 D3
le's Ct. TN5 .... 174 F4
cken Hill Rd. TN27 ..... 127 C2
ckenhall Way. DA13 ... 29 E1
ckenhill Cty Prim Sch.
                            .... 39 C3
ckenhill Hill. BR5 .... 38 D4
ckenhill Rd. BR8 .... 40 C2
ckenhill Rd. BR5 & BR8 . 38 E4
ckers Hatch Cnr. TN3 . 147 D2
ckham Hill CE Prim Sch.
                            .... 96 C2
ckham Way. SE9 .... 23 A4
t Cl. Chatham ME5 .... 62 C1
t Cl. Chislehurst BR7 .... 22 F3
t Cl. Erith DA17 .... 3 F1
t Cl. Tonbridge TN10 ... 117 F5
t Ct. TN8 .... 112 C1
t Gdns. ME17 .... 111 D4
t La. TN8 .... 112 C1
t Rd. Bromley BR1 ...... 22 A2
t Rd. Westerham TN16 .. 81 C1
t The. Leybourne ME20 .. 74 E2
t The. Swanley BR8 ...... 39 C6

Croft Way. Sevenoaks TN13 . 83 F2
Croft Way. Sidcup DA15 ... 23 E5
Crofters The. ME8 .... 63 F7
Crofton Ave. Orpington BR6 . 51 C8
Crofton Ave. Sidcup DA5 .. 24 D8
Crofton Inf Sch. BR5 .... 37 D2
Crofton Jun Sch. BR5 ...... 37 D2
Crofton La. BR5 & BR6 ..... 37 D2
Crofton Rd. BR6 .... 51 B8
Croftside. DA13 .... 73 A8
Cromarty Ct. **5** BR1 ...... 36 C7
Crombie Rd. DA15 .... 23 D7
Cromer Pl. **5** BR6 .... 37 D1
Cromer Rd. ME2 .... 47 B8
Cromer St. TN9 .... 117 A1
Cromford Cl. BR6 .... 51 E7
Cromlix Cl. BR7 .... 37 B7
Cromwell Ave. BR2 .... 36 B5
Cromwell Rd.
Maidstone ME14 .... 92 B5
Cromwell Rd.
Royal Tunbridge Wells
TN2 .... 149 C3
Cromwell Terr. ME14 ...... 48 A3
Cronin Cl. **2** ME20 .... 74 F4
Crook Log. DA6 .... 7 D3
Crook Log Prim Sch. DA6 ... 7 D3
Crook Log Sports Ctr. DA16 . 7 D4
Crook Rd. TN12 .... 136 D1
Crooked La. DA11 .... 13 B1
Crookston Rd. SE9 .... 6 A4
Coombs Rd. E16 .... 1 C8
Crosby House. DA11 .... 9 A1
Crosley Rd. ME7 .... 48 D3
Cross Ct. **11** SE28 .... 3 B6
Cross Dr. ME17 .... 109 B1
Cross Keys. Maidstone ME14 93 C4
Cross Keys. Sevenoaks TN13 99 A8
Cross Keys Cl. TN13 .... 99 A8
Cross La. Sidcup DA5 ...... 24 F8
Cross La. Ticehurst TN5 .. 176 D2
Cross La E. DA12 .... 30 B6
Cross La W. DA11 .... 30 B6
Cross Lane Gdns. TN5 .... 176 D1
Cross Rd. Dartford DA1 .... 9 C1
Cross Rd. Hawley DA2 .... 26 F4
Cross Rd. Keston Mark BR2 .. 50 E8
Cross Rd. Northfleet DA11 . 12 F1
Cross Rd. Orpington BR5 .. 38 B4
Cross Rd. Sidcup DA14 .... 24 B4
Cross St. Chatham ME4 .... 48 A4
Cross St. Erith DA8 .... 8 E8
Cross St. Gillingham ME7 ... 48 E6
Cross St. **24**
Gravesend DA11 .... 13 B1
Cross St. Maidstone ME14 ... 92 A6
Cross St. Rochester ME2 .... 47 B8
Cross Way. ME5 .... 5 E4
Crossbrook Rd. SE3 .... 5 E4
Crossmead. SE9 .... 22 F7
Crossway. Chatham ME5 ... 61 E6
Crossway. Erith SE28 .... 3 D7
Crossway. Orpington BR5 .. 37 D4
Crossway The.
Chislehurst SE9 .... 22 D6
Crossway The.
Royal Tunbridge Wells
TN4 .... 148 D2
Crossways.
Chart Sutton ME17 ...... 108 B1
Crossways. Dartford DA9 .. 10 C3
Crossways Bvd. DA9 .... 10 C3
Crouch Croft. SE9 .... 23 A5
Crouch House Cotts. TN8 . 112 B2
Crouch House Rd. TN8 ... 112 B2
Crouch La. Crouch TN15 ... 87 B6
Crouch La. Linkhill TN18 .. 186 D6
Crow Cnr. ME1 .... 47 C5
Crow Dr. TN14 .... 97 A4
Crow Hill. TN15 .... 87 A7
Crow Hill Rd. TN15 .... 87 A7
Crow La. ME1 .... 47 C5
Crowden Way. SE28 .... 3 C6
Crowhurst La. Basted TN15 . 86 E4
Crowhurst La.
West Kingsdown TN15 ... 56 B4
Crowhurst Oast. TN12 .... 103 D1
Crowhurst Rd. TN15 .... 86 F6
Crowhurst Way. BR5 ...... 38 C4
Crown Acres. TN12 .... 120 A6
Crown Cl. BR6 .... 52 A6
Crown Ct. Bromley BR1 .... 36 E4
Crown Ct. Cranbrook TN17 169 C5
Crown Ct. Eltham SE12 .... 5 B1
Crown Ct. Tilbury RM18 .... 13 A5
Crown Gn. DA12 .... 31 E3
Crown La. Bromley BR2 .... 36 D4
Crown La. Chislehurst BR7 . 37 C8
Crown La. Shorne DA12 .... 31 E4
Crown Lane Spur. BR2 .... 36 D3
Crown Rd. Grays RM17 .... 12 A8

Crown Rd. Marlpit Hill TN8 112 D4
Crown Rd. Orpington BR6 ... 52 A5
Crown Rd. Shoreham TN14 .. 53 F1
Crown St. ME7 .... 48 D6
Crown Woods Sch. SE9 ..... 6 C2
Crown Woods Way. SE9 ..... 6 D2
Crownfields.
Maidstone ME14 .... 92 F4
Crownfields.
Sevenoaks TN13 .... 84 B2
Crowther Cl. TN12 .... 139 E4
Croxley Cl. BR5 .... 38 B7
Croxley Gn. BR5 .... 38 B8
Croyde Cl. SE9 .... 23 D8
Croydon Cl. ME5 .... 62 C4
Croydon Rd. Keston Mark
BR2 & BR4 & BR6 .... 50 C7
Croydon Rd.
Westerham TN16 .... 81 B2
Crozier House. SE3 .... 5 B4
Cruden Rd. DA12 .... 30 F6
Crump's La. ME17 .... 126 B4
Crumpsall St. SE2 .... 3 C2
Crundale. **2** ME14 .... 92 A5
Crundale Rd. ME8 .... 49 C3
Crundale Tower. BR5 ...... 38 C1
Crundwell Rd. TN4 .... 132 F1
Crusader Cl. ME7 .... 63 B8
Crusader Ct. DA1 .... 9 F3
Crusoe Rd. DA8 .... 4 D1
Crutches La. ME2 .... 32 B1
Cryals Ct. TN12 .... 151 E5
Cryals Rd. TN12 .... 151 D5
Crystal House. SE18 .... 2 F1
Cuckmere Ct. **18** BR5 ..... 38 D1
Cuckmere House. **3**
                            .... 107 E8
Cuckold's Cnr. ME3 .... 32 C6
Cuckolds Cnr. DA3 .... 57 B7
Cuckolds Green Rd. ME3 .. 19 B5
Cuckoo La. Lamberhurst Quarter
TN12 & TN3 .... 152 A2
Cuckoo La.
Tonbridge TN10 & TN11 .. 118 A7
Cuckoowood Ave. ME14 ... 76 F1
Cudham CE Prim Sch.
TN16 .... 66 A3
Cudham Cl. ME14 .... 92 C6
Cudham La N. TN14 & BR6 .. 66 D7
Cudham La S.
TN14 & TN16 .... 66 D2
Cudham Park Rd. TN14 .... 51 E1
Cudham Rd. BR6 .... 66 B7
Cuff Cres. SE9 .... 5 D1
Cugley Rd. DA2 .... 27 C8
Culcroft. DA3 .... 42 F6
Culpeper Cl.
Hollingbourne ME17 ...... 94 E2
Culpeper Cl. Rochester ME2 47 E6
Culpepers. TN17 .... 167 E7
Culpeper Rd.
Coxheath ME17 .... 106 B3
Culpepper Rd.
Gillingham ME8 .... 63 D4
Culverden Ave. TN4 ...... 149 A6
Culverden Down. TN4 ... 148 F5
Culverden Park Rd. TN4 . 148 F5
Culverden Pk. TN4 .... 148 F5
Culverden Sq. TN1 & TN4 . 149 A5
Culverden St. TN1 .... 149 A4
Culverstone Green Cty Prim Sch.
DA13 .... 57 F4
Culverstone House. BR5 .. 38 B6
Culverton Ct. **5** DA14 ... 24 A4
Culvey Cl. DA3 .... 42 E4
Cumberland Ave.
Bexley DA16 .... 6 F3
Cumberland Ave.
Gravesend DA11 .... 30 C8
Cumberland Ave.
Maidstone ME15 .... 107 D8
Cumberland Ct. TN11 ... 117 A4
Cumberland Dr.
Dartford DA1 .... 26 F8
Cumberland Dr. Erith DA7 .. 7 E7
Cumberland Gdns. **10**
TN1 .... 149 A2
Cumberland Mews.
TN1 .... 149 A2
Cumberland Rd.
Gillingham ME4 & ME7 ... 48 B7
Cumberland Rd.
Gillingham ME7 .... 48 C7
Cumberland Rd.
Newham E13 .... 1 B8
Cumberland Sch. E16 ...... 1 A8
Cumberland Wlk. TN1 .... 149 A2
Cumberland Yd. **11** TN1 .. 149 A2
Cumberland Ave. DA7 ...... 8 E5
Cundy Rd. E16 .... 1 C7
Cunningham Cl. TN4 ..... 149 B7

Cunningham Cres. ME5 ..... 62 A8
Cunningham House. ME1 ... 47 B4
Cunningham Rd. TN4 ..... 149 B7
Cupola Cl. BR1 .... 22 B3
Curlew Cl. SE28 .... 3 D6
Curlew Cres. ME2 .... 46 C6
Curlews The. DA12 .... 30 D6
Curran Ave. DA15 .... 6 F2
Currie Rd. TN4 .... 149 A5
Curteis Rd. TN30 .... 173 B1
Curtis Way. **7** SE28 .... 3 B6
Curtismill Cl. BR5 .... 38 B6
Curtismill Way. BR5 .... 38 B6
Curzon Cl. BR6 .... 51 D6
Curzon Rd. ME5 .... 62 C3
Curzon Rd. RM17 .... 12 C7
Curzon Rd. Chatham ME4 .. 47 F3
Curzon Rd. Maidstone ME14 92 A6
Custom House Sta. E16 .... 1 B6
Cut The. TN27 .... 158 E8
Cutbush Almshouses. **2**
ME15 .... 92 A3
Cutbush and Corrall Cl.
ME14 .... 92 B4
Cutmore St. DA11 .... 30 B8
Cutter Ridge Rd. DA13 .... 45 A1
Cutty Sark Cl. DA9 .... 11 A2
Cuxton. BR5 .... 37 C4
Cuxton Cl. DA6 .... 7 E2
Cuxton Cty Inf Sch. ME2 .. 46 B2
Cuxton Cty Jun Sch. ME2 . 46 B2
Cuxton Ind Est. ME2 ...... 46 C2
Cuxton Rd.
Park Wood ME15 .... 107 F5
Cuxton Rd. Rochester ME2 . 46 F5
Cuxton Sta. ME2 .... 46 C2
Cyclamen Rd. BR8 .... 39 D5
Cygnet Cl. ME20 .... 75 A2
Cygnet Gdns. DA11 .... 29 F6
Cygnet L Ctr. DA11 .... 29 E6
Cygnet Rd. ME5 .... 62 C2
Cypress Ave. ME3 .... 34 E3
Cypress Cl. ME7 .... 48 F6
Cypress Gr. TN2 .... 163 C8
Cypress Rd. ME2 .... 33 C1
Cypress Tree Cl. DA15 .... 23 F7
Cyprus Pl. E6 .... 2 A6
Cyprus Sta. E6 .... 2 A6
Cyril Lodge. **2** DA14 .... 24 A4
Cyril Rd. Bexley DA7 .... 7 E5
Cyril Rd. Orpington BR6 ... 38 A2

D'arcy Pl. BR2 .... 36 A5
Dabbling Cl. DA8 .... 9 B7
Dabells. TN17 .... 169 D4
Daerwood Cl. BR2 .... 36 F1
Daffodil Rd. ME2 .... 46 F7
Dagenham Cl. ME14 .... 92 C6
Dagnet Gdns. **2** BR1 .... 22 A5
Dagonet Rd. BR1 .... 22 A5
Dahlia Dr. BR8 .... 39 F7
Dahlia Rd. SE2 .... 3 B2
Dainton Cl. **2** BR1 .... 36 B8
Daintons Cotts. **2** TN18 . 178 F2
Dairsie Cl. **2** BR1 .... 36 C7
Dairsie Rd. SE9 .... 6 A4
Dairy Cl. DA4 .... 27 B1
Dairy La. Chainhurst TN12 121 F4
Dairy La. Crockham Hill TN8 . 96 B1
Dairy La. Woolwich SE18 .... 1 F2
Dairy Pl. TN12 .... 121 F4
Dakota Gdns. E6 .... 1 E8
Dalberg Way. SE2 .... 3 D3
Dale Cl. Crayford DA1 .... 8 F1
Dale Cl. Greenwich SE3 .... 5 A4
Dale End. DA1 .... 8 F1
Dale Rd. Crayford DA1 ...... 8 F1
Dale Rd. Rochester ME1 .... 47 C3
Dale Rd. Southfleet DA13 .. 29 A4
Dale Rd. Swanley BR8 ..... 39 C6
Dale St. Chatham ME4 ...... 47 F4
Dale St. Royal Tunbridge Wells
TN1 .... 149 B4
Dale The. BR2 .... 50 D6
Dale View. DA8 .... 8 F5
Dale Wlk. DA2 .... 27 C7
Dale Wood Rd. BR6 .... 37 E1
Daleside. SE2 .... 3 C2
Daleside Cl. BR6 .... 52 A4
Dalison Ct. ME2 .... 60 A4
Dallin Rd. Bexley DA6 .... 7 D3
Dallin Rd. Woolwich SE18 ... 6 B7
Dalmeny Rd. DA7 & DA8 ... 8 B6
Dalton Cl. BR6 .... 51 E7
Dalton St. ME7 .... 48 C6
Daltons Rd. BR8 & BR6 .... 53 C7
Damiem Cl. ME4 .... 48 A2
Damigos Rd. DA12 .... 30 F7
Damon Cl. DA14 .... 24 B5
Damon Ct. DA14 .... 24 B5
Damson Ct. BR8 .... 39 D5

Damson Dr. ME3 .... 34 E3
Danaway Cotts. ME9 .... 65 C3
Dando Cres. SE3 .... 5 B4
Dandridge Cl. SE10 .... 1 A1
Dane Cl. Chatham ME5 ..... 62 C2
Dane Cl. Hartlip ME9 .... 64 D6
Dane Cl. Orpington BR6 .... 51 D5
Dane Cl. Sidcup DA5 .... 25 A8
Dane Ct. ME17 .... 106 C2
Dane La. ME9 .... 64 D6
Dane Rd. TN14 .... 68 F2
Danecourt Sch The. ME8 .. 49 A2
Danefield Ct.
Maidstone ME14 .... 93 B4
Danefield Ct.
Sevenoaks TN13 .... 83 C4
Danehill Wlk. DA14 .... 24 A5
Danemore. TN30 .... 183 B8
Danes Cl. DA11 .... 29 C5
Danes Hill. ME7 .... 49 A6
Danescombe. SE12 .... 22 A7
Danns La. ME18 .... 89 A1
Dansington Rd. DA16 .... 7 A3
Danson Cres. DA16 .... 7 B4
Danson La. DA16 .... 7 B3
Danson Mead. DA16 .... 7 C4
Danson Prim Sch. DA16 .... 7 A3
Danson Rd. Bexley DA6 .... 7 D2
Danson Rd. Sidcup DA5 .... 7 C1
Danson Underpass. DA5 ... 7 C1
Danson Way. ME8 .... 49 D2
Danvers Rd. TN9 .... 117 B1
Darby's La. TN5 .... 175 B2
Darby Gdns. ME3 .... 32 B3
Darby's La. TN13 .... 83 C5
Darent Ind Pk. DA8 .... 9 D8
Darent Mead. DA4 .... 41 B8
Darent Valley Golf Course.
                            .... 69 A6
Darenth Ave. TN10 .... 117 C5
Darenth Cotts. TN14 .... 68 F8
Darenth Ct. **5** BR5 .... 38 D1
Darenth Cty Prim Sch. DA2 27 E2
Darenth Dr. DA12 .... 31 B7
Darenth Gdns. TN16 .... 81 D1
Darenth Hill. DA2 & DA4 .. 27 C3
Darenth House. **2** ME15 . 107 D8
Darenth La. TN13 .... 83 E6
Darenth Rd. Bexley DA16 .. 7 A6
Darenth Rd. Dartford DA1 . 26 F7
Darenth Rd. S. DA2 .... 26 F7
Darenth Rise. ME5 .... 62 B3
Darenth Way. TN14 .... 69 A8
Darenth Wood Rd.
Dartford DA2 .... 27 E6
Darenth Wood Rd.
Lane End DA2 .... 27 E5
Dargate Cl. ME16 .... 91 D7
Dargets Rd. ME5 .... 62 A3
Daria Dr. DA12 .... 30 F5
Darland Ave. ME7 .... 48 E1
Darlton Cl. DA1 .... 8 F4
Darman La. TN12 .... 120 D3
Darnets Field. TN14 .... 68 F2
Darnley Cl. ME2 .... 46 D6
Darnley Dr. TN4 .... 132 E4
Darnley Rd.
Gravesend DA11 .... 30 A8
Darnley Rd. **1** Grays RM17 12 B8
Darnley Rd. Maidstone ME2 . 46 E6
Darnley St. DA11 .... 30 B8
Darns Hill. BR8 .... 39 C2
Darrick Wood House. BR6 .. 51 C7
Darrick Wood Inf Sch. BR6 51 B7
Darrick Wood Jun Sch.
BR6 .... 51 B6
Darrick Wood Rd. BR6 ..... 51 C8
Darrick Wood Sch. BR6 .... 51 B7
Darrick Wood Sports Ctr.
BR6 .... 51 B8
Dart Cl. ME2 .... 46 F7
Dartford Golf Club. DA1 ... 26 C8
Dartford Gram Sch. DA1 ... 9 C1
Dartford Gram Sch for Girls.
DA1 .... 26 C8
Dartford Rd. Coldblow DA5 . 25 C7
Dartford Rd. Dartford DA1 ... 9 B1
Dartford Rd.
Farningham DA4 .... 41 A5
Dartford Rd.
Sevenoaks TN13 .... 84 C3
Dartford Sta. DA1 .... 9 E1
Dartford Trad Pk. DA1 .... 26 F6
Dartmouth Rd. BR2 .... 36 A2
Darwin Ct. BR5 .... 51 D5
Darwin Dr. SE9 .... 6 A1
Darwin Dr. TN10 .... 117 D6
Darwin Rd. Bexley DA16 ... 6 F4

Darwin Rd. Tilbury RM18 ...... 12 F6
Dashmonden Cl. ME2 .... 33 C2
Dashwood Cl. DA6 .... 8 A2
Dashwood Rd. DA11 .... 30 A6
Davall House. 10 RM17 ...... 12 E8
Davenport Ave. ME7 .... 48 E7
Davenport Rd. DA14 .... 24 E6
David Coffer Ct. DA17 .... 4 B2
David Saloman's House.
TN3 .... 148 D8
Davidson Tower. BR1 .... 22 B3
Davis Ave. DA11 .... 29 F7
Davis Cl. TN13 .... 84 C5
Davy's Pl. DA12 .... 30 E2
Dawborns. TN30 .... 173 B3
Dawes Cl. DA9 .... 10 F2
Dawes St. ME7 .... 48 C5
Dawn Rise. BR5 .... 38 B7
Dawson Cl. SE18 .... 2 C2
Dawson Dr. BR8 .... 25 E1
Days La. DA15 .... 23 E8
Days Lane Prim Sch. DA15 .... 6 F1
Dayton Dr. DA8 .... 9 D8
De Lapre Cl. BR5 .... 38 D2
De Luci Rd. DA8 .... 4 C1
De Lucy Prim Sch. SE2 .... 3 B4
De Lucy St. SE2 .... 3 B2
De Mere Cl. ME8 .... 63 D6
De Warren House. DA11 ..... 12 D1
Deacon Cl. ME2 .... 46 E8
Deacon Est The. ME20 .... 76 A2
Deacon Trad Ctr. ME2 .... 47 A6
Deacon Trad Est. TN9 .... 117 D1
Deacons Leas. BR6 .... 51 D6
Deakin Leas. TN11 & TN9 .. 133 B7
Dean & Chapter Cotts.
DA13 .... 29 B2
Dean La. DA13 .... 58 C5
Dean Rd. Luddesdown DA13 58 E8
Dean Rd. Rochester ME2 ..... 46 F8
Dean St. ME15 .... 106 C6
Dean Wood Cty Prim Inf Sch.
ME8 .... 63 D3
Dean Wood Cty Prim Jun Sch.
ME8 .... 63 D4
Deanery Rd. TN8 .... 96 C2
Deangate Ridge Sports Ground.
ME3 .... 34 D8
Deans Ct. 6 TN9 .... 133 B8
Deans Hill Rd. ME9 .... 80 D5
Deansfield Inf Sch. SE9 .... 6 A4
Deansfield Jun Sch. SE9 ...... 6 A4
Deanwood Cl. ME8 .... 63 D6
Deanwood Dr. ME8 .... 63 E4
Debrabant Cl. DA8 .... 8 D8
Decoy Hill Rd. ME23 .... 17 F6
Deepdene. TN5 .... 175 A6
Deepdene Rd. DA16 .... 7 A4
Deerhurst Cl. DA3 .... 43 C6
Deerhurst Gdns. ME16 .... 91 D4
Deerleap La. TN14 .... 67 E6
Defiance Wlk. SE18 .... 1 F3
Defiant Cl. ME5 .... 62 B6
Defoe Cl. Chatham ME5 ...... 62 B6
Defoe Cl. Erith DA8 .... 4 B8
Degema Rd. BR7 .... 23 B3
Deidre Chapman House.
DA10 .... 11 E1
Delacourt Rd. SE3 .... 5 B7
Delafield Rd. SE7 .... 1 C1
Delagarde Rd. TN16 .... 81 C1
Delamere Gdns. 3 ME6 ...... 75 A8
Delamere Rd. ME6 .... 75 A8
Delaware Cotts. TN8 .... 128 F8
Delce Cty Inf Sch. ME1 .... 47 D2
Delce Cty Jun Sch. ME1 ...... 47 C2
Delce Rd. ME1 .... 47 D4
Delius Dr. TN10 .... 117 F6
Dell Dr. TN2 .... 149 D4
Dell The. Maypole DA5 .... 25 E7
Dell The. Woolwich SE2 .... 3 A1
Delme Cres. SE3 .... 5 B5
Delmonden Rd. TN18 .... 178 B1
Delves Ave. TN2 .... 149 C1
Delvon Cl. SE18 .... 2 A4
Den Cross. TN8 .... 128 D6
Den La. TN12 .... 121 C3
Denbeigh Dr. TN10 .... 117 D6
Denberry Dr. DA14 .... 24 B5
Denbigh Ave. ME8 .... 49 D1
Denbigh Cl. BR7 .... 22 F2
Denbigh Rd. TN4 .... 149 C7
Denbridge Rd. BR1 & BR7 .. 36 F7
Dene Ave. DA15 .... 24 B8
Dene Cl. DA2 .... 25 E4
Dene Dr. New Barn DA3 ..... 43 E7
Dene Dr. Orpington BR6 ..... 52 B7
Dene Holm Rd. DA11 .... 29 E5

Dene Lodge Cl. TN15 .... 86 F7
Dene Rd. DA1 .... 26 F8
Dene The. TN13 .... 84 B1
Dene Way. TN13 .... 148 A7
Dene Wlk. DA3 .... 42 E6
Denecourt. BR5 .... 38 C1
Denesway. DA13 .... 44 B3
Denham Rd. ME9 .... 65 B7
Denham St. SE10 .... 1 A1
Denison Mews. ME3 .... 19 C4
Deniston Ave. DA5 .... 24 E7
Denmark House. 9 SE7 ...... 1 E2
Denmark Rd. BR1 .... 36 B8
Denmark St. E13 .... 1 B8
Dennard Way. BR6 .... 51 A6
Dennettsland Rd. TN8 .... 96 C1
Dennington Ct. TN4 .... 133 A2
Dennis Cadman House. 4
ME20 .... 75 A8
Dennis Rd. DA11 .... 30 B5
Dennis Willocks Cl. ME9 ..... 65 B6
Denny Cl. 12 E6 .... 1 E7
Denny Ct. 1 DA2 .... 10 B1
Denstead Wlk. 11 ME15 ... 107 F6
Denton Cl. ME15 .... 107 E8
Denton Court Rd. DA12 ..... 30 E8
Denton Rd. Bexley DA6 .... 7 C7
Denton Rd. Dartford DA1 ... 25 E8
Denton Rd. Maypole DA5 ... 25 E8
Denton St. DA12 .... 30 E8
Denton Terr. DA5 .... 25 E6
Denver Cl. BR6 .... 37 E3
Denver Ind Est. RM13 .... 4 F8
Denver Rd. DA1 .... 26 A8
Derby Cl. TN11 .... 116 E6
Derby Rd. Chatham ME5 ..... 48 E2
Derby Rd. Gillingham ME5 .. 48 E2
Derby Rd. Grays RM17 .... 12 B8
Derby Rd. Maidstone ME15 107 C8
Derby Road Bridge. RM17 .. 12 B8
Derifall Cl. E6 .... 1 F8
Dering Way. DA12 .... 30 F7
Deringwood Dr. ME15 .... 92 F1
Dernier Rd. TN10 & TN9 .. 117 C4
Derrick Gdns. SE7 .... 1 C2
Derry Downs. BR5 .... 38 C3
Derwent Cl. DA1 .... 26 B7
Derwent Cres. DA7 .... 8 A5
Derwent Dr. Orpington BR5 . 37 D2
Derwent Dr. Royal Tunbridge Wells
TN4 .... 148 E5
Derwent House. 5 ME15 . 107 E7
Derwent Lodge Sch. TN1 . 149 B4
Derwent Rd. TN10 .... 117 C5
Derwent Way. ME8 .... 63 D8
Detling CE Prim Sch. ME14 . 78 A1
Detling Cl. ME8 .... 49 C2
Detling Hill. ME14 .... 78 B2
Detling Rd. Bromley BR1 .... 22 A3
Detling Rd. Erith DA8 .... 8 D7
Detling Rd. Northfleet DA11 29 D7
Devalls Cl. E6 .... 2 A6
Devema Cl. BR7 .... 37 A8
Devenish Rd. SE2 .... 3 A4
Devon Cl. Chatham ME5 ..... 62 C7
Devon Cl. Gillingham ME8 ... 49 F1
Devon Ct. DA4 .... 41 B8
Devon Rd.
Maidstone ME15 .... 107 C8
Devon Rd.
Sutton at Hone DA4 .... 41 C8
Devonshire Ave. DA1 .... 9 N1
Devonshire Cl. TN2 .... 162 F8
Devonshire Rd. Bexley DA6 .. 7 E3
Devonshire Rd.
Chislehurst SE9 .... 22 C6
Devonshire Rd.
Gillingham ME7 .... 48 D7
Devonshire Rd.
Gravesend DA12 .... 30 B6
Devonshire Rd. Newham E16 1 B7
Devonshire Sq. BR2 .... 36 B5
Dewberry Gdns. E6 .... 1 E8
Dewhurst Cotts. TN5 .... 174 A7
Dewhurst La. TN5 .... 174 A8
DeWinter House. TN13 ...... 84 A3
Dewlands Ave. DA2 .... 27 B8
Dexter House. 2 DA18 .... 3 E3
Dhekelia Cl. ME14 .... 92 A7
Dial Cl. Gillingham ME7 ...... 48 F6
Dial Cl. Swanscombe DA9 .. 11 D2
Dial Rd. ME7 .... 48 F6
Diameter Rd. BR5 .... 37 C3
Diamond Field. TN12 .... 152 F3
Diana Cl. DA8 .... 4 B8
Dianne Ct. SE12 .... 22 A7
Dianthus Cl. SE2 .... 3 B1
Dibden La. TN13 & TN14 ... 98 E8
Dornden Gdns. ME5 .... 62 B2

Dickens Ave. Tilbury RM18 .... 13 B6
Dickens Cl. Erith DA8 .... 8 B7
Dickens Cl. Hartley DA3 ...... 42 F4
Dickens Cl.
Langley Heath ME17 ...... 108 E4
Dickens Cl. ME2 .... 47 D8
Dickens Dr. Chislehurst BR7 23 C2
Dickens Dr.
East Malling ME19 .... 74 F1
Dickens House. 3 DA17 .... 3 F1
Dickens Rd.
Gravesend DA12 .... 30 E7
Dickens Rd.
Maidstone ME14 .... 91 E8
Dickens Rd. Rochester ME1 . 47 C2
Dickens Way. TN18 .... 179 A2
Dickensian Cl. ME3 .... 19 A2
Dickley La. ME17 .... 111 A6
Dickson House. SE18 .... 5 E6
Dickson Rd. SE9 .... 5 E4
Digdog La. TN17 .... 156 D3
Dignals Cl. ME8 .... 49 F2
Dilhorne Cl. SE12 .... 22 B5
Dillon Way. TN1 .... 149 D6
Dillywood Cotts. ME3 .... 32 F2
Dillywood La. ME3 .... 32 F2
Dimmock Cl. TN12 .... 136 B7
Dingleden La. TN17 .... 180 F2
Dippers Cl. TN15 .... 69 F2
Dislingbury Rd. TN11 .... 134 C4
Disraeli Cl.
Park Wood ME15 .... 107 E5
Disraeli Cl. Woolwich SE28 ... 3 C5
Dittisham Rd. SE9 .... 22 E4
Ditton CE Jun Sch. ME20 ... 75 C1
Ditton Court Cl. ME19 .... 75 B1
Ditton Cty Inf Sch. ME20 ... 75 B1
Ditton Pl. ME19 & ME20 .... 75 B1
Ditton Rd. DA6 .... 7 D2
Dixon Cl. Maidstone ME15 .. 91 F2
Dixon Cl. 4 Newham E6 .... 1 F7
Dixon House. SE2 .... 3 C1
Dixwell Cl. ME8 .... 63 D5
Dobell Rd. SE9 .... 5 F2
Dobson Rd. DA12 .... 30 E3
Dock Approach Rd. RM17 .. 12 E8
Dock Head Rd. ME4 .... 48 A8
Dock Rd. Chatham ME4 .... 47 F6
Dock Rd. Gillingham ME4 ... 48 A7
Dock Rd. Grays RM17 .... 12 D8
Dock Rd. Grays RM17 .... 12 E7
Dock Rd. Tilbury RM18 .... 13 A4
Dock Rd. Tilbury RM18 .... 13 A4
Dockland St. Newham E16 .... 2 A4
Dockland St. Newham E16 .... 2 A3
Doctor Hope's Rd. TN17 ... 169 D4
Dodd Rd. TN10 .... 117 E5
Doddington Cl. ME16 .... 91 E5
Doddington Rd. ME8 .... 49 D3
Doebury Wlk. SE18 .... 2 F7
Dog Cotts. RH19 .... 144 B1
Doggett's Sq. ME2 .... 47 C7
Doggetts Row. ME3 .... 32 B1
Dogwood Cl. Chatham ME5 . 62 D1
Dogwood Cl.
Northfleet DA11 .... 29 F4
Dolphin Cl. SE28 .... 3 D7
Dolphin Dr. ME8 .... 63 F1
Dombey Cl. Higham ME3 .... 32 C3
Dombey Cl. Rochester ME1 . 47 C3
Domonic Dr. SE9 .... 23 B5
Donaldson Rd. SE18 .... 6 A6
Doncaster Cl. 7 ME15 ...... 107 F6
Donet Cl. ME8 .... 63 C5
Dongola Rd. ME2 .... 33 B1
Donkey Field. TN11 .... 115 E1
Donkey La. DA4 .... 55 B8
Donnington Rd. TN13 .... 83 D8
Doon Brae. TN4 .... 133 A2
Dorado Gdns. BR6 .... 52 D7
Doran Gr. SE18 .... 6 E7
Dorchester. TN4 .... 149 B6
Dorchester Ave. DA5 .... 24 D8
Dorchester Cl.
Cliffe Woods ME3 .... 33 B7
Dorchester Cl. Dartford DA1 10 D5
Dorchester Cl.
St Paul's Cray BR5 .... 24 B1
Dorchester Rd. DA12 .... 30 D5
Dorcis Ave. DA7 .... 7 E5
Doric Ave. TN4 .... 132 F1
Doric Cl. TN4 .... 132 F1
Dorin Ct. TN2 .... 149 C3
Doris Ave. DA7 .... 8 C6
Dorking Rd. TN1 .... 149 C6
Dorland House. SE9 .... 6 D1
Dormers Dr. DA13 .... 44 B2
Dornberg Cl. SE3 .... 5 A7
Dornberg Cl. SE3 .... 5 B7
Downs Wood. DA13 .... 72 F8
Downside. ME2 .... 47 A7
Downsview. Chatham ME5 .. 62 C8

Dorne Cotts. TN27 .... 127 E6
Dorney Rise. BR5 .... 37 F5
Dorothy Ave. TN17 .... 169 E4
Dorothy Evans Cl. DA7 .... 8 B3
Dorrit Way. Chislehurst
BR7 .... 23 C2
Dorrit Way. Rochester ME1 . 47 D2
Dorset Ave. DA16 .... 6 F3
Dorset Cotts. TN7 .... 160 B4
Dorset Cres. DA12 .... 30 E4
Dorset Rd. Chislehurst SE9 . 22 E6
Dorset Rd. Royal Tunbridge Wells
TN2 .... 149 D2
Dorset Road Inf Sch. SE9 ... 22 E6
Dorset Sq. ME8 .... 49 D1
Dorset St. TN13 .... 84 C2
Dorset Way. ME15 .... 107 C8
Dorton Coll. TN15 .... 84 F5
Dorton Dr. TN15 .... 84 F5
Dorton House (Royal London
Society Sch for the Blind).
TN15 .... 84 F5
Dorville Rd. SE12 & SE13 ..... 5 A2
Dothill Rd. SE18 .... 6 C7
Dotterel Cl. ME5 .... 62 D2
Doubleton La. TN11 .... 131 A5
Doug Siddons Ct. 7 RM17 . 12 C8
Douglas Almshouses.
ME17 .... 111 D5
Douglas Bldgs. TN12 .... 139 E5
Douglas Rd. Bexley DA16 .... 7 B6
Douglas Rd. Lenham ME17 111 D5
Douglas Rd.
Maidstone ME16 .... 91 E3
Douglas Rd. 6 Newham E16 1 A8
Douglas Rd.
Tonbridge TN9 .... 133 A8
Dove App. E6 .... 1 F8
Dove Cl. ME5 .... 62 B6
Dove Rd. TN10 .... 117 C6
Dovedale Cl. DA16 .... 7 A5
Dovedale Rd. DA2 .... 27 C7
Doveney Cl. BR5 .... 38 D6
Dover House. ME2 .... 33 C1
Dover Patrol. SE3 .... 5 C6
Dover Rd. Northfleet DA11 . 29 D8
Dover Rd. Woolwich SE18 .... 6 C5
Dover Rd E. DA11 .... 29 E7
Dover Road Cty Prim Jun Sch.
DA11 .... 29 E7
Dover St. ME16 .... 91 C2
Doves Cl. BR2 .... 50 E8
Dowding Wlk. 3 DA11 ...... 29 E5
Dower House Cres. TN4 ... 132 E3
Dowgate Cl. TN9 .... 133 D7
Dowlerville Rd. BR6 .... 51 F4
Dowling Cl. ME6 .... 74 E7
Dowling House. DA17 .... 3 F3
Down Ave. TN3 .... 166 A4
Down House. BR6 .... 66 A7
Down La. TN3 .... 163 C1
Down's Cl. TN27 .... 141 E5
Downage The. DA11 .... 30 A6
Downash Ct. TN5 .... 177 A3
Downash House. TN5 .... 177 A3
Downbank Ave. DA7 .... 8 D5
Downderry Way. ME19 ...... 75 B1
Downe Ave. TN14 .... 66 D8
Downe Cl. DA16 .... 7 C7
Downe House. 9 SE7 .... 5 D8
Downe Prim Sch. BR6 .... 66 A8
Downe Rd.
Cudham BR6 & TN14 .... 66 C5
Downe Rd.
Farthing Street BR2 .... 50 C2
Downend. SE18 .... 6 B7
Downer Ct. ME4 .... 61 E8
Downham Way.
BR1 & SE12 .... 22 A4
Downings. E6 .... 2 A7
Downlands. ME17 .... 110 F6
Downleys Cl. SE9 .... 22 F6
Downman Rd. SE9 .... 5 E4
Downs Ave. Chislehurst BR7 23 F3
Downs Ave. Dartford DA1 ... 27 A8
Downs Cl. ME14 .... 92 B8
Downs Rd.
Istead Rise DA13 .... 29 D3
Downs Rd. Maidstone ME14 92 B8
Downs Rd. Yalding ME18 ... 105 A1
Downs The. ME5 .... 61 D1
Downs Valley. DA3 .... 42 E5
Downs View. Burham ME1 .. 60 F1
Downs View.
West Malling ME19 .... 89 B8
Downs View Cl. BR6 .... 52 C1
Downs View Rd. ME14 .... 92 B8

Downsview.
Trottiscliffe ME19 .... 73 A4
Downsview Cl. BR8 .... 39 E6
Downsview Cty Prim Sch.
BR8 ....
Downsway. DA13 ....
Doyle Cl. DA8 ....
Doyle Way. RM18 ....
Drage Rd. TN12 .... 1..
Drake Cres. SE28 ....
Drake Cl. BR5 ....
Drake's Ave. ME2 ....
Draper Cl. DA17 ....
Draper Ct. BR1 ....
Draper St. 3 TN4 ....
Drawell Cl. SE18 ....
Dray Corner Rd. TN27 ....
Dray Ct. TN11 ....
Drays Cotts. DA4 ....
Drayton Ave. BR6 ....
Drayton Rd. TN9 ....
Drew Prim Sch. E16 ....
Drew Rd. Newham E16 ....
Drewery Dr. ME8 ....
Driffield Gdns. TN9 ....
Drift The. BR2 ....
Drive The. Bexley DA5 ....
Drive The. Chislehurst BR7 . ..
Drive The. Erith DA8 ....
Drive The. Gravesend DA12 . ..
Drive The. New Barn DA3 ... ..
Drive The. Orpington BR6 ... ..
Drive The. Royal Tunbridge We
TN2 .... 14..
Drive The. Sevenoaks TN13 . ..
Drive The. Sidcup DA14 ..... 1..
Drive The.
St Paul's Cray BR7 ....
Drive The. Tonbridge TN9 . 1..
Drove Way The. DA13 ....
Drudgeon Way. DA2 ....
Drummond Cl. DA8 ....
Drummond House. 11
SE18 ....
Drury Rd. TN30 .... 1..
Dry Bank Ct. TN10 ....
Dry Bank Rd. TN10 ....
Dry Hill Park Cres. TN10 ... 1..
Dry Hill Park Rd. TN10 ...... 1..
Dry Hill Rd. TN10 ....
Dryden House. BR2 ....
Dryden Pl. RM18 ....
Dryden Rd. DA16 ....
Dryden Way. BR6 ....
Dryhill La. TN14 ....
Dryhill Rd. DA17 ....
Dryland Ave. 5 BR6 ....
Dryland Rd.
Borough Green TN15 ....
Dryland Rd. Snodland ME6 .. ..
Duchess Cl. ME2 ....
Duchess of Kent Ct The. 1
ME20 ....
Duchess of Kent Dr. ME5 .... ..
Duchess Wlk. TN15 ....
Ducie House. 8 SE7 ....
Ducketts Rd. DA1 ....
Duddington Cl. SE9 ....
Dudely Rd. DA11 ....
Dudley Lodge. TN2 .... 14..
Dudley Rd. TN1 .... 14..
Dudsbury Rd. DA1 ....
Dukes Meadow. TN11 .... 11..
Dukes Meadow Dr. ME7 ....
Dukes Orch. DA5 ....
Dukes Rd. TN1 .... 14..
Dukes Wlk. 5 ME15 .... 9..
Dulverton Prim Sch. DA15 .. 2..
Dulverton Rd. SE9 .... 2..
Dumbreck Rd. SE9 ....
Dunblane Rd. SE9 ....
Duncan Rd. ME7 ....
Duncans Cotts. 3 TN16 .... 8..
Duncroft. SE18 ....
Dundale Rd. TN12 & TN3 . 15..
Dundonald Cl. 6 E6 ....
Dunedin House. 8 RM18 .. 1..
Dunera Dr. ME14 ....
Dunk's Green Rd. TN11 ..... 1..
Dunkery Rd. SE12 & SE9 .... 2..
Dunkin Rd. DA1 ....
Dunkirk Cl. DA12 ....
Dunkirk Dr. ME5 ....
Dunkley Villas. TN15 ....
Dunlop Ct. 1 TN18 .... 17..
Dunlop Point. E16 ....
Dunlop Rd. RM18 ....
Dunn Street Rd. ME7 ....
Dunning's La. ME1 ....

nnings The. ME16 .... 91 A2
nnock Rd. E6 .... 1 E7
nose Cl. TN14 .... 10 B8
hoon Cotts. BR6 .... 66 A5
horlan Farm Cotts.
   .... 149 E4
nstable Ct. 4 SE3 .... 5 A7
nstall Welling Est. DA16 .. 7 B5
nstan Glade. BR5 .... 37 D3
nstan Gr. TN4 .... 149 B6
nstan Terr. TN4 .... 149 B6
nster Ct. 4 DA2 .... 10 B1
rton Green Cty Prim Sch.
   N13 .... 83 E7
rton Green Sta. TN13 .... 83 E7
rvegan Rd. SE9 .... 5 F3
rwich Rd. DA7 .... 7 F6
oree Rd. SE7 .... 1 B1
rant Rd. BR8 .... 26 A2
ham House. 7 ME15 .... 107 E5
ham Rd. Bromley BR2 .. 36 A5
ham Rd. Gillingham ME8 63 C7
ham Rd. Sidcup DA14 .... 24 B3
ham Rise. SE18 .... 2 D1
riun Way. DA8 .... 9 F7
ley Gdns. BR6 .... 52 B7
ndale La.
   orthfleet DA11 .... 29 E4
ndale La.
   orthfleet DA11 .... 29 F5
rant Way.
rpington BR6 .... 51 D5
rant Way.
rwanscombe DA10 ...... 28 E8
rrell Gdns. ME5 .... 48 C1
sley Cl. SE3 .... 5 C5
sley Gdns. SE3 .... 5 D6
sley Rd. SE3 .... 5 C5
sler Rd. ME1 .... 61 E8
vard's Pl. ME9 .... 65 F1
Hill. TN15 .... 101 F8
x La. TN15 .... 86 A2
xberry Cl. BR2 .... 36 E4
xford House. 12 SE2 ...... 3 D4
ce Dr. BR5 .... 38 C2
xewood Cl. DA5 .... 25 E5
an Rd. DA17 .... 4 A3
nchurch Cl. BR6 .... 51 E6
ward Rd. SE12 .... 22 C5
nes Rd. TN14 & TN15 .... 69 E2
nevor Rd. TN4 .... 149 C7
gle Cl. ME20 .... 75 A2
gle House. RM17 .... 11 C8
gle Way. DA11 .... 12 A2
gle Rd. DA8 .... 11 B2
glesfield Rd. SE18 .... 6 B6
glesfield Sch. SE18 .... 6 A6
glestone Cl. TN15 .... 87 A8
dham Prim Sch. SE9 ...... 5 C3
dham Sq. SE9 .... 5 C5
gham Cl. ME5 .... 62 C4
demont Cl. DA1 .... 8 F3
dley Point. 9 SE18 .... 2 B2
dley Rd. Erith DA17 .... 4 A3
dley Rd. Sevenoaks TN13 84 B3
d Cl. ME5 .... 62 B4
d Rd. DA11 .... 29 E6
d Rise. SE18 .... 2 D2
t St. ME14 .... 91 F4
l's Rd. TN4 .... 148 F4
shall Rd. SE9 .... 6 A3
son Villas. TN12 .... 138 D6
t Becton District Ctr.
   16 .... 1 F8
t Borough Cty Prim Sch.
   ME14 .... 92 B5
t Cliff Rd. TN4 .... 149 A6
t Crescent Rd. DA11 .... 13 C1
t Cross. TN30 .... 183 B7
t Dr. BR5 .... 38 B8
t Farleigh Cty Prim Sch.
   ME15 .... 106 B6
t Farleigh Sta. ME16 .. 106 B8
t Hall Hill. ME17 .... 123 E7
t Hall Rd. BR5 .... 38 F2
t Ham Ind Est. E16 .... 1 C8
t Ham Manor Way. E6 .... 2 A7
t Hill. Dartford DA1 .... 26 F8
t Hill. South Darenth DA4 41 D7
t Hill. Tenterden TN30 .. 183 B8
t Hill Dr. DA1 .... 26 F8
t Hill Rd. TN15 .... 70 B7
t Holme. DA8 .... 8 E8
t Kent Ave. DA11 .... 12 C1
t Malling Research Sta
   Horticultural). ME19 .... 90 C6
t Malling Sta. ME19 .... 90 A6
t Mascalls. 18 SE27 ...... 3 C4
t Mill. DA12 .... 12 F1

East Milton Rd. DA12 ...... 30 D8
East Park Rd. ME20 .... 91 A8
East Peckham Cty Prim Sch.
   TN12 .... 119 F6
East Rd. Bexley DA16 ...... 7 B5
East Rd. Chatham ME4 .... 48 A7
East Rd. Gillingham ME4 .. 48 A8
East Rochester Way.
   Coldblow DA1 .... 25 D8
East Rochester Way.
   Sidcup SE9 .... 7 C1
East Row. ME1 .... 47 C5
East St. Addington ME19 .. 73 D3
East St. Bexley DA7 .... 8 A3
East St. Bromley BR1 ...... 36 A7
East St. Chatham ME4 .... 48 A3
East St. Gillingham ME7 .. 48 B6
East St. Grays RM16 .... 11 E8
East St. Harrietsham ME17 110 E5
East St. Hunton ME15 .... 121 F7
East St. Snodland ME6 .... 75 B8
East St. Tonbridge TN9 .. 117 C2
East Street N. ME19 .... 73 D3
East Sutton Park (HM Young
   Offender Inst & Prison).
   ME17 .... 125 B7
East Sutton Rd.
   Hearnden Green ME17 .. 125 A7
East Sutton Rd.
   Sutton Valence ME17 .... 125 A7
East Terr. Gravesend DA11 .. 13 C1
East Terr. Sidcup DA15 .... 23 F7
East Thurrock Rd. RM17 .. 12 C8
East Weald Dr. TN30 .... 173 B1
East Wickham Inf Sch.
   DA16 .... 6 F6
East Wickham Jun Sch.
   DA16 .... 6 F6
East Woodside. DA5 ...... 24 E7
Eastbrook Rd. SE3 .... 5 B6
Eastbury Rd. Newham E6 .. 2 A8
Eastbury Rd. Orpington BR5 37 D3
Eastcombe Ave. SE7 .... 5 B8
Eastcote. BR6 .... 37 F1
Eastcote Prim Sch. DA16 .. 6 D4
Eastcote Rd. DA16 .... 6 D5
Eastcourt Gn. ME8 .... 49 B4
Eastcourt La.
   Gillingham ME8 .... 49 B3
Eastcourt La.
   Gillingham,Lower Twydall
   ME7 & ME8 .... 49 B4
Easterfields. ME16 & ME19 .. 90 C5
Eastern Rd. ME7 .... 48 F6
Eastern Way. Erith SE28 .. 3 D5
Eastern Way. 1
   Grays RM17 .... 12 A8
Eastfield Gdns. TN10 .... 117 E5
Eastfield Cl. SE18 .... 6 B6
Eastfield Sch. SE18 .... 6 A6
Eastgate. ME1 .... 47 D5
Eastgate Cl. SE28 .... 3 D7
Eastgate Ct. ME1 .... 47 C5
Eastgate Rd. TN30 .... 183 C8
Eastgate Terr. ME1 .... 47 C5
Eastlands CI. TN2 & TN4 .. 162 E8
Eastlands Rd. TN4 .... 148 E1
Eastleigh Rd. DA7 .... 8 C4
Eastling Cl. ME8 .... 49 B3
Eastling House. 8 BR5 .... 38 D1
Eastmead Cl. BR1 .... 36 E7
Eastmoor Pl. SE18 & SE7 .. 1 D3
Eastmoor St. SE7 .... 1 D3
Eastnor Rd. SE9 .... 8 A7
Eastry Cl. ME16 .... 91 C7
Eastry Rd. DA8 .... 8 A7
Eastview Ave. SE18 .... 6 E7
Eastway. BR2 .... 36 A2
Eastwell. 3 TN30 .... 183 A7
Eastwell Barn Mews.
   TN30 .... 183 A8
Eastwell Cl.
   Maidstone ME14 .... 92 C5
Eastwell Cl.
   Paddock Wood TN12 .... 135 E6
Eastwell Meadows. TN30 .. 183 A8
Eaton Cl. BR7 .... 23 C2
Eaton Rd. DA14 .... 24 D6
Eaton Sq. DA3 .... 42 D6
Ebbsfleet Ind Est. DA11 .. 12 B2
Ebbsfleet Wlk. DA11 ...... 12 B1
Ebdon Way. SE3 .... 5 B8
Ebury Cl. BR2 .... 50 E7
Eccles Row. ME20 .... 75 F6
Eccleston Cl. BR6 .... 37 D1
Eccleston Rd. ME15 .... 91 F2
Echo Cl. ME15 .... 107 F6
Echo Ct. DA12 .... 30 C6
Eclipse Rd. E13 .... 1 B8
Edam Ct. 11 DA14 .... 24 A5
Eddington Cl. ME15 ...... 107 B6
Eden Ave. ME5 .... 62 A7

Eden Cl. DA5 .... 25 D4
Eden Ct. 1
   Hawkhurst TN18 .... 178 F2
Eden Ct. 17 Orpington BR5 .. 38 D1
Eden Pl. DA11 .... 30 B8
Eden Rd.
   High Halstow ME23 ...... 17 E4
Eden Rd.
   Joyden's Wood DA5 ...... 25 D4
Eden Rd. Royal Tunbridge Wells
   TN1 .... 149 A2
Eden Valley Sch. TN8 .... 112 C2
Eden Villas. TN8 .... 128 D7
Edenbridge Cl. BR5 .... 38 D5
Edenbridge Cty Prim Sch.
   TN8 .... 112 D1
Edenbridge & District
   War Meml Hospl. TN8 .. 128 D7
Edenbridge Golf & Country Club.
   TN8 .... 112 A2
Edenbridge Rd.
   TN8 & TN7 .... 145 E2
Edenbridge Sta. TN8 .... 112 C3
Edenbridge Town Sta.
   TN8 .... 112 D2
Edenbridge Trad Ctr. TN8 128 D8
Edendale Rd. DA7 .... 8 D6
Edensmuir Ct. SE3 .... 5 A7
Edgar Cl. BR8 .... 39 F6
Edgar Rd. TN14 .... 69 E2
Edge Hill. SE18 .... 6 B8
Edge Hill Ct. DA14 .... 23 F4
Edgeborough Way. BR1 .. 36 D8
Edgebury. BR7 & SE9 ...... 23 B4
Edgebury Prim Sch. BR7 .. 23 C4
Edgebury Wlk. BR7 .... 23 C5
Edgefield Cl. DA1 .... 27 B7
Edgehill Gdns. DA13 ...... 43 F8
Edgehill Rd. BR7 .... 23 C4
Edger Pl. 3 ME15 .... 92 A4
Edgewood Dr. BR6 .... 52 A5
Edgeworth Rd. SE9 .... 5 D3
Edgington Way. DA14 .... 24 D1
Edinburgh Ct. DA8 .... 8 D7
Edinburgh Mews. RM18 .. 13 B5
Edinburgh Rd.
   Chatham ME4 .... 48 C2
Edinburgh Rd.
   Gillingham ME7 .... 48 D5
Edinburgh Rd. Grain ME3 .. 21 B5
Edinburgh Sq.
   Maidstone ME15 .... 107 C7
Edinburgh Sq.
   Maidstone ME15 .... 107 D6
Edington Rd. SE2 .... 3 B3
Edison Gr. SE18 .... 6 F7
Edison Rd. Bexley DA16 .. 6 F6
Edison Rd. Bromley BR2 .. 36 A7
Edith Pond Ct. SE9 .... 23 B6
Edith Rd. BR6 .... 52 A5
Ediva Rd. DA13 .... 44 A4
Edmund Cl.
   Maidstone ME16 .... 91 A3
Edmund Cl.
   Meopham Station DA13 .. 44 A4
Edmund Rd. Bexley DA16 .. 7 A4
Edmund Rd. Orpington BR5 .. 38 C3
Edmunds Ave. BR5 .... 38 D6
Edmundson House. 10
   SE18 .... 2 A2
Edna Rd. ME14 .... 91 F8
Edward Ct. Chatham ME5 .. 48 C1
Edward St. 2 Newham E16 .. 1 A8
Edward Harvey Ct. DA17 .. 3 F1
Edward Rd. Bromley BR1 .. 22 C1
Edward Rd. Chislehurst BR7 23 B3
Edward St. Chatham ME4 .. 48 A3
Edward St. Rochester ME2 .. 47 B7
Edward St. Royal Tunbridge Wells
   TN4 .... 148 F8
Edward St. Rusthall TN4 .. 148 C4
Edward Tyler Rd. SE12 .... 22 C6
Edwards Cl. ME8 .... 63 C5
Edwards Gdns. BR8 .... 39 D5
Edwards Rd. DA17 .... 4 A2
Edwin Arnold Ct. DA15 .. 23 F4
Edwin Cl. DA7 .... 7 F8
Edwin Petty Pl. DA2 .... 27 B7
Edwin Rd. Gillingham ME8 .. 63 C8
Edwin Rd. Wilmington DA2 .. 26 D7
Edwin St. Gravesend DA11 .. 30 B8
Edwin St. Newham E16 .... 1 A8
Edwina Pl. ME9 .... 65 C7
Egdean Wlk. TN13 .... 84 C4
Egerton Ave. BR8 .... 39 F8
Egerton CE Prim Sch.
   TN27 .... 127 F3
Egerton Cl. DA1 .... 26 B7
Egerton House Rd. TN27 127 E4
Egerton Rd. ME14 .... 91 E7

Eggpie La. TN11 .... 115 E7
Egham Rd. E13 .... 1 B8
Eglantine La. DA4 .... 41 B3
Eglinton Hill. SE18 .... 6 B7
Eglinton Inf Sch. SE18 .... 6 A8
Eglinton Jun Mix Sch. SE18 .. 6 A8
Eglinton Rd.
   Swanscombe DA10 .... 11 F1
Eglinton Rd. Woolwich SE18 .. 6 B8
Egremont Rd. ME15 .... 92 F2
Eight Dock East Rd. ME4 .. 34 A1
Eileen Ct. BR7 .... 23 A3
Eisenhower Dr. E6 .... 1 E8
Elaine Ave. ME2 .... 46 E7
Elaine Ct. ME2 .... 46 E6
Elaine Prim Sch. ME2 ...... 46 E6
Elbourne Trad Est. DA17 .... 4 B2
Elbury Dr. E16 .... 1 A7
Elder Cl.
   Hoo St Werburgh ME3 .... 34 E3
Elder Cl. Kingswood ME17 . 109 D2
Elder Cl. Sidcup DA15 ...... 23 F7
Elder Ct. ME8 .... 63 B6
Elderslie Rd. SE9 .... 6 A2
Eldon St. ME4 .... 48 A4
Eldon Way. TN12 .... 135 F7
Eldred Dr. BR5 .... 52 D8
Eleanor Wlk. 25 SE18 ...... 1 F7
Elford Cl. SE3 .... 5 C3
Elgal Cl. BR6 .... 51 B5
Elgar Cl. TN10 .... 117 E6
Elgar Gdns. RM18 .... 13 B6
Elgin Gdns. ME2 .... 46 D5
Elham Cl. Bromley BR1 .... 22 D1
Elham Cl. Gillingham ME8 .. 49 B3
Elibank Rd. SE9 .... 6 A3
Eling Ct. ME15 .... 107 A8
Eliot Rd. DA1 .... 10 B2
Elizabeth Cl. RM18 .... 13 B5
Elizabeth Ct. Chatham ME5 .. 62 A7
Elizabeth Ct. Erith DA8 .... 4 A2
Elizabeth Ct.
   Gillingham ME8 .... 49 C1
Elizabeth Ct.
   Gravesend DA11 .... 13 A1
Elizabeth Garlick Ct. 1
   TN1 .... 149 B4
Elizabeth Garrett Anderson
   House. 9 DA17 .... 4 A3
Elizabeth Huggins Cotts.
   DA11 .... 30 B6
Elizabeth Pl. DA4 .... 40 E3
Elizabeth Raybould Ctr (Univ of
   Greenwich) The. DA2 .. 10 E1
Elizabeth Smith's Ct. ME19 . 89 F7
Elizabeth St. DA9 .... 10 E2
Elizabeth Terr. SE9 .... 5 F1
Elizabeth Way. BR5 .... 38 C4
Ellen Cl. BR1 .... 36 D6
Ellen Wilkinson Prim Sch.
   E16 .... 1 A7
Ellen's Pl. ME9 .... 65 C6
Ellenborough Rd. DA14 .. 24 E3
Ellenswood Cl. ME15 ...... 93 A1
Ellerman Rd. RM18 .... 12 F3
Ellerslie. DA12 .... 30 D8
Ellesmere Ct. SE12 .... 22 A7
Ellingham Leas. ME15 .. 107 C7
Elliott Rd. BR2 .... 36 D5
Elliott St. DA12 .... 30 D8
Elliotts La. TN14 & TN16 .. 82 C3
Ellis Cl. SE9 .... 23 C6
Ellis Cl. DA1 .... 27 B7
Ellis Way. DA1 .... 26 F6
Elliscombe Mount. 11 SE7 .. 5 C8
Elliscombe Rd. SE7 .... 5 C8
Ellison Rd. DA15 .... 23 D7
Elliston House. 14 SE18 .... 2 A2
Elm Ave. Chatham ME4 .... 47 E1
Elm Ave. Chattenden ME3 .. 34 A4
Elm Cl. Dartford DA1 ...... 26 C7
Elm Cl. Egerton TN27 .... 127 F3
Elm Cl. Higham ME3 .... 32 C3
Elm Cotts. BR8 .... 40 B8
Elm Court Ind Est. ME7 .... 62 E3
Elm Cres. ME19 .... 89 F8
Elm Ct. BR8 .... 39 D7
Elm Gr. Erith DA8 .... 8 E7
Elm Gr.
   Hildenborough TN11 .. 116 F5
Elm Gr. Maidstone ME15 .. 92 B3
Elm Gr. Orpington BR6 .... 37 F1
Elm La. TN18 & TN9 ...... 117 C3
Elm Rd. Dartford DA1 ...... 26 D7
Elm Rd. Erith DA8 .... 9 A6
Elm Rd. Gillingham ME7 .. 48 E6
Elm Rd. Gravesend DA12 .. 30 C5
Elm Rd. Grays RM17 ...... 12 C8
Elm Rd.
   Hoo St Werburgh ME3 .. 34 E3

Elm Rd. Orpington BR6 .... 52 A3
Elm Rd. Royal Tunbridge Wells
   TN4 .... 132 F1
Elm Rd. Sidcup DA14 ...... 24 A4
Elm Rd. Stone DA9 .... 10 E1
Elm Rd. Westerham TN16 .. 81 E2
Elm Terr. 3 Eltham SE9 .... 6 A1
Elm Terr.
   West Thurrock RM16 .... 11 B8
Elm Tree Cotts. ME13 .... 19 A3
Elm Tree Ct. 18 SE7 .... 5 C8
Elm Tree Dr. ME1 .... 47 A2
Elm Wlk. Aylesford ME20 .. 75 E1
Elm Wlk. Orpington BR6 .. 50 F7
Elmbank Dr. BR1 .... 36 D7
Elmbourne Dr. DA17 .... 4 B2
Elmcroft. BR6 .... 52 B5
Elmcroft Ave. DA15 .... 7 A1
Elmcroft Rd. BR6 .... 52 B5
Elmdene Rd. SE18 .... 2 B1
Elmfield. Gillingham ME8 . 49 E2
Elmfield. Tenterden TN30 .. 183 B8
Elmfield Cl.
   Gravesend DA11 .... 30 B7
Elmfield Cl.
   Sevenoaks Weald TN14 .. 99 B3
Elmfield Ct. Bexley DA16 .. 7 B6
Elmfield Ct.
   Coxheath ME17 .... 106 C3
Elmfield Ct.
   Tenterden TN30 .... 183 B8
Elmfield Pk. BR1 .... 36 A6
Elmfield Rd. BR1 .... 36 A6
Elmhurst. Erith DA17 .... 7 E8
Elmhurst. Swanscombe
   .... 11 B1
Elmhurst Ave. TN2 .... 150 D8
Elmhurst Gdns. ME1 .... 47 E3
Elmhurst Rd. SE9 .... 22 E5
Elmington Cl. DA5 .... 8 B2
Elmlea Cl. BR7 .... 22 F2
Elmley Cl. 15 E6 .... 1 E8
Elmley St. SE18 .... 2 D2
Elmshurst Gdns. TN10 .. 117 C7
Elmslie Ct. SE9 .... 6 A1
Elmstead Ave. BR7 .... 22 F3
Elmstead Cl. TN13 .... 83 E5
Elmstead Glade. BR7 ...... 22 F2
Elmstead La. BR7 & SE9 .. 22 F3
Elmstead Rd. DA8 .... 8 F8
Elmstead Woods Sta. BR7 .. 22 E2
Elmsted Cres. DA16 .... 7 C8
Elmstone Cl. ME16 .... 91 B2
Elmstone Hole Rd. ME17 .. 126 D8
Elmstone La. ME16 .... 91 B8
Elmstone Rd. ME8 .... 63 D7
Elmtree Terr. 3 BR5 .... 38 C5
Elmtree Cotts. TN14 ...... 67 D4
Elmwood Dr. DA5 .... 24 E8
Elmwood Rd. ME3 .... 33 F6
Elphick's Pl. TN2 .... 163 B8
Elrick Cl. DA8 .... 8 E8
Elsa Rd. DA16 .... 7 C5
Elsinore House. 7 SE7 ...... 1 E2
Elstow Cl. Eltham SE9 ...... 5 F2
Elstow Cl. Gillingham ME8 .. 49 B4
Elstree Gdns. DA17 .... 3 F2
Eltham CE Prim Sch. SE9 .. 5 F2
Eltham Coll. SE9 .... 22 D6
Eltham Green Rd. SE9 ...... 5 C3
Eltham Green Sch. SE9 .... 5 C3
Eltham High St. SE9 .... 5 F1
Eltham Hill. SE9 .... 5 E1
Eltham Hill Sch. SE9 .... 5 E1
Eltham & Mottingham
   Hospl (General). SE9 .... 5 F1
Eltham Palace. SE9 .... 22 D8
Eltham Palace Rd.
   SE12 & SE9 .... 5 D1
Eltham Park Gdns. SE9 .... 6 A3
Eltham Rd. SE12 & SE9 .... 5 B2
Eltham Sta. SE9 .... 5 F2
Eltham Warren Golf Course.
   SE9 .... 6 B2
Elvington Cl. ME16 .... 91 D5
Elwick Ct. DA1 .... 9 A3
Elwill Way. DA13 .... 43 F8
Elwyn Gdns. SE12 .... 22 A8
Ely Cl. Erith DA8 .... 8 F5
Ely Cl. Gillingham ME8 .... 49 E2
Ely Ct. TN2 .... 149 B4
Ely Gdns. TN10 & TN9 .. 117 D4
Elysian Ave. BR5 .... 37 F3
Embassey Ct. DA14 .... 24 B5
Embassy Ct. ME7 .... 48 F1
Embassy Ct. DA16 .... 7 B4
Ember Cl. BR5 .... 37 C2
Emerald Cl. Chatham ME1 .. 61 D7

Emerald Cl. Newham E16 ..... 1 E7
Emersons Ave. BR8 .... 25 F1
Emerton Cl. DA6 .... 7 E3
Emes Rd. DA8 .... 8 E7
Emily Jackson Cl. TN13 .... 84 B3
Emily Rd. ME5 .... 62 B6
Emmett Hill La. ME18 .... 120 F5
Emmetts Garden (NT).
TN14 .... 97 D5
Emmetts Rd. TN14 & TN16 .. 97 D6
Empress Dr. BR7 .... 23 B2
Empress Rd. DA12 .... 30 E8
Emsworth Gr. ME14 .... 92 D6
Enderfield Ct. BR7 .... 37 A8
Engineer Cl. SE18 .... 6 A8
Englefield Ct. BR5 .... 37 F5
Englefield Cres.
Cliffe Woods ME3 .... 33 B7
Englefield Cres.
Orpington BR5 .... 38 A5
Englefield Path. BR5 .... 38 A5
English Martyrs' RC Prim Sch.
ME2 .... 47 B8
Ennerdale Rd. DA7 .... 8 A6
Ennis Rd. SE18 .... 6 C8
Ensfield Rd. Leigh TN11 .. 115 E1
Ensfield Rd. Upper Hayesden
TN11 & TN3 .... 132 A6
Ensign House. RM17 .... 11 F8
Enslin Rd. SE9 .... 23 A8
Enterprise Bsns Est. ME2 .... 47 E7
Enterprise Cl. ME2 .... 47 D8
Enterprise Ctr The. ME5 .... 77 C8
Enterprise Rd. ME15 .... 92 A1
Enterprise Way. TN8 ...... 112 C3
Epaul La. ME1 .... 47 C2
Epsom Cl. Bexley DA7 ...... 8 B4
Epsom Cl. Maidstone ME15 107 F6
Epsom Cl. New Town ME19 .. 89 B8
Epstein Rd. SE28 .... 3 B5
Erica Cl. BR8 .... 39 E5
Eridge Green Cl. BR5 .... 38 C1
Eridge Rd. TN2 & TN4 ... 148 E1
Eridge Sta. TN3 .... 161 E2
Erindale. SE18 .... 6 D8
Erindale Terr. SE18 .... 6 D8
Erith Cl. ME14 .... 92 A8
Erith & District Hospl. DA8 .. 8 D8
Erith High St. Erith DA8 .... 8 F8
Erith Rd. Bexley DA7 .... 8 B4
Erith Rd. Erith DA17 .... 4 B1
Erith Sch. DA8 .... 8 C7
Erith Sch West. DA8 .... 8 B7
Erith Sta. DA8 .... 8 E7
Ermington Rd. BR7 & SE9 .. 23 C4
Ernest Dr. ME16 .... 91 B5
Ernest Rd. ME4 .... 48 A3
Erskine House. **7** SE7 ..... 5 C8
Erskine Park Rd. TN4 ..... 148 C4
Erskine Rd. DA13 .... 73 B8
Erwood Rd. SE7 .... 1 E1
Escott Gdns. SE9 .... 22 E4
Escreet Gr. SE18 .... 2 A2
Eshcol Rd. ME3 .... 35 C6
Esher Cl. DA5 .... 24 E7
Eskdale Cl. DA2 .... 27 C7
Eskdale Rd. DA7 .... 8 A6
Esplanade. ME1 .... 47 B5
Essenden Rd. DA17 .... 4 A1
Essex Cl. TN2 .... 162 F8
Essex Rd. **1** Dartford DA1 .. 9 D1
Essex Rd. Gravesend DA11 .. 30 A7
Essex Rd. Halling ME2 .... 60 A6
Essex Rd. Longfield DA3 .. 42 D7
Essex Rd. Maidstone ME15 . 107 E6
Essex Rd.
West Thurrock RM16 ..... 11 A8
Essex St. SE18 .... 2 C3
Estelle Cl. ME1 .... 61 D7
Estridge Way. TN10 .... 117 F5
Etfield Gr. DA14 .... 24 B3
Ethel Brooks House. SE18 .... 6 B8
Ethel Rd. E16 .... 1 C7
Ethel Terr. BR6 .... 52 C2
Ethel-Maud Ct. ME7 .... 48 D7
Ethelbert Cl. BR1 .... 36 A6
Ethelbert Rd.
Bromley BR1 & BR2 ...... 36 A6
Ethelbert Rd. Erith DA8 .... 8 C7
Ethelbert Rd.
Rochester ME1 .... 47 C4
Ethelbert Rd.
St Paul's Cray BR5 .... 38 D6
Ethelbery Rd. DA2 .... 26 E3
Etherington Hill. TN3 ..... 148 E8
Ethnam La. TN18 .... 186 E4
Ethronvi Rd. DA7 .... 7 E4

Eton Cl. ME5 .... 61 F4
Eton Rd. BR6 .... 52 B6
Eton Way. DA1 .... 9 C3
Europa Trad Est. DA8 .... 4 D1
Europe Rd. SE18 .... 1 F3
Euroway. ME20 .... 90 E8
Eustace Pl. SE18 .... 1 F2
Eva Rd. ME7 .... 48 D3
Evans Cl. DA9 .... 11 A2
Evelyn Denington Rd. E6 .... 1 F8
Evelyn Rd. Maidstone ME16 . 91 E3
Evelyn Rd. Newham E16 .... 1 B5
Evelyn Rd. Otford TN14 .... 69 C2
Evenden House. TN17 .... 169 D5
Evenden Rd. DA13 .... 44 A2
Evenlode House. **5** SE2 .. 3 C4
Everard Ave. BR2 .... 36 A1
Everest Cl. **1** DA11 .... 29 E5
Everest Ct. SE9 .... 22 E6
Everest Dr. ME3 .... 34 E4
Everest La. ME2 .... 33 B1
Everest Mews. ME3 .... 34 E4
Everest Pl. BR8 .... 39 D5
Everest Rd. SE9 .... 5 F2
Everett Wlk. DA17 .... 3 F1
Everglades Cl. DA3 .... 42 F5
Everglades The. ME7 .... 62 F6
Evergreen Cl.
Gillingham ME7 .... 63 A5
Evergreen Cl.
Leybourne ME19 .... 74 E2
Eversfield Ct. SE12 .... 22 B6
Eversley Ave. DA7 & DA8 .... 8 E5
Eversley Cl. ME16 .... 91 C6
Eversley Cross. DA7 .... 8 E5
Eversley Rd. SE7 .... 5 B8
Evesham Rd. DA12 .... 30 D6
Evry Rd. DA14 .... 24 C2
Ewart Rd. ME4 .... 47 E1
Ewehurst La. TN3 .... 147 F6
Ewell Ave. ME19 .... 89 A8
Ewell La. ME15 .... 105 D5
Ewins Cl. TN12 .... 136 A6
Exedown Rd. TN15 .... 71 C4
Exeter Cl.
Tonbridge TN10 & TN9 .. 117 D4
Exeter Rd. Bexley DA16 .... 6 F5
Exeter Rd. Gravesend DA12 . 30 D5
Exeter Rd. Newham E16 .... 1 A8
Exeter Wlk. ME1 .... 61 C7
Exford Gdns. SE12 .... 22 B7
Exford Rd. SE12 .... 22 B7
Exmouth Rd. Bexley DA16 .. 7 C7
Exmouth Rd. Bromley BR2 . 36 B6
Exmouth Rd.
Gillingham ME7 .... 48 C7
Exmouth Rd. Grays RM17 . 12 B8
Exton Cl. ME5 .... 62 C2
Exton Gdns. ME14 .... 92 F5
Eyhorne St. ME17 .... 94 D2
Eylesden Court Sch. ME14 . 93 B4
Eynsford Castle. DA4 .... 54 B8
Eynsford Cl. BR5 .... 37 C3
Eynsford Cres. DA5 .... 24 D7
Eynsford Rd.
Crockenhill BR8 .... 39 E3
Eynsford Rd. Eynsford DA4 . 40 F1
Eynsford Rd.
Maidstone ME16 .... 91 D7
Eynsford Rd.
Swanscombe DA9 .... 11 C2
Eynsford Rise. DA4 .... 54 D6
Eynsford Sta. DA4 .... 54 D6
Eynsham Dr. SE2 .... 3 B3
Eynswood Dr. DA14 .... 24 C3

F Ave. SE18 .... 2 B3
Fackenden La. TN14 .... 69 C7
Factory Rd. Newham E16 .... 1 E5
Factory Rd. Northfleet DA11 . 12 C1
Faesten Way. DA5 .... 25 F5
Fagus Cl. ME5 .... 62 B1
Fair Acres. BR2 .... 36 A4
Fair View. TN5 .... 175 A6
Fair View Jun & Inf Schs.
ME8 .... 63 C5
Faircire Pl. DA3 .... 42 E6
Fairbank Ave. BR6 .... 51 B8
Fairbourne Heath Cotts.
ME17 .... 110 B1
Fairbourne La. ME17 ...... 110 C4
Fairby La. DA3 .... 42 E3
Fairby Rd. SE12 .... 5 B2
Faircroft La. TN5 .... 174 B5
Fairfax Bsns Ctr. ME15 ... 107 F4
Fairfax Cl. ME8 .... 63 D5
Fairfax Gdns. SE3 .... 5 C6
Fairfax Rd. RM18 .... 12 F6
Fairfield Ave. TN1 & TN2 . 149 C5

Fairfield Cl. Kemsing TN15 .. 70 A1
Fairfield Cl. Sidcup DA15 .... 6 F1
Fairfield Cres. TN9 .... 133 C8
Fairfield Gr. SE7 .... 5 D8
Fairfield Rd. Bexley DA7 .... 7 F5
Fairfield Rd.
Borough Green TN15 ..... 86 F8
Fairfield Rd. Bromley BR1 . 22 A1
Fairfield Rd. Orpington BR5 . 37 D3
Fairfield Way. TN11 .... 116 F5
Fairfields. DA12 .... 30 E3
Fairford Ave. DA7 .... 8 D6
Fairglen Cotts. TN5 .... 174 B4
Fairglen Rd. TN5 .... 174 B4
Fairhurst Dr. ME15 .... 106 B4
Fairings The. TN30 .... 183 B8
Fairland House. BR2 .... 36 A5
Fairlands St. **8** SE9 .... 6 A1
Fairlawn. SE7 .... 5 A8
Fairlawn Ave. DA16 .... 7 D5
Fairlawn Cl. ME16 .... 105 A8
Fairlawn Ct. SE7 .... 5 C7
Fairlead Rd. ME1 .... 47 D1
Fairlight Cl. TN4 .... 133 A2
Fairlight Cross. DA3 .... 43 C6
Fairlight Ct. TN10 .... 117 B4
Fairman's La. TN12 .... 152 B6
Fairmead. BR1 .... 36 F5
Fairmead Cl. BR1 .... 36 F5
Fairmead Rd. TN8 .... 112 C5
Fairmeadow. ME14 .... 91 F4
Fairmile House. BR5 .... 38 A7
Fairmile Rd. TN2 .... 149 E5
Fairmont Cl. DA17 .... 3 F1
Fairoak Cl. BR5 .... 37 B2
Fairoak Dr. SE9 .... 6 D2
Fairseat La. Fairseat TN15 . 72 B5
Fairseat La. Stansted TN15 . 57 A1
Fairthorn Rd. SE10 & SE7 .. 1 A1
Fairtrough Rd. BR6 .... 67 B7
Fairview. Erith DA8 .... 8 F7
Fairview.
Fawkham Green DA3 ..... 56 B7
Fairview Ave. ME8 .... 63 B5
Fairview Cl. TN9 .... 133 B7
Fairview Cotts. ME15 ..... 106 F5
Fairview Dr. Higham ME3 . 32 B4
Fairview Dr. Orpington BR6 . 51 D6
Fairview Gdns. DA13 .... 44 A4
Fairview Ind Est. RM9 ...... 4 D8
Fairview Rd. DA13 .... 29 E1
Fairwater Ave. DA16 .... 7 A3
Fairway. Bexley DA6 .... 7 F3
Fairway. Orpington BR5 ... 37 D4
Fairway Cl. ME1 .... 47 C1
Fairway Ct. **12** SE9 .... 6 A1
Fairway Dr. DA2 .... 27 B8
Fairway The.
Bromley BR1 & BR2 ...... 36 F4
Fairway The.
Gravesend DA11 .... 30 C8
Fairway The. Rochester ME1 . 47 C1
Fairways The. TN4 .... 149 A7
Falcon Ave. Bromley BR1 ... 36 C5
Falcon Ave. Grays RM17 ... 12 C7
Falcon Cl. DA1 .... 9 F4
Falcon Gn. ME20 .... 74 F1
Falcon Mews. DA11 .... 29 E7
Falconwood Ave. DA16 ..... 6 E5
Falconwood Par. DA16 ...... 6 F3
Falconwood Sta. SE9 .... 6 D3
Falkland Pl. ME5 .... 61 E1
Fallowfield. ME5 .... 62 B8
Fallowfield Cl. ME14 .... 92 E4
Falmouth Pl. TN12 .... 135 C7
Fanconi Rd. ME8 .... 62 B3
Fancy Row. ME14 .... 93 C5
Fane Way. ME8 .... 63 D4
Fant La. ME16 .... 91 B2
Faraday Ave. DA14 .... 24 B6
Faraday Rd. Bexley DA16 .... 7 A4
Faraday Rd.
Maidstone ME14 .... 92 C7
Faraday Ride. TN10 .... 117 D7
Faraday Way.
Greenwich SE10 .... 1 D3
Faraday Way.
Orpington BR5 .... 38 B5
Fareham Wlk. **10** ME15 .. 107 F6
Faringdon Ave. BR2 .... 37 A3
Farjeon Rd. SE18 & SE3 .... 5 D6
Farleigh Ave. BR2 .... 36 A2
Farleigh Ct. ME16 .... 91 A2
Farleigh Hill. ME15 .... 91 E1
Farleigh Hill Ret Pk. ME15 . 91 E1
Farleigh La. ME16 .... 91 A2
Farleigh Trad Est. ME15 ... 91 E1
Farley Cl. ME5 .... 62 D2
Farley La. TN16 .... 96 B8
Farley Rd. DA12 .... 30 F7

Farleycroft. TN16 .... 81 C1
Farlow Cl. DA11 .... 29 F5
Farm Ave. BR8 .... 39 C6
Farm Holt. DA3 .... 42 F1
Farm La. TN11 .... 117 A4
Farm Pl. DA1 .... 9 A3
Farm Rd. Chatham ME5 .... 61 E3
Farm Rd. Sevenoaks TN14 . 84 C7
Farm Vale. DA5 .... 8 B1
Farmcombe Cl. TN1 .... 149 B2
Farmcombe La. TN1 .... 149 B2
Farmcombe Rd.
TN1 & TN2 .... 149 C2
Farmcote Rd. SE12 .... 22 A7
Farmcroft. DA11 .... 30 A6
Farmdale. ME1 .... 46 F3
Farmdale Ave. ME1 .... 46 F2
Farmdale Rd. SE10 .... 1 A1
Farmer Cl. ME17 .... 109 A6
Farmland Wlk. BR7 .... 23 B3
Farmstead Dr. TN8 .... 112 D3
Farnaby Dr. TN13 .... 84 A1
Farnaby Rd. SE9 .... 5 D5
Farnborough Cl. ME16 .... 91 C2
Farnborough Comm.
Keston Mark BR2 & BR6 . 50 F7
Farnborough Comm.
Orpington BR6 .... 51 A6
Farnborough Ct. **2** BR6 . 51 C5
Farnborough Hill. BR6 .... 51 E5
Farnborough Hospl. BR6 . 51 A6
Farnborough Prim Sch.
BR6 .... 51 C5
Farnborough Way. BR6 ... 51 D5
Farne Cl. ME15 .... 107 A6
Farnham Beeches. TN3 ... 148 A4
Farnham Cl. Gillingham ME8 . 64 A8
Farnham Cl.
Langton Green TN3 ...... 148 A3
Farnham La. TN3 .... 148 A4
Farnham Rd. DA16 .... 7 C5
Farningham Cl. ME14 ...... 92 C6
Farningham Hill Rd. DA4 .. 40 D3
Farningham Road Sta.
DA4 .... 41 B7
Farnol Rd. DA1 .... 10 A3
Faro Cl. BR1 .... 37 A7
Farraday Cl. ME1 .... 61 D8
Farrant Cl. BR6 .... 52 A3
Farrier Cl. ME14 .... 92 E5
Farriers Cl. DA12 .... 30 F7
Farriers Ct. ME8 .... 64 C8
Farringdon Ave. BR5 .... 38 B6
Farrington House. **12** SE18 . 2 A2
Farrington Pl. BR7 .... 23 D1
Farringtons Sch. BR7 ...... 23 D1
Fartherwell Ave. ME19 .... 89 A8
Fartherwell Rd. ME19 ..... 89 A8
Farthing Cl. DA1 .... 9 F3
Farthing Cnr. ME9 .... 63 E3
Farthing Hill. TN5 .... 176 E1
Farthing St. BR6 .... 50 F2
Farthingfield. TN15 .... 72 A3
Farthings Cotts. ME14 .... 76 F1
Farwell Rd. DA14 .... 24 C4
Farwig La. BR1 .... 36 A8
Fashoda Rd. BR2 .... 36 D5
Fauchon's Cl. ME14 .... 92 F3
Fauchon's La. ME14 .... 92 F4
Faversham Rd. ME7 .... 111 E7
Fawkham Ave. DA3 .... 43 C6
Fawkham CE Prim Sch.
DA3 .... 42 B1
Fawkham Green Rd. TN15 . 56 B7
Fawkham House. **10** BR5 . 38 D1
Fawkham Manor Hospl.
DA3 .... 42 C1
Fawkham Rd. Longfield DA3 . 42 D6
Fawkham Rd.
West Kingsdown TN15 ... 56 A4
Fawley Cl. ME14 .... 91 E7
Faygate Cres. DA6 .... 8 A2
Fazan Ct. TN5 .... 174 F4
Fearon St. SE10 .... 1 A1
Featherby Cty Prim Inf Sch.
ME8 .... 49 A3
Featherby Jun Sch. ME8 ... 49 A3
Featherby Rd. Gillingham,
Lower Twydall ME7 .... 49 A3
Featherby Rd.
Gillingham,Twydall ME8 . 49 A3
Federation Rd. SE2 .... 3 C2
Feenan Highway. RM18 ... 13 B6
Felderland Cl. ME17 .... 107 E5
Felderland Dr. ME17 ...... 107 E5
Felderland Rd. ME17 ...... 107 E5
Feldspar Cl. ME5 .... 62 A1
Felhampton Rd. SE9 .... 23 B5
Felix Manor. BR7 .... 23 E2
Felixstowe Rd. SE2 .... 3 B3
Fell Mead. TN12 .... 119 F6

Fellowes Way. TN11 .... 118 [?]
Fellows Cl. ME8 .... 6 [?]
Felltram Way. SE7 ....
Felspar Cl. SE18 ....
Felstead Rd. BR6 .... 5 [?]
Felsted Rd. E16 ....
Felton Cl. BR5 .... 3 [?]
Felton House. SE13 ....
Felton Lea. DA14 ....
Fen Gr. DA15 ....
Fen Meadow. TN15 .... 7 [?]
Fen Pond Rd. TN15 .... 8 [?]
Fendyke Rd. SE2 ....
Fenn Cl. BR1 ....
Fennell St. SE18 ....
Fens Way. BR8 ....
Fenton Cl. BR7 ....
Fenwick Cl. **16** SE18 .....
Ferbies. TN3 .... 14[?]
Ferbies Cotts. TN3 .... 14[?]
Ferby Ct. DA15 ....
Ferdinand Terr. TN3 .... 16[?]
Ferguson Ave. DA12 .... 3 [?]
Fern Cl. DA8 ....
Fern Down. DA13 .... 7 [?]
Fern Hill Pl. **3** BR6 .... 5 [?]
Fernbank Cl. ME5 .... 6[?]
Ferndale. Bromley BR1 ....
Ferndale. Royal Tunbridge Well[?]
TN2 ....
Ferndale. Sevenoaks TN13 . 8[?]
Ferndale Cl. Bexley DA7 ....
Ferndale Cl. Royal Tunbridge W[?]
TN2 .... 14[?]
Ferndale Point. TN2 .... 14[?]
Ferndale Rd.
Gillingham ME7 ....
Ferndale Rd.
Gravesend DA12 .... 3[?]
Ferndale St. E6 ....
Ferndale Way. BR6 ....
Ferndell Ave. DA5 ....
Ferndene. DA3 .... 4[?]
Ferndown Cl.
Gillingham ME7 .... 6[?]
Ferndown Cl.
Orpington BR6 .... 3[?]
Ferndown Rd. SE9 ....
Fernheath Way. DA2 2
Fernhill Rd. ME16 ....
Fernhill St. E16 ....
Fernholt. TN10 .... 11[?]
Fernhurst Cres. TN4 .... 14[?]
Fernleigh Rise. ME20 ...... 7[?]
Ferns The. Larkfield ME20 . 7[?]
Ferns The. Platt TN15 ..... 8[?]
Ferns The. Royal Tunbridge Well[?]
TN1 .... 14[?]
Fernside La. TN13 .... 9[?]
Fernwood Cl. BR1 .... 3[?]
Ferranti Cl. SE18 ....
Ferrier Cl. ME8 .... 6[?]
Ferrier Point. **8** E16 ......
Ferry La. Rainham RM13 ...
Ferry La. Wouldham ME1 .. 6[?]
Ferry Rd. Halling ME2 ..... 6[?]
Ferry Rd. Tilbury RM18 ... 1[?]
Festival Ave. DA3 4
Festival Cl. Erith DA8 ....
Festival Cl. Sidcup DA15 .. 2[?]
Ffinch Cl. ME20 .... 9[?]
Fiddlers Cl. DA9 1
Field Cl. Bromley BR1 ..... 3[?]
Field Cl. Chatham ME5 .... 6[?]
Field Dr. TN8 .... 11[?]
Field Rd. DA13 & TN15 .... 5[?]
Fieldfare Rd. SE28 ....
Fielding Ave. RM18 1
Fielding Dr. ME20 .... 7[?]
Fields La. ME18 .... 10[?]
Fieldside Cl. BR6 .... 5[?]
Fieldway. BR5 .... 3[?]
Fieldways. TN18 .... 17[?]
Fieldworks Rd. ME4 & ME7 . 4
Fiennes Way. TN13 9
Fiesta Dr. RM9 ....
Fife Rd. E16 ....
Fifteenpenny Fields. SE9 .... 6[?]
Fifth Ave. RM16 1
Fiji Terr. ME14 9
Filborough Way. DA12 ..... 3[?]
Filmer La.
TN13 & TN14 & TN15 ... 8[?]
Filston La. TN13 & TN14 .. 6[?]
Filston Rd. DA8 ....
Finch Cl. ME14 9
Finchale Rd. SE2 ....
Finchley Cl. DA1 ....
Finchley Rd. RM17 .... 1[?]
Findlay Cl. ME8 .... 6[?]
Finglesham Cl. BR5 .... 3[?]

...sham Ct. ME15 .... 107 C8
...ury Way. DA5 .... 7 F1
...agh Dr. ME14 .... 92 B6
...ane Dr. BR5 .... 38 C2
...ee Rd. BR5 .... 51 A7
...ee Cl.
  ...enborough TN11 .... 116 E5
...ee Cl. 5
  ...ington BR6 .... 51 F5
...ee Cl.
  ...lehurst TN12 .... 139 F3
...ee Gr. Bredhurst ME7 ... 63 B1
...ee Gr. Chatham ME5 ..... 62 D1
...ee Rd. TN14 .... 148 F3
...ck Cl. E16 .... 1 A8
...ft Way. TN8 .... 112 C3
...st Cl. DA3 .... 43 B6
...orn Cl. ME7 .... 48 E6
...e Rd. DA1 .... 9 C2
...ngers Rd. BR6 .... 53 C5
...l. ME20 .... 75 E1
...t. TN4 .... 148 F6
...he. Coldblow DA5 ... 25 D7
...he. Sidcup DA15 ..... 23 F5
...e Gr. DA15 .... 23 F7
Ave. Bexley DA7 .... 7 C7
Ave. Chatham ME4 ..... 48 C2
Ave. Gillingham ME7 .... 48 E3
Ave. Northfleet DA11 ... 29 E7
Ave.
  ...st Thurrock RM16 ... 11 A8
...a. ME15 .... 93 E2
...st. TN3 .... 147 F3
...r House. 13 SE18 ... 2 A2
...ee. ME5 .... 62 B7
...r St. Maidstone ME14 ... 92 A6
...St. Newham E16 ..... 1 A8
...r's Gate Cotts. TN7 ... 160 A1
...r's Way. DA17 .... 4 C5
...ermans Wlk. SE28 ..... 2 E4
...rmen's Hill. DA11 ... 12 B2
...s Cl. TN12 .... 139 F5
...rs Rd. TN12 .... 139 F5
...onds Rd. BR2 .... 50 D5
...s Rd. E16 .... 1 A5
...ay Ct. DA1 .... 27 B7
...orold House. ME7 ..... 48 E7
...lliam Mews. E16 ..... 1 A5
...ham Rd. ME14 .... 92 F5
...Acre Wood Sch.
  ...5 .... 107 B7
...Bells La. ME1 .... 47 D4
...Elms Rd. BR2 .... 50 C7
...Oak Green Rd. Five Oak Green
1 & TN12 .... 134 D6
Oak Green Rd.
  ...bridge TN9 .... 133 F7
...Oak La. TN12 .... 139 B1
...Wents. BR8 .... 40 A7
...sh Rd. DA11 .... 29 E8
...rays. TN1 .... 149 A4
...s Cl. TN7 .... 160 A1
...rs Ct. ME4 .... 48 A4
...Gdns. ME3 .... 34 E5
...ngo Cl. ME5 .... 62 A7
...steed Rd. SE7 .... 1 E1
...The. DA9 .... 11 C2
...han Ct. Erith DA17 ... 4 A1
...han Ct. 7
  ...ingham ME7 .... 48 A6
...ham Rd. ME16 .... 91 C6
...hore Ct. DA7 .... 8 B4
...hers Cl. BR2 .... 36 B5
...hore Pl. TN4 .... 133 A2
...Rd. SE18 .... 6 E7
...Ave. DA2 .... 27 C7
...Dale Par. DA2 .... 27 C7
...Rd. Dartford DA2 ... 27 C7
...Rd. Northfleet DA11 ... 29 C6
...Rd. Rochester ME1 ... 47 D1
...down City Prim Sch.
  ...2 .... 27 C6
...wood Cl. E16 .... 1 D8
...wood Cl. 1
  ...ham E6 .... 1 F8
...wood Cl.
  ...ington BR6 .... 51 A6
...ing Gdns. RM18 .... 13 C6
...ing Way. Erith SE28 ... 3 D6
...ing Way.
  ...bridge TN10 .... 117 E7
...her Rd. TN12 .... 139 E3
...hers Cl. BR2 .... 36 B5
...thing Rd. SE7 .... 5 D8
...well Bird Pk. TN19 ... 177 E2
...well Cl. TN5 .... 177 D4
...Cl. 8 BR6 .... 51 F4
...Gn. ME5 .... 62 C3
...La. ME17 .... 111 C8
...St. RM16 .... 11 B8
...mill Cres. SE3 & SE9 ... 5 E5
...s The. TN13 .... 83 E6
...d Hatch. ME15 .... 91 D2

Flora St. DA17 .... 3 F1
Florance La. TN3 .... 161 B6
Florence Cl. RM17 & RM16 ... 11 E8
Florence Cotts. TN8 .... 112 C1
Florence Farm Mobile Home Pk.
TN15 .... 55 D4
Florence House. SE18 .... 5 F6
Florence Rd. Bromley BR1 ... 36 A8
Florence Rd. Erith SE2 .... 3 C2
Florence Rd.
  Maidstone ME16 .... 91 E3
Florence St. ME2 .... 47 B8
Flower Rise. ME14 .... 91 F7
Flowerfield. TN14 .... 68 F2
Flowerhill Way. DA13 .... 29 E1
Floyd Rd. SE7 .... 1 C1
Flume End. ME16 .... 91 D2
Flyers Way The. TN16 .... 81 D1
Foalhurst Cl. TN10 .... 117 E4
Foley Ct. DA1 .... 27 B7
Foley St. ME14 .... 92 A5
Folkstone House. 4
ME15 .... 107 F6
Fontwell Cl. 6 ME15 ... 107 F6
Fontwell Dr. BR2 .... 37 A4
Foord Almshouses. ME1 ... 47 B3
Foord Rd. DA11 .... 11 D5
Foord St. ME1 .... 47 D4
Footbury Hill Rd. BR6 .... 38 A2
Foots Cray High St. DA14 ... 24 D2
Foots Cray La. DA5 & DA14 . 24 C7
Footscray Rd. BR7 & SE9 ... 23 C7
Force Green La. TN16 .... 81 E4
Ford House. 2 SE18 .... 2 B1
Ford La. Trottiscliffe ME19 ... 73 A4
Ford La.
  Wrotham Heath TN15 .... 72 F2
Ford Rd. DA11 .... 12 B2
Fordcombe CE Prim Sch.
TN3 .... 147 B5
Fordcombe Cl. ME15 .... 107 F7
Fordcombe La. TN3 .... 147 C5
Fordcombe Rd.
  Fordcombe TN3 .... 147 C4
Fordcombe Rd.
  Penshurst TN11 .... 131 A3
Fordwich Cl.
  Maidstone ME16 .... 91 B7
Fordwich Cl. Orpington BR6 . 37 F2
Fordwich Rd. ME8 .... 49 C3
Foreland St. SE18 .... 2 D2
Foremans Barn Rd. ME15 ... 105 F3
Forest Cl. BR7 .... 37 A8
Forest Dr. Chatham ME5 ... 61 F2
Forest Dr. Keston Mark BR2 . 50 E7
Forest Gr. TN10 .... 117 C5
Forest Hill Rd. DA7 .... 8 B4
Forest Lawns. BR1 .... 36 C8
Forest Rd. Erith DA8 .... 9 A6
Forest Rd.
  Paddock Wood TN12 .... 136 A6
Forest Rd. Royal Tunbridge Wells,
  Hawkenbury TN12 .... 149 C1
Forest Rd. Royal Tunbridge Wells,
  Rumbers Hill TN12 .... 163 A8
Forest Ridge. BR2 .... 50 F6
Forest Way. Kings Hill ME19 . 89 A3
Forest Way. Orpington BR5 .. 38 A4
Forest Way. Pembury TN2 ... 150 D8
Forest Way. Royal Tunbridge Wells
TN2 .... 149 D1
Forest Way. Sidcup SE9 ...... 23 D8
Forestdale Rd. ME5 .... 77 A8
Foresters Cl. ME5 .... 61 F2
Foresters Cres. DA7 .... 8 B3
Forge Cl. Hayes BR2 .... 36 A1
Forge Cl. Penshurst TN11 .. 131 B4
Forge Cotts. ME18 .... 104 C2
Forge Croft. TN8 .... 112 D1
Forge La. Benover ME18 ... 121 B4
Forge La. Boxley ME14 ...... 77 C2
Forge La. Bredhurst ME7 .... 63 A1
Forge La.
  Dean Street ME15 .... 106 C7
Forge La.
  Egerton Forstal TN27 ...... 127 C1
Forge La. Gillingham ME7 .... 48 E7
Forge La. Gravesend DA12 ... 30 F6
Forge La. Headcorn TN27 .. 141 D5
Forge La.
  High Halstow ME23 ...... 17 E3
Forge La. Higham ME3 ...... 32 C3
Forge La. Horton Kirby DA4 .. 41 C5
Forge La. Leeds ME17 ...... 108 F7
Forge La.
  Rabbit's Cross TN12 ...... 123 F3
Forge La. Shorne DA12 ..... 31 E3

Forge La.
  West Kingsdown TN15 ...... 56 A1
Forge La.
  West Peckham ME18 ...... 103 A6
Forge Lane Cty Inf Sch.
ME7 .... 48 E6
Forge Mdw. ME17 .... 110 D6
Forge Meadows. TN27 ..... 141 D5
Forge Meadows. TN30 ..... 189 E3
Forge Rd.
  Groombridge TN3 & TN6 .. 161 C2
Forge Rd. Royal Tunbridge Wells
TN4 .... 133 A1
Forge Sq. TN11 .... 115 F2
Forge The. TN12 .... 135 B7
Forge View. TN15 .... 100 B5
Forge Way.
  Paddock Wood TN12 ...... 136 A7
Forge Way. Shoreham TN14 . 68 F8
Forgefield Ct. BR5 .... 38 C4
Formby Rd. ME2 .... 60 A7
Formby Terr. ME2 .... 60 A6
Forsham La. ME17 .... 124 C5
Forson Cl. TN30 .... 183 B8
Forstal Cl. BR2 .... 36 A6
Forstal Cotts. ME20 .... 76 B2
Forstal La. ME17 .... 106 D4
Forstal Rd.
  Egerton Forstal TN27 ...... 127 C1
Forstal Rd. Forstal ME20 ... 76 C2
Forstal The. Cobbarn TN3 . 161 F3
Forstal The. Hadlow TN11 .. 118 F8
Forstal The. Pembury TN2 . 150 E8
Forstall. TN3 .... 148 A4
Forstall The. TN11 .... 116 A2
Forsters. ME17 .... 108 E4
Fort Luton (Mus). ME4 ...... 48 A1
Fort Pitt Gram Sch. ME1 ... 47 E4
Fort Pitt Hill. ME1 & ME4 ... 47 E4
Fort Pitt St. ME4 .... 47 E3
Fort Rd.
  Shepham Heath TN14 ...... 68 C4
Fort Rd. Tilbury RM18 ...... 13 C5
Fort St. Newham E16 .... 1 B5
Fort St. Rochester ME1 ...... 47 D4
Fortis. E16 .... 1 C7
Fortrye Cl. DA11 .... 29 E6
Fortuna Cl. DA3 .... 42 F5
Forty Acre La. E16 .... 1 A8
Fossdene Prim Sch. SE7 ... 1 B1
Fossdene Rd. SE7 .... 1 B1
Fosse Bank. TN9 .... 133 A7
Fosse Bank New Sch.
TN11 .... 116 E7
Fosse Rd. TN9 .... 117 B2
Fossington Rd. DA17 .... 3 D2
Fosten La. TN27 .... 171 E7
Foster Clark Est. ME15 ...... 92 B2
Foster St. ME15 .... 92 A3
Fosters Cl. BR7 .... 22 F3
Fosters VC Prim Sch. DA16 .. 7 B5
Fostington Way. ME5 .... 61 F1
Foulds Cl. ME8 .... 63 B5
Founder Cl. E6 .... 2 B7
Fountain Ct. Eynsford DA4 ... 54 E8
Fountain Ct. Sidcup DA15 ... 7 B1
Fountain Ent Pk. ME15 ...... 92 A1
Fountain La. ME15 .... 91 A2
Fountain Rd. ME2 .... 32 E1
Fountain Wlk. DA11 .... 12 F1
Four Acres. ME19 .... 90 B5
Four Elms Cty Prim Sch.
TN8 .... 113 B5
Four Elms Hill. ME3 .... 33 E4
Four Elms Rd. TN8 .... 112 D4
Four Oaks Rd.
TN12 & TN27 .... 140 E7
Four Wents.
  Langley Heath ME17 ...... 108 E3
Four Wents. Marlpit ME17 . 107 F2
Fouracre Cotts. ME9 .... 64 F6
Fourth Ave. Gillingham ME7 . 48 E4
Fourth Ave.
  West Thurrock RM16 ...... 11 A8
Fourwents Rd. ME3 .... 34 D7
Fowey Cl. ME5 .... 62 C5
Fowler Cl. Gillingham ME8 ... 63 C3
Fowler Cl. Sidcup DA14 ...... 24 E3
Fox Cl. Newham E16 .... 1 A8
Fox Cl. Orpington BR6 ...... 52 A5
Fox Hollow Dr. DA16 .... 7 D4
Fox House Rd. DA17 .... 4 B1
Fox In The Wood. TN5 ...... 174 C6
Fox La. BR2 .... 50 C5
Fox St. ME7 .... 48 C6
Foxburrow Cl. ME8 .... 63 D5
Foxburrow. DA3 .... 56 E7
Foxbury Ave. BR7 .... 23 D2
Foxbury Cl. Bromley BR1 ... 22 B2
Foxbury Cl. Orpington BR6 .. 52 A5

Foxbury Dr. BR6 .... 52 A4
Foxbury Rd. BR1 .... 22 B2
Foxbush. TN11 .... 116 C6
Foxcroft Rd. SE18 .... 6 B6
Foxden Dr. ME15 .... 92 F1
Foxendown La. DA13 ...... 44 B5
Foxes Dale. SE3 .... 5 A4
Foxfield Prim Sch. SE18 ... 2 C2
Foxfield Rd. BR6 .... 51 D8
Foxglove Cl. 9 TN8 ...... 112 D3
Foxglove Cres. ME5 .... 61 E4
Foxglove Rise. ME14 ...... 91 E7
Foxhole La.
  Four Throws TN18 .... 179 E1
Foxhole La. Matfield TN12 . 151 C8
Foxhole La. Wadhurst TN5 . 175 B4
Foxhole Rd. SE9 .... 5 E2
Foxhome Cl. BR7 .... 23 A2
Foxton House. E16 .... 2 A4
Foxton Rd. RM16 .... 11 D8
Foxwood Gr. BR6 .... 52 C1
Foxwood Rd. DA2 .... 28 B5
Foxwood Way. DA3 .... 43 D7
Framley Rd. TN10 .... 117 F5
Framlingham Cres. SE9 ... 22 F4
Frances St. SE18 .... 1 F2
Francis Ave. DA7 .... 8 A5
Francis Dr. ME5 .... 62 A2
Francis La. ME15 .... 107 F5
Francis Rd. Dartford DA1 ... 9 D2
Francis Rd.
  Hildenborough TN11 ...... 116 D6
Francis Rd.
  St Paul's Cray BR5 .... 38 D6
Frank Burton Cl. 4 SE7 ... 1 B1
Frank Woolley Rd. TN10 ... 117 F5
Frank's Hollow Rd.
TN14 .... 132 C2
Frankapps Cl. ME9 .... 65 B6
Frankfield Rise. TN2 .... 149 A1
Franklin Dr. ME14 .... 92 D4
Franklin Rd. Bexley DA7 ...... 7 E6
Franklin Rd. Gillingham ME7 . 48 D5
Franklin Rd.
  Gravesend DA12 .... 30 D3
Franklins Cotts. ME15 ...... 106 C5
Franks Cl. ME8 .... 49 B2
Franks La. DA4 .... 41 B4
Franks Wood Ave.
BR2 & BR5 .... 37 C4
Frant CE Prim Sch. TN3 ... 163 B4
Frant Field. TN8 .... 112 C1
Frant Rd. TN2 & TN3 ...... 163 A7
Frant Sta. TN3 .... 163 F5
Fraser Cl. Coldblow DA5 ... 25 C7
Fraser Cl. 3 Newham E16 . 1 E7
Fraser House. 3 SE18 ...... 2 A2
Fraser Rd. DA8 .... 4 D1
Frederick House. SE7 ...... 1 E3
Frederick Andrews Ct.
RM17 .... 12 D8
Frederick Pl. SE18 .... 2 B1
Frederick Rd. ME7 .... 48 C4
'Free Heath Rd. TN3 & TN5 . 165 C3
Freehold. TN12 .... 119 F6
Freehold The. TN11 .... 102 D1
Freeland Way. DA8 .... 9 A6
Freelands Gr. BR1 .... 36 B8
Freelands Rd. Bromley BR1 . 36 B8
Freelands Rd. Snodland
ME6 .... 74 F8
Freeman Gdns. ME4 .... 47 F2
Freeman Rd. DA12 .... 30 E5
Freeman Way. ME15 ...... 107 E7
Freemasons Rd. E16 .... 1 B7
Freesia Cl. Orpington BR6 ... 51 F5
Freight La. TN17 .... 169 C3
Fremantle House. RM18 ... 12 F6
Fremantle Rd. DA17 .... 4 A2
Fremlin Cl. TN4 .... 148 B4
Fremlins Rd. ME14 .... 93 C4
Frensham Rd.
  Rolvenden Layne TN17 ... 182 A1
Frensham Rd. Sidcup DA15 . 23 D6
Frensham Wlk. ME16 .... 61 F1
Freshland Rd. ME16 .... 91 B4
Freshwater Rd. ME5 .... 62 B7
Freta Rd. DA6 .... 7 F2
Frewing Ct. BR7 .... 23 A3
Friar Rd. BR5 .... 38 A4
Friars Ave. ME15 .... 61 F2
Friars Mews. SE9 .... 6 A2
Friars Way. TN2 .... 149 D6
Friars Wlk. SE2 .... 3 D1
Friary Pl. 3 ME2 .... 47 B7
Friary Prec. ME2 .... 47 B7
Friday Rd. DA8 .... 4 D1
Friday St. ME17 .... 125 B6
Friezland Rd. TN14 .... 148 D1
Friezley La. TN17 .... 155 C1

Frimley Ct. DA14 .... 24 C3
Frindsbury Hill. ME2 .... 33 C1
Frindsbury Rd. ME2 .... 47 B8
Frinstead Cl. BR5 .... 38 D5
Frinstead Wlk. ME16 .... 91 B7
Frinsted Cl. ME8 .... 49 C3
Frinsted Rd. DA8 .... 8 D7
Frinton Rd. DA14 .... 24 E6
Friston Way. ME1 .... 61 D8
Friswell Pl. 1 DA7 .... 8 A3
Frithwood Cl. ME5 .... 92 F1
Frittenden Rd.
  Rochester ME2 .... 33 D2
Frittenden Rd.
  Staplehurst TN12 .... 140 B2
Frobisher Gdns. ME1 .... 47 C2
Frobisher Rd. Erith DA8 ...... 9 A7
Frobisher Rd. Newham E6 ... 2 A7
Frobisher Way. DA12 .... 30 E3
Frog La. Rainham RM9 ...... 4 D8
Frog La. Royal Tunbridge Wells
TN1 .... 149 A2
Frog La. West Malling ME19 . 89 C8
Frog's La. TN17 .... 181 E1
Froghole La. TN16 & TN8 ... 96 D2
Frogmore Wlk. ME17 ...... 111 C5
Frognal Ave. DA14 .... 24 A2
Frognal Pl. DA14 .... 24 A3
Frognall Cnr. BR7 .... 23 F2
Frogs Hole La. TN17 ...... 171 E3
Froissart Rd. SE9 .... 5 E2
Fromandez Dr. TN12 ...... 152 F5
Frome Ct. TN10 .... 117 B5
Front Cotts. TN5 .... 174 F6
Frost Cres. ME5 .... 62 A7
Froyle Cl. ME16 .... 91 C6
Fruitfields. TN5 .... 177 C3
Fry Cl. ME3 .... 21 A6
Fry's Cotts. ME4 .... 19 C4
Frythe Cres. TN17 .... 169 D4
Frythe Rd. TN17 .... 169 D4
Frythe Wlk. TN17 .... 169 D4
FTA (Trng Ctr). TN5 .... 174 D6
Fuchsia St. SE2 .... 3 B1
Fuggles Cl. TN12 .... 135 E6
Fuggles Ct. TN17 .... 180 D6
Fulbert Dr. ME14 .... 92 F5
Fuller Cl. Durgates TN5 ...... 174 E5
Fuller Cl. Orpington BR6 ...... 51 F5
Fullers St. ME9 .... 93 A4
Fullers Hill. 4 TN16 .... 81 D1
Fulmar Rd. ME2 .... 46 D6
Fulmer Rd. E16 .... 1 D8
Fulthorp Rd. SE3 .... 5 A5
Fulwich Rd. DA1 .... 9 F1
Furfield Cl. ME17 .... 107 E5
Furnace Ave. TN3 .... 166 A3
Furnace La.
  Hook Green TN3 .... 165 E4
Furnace La.
  Horsmonden TN12 .... 152 F7
Furner Cl. DA1 .... 8 F4
Furness Sch. BR8 .... 25 F2
Furnival Ct. TN2 .... 162 F8
Furrell's Rd. ME1 .... 47 D5
Furze Bank. ME16 .... 113 B5
Furzefield Ave. TN3 .... 148 A8
Furzefield Cl. BR7 .... 23 B2
Furzefield Rd. SE3 & SE7 ... 5 B7
Furzehill Sq. BR5 .... 38 B5
Fyfe Way. BR1 .... 36 A7
Gable Cl. DA1 .... 9 A2
Gables Cl. SE12 .... 22 A7
Gables The. Bromley BR1 ... 22 B1
Gables The. New Barn DA3 . 43 C6
Gabriel Gdns. DA12 .... 30 E3
Gabriel Spring Road (East).
DA3 & DA4 .... 55 F8
Gabriel's Hill.
ME14 & ME15 .... 92 A4
Gabrielspring Rd. DA4 ...... 55 D8
Gads Hill. ME7 .... 48 F6
Gads Hill Sch. ME3 .... 32 C2
Gadsby La. TN27 .... 159 F3
Gadwall Cl. E16 .... 1 B7
Gadwall Way. SE28 .... 2 D4
Gafford's Bridge Cotts.
TN12 .... 137 C4
Gagetown Terr. ME14 ...... 91 F7
Gainsborough Ave.
  Dartford DA1 .... 9 C2
Gainsborough Ave.
  Tilbury RM18 .... 13 B6
Gainsborough Cl. ME8 ...... 63 D6
Gainsborough Dr.
  Maidstone ME16 .... 91 B4

Gainsborough Dr.
Northfleet DA11 .... 29 D5
Gainsborough Gdns.
TN10 .... 117 E5
Gainsborough House. ME1 . 47 D5
Gainsborough Sq. DA7 .... 7 D4
Gaitskell Rd. SE9 .... 23 C7
Galahad Ave. ME4 .... 46 E6
Galahad Rd. BR1 .... 22 A4
Galena Cl. ME5 .... 62 A1
Galena House. SE18 .... 2 F1
Gallants La. ME15 .... 105 F6
Galleon Bvd. DA9 .... 10 D3
Galleon Cl. Chatham ME1 .... 61 C8
Galleon Cl. Erith DA8 .... 4 D2
Galley Hill Rd. DA11 .... 11 F2
Galley Hill Trad Est. DA10 ... 11 E2
Gallions Mount Prim Sch.
SE18 .... 2 F1
Gallions Rd. Greenwich SE7 .. 1 A2
Gallions Rd. Newham E16 .... 2 C6
Gallions Reach Sta. E16 ...... 2 B6
Gallon Cl. SE7 .... 1 C2
Gallops The. DA13 .... 72 F7
Gallosson Rd. SE18 .... 2 E2
Gallus Sq. SE3 .... 5 B4
Galsworthy Cl. SE28 .... 3 B5
Galsworthy Cres. SE3 .... 5 C6
Galsworthy Rd. RM18 .... 13 C6
Galton House. SE18 .... 5 F6
Games House. 6 SE7 .... 5 C8
Gamma Rd. ME3 .... 35 D7
Gandy's La. ME17 .... 107 C2
Garden Ave. DA7 .... 8 A4
Garden Cl. Lewisham SE12 .. 22 B5
Garden Cl.
Maidstone ME15 .... 107 E7
Garden Cl. Toy's Hill TN16 ... 97 C3
Garden Cotts. Leigh TN11 . 116 A2
Garden Cotts.
St Paul's Cray BR5 .... 38 C7
Garden Cl. 10 SE9 .... 6 A3
Garden La. BR1 .... 22 B2
Garden of England Pk
(Mobile Home Pk). ME17 110 B7
Garden Pl. DA2 .... 26 D5
Garden Rd. Bromley BR1 ..... 22 B2
Garden Rd. Royal Tunbridge Wells
TN1 .... 149 B4
Garden Row. DA11 .... 29 F5
Garden St. Gillingham ME7 .. 48 A6
Garden St. Royal Tunbridge Wells
TN1 .... 149 B4
Garden Terr. TN15 .... 85 A6
Garden Way. ME18 .... 88 F2
Gardenia Cl. ME2 .... 33 B2
Gardens The. ME7 .... 106 C3
Gardiner Cl. BR5 .... 38 C7
Gardiner House. SE18 .... 5 F7
Gardiner St. ME7 .... 48 C6
Gardyne Mews. 9 TN9 ..... 133 B8
Gareth Gr. BR1 .... 22 A4
Garfield Rd. ME7 .... 48 D6
Gargany Wlk. SE28 .... 3 D5
Garibaldi St. SE18 .... 2 E2
Garland Rd. SE18 .... 6 D7
Garlands. TN11 .... 116 D8
Garlinge Rd. TN4 .... 133 A1
Garnet Wlk. 6 E6 .... 1 E8
Garnett Cl. SE9 .... 5 F4
Garrard Cl. Bexley DA7 .... 8 A4
Garrard Cl. Chislehurst BR7 . 23 B3
Garrick Dr. SE18 .... 2 D3
Garrick St. 15 DA11 .... 13 B1
Garrington Cl. ME14 .... 92 C6
Garrison Cl. SE18 .... 6 A7
Garrison Rd. ME12 .... 21 F3
Garrolds Cl. BR8 .... 39 D7
Garrow. DA3 .... 43 B6
Garside Cl. SE28 .... 2 D3
Garth Rd. TN13 .... 99 C7
Garvary Rd. E16 .... 1 B7
Garvock Dr. TN13 .... 84 A1
Gas House Rd. ME1 .... 47 C6
Gascoyne Dr. DA1 .... 9 F4
Gasoline Alley. TN15 .... 72 D2
Gasson Rd. DA10 .... 11 E1
Gassons Rd. ME6 .... 74 E8
Gatcombe Cl. Chatham ME5 62 A5
Gatcombe Cl.
Maidstone ME16 .... 91 B5
Gate Farm Rd. TN8 & TN4 . 132 C4
Gateacre Ct. DA14 .... 24 A4
Gatefield Cotts. TN17 .... 181 F4
Gatehouse Farm Cotts.
TN4 .... 132 C4

Gates Green Rd.
BR2 & BR4 .... 50 A6
Gateway Par. DA12 .... 30 F4
Gatland La. ME16 .... 91 B2
Gatling Rd. SE18 & SE2 .... 3 A1
Gaton Rd. SE2 .... 3 A3
Gattons Way. DA14 .... 24 F4
Gatwick Farm Cotts.
RH19 .... 144 A4
Gatwick Rd. DA12 .... 30 B6
Gault Cl. ME15 .... 93 A2
Gautrey Sq. 6 E6 .... 1 F7
Gavestone Cres. SE12 .... 22 B8
Gavestone Rd. SE12 .... 22 B8
Gavin House. SE18 .... 2 E2
Gayhurst Cl. ME8 .... 63 D6
Gaylor Rd. RM18 .... 12 F6
Gaza Trad Est. TN11 .... 115 D7
Gazelle Glade. DA12 .... 30 F3
Gean Cl. ME5 .... 77 A8
Geddes Pl. 3 DA7 .... 8 A3
Gedge's Hill. TN12 .... 135 F3
Geffery's St. SE9 .... 22 E5
General Gordon Pl. SE18 .... 2 B2
Genesta Glade. DA12 .... 31 A3
Genesta Rd. SE18 .... 6 C8
Geneva Ave. ME8 .... 49 A2
Gentian Cl. 4
Chatham ME5 .... 61 E4
Gentian Cl. Maidstone ME14 92 E5
George Akass House. 3
SE18 .... 2 C1
George Crooks House. 7
RM17 .... 12 B8
George La. Hayes BR2 .... 36 B1
George La. Leeds ME17 ..... 109 B7
George La. Rochester ME1 .. 47 C6
George Marsham House.
ME15 .... 106 F3
George St.
Chainhurst ME15 .... 122 A7
George St. Grays RM17 ...... 12 A8
George St. Maidstone ME15 . 92 A3
George St. Royal Tunbridge Wells
TN2 .... 149 C3
George St.
Sparrow's Green TN5 .... 174 F5
George St.
Staplehurst TN12 .... 139 E6
George St. Tonbridge TN9 . 133 B8
George Summers Cl. ME2 ... 47 E8
Georges Cl. BR5 .... 38 C6
Georgian Cl. BR2 .... 36 B1
Georgian Cl. ME17 .... 106 D3
Georgian Way. ME8 .... 63 C4
Geraint Rd. BR1 .... 22 A4
Gerald Ave. ME4 .... 47 F2
Gerald Rd. DA12 .... 30 E8
Gerda Rd. SE9 .... 23 C6
Gerdview Dr. DA2 .... 26 C5
Gerrard Ave. ME1 .... 61 E8
Gertrude Rd. DA17 .... 4 A2
Gibbet La. TN12 .... 152 F6
Gibbetts. TN3 .... 147 F1
Gibbs Hill. Headcorn TN27 . 141 E5
Gibbs Hill.
Nettlestead ME18 .... 104 B5
Gibraltar Ave. ME7 .... 48 B7
Gibraltar Hill. ME4 .... 47 F4
Gibraltar La. ME14 .... 91 F8
Gibson Cl. DA11 .... 29 F5
Gibson Dr. ME19 .... 88 A8
Gidd's Pond Cotts. ME14 .... 92 E6
Giddyhorn La. ME15 .... 91 C5
Gideon Cl. DA17 .... 4 B2
Gifford Cl. ME8 .... 49 C3
Giggs Hill. BR5 .... 38 A8
Gighill Rd. ME20 .... 74 F4
Gilbert Cl. Eltham SE18 .... 5 F6
Gilbert Cl. Gillingham ME7 .. 63 A5
Gilbert Cl.
Swanscombe DA10 .... 11 D1
Gilbert Rd. Bromley BR1 ..... 22 A1
Gilbert Rd. Erith DA17 .... 4 A3
Gilbert Terr. ME1 .... 91 F7
Gilbourne Rd. SE18 .... 6 E8
Gilchrist Cotts. TN14 .... 99 C2
Gildenhill Rd. BR8 .... 26 C1
Gildersome St. SE18 .... 6 A8
Gill Ave. Newham E16 .... 1 A7
Gill Ave. Rochester ME2 ...... 33 C1
Gill Cres. DA11 .... 29 F5
Gill Ct. SE18 .... 2 C2
Gill The. TN2 .... 150 E8
Gill's Rd.
Green Street Green DA2 .. 28 B1
Gill's Rd. South Darenth DA4 41 F8
Gillan Ct. SE12 .... 22 B5
Gilletts La. ME19 .... 90 A6
Gillies Cl. DA14 .... 23 E4
Gillies Rd. TN15 .... 55 E5

Gillingham Gn. ME7 .... 48 E6
Gillingham Rd. ME7 .... 48 D5
Gillingham Sta. ME7 .... 48 D5
Gillmans Rd. BR5 & BR6 ...... 38 B1
Gilroy Way. BR5 .... 38 B2
Gimble Way. TN2 .... 134 D1
Gingerbread La. TN18 .... 177 F2
Ginsbury Cl. ME2 .... 47 E6
Gipps Cross La. TN3 .... 147 F3
Gipsy La. RM17 .... 12 C8
Gipsy Rd. DA16 .... 7 D5
Giralda Cl. E16 .... 1 D8
Glade Bsns Ctr The. RM16 .. 10 F8
Glade The. Bromley BR1 ...... 36 D7
Glade The. Chatham ME5 .... 62 A2
Glade The. Greenwich SE7 ... 5 C7
Glade The. Sevenoaks TN13 . 84 B4
Glades Sh Ctr The. BR1 ...... 36 A7
Glades The. DA12 .... 30 D2
Gladeswood Rd. DA17 .... 4 B2
Gladstone Rd. Chatham ME4 47 E2
Gladstone Rd. Dartford DA1 .. 9 F1
Gladstone Rd.
Maidstone ME14 .... 92 A6
Gladstone Rd.
Orpington BR6 .... 51 C5
Gladstone Rd.
Rusthall TN4 .... 148 B4
Gladstone Rd.
Tonbridge TN9 .... 117 B1
Gladwell Rd. BR1 .... 22 A2
Gladwyn Cl. ME8 .... 63 D4
Glamford Rd. ME2 .... 46 D5
Glamis Cl. ME5 .... 62 A5
Glanville Rd. Bromley BR2 ... 36 B6
Glanville Rd.
Gillingham ME7 .... 48 D5
Glanville Rd. Rochester ME2 47 A8
Glasbrook Rd. SE9 .... 22 C8
Glasgow House. 7 ME15 . 107 E7
Glass St. SE18 .... 2 A3
Glassmill La. BR2 .... 36 A7
Gleaming Wood Dr. ME5 ..... 77 D8
Gleaners Cl. ME14 .... 92 E4
Glebe Cl. TN27 .... 143 B2
Glebe Cotts. TN16 .... 82 B4
Glebe Gdns. ME17 .... 111 E5
Glebe House. 7 SE18 .... 2 A2
Glebe House Dr. BR2 .... 36 B1
Glebe La. Maidstone ME16 .. 91 A1
Glebe La. Sevenoaks TN13 .. 84 B1
Glebe Meadow. ME18 .... 104 E7
Glebe Pl. DA4 .... 41 C5
Glebe Rd. Bromley BR1 .... 36 A8
Glebe Rd. Gillingham ME7 ... 48 D5
Glebe Rd. Gravesend DA11 .. 29 F7
Glebe Rd.
Sevenoaks Weald TN14 ... 99 B3
Glebe The.
Bidborough TN4 .... 132 C3
Glebe The. Chislehurst BR7 . 37 C8
Glebe The. Cuxton ME2 ...... 46 C2
Glebe The. Pembury TN2 .. 150 D8
Glebe The.
Penshurst TN11 .... 131 A3
Glebe Way. DA8 .... 8 B7
Glebefield The. TN13 .... 83 F4
Glebeland. TN27 .... 127 F4
Glebelands.
Bidborough TN3 & TN4 .. 132 C3
Glebelands.
Biddenden TN27 .... 157 F1
Glebelands. Crayford DA1 .... 8 F3
Glebelands.
Penshurst TN11 .... 131 A3
Gleeson Dr. BR6 .... 51 F6
Glen Cl. DA14 .... 24 A4
Glen Dunlop House The.
TN13 .... 84 C5
Glen House. 6 E16 .... 1 E2
Glen The. BR6 .... 51 A7
Glen View. DA3 .... 30 C7
Glen View Rd. BR1 .... 36 D7
Glenalvon Way. 6 SE7 .... 1 E2
Glenbarr Cl. SE9 .... 6 B4
Glencairne Cl. E16 .... 1 D8
Glencoe Cty Inf Sch. ME4 ... 48 A2
Glencoe Cty Prim Sch.
ME4 .... 48 A2
Glendale. BR8 .... 39 F4
Glendale Cl. SE9 .... 6 A4
Glendale Cl. TN1 .... 149 D6
Glendale Rd. Erith DA8 .... 4 C2
Glendale Rd.
Northfleet DA11 .... 29 E5
Glendale Way. SE28 .... 3 C6
Glendower Cres.
BR5 & BR6 .... 38 A1
Glendown Rd. SE2 .... 3 A1
Gleneagles Cl. BR6 .... 37 D1

Gleneagles Ct. ME5 .... 61 F2
Gleneagles Dr. ME15 .... 92 A1
Gleneagles Gn. 1 BR6 ...... 37 D1
Glenesk Rd. SE9 .... 6 B3
Glengall Rd. DA7 .... 7 E4
Glenhead Cl. SE9 .... 6 B4
Glenhouse Rd. SE9 .... 6 A2
Glenhurst Ave. DA5 .... 24 F7
Glenister St. E16 .... 2 A5
Glenlea Rd. SE9 .... 6 A3
Glenlee Rd. SE3 .... 5 A8
Glenlyon Rd. SE9 .... 6 B3
Glenmore Pk. TN2 .... 162 F8
Glenmore Rd. DA16 .... 6 F6
Glenmount Path. 1 SE18 .... 2 C1
Glenrosa Gdns. DA12 .... 30 F3
Glenrose Ct. DA14 .... 24 B3
Glenshiel Rd. SE9 .... 6 A2
Glentrammon Ave. BR6 ...... 51 F4
Glentrammon Cl. BR6 .... 51 F5
Glentrammon Gdns. BR6 ... 51 F4
Glentrammon Rd. BR6 .... 51 F4
Glenure Rd. SE9 .... 6 A2
Glenview. SE2 .... 7 D8
Glenwood. Dr. Sidcup DA14 . 24 A4
Glenwood Cl. Chatham ME5 48 C1
Glenwood Cl.
Gillingham ME7 .... 63 A5
Glenwood Cl.
Maidstone ME16 .... 91 C5
Glenwood Cl.
St Michaels TN30 .... 173 B3
Glenwood Cl. 4 DA14 .... 24 A4
Glimpsing Gn. DA18 .... 3 E3
Glistening Glade. ME8 .... 63 E6
Gload Cres. BR5 .... 52 D8
Globe La. ME4 .... 47 F5
Globe Yd. 11 DA11 .... 13 B1
Gloucester Ave. Bexley DA16 6 F3
Gloucester Ave.
Sidcup DA15 .... 23 E6
Gloucester Cl. ME8 .... 64 A8
Gloucester Ct. RM18 .... 12 F5
Gloucester Par. DA15 .... 7 A2
Gloucester Rd.
Dartford DA1 .... 26 B8
Gloucester Rd. Erith DA17 ... 3 F1
Gloucester Rd.
Gravesend DA12 .... 30 C4
Gloucester Rd.
Maidstone ME15 .... 107 D8
Gloucester Rd.
Sparrow's Green TN5 .... 174 F6
Glover Cl. SE2 .... 3 C2
Gloxinia Rd. DA13 .... 29 B2
Glyn Davies Cl. TN13 .... 83 E7
Glyn Dr. DA14 .... 24 B4
Glynde Rd. DA7 .... 7 E4
Glyndebourne Pk. BR6 .... 51 B8
Glyndon Rd. SE18 .... 2 D2
Goad Ave. ME5 .... 62 B3
Goddard's Green Cotts.
TN17 .... 170 F1
Goddards Cl. TN17 .... 169 B4
Godden Rd. ME6 .... 74 F8
Goddings Dr. ME1 .... 47 A3
Goddington Chase. BR6 ...... 52 A6
Goddington House. BR6 ...... 52 C7
Goddington La.
Harrietsham ME17 .... 110 B6
Goddington La.
Orpington BR6 .... 52 A7
Goddington Rd. ME2 .... 47 B8
Godfrey Cl. ME2 .... 32 F1
Godfrey Evans Cl. TN10 .... 117 F5
Godfrey Hill. SE18 .... 1 E2
Godfrey Rd. SE18 .... 1 F2
Godstow Rd. SE2 .... 3 C4
Godwin House. SE18 .... 5 F6
Godwin Rd. BR1 & BR2 .... 36 C6
Gold St. DA12 .... 44 C6
Goldace. RM17 .... 11 F8
Goldcrest Cl. Newham E16 ... 1 D8
Goldcrest Cl. Woolwich SE28 . 3 C6
Golden Plover Cl. E16 .... 1 A7
Golden Sq. TN30 .... 183 B8
Golden Wood Cl. ME5 .... 77 D8
Goldfinch Cl. Larkfield ME20 75 A2
Goldfinch Cl. Orpington BR6 52 A5
Goldfinch Cl.
Paddock Wood TN12 ..... 136 A5
Goldfinch Rd. SE28 .... 2 D3
Goldie Leigh Hospl. SE2 .... 7 C8
Golding Cl. ME20 .... 75 C1
Golding Gdns. TN12 .... 120 A6
Golding Rd. TN13 .... 84 C5
Goldings. TN12 .... 135 E5
Goldings The. ME8 .... 63 C8
Goldmark House. SE3 .... 5 A4
Goldsel Rd. BR8 .... 39 E5
Goldsmid Rd. TN9 .... 133 C8

Goldsmid St. SE18 .... [?]
Goldsmith. MR17 .... [?]
Goldsmith's Bottom. TN14 .. [?]
Goldstone Wlk. ME5 .... [?]
Goldsworth Dr. ME2 .... [?]
Goldthorne Cl. ME14 .... [?]
Goldwing Cl. E16 .... [?]
Golf Links Ave. DA11 .... [?]
Golf Rd. BR1 .... [?]
Golford Rd. TN17 .... 1[?]
Gollogly Terr. 9 SE7 .... [?]
Goodall Cl. ME8 .... [?]
Goodbury Rd. TN15 .... [?]
Gooding House. 4 SE7 .... [?]
Goodley Stock Rd.
TN16 & TN8 .... [?]
Goodmead Rd. BR6 .... [?]
Goods Hill. TN30 .... 18[?]
Goods Station Rd. TN1 ..... 14[?]
Goodtrees La. TN8 .... 14[?]
Goodwin Dr.
Maidstone ME14 .... [?]
Goodwin Dr. Sidcup DA14 ... [?]
Goodwin Rd. ME3 .... [?]
Goodwins The. TN2 .... 14[?]
Goodwood Cl.
High Halstow ME23 .... [?]
Goodwood Cl.
Maidstone ME15 .... 1[?]
Goodwood Cres. DA12 .... [?]
Goodworth Rd. TN15 .... [?]
Goosander Way.
SE18 & SE28 .... [?]
Goose Cl. ME5 .... [?]
Goose Green Cl. BR5 .... 3[?]
Goose Sq. 8 E6 .... [?]
Gooseneck La. TN27 .... 14[?]
Gordon Cl. ME17 .... 1[?]
Gordon Cty Jun Sch. ME2 ... [?]
Gordon House. SE12 .... [?]
Gordon Pl. DA11 .... [?]
Gordon Prim Sch. SE9 .... [?]
Gordon Rd. Chatham ME4 .... [?]
Gordon Rd. Dartford DA1 .... [?]
Gordon Rd. Erith DA17 .... [?]
Gordon Rd. Gillingham ME7 . [?]
Gordon Rd.
Gillingham,Brompton ME7 . [?]
Gordon Rd.
Hoo St Werburgh ME3 ...... 3[?]
Gordon Rd. Northfleet DA11 . 3[?]
Gordon Rd. Rochester ME2 ... [?]
Gordon Rd. Royal Tunbridge W
TN4 .... 14[?]
Gordon Rd. Sevenoaks TN13 8[?]
Gordon Rd. Sidcup DA15 ..... [?]
Gordon Terr. ME1 .... [?]
Gordon Way. BR1 .... [?]
Gore Cotts. DA2 .... [?]
Gore Court Rd. ME15 .... 1[?]
Gore Farm Cotts. DA2 .... [?]
Gore Green Rd. ME3 .... [?]
Gore La. TN17 .... 15[?]
Gore Rd. Dartford DA2 .... [?]
Gore Rd. Silver Street ME9 .. 8[?]
Gorham Cl. ME6 .... [?]
Gorham Dr.
Maidstone ME15 .... [?]
Gorham Dr. Tonbridge TN9 13[?]
Gorman Rd. SE18 .... [?]
Gorringe Ave. DA4 .... 4[?]
Gorse Ave. ME5 .... 6[?]
Gorse Cl. E16 .... [?]
Gorse Cres. ME20 .... 9[?]
Gorse Rd. Orpington BR5 .... 5[?]
Gorse Rd. Rochester ME2 .... [?]
Gorse Rd. Royal Tunbridge Wel
TN2 .... 14[?]
Gorse Way. DA3 .... [?]
Gorse Wood Rd.
Hartley DA3 .... [?]
Gorse Wood Rd.
New Barn DA3 .... [?]
Goss Hill. BR8 .... 2[?]
Gossage Rd. SE18 .... 2[?]
Gosshill Rd. BR7 .... 3[?]
Gossington Cl. BR7 .... 2[?]
Gothic Cl. DA1 .... 2[?]
Goudhurst Cl. ME16 .... [?]
Goudhurst & Kilndown
CE Prim Sch. TN17 .... 1[?]
Goudhurst Rd.
Gillingham ME8 .... [?]
Goudhurst Rd.
Horsmonden TN12 .... 15[?]
Goudhurst Rd.
Knox Bridge TN12 & TN17 15[?]
Goudhurst Rd.
Wilsley Pound TN17 ...... 16[?]
Gouge Ave. DA11 .... 2[?]

d Rd. ME5 .... 62 B3
dhurst Rd. TN12 .... 138 B5
ock Rd. SE9 .... 6 A2
he Rd. TN11 .... 102 E6
e Ave. Bexley DA7 ...... 7 F5
e Ave. Maidstone ME16 91 D6
e Cl. SE9 .... 22 D5
ous La. TN13 .... 99 B5
ious Lane Bridge.
13 .... 99 A6
ous Lane End. TN14 ... 98 F5
con Ave. ME1 .... 61 E8
am Ct. BR1 .... 22 B1
am House. SE18 .... 6 B7
am Rd. DA7 .... 8 A3
n Rd. Gillingham ME8 ... 63 C3
n Rd. Grain ME3 .... 20 D3
hey Field. ME9 .... 64 E4
nger Wlk. TN10 .... 117 E6
n Sch for Girls Wilmington.
.... 26 B5
pian Cl. Orpington BR6 37 F3
pian Cl.
ral Tunbridge Wells
.... 149 D5
narp Way. ME15 .... 93 A1
ada House. ME15 .... 92 A4
ada St. ME15 .... 92 A4
ary. TN12 .... 136 B6
ary Cl. Gillingham ME8 . 49 F1
ary Cl. Maidstone ME14 92 E5
by House. ME14 SE18 ...... 1 F2
by Rd. Eltham SE9 .... 5 F4
by Rd. Northfleet DA11 . 12 D1
by Rd. Woolwich SE18 ... 2 B3
nd Depot Rd. SE18 .... 2 A1
dshire Gdns. ME3 ...... 34 E6
dshire La. TN17 .... 156 B5
ge Cl. Edenbridge TN8 112 C1
ge Cl. Leybourne ME19 . 74 C2
ge Cl. Sidcup DA14 ...... 24 A5
ge Cotts. TN11 .... 101 D5
ge Cres. Erith SE28 .... 3 C7
ge Cres.
lichaels TN30 .... 173 A3
ge Dr. Chislehurst BR7 . 22 F2
ge Dr.
tt's Bottom BR6 .... 52 C2
ge Gdns. TN4 .... 148 D4
ge Hill. Chatham ME4 ... 48 B3
ge Hill. Plaxtol TN15 .. 101 E8
ge House. Erith DA8 ...... 9 A5
ge House.
avesend DA11 .... 30 A8
ge House.
idstone ME16 .... 91 A2
ge La. Hartley DA3 ..... 43 B2
ge La. Maidstone ME5 .. 77 A1
ge Rd. Gillingham ME7 . 49 B5
ge Rd. Gravesend DA11 30 A8
ge Rd. Grays RM17 ..... 12 B8
ge Rd. Orpington BR6 .. 51 C8
ge Rd. Platt TN15 .... 87 C7
ge Rd. Rochester ME2 .. 47 B7
ge Rd. Rusthall TN4 ... 148 D4
ge Rd. Sevenoaks TN13 99 A8
ge Rd.
Michaels TN30 .... 172 F3
ge The.
t Malling ME19 .... 90 A7
ge The.
uth Darenth DA4 ...... 41 D8
ge The.
st Kingsdown TN15 ..... 55 F2
ge The.
esterham TN16 .... 81 C1
ge Way. Erith DA8 .... 9 B7
ge Way. Hartley DA3 .... 42 F3
ge Way.
hester ME1 .... 47 C3
gehill Pl. SE9 .... 5 F4
gehill Rd. SE9 .... 5 F3
gelands Cl. DA11 .... 29 F4
geywood. DA5 .... 24 F7
aite St. SE18 .... 2 F1
t Cl. ME7 .... 49 B1
t's Cotts. ME17 .... 111 B5
ton Rd. DA14 .... 24 C2
ville Ct. TN13 .... 84 A3
ville Mews. DA14 .... 24 A4
ville. Bexley DA6 .... 7 C4
ville Rd.
ingham ME7 .... 48 E5
ville Rd.
avesend DA11 .... 29 F7
ville Rd.
idstone ME14 .... 92 A6
ville Rd.
ral Tunbridge Wells
.... 149 C5

Granville Rd.
Sevenoaks TN13 .... 84 A3
Granville Rd. Sidcup DA14 .. 24 B4
Granville Rd.
Westerham TN16 .... 81 C1
Granville Sch The. TN13 .. 84 A4
Grapple Rd. ME14 .... 92 A7
Grasdene Rd. SE18 & SE2 .. 7 A7
Grasmere Ave. BR6 ...... 51 B7
Grasmere Gdns. BR6 .... 51 B7
Grasmere Gr. ME2 .... 33 C2
Grasmere Rd. Bexley DA7 .. 8 C5
Grasmere Rd.
Orpington BR6 .... 51 B7
Grassington Rd. DA14 ... 24 A4
Grasslands. ME17 .... 108 E4
Grassmere. ME20 .... 74 F2
Grassy Glade. ME7 .... 63 B6
Grassy La. TN13 .... 99 B8
Gravel Hill. DA6 .... 8 B2
Gravel Hill Cl. DA5 .... 8 B1
Gravel Hill Prim Sch. DA6 ... 8 B3
Gravel Pit Way. BR6 ..... 38 A1
Gravel Rd. Keston Mark BR2 50 E8
Gravel Rd.
Sutton at Hone DA4 ..... 27 B1
Gravel Wlk. ME1 .... 47 D5
Gravelly Bottom Rd.
ME17 .... 109 B2
Gravelly Ways. TN12 ... 120 D5
Gravelwood Cl. BR7 ..... 23 C5
Graveney Cl. ME3 .... 33 C7
Graveney Rd. ME15 .... 107 F7
Graves Est. DA14 .... 7 B5
Gravesend Gram Sch for Boys.
DA12 .... 30 A7
Gravesend Gram Sch for Girls.
Gravesend DA11 .... 30 A8
Gravesend Gram Sch for Girls.
Gravesend DA11 .... 13 A1
Gravesend Rd. Gadshill
ME2 & ME3 & DA12 ...... 32 C2
Gravesend Rd.
Rochester ME2 .... 46 F8
Gravesend Rd. Shorne DA12 31 D5
Gravesend Rd.
Vigo Village TN15 .... 72 D6
Gravesend Sta. DA11 ... 13 B1
Gravesham Ct. DA11 ..... 30 B8
Grayland Cl. BR1 .... 36 D8
Graylands. RM17 .... 11 E8
Grayne Ave. ME3 .... 21 B5
Grays Farm Prim Sch. BR5 . 38 B8
Grays Farm Production Village.
BR5 .... 38 B8
Grays Farm Rd. BR5 ...... 38 B8
Grays Rd. TN14 & TN16 . 81 D7
Grays Sh Ctr. RM17 ...... 12 A8
Grays Sta. RM17 .... 12 A8
Grazeley Cl. DA6 .... 8 C2
Great Basin Rd. ME12 ... 21 F2
Great Bounds Dr. TN4 .. 132 E3
Great Brooms Rd. TN4 .. 149 C8
Great Courtlands. TN3 .. 148 A3
Great Elms. TN11 .... 102 E1
Great Elms Rd. BR2 .... 36 C5
Great Footway. TN3 .... 147 F3
Great Hall Arc. ❸ TN1 . 149 B3
Great Harry Dr. SE9 ...... 23 A5
Great Ivy Mill Cotts.
ME15 .... 106 F7
Great Lines. ME7 .... 48 B5
Great Lodge Cotts. TN2 133 E2
Great Maytham Hall.
TN17 .... 181 F2
Great Oak. TN19 .... 184 A3
Great Queen St. DA1 ...... 9 F1
Great South Ave. ME4 ... 48 A1
Great Thrift. BR5 .... 37 C5
Greatness La. TN14 ...... 84 C6
Greatness Rd. TN13 & TN14 84 C6
Greatwood. BR7 .... 23 A1
Grebe Apartments. ❸
ME15 .... 107 E5
Grebe Cl. ME3 .... 19 C4
Grebe Ct. ME20 .... 74 F1
Grecian Rd. TN1 .... 149 B2
Grecian St. ME14 .... 92 A6
Green Acres. DA14 .... 23 F4
Green Bank Cl. ME7 ...... 63 A5
Green Cl. ME1 .... 47 D2
Green Court Rd. BR8 .... 39 D3
Green Farm Cl. BR6 ...... 51 F5
Green Farm La. DA12 ... 31 E5
Green Gdns. BR6 .... 51 C5
Green Hedges. TN30 ... 183 B8
Green Hill. Maidstone ME15 . 93 B1
Green Hill. Woolwich SE18 ... 1 F1
Green Hill La. ME17 .... 110 D1

Green La. Boughton Monchelsea
ME17 .... 107 C3
Green La. Cliffe ME3 ...... 16 B6
Green La.
Collier Street TN12 ..... 137 E8
Green La.
Devil's Den ME17 .... 124 B4
Green La. East End TN17 . 171 C2
Green La. Eltham BR7 & SE9 23 B5
Green La. Four Elms TN8 . 113 C7
Green La. Grain ME3 ..... 21 B5
Green La.
Langley Heath ME17 .... 108 E3
Green La.
Meopham Station DA13 . 44 B2
Green La.
Platt's Heath ME17 ..... 110 F2
Green La. Smarden TN27 . 143 A1
Green La. Stockbury ME9 .. 64 F1
Green La. Trottiscliffe ME19 . 73 A5
Green La. Withyham TN26 . 159 F3
Green La. The. TN11 .... 115 F1
Green Lands. DA13 ...... 44 D4
Green Lane Bsns Pk. SE9 ... 23 A6
Green Lane Cotts.
Collier Street TN12 ..... 121 D1
Green Lane Cotts.
Langley Heath ME17 .... 108 E3
Green Lawns. ❸ SE18 ..... 2 B2
Green Pl. DA1 .... 8 E2
Green Rd. TN12 .... 153 A6
Green Sands. ME14 ...... 77 C8
Green Sq. TN5 .... 174 F5
Green St. ME7 .... 48 C5
Green Street Green Prim Sch.
BR6 .... 51 F4
Green Street Green Rd.
DA1 .... 26 D1
Green The.
Bexley,Bexley Heath DA7 .. 8 A6
Green The.
Bexley,Falconwood DA16 .... 6 E3
Green The.
East Farleigh ME15 .... 106 B7
Green The. Hayes BR2 ... 36 A2
Green The.
Langton Green TN3 ..... 147 E3
Green The. Leigh TN11 .. 115 F1
Green The. Lewisham BR1 .. 22 A5
Green The. Sevenoaks TN13 84 D5
Green The. Sidcup DA14 . 24 A4
Green The.
St Paul's Cray BR5 .... 24 B1
Green The.
Westerham TN16 .... 81 D1
Green Vale. DA6 .... 7 D2
Green View Ave. TN11 .. 116 A1
Green Way. Bromley BR2 36 E3
Green Way. Eltham SE9 ... 5 D2
Green Way. Hartley DA3 . 42 E4
Green Way.
Maidstone ME16 .... 91 B3
Green Way. Royal Tunbridge Wells
TN2 .... 149 E8
Green Wlk. DA1 .... 8 F3
Green's Cotts. ME15 .... 106 A4
Greenacre. DA1 .... 26 D6
Greenacre Cl. Chatham ME5 62 A5
Greenacre Cl. Swanley BR8 . 39 E5
Greenacre Sch. ME5 ...... 61 F5
Greenacre. SE9 .... 6 A1
Greenacres Cl. BR6 ...... 51 C6
Greenacres Prim Sch & Language
Impairment Unit. SE9 .. 23 A6
Greenbank. ME5 .... 62 B8
Greenbank Lodge. ❷ BR7 . 37 A8
Greenbanks. DA1 .... 26 E6
Greenbay Rd. SE7 .... 5 D7
Greenborough Cl. ME15 107 E6
Greencourt Rd. BR6 ...... 37 E4
Greencroft Cl. E16 .... 1 D8
Greendale Wlk. ❹ DA11 . 29 E5
Greenfield. TN8 .... 112 D1
Greenfield Cl. Eccles ME20 .. 76 A6
Greenfield Cl.
Rusthall TN4 .... 148 C5
Greenfield Cotts. ME14 . 77 C3
Greenfield Gdns. BR5 ... 37 D2
Greenfield Rd.
Gillingham ME7 .... 48 D6
Greenfield Rd.
Joyden's Wood DA2 ..... 25 D3
Greenfields. ME15 ...... 107 E8
Greenfields Cl. ME3 ...... 33 D3
Greenfinches.
Gillingham ME7 .... 62 F6
Greenfinches.
New Barn DA3 .... 43 B6
Greenfrith Dr. TN10 .... 117 B6
Greenhill Cts. SE7 .... 1 F1
Greenhill La. TN27 ...... 143 F7

Greenhill Rd.
Northfleet DA11 .... 29 F6
Greenhill Rd. Otford TN14 . 69 C5
Greenhill Terr. SE18 .... 1 F1
Greenhithe. ❸ ME15 .... 92 A3
Greenhithe Cl. SE9 .... 23 E8
Greenhithe Sta. DA9 .... 11 A2
Greenholm Rd. SE9 .... 6 B2
Greening St. SE2 .... 3 C2
Greenlands. TN15 .... 87 C7
Greenlands Rd. TN15 .... 85 B8
Greenlaw St. SE18 .... 2 A3
Greenleas. TN2 .... 150 C6
Greenleigh Ave. BR5 .... 38 B5
Greens End. SE18 .... 2 B2
Greensand Rd. ME15 .... 93 A2
Greenshields Ind Est. E16 .. 1 B5
Greenside.
High Halden TN26 ...... 173 E7
Greenside. Maidstone ME15 92 B3
Greenside. Sidcup DA5 .. 24 E7
Greenside. Swanley BR8 . 39 D7
Greenslade Prim Sch. SE18 . 6 D8
Greentrees Ave. TN10 . 117 F5
Greenvale Gdns. ME8 ... 49 B2
Greenvale Rd. SE9 .... 6 A3
Greenview Cres. TN11 . 116 E4
Greenview Wlk. ME8 ..... 49 A4
Greenway. Chatham ME5 .. 61 D6
Greenway. Chislehurst BR7 .. 23 B3
Greenway.
Cranbrook TN17 .... 169 B4
Greenway Court Farm Cotts.
ME17 .... 95 A1
Greenway Court Rd. ME17 .. 95 A1
Greenway La. ME17 .... 110 A7
Greenway The. BR5 ...... 38 B3
Greenways.
Maidstone ME14 .... 92 F5
Greenways. New Barn DA3 .. 43 D6
Greenways The. TN12 .. 135 F5
Greenwich Cl.
Chatham ME5 .... 62 B4
Greenwich Cl.
Maidstone ME16 .... 91 B3
Greenwich Com Coll. SE9 .. 5 E1
Greenwich Cres. E6 .... 1 E8
Greenwich Educ Tuition Ctr
(Foxhill Ctr). SE18 .... 6 B8
Greenwich Ind Est. SE7 .. 1 B2
Greenwood Cl.
Orpington BR5 & BR6 ... 37 E3
Greenwood Cl. Sidcup DA14 23 A6
Greenwood House. ❸
RM17 .... 12 B8
Greenwood Pl. TN15 .... 72 A2
Greenwood Rd. DA5 ..... 25 D4
Greenwood Sch. SE18 .... 6 E6
Greenwood Way. TN13 .. 83 F2
Greggs Wood Rd.
TN1 & TN2 .... 149 E7
Gregor Mews. SE3 .... 5 A7
Gregory Cl. ME8 .... 63 E4
Gregory Cres. SE9 .... 22 D8
Gregory House. SE3 .... 5 B5
Grenada Rd. SE7 .... 5 C7
Grenadier St. E16 .... 2 A5
Grenville Cl. DA3 .... 58 A8
Gresham Ave. DA3 .... 42 F4
Gresham Cl. DA5 .... 7 F1
Gresham Rd.
Coxheath ME17 .... 106 D3
Gresham Rd. Hartley DA3 42 F5
Gresham Rd. Newham E16 .. 1 B7
Gresswell Cl. DA14 ...... 24 A5
Grey Wethers. ME14 .... 76 E4
Greybury La. TN8 .... 128 B3
Greyfriars Cl. ME16 ..... 91 D5
Greyhound Way. DA1 ..... 8 E1
Greys Park Cl. BR2 ...... 50 D5
Greystone Pk. TN14 ..... 82 E2
Greystones Cl.
TN14 & TN15 .... 69 E2
Greystones Rd. ME15 ... 93 A2
Greystone Bridge La. TN27 .. 172 B5
Grieves Rd. DA11 .... 29 F5
Grieveson House. ME14 .. 48 A4
Griffin Manor Sch. SE18 .. 6 E6
Griffin Manor Way. SE28 ... 2 D3
Griffin Rd. SE18 .... 2 D1
Griffin Way. SE28 .... 2 E3
Griffin Wlk. DA9 .... 10 F2
Griffiths House. ❷ SE18 .. 6 B8
Grigg La. TN27 .... 142 C7
Grigg's Cross. BR5 .... 38 D3
Griggs Way. TN15 .... 87 A7
Grinling House. ❻ SE18 .. 1 F2
Grizedale Cl. ME5 .... 61 D8
Gromenfield. TN3 .... 161 C7
Groombridge Cl. DA16 ... 7 A2
Groombridge Hill. TN3 . 147 D1

Groombridge Place. TN3 . 161 E3
Groombridge Rd. TN3 .. 147 A1
Groombridge Sq. ❸
ME15 .... 107 F6
Grosmont Rd. SE18 .... 2 F1
Grosvenor Ave. ME1 & ME4 . 47 E3
Grosvenor Bridge.
TN1 & TN4 .... 149 B5
Grosvenor Cres. DA1 ...... 9 D2
Grosvenor Pk. TN1 & TN4 . 149 A4
Grosvenor Rd. Bexley DA6 .. 7 E2
Grosvenor Rd. Erith DA17 .. 8 A8
Grosvenor Rd.
Gillingham ME7 .... 49 A1
Grosvenor Rd.
Orpington BR5 & BR6 ... 37 E3
Grosvenor Rd.
Royal Tunbridge Wells
TN1 .... 149 A4
Grosvenor Sq. DA3 .... 42 E6
Grove Ave. TN1 .... 149 A4
Grove Ave. TN1 .... 149 A2
Grove Cl. BR2 .... 50 A8
Grove Cotts. TN30 ...... 183 B6
Grove Green La. ME14 ... 92 E5
Grove Green Rd. ME14 .. 92 F5
Grove Hill Gdns. TN1 .. 149 B2
Grove Hill Rd. TN1 & TN2 . 149 B3
Grove Market Pl. SE9 ...... 5 F1
Grove Park Rd. SE12 & SE9 . 22 D6
Grove Park Sta. SE12 .... 22 B5
Grove Rd. Bexley DA7 ...... 8 C3
Grove Rd. Chatham ME4 . 48 B2
Grove Rd. ❸ Erith DA17 ... 7 F8
Grove Rd. Gillingham ME7 ... 49 A6
Grove Rd. Grays RM17 ... 12 C8
Grove Rd. Maidstone ME15 107 B2
Grove Rd. Northfleet DA11 . 12 B7
Grove Rd.
Penshurst TN11 & TN8 .. 130 C2
Grove Rd. Rochester ME2 .. 47 B8
Grove Rd. Seal TN15 ..... 85 B5
Grove Rd.
Sevenoaks TN13 & TN14 .. 84 C6
Grove Rd.
Upper Halling ME2 .... 59 E5
Grove The. Bexley DA6 .... 7 D3
Grove The. Gravesend DA11 30 B8
Grove The. Maidstone ME14 93 A3
Grove The. Pembury TN2 . 150 D8
Grove The. Sidcup DA14 .. 24 E4
Grove The. Swanley BR8 . 39 F6
Grove The.
Swanscombe DA10 .... 11 F2
Grove The.
West Kingsdown TN15 ... 55 F1
Grove Vale. BR7 .... 23 A2
Grove Wood Cotts. TN11 . 100 A1
Groveburry Cl. DA8 .... 8 D8
Groveburry Ct. DA6 .... 8 B2
Groveburry Rd. SE2 .... 3 B4
Grovehurst La. TN12 .... 153 C5
Grovelands. ME17 ...... 111 E5
Grovelands Rd. BR5 ...... 24 C1
Grovelands Way. RM17 ... 11 F8
Grover St. ❸ TN1 .... 149 B4
Groves The. ME6 .... 74 F7
Grovewood Dr. ME14 ..... 92 E4
Guardian Ct. ME8 .... 49 C1
Guardian Ind Est. TN12 . 138 C7
Guestwick. TN10 .... 117 F5
Guibal Rd. SE12 .... 22 B7
Guild Rd. Erith DA8 .... 8 F7
Guild Rd. Greenwich SE7 .. 5 D8
Guildford Gdns. ME2 .... 46 C6
Guildford Rd. Newham E6 .. 1 F7
Guildford Rd. ❼
Royal Tunbridge Wells
TN1 & TN2 .... 149 B3
Gullands. ME17 .... 108 E4
Gulliver Rd. DA15 .... 23 E6
Gumley Rd. RM16 .... 11 E8
Gumping Rd. BR5 .... 51 C8
Gun Hill. RM18 .... 13 D8
Gun La. Horsmonden TN12 153 A5
Gun La. Rochester ME2 .. 47 B7
Gundulph Rd. Bromley BR2 . 36 C6
Gundulph Rd.
Chatham ME1 & ME4 .... 47 E4
Gundulph Sq. ME1 .... 47 C6
Gunfleet Cl. DA12 .... 30 E8
Gunlands. TN12 .... 153 A6
Gunn Rd. DA10 .... 11 E1
Gunner La. SE18 .... 2 A1
Gunning St. SE18 .... 2 E2
Gunnis Cl. ME8 .... 63 D4
Gurdon Rd. SE7 .... 1 A1
Guston Rd. ME14 .... 92 C6

Guy Barnett Gr. SE3 .... 5 A4
Gwillim Cl. DA15 .... 7 A2
Gwynn Rd. DA11 .... 29 C6
Gybbon Rise. TN12 .... 139 E3
Gybbons Rd. TN17 .... 181 F3

Ha-Ha Rd. SE18 & SE7 .... 5 F8
Hackney Rd. ME16 .... 91 C2
Hadden Rd. SE28 .... 2 E3
Haddon Gr. DA15 .... 24 A8
Haddon Rd. BR5 .... 38 C4
Hadleigh Ct. ME7 .... 63 B3
Hadleigh Wlk. **1** E6 .... 1 E7
Hadley Cl. DA13 .... 58 B8
Hadley Ct. TN4 .... 148 F6
Hadley Gdns. ME17 .... 94 E2
Hadley House. BR5 .... 37 F7
Hadley Rd. DA17 .... 3 F2
Hadlow Coll of Agriculture &
  Horticulture. TN11 .... 118 D8
Hadlow City Prim Sch.
  TN11 .... 118 E8
Hadlow Pk. TN11 .... 102 E1
Hadlow Rd. Bexley DA16 .... 7 C7
Hadlow Rd.
  Maidstone ME14 .... 92 C5
Hadlow Rd. Sidcup DA14 ...... 24 A4
Hadlow Rd. Tonbridge TN9 117 D3
Hadlow Rd.Tonbridge,
  Higham Wood TN10 .... 118 A5
Hadlow Stair Rd. TN10 ...... 117 F4
Hadlow Way. DA13 .... 29 E1
Haffenden Cl. TN12 .... 138 D6
Haffenden Rd. TN30 .... 173 B1
Haig Ave. Chatham ME1 .... 47 D1
Haig Ave.
  Chatham,Luton ME4 .... 48 A2
Haig Ave. Gillingham ME7 .... 48 E4
Haig Ct. BR7 .... 23 B3
Haig Gdns. DA12 .... 30 C8
Haig Villas. ME3 .... 34 A5
Hailey Rd. DA18 .... 4 A4
Haileybury Rd. BR6 .... 52 A6
Hailstone Cl. TN11 .... 118 E8
Haimo Prim Sch. SE9 .... 5 D2
Haimo Rd. SE9 .... 5 D2
Hainault St. SE9 .... 23 B7
Halcot Ave. DA6 .... 8 C2
Haldane Gdns. DA11 .... 29 C7
Haldane Rd. SE28 .... 3 D6
Halden Cl. ME15 .... 107 F6
Halden La. TN17 .... 181 F6
Hale Cl. BR6 .... 51 C6
Hale Cotts. DA9 .... 11 C2
Hale Ct. TN12 .... 120 A7
Hale La. TN14 .... 68 F2
Hale Oak Rd.
  Hall's Green TN14 & TN8 . 114 E4
Hale Oak Rd.
  Sevenoaks Weald TN14 ..... 99 B1
Hale Rd. ME3 .... 33 C7
Hale St. TN12 .... 120 A7
Hales Cl. TN30 .... 183 B8
Hales Ct. TN30 .... 183 B8
Haleys Pl. ME1 .... 76 A8
Half Moon La. TN11 .... 116 D6
Halfpence La. DA12 .... 45 B7
Halfpenny Cl. ME16 .... 91 A2
Halfway St. DA15 .... 23 E7
Halifax Cl. ME5 .... 62 B6
Halifield Dr. DA17 .... 4 A2
Hall Hill. TN15 .... 85 C4
Hall Place Cres. DA1 & DA5 ... 8 D2
Hall Rd. Aylesford ME20 ...... 75 F1
Hall Rd. Chatham ME5 .... 62 C3
Hall Rd. Dartford DA1 .... 9 F3
Hall Rd. Northfleet,Pepper Hill
  DA11 &DA13 .... 29 C5
Hall Rd. Northfleet,Wombwell Park
  DA11 .... 29 D6
Hall Rd. St Mary Hoo ME3 ... 18 C6
Hall Rd. Wouldham ME1 .... 60 C3
Hall The. SE3 .... 5 A4
Hall View. SE9 .... 22 C8
Hall's Grove Rd. TN2 .... 149 D2
Hall's Hole Rd. TN2 .... 149 E4
Hallam Cl. BR7 .... 22 F3
Hallford Way. DA1 .... 9 C2
Hallgate. SE3 .... 5 A4
Halling Cty Prim Sch. ME2 .. 59 F5
Halling Sta. ME2 .... 60 A5
Halls Cotts. TN5 .... 174 F5
Hallsfield Rd. ME15 .... 61 D2
Hallsville Prim Sch. E16 .... 1 A7
Hallwards. TN12 .... 139 F2
Hallwood Cl. ME8 .... 63 D5
Hallwood House. ME5 .... 62 C2
Hallywell Cres. E6 .... 1 F8

Halons Rd. SE9 .... 23 A8
Halsbrook Rd. SE3 .... 5 D8
Halstead Cty Prim Sch.
  TN14 .... 67 F7
Halstead La. TN14 .... 67 E5
Halstead Place Sch. TN14 ... 67 E8
Halstead Rd. DA8 .... 8 E6
Halstead Wlk. ME16 .... 91 C7
Halstow Cl. ME15 .... 107 B6
Halstow Prim Sch. SE10 .... 1 A1
Halstow Rd. SE10 & SE3 .... 1 A1
Halt Robin La. DA17 .... 4 B2
Halt Robin Rd. Erith DA17 ..... 4 A2
Halt Robin Rd. Erith DA17 ..... 4 B2
Ham La. Gillingham ME5 ...... 62 B7
Ham La. Lenham ME17 .... 111 C5
Ham River Hill. ME3 .... 33 A6
Ham Shades Cl. **1** DA15 ... 24 A5
Hamble Rd. TN10 .... 117 B5
Hambledon Cl. ME16 .... 91 B3
Hambledown Rd. SE9 .... 23 E8
Hambro Ave. BR2 .... 36 A1
Hamble Rd. ME7 .... 48 B8
Hamerton Rd. DA11 .... 12 B2
Hamilton Cl. TN4 .... 149 A5
Hamilton House.
  Coxheath ME17 .... 106 C3
Hamilton House.
  Royal Tunbridge Wells
  TN4 .... 149 A5
Hamilton Rd. Bexley DA7 ...... 7 E5
Hamilton Rd.
  Gillingham ME7 .... 48 D7
Hamilton Rd. Sidcup DA15 ... 24 A4
Hamilton Wlk. DA8 .... 8 F7
Hamlea Cl. SE12 .... 5 A2
Hamlet House. Eltham SE9 .... 6 A2
Hamlet House. **5** Erith DA8 . 8 E7
Hamlin Rd. TN13 .... 83 E6
Hamlyn Cl. TN13 .... 83 E6
Hammelton Rd. BR1 .... 36 A8
Hammerwood Pk. RH19 .... 144 C2
Hammond Way. **2** SE28 ...... 3 B6
Hammonds. **9** TN18 .... 179 A2
Hammonds Sq. ME6 .... 75 A8
Hamond Hill. ME4 .... 47 E4
Hampden Way. ME19 .... 88 F3
Hampshire Cl. ME5 .... 62 C7
Hampshire Dr. ME15 .... 107 C8
Hampson Way. ME14 .... 93 A4
Hampstead Cl. SE28 .... 3 B5
Hampstead La. ME18 .... 104 C1
Hampton Cl. ME5 .... 62 A5
Hampton Cotts. TN14 .... 67 F4
Hampton Cres. DA12 .... 30 E6
Hampton House. DA7 .... 8 B5
Hampton Rd. ME14 .... 92 C6
Hamptons Rd. TN11 .... 102 B5
Hamwick Gn. ME5 .... 62 C1
Hanameel St. E16 .... 1 B5
Hanbury Cl. ME18 .... 104 E7
Hanbury Wlk. DA5 .... 25 E5
Handel Cres. RM18 .... 13 A7
Handel Wlk. TN10 .... 117 E6
Hands Wlk. E16 .... 1 A7
Hang Grove Hill. BR6 .... 66 B6
Hangmans Cnr. BR7 .... 37 B8
Hanmer Way. TN12 .... 139 E2
Hanover Ave. E16 .... 1 A5
Hanover La. ME14 .... 92 B5
Hanover Dr. Chislehurst BR7 23 C4
Hanover Dr. Gillingham ME8 63 C4
Hanover Gn. ME20 .... 74 F3
Hanover Pl. DA3 .... 56 F8
Hanover Rd.
  Coxheath ME17 .... 106 C3
Hanover Rd. Royal Tunbridge Wells
  TN1 .... 149 A4
Hanover Way. DA7 .... 7 D4
Hansol Rd. DA6 .... 7 E2
Hansom Terr. **1** BR1 .... 36 B8
Hanway. ME8 .... 49 A2
Harbex Cl. DA5 .... 25 B8
Harbledown Manor. ME8 .... 49 B3
Harbledown Pl. **7** BR5 .... 38 C5
Harborough Ave. DA15 .... 23 F8
Harbour The. ME17 .... 124 E5
Harbourland Cl. ME14 .... 92 B8
Harbourne La.
  TN26 & TN30 .... 173 E5
Harcourt Ave. DA5 & DA15 .. 24 C8
Harcourt Gdns. ME8 .... 63 E4
Harcourt Rd. DA6 & DA7 .... 7 E3
Harden Cl. **1** SE7 .... 1 E2
Harden Rd. DA11 .... 29 F6
Hardens Manorway. SE18 ...... 1 D2
Hardie Cl. ME19 .... 74 F1
Harding House. **16** SE18 ...... 1 F2
Harding Rd. DA7 .... 8 A4
Hardinge Ave. TN4 .... 132 E3
Hardinge Cl. ME8 .... 63 D4

Hardinge St. SE18 .... 2 C3
Hardman Rd. SE7 .... 1 B1
Hardres Terr. BR5 .... 52 D8
Hards Town. ME4 .... 48 A4
Hardwick Cres. DA2 .... 10 B1
Hardwick Ct. DA8 .... 8 D8
Hardwick House. **1**
  ME15 .... 107 E8
Hardwick Rd. TN11 .... 116 E6
Hardy Ave. DA11 .... 29 E6
Hardy Cl. ME5 .... 62 B6
Hardy Gr. DA1 .... 10 A3
Hardy Rd. **2** SE3 .... 5 A5
Hardy St. ME14 .... 92 A6
Hare St. **2** Chatham ME4 .... 48 B3
Hare St. Woolwich SE18 .... 2 A3
Hardwell Cl. **3**
  Chatham ME5 .... 61 F4
Harebell Cl.
  Maidstone ME14 .... 92 E5
Harebell Dr. E6 .... 2 A8
Haredale Cl. ME1 .... 61 D7
Harefield Rd. DA14 .... 24 B5
Harenc Sch Trust. DA14 ...... 24 C3
Harescroft. TN2 .... 162 F7
Harfst Way. BR8 .... 39 C6
Hargate Cl. TN2 .... 162 F8
Hargood Rd. SE3 .... 5 C6
Harland Ave. DA15 .... 23 E6
Harland Rd. SE12 .... 22 A7
Harland Way. TN4 .... 132 F4
Harlands Gr. BR6 .... 51 B6
Harlech Cl. ME2 .... 32 F1
Harlequin House. **1** DA18 ... 3 E3
Harley Gdns. BR6 .... 51 E6
Harleyford. BR1 .... 36 C8
Harlington Rd. DA7 .... 7 E4
Harman Ave. DA11 .... 30 B3
Harman Ct. ME5 .... 62 B3
Harman Dr. DA15 .... 6 F1
Harmer Ct. TN4 .... 133 A2
Harmer Rd. DA10 .... 11 F1
Harmer St. DA11 .... 13 C1
Harness Rd. SE28 .... 3 A4
Harmony St. TN4 .... 148 D4
Harness Rd. SE28 .... 3 A4
Harold Ave. Erith DA17 .... 3 F1
Harold Ave.
  Gillingham ME7 .... 48 E4
Harold Gibbons Ct. **12** SE7 .. 5 C8
Harold Rd. Cuxton ME2 .... 46 C3
Harold Rd. Hawley DA2 .... 26 F4
Harp Farm Rd. ME14 .... 77 C6
Harper Rd. E6 .... 1 F7
Harple La. ME14 .... 77 F5
Harpswood. ME17 .... 94 F1
Harptree Dr. ME5 .... 61 F5
Harraden Rd. SE3 .... 5 C6
Harrier Mews. SE28 .... 2 D4
Harrier Way. E6 .... 1 F8
Harriers Rd. TN1 & TN2 ..... 149 E7
Harrietsham Sta. ME17 ...... 110 D6
Harrington Way. SE18 .... 1 D3
Harris Cl. DA11 .... 29 F5
Harris Rd. DA7 .... 7 F6
Harrison Dr. ME23 .... 17 E4
Harrison Rd. TN15 .... 86 F7
Harrison Way. TN13 .... 84 A5
Harrow Cl. TN8 .... 112 D3
Harrow Ct. Chatham ME5 ..... 62 C4
Harrow Ct. Stockbury ME9 ... 79 D8
Harrow Gdns. BR6 .... 52 B6
Harrow Manor Way. SE2 .... 3 C3
Harrow Rd. Gillingham ME7 . 62 F6
Harrow Rd.
  Knockholt Pound TN14 ..... 67 E4
Harrow Way. ME14 .... 92 F5
Harrowby Gdns. DA11 .... 29 E6
Hart Dyke Cres. BR8 .... 39 D6
Hart Dyke Rd.
  Orpington BR5 .... 38 C1
Hart Dyke Rd. Swanley BR8 . 39 D6
Hart Shaw. DA3 .... 43 B7
Hart St. ME16 .... 91 F3
Hart St Commercial Ctr.
  ME16 .... 91 F3
Hartfield Cl. TN10 .... 117 E5
Hartfield Cres. BR4 .... 50 A7
Hartfield Pl. DA11 .... 29 D8
Hartfield Rd. Hayes BR4 ...... 50 A6
Hartfield Rd. Stick Hill TN8 129 A4
Hartford Rd. DA5 .... 8 A1
Hartford Wlk. **12** DA17 .... 4 A1
Harting Rd. SE9 .... 22 E5
Hartington Cl. BR6 .... 51 C5
Hartington Rd. E16 .... 1 B7
Hartington St. ME4 .... 48 A3
Hartlake Rd. TN11 .... 118 D3
Hartlands Cl. DA5 .... 7 F1
Hartley Bottom Rd. DA3 ...... 43 C2
Hartley Cl. Bromley BR1 ...... 36 F7

Hartley Cl.
  Maidstone ME15 .... 107 F6
Hartley Court Gdns. TN17 .. 169 A3
Hartley Cty Prim Sch. DA3 .. 42 E3
Hartley Hill. DA3 .... 43 A1
Hartley Rd. Bexley DA16 .... 7 C7
Hartley Rd. Hartley TN17 ... 169 A3
Hartley Rd. Longfield DA3 .. 42 E7
Hartley Rd.
  Westerham TN16 .... 81 D2
Hartlip Endowed CE Prim Sch.
  ME9 .... 64 D5
Hartlip Hill. ME9 .... 64 F7
Hartmann Rd. E16 .... 1 E5
Hartnokes. TN18 .... 179 A2
Hartnup St. ME16 .... 91 C2
Harton Cl. BR1 .... 36 D8
Hartpiece Cl. ME8 .... 49 F2
Hartshill Rd. DA11 .... 29 F6
Hartsland Rd. TN13 .... 84 C4
Hartslock Dr. SE2 .... 3 D4
Hartsmead Rd. SE9 .... 22 F6
Hartville Rd. SE18 .... 2 E2
Hartwell House. **2** SE7 .... 1 B1
Harty Ave. ME8 .... 63 C3
Harvard Ct. **8** SE9 .... 6 A1
Harvel Ave. ME2 .... 46 F7
Harvel Ct. BR5 & BR7 .... 38 A6
Harvel Cres. SE2 .... 3 D1
Harvel La. DA13 .... 58 B2
Harvel Rd. DA13 .... 73 A8
Harvel St. DA13 .... 58 C3
Harvest Bank Rd. BR4 .... 50 A7
Harvest Rd. TN10 .... 117 D6
Harvest Ridge. ME19 .... 74 D2
Harvest Way. BR8 .... 39 D2
Harvesters Cl. ME8 .... 63 E7
Harvesters Way. ME14 .... 92 D4
Harvey Gdns. SE7 .... 1 C1
Harvey Point. **9** E16 .... 1 A8
Harvey Rd. ME8 .... 63 E8
Harvill Rd. DA14 .... 24 E3
Harwood Ave. BR1 .... 36 B7
Harwood Ct. **3** RM17 .... 12 C8
Haslemere Est. ME15 .... 107 F5
Haslemere Rd. DA7 .... 8 A5
Hasler Cl. SE28 .... 3 C5
Hasletts Cl. TN4 .... 149 B6
Haslewood Cl. TN27 .... 143 B2
Hassendean Rd. SE3 & SE7 .. 5 B7
Hassock Wood. BR2 .... 50 E6
Hassop Wlk. SE9 .... 22 E4
Haste Hill Cl. ME17 .... 107 B3
Haste Hill Rd. ME17 .... 107 B3
Hasted Cl. DA9 .... 11 C1
Hasted Rd. Greenwich SE7 ... 1 D1
Hasted Rd. Newington ME9 .. 65 B7
Hasteds. ME17 .... 94 D2
Hastings House. **11** SE18 .... 1 F2
Hastings Rd.
  Keston Mark BR2 .... 50 E8
Hastings Rd.
  Maidstone ME15 .... 92 B3
Hastings Rd.
  Newenden TN17 & TN18 ... 187 C6
Hastings Rd. Pembury TN2 150 D6
Hastings Rd.
  The Moor TN18 .... 184 F6
Hastings St. SE18 .... 2 C3
Hatch Rd. ME17 .... 111 C5
Hatches La. TN11 & TN12 . 119 D6
Hatfield Cl. SE3 .... 5 A7
Hatfield Rd. ME2 .... 47 A8
Hatham Green La. TN15 ...... 56 D1
Hathaway Cl. BR2 .... 36 F1
Hathaway Ct.
  Gillingham ME8 .... 63 D8
Hathaway Ct.
  Rochester ME1 .... 47 B5
Hatherall Rd. ME14 .... 92 B6
Hatherley Cress. DA14 .... 24 A6
Hatherley Rd. DA14 .... 24 A5
Hatten Gdns. SE9 .... 23 A4
Hattersfield Cl. DA17 .... 3 F2
Hatton Cl. Northfleet DA11 .. 29 E5
Hatton Cl. Woolwich SE18 .... 6 D7
Hatton Ct. BR7 .... 22 E1
Hatton Rd. ME5 .... 62 C3
Havant Wlk. **8** ME15 .... 107 F6
Havelock Rd. Bromley BR2 .. 36 C5
Havelock Rd. Dartford DA1 .... 9 B1
Havelock Rd. Erith DA17 .... 3 F2
Havelock Rd.
  Gravesend DA11 .... 29 F7
Havelock Rd.
  Tonbridge TN9 .... 117 B2
Haven Cl. Chislehurst SE9 ... 22 F5

Haven Cl. Istead Rise DA13 .
Haven Cl. Rochester ME1 .....
Haven Cl. Sidcup DA14 ....
Haven Cl. Swanley BR8 ....
Haven Hill. TN15 ....
Haven Lodge. **7** SE18 ....
Haven Way. ME4 ....
Havengore Ave. DA12 ....
Haverstock Ct. **2** BR5 ....
Haverthwaite Rd. BR6 ....
Havisham Cl. ME1 ....
Havisham Rd. DA12 ....
Havock La. **1** ME14 ....
Hawbeck Rd. ME8 ....
Hawden Cl. TN11 ....
Hawden La. TN11 ....
Hawden Rd. TN9 ....
Hawes Rd. BR1 ....
Hawfield Bank. BR6 ....
Hawkenbury Ct. TN2 ....
Hawkenbury Mead. TN2 ... 1
Hawkenbury Rd.
  Hawkenbury TN12 ....
Hawkenbury Rd.
  Royal Tunbridge Wells
  TN2 & TN3 ....
Hawkes Cl. RM17 ....
Hawkes Rd. ME20 ....
Hawkhurst CE Prim Sch.
Hawkhurst TN18 ....
Hawkhurst CE Prim Sch.
  The Moor TN18 ....
Hawkhurst Cottage Hospl.
  TN18 ....
Hawkhurst Rd. Flimwell
  TN18 & TN19 & TN5 ....
Hawkhurst Rd.
  Gillingham ME8 ....
Hawkhurst Rd.
  Hartley TN17 & TN18 .....
Hawkinge Wlk. BR5 ....
Hawkins Ave. DA12 ....
Hawkins Cl. ME4 ....
Hawksmoor Cl. **2**
  Newham E6 ....
Hawksmoor Cl.
  Woolwich SE18 ....
Hawksmoor Prim Sch. SE28
Hawkwell Cotts. TN2 ....
Hawkwood Cl. ME16 ....
Hawkwood La. ME1 ....
Hawkwood La. BR7 ....
Hawley Cl. ME16 ....
Hawley Rd. DA1,DA2 & DA4 .
Hawley Terr. DA2 ....
Hawley Vale. DA2 ....
Hawser Rd. ME1 ....
Hawthorn La. BR6 ....
Hawthorn Cl.
  Edenbridge TN8 1
Hawthorn Cl.
  Gravesend DA12 ....
Hawthorn Cl. Orpington BR5
Hawthorn House. **5** ME5 ...
Hawthorn Pl. DA8 ....
Hawthorn Rd. Bexley DA6 ...
Hawthorn Rd. Dartford DA1 .
Hawthorn Rd.
  Rochester ME2 ....
Hawthorn Terr. DA15 ....
Hawthorn Wlk.
  Royal Tunbridge Wells
  TN2 1
Hawthorn Wlk.
  Tonbridge TN10 1
Hawthorndene Cl. BR2 ....
Hawthorndene Rd. BR2 ......
Hawthorne Ave. ME8 ....
Hawthorne Cl. BR1 ....
Hawthorne Rd. BR1 ....
Hawthorns. Chatham ME5 ...
Hawthorns. Hartley DA3 .....
Hawthorns. The. ME20 ....
Haxted Rd. BR1 ....
Hay's Mead. DA13 ....
Hayday Rd. E16 ....
Hayday Cl. BR5 ....
Haydens Mews. TN9 ....
Haydens The. TN9 1
Hayes Cl. Hayes BR2 ....
Hayes Cl. Higham ME3 ....
Hayes Cl.
  West Thurrock RM16 ....
Hayes Garden. BR2 ....
Hayes La. Hayes BR2 ....
Hayes La. Stockbury ME9 ....
Hayes Prim Sch. BR2 ....
Hayes Rd. Hayes BR2 ....
Hayes Rd. Stone DA2 ....

Sch. BR2 50 B8
St. BR2 36 B1
Sta. BR2 36 A1
Terr. DA12 31 E3
Wood Ave. BR2 36 B1
brook Sch. TN9 133 A8
den La.
& TN3 & TN4 132 B5
ford Park Dr. BR2 36 A4
eld. ME19 74 E2
eld Rd. BR5 38 A4
elds. ME5 62 D2
Mill Cotts. ME15 106 F8
Mill Rd. ME15 106 F8
Rd. ME15 92 A3
Cl. ME2 46 C2
an Wlk. ME20 75 F6
ans Hill. TN12 153 C7
en St. ME4 47 E3
es Rd. DA11 29 F5
ck Cl. ME14 92 E5
Rd. ME6 74 F6
den Ctry Pk. TN11 132 D8
ain Cl.
dstone ME14 92 F4
ain Cl.
ock Wood TN12 136 A5
ard Ave. ME2 47 B8
ard Cl. DA1 8 D2
ard Dr. DA1 26 F6
ood Rd. BR2 36 D5
ood Rise. BR6 51 E5
Ave.
St Werburgh ME3 34 E3
Ave. Maidstone ME16 91 C5
Cotts. TN14 68 A6
Dr. DA8 9 B6
End. BR8 39 E4
Gr. Chatham ME5 62 B8
Gr. Orpington BR6 51 B8
Rd. Dartford DA1 26 D6
Rd. Erith DA8 9 A6
Shaw. TN10 117 D7
Street Rd. ME9 80 A4
Wlk. BR2 37 A3
bank. TN3 147 F3
den Cl. TN15 56 A2
dene Rd. DA16 7 C5
mere Rd. BR5 37 D5
mere Way. BR2 36 A3
s The. ME8 63 B5
wood Cl. TN2 149 E8
wood Cotts. TN5 176 D1
wood Dr. ME16 91 B4
wood Rd. TN14 66 D8
mere Dr. ME7 49 A5
t Ct. 4 SE28 3 C5
t Dr. ME16 91 D5
Race The. ME15 91 D2
corn Cty Prim Sch.
7 141 C5
corn Rd. Bromley BR1 22 A3
corn Rd.
ngham ME8 49 B4
corn Rd.
's Heath ME17 110 F1
corn Rd.
rden Bell TN27 142 C3
corn Rd.
nden TN27 158 A5
corn Rd.
lehurst TN12 140 B4
corn Rd.
Harbour ME17 124 E4
corn Rd.
mbe ME17 125 F5
corn Sta. TN27 141 D4
ingley Rd. ME16 91 B6
ley Ct. TN8 112 C2
ley House. 5 BR5 38 B7
Dr. 1 BR6 51 F6
sill La. TN18 184 E8
ns Cl. BR5 38 C5
ns Rd. BR5 38 C5
ns Rise. BR5 38 D5
enoak Rd. TN18 179 B3
Ave. DA7 7 D8
Cl. Orpington BR5 38 C3
Cl. Swanley BR8 39 E7
Gdns. DA1 26 C7
Gr. ME16 91 A2
House. DA15 23 F4
La. Dartford DA1 26 C7
La. Dartford,Dartford Heath
26 B7
Park Dr. BR1 36 E6
Rd. Coldblow DA5 25 C7
Rd. Coxheath ME17 106 C3
Rd. Crayford DA1 8 F1
Rd.
gley Heath ME17 108 E4

Heath Rd. Maidstone ME16 90 F3
Heath Rise. BR2 36 A3
Heath Side. BR5 37 C2
Heath St. DA1 26 D8
Heath Terr. TN12 153 A6
Heath The. ME19 89 F5
Heath View Dr. SE2 7 D8
Heath Villas. SE18 2 F1
Heath Way. DA7 & DA8 8 D6
Heathclose Ave. DA1 26 B8
Heathclose Rd. DA1 26 B7
Heathcote Cl. ME20 75 F2
Heathdene Dr. DA17 4 B2
Heathend Rd. DA5 25 E7
Heather Cl. Chatham ME5 61 F4
Heather Cl. Newham E6 2 A7
Heather Dr. Dartford DA1 26 A8
Heather Dr.
Maidstone ME15 92 B2
Heather Dr.
St Michaels TN30 173 B3
Heather End. BR8 39 D5
Heather Rd. SE12 22 A7
Heather Wlk. TN10 117 B6
Heatherbank.
Chislehurst BR7 37 A7
Heatherbank. Eltham SE9 5 F5
Heatherbank Cl. DA1 8 E1
Heatherside Rd. DA14 24 C5
Heatherwood Cl. ME17 109 E2
Heathfield. Chislehurst BR7 23 C2
Heathfield.
Langley Heath ME17 108 E4
Heathfield Ave. ME14 92 C7
Heathfield Cl. Chatham ME5 62 B7
Heathfield Cl. Keston BR2 50 C5
Heathfield Cl.
Maidstone ME14 92 B7
Heathfield Cl. Newham E16 1 D8
Heathfield Ct. DA14 24 B3
Heathfield La. BR7 23 C2
Heathfield Rd. Bexley DA6 7 F3
Heathfield Rd. Keston BR2 50 D5
Heathfield Rd.
Maidstone ME14 92 C7
Heathfield Rd.
Sevenoaks TN13 83 F5
Heathfield Terr.
Swanley BR8 39 D7
Heathfield Terr.
Woolwich SE18 6 F8
Heathfields. TN2 149 D4
Heathlands Rise. DA1 9 B1
Heathlee Rd. DA1 8 E1
Heathley End. BR7 23 C2
Heathorn St. ME14 92 B5
Heathside Ave. Bexley DA7 7 E5
Heathside Ave.
Coxheath ME17 106 C4
Heathview. TN4 132 F2
Heathview Ave. DA1 8 E1
Heathview Cres. DA1 26 B7
Heathway. SE3 5 A7
Heathwood Gdns.
Swanley BR8 39 C7
Heathwood Gdns.
Woolwich SE7 1 E1
Heathwood Wlk. DA5 25 E7
Heaverham Rd. TN15 70 C2
Heavitree Cl. SE18 2 D1
Heavitree Rd. SE18 2 D1
Hector St. SE18 2 E2
Hectorage Rd. TN9 133 D8
Hedge Place Rd. DA9 11 A1
Hedgerow The. ME14 92 E5
Hedgerows The. DA11 29 E6
Hedges The. ME14 92 A7
Hedley Ave. RM16 11 C8
Hedley St. ME14 92 A5
Heights The. SE7 1 C1
Helen Allison Sch The.
DA13 44 A2
Helen Cl. DA1 26 B8
Helen Keller Ct. TN10 117 D4
Helen St. SE18 2 B2
Helverswood. TN14 53 A2
Hemmings Cl. DA14 24 B6
Hempstead Cty Jun Sch.
ME7 63 A5
Hempstead Cty Prim Sch.
ME7 63 A5
Hempstead Rd.
Gillingham ME7 63 A5
Hempstead Rd.
Gillingham ME7 63 B6
Hempstead Valley Dr. ME7 63 A4
Hempstead Valley Sh Ctr.
ME7 63 A3
Hemsted Rd. DA8 8 E7
Henbane Cl. ME14 92 E5
Henderson Dr. DA1 10 A3

Hendley Dr. TN17 169 C5
Hendry House. ME3 33 F6
Hendy Rd. ME6 75 B8
Henfield Cl. DA5 8 A1
Hengist Rd. Eltham SE12 22 B8
Hengist Rd. Erith DA8 8 C7
Hengrove Ct. DA5 24 E7
Henham Gdns. TN12 120 A6
Henhurst Hill. DA13 44 D8
Henhurst Rd.
Gravesend DA13 30 E1
Henhurst Rd.
Henhurst DA12 44 E8
Heniker La. ME17 125 A4
Henley Bsns Pk. ME2 47 D7
Henley Cl. Chatham ME5 62 A6
Henley Cl. Gillingham ME8 63 D8
Henley Cl. Royal Tunbridge Wells
TN2 149 C4
Henley Deane. DA11 29 E4
Henley Fields.
Maidstone ME14 92 E6
Henley Fields.
St Michaels TN30 173 B2
Henley Meadows. TN30 173 A2
Henley Rd. Newham E16 1 F4
Henley Rd.
Paddock Wood TN12 136 A7
Henley St. DA13 44 F3
Henley View. TN30 173 B2
Henniker Cotts. TN17 169 A3
Henry Cooper Way. SE12 22 D4
Henry St. Bromley BR1 36 B8
Henry St. Chatham ME4 48 B3
Henry St. 9 Grays RM17 12 C8
Henson Cl. BR6 51 B8
Henville Rd. BR1 36 B8
Henwick Prim Sch. SE9 5 E4
Henwick Rd. SE9 5 E4
Henwood Green Rd.
TN12 & TN2 150 E6
Henwoods Cres. TN2 150 D6
Henwoods Mount. TN2 150 E6
Herald Wlk. DA1 9 F2
Herbert Pl. SE18 6 B8
Herbert Rd. Bexley DA7 7 E5
Herbert Rd. Bromley BR2 36 E4
Herbert Rd. Chatham ME4 48 A3
Herbert Rd. Gillingham ME8 63 E8
Herbert Rd. Hextable BR8 26 B2
Herbert Rd.
Swanscombe DA10 11 F1
Herbert Rd. Woolwich SE18 6 B8
Herdsdown. ME3 34 D5
Hereford Cl. ME8 49 D2
Hereford House. 7 SE18 1 F2
Hereford Rd. ME15 107 D7
Heritage Dr. ME7 48 F1
Heritage Hill. BR2 50 C5
Heritage Rd. ME5 62 A6
Heritage The. BR6 38 A2
Herman Terr. ME4 48 A3
Hermitage Ct. ME16 90 F5
Hermitage La. Detling
ME14 78 B4
Hermitage La.
Maidstone ME16 & ME20 90 F6
Hermitage La.
Rabbit's Cross ME17 123 E6
Hermitage Rd. ME3 32 E4
Herne Rd. ME8 49 C2
Hero Wlk. ME1 61 C7
Heron Apartments. 3
ME15 107 F5
Heron Cl. TN8 112 C3
Heron Cotts. TN18 187 D3
Heron Cres. DA14 23 E4
Heron Ct. BR2 36 C5
Heron Hill. DA17 3 F2
Heron Hill La. DA13 58 A4
Heron Rd. ME20 74 F1
Heron Way. Chatham ME5 62 B7
Heron Way.
Lower Stoke ME3 19 C4
Heronden Rd. ME15 107 F4
Herongate Rd. BR8 25 E2
Herons Way. TN2 150 E8
Heronsgate Prim Sch. SE28 2 D3
Herringham Rd. SE7 1 C3
Herts Cres. ME15 106 F3
Hervey Rd. SE3 & SE7 5 B6
Hesketh Ave. DA2 27 B7
Heskett Pk. TN2 150 E6
Hever Ave. TN15 55 E4
Hever Castle. TN8 129 D7
Hever CE Prim Sch. TN8 129 D6
Hever Cl. ME15 107 F6
Hever Court Rd. DA12 30 D2
Hever Croft. Eltham SE9 23 A4
Hever Croft. Rochester ME2 46 F5
Hever Gdns. Bromley BR1 37 A7

Hever Gdns.
Maidstone ME16 91 E3
Hever Hotel & Golf Club.
TN8 113 D1
Hever House. ME2 33 C1
Hever Rd. Hever TN8 129 B7
Hever Rd.
West Kingsdown TN15 55 E4
Hever Road Cotts. TN8 113 E2
Hever Sta. TN8 129 B6
Hever Wood Rd. TN15 55 E4
Heverham Rd. SE18 2 E2
Heversham Rd. DA7 8 A6
Hewett House. 7 SE18 2 B1
Hewett Pl. BR8 39 D5
Hewitt Cl. ME7 48 F6
Hewitts Rd. BR6 & TN14 52 F3
Hextable Cl. ME16 91 D7
Hextable Cty Inf Sch. BR8 25 F2
Hextable Cty Jun Sch. BR8 25 F2
Hextable Sch. BR8 39 F8
Hibbs Cl. BR8 39 D7
Hibernia Dr. DA12 30 F5
Hibernia Point. 11 SE2 3 D4
Hickin Cl. SE7 1 D2
Hickman Cl. E16 1 D8
Hickory Dell. ME7 63 A5
Hide. E6 2 A7
Higgins' La. ME4 47 F5
High Banks. Loose ME15 106 F5
High Banks. Rochester ME1 47 D2
High Beeches.
Orpington BR6 52 A4
High Beeches.
Royal Tunbridge Wells
TN2 149 D6
High Beeches. Sidcup DA14 24 E3
High Broom Ind Pk. TN4 149 C8
High Brooms Rd. TN4 149 C7
High Brooms Sta. TN1 149 C7
High Croft Cotts. BR8 40 A5
High Cross Rd. TN15 86 B1
High Dewar Rd. ME8 64 A8
High Elms. ME8 49 E1
High Elms Public Golf Course.
BR6 51 D3
High Elms Rd. BR6 51 C2
High Firs. BR8 39 E5
High Firs Cty Prim Sch.
BR8 39 F5
High Gr. Bromley BR1 36 D8
High Gr. Woolwich SE18 6 D6
High Halden Parochial
CE Prim Sch. TN26 173 E7
High Halden Rd. TN27 158 C2
High Halstow Cty Prim Sch.
ME23 17 E3
High Hilden Cl. TN11 117 A4
High House La. TN11 102 C2
High Meads Rd. E16 1 D7
High Oak Hill. ME9 65 D8
High Point. SE9 23 B5
High Rd. DA2 26 C5
High Ridge. TN17 167 E8
High Rocks. TN3 148 B1
High Rocks La. TN3 & TN4 148 C1
High St. Aylesford ME20 75 F3
High St. Bean DA2 28 B5
High St. Bidborough TN4 132 C3
High St. Biddenden TN27 157 F1
High St.
Borough Green TN15 86 F7
High St.
Brasted TN14 & TN16 82 C3
High St. Brenchley TN12 152 B8
High St. Bromley BR1 36 A7
High St. Chatham ME4 47 E4
High St. Chatham ME4 48 A4
High St. Cowden TN8 145 B5
High St. Cranbrook TN17 169 C4
High St. Dartford DA1 9 E1
High St. Downe BR6 66 A8
High St. East Malling ME19 90 A6
High St. Edenbridge TN8 112 C1
High St. Eynsford DA4 54 E8
High St. Farningham DA4 40 F2
High St. Flimwell TN5 177 C3
High St. Frant TN3 163 C4
High St. Gillingham ME7 48 B6
High St. Gillingham ME7 48 C5
High St.
Gillingham,Brompton ME4 48 A6
High St.
Gillingham,Rainham ME8 63 F8
High St. Goudhurst TN17 167 E8
High St. Grain ME3 21 B6
High St. Gravesend DA11 13 B1
High St. 3 Grays RM17 12 A8
High St. Hadlow TN11 118 E8
High St. Halling ME2 60 A4
High St. Headcorn TN27 141 C5

High St. High Street TN18 178 E2
High St. Kemsing TN15 70 B2
High St. Lamberhurst TN3 166 B5
High St. Leigh TN11 115 F1
High St. Lenham ME17 111 D5
High St. Maidstone ME14 91 F4
High St. Marden TN12 138 D6
High St. Newington ME9 65 C6
High St. Northfleet DA11 12 C1
High St. Orpington BR6 38 A1
High St. Orpington,Farnborough
BR6 51 C5
High St. Orpington,
Green Street Green BR6 51 F4
High St. Orpington,
St Mary Cray BR5 38 C4
High St. Otford TN14 69 A3
High St. Pembury TN2 150 C6
High St. Penshurst TN11 131 B4
High St. Rochester ME2 47 B7
High St. Rochester ME1 47 C6
High St. Rochester ME4 47 E4
High St. Rolvenden TN17 181 E4
High St. Royal Tunbridge Wells
TN1 149 A2
High St. Seal TN15 84 F6
High St. Sevenoaks TN13 84 C2
High St.
Sevenoaks,Chipstead TN13 83 C5
High St. Shoreham TN14 53 F1
High St. Sidcup DA14 24 A4
High St. Smarden TN27 143 A1
High St. Snodland ME6 75 A8
High St. Staplehurst TN12 139 F3
High St.
Sutton Valence ME17 124 E7
High St. Swanley BR8 39 F5
High St. Swanscombe DA10 11 F2
High St. Swanscombe,Greenhithe
DA9 11 B3
High St. Tenterden TN30 183 A7
High St. Ticehurst TN5 176 C1
High St. Tonbridge TN9 117 C2
High St. Upper Upton ME2 33 F1
High St. Wadhurst TN5 174 F4
High St. West Malling ME19 89 C8
High St. Westerham TN16 96 C8
High St. Wouldham ME1 60 C5
High St. Wrotham TN15 72 A3
High St. Yalding ME18 104 F1
High Tor Cl. BR1 22 B1
High View. ME3 32 C4
High Woods La. TN2 150 B3
Higham Cl. ME15 91 E2
Higham Cty Prim Sch. ME3 32 C5
Higham Gdns. TN10 117 F5
Higham La. TN10 117 F6
Higham Rd. Cliffe ME3 16 A4
Higham Rd. Rochester ME3 33 D3
Higham School Rd. TN10 117 E6
Higham Sta. ME3 32 D6
Higham View. ME14 76 E4
Highbanks Cl. DA16 7 B7
Highberry. ME19 74 E2
Highbrook Rd. SE3 5 D4
Highbury La. TN30 183 A7
Highcombe. SE7 5 B8
Highcombe Cl. SE9 22 E7
Highcroft Gn. ME15 107 F4
Highcross Rd. DA13 28 D2
Highdown Cotts. TN17 166 F3
Highfield Ave. Erith DA8 8 B8
Highfield Ave.
Orpington BR6 51 F5
Highfield Cl.
Gillingham ME8 63 D7
Highfield Cl.
Hawkhurst TN18 179 A1
Highfield Cl. Pembury TN2 150 D6
Highfield Cotts. BR8 26 B2
Highfield Rd. Bexley DA6 7 F2
Highfield Rd. Bromley BR1 36 F5
Highfield Rd. Dartford DA1 26 D8
Highfield Rd.
Gillingham ME8 63 D7
Highfield Rd. Kemsing TN14 69 F3
Highfield Rd.
Royal Tunbridge Wells TN4 149 C7
Highfield Rd.
St Paul's Cray BR5 & BR7 37 F6
Highfield Rd N. DA1 9 D1
Highfield Rd S. DA1 26 D7
Highfields Rd. TN8 112 C4
Highgate Ct. 8 TN18 178 F2
Highgate Hill. TN18 178 F1
Highgrove. TN2 163 A8
Highgrove Cl. BR7 36 E8
Highgrove Rd. ME5 62 A5

Highland Rd.
  Badgers Mount TN14 ...... 68 B8
Highland Rd. Bexley DA6 ...... 8 A3
Highland Rd.
  Maidstone ME15 ...... 107 E6
Highlands Cl. ME2 ...... 46 D5
Highlands Hill. BR8 ...... 40 A8
Highlands Pk. TN15 ...... 84 E6
Highlands Rd. BR5 ...... 38 C2
Highmead. SE18 ...... 6 F7
Highridge. ME7 ...... 48 F1
Highridge Cl. ME14 ...... 92 F5
Highstead Cres. DA8 ...... 8 E7
Highview. Vigo Village DA13 73 B8
Highview. Woolwich SE18 ...... 6 B7
Highview Cl. ME15 ...... 107 A8
Highview Dr. ME5 ...... 61 D5
Highview Rd. DA14 ...... 24 B4
Highway Prim Sch. BR6 ...... 52 C5
Highway The. BR6 ...... 52 C5
Highwood Cl. BR6 ...... 51 C8
Highwood Dr. BR6 ...... 51 C8
Highwoods Cl. ME3 ...... 32 C4
Hilary Cl. DA7 ...... 8 C6
Hilary Gdns. ME1 ...... 46 F1
Hilbert Cl. TN2 ...... 149 C5
Hilborough Way. BR6 ...... 51 D5
Hilda May Ave. BR8 ...... 39 E7
Hilda Rd. ME4 ...... 48 A3
Hilda Vale Cl. BR6 ...... 51 A6
Hilda Vale Rd. BR6 ...... 51 B6
Hilden Ave. TN11 ...... 116 F4
Hilden Dr. DA8 ...... 9 B7
Hilden Grange Sch. TN10 . 117 B4
Hilden Oaks Sch. TN10 ...... 117 B3
Hilden Park Rd. TN11 ...... 116 F4
Hildenborough CE Prim Sch.
  TN11 ...... 116 D6
Hildenborough Cres. ME16 . 91 C7
Hildenborough Rd.
  Leigh TN11 ...... 116 A2
Hildenborough Rd.
  Shipbourne TN11 & TN15 . 100 E4
Hildenborough Sta. TN11 . 116 B6
Hilders Cl. TN8 ...... 112 B4
Hilders La. TN8 ...... 112 A4
Hill Brow. Bromley BR1 ...... 36 D8
Hill Brow. Crayford DA1 ...... 8 D8
Hill Brow. Maidstone ME14 ... 93 A5
Hill Chase. ME5 ...... 61 E3
Hill Cl. Chislehurst BR7 ...... 23 B3
Hill Cl. Istead Rise DA13 ...... 29 E1
Hill Cres. Coldblow DA5 ...... 25 C7
Hill Cres. Lenham ME17 ...... 111 D5
Hill Crest. Royal Tunbridge Wells
  TN4 ...... 149 B8
Hill Crest. Sevenoaks TN13 .. 84 A5
Hill Crest. Sidcup DA15 ...... 24 B8
Hill Cut. ME3 ...... 33 F4
Hill End. Orpington BR6 ...... 51 F8
Hill End. Woolwich SE18 ...... 6 A6
Hill Farm Ave. ME2 ...... 32 F1
Hill Farm Cl. ME23 ...... 17 E3
Hill Green Rd. ME9 ...... 79 D8
Hill House Rd. DA2 ...... 27 C8
Hill Rd. Dartford DA1 ...... 26 E6
Hill Rd. Rochester ME1 ...... 47 A2
Hill Rd. Wouldham ME1 ...... 60 F5
Hill Rise. DA2 ...... 27 E3
Hill Sch The. TN16 ...... 81 B4
Hill Shaw. DA3 ...... 42 F3
Hill St. TN1 ...... 149 B5
Hill The. Cranbrook TN17 .. 169 D4
Hill The. Northfleet DA11 ...... 12 C1
Hill Top. TN17 ...... 154 E5
Hill Top Cotts. ME17 ...... 106 E2
Hill View. Basted TN15 ...... 86 F4
Hill View.
  Borough Green TN15 ...... 87 A7
Hill View Cl. TN15 ...... 87 A7
Hill View Dr. DA16 ...... 6 E5
Hill View Rd.
  Hildenborough TN11 ...... 116 F5
Hill View Rd. New Barn DA3 43 B6
Hill View Rd. Orpington BR6 51 F8
Hill View Rd. Rusthall TN4 . 148 C4
Hill View Way. ME5 ...... 61 E5
Hill's Terr. ME4 ...... 47 F3
Hillary Ave. DA11 ...... 29 E5
Hillary Ct. SE9 ...... 22 E6
Hillary Rd. ME14 ...... 92 A7
Hillbert Rd. TN1 & TN2 ... 149 C5
Hillborough Ave.
  TN13 & TN15 ...... 84 D5
Hillborough Gr. ME5 ...... 62 A3
Hillbrow Cl. DA5 ...... 25 D4
Hillbury Gdns. TN5 ...... 176 D1
Hillcrest. TN8 ...... 113 B5

Hillcrest Ave. RM16 ...... 11 A8
Hillcrest Dr. Cuxton ME2 ...... 46 C2
Hillcrest Dr. Royal Tunbridge Wells
  TN1 ...... 149 D7
Hillcrest Dr.
  Swanscombe DA9 ...... 11 A2
Hillcrest Rd. Bromley BR1 ... 22 A4
Hillcrest Rd. Chatham ME4 .. 47 F2
Hillcrest Rd. Dartford DA1 ... 25 F8
Hillcrest Rd.
  Marlpit Hill TN8 ...... 112 C4
Hillcrest Rd. Orpington BR6 . 52 A8
Hillcroft Rd. E6 ...... 2 B8
Hillden Shaw. ME15 ...... 107 A8
Hilldown Lodge. BR6 ...... 52 B8
Hilldrop Rd. BR1 ...... 22 B2
Hillfield Rd. TN13 ...... 83 E7
Hillfield Villas. TN26 ...... 173 F8
Hillgarth. TN4 ...... 149 A8
Hillingdon Ave. TN13 ...... 84 D6
Hillingdon Rd. Bexley DA7 ... 8 C4
Hillingdon Rd.
  Gravesend DA11 ...... 30 B6
Hillingdon Rise. TN13 ...... 84 D5
Hillreach. SE18 & SE7 ...... 1 F1
Hills La. TN15 ...... 70 C7
Hillsgrove Cl. DA16 ...... 7 C7
Hillsgrove Prim Sch. DA16 ... 7 C7
Hillside. Chatham ME2 ...... 46 D5
Hillside. Erith DA17 ...... 4 C2
Hillside. Farningham DA4 ...... 40 F2
Hillside. Lane End DA2 ...... 27 E3
Hillside. Tonbridge TN9 ... 133 A7
Hillside Ave.
  Gravesend DA12 ...... 30 D6
Hillside Ave. Rochester ME2 47 B8
Hillside Cotts. TN5 ...... 175 B8
Hillside Cl. [1]
Hillside Ct.
  Rochester ME2 ...... 47 A7
Hillside Ct. Swanley BR8 ...... 40 A5
Hillside Ct.
  Wateringbury ME18 ...... 104 F7
Hillside Dr. DA12 ...... 30 D6
Hillside Rd. DA2 ...... 50 A8
Hillside Rd. Chatham ME4 .... 48 A4
Hillside Rd. Crayford DA1 ...... 9 A1
Hillside Rd. Kemsing TN14 .. 69 F2
Hillside Rd.
  Sevenoaks TN13 ...... 84 D4
Hillside The. BR6 ...... 52 B2
Hillside. Tonbridge TN9 ... 133 B7
Hilltop.
  West Farleigh ME15 ...... 105 D3
Hilltop Gdns. Dartford DA1 ... 9 F2
Hilltop Gdns. Orpington BR6 51 E8
Hilltop Prim Sch. ME2 ...... 33 C1
Hilltop Rd. Rochester ME2 ... 33 C1
Hilltop Rd.
  West Thurrock RM16 ...... 11 B8
Hillview Cres. BR6 ...... 37 F1
Hillview Rd. BR7 & SE9 ...... 23 A4
Hillview Sch for Girls.
  TN9 ...... 133 D8
Hillydeal Rd. TN14 ...... 69 C4
Hillyfield Cl. ME2 ...... 32 F1
Hillyfields Cty Jun Sch.
  ME7 ...... 48 E6
Hilton Rd. ME3 ...... 33 B7
Hind Cres. DA8 ...... 8 D7
Hines Terr. ME5 ...... 48 C1
Hinksden Rd.
  TN17 & TN18 ...... 179 F3
Hinksey Path. SE2 ...... 3 D3
Hinstock Rd. SE18 ...... 6 C7
Hinton Cl. SE9 ...... 22 E7
Hinton Cres. ME7 ...... 63 A6
Hitchen Hatch La. TN13 ...... 84 B4
Hither Chantlers. TN3 ...... 148 A2
Hive La. DA11 ...... 12 B2
Hive The. DA11 ...... 12 B1
Hoath Cl. ME7 ...... 63 B7
Hoath La. ME8 ...... 63 B7
Hoath Meadow. TN12 ...... 153 A6
Hoath Way. ME7 & ME8 ...... 63 B5
Hobart Rd. RM18 ...... 13 A6
Hoblands End. BR7 ...... 23 E2
Hockenden La. BR5 & BR8 . 39 B7
Hockers Cl. ME14 ...... 93 A8
Hockers La. ME14 ...... 93 A7
Hoddesdon Rd. DA17 ...... 4 A1
Hodgkins Cl. SE28 ...... 3 D6
Hodgson Cres. ME6 ...... 60 A1
Hodsoll Ct. BR5 ...... 38 D4
Hodsoll St. TN15 ...... 57 D1
Hodson Cres. BR5 ...... 38 D3
Hog Hill. ME14 ...... 93 B5
Hog La. DA11 ...... 29 D5
Hogarth Cl. E16 ...... 1 D8
Hogbarn La. ME17 ...... 95 F2
Hoghole La. TN3 ...... 165 F2
Hognore La. TN15 ...... 72 D6

Hogtrough Hill.
  TN16 & TN14 ...... 82 A5
Holbeach Gdns. DA15 ...... 6 F1
Holborn La. ME4 ...... 47 F5
Holborn Rd. E13 ...... 1 B8
Holborough Rd. ME6 ...... 60 A1
Holbrook House. BR7 ...... 37 D8
Holbrook La. BR7 ...... 23 D1
Holbrook Way. BR2 ...... 36 F4
Holburne Cl. SE3 ...... 5 C6
Holburne Gdns. SE3 ...... 5 D6
Holburne Rd. SE3 ...... 5 D6
Holcombe Rd.
  Chatham ME4 ...... 47 F2
Holcombe Rd.
  Rochester ME1 ...... 47 C3
Holcote Cl. DA17 ...... 3 E3
Holden Cnr. TN4 ...... 132 F1
Holden Park Rd. TN4 ...... 149 A8
Holden Rd. TN4 ...... 132 F1
Holden Cl. ME5 ...... 62 C6
Holding St. ME8 ...... 49 F1
Hole La. TN8 ...... 112 A6
Holford St. [1] TN9 ...... 117 B1
Holgate St. SE7 ...... 1 D3
Holland House. ME1 ...... 47 D5
Holland Rd. Chatham ME5 ... 61 E4
Holland Rd.
  Maidstone ME14 ...... 92 B5
Hollands Cl. DA12 ...... 31 E3
Hollies Ave. DA15 ...... 23 F7
Hollies The. DA12 ...... 30 D2
Holligrave Rd. BR1 ...... 36 A8
Hollin Cl. TN4 ...... 148 F4
Hollingbourne Ave. DA7 ...... 7 F6
Hollingbourne Cty Prim Sch.
  ME17 ...... 94 C2
Hollingbourne Hill. ME17 ... 94 F4
Hollingbourne Rd. ME8 ...... 49 C2
Hollingbourne Sta. ME17 ... 94 C3
Hollingbourne Tower. [4]
  BR5 ...... 38 D1
Hollington Ct. BR7 ...... 23 B2
Hollingworth Rd.
  Orpington BR2 & BR5 ...... 37 B2
Hollingworth Rd.
  Park Wood ME15 ...... 107 F5
Hollingworth Way. TN16 ... 81 D1
Hollow La. Hartlip ME9 ...... 64 E5
Hollow La. Snodland ME6 ... 74 F6
Hollow Trees Dr. TN11 ...... 116 A1
Holly Bank. TN12 ...... 152 B8
Holly Bush La. TN13 ...... 84 C3
Holly Cl. Chatham ME5 ...... 62 C8
Holly Cl. Gillingham ME7 ...... 48 E6
Holly Cotts. TN8 ...... 112 B2
Holly Ct. DA14 ...... 24 B4
Holly Farm Rd. ME15 ...... 108 C6
Holly Hill. DA13 ...... 58 F3
Holly Hill Rd. DA17 ...... 4 B1
Holly Rd. Dartford DA1 ...... 26 D7
Holly Rd. Orpington BR6 ...... 52 A3
Holly Rd.
  Rochester,Strood ME2 ...... 46 E5
Holly Rd.
  Rochester,Wainscott ME2 .. 33 D2
Holly Tree Cl. ME17 ...... 109 E2
Hollybrake Cl. BR7 ...... 23 D1
Hollybush Cl. TN13 ...... 84 C3
Hollybush Cl. TN13 ...... 84 C3
Hollybush La. BR6 ...... 53 A4
Hollybush Rd. DA12 ...... 30 C6
Hollycroft. ME2 ...... 46 C2
Hollydale Dr. BR2 ...... 50 F7
Hollydene Rd. TN5 ...... 174 F6
Hollyshaw Cl. TN2 ...... 149 C2
Hollytree Ave. BR8 ...... 39 E7
Hollytree Dr. ME3 ...... 32 B3
Hollywood La.
  Knockmill TN15 ...... 70 F8
Hollywood La.
  Rochester ME2 ...... 33 C2
Hollywood Manor. TN15 ...... 70 F7
Hollywood Way. DA8 ...... 9 B6
Holm Cl. SE12 ...... 22 B5
Holm Mill La. ME17 ...... 110 B6
Holmbury Manor. [6] DA14 . 24 A4
Holmbury Pk. BR7 ...... 22 E1
Holmcroft Way. BR2 ...... 36 F4
Holmdale Rd. BR7 ...... 23 C3
Holmdene Ct. BR1 ...... 36 E6
Holmes Cl. ME19 ...... 73 F4
Holmesdale Cl.
  Durgates TN5 ...... 174 C5
Holmesdale Cl.
  Loose ME15 ...... 106 F3
Holmesdale Com Sch. ME4 74 F7
Holmesdale Hill. DA4 ...... 41 D8
Holmesdale Rd. Bexley DA7 7 D5
Holmesdale Rd.
  Sevenoaks TN13 ...... 84 D4

Holmesdale Rd.
  South Darenth DA4 ...... 41 C8
Holmesdale Sch (Farm Annex).
  ME6 ...... 74 F6
Holmewood House. TN3 .. 148 A2
Holmewood Rd. TN4 ...... 149 C7
Holmewood Ridge. TN3 .... 147 F3
Holmhurst Cl. TN4 ...... 148 F4
Holmhurst Rd. DA17 ...... 4 B1
Holmleigh Ave. DA1 ...... 9 C2
Holmoaks. Gillingham ME8 ... 49 E2
Holmoaks. Maidstone ME14 . 92 C5
Holmsdale Gr. DA1 & DA7 .. 8 E4
Holmside. ME7 ...... 48 E3
Holmwood Cotts. BR6 ...... 52 C1
Holmwood Cl. DA14 ...... 23 F3
Holstein Way. [6] DA18 ...... 3 E3
Holt Cl. SE28 ...... 3 C6
Holt Rd. E16 ...... 1 E5
Holt Wood Ave. ME20 ...... 90 E8
Holtwood Cl. ME8 ...... 63 D6
Holtye Cres. ME15 ...... 92 B2
Holtye Golf Club. TN8 ...... 144 F3
Holtye Rd. RH19 ...... 144 A3
Holwood Park Ave.
  BR2 & BR6 ...... 50 F6
Holy Family RC Prim Sch.
  SE9 ...... 5 C3
Holy Family RC Prim Sch The.
  ME15 ...... 107 F4
Holy Innocents RC Prim Sch.
  BR6 ...... 51 F7
Holy Trinity CE Prim Sch.
  Dartford DA1 ...... 9 C2
Holy Trinity CE Prim Sch.
  Dartford DA1 ...... 9 D1
Holy Trinity Coll & Prep Sch.
  BR1 ...... 36 C8
Holy Trinity Lamorbey
  CE Prim Sch. DA15 ...... 24 A7
Holyhead Cl. [3] E6 ...... 1 F8
Holyoake Terr. TN13 ...... 84 A3
Holywell Cl. SE3 ...... 5 A8
Home Farm Cl. TN11 ...... 116 A3
Home Farm Cotts. BR5 ...... 38 D8
Home Farm Ct. TN3 ...... 163 C4
Home Farm La.
  Royal Tunbridge Wells
  TN11 & TN2 ...... 133 F1
Home Farm La.
  Royal Tunbridge Wells TN2 149 E8
Home Gdns. DA1 ...... 9 E1
Home Hill. BR8 ...... 25 F1
Home Lea. BR6 ...... 51 F5
Home Mead Cl. [6] DA11 .... 30 B8
Homedean Rd. TN13 ...... 83 C4
Homefield Cl.
  St Paul's Cray BR5 ...... 38 B5
Homefield Cl. Swanley BR8 . 39 F6
Homefield Rd. Bromley BR1 36 C8
Homefield Rd.
  Sevenoaks TN13 ...... 83 E5
Homefield Rise. BR6 ...... 38 A1
Homemead. [7]
  Gravesend DA11 ...... 30 B8
Homemead.
  Swanscombe DA9 ...... 11 B1
Homemead Rd. BR2 ...... 36 F4
Homer Cl. DA7 ...... 8 C6
Homesdale Rd.
  Bromley BR1 & BR2 ...... 36 C6
Homesdale Rd.
  Orpington BR5 & BR6 ...... 37 E2
Homestead Rd.
  Marlpit Hill TN8 ...... 112 B5
Homestead Rd.
  Orpington BR6 ...... 52 B4
Homestead The.
  Crayford DA1 ...... 8 E2
Homestead The.
  Dartford DA1 ...... 9 C1
Homestead The.
  Groombridge TN3 ...... 161 C7
Homevale Cotts. TN14 ...... 67 E4
Homewards Rd. ME3 ...... 19 B8
Homewood Cotts. BR7 ...... 31 E1
Homewood Cres. BR7 ...... 23 E2
Homewood Rd.
  Langton Green TN3 ...... 147 F3
Homewood Rd.
  Tenterden TN30 ...... 173 B1
Homewood Sch. TN30 ...... 173 B1
Homoeopathic Hospl. TN1 . 149 A3
Honduras Terr. [8] ME14 .... 92 A7
Hone St. ME2 ...... 47 B8
Honey Bee Glade. ME8 ...... 63 E6
Honey Cl. ME7 ...... 63 A3
Honey La. ME15 ...... 108 B6
Honey Pot La. ME3 ...... 37 D1
Honeycrest Ind Pk. TN12 .. 139 E5
Honeycrock Hill. ME9 ...... 79 F8

Honeyden Rd. DA14 ......
Honeypot Cl. ME2 ......
Honeypot La.
  Hodsoll Street TN15 ......
Honeypot La.
  Noah's Ark TN15 ......
Honeysuckle Cl. [3]
  Chatham ME5 ......
Honeysuckle Cl.
  Gillingham ME7 ......
Honeysuckle Cl. [4] SE12 ...
Honiton Rd. DA16 ......
Honywood Rd. ME17 ......
Hoo Comm Rd. ME3 ......
Hoo Rd. ME2 & ME3 ......
Hoo St Werburgh Cty Prim
  ME3 ......
Hoo St Werburgh Mid Sch.
  ME3 ......
Hood Ave. BR5 ......
Hook Cl. ME5 ......
Hook Farm Rd. BR2 ......
Hook Green Cl. DA13 ......
Hook Green La. DA2 ......
Hook Green Rd. DA13 ......
Hook Hill. TN5 ......
Hook La. Bexley DA16 ......
Hook La.
  Harrietsham ME17 ......
Hook Lane Prim Sch. DA16
Hook Rd. ME6 ......
Hook St. ME17 ......
Hookfields. DA11 ......
Hookstead. TN26 ......
Hookwood Cotts. TN14 ......
Hookwood Rd. BR6 & TN14
Hooper Rd. E16 ......
Hooper's Pl. ME1 ......
Hooper's Rd. ME1 ......
Hoopers Cnr. ME15 ......
Hoopers Yd. TN15 ......
Hop Pocket Cl. TN17 ......
Hop Pocket La. TN12 ......
Hope Ave. TN11 ......
Hope Cl. SE12 ......
Hope Cotts. DA2 ......
Hope Rd. DA10 ......
Hope St. Chatham ME4 ......
Hope St. Maidstone ME14 ...
Hope Terr. ME3 ......
Hopedale Rd. SE7 ......
Hopehouse La.
Hopes Gr. TN26 ......
Hopewell Dr. Chatham ME5
Hopewell Dr.
  Gravesend DA12 ......
Hopgarden Cl. [12] TN8 ......
Hopgarden La. TN13 ......
Hopgarden Oast. ME18 ......
Hopgarden Rd. TN10 ......
Hoppers Cnr. ME15 ......
Hopton Ct. BR2 ......
Hopton Rd. SE18 ......
Hopwood Gdns. TN4 ......
Horizon Cl. TN4 ......
Horley Cl. DA6 ......
Horley Rd. SE9 ......
Horn La. SE10 ......
Horn Park Cl. SE12 ......
Horn Park La. SE12 ......
Horn Park Prim Sch. SE12 ..
Horn'd. [6] DA11 ......
Horn's Oak Rd. DA13 ......
Hornbeam Ave.
  Chatham ME5 ......
Hornbeam Ave.
  Royal Tunbridge Wells
  TN2 ......
Hornbeam Cl.
  Larkfield ME20 ......
Hornbeam Cl.
  Putlands TN12 ......
Hornbeam House. [6] DA15
Hornbeam La. DA7 ......
Hornbeam Way. BR2 ......
Hornbeams. DA13 ......
Horncastle Cl. SE12 ......
Horncastle Rd. SE12 ......
Horne House. SE18 ......
Hornetts Cl. BR8 ......
Hornfair Rd. SE7 ......
Hornfield Cotts. DA13 ......
Horning Cl. SE9 ......
Horns La. ME18 ......
Horns Lodge La. TN11 ......
Horns Rd. TN18 ......
Horsa Rd. Eltham SE12 ......
Horsa Rd. Erith DA8 ......
Horse Leaze. E6 ......
Horsecroft Cl. BR6 ......

grove Ave. TN5 .... 176 F1
l Rd. BR5 .... 38 B8
shoe Cl.
ghams ME7 .... 62 F5
shoe Cl.
stone ME14 .... 92 E5
shoes La. ME17 .... 108 E4
wash La. ME1 .... 47 C6
ld Gdns. SE9 .... 5 E2
ld Rd. SE9 .... 5 D2
lam Cl. DA2 .... 27 C8
am Rd. DA6 .... 8 A2
y Rd. Bromley BR1 ..... 36 B8
y Rd. Rochester ME1 .. 47 B4
onden Cl. BR6 .... 37 F2
onden Cty Prim Sch.
.... 153 A6
onden Rd. TN12 .... 152 D6
led Ave. ME4 .... 47 E1
ed Cty Inf Sch. ME4 .... 61 D5
ed Cty Jun Sch. ME5 ... 61 D5
led Way. ME1 .... 61 D7
h Downs. ME15 .... 92 F1
h Kirby CE Prim Sch.
.... 41 C6
h La. PL TN16 .... 81 D1
h Rd. DA4 .... 41 C6
n Tower. 2 BR5 .... 38 C5
h Way. DA4 .... 40 F2
ns Way. 1 TN16 .... 81 D1
hs La. ME1 .... 61 B8
nds View. DA3 .... 42 E5
k Ave. SE12 .... 22 A6
k Common La. TN16 .... 96 F5
k Common Rd.
. & TN8 .... 96 D5
h Hill. TN16 .... 96 E8
ls Cl. E16 .... 1 C7
al La. ME1 .... 47 E4
rl Rd.
hgbourne ME17 .... 109 E8
al Rd.
noaks TN13 .... 84 C6
Rd. ME8 .... 49 A2
n Cl.
t an Hone DA4 .... 27 B1
m Cl.
ley Village BR8 .... 40 B8
ield Rd. ME8 .... 49 F1
ield. DA3 .... 42 E6
am House. 11 BR5 .... 38 D1
ton Ave. ME7 .... 63 B3
lands Rd. TN9 .... 117 B2
l. RM17 .... 12 A8
dens. TN17 .... 170 A8
n Rd. SE28 .... 3 C7
Green La. TN8 .... 113 C2
d Ave.
ester ME1 .... 47 D3
d Ave. Sidcup DA5 ..... 24 C8
d Dr. ME16 .... 91 B5
d Gdns. TN2 .... 149 A1
d Rd. Bromley BR1 .... 22 A1
d Rd. Dartford DA1 ..... 10 A1
d Rd.
Malling ME19 .... 89 F8
d Sch The. ME8 .... 63 D8
th Rd. SE2 .... 3 A2
ury La. DA2 .... 9 A5
ury Rd. DA1 & DA8 ...... 9 A5
ury Wlk. ME8 .... 63 D4
en Cl. SE28 .... 3 D6
js Cl. TN15 .... 55 E4
s Cotts. TN18 .... 184 F8
k Cl. ME20 .... 90 F8
nd Rd. TN12 .... 138 E6
mere Cl. ME2 .... 60 B3
ard's Hill.
.... 117 D6
es Dr. ME2 .... 33 D2
wood Cl. DA2 .... 26 B5
ns Ct. 1 TN18 .... 179 A2
er Cres. ME2 .... 46 F7
er House. 5 ME15 .... 107 E8
er Rd. Dartford DA1 ..... 9 D2
er Rd. 4
wich SE10 .... 1 A1
er Rd. Greenwich SE3 ... 5 A8
er Rd. ME18 .... 105 A7
oldt Ct. TN7 .... 160 A8
s Ave. RM18 .... 13 B5
CL RM18 .... 13 A4
hreys. TN12 .... 151 F6
ed of Hoo Sch. ME2 ... 34 C5

Hungershall Pk. TN4 ..... 148 E2
Hunsdon Dr. TN13 .... 84 B4
Hunstanton Cl. ME8 .... 63 E3
Hunt Rd. Northfleet DA11 ... 29 F5
Hunt Rd. Tonbridge TN10 ... 117 E6
Hunt St. Nettlestead ME18 ... 104 F5
Hunt St. West Farleigh
ME15 & ME18 .... 105 B5
Hunter's Gr. BR6 .... 51 C6
Hunters Cl. DA5 .... 25 E5
Hunters Ct. ME4 .... 48 C7
Hunters Lodge. 10 DA15 ... 24 A5
Hunters Way.
Gillingham ME7 .... 48 E1
Hunters Way.
Royal Tunbridge Wells
TN2 148 F1
Hunters Way W.
ME5 & ME7 .... 48 E1
Hunters Wlk. TN14 .... 67 E5
Huntersfield Cl. ME5 ..... 62 C1
Huntingdon Wlk. 4
.... 107 E7
Huntingfield Rd. DA13 ... 44 A2
Huntington Cl. TN17 .... 169 D4
Huntington Rd. ME17 ... 106 B3
Huntley Ave. DA11 .... 12 C1
Huntley Mill Rd. TN5 ... 176 E3
Huntleys Pk. TN4 .... 148 F5
Hunton CE Prim Sch.
.... 121 D7
Hunton Hill. ME15 .... 105 F1
Hunton House. 4 BR5 ... 38 C4
Hunton Rd. TN12 .... 122 A3
Hunts Cl. SE3 .... 5 A5
Hunts Farm Cl. TN15 ... 87 A7
Hunts Mead Cl. BR7 ...... 22 F1
Huntsman La.
Maidstone ME14 .... 92 B4
Huntsman La.
Wrotham Heath TN15 ... 72 E1
Huntsman's Cnr. ME4 .... 61 E8
Huntsmans Cl. ME4 .... 47 E1
Huntsmoor House. BR5 ... 38 B5
Hurlfield. DA2 .... 26 C5
Hurlingham Rd. DA7 .... 7 F7
Huron Cl. 5 BR6 .... 51 F4
Hurricane Rd. ME19 ...... 88 F3
Hurst Cl. Chatham ME5 ... 61 E6
Hurst Cl. Staplehurst TN12 ... 139 F4
Hurst Prim Sch. DA5 ..... 24 D7
Hurst Rd. Erith DA8 .... 8 C7
Hurst Rd. Sidcup DA5 .... 24 D7
Hurst Springs. DA5 .... 24 D7
Hurst The. Crouch ME18 ... 102 D7
Hurst The.
Plaxtol Spoute TN15 ...... 87 C1
Hurst The. Royal Tunbridge Wells
TN2 .... 149 E7
Hurst Way. Maidstone ME16 ... 90 F2
Hurst Way. Sevenoaks TN13 ... 99 C8
Hurstbourne Cotts. DA5 ... 25 B8
Hurstfield. ME2 .... 36 A4
Hurstings The. ME16 ..... 91 D2
Hurstmere Sch. DA15 .... 24 C7
Hurstwood. ME5 .... 61 E4
Hurstwood Ave.
Erith DA7 & DA8 .... 8 E6
Hurstwood Ave. Sidcup DA5 ... 24 E7
Hurstwood Dr. ME1 .... 36 F6
Hurstwood La. TN4 ...... 148 F3
Hurstwood Pk. TN4 ...... 148 F3
Hurstwood Rd.
Bredhurst ME14 .... 63 B1
Hurstwood Rd.
Detling ME14 .... 78 B7
Husheath Hill. TN17 .... 154 F6
Husseywell Cres. BR4 ... 36 A1
Hutchings Cl. ME8 .... 63 D5
Hutson Terr. RM16 .... 10 D8
Huxley Cl. ME1 .... 47 D4
Huxley House. SE2 .... 3 D1
Huxley Rd. DA16 .... 6 F4
Hyacinth Rd. ME2 .... 46 E6
Hybrid Cl. ME1 .... 47 D1
Hyde Dr. BR5 .... 38 B5
Hyde Rd. Bexley DA7 .... 7 F5
Hyde Rd. Maidstone ME16 ... 91 B6
Hyde's Orch. TN27 ...... 141 E5
Hylton St. SE18 .... 2 F2
Hyperion Dr. ME2 .... 32 F1

Hythe Ave. DA7 .... 7 F7
Hythe Cl. Orpington BR5 ... 38 C5
Hythe Cl. Royal Tunbridge Wells
TN4 .... 133 A1
Hythe St. DA1 .... 9 E1

Ickleton Rd. SE9 .... 22 E4
Icough Ct. SE3 .... 5 B7
Iddenden Cotts. TN18 ... 178 D2
Ide Hill CE Prim Sch. TN14 ... 97 F4
Ide Hill Rd. TN14 .... 97 F2
Iden Cres. TN12 .... 139 F2
Iden Rd. ME2 .... 33 C1
Idenwood Cl. ME8 .... 63 D6
Idleigh Court Rd.
DA3 & DA13 .... 57 C8
Ifield Cl. ME15 .... 107 F7
Ifield Cotts. DA12 .... 31 C2
Ifield Sch. DA12 .... 30 D2
Ifield Way. DA12 .... 30 D2
Ightham By-Pass. TN15 ... 86 C7
Ightham Cotts. DA12 ...... 28 B6
Ightham Cty Prim Sch.
.... 86 B6
Ightham Mote (NT). TN15 ... 101 A7
Ightham Rd. Erith DA8 ..... 8 A7
Ightham Rd.
Shipbourne TN11 & TN15 ... 101 C5
Ilkley Rd. E16 .... 1 C8
Illustrious Cl. ME5 .... 62 A6
Imber Ct. 4 SE9 .... 6 A1
Impala Gdns. TN4 .... 149 B6
Imperial Bsns Pk. DA11 ... 12 F1
Imperial Dr. DA12 .... 30 F3
Imperial Rd. ME7 .... 48 C3
Imperial Ret Pk. DA11 ... 13 A1
Imperial Way. BR7 & SE9 ... 23 C5
Impton La. ME5 .... 62 A1
Ince Dr. SE9 .... 23 B8
Indus Rd. SE7 .... 5 C7
Ingle Rd. ME4 .... 47 F2
Ingleby Way. BR7 .... 23 A3
Ingleden Park Rd. TN30 ... 173 C1
Ingleden Rd. SE18 .... 2 D5
Ingleside. 2 SE3 .... 5 A8
Ingleton Ave. DA16 .... 7 A8
Inglewood. Chislehurst BR7 ... 23 D2
Inglewood. Swanley BR8 ... 39 E7
Inglewood Copse. BR1 ... 36 F7
Ingoldsby Rd. DA12 .... 30 D3
Ingram Rd. Dartford DA1 ... 26 E7
Ingram Rd. Gillingham ME7 ... 48 E6
Ingress Gdns. DA9 & DA11 ... 11 D2
Ingress Terr. DA13 .... 28 F4
Inigo Jones Rd. SE7 .... 5 E7
Institute Rd. ME4 .... 48 A4
Instone Rd. DA1 .... 26 D8
Inverary Pl. SE18 .... 6 D8
Inverine Rd. SE7 .... 1 B1
Invermore Pl. SE18 .... 2 C2
Inverness House. 6
ME15 .... 107 E7
Invicta Cl. BR7 .... 23 A3
Invicta Gram Sch for Girls.
.... 94 C4
Invicta Inf Sch. SE3 .... 5 B7
Invicta Rd. Dartford DA2 ... 10 B1
Invicta Rd.
Greenwich SE3 & SE7 ...... 5 A8
Invicta Villas. ME14 .... 93 C4
Iona Cl. ME5 .... 62 D1
Iona Rd. ME15 .... 107 E8
Ireland Cl. E6 .... 1 F8
Irene Rd. BR6 .... 37 F1
Iris Ave. DA5 .... 7 E1
Iris Cl. ME5 .... 77 A8
Iris Cres. DA7 .... 7 F8
Iron Mill La. DA1 .... 8 F3
Iron Mill Pl. DA1 .... 8 F3
Ironside Cl. ME5 .... 62 A6
Ironstones. TN3 .... 148 B3
Irvine Rd. ME3 .... 32 B3
Irvine Way. BR6 .... 37 F2
Irving House. TN1 .... 149 B5
Irving Wlk. DA10 .... 28 E8
Irwin Ave. SE18 .... 6 E8
Isabella Dr. BR6 .... 51 C6
Isla Rd. SE18 .... 6 C1
Islehurst Cl. BR7 .... 37 A8
Ismays Rd. TN15 .... 86 C3
Istead Rise. DA13 .... 29 F1
Istead Rise Cty Prim Sch.
DA13 .... 43 E8
Ivedon Rd. DA16 .... 7 C5
Ivens Way. ME17 .... 110 D6
Iverhurst Cl. DA6 .... 7 D2
Iversgate Cl. ME8 .... 49 F2
Ives Rd. TN9 .... 116 F1
Ivor Gr. SE9 .... 23 B7

Ivorydown. BR1 .... 22 A4
Ivy Bower Cl. DA9 .... 11 B2
Ivy Cl. Dartford DA1 .... 27 A8
Ivy Cl. Gravesend DA12 ... 30 D5
Ivy Cl. Kingswood ME17 ... 109 D2
Ivy House La. TN13 .... 68 E2
Ivy La. TN14 .... 67 E3
Ivy Rd. E16 .... 1 A7
Ivy St. ME8 .... 63 F8
Ivy Villas. DA9 .... 11 B2
Ivybridge Ct. 1 BR7 ...... 37 A8
Izane Rd. DA6 .... 7 F3

Jack Lobley Cty Prim Sch.
RM18 .... 12 F6
Jackass La. BR2 .... 50 C4
Jacklin Cl. ME5 .... 61 F2
Jackson Ave. ME1 .... 61 E8
Jackson Cl. Gillingham ME8 ... 49 C1
Jackson Cl. Stone DA9 .... 11 A2
Jackson Rd. BR2 .... 50 F8
Jackson St. SE18 .... 6 A8
Jackson Way. TN17 .... 171 C3
Jacksons La. 5 TN30 ..... 183 A7
Jacob House. 5 DA18 ...... 3 D4
Jacob's La. ME3 .... 35 B6
Jade Cl. E16 .... 1 D9
Jaffray Rd. BR2 .... 36 D5
Jaggard Way. TN12 .... 139 E3
Jago Cl. SE18 .... 6 C8
Jago Ct. DA2 .... 27 C8
Jail La. TN16 .... 66 A3
Jamaica Terr. ME16 .... 92 A7
James Newman Ct. SE9 ... 23 A5
James Rd. Cuxton ME2 ... 46 C2
James Rd. Dartford DA1 ... 26 A8
James St. Chatham ME4 ... 47 F4
James St. Gillingham ME7 ... 48 C6
James St. Maidstone ME14 ... 92 A5
James St. Rochester ME1 ... 47 C4
James Whatman Way.
ME14 .... 91 F5
Janet Ct. 4 DA7 .... 8 A3
Japonica Cl. ME5 .... 62 C2
Jaquets Ct. DA5 .... 25 A6
Jarrah Cotts. RM16 .... 11 B8
Jarrett Ave. ME2 .... 33 C2
Jarvis Cl. ME19 .... 154 B3
Jarvis Pl. TN30 .... 173 B3
Jashada House. SE18 .... 2 A1
Jasmine Cl. 2
Chatham ME5 .... 61 F4
Jasmine Cl.
East Malling ME19 .... 89 F8
Jasmine Cl. Orpington BR6 ... 51 B8
Jasmine Cotts. TN3 .... 161 C7
Jasmine Rd. SE18 .... 6 C8
Jason Wlk. SE9 .... 23 A4
Jasper Ave. ME1 .... 47 D2
Jasper Rd. E16 .... 1 D7
Javelin Rd. ME19 .... 88 F3
Jay Gdns. BR7 .... 22 F3
Jefferson Dr. ME8 .... 49 C1
Jefferson Wlk. 13 SE18 ... 6 A8
Jeffery St. ME7 .... 48 C6
Jeffrey Cl. TN12 .... 139 E4
Jeffrey Row. SE12 .... 5 B2
Jeffrey St. ME14 .... 92 A5
Jeken Rd. SE9 .... 5 C3
Jellicoe Ave. DA12 .... 30 C5
Jellicoe Ave W. DA12 ..... 30 C5
Jenkins' Dale. ME4 .... 47 F3
Jenkins Dr. ME15 .... 107 E5
Jenner House. 4 DA17 ..... 4 A1
Jenner Rd. ME1 .... 47 C4
Jenner Way. ME20 .... 75 F6
Jennifer Ct. ME3 .... 34 E5
Jenningtree Rd. DA8 .... 9 B7
Jenningtree Way. DA17 .... 4 C4
Jenton Ave. DA7 .... 7 E5
Jerome Rd. ME20 .... 74 F4
Jersey Dr. BR5 .... 37 C3
Jersey Rd. Newham E16 ... 1 C7
Jersey Rd. Rochester ME7 ... 47 A8
Jeskyns Rd. DA2 .... 44 E6
Jessamine Pl. DA2 .... 27 C8
Jessamine Terr. BR8 .... 39 C8
Jessup Cl. SE18 .... 2 C2
Jetty Rd. Kingsnorth ME3 ... 35 D7
Jetty Rd. Sheerness ME12 ... 21 F3
Jetty Wlk. 4 RM17 .... 12 A8
Jevington Way. SE12 ...... 22 B2
Jewell Gr. TN12 .... 138 D5
Jeyes Rd. ME7 .... 48 C4
Jezreels Rd. ME7 .... 48 D3
Jim Bradley Cl. 16 SE18 ... 2 A2
Jiniwin Rd. ME1 .... 61 D7
Joan Cres. SE9 .... 22 D8
Jockey La. TN17 .... 169 D5
Johannesburg House. 2
ME15 .... 107 F5

John Hunt Ct. SE9 .... 22 E6
John Mayne CE Prim Sch.
TN27 .... 157 F1
John Newton Ct. DA16 ..... 7 B4
John Spare Ct. TN4 .... 149 A6
John St. Grays RM17 ...... 12 C8
John St. Maidstone ME14 ... 92 A6
John St. Rochester ME1 ... 47 C4
John St. Royal Tunbridge Wells
TN4 .... 149 A5
John Wilson St. SE18 .... 2 A2
John's Rd. DA13 .... 43 F4
Johns Cl. DA3 .... 42 F4
Johnson Ave. ME7 .... 48 C7
Johnson Cl. DA11 .... 29 D5
Johnson Rd. BR2 .... 36 D4
Johnsons Ave. TN14 .... 53 B1
Johnsons Way. DA9 .... 11 C1
Joiners Ct. ME4 .... 48 B2
Jonas Dr. TN5 .... 174 E5
Jonas La. TN5 .... 174 E5
Jones Rd. E13 .... 1 B8
Jordan Cl. ME15 .... 107 E5
Joy Rd. DA12 .... 30 C7
Joyce Cl. TN17 .... 169 C5
Joyce Dawson Way. SE28 ... 3 A6
Joyce Green Hospl. DA1 ... 9 F5
Joyce Green La.
Dartford DA1 .... 9 E6
Joyce Green La.
Dartford,Temple Hill DA1 ... 9 F3
Joyce Green Wlk. DA1 ..... 9 F3
Joyce Page Cl. SE7 .... 5 D8
Joyden's Wood Rd. DA5 ... 25 E5
Joydens Wood Cty Jun Sch.
DA5 .... 25 E4
Joydens Wood Cty Prim Inf Sch.
DA5 .... 25 E4
Jubilee Ctry Pk. BR2 ...... 37 B4
Jubilee Cl. DA12 .... 11 C1
Jubilee Cnr. ME17 .... 125 E3
Jubilee Cres.
Gravesend DA12 .... 30 E6
Jubilee Cres. Ightham TN15 ... 86 C6
Jubilee Ct. DA1 .... 26 D8
Jubilee Field. TN30 ...... 189 E4
Jubilee Prim Sch. SE28 ..... 3 C6
Jubilee Rd. Maypole BR6 ... 53 A4
Jubilee Rd.
West Thurrock RM16 ..... 11 B8
Jubilee Rise. TN15 .... 84 F6
Jubilee Terr. ME7 .... 48 C6
Jubilee Way. DA14 .... 24 A6
Judd Rd. TN9 .... 133 B7
Judd Sch The. TN9 .... 133 A8
Judeth Gdns. DA12 .... 30 E3
Judkins Cl. ME5 .... 62 C6
Juglans Rd. BR6 .... 38 A1
Julian Rd. BR6 .... 52 A4
Julians Cl. TN13 .... 99 A8
Julians Way. TN13 .... 99 A8
Junction Rd.
Bodiam TN18 & TN32 ... 185 A3
Junction Rd. Dartford DA1 ... 9 D1
Junction Rd.
Gillingham ME7 .... 48 D4
Juniper Cl. Chatham ME5 ... 62 A4
Juniper Cl. Royal Tunbridge Wells
TN2 .... 133 D1
Juniper La. E6 .... 1 E8
Juniper Wlk. BR8 .... 39 D7
Jury St. 10 DA11 .... 13 B1
Jutland Cl. ME3 .... 19 D7
Jutland House. 10 SE7 ..... 1 E2

Kale Rd. DA18 .... 3 E4
Kashgar Rd. SE18 .... 2 F2
Kashmir Rd. SE7 .... 5 D7
Katherine Ct. ME5 .... 62 B2
Katherine Gdns. SE9 .... 5 C3
Katherine Rd. TN8 .... 128 C5
Katie Rance Ct. 8 SE18 ... 1 F2
Kay St. DA16 .... 7 B6
Keary Rd. DA10 .... 28 F8
Keats Gdns. RM18 .... 13 B5
Keats House. DA1 .... 8 E2
Keats Rd. Bexley DA16 ..... 6 F6
Keats Rd. Erith DA17 .... 4 C3
Keats Rd. Lunsford ME20 ... 74 F3
Kechill Gdns. BR2 .... 36 A2
Keddleston Dr. BR5 .... 37 F4
Keeble Cl. SE18 .... 6 B8
Keedonwood Rd. BR1 ..... 22 A3
Keefe Cl. ME5 .... 62 B1
Keel Gdns. TN4 .... 148 E8
Keeling Rd. SE9 .... 5 D2
Keemor Cl. SE18 .... 6 A7
Keep The. SE3 .... 5 A5

Keightley Dr. SE9 .... 23 C7
Keir Hardy House. **7** DA17 .. 4 A3
Keith Ave. DA4 .... 27 B2
Keith Sutton House. SE9 ...... 23 C6
Kelbrook Rd. SE3 & SE9 .... 5 E4
Kelchers La. TN11 .... 118 F5
Kelham House. **10** SE18 .... 6 B8
Kellaway Rd. Chatham ME5 . 62 A2
Kellaway Rd. Greenwich SE3 . 5 D5
Kellner Rd. SE28 .... 2 F3
Kelly Dr. ME7 .... 48 C7
Kelly House. ME1 .... 61 C7
Kelsall Cl. SE3 .... 5 B5
Kelsey Rd. BR5 .... 38 B7
Kelso Dr. DA12 .... 30 F4
Kelvin Cl. TN10 .... 117 D7
Kelvin House. **3** DA17 .... 4 A3
Kelvin Par. SE18 .... 37 E1
Kelvin Rd. Bexley DA16 .... 7 A4
Kelvin Rd. Tilbury RM18 ...... 13 A5
Kemble Cl. TN2 .... 149 E7
Kemble Dr. BR2 .... 50 C7
Kemnal Rd. BR7 .... 23 D3
Kemnal Tech Coll. BR5 .... 24 B1
Kemnal Warren. BR7 .... 23 D2
Kemp Cl. ME5 .... 61 E4
Kempley Ct. **2** RM17 .... 12 D8
Kempt St. SE18 .... 6 A8
Kempton Cl. Chatham ME5 .. 62 C2
Kempton Cl. Erith DA8 .... 8 C8
Kemsing Cl. DA5 .... 24 E8
Kemsing Cty Prim Sch.
  TN15 .... 70 A2
Kemsing Rd. Greenwich SE10 1 A1
Kemsing Rd. Wrotham TN15 71 C3
Kemsing Sta. TN15 .... 85 D8
Kemsley Cl. Northfleet DA11 29 F4
Kemsley Cl.
  Swanscombe DA9 .... 11 B1
Kemsley Street Rd. ME14 .... 63 C1
Kendal Dr. TN9 .... 117 C2
Kendal Pk. TN4 .... 148 E5
Kendal Way. ME8 .... 63 D8
Kendall Ct. DA15 .... 24 A5
Kendall Lodge. **5** BR1 .... 36 B8
Kendon Bsns Pk. ME2 .... 47 D8
Kenia Wlk. DA12 .... 30 F5
Kenilworth Dr. ME8 .... 63 D6
Kenilworth Gdns.
  Gillingham ME8 .... 63 A7
Kenilworth Gdns.
  Woolwich SE18 .... 6 B5
Kenilworth House. ME16 ...... 91 B2
Kenilworth Rd. BR5 .... 37 C3
Kenley Cl. Sidcup DA5 .... 25 A8
Kenley Cl.
  St Paul's Cray BR7 .... 37 E6
Kenley House. **6** BR5 .... 38 B7
Kenmere Rd. DA16 .... 7 C5
Kennard Cl. ME1 .... 46 F2
Kennard St. E16 .... 1 F5
Kennedy Cl. BR5 .... 37 D1
Kennedy Gdns. TN13 .... 84 D5
Kennedy House. TN17 .... 180 E6
Kennel Barn Rd. ME9 .... 80 C5
Kennet Cl. **2** BR8 .... 39 E6
Kennet Rd. Crayford DA1 ...... 9 A4
Kennet Rd. Tonbridge TN10 117 C5
Kennett Ct. **16** BR5 .... 38 D1
Kennington Cl.
  Gillingham ME8 .... 49 B4
Kennington Cl.
  Maidstone ME15 .... 107 F7
Kensington Ct. **4** RM17 .. 12 C8
Kensington House. ME16 .... 91 A2
Kent Ave. Bexley DA16 .... 6 F2
Kent Ave. Maidstone ME15 .. 92 C1
Kent Cl. Chatham ME1 .... 61 C8
Kent Cl. Orpington BR6 .... 51 E4
Kent Cl.
  Paddock Wood TN12 .... 136 A6
Kent Coll. TN2 .... 134 D3
Kent County Opthalmic &
  Aural Hospl. ME14 .... 92 A4
Kent County Show Gd.
  ME14 .... 92 B7
Kent & East Sussex Rly.
  TN17 .... 188 D5
Kent Hatch Rd. TN8 & RH8 .. 96 B4
Kent House. TN18 .... 179 A2
Kent Inst of Art & Design.
  Chatham ME1 .... 47 E4
Kent Inst of Art & Design.
  Maidstone ME16 .... 91 C3
Kent Kraft Ind Est. DA11 .... 11 F2
Kent Music Sch. TN9 .... 133 B8
Kent Rd. Dartford DA1 .... 9 E1
Kent Rd. Gravesend DA11 .... 30 A7

Kent Rd. Grays RM17 .... 12 C8
Kent Rd. Halling ME2 .... 60 A6
Kent Rd. Longfield DA3 .... 42 D2
Kent Rd. Orpington BR5 ...... 38 B3
Kent Rd. Royal Tunbridge Wells
  TN4 .... 149 A6
Kent Rd. Snodland ME6 .... 75 A6
Kent St. ME18 .... 88 E2
Kent & Sussex Hospl.
  Lower Higham ME3 .... 32 D7
Kent Terr.
  Meopham Green DA13 ...... 58 A7
Kentish Gdns. TN2 .... 162 E8
Kentish Rd. DA17 .... 4 A2
Kentish Way. BR1 & BR2 ..... 36 B6
Kentmere Rd. SE18 .... 2 E2
Kenward Ct. TN11 .... 118 E8
Kenward Rd. Eltham SE9 ...... 5 D2
Kenward Rd.
  Maidstone ME16 .... 91 D6
Kenward Rd. Yalding ME18 104 E2
Kenwood Ave.
  Chatham ME5 .... 62 A4
Kenwood Ave.
  New Barn DA3 .... 43 C6
Kenwyn Rd. DA1 .... 9 D2
Kenya Rd. SE7 .... 5 D7
Kenya Terr. **7** ME14 .... 92 A7
Kenyon Wlk. ME8 .... 63 B3
Kerry Cl. E16 .... 1 B7
Kersey Gdns. SE9 .... 22 E4
Kesteven Cl. ME2 .... 60 B5
Kestlake Rd. DA5 .... 7 C1
Kester Ind Est. DA9 .... 11 A3
Keston Ave. BR2 .... 50 C5
Keston CE Prim Sch. BR2 .... 50 D5
Keston Cl. DA16 .... 7 C7
Keston Ct. DA5 .... 24 F8
Keston Gdns. BR2 .... 50 C6
Keston Park Cl. BR2 .... 50 F7
Kestrel Ave. E6 .... 1 E8
Kestrel Cl. TN8 .... 112 D3
Kestrel House. **3** ME7 ..... 48 A6
Kestrel Rd. ME5 .... 62 C2
Keswick Cl. TN9 .... 117 C2
Keswick Dr. ME16 .... 91 B5
Keswick Rd. Bexley DA7 .... 8 A6
Keswick Rd. Orpington BR6 .. 38 A2
Ketridge La. ME19 .... 89 D2
Kettle La. ME15 .... 105 E6
Kettlewell Ct. BR8 .... 39 F7
Kevington Cl. BR5 .... 37 F5
Kevington Dr. BR5 & BR7 .... 37 F5
Kevington Prim Sch. BR5 .... 38 D4
Kewlands. ME11 .... 92 C6
Keycol Hill. ME9 .... 65 F5
Keycol Hospl. ME9 .... 65 E6
Keyes Ave. ME4 .... 47 F2
Keyes Gdns. TN9 .... 132 F7
Keyes Rd. DA1 .... 10 A3
Keynes Ct. **9** SE28 .... 3 B6
Keynsham Gdns. SE9 .... 5 E2
Keynsham Rd. SE9 .... 5 E2
Keyworth Cl. TN12 .... 135 F6
Khartoum Rd. Chatham ME4 47 F5
Khartoum Rd.
  Gillingham ME4 .... 48 A6
Khyber Rd. ME4 & ME7 ...... 48 B7
Kibbles La. TN4 .... 148 E8
Kidbrooke Gdns. SE3 .... 5 A6
Kidbrooke Gr. SE3 .... 5 B6
Kidbrooke La. SE9 .... 5 E3
Kidbrooke Park Cl. SE3 .... 5 B6
Kidbrooke Park Prim Sch.
  SE3 .... 5 C6
Kidbrooke Park Rd.
  SE12 & SE3 & SE9 .... 5 B4
Kidbrooke Sch. SE3 .... 5 D5
Kidbrooke Sta. SE3 .... 5 B4
Kidbrooke Way. SE3 .... 5 B5
Kidd Pl. SE7 .... 1 E1
Kiddens. BR8 .... 39 B7
Kildare Rd. E16 .... 1 A8
Killewarren Way. BR5 .... 38 C3
Killick Cl. TN13 .... 83 F1
Killick Rd. ME3 .... 34 D5
Killicks Cotts. ME18 .... 120 F8
Kiln Barn Rd.
  ME16 & ME19 & ME20 ...... 90 C7
Kiln Field. TN30 .... 183 C7
Kiln La. TN11 .... 115 F1
Kiln Way. TN12 .... 136 A5
Kilndown. DA12 .... 30 D2
Kilndown Cl. ME16 .... 91 C7
Kilnfields. BR6 .... 53 A4
Kilnwood. TN14 .... 67 F6
Kimber House. **11** SE18 .... 6 B8
Kimberley Dr. DA14 .... 24 D6
Kimberley Rd. ME7 .... 48 D3

Kimmeridge Gdns. SE9 .... 22 E4
Kimmeridge Rd. SE9 .... 22 E4
Kincraig. BR7 .... 37 A8
Kincraig Dr. TN13 .... 84 B4
Kinder Cl. SE28 .... 3 D6
King and Queen Cl. SE9 ...... 22 E4
King Arthur's Dr. ME2 .... 33 A1
King Edward Ave. DA1 .... 9 D1
King Edward Rd.
  Chatham ME4 .... 47 F2
King Edward Rd.
  Gillingham ME7 .... 48 F6
King Edward Rd.
  Maidstone ME15 .... 91 F2
King Edward Rd.
  Rochester ME1 .... 47 C5
King Edward Rd. Stone DA9 11 A2
King Edward VII Ave. SE18 .... 1 C3
King George Ave. E16 .... 1 D7
King George Rd. ME5 .... 61 E4
King George V Hill. TN1 ...... 149 B4
King George V Memorial Houses.
  ME8 .... 49 C2
King Harolds Way. DA7 .... 7 E7
King Henry Mews. **7** BR6 . 51 F5
King Hill. ME19 .... 89 A5
King John's Wlk. SE9 .... 5 E1
King St. Chatham ME4 .... 48 A4
King St. Gillingham ME7 ...... 48 C6
King St. Gravesend DA11 .... 13 B1
King St.
  Maidstone ME14 & ME15 .. 92 A4
King St. Rochester ME1 .... 47 C5
King St. West Malling ME19 . 89 C8
King William Rd. **5** ME7 .. 48 C7
King's Ave. ME1 .... 47 C3
King's Bastion. ME7 .... 48 A5
King's Cotts. ME18 .... 104 D6
King's Highway. SE18 & SE2 . 6 F8
King's Orch. Eltham SE9 .... 5 E3
King's Orch. Rochester ME1 . 47 C5
King's Rd. Chatham ME5 ..... 48 D1
King's Rd. Tonbridge TN9 .. 133 D7
King's Sch. ME1 .... 47 C5
King's Standing Ind Est.
  TN2 .... 133 F2
Kingfisher Apartments. **11**
  ME15 .... 107 E5
Kingfisher Cl. Erith SE28 ...... 3 E6
Kingfisher Cl.
  St Paul's Cray BR5 .... 38 D5
Kingfisher Ct. TN15 .... 55 E3
Kingfisher Dr. ME5 .... 62 C7
Kingfisher Drive Cty Prim Sch.
  ME5 .... 62 B7
Kingfisher Pl. DA4 .... 41 C7
Kingfisher Rd. ME20 .... 75 A2
Kingfisher St. E6 .... 1 E8
Kings Acre. ME15 .... 93 A1
Kings Ave. BR1 .... 22 A2
Kings Cl. DA1 .... 8 E3
Kings Cotts. Leeds ME17 .... 108 F6
Kings Cotts.
  Wilsley Green TN17 .... 169 D6
Kings Ct. TN12 .... 153 A6
Kings Dr. DA12 .... 30 B5
Kings Farm Cty Prim Sch.
  DA12 .... 30 C3
Kings Hill Ave. ME19 .... 89 A4
Kings Hill Sch. ME19 .... 89 A4
Kings Pk. TN2 .... 149 D3
Kings Rd. Headcorn TN27 .. 141 C5
Kings Rd. Orpington BR6 .... 51 F6
Kings Standing Way. TN2 .. 133 F1
Kings Toll Rd. TN12 & TN2 . 151 A6
Kings Wlk. RM17 .... 12 A8
Kingsand Rd. SE12 .... 22 A6
Kingsdale Cl. Chatham ME5 . 48 C1
Kingsdale Cl.
  Swanscombe DA10 .... 11 E1
Kingsdale Rd. SE18 .... 6 F8
Kingsdown Cl.
  Gillingham ME7 .... 63 B4
Kingsdown Cl.
  Gravesend DA12 .... 30 F7
Kingsdown Cl.
  Maidstone ME16 .... 91 E4
Kingsdown Way. BR2 .... 36 A3
Kingsfield House. SE9 .... 22 D8
Kingsford Cotts. TN17 ...... 180 D6
Kingsford Way. E6 .... 1 F8
Kingsgate Cl. Bexley DA7 ..... 7 E6
Kingsgate Cl.
  St Paul's Cray BR5 .... 38 C6
Kingsgate La. TN30 .... 189 C5
Kingshill Dr. ME3 .... 34 D6
Kingsholm Gdns. SE9 .... 5 E3
Kingshurst Rd. SE12 .... 22 A8
Kingsingfield Cl. TN15 .... 55 E3

Kingsingfield Rd. TN15 .... 55 E2
Kingsland Gr. TN27 .... 141 D5
Kingsland La. TN27 .... 127 E1
Kingsley Ave. DA1 .... 10 A2
Kingsley Cl. Bexley DA6 .... 8 A3
Kingsley Ct. Wadhurst TN5 175 A4
Kingsley Ct. **1**
  Woolwich SE18 .... 3 C5
Kingsley Mews. BR7 .... 23 B2
Kingsley Rd.
  Maidstone ME15 .... 92 A3
Kingsley Rd. Orpington BR6 . 51 F3
Kingsley Wood Dr. SE9 .... 22 F5
Kingsman Par. SE18 .... 1 F2
Kingsman St. SE18 .... 1 F2
Kingsmead Cl. DA15 .... 24 A6
Kingsmere. BR7 .... 36 E8
Kingsnorth Ct. BR8 .... 39 C3
Kingsnorth Rd. ME8 .... 49 C4
Kingsridge Gdns. DA1 .... 9 D1
Kingston Cres. ME5 .... 62 C4
Kingston Ct. DA11 .... 12 B1
Kingston Dr. ME15 .... 107 A8
Kingsway. Chatham ME5 ..... 48 D1
Kingsway. Gillingham ME7 ... 48 E1
Kingsway. Orpington BR5 ... 37 D4
Kingswood Ave.
  Chatham ME4 .... 47 F2
Kingswood Ave. Erith DA17 .. 3 F2
Kingswood Cl.
  Swanley BR8 .... 39 F6
Kingswood Cl. Dartford DA1 . 9 C1
Kingswood Cl.
  Orpington BR6 .... 37 D2
Kingswood Cty Prim Sch.
  ME17 .... 109 E2
Kingswood Rd.
  Gillingham ME7 .... 48 D6
Kingswood Rd.
  Kit's Coty ME1 & ME20 ..... 76 D8
Kingswood Rd.
  Royal Tunbridge Wells TN2 149 C3
Kingswood Rd.
  Sevenoaks TN13 .... 83 E7
Kinlet Rd. SE18 .... 6 C6
Kinnings Row. TN9 .... 117 C2
Kinross Cl. ME5 .... 62 B7
Kinveachy Gdns. SE7 .... 1 E1
Kipling Ave. RM18 .... 13 C6
Kipling Dr. ME20 .... 74 F4
Kipling Rd. Bexley DA7 .... 7 E6
Kipling Rd. Dartford DA1 .... 10 B2
Kippington Cl. TN13 .... 83 F3
Kippington Dr. SE9 .... 22 D7
Kippington Rd. TN13 .... 84 A2
Kirby Cl. TN17 .... 169 D4
Kirby Rd. Chattenden ME3 .. 33 F5
Kirby Rd. Dartford DA2 .... 27 D8
Kirk La. SE18 .... 6 C5
Kirkcourt. TN13 .... 84 A4
Kirkdale. ME15 .... 106 F5
Kirkdale Cl. ME5 .... 62 D1
Kirkdale Cotts. ME15 .... 106 F5
Kirkdale Rd.
  Maidstone ME15 .... 106 F6
Kirkdale Rd. Royal Tunbridge Wells
  TN1 .... 149 B4
Kirkham Rd. E6 .... 1 E7
Kirkham St. SE18 .... 6 E8
Kirkins Cl. TN12 .... 153 A6
Kirkland Cl. DA15 .... 6 E1
Kirkman Ct. TN12 .... 139 E3
Kirkside Rd. SE3 .... 5 A8
Kit Hill Ave. ME5 .... 62 A1
Kit's Coty House. ME20 ...... 76 C6
Kitchener Ave.
  Gravesend DA12 .... 30 C3
Kitchener Cotts. ME3 .... 19 C4
Kitchener Rd.
  Chattenden ME3 .... 33 F4
Kitchener Rd.
  Rochester ME2 .... 47 A8
Knatts La. TN15 .... 70 D8
Knatts Valley Rd. TN15 .... 55 D1
Knave Wood Rd. TN14 .... 69 E2
Knaves Acre. TN27 .... 141 D5
Knavescare Ct. ME8 .... 63 D5
Knee Hill. SE2 .... 3 C1
Knee Hill Cres. SE2 .... 3 C2
Knight Ave. ME7 .... 48 D7
Knight Rd. Rochester ME2 ... 47 A6
Knight Rd. Tonbridge TN10 117 E6
Knight's Cl. DA8 .... 8 F7
Knight's Ridge. TN2 .... 150 D7
Knight's Way. TN27 .... 141 D6
Knighton Rd. TN14 .... 68 F2
Knightrider Ct. ME15 .... 92 A3

Knightrider St. **1** ME15 ......
Knights Cl.
  Hoo St Werburgh ME3 ......
Knights Cl. Pembury TN2 .. 1
Knights Croft. DA3 ....
Knights Manor Way. DA1 .....
Knights Pk. ME2 ....
Knights Rd.
  Hoo St Werburgh ME3 ......
Knights Rd. Newham E16 ....
Knights Ridge. BR6 ....
Knightsbridge Cl. TN4 ....
Knightsbridge Mews. BR7 ...
Knock Mill La. TN15 ....
Knockhall Chase. DA9 ....
Knockhall Cty Prim Sch.
  DA9 ....
Knockhall Rd. DA9 ....
Knockhall CE Prim Sch.
  TN14 ....
Knockholt Rd. Eltham SE9 ..
Knockholt Rd.
  Halstead TN14 ....
Knockholt Sta. TN14 ....
Knockhurst Ct. TN30 ....
Knockwood Rd. TN30 1
Knole. TN15 ....
Knole Ave.
  Chatham ME4 ....
Knole Gate. DA15 ....
Knole La. TN13 & TN15 ....
Knole Park Golf Course.
  TN15 ....
Knole Rd. Chatham ME5 ......
Knole Rd. Dartford DA1 ......
Knole Rd. Sevenoaks TN13 ...
Knole The. Eltham SE9 ....
Knole Rd. Istead Rise DA13 ...
Knole Way. TN15 ....
Knole Rd. Sidcup DA14 ....
Knoll Rd.
  Sidcup,Old Bexley DA5 .....
Knoll Rise. BR6 ....
Knoll The. BR2 ....
Knotley Hall Cotts. TN11 .. 1
Knott Ct. ME14 ....
Knotts Pl. TN13 ....
Knowle Ave. DA7 ....
Knowle Cl. TN3 ....
Knowle Cotts. TN13 1
Knowle La. TN12 ....
Knowle Rd.
  Castle Hill TN12 1
Knowle Rd.
  Keston Mark BR2 ....
Knowle Rd. Maidstone ME14
Knowle Rd. Wouldham ME1 ..
Knowles Gdns. TN27 1
Knowles Wlk. TN12 ....
Knowlton Gdns. ME16 ....
Knowlton Gn. BR2 ....
Knowsley Way. TN11 ....
Knox Ct. TN15 ....
Kydbrook Cl. BR5 ....
Kyetop Wlk. ME8 ....
Kynaston Rd. Bromley BR1 ..
Kynaston Rd. Orpington BR5

La Tourne Gdns. BR6 ....
Labour-in-Vain Rd. TN15 ....
Laburnham Pl. SE9 ....
Laburnum Ave.
  Dartford DA1 ....
Laburnum Ave.
  Swanley BR8 ....
Laburnum Ct. TN1 1
Laburnum Dr. ME20 ....
Laburnum Gr. DA11 ....
Laburnum Rd. ME2 ....
Laburnum Way. BR2 ....
Lacebark Cl. DA15 ....
Lacey Cl. ME17 1
Laceys La. ME17 1
Ladbrooke Cres. DA14 ......
Laddingford CE Prim Sch.
  ME18 1
Laddingford Farm Ind Est.
  ME18 1
Ladds Cnr. ME7 ....
Ladds La. ME6 ....
Ladds Way. BR8 ....
Ladham Rd. TN17 1
Ladies Mile. TN3 1
Lady Amherst's Dr. TN4 ......
Lady Boswell's CE Prim Sch.
  TN15 ....
Lady Oak La.
  TN17 & TN18 & TN5 1
Lady Vane Cl. TN11 1
Ladycroft Wlk. TN2 ....
Lady's Gift Rd. TN4 ....
Ladyclose Ave. ME3 ....
Ladycroft Gdns. **6** BR6 ..

croft Way. BR6 .... 51 C5
ern Ct. TN2 .... 149 C4
fields. Chatham ME5 ...... 62 D2
fields. Northfleet DA11 . 29 F4
smith Rd. SE9 .... 6 A1
View Rd. BR5 .... 38 B7
ork Rd. BR5 .... 37 E4
wood Rd. Cuxton ME2 .. 46 B2
wood Rd. Lane End DA2 27 E3
nda Way. DA1 .... 9 C3
n Rd. BR5 .... 38 B4
Ave. BR1 .... 22 A2
Dr. ME3 .... 32 C6
Rd. Ditton ME20 .... 90 E8
Rd. Royal Tunbridge Wells
.... 148 E4
Way Rd. TN13 .... 84 A4
dale Rd. SE18 .... 2 E1
ands.
rietsham ME17 .... 110 E6
ands.
dstone ME15 .... 107 A7
Rd. ME1 .... 61 C6
Rd. BR2 .... 50 C5
ide. Royal Tunbridge Wells
.... 149 E6
ide. Snodland ME6 .... 74 F6
ide Ave. SE28 .... 3 A5
ide Cl.
gh Beech TN8 .... 113 F4
Cl. Sidcup DA15 .... 7 C2
Dr. BR2 .... 50 E7
ide Pk. ME2 .... 47 E7
wood Rd. BR5 .... 37 C3
view Cl. ME6 .... 75 A6
ide Rd. TN13 .... 7 B3
wood Dr. ME8 .... 63 C6
Cl. RM18 .... 13 C5
's Cross. ME17 .... 124 A5
arde House. 6 ME14 ..... 92 A5
arde Ave. SE9 .... 23 A4
arde Cl. ME2 .... 60 A4
arde Dr. TN13 .... 84 A4
arde Cl. TN13 .... 84 A5
ardes. DA3 .... 56 F7
erhurst CE Prim Sch.
.... 166 B6
erhurst Cl. 14 BR5 ...... 38 D1
erhurst Gn. ME8 .... 49 B3
erhurst Golf Course.
.... 166 C5
erhurst Rd.
smonden TN12 & TN3 . 152 E3
urborne ME16 .... 91 B7
ersart Cl.
al Tunbridge Wells
& TN4 .... 133 D1
Cl. DA8 .... 8 C8
ert Mews. 4 ME6 .... 75 A8
ert Rd. E16 .... 1 B7
ert's Yd. TN9 .... 117 B1
erts Rd. TN1 & TN2 ... 149 D8
ert Cl. ME5 .... 62 B4
ourn Dr.
8 & ME19 .... 89 A2
ourn Way.
tham ME5 .... 62 C2
ourn Way.
al Tunbridge Wells
.... 149 D1
ourne Pl. SE3 .... 5 B6
ourne Rd. ME15 .... 92 F2
s Bank. TN9 .... 133 B7
scroft Ave.
2 & SE9 .... 22 D5
sfrith Gr. ME7 .... 63 B3
rbey Cl. DA15 .... 23 F6
rna Ave. DA12 .... 30 D6
Cl. BR6 .... 38 A2
ington Row. TN3 .... 147 E3
lighters Cl. 2
tford DA1 .... 9 F1
lighters Cl.
gham ME7 .... 62 F5
ort Cl. SE18 .... 1 F2
on Rd. RM13 .... 4 F8
shire Rd. ME15 .... 107 E7
aster Ct.
gham ME8 .... 63 C7
aster Ct.
esend DA12 .... 30 C5
aster Way. ME19 .... 88 F3
e Croft. DA3 .... 56 F8
elot Ave. ME2 .... 46 E7
elot Cl. ME2 .... 46 E6
elot Rd. DA16 .... 86 E8
elot Rd. DA16 .... 7 A4
es Cl. DA13 .... 44 A2
et La. ME15 .... 107 A6
es Cl. SE7 .... 1 E2

Lancing Rd. BR6 .... 52 B8
Land Way. ME3 .... 32 D5
Landale Gdns. DA1 .... 26 C8
Landale Ct. ME7 .... 63 A3
Landseer Ave. DA11 .... 29 D5
Landseer Cl. TN10 ...... 117 E6
Landstead Rd. SE18 .... 6 D7
Landway. TN15 .... 84 F7
Landway. The.
Borough Green TN15 ... 86 F7
Landway. The.
Kemsing TN15 .... 70 A2
Landway. The.
Maidstone ME14 .... 93 A4
Landway. The.
St Paul's Cray BR5 .... 38 C6
Lane End. DA7 .... 8 B4
Lane. The. SE3 .... 5 A6
Lanes Ave. DA11 .... 30 A5
Laneside. BR7 .... 23 C3
Langafel CE (VC) Prim Sch.
DA3 .... 43 A6
Langafel Cl. DA3 .... 42 E7
Langbrook Rd. SE3 .... 5 D5
Langdale Cl.
Gillingham ME8 .... 49 F1
Langdale Cl. Orpington BR6 . 51 B7
Langdale Cres. DA7 .... 8 A6
Langdale Rise. ME16 .... 91 C5
Langdale Wlk. 5 DA11 .. 29 F5
Langdon Rd. Bromley BR2 .. 36 B6
Langdon Rd. Rochester ME1 47 C4
Langdon Shaw. DA14 ... 23 F3
Langford Pl. DA14 .... 24 A5
Langham Gr. ME16 .... 91 C4
Langholm Rd. TN3 ...... 147 F3
Langhorne House. 3 SE7 .... 5 C8
Langlands Dr. DA2 .... 27 E3
Langley Gdns. BR5 .... 37 B3
Langley House. BR1 ..... 22 B1
Langley Rd. DA16 .... 7 C8
Langmore Ct. DA7 .... 7 D4
Langton Cl. ME14 .... 92 C5
Langton Green Cty Prim Sch.
TN3 .... 147 E4
Langton Rd.
Rusthall TN3 & TN4 ... 148 C3
Langton Rd.
Speldhurst TN3 .... 148 A7
Langton Ridge. TN3 .... 148 B3
Langton Way. SE3 .... 5 B7
Langworth Cl. DA2 .... 26 D5
Lankester Parker Rd. ME1 .. 61 C6
Lannoy Rd. SE9 .... 23 C7
Lanridge Rd. SE2 .... 3 D3
Lansbury Cres. DA1 ...... 10 A2
Lansbury Ct. SE28 .... 3 B6
Lansbury Gdns. RM18 .. 13 A6
Lansbury House. 5 DA17 .. 3 F1
Lansdown Rd.
Northfleet DA11 .... 29 F7
Lansdown Rd. Sidcup DA14 . 24 B5
Lansdown Rd. Tilbury RM18 12 F5
Lansdowne. Bexley DA7 . 7 D7
Lansdowne Ave.
Maidstone ME15 .... 107 C6
Lansdowne Ave.
Orpington BR6 .... 37 B1
Lansdowne Ct. 2 ME4 .. 47 F4
Lansdowne La. SE7 .... 1 D1
Lansdowne Mews. SE7 .. 1 D1
Lansdowne Prim Sch.
RM18 .... 12 F5
Lansdowne Rd.
Bromley BR1 .... 22 B1
Lansdowne Rd.
Chatham ME4 .... 47 E2
Lansdowne Rd.
East Malling ME19 .... 89 F8
Lansdowne Rd.
Royal Tunbridge Wells
TN1 & TN2 .... 149 B4
Lansdowne Rd.
Sevenoaks TN13 .... 84 D5
Lansdowne Rd.
Tonbridge TN9 .... 117 B2
Lansdowne Sq.
Northfleet DA11 .... 12 F1
Lansdowne Sq. 8
Royal Tunbridge Wells
TN1 .... 149 B4
Lansdowne Rd.
Sevenoaks TN13 .... 84 D5
Lansdowne Rd.
Tonbridge TN9 .... 117 B2
Lapins La. ME18 .... 88 F2
Lapis Cl. DA12 .... 31 B7
Lapwing Cl. DA8 .... 9 B7
Lapwing Rd. ME3 .... 21 B5
Lapwings. DA3 .... 43 B6
Lapwoods. The. DA12 ... 30 D6
Lapworth Cl. BR6 .... 52 C8
Larch Cl. ME20 .... 75 B2
Larch Cres.
Hoo St Werburgh ME3 34 E3
Larch Cres.
Tonbridge TN10 .... 117 C6

Larch Dene. BR6 .... 51 A8
Larch Gr.
Paddock Wood TN12 .. 135 F6
Larch Gr. Sidcup DA15 .. 23 F7
Larch Rd. DA1 .... 26 D7
Larch Way. BR2 .... 37 A2
Larch Wlk. BR8 .... 39 D7
Larch Wood Cl. ME5 ..... 62 D1
Larchcroft. ME5 .... 62 A4
Larches The. ME3 .... 32 C3
Larchwood Rd. SE9 ...... 23 B6
Larkfield. TN12 .... 135 A7
Larkfield Ave. ME7 .... 48 E4
Larkfield Brookfield
Cty Prim Schs. ME20 .. 75 A2
Larkfield Cl. Hayes BR2 .. 50 A8
Larkfield Cl. Larkfield ME20 . 75 A1
Larkfield Cl. Larkfield ME20 75 B1
Larkfield Rd.
Sevenoaks TN13 .... 83 C4
Larkfield Rd. Sidcup DA14 . 23 F5
Larkfield Trad Est. ME20 .. 75 B5
Larkfields. DA11 .... 29 E5
Larkin Cl. ME2 .... 33 B2
Larks Field. DA3 .... 42 F5
Larkspur Cl.
East Malling ME19 .... 75 A1
Larkspur Cl. 4 Newham E16 1 E8
Larkspur Cl. Orpington BR6 52 C7
Larkspur Rd. Chatham ME5 .. 61 E4
Larkspur Rd.
East Malling ME19 .... 74 F1
Larkstore Pk. TN12 ...... 139 E5
Larkswood Cl. DA8 .... 9 A6
Larkwell La. DA3 .... 42 F5
Larner Rd. DA8 .... 8 E7
Laser Quay. ME2 .... 47 D6
Lashenden Air Warfare Mus.
TN27 .... 142 A2
Lassa Rd. SE9 .... 5 F2
Latham Cl. E6 .... 1 E7
Latham Rd. DA6 .... 8 A2
Latimer Pl. 3 ME7 .... 48 C7
Latona Rd. DA12 .... 30 F3
Latymers. TN11 .... 131 B4
Launcelot Prim Sch. BR1 .. 22 A4
Launcelot Rd. BR1 & SE12 .. 22 A4
Launder Way. ME15 ...... 91 E2
Laura Dr. BR8 .... 26 A1
Laurel Ave. DA12 .... 30 C6
Laurel Bank. Royal Tunbridge Wells
TN4 .... 149 B8
Laurel Bank.
Wadhurst TN5 .... 175 A4
Laurel Cl. Dartford DA1 . 26 C7
Laurel Cl. Sidcup DA14 .. 24 A5
Laurel Gr. ME17 .... 109 D2
Laurel Rd. Gillingham ME7 .. 48 C7
Laurel Rd. Royal Tunbridge Wells
TN1 .... 149 D7
Laurel Way. TN1 .... 149 D7
Laurel Wlk. ME8 .... 63 E6
Laurels The. Bromley BR2 .. 36 A5
Laurels The. 3
Bromley,Widmore BR1 .. 36 B8
Laurels The.
Maidstone ME16 .... 91 C1
Laurels The. New Barn DA3 . 43 D6
Laurels The.
Wilmington DA2 .... 26 C5
Laurie Gray Ave. ME5 ... 61 D1
Lavenda Cl. ME7 .... 63 A4
Lavender Cl. Bromley BR2 .. 36 E3
Lavender Cl. 1
Chatham ME5 .... 61 C4
Lavender Cl.
East Malling ME19 .... 89 F8
Lavender Gdns. TN5 .... 176 F1
Lavender Hill. Swanley BR8 . 39 D6
Lavender Hill.
Tonbridge TN9 .... 133 C8
Lavender Rd. ME19 .... 89 F8
Lavender Sq. 6 ME19 . 179 A2
Lavenders Rd. ME19 ..... 89 C6
Lavernock Rd. DA7 .... 8 A5
Laverstoke Rd. ME16 .... 91 C8
Lavidge Rd. SE9 .... 22 F6
Lavinia Rd. 1 DA1 .... 9 F1
Lavisham House. BR1 ... 22 B3
Lawford Gdns. DA1 .... 9 C2
Lawn Cl. Bromley BR1 ... 22 B1
Lawn Cl. Chatham ME4 .. 48 B2
Lawn Cl. Swanley BR8 ... 39 C7
Lawn Cl. Tenterden TN30 .. 182 F7
Lawn Cty Prim Sch. DA11 .. 12 C1
Lawn Pk. TN13 .... 99 B8
Lawn Rd. Northfleet DA11 .. 12 C1
Lawn Rd. Tonbridge TN9 .. 133 B8
Lawns Cres. RM17 .... 12 D8
Lawns The.
Brenchley TN12 .... 152 B8

Lawns The. Sidcup DA14 .. 24 B4
Lawrance Sq. DA11 .... 29 F5
Lawrence Cl. ME15 ...... 107 A7
Lawrence Ct. DA12 .... 45 A5
Lawrence Gdns. RM18 .. 13 B7
Lawrence Hill Gdns. DA1 .. 9 C1
Lawrence Hill Rd. DA1 .... 9 C1
Lawrence Rd. Erith DA8 .. 8 B7
Lawrence Rd. Hayes BR4 .. 50 A6
Lawrence Rd.
Tonbridge TN10 .... 117 E6
Lawrence St. ME7 .... 48 C5
Lawson Cl. E16 .... 1 C8
Lawson Gdns. DA1 .... 9 D3
Lawson House. 1 SE18 .. 6 A8
Lawson Rd. DA1 .... 9 D3
Laxey Rd. BR6 .... 51 F4
Laxey The. ME15 .... 91 E1
Laxton Cl. ME15 .... 92 F3
Laxton Dr. ME17 .... 108 A1
Laxton Gdns. TN12 ...... 135 E7
Layfield House. 1 SE10 .. 1 A1
Layfield Rd. ME7 .... 48 F7
Layhams Rd. BR2 .... 50 A3
Laymarsh Cl. DA1 .... 3 F3
Layzell Wlk. SE9 .... 22 D7
Le May Ave. SE12 .... 22 B5
Le Temple Rd. TN12 ... 136 B6
Lea Ct. ME4 .... 47 E1
Lea Rd. TN13 .... 99 C8
Lea Vale. DA1 & DA7 ...... 8 D3
Leafield La. DA14 .... 24 F5
Leafy Glade. ME8 .... 63 B6
Leafy Gr. BR2 .... 50 C5
Leafy La. DA13 .... 58 A3
Leafy Oak Rd. SE12 ...... 22 C5
Lealands Ave. TN11 ..... 116 A1
Lealands Cl. TN3 .... 161 C6
Leamington Ave.
Bromley BR1 .... 22 C3
Leamington Ave.
Orpington BR6 .... 51 E6
Leamington Cl. BR1 ...... 22 C3
Leamouth Rd. E6 .... 1 E8
Leander Dr. DA12 .... 30 F4
Leander Rd. ME1 .... 61 C7
Learoyd Gdns. E6 .... 2 A6
Leas Dale. SE9 .... 23 A5
Leas Gn. BR7 .... 23 F2
Leas The.
Turner's Green TN5 ... 175 A6
Leas The. Woolwich SE18 .. 6 B6
Leatherbottle Gn. DA18 .. 3 F3
Leaves Green Rd. BR2 .. 50 D1
Lebrun Sq. SE3 .... 5 B4
Leckwith Ave. DA17 .... 7 E8
Leclair House. SE3 .... 5 B4
Leconfield Cl. TN9 .... 132 F7
Leda Rd. SE18 .... 1 F3
Lee Gn. BR5 .... 38 A4
Lee Green Rd. ME3 .... 33 D4
Lee Rd. ME6 .... 75 A8
Lee Sta. SE12 .... 5 A1
Leechcroft Ave. Sidcup DA15 .. 6 F2
Leechcroft Ave.
Swanley BR8 .... 39 F6
Leeds & Broomfield CE Prim Sch.
ME17 .... 109 D7
Leeds Castle. ME17 ...... 109 D7
Leeds Cl. BR6 .... 52 D8
Leeds House. ME2 .... 33 C1
Leeds Rd. ME17 .... 108 E3
Leeds Sq. ME8 .... 49 B3
Lees Rd. ME18 .... 120 E7
Leesons Hill. BR5 & BR7 .. 38 A6
Leesons Rd. BR5 .... 38 B6
Leesons Way. BR5 .... 37 F7
Leet Cl. ME7 .... 48 E6
Leeward Rd. ME7 .... 47 C1
Leewood Cl. SE12 .... 5 A1
Leewood Pl. BR8 .... 39 D5
Legatt Rd. SE9 .... 5 D2
Legge La. ME19 .... 74 D6
Leggs' La. TN3 .... 147 E5
Leghorn Rd. SE18 .... 2 D1
Leicester Dr. TN2 .... 162 F8
Leicester Rd.
Maidstone ME15 .... 107 D7
Leicester Rd.
Tilbury RM18 .... 12 F6
Leigh Ave. ME15 .... 107 B6
Leigh City Tech Coll The.
DA1 .... 27 A7
Leigh Cty Prim Sch. TN11 . 115 F1
Leigh Green Ind Est.
TN30 .... 183 B6
Leigh Halt. TN11 .... 115 F1
Leigh Pl. DA16 .... 7 A5
Leigh Rd. Gravesend DA11 .. 30 B6
Leigh Rd.
Powder Mills TN11 .... 116 B3

Leigh Terr. 2
St Paul's Cray BR5 .... 38 B6
Leigh Terr. Teston ME18 .. 90 A1
Leighton Cl. TN4 .... 149 A7
Leighton Gdns. RM18 .. 13 A7
Leila Parnell Pl. 14 SE7 .. 5 C8
Leith Hill. BR5 .... 38 A8
Leith Hill Gn. BR5 .... 38 A8
Leith Park Rd.
Gravesend DA12 .... 30 B7
Lelland House. 8 SE7 ..... 1 E2
Lemonwell Ct. SE9 .... 6 C2
Lemonwell Dr. SE9 .... 6 C2
Len Clifton House. 13
SE18 .... 1 F2
Len Valley Wlk. ME15 ... 92 F1
Lenderyou Ct. DA1 .... 26 E8
London Rd. TN15 .... 86 F6
Leneda Dr. TN2 .... 162 E8
Leney Rd. ME18 .... 104 E7
Lenfield Ave. ME14 ...... 92 B4
Lenham Cty Prim Sch.
ME17 .... 111 C5
Lenham Heath Rd. ME17 .. 111 C2
Lenham House.
Lenham ME17 .... 111 E5
Lenham House. 13
Orpington BR5 .... 38 D1
Lenham Rd.
Broadstone TN27 & ME17 126 D3
Lenham Rd. Erith DA7 .... 7 F8
Lenham Rd.
Fairbourne Heath ME17 .. 110 C1
Lenham Rd.
Headcorn TN27 .... 141 E6
Lenham Sta. ME17 ...... 111 C4
Lenham Way. ME8 .... 49 A3
Lennard Rd.
Keston Mark BR2 .... 36 F1
Lennard Rd.
Sevenoaks TN13 .... 83 E7
Lennox Ave. DA11 .... 13 A1
Lennox House. 6 DA17 .. 4 A3
Lennox Rd. DA11 .... 29 F8
Lennox Rd E. DA11 .... 30 A8
Lenor Cl. DA6 .... 7 E3
Lensbury Way. SE2 .... 3 D3
Lenside Dr. ME15 .... 93 A2
Lenton St. SE18 .... 2 D2
Leonard Ave. Otford TN14 .. 69 B3
Leonard Ave.
Swanscombe DA10 ...... 28 E8
Leonard Cl. ME16 .... 91 B6
Leonard Judge House.
DA2 .... 27 E3
Leonard Rd. ME3 .... 34 B3
Leonard Robbins Path. 3
SE28 .... 3 B6
Leonard St. E16 .... 1 E5
Leopold Rd. 2 ME4 .... 48 A3
Lesley Cl. Istead Rise DA13 .. 43 F8
Lesley Cl. Sidcup DA5 ... 25 B8
Lesley Cl. Swanley BR8 .. 39 D6
Lesley Tew Ct. TN10 .... 117 C5
Leslie Cres. TN30 .... 173 B2
Leslie Pl. ME16 .... 91 E5
Leslie Rd. Gillingham ME7 .. 48 D7
Leslie Rd. Newham E16 .. 1 B7
Leslie Smith Sq. 7 SE18 ... 6 A8
Lesnes Abbey (remains of).
SE2 .... 3 C2
Lesney Park Prim Sch. DA8 .. 8 D8
Lesney Park Rd. DA8 ...... 8 D8
Lesney Pk. DA8 .... 8 D8
Lessness Ave. DA7 .... 7 D7
Lessness Heath Prim Sch.
DA17 .... 4 A1
Lessness Pk. DA17 .... 4 A1
Lessness Rd. 3 DA17 ...... 4 A1
Lester Cl. ME13 .... 63 C2
Lester Rd. ME4 .... 48 A3
Lestock House. SE3 .... 5 D6
Letchworth Ave. ME4 .... 47 F1
Letchworth Cl. BR2 .... 36 A4
Letchworth Dr. BR2 .... 36 A4
Letter Box La. TN13 .... 99 C6
Leverholme Gdns. SE9 .. 23 A4
Levett Cl. ME3 .... 21 D8
Levetts La. TN32 .... 185 D1
Lewd La. TN27 .... 143 A3
Lewes Cl. RM17 .... 12 A8
Lewes Rd. BR1 .... 36 D7
Lewin Rd. DA6 .... 7 E3
Lewing Cl. BR6 .... 37 E1
Lewis Ave. ME8 .... 49 B2
Lewis Court Dr. ME17 .. 107 C3
Lewis Cl. DA11 .... 29 F6
Lewis King House. BR1 .. 22 B1

Lewis Rd. Bexley DA16 .... 7 C4
Lewis Rd. Istead Rise DA13 .. 43 F8
Lewis Rd. Sidcup DA14 .... 24 C5
Lewis Rd.
  Swanscombe DA10 .... 11 E1
Leybank. TN11 .... 116 F4
Leybourne CE (VA) Prim Sch.
  ME19 .... 74 E2
Leybourne Cl. Chatham ME5 62 A2
Leybourne Cl. Hayes BR2 ..... 36 A3
Leybourne Dell. TN17 .... 180 E6
Leybourne Rd. ME2 .... 46 F8
Leybourne Way. ME20 .... 74 F4
Leybridge Ct. SE12 .... 5 A2
Leybourne House. SE18 .... 5 E7
Leycroft Gdns. DA8 .... 9 B6
Leydenhatch La. BR8 .... 39 D8
Leyes Rd. E16 .... 1 D7
Leyhill Cl. BR8 .... 39 E4
Leyland Rd. SE12 .... 5 A2
Leysdown Ave. DA7 .... 8 E3
Leysdown Rd. SE9 .... 22 F6
Leyton Ave. ME7 .... 48 E1
Leyton Cross. DA2 .... 26 A6
Leyton Cross Rd. DA2 .... 25 F5
Leywood Rd. DA13 .... 58 D3
Lezayre Rd. BR6 .... 51 F4
Libya Terr. 6 ME14 .... 92 A7
Lichdale Cl. 7 BR6 .... 51 F6
Lichfield Cl. ME8 .... 49 D2
Liddon Rd. BR1 .... 36 D6
Lidsing Rd. ME14 .... 77 E6
Lidwells La. TN17 .... 153 E1
Lieth Park Rd. DA12 .... 30 C7
Liffler Rd. SE18 .... 2 E1
Lightfoot Gn. TN18 .... 178 E3
Lila Pl. BR8 .... 39 E5
Lilac Cres. ME2 .... 46 E6
Lilac Gdns. BR8 .... 39 D6
Lilac Pl. DA13 .... 44 B2
Lilac Rd. ME2 .... 46 E5
Lilburne Gdns. SE9 .... 5 E2
Lilburne Rd. SE9 .... 5 E2
Lilian Barker Cl. SE12 .... 5 A2
Lilk Hill. ME14 .... 93 C3
Lillechurch Rd. ME3 .... 32 F7
Lillesden Cotts. TN18 .... 184 E8
Lillieburn. ME19 .... 74 D2
Limavady House. 18 SE18 ...... 2 A2
Lime Ave. DA11 .... 29 D8
Lime Cl. Bromley BR1 .... 36 E5
Lime Cl. Frant TN3 .... 163 E3
Lime Cl. Marden TN12 .... 138 C6
Lime Cotts. TN12 .... 139 F3
Lime Cres. ME19 .... 90 A7
Lime Ct. ME8 .... 63 C3
Lime Gr. Orpington BR6 .... 51 B8
Lime Gr. Sidcup DA15 .... 6 F1
Lime Hill Rd. TN1 .... 149 A4
Lime Kiln Dr. SE7 .... 5 B8
Lime Pit La. TN14 .... 68 C2
Lime Rd. BR8 .... 39 D6
Lime Row. DA18 .... 3 F3
Lime Tree Cl. TN9 .... 117 C2
Lime Tree Wlk. TN13 .... 84 B2
Limepits Cross. ME9 .... 65 F3
Limes Cl. TN30 .... 183 C8
Limes Gr. TN18 .... 178 F5
Limes Row. BR6 .... 51 A5
Limes The. Edenbridge TN8 112 C1
Limes The.
  Frittenden TN17 .... 156 E6
Limes The. Keston Mark BR2 50 E8
Limes The. Lenham ME17 ... 111 D5
Limetree Cl. ME5 .... 62 B8
Limetree Terr. ME17 .... 111 E6
Limewood Rd. DA8 .... 8 C7
Linchmere Rd. SE12 .... 22 A8
Linclon Cl. DA8 .... 9 B5
Lincoln Cl. ME2 .... 46 D6
Lincoln Cl. SE12 .... 22 C5
Lincoln Green Rd. BR5 .... 37 F4
Lincoln Rd. Erith DA8 .... 8 F5
Lincoln Rd.
  Maidstone ME15 .... 107 D8
Lincoln Rd. Sidcup DA14 .... 24 B3
Lincolnshire Terr. DA2 .... 27 D4
Lincon Rd. ME7 .... 48 E5
Linden Ave. DA1 .... 26 C7
Linden Chase Rd. TN13 .... 84 B5
Linden Cl. Orpington BR6 .... 52 A5
Linden Cl.
  Paddock Wood TN12 ...... 136 A6
Linden Cl. Purfleet RM16 .... 10 C8
Linden Ct. Royal Tunbridge Wells
  TN2 .... 149 A2
Linden Ct. Sidcup DA14 ...... 23 E4
Linden Ct. Tonbridge TN10 117 B7

Linden Gdns. TN2 .... 148 F1
Linden House. 5 ME5 .... 61 F4
Linden Park Rd. TN2 .... 149 A2
Linden Rd. Coxheath ME17 106 C4
Linden Rd. Gillingham ME7 .. 48 E5
Linden Sq. TN13 .... 83 E5
Lindenfield. BR7 .... 37 B7
Lindens The. ME20 .... 75 E1
Lindisfarne Cl. DA12 .... 30 E6
Lindridge La. TN12 .... 139 C5
Lindsay House. 3 SE18 .... 2 A2
Lindsey Cl. BR1 .... 36 E6
Lindwood Cl. 8 E6 .... 1 F8
Lineacre Cl. ME8 .... 63 D6
Lines Terr. ME4 .... 48 A4
Ling Rd. Erith DA8 .... 8 E8
Ling Rd. Newham E16 .... 1 A8
Lingey Cl. DA15 .... 23 F6
Lingfield Ave. DA2 .... 27 B8
Lingfield Cres. SE9 .... 6 D3
Lingfield Rd.
  Borough Green TN15 ...... 87 B7
Lingfield Rd.
  Edenbridge TN8 .... 128 A8
Lingfield Rd.
  Gravesend DA12 .... 30 B6
Lingley Dr. ME2 .... 33 C2
Lingwood. DA7 .... 8 B5
Link Field. ME2 .... 36 A3
Link Hill La. TN27 .... 127 D3
Link The. Eltham SE9 .... 23 A5
Link The.
  New Ash Green DA3 .... 56 F8
Link Way. Bromley BR2 .... 36 E2
Link Way. Royal Tunbridge Wells
Linkden Cotts. TN18 .... 186 E5
Links The. Addington ME19 .. 73 E2
Links The. Chatham ME5 .... 62 B8
Links View. Dartford DA1 .... 26 C7
Links View. Woolwich SE18 .. 6 B6
Linkway. ME20 .... 75 C1
Linley Cl. RM18 .... 14 D7
Linnet Ave. TN12 .... 136 A5
Linnet Cl. SE28 .... 3 C6
Linslade Rd. BR6 .... 52 A4
Linsted Ct. SE9 & DA15 .... 6 E1
Linton Cl. Bexley DA16 .... 7 B6
Linton Cl. 2 Greenwich SE7 .. 1 C1
Linton Dann Cl. ME3 .... 34 D6
Linton Gdns. E6 .... 1 E7
Linton Gore. ME17 .... 106 D3
Linton Hill. TN12 .... 122 F6
Linton Hospl. ME17 .... 106 C2
Linton Mead Prim Sch. SE28 3 B6
Linton Rd. ME15 .... 106 F4
Lintorn Symonds Rd. ME3 .. 33 F5
Linwood Ave. ME2 .... 46 E8
Linzee Rd. Bexley DA6 .... 7 F3
Lion Rd. Newham E6 .... 1 F8
Lionel Gdns. SE9 .... 5 D2
Lionel Oxley House. 5
  RM17 .... 12 B8
Lionel Rd. Eltham SE9 .... 5 D2
Lionel Rd. Tonbridge TN9 .. 133 A8
Lions Cl. SE12 .... 22 D5
Liphook Way. ME16 .... 91 C8
Lipscombe Rd. TN2 .... 149 D6
Lipton Cl. SE28 .... 3 C6
Liptraps La. TN1 & TN2 ..... 149 D7
Lipwell Hill. ME23 .... 17 B4
Liskeard Cl. BR7 .... 23 C2
Liskeard Gdns. SE3 .... 5 A6
Lisle Cl. DA12 .... 31 B6
Lismore Cl. ME15 .... 107 A7
Lister Cl. ME19 .... 89 F8
Lister Rd. RM18 .... 13 A5
Lister Wlk. SE28 .... 3 D6
Listmas Rd. ME4 .... 48 B3
Little Alley. TN8 .... 128 B5
Little Bayham Cotts. TN3 .. 164 F4
Little Birches. DA15 .... 23 E6
Little Boundes Cl. TN4 ...... 132 F3
Little Browns La. TN8 .... 112 A4
Little Buckland Ave. ME16 .. 91 D6
Little Ct. ME16 .... 91 D2
Little Footway. TN3 .... 147 F3
Little Heath. SE7 .... 1 E1
Little Heath Rd. DA7 .... 7 F7
Little Hill. TN30 .... 174 C5
Little Iridge Farm Cotts.
  TN19 .... 184 C1
Little Job's Cross. TN17 ..... 181 F1
Little John Ave. ME5 .... 62 A1
Little Julians Hill. TN13 ...... 99 B8
Little Kit's Coty House.
  ME20 .... 76 C8
Little Mallett. TN3 .... 147 F3
Little Market Row. ME19 ..... 74 E2
Little Mount Sion. TN1 ...... 149 A2

Little Oakham Ct. ME3 .... 19 C4
Little Orch. ME17 .... 106 D3
Little Oxley. ME20 .... 74 E2
Little Pk. TN5 .... 174 E5
Little Queen St. DA1 .... 26 F8
Little Redlands. BR1 .... 36 E7
Little Sheephurst Cotts.
  TN12 .... 137 E5
Little Thrift. BR5 .... 37 C5
Little Wood. TN13 .... 84 D5
Littlebourne Ave. ME8 .... 49 B4
Littlebourne Rd. ME14 .... 92 C6
Littlebrook Manor Way.
  DA1 .... 10 A2
Littlecombe. SE7 .... 5 B8
Littlecourt Rd. TN13 .... 84 A3
Littlecroft. Eltham SE9 .... 6 A4
Littlecroft. Istead Rise DA13 29 E1
Littledale. Darenth DA2 .... 27 C5
Littledale. Woolwich SE2 .... 7 A8
Littlefield. TN11 .... 118 E8
Littlejohn Rd. BR5 .... 38 B4
Littlemede. SE9 .... 22 F5
Littlemore Rd. SE2 .... 3 A4
Livesey St. ME18 .... 90 A1
Livingstone Circ. ME7 .... 48 D5
Livingstone Gdns. DA12 ...... 30 D3
Livingstone Hospl. DA1 .... 26 F8
Livingstone Rd.
  Gillingham ME7 .... 48 D5
Livingstone Rd.
  Gravesend DA12 .... 30 D3
Livingstone Wlk. 4 ME15 107 F5
Lizban St. SE3 .... 5 B7
Llanover Rd. SE18 .... 6 A7
Lloyd House. 10 SE18 .... 1 F2
Lloyds Gn. TN30 .... 189 D4
Loaland Bsns Ctr. ME2 .... 47 D8
Loam Ct. DA1 .... 26 A7
Loampits Cl. TN9 .... 117 D3
Lobelia Cl. Gillingham ME7 .. 48 E6
Lobelia Cl. 5 Newham E6 ..... 1 E8
Locarno Ave. ME8 .... 49 A2
Lochat Rd. ME3 .... 33 E6
Lochmere Cl. DA8 .... 8 B8
Lock La. ME14 & ME16 .... 76 D1
Lock St. ME7 .... 48 C5
Lock's Yd. TN15 .... 84 C2
Lockesley Dr. BR5 .... 38 A3
Lockington Cl. TN9 .... 132 F7
Lockington Gr. ME1 .... 47 C5
Locknut Cotts. DA13 .... 57 E2
Lockside. TN9 .... 117 C2
Locksley Cl. ME5 .... 61 E2
Lockswood. ME16 .... 91 D7
Lockyer Rd. RM16 .... 10 C8
Lockyers Hill. DA13 .... 58 F5
Lodden Ct. 18 BR5 .... 38 D1
Loddington La. ME17 .... 123 A8
Lodder Cl. ME17 .... 111 B5
Lodge Ave. DA1 .... 9 C1
Lodge Cl. Orpington BR6 ..... 38 B1
Lodge Cl.
  Wateringbury ME18 .... 104 D8
Lodge Cres. BR6 .... 38 B1
Lodge Ct. DA12 .... 31 E2
Lodge Gdns. ME17 .... 125 F6
Lodge Hill La. ME3 .... 7 B7
Lodge Hill La. ME3 .... 33 F7
Lodge La. Cobham DA12 ...... 45 B5
Lodge La. Sidcup DA6 .... 7 D1
Lodge La. Westerham TN16 .. 96 C8
Lodge Oak La. TN9 .... 133 D8
Lodge Rd. Bromley BR1 ...... 22 C1
Lodge Rd. Maidstone ME14 .. 92 D5
Lodge Rd.
  Staplehurst TN12 .... 139 E5
Lodge Rd. Tonbridge TN9 .. 117 B2
Lodgewood Cotts. TN8 ...... 113 D2
Logs Hill. BR1 & BR7 .... 36 E8
Logs Hill Cl. BR7 .... 36 E8
Lomaria Ct. TN9 .... 149 C4
Lomas La. TN18 .... 186 F5
Lombard St. DA4 .... 41 C5
Lombard Trad Est. SE7 .... 1 B2
Lombard Wall. SE7 .... 1 B2
Lombardy Cl. ME7 .... 63 A6
Lombardy Dr. ME14 .... 92 C5
London City Airport. E16 ...... 1 C5
London Golf Course. TN15 .. 56 D4
London Ind Pk The. E6 .... 2 A8
London La. Bromley BR1 ..... 22 A1
London La.
  Cranbrook Common TN17 156 A2
London Rd.
  Addington ME19 .... 73 D2
London Rd.
  Bidborough TN4 .... 132 F3
London Rd. Bromley BR1 ... 36 A8
London Rd. Crayford DA1 .... 8 B2
London Rd. Ditton ME20 ..... 75 C1

London Rd.
  Farningham DA4 .... 40 D3
London Rd. Flimwell TN5 .. 177 D3
London Rd. Gillingham ME8 . 49 C1
London Rd.
  Grays RM17 & RM16 ...... 11 E8
London Rd.
  Hartlip Hill ME8 & ME9 ... 64 D7
London Rd.
  Hurst Green TN19 .... 184 A3
London Rd.
  Knockholt Pound TN14 ... 67 E4
London Rd. Maidstone ME16 91 C6
London Rd.
  Maypole BR6 & TN14 ..... 52 F2
London Rd. Newington ME9 . 65 A6
London Rd. Northfleet DA11 12 E1
London Rd. Rochester ME2 .. 47 A7
London Rd.
  Royal Tunbridge Wells,Mount Sion
  TN1 & TN2 & TN4 .... 149 A3
London Rd. Sevenoaks TN13 84 B2
London Rd. Sevenoaks,
  Dunton Green TN13 .... 83 E7
London Rd.
  Shepham Heath TN14 ..... 68 C6
London Rd. Swanley BR8 ... 39 E6
London Rd.
  Swanley,White Oak BR8 .. 39 D7
London Rd.
  Swanscombe DA9 .... 11 C2
London Rd. Tilbury RM18 ... 13 B5
London Rd.
  Tonbridge TN10 & TN11 .. 117 B3
London Rd.
  Twitton TN13 & TN14 ..... 68 D1
London Rd. Watt's Cross
  TN11 & TN13 & TN15 ... 116 B7
London Rd.
  West Kingsdown TN15 ..... 56 A1
London Rd.
  Westerham TN16 .... 81 D3
London Rd.
  Wrotham TN15 .. 72 B3
London Rd.
  Wrotham Heath TN15 ..... 72 F1
London Rd E. ME20 .... 90 F8
London Road Purfleet.
  RM16 .... 10 C8
London Road West Thurrock.
  RM16 .... 11 A8
Londonderry Par. DA8 .... 8 D7
Lonewood Way. TN11 .... 102 F2
Long Acre. BR5 & BR6 .... 52 D8
Long Barn Rd. TN14 .... 99 B2
Long Catlis Rd. ME8 .... 63 D4
Long Cl. DA9 .... 11 E1
Long Meadow. ME2 .... 46 C8
Long Street La. RM18 .... 3 B3
Long Ave. E16 .... 1 A8
Lower Bell La. ME7 7
Lower Boxley Rd. 8 ME14 . 9
Lower Camden. BR7 3
Lower Church Hill. DA9 1
Lower Croft. BR8 2
Lower East Rd. ME4 4
Lower Fant Rd. ME16 9
Lower Farm Rd. ME17 12
Lower Gn. TN11 1
Lower Gravel Rd. BR2 3
Lower Green Rd.
  Pembury TN2 15
Lower Green Rd.
  Rusthall TN3 & TN4 14
Lower Haysden La.
  TN11 & TN4 & TN9 13
Lower Hartlip Rd. ME9 6
Lower Hazelhurst. TN5 17
Lower High St. TN5 17
Lower Higham Rd. DA12 3
Lower Park Rd. DA17 ....
Lower Platts. TN5 17
Lower Rainham Rd. ME7 4
Lower Range Rd. DA12 3
Lower Rd. Erith DA8 ....
Lower Rd.
  Erith,Belvedere DA17 ......
Lower Rd. Hextable BR8 2
Lower Rd.
  Orpington BR5 & BR6 .....
Lower Rd.
  Sutton Valence ME17 12
Lower Rd. Tilbury RM18 1
Lower Rd.
  West Farleigh ME15 10

Longmead Dr. DA14 ....
Longmeadow Rd. DA15 ....
Longparish Cl. ME15 ....
Longreach Rd. DA8 ....
Longshaw Rd. ME1 ....
Longspring Wood. TN13 .....
Longten's Cotts. DA12 ....
Longtown Ct. 7 DA2 ....
Longview Way. TN1 ....
Longwalk. DA13 ....
Longwood. ME5 ....
Longworth Cl. SE28 ....
Lonsdale Cl. SE12 & SE9 ....
Lonsdale Cres. DA2 ....
Lonsdale Dr. ME8 ....
Lonsdale Gdns. TN1 & TN2 1
Lonsdale Rd. DA7 ....
Loop Rd. BR7 ....
Loose Cty Prim Sch.
  ME15 10
Loose Rd. ME15 10
Loraine Ct. BR7 ....
Lord Chatham's Ride.
  TN14 6
Lord Roberts Terr. SE18 .....
Lord Romney's Hill. ME14 .. 9
Lord St. Gravesend DA11 3
Lord St. Newham E16 ....
Lord Warwick St. SE18 ....
Lords Wood Cl. ME5 ....
Lords Wood La. ME5 ....
Lordswood Cl. DA2 ....
Lordswood Cty Prim Sch.
  ME5 ....
Lordswood Ind Est. ME5 ......
Lorenden Pk. TN18 1
Lorimar Bsns Ctr. RM13 .....
Lorton Cl. DA12 ....
Lossenham La. TN18 18
Louisville Ave. ME7 ....
Louvain Rd. DA2 ....
Lovage App. E6 ....
Love La. East End TN27 14
Love La. East Tilbury RM18 ..
Love La. Rochester ME1 ....
Love La. Sidcup DA15 ....
Love La.
  Wateringbury ME18 10
Love La. Woolwich SE18 ......
Lovel Ave. DA16 ....
Lovelace Ave. BR2 ....
Lovelace Cl. Gillingham ME8 6
Lovelace Cl.
  West Kingsdown TN15 .....
Lovelace Gn. SE9 ....
Lover's La. DA9 ....
Lovers La. TN17 1
Lovibonds Ave. BR6 ....
Low Cl. DA9 ....
Low Meadow. ME2 ....
Low Street La. RM18 ....
Lowe Ave. E16 ....

Marden Sta. TN12 .... 138 C6
Marechal Niel Ave. DA15 ...... 23 D5
Marechal Niel Par. DA15 ...... 23 D5
Margaret Gardner Dr. SE9 .. 22 F6
Margaret Rd. DA5 .... 7 D1
Margate Cl. ME7 .... 48 E6
Margetts La. ME1 .... 60 D1
Margetts Pl. ME2 .... 34 A3
Marian Sq. TN12 .... 139 F4
Marina Cl. **1** BR2 .... 36 A6
Marina Dr. Bexley DA16 .... 6 E5
Marina Dr. Dartford DA1 ...... 27 A7
Marina Dr. Northfleet DA11 .. 12 F1
Marine Dr.
  Hoo St Werburgh ME3 ...... 34 E3
Marine Dr. **5** Woolwich SE18 .. 1 F2
Marine View. ME4 .... 34 B1
Mariners Cl. DA9 .... 11 B3
Mariners Wlk. DA8 .... 8 F8
Marion Cl. ME5 .... 62 A2
Marion Cres.
  Maidstone ME15 .... 107 B8
Marion Cres. Orpington BR5 38 B4
Maritime Cl. Rochester ME2 47 D8
Maritime Cl.
  Swanscombe DA9 .... 11 B2
Maritime Ind Est. SE7 .... 1 B2
Maritime Way. ME4 .... 48 A8
Marjorie McClure Sch. BR7 . 37 C8
Mark Cl. Bexley DA7 .... 7 E6
Mark Cl. Keston BR2 .... 50 E6
Mark La. DA12 .... 13 E1
Mark Way. BR8 .... 40 A4
Market Alley. **3** DA11 .... 13 B1
Market Bldgs. **4** ME14 .... 91 F4
Market Colonnade. **3**
  ME14 .... 91 F4
Market Meadow. BR5 .... 38 C5
Market Pl. **2** Bexley DA7 ..... 8 A3
Market Pl. Dartford DA1 .... 26 E8
Market Pl. **14**
  Royal Tunbridge Wells TN2 149 A2
Market Pl. **1** Tilbury RM18 .. 13 A5
Market Sq. Bromley BR1 ...... 36 A7
Market Sq. Royal Tunbridge Wells
  TN2 .... 149 B4
Market Sq.
  Westerham TN16 .... 81 D1
Market St. Dartford DA1 .... 26 E8
Market St. **2**
  Maidstone ME14 .... 91 F4
Market St. **13**
  Royal Tunbridge Wells TN2 149 A2
Market St.
  Staplehurst TN12 .... 139 F5
Market St. Woolwich SE18 .... 2 A2
Market Way. **2** TN16 .... 81 D1
Marks Sq. DA11 .... 29 F4
Marlborough Cl.
  Orpington BR5 .... 37 F3
Marlborough Cl.
  Royal Tunbridge Wells TN4 148 E4
Marlborough Cres. TN13 ...... 83 E3
Marlborough Ct. TN16 .... 81 C1
Marlborough House. ME8 .... 63 F8
Marlborough House Sch.
  TN18 .... 178 E2
Marlborough La. SE7 .... 5 C7
Marlborough Park Ave.
  DA15 .... 24 A7
Marlborough Rd.
  Bexley DA16 .... 7 D4
Marlborough Rd.
  Bromley BR2 .... 36 C5
Marlborough Rd.
  Dartford DA1 .... 9 C1
Marlborough Rd.
  Gillingham ME7 .... 48 B5
Marlborough Rd.
  Woolwich SE18 .... 2 C3
Marlborough Sch. DA15 ...... 24 A8
Marle Place Rd. TN12 .... 152 C4
Marler House. DA8 .... 8 F5
Marley Ave. DA7 .... 7 D8
Marley La. TN27 .... 142 C3
Marley Rd.
  Harrietsham ME17 .... 110 F6
Marley Rd.
  Hoo St Werburgh ME3 ...... 34 D6
Marley Way. ME1 .... 47 C2
Marlhurst. TN8 .... 112 B4
Marling Way. DA12 .... 30 E3
Marlings Cl. BR7 .... 37 E5
Marlings Park Ave. BR7 .... 37 E6
Marlow Copse. ME5 .... 61 F1
Marlowe Cl. BR7 .... 23 D2
Marlowe Gdns. SE9 .... 6 A1
Marlowe Rd. ME20 .... 75 A3

Marlowes The. DA1 .... 8 D3
Marlpit Cl. TN8 .... 112 C4
Marlpit Cotts. ME17 .... 107 E2
Marlpit Gdns. TN5 .... 176 E1
Marlpit The. TN5 .... 174 E5
Marlwood Cl. DA15 .... 23 E6
Marmadon Rd. SE18 & SE2 ... 2 F7
Marne Ave. DA16 .... 7 A4
Marquis Dr. ME7 .... 63 B3
Marrabon Cl. DA15 .... 24 A7
Marram Ct. RM17 .... 12 E8
Marriott Rd. DA1 .... 27 A8
Marsden Way. **2** BR6 .... 51 F6
Marsh Cres. ME23 .... 17 E4
Marsh Green Rd. TN8 .... 128 C5
Marsh La. ME3 .... 16 B6
Marsh Quarter La. TN18 .... 186 C3
Marsh Rd. ME2 .... 60 B5
Marsh St. Dartford DA1 .... 10 A5
Marsh St. Rochester ME2 .... 47 B7
Marsh Way.
  New Hythe ME20 .... 75 A4
Marsh Way. Rainham RM9 .... 4 D8
Marshall Gdns. TN11 .... 102 E1
Marshall Path. **10** SE28 ...... 3 B6
Marshall Rd. ME8 .... 63 C8
Marshalls Gr. SE18 .... 1 E2
Marshalls Land. TN30 .... 173 A3
Marsham Cl. BR7 .... 23 B3
Marsham Cres. ME17 .... 108 B1
Marsham St. ME14 .... 92 A4
Marsham Way. ME2 .... 60 A5
Marshbrook Cl. SE3 .... 5 D4
Marshland View. ME3 .... 19 C5
Marston Cl. ME1 .... 61 E3
Marston Ct. DA14 .... 23 F4
Marston Dr. ME14 .... 92 C5
Marston House. RM17 .... 12 A8
Marston Wlk. ME5 .... 61 E3
Martens Ave. DA7 .... 8 C3
Martens Cl. DA7 .... 8 C3
Martham Cl. SE28 .... 3 D6
Martin Bowes Rd. SE9 .... 5 F4
Martin Cl. ME7 .... 63 A3
Martin Dene. DA6 .... 7 F2
Martin Dr. DA2 .... 10 C1
Martin Hardie Way. TN10 .. 117 E5
Martin House. DA11 .... 29 F6
Martin Rd. Rochester ME2 ... 47 B8
Martin Rd. Wilmington DA2 . 26 C5
Martin Rise. DA6 .... 7 F2
Martin Sq. ME20 .... 75 A2
Martin's Shaw. TN13 .... 83 C5
Martindale Ave. Newham
  E16 .... 1 A6
Martindale Ave.
  Orpington BR6 .... 52 A5
Martins Cl.
  Lower Higham ME3 .... 32 D6
Martins Cl.
  St Paul's Cray BR5 .... 38 C5
Martins Cl.
  Tenterden TN30 .... 183 C8
Martins La. TN12 .... 103 E2
Martyn House. SE2 .... 7 D8
Marvels Cl. SE12 .... 22 B6
Marvels La. SE12 .... 22 C5
Marvels Lane Prim Sch.
  SE12 .... 22 D4
Marvin Ct. TN12 .... 119 F6
Marwell. TN16 .... 81 B1
Marwood Cl. DA16 .... 7 B4
Mary Burrows Gdns. TN15 .. 70 B2
Mary Day's. TN17 .... 167 E7
Mary Lawrenson Pl. **2** SE3 .. 5 A7
Mary Macarthur House. **3**
  DA17 .... 4 A3
Mary Magdalene House. **7**
  TN9 .... 133 B8
Mary Rose Hall. E6 .... 1 F8
Marybank. SE18 .... 1 F2
Maryfield Cl. DA5 .... 25 E5
Maryland Cl. ME8 .... 63 E5
Maryland Dr. ME16 .... 90 F2
Maryland Rd. TN2 .... 149 D1
Maryon Ct. BR5 .... 38 B5
Maryon Gr. SE7 .... 1 E2
Maryon Rd. SE7 .... 1 E2
Maryville. DA16 .... 6 F5
Mascall's Court La. TN12 .. 136 B4
Mascall's Court Rd. TN12 .. 136 A4
Mascalls Cl. **13** SE7 .... 5 C8
Mascalls Pk. TN12 .... 135 F5
Mascalls Rd. SE7 .... 5 C8
Mascalls Sch. TN12 .... 136 A4
Masefield Cl. DA8 .... 8 F6
Masefield Dr. ME3 .... 33 B8
Masefield Rd. Dartford DA1 .. 10 B2
Masefield Rd.
  Lunsford ME20 .... 74 F4

Masefield Rd.
  Northfleet DA11 .... 29 D5
Masefield View. BR6 .... 51 C7
Masefield Way. TN9 .... 132 F7
Masham House. **6** DA18 ...... 3 D4
Mason Cl. DA7 .... 8 B4
Masons Hill. Bromley BR2 ... 36 B5
Masons Hill. Woolwich SE18 .. 2 B2
Masser Gunners' Pl. SE18 ..... 5 E7
Masters La. ME19 .... 74 B5
Masthead Cl. DA9 .... 10 C3
Matchless Dr. SE18 .... 6 A7
Mate Hall Villas. ME14 .... 93 C4
Matfield Cl. BR2 .... 36 A4
Matfield Cres. ME14 .... 92 C5
Matfield Rd. DA17 .... 8 A8
Matilda Cl. ME7 .... 63 B8
Matrix Bens Ctr. DA1 .... 9 E2
Matterdale Gdns. ME16 ...... 90 E2
Matthews La. TN11 .... 102 F4
Mattinson Pl. ME9 .... 95 F7
Matts Hill Rd. ME9 .... 64 E2
Maud Cashmore Way. SE18 .. 1 F3
Maude Rd. BR8 .... 26 A2
Maudslay Rd. SE9 .... 5 F4
Maundene Cty Prim Sch.
  ME5 .... 62 B5
Maunders Cl. ME5 .... 62 C8
Mavelstone Cl. BR1 .... 36 E8
Mavelstone Rd. BR1 .... 36 E8
Mavis Wlk. **9** E6 .... 1 E8
Maxey Rd. SE18 .... 2 C2
Maxim Rd. Crayford DA1 ...... 8 E2
Maxim Rd. Erith DA8 .... 4 E2
Maxinfeldt Rd. DA8 .... 4 E1
Maximilian Dr. ME2 .... 60 B4
Maxton Cl. ME14 .... 92 F5
Maxwell Dr. ME16 .... 91 B6
Maxwell Gdns. BR6 .... 51 F7
Maxwell House.
  Chislehurst BR7 .... 23 B1
Maxwell House. **12**
  Woolwich SE18 .... 6 B8
Maxwell Rd. Bexley DA16 ..... 7 A4
Maxwell Rd. Gillingham ME7 48 A6
May Ave. Northfleet DA11 ... 29 F7
May Ave. Orpington BR5 ..... 38 B4
May Avenue Est. **1** DA11 ... 29 F7
May Ct. RM17 .... 12 E8
May Pl. DA13 .... 44 D4
May Rd. Gillingham ME7 ..... 48 C4
May Rd. Hawley DA2 .... 26 F4
May Rd. Rochester ME1 .... 47 C3
May St. Cuxton ME2 .... 46 B2
May St. Snodland ME6 .... 75 B8
May Terr. **2** ME4 .... 48 A7
May Wynne House. E16 .... 1 B7
Maybury Ave. DA2 .... 27 C7
Maybury Cl. BR5 .... 37 B4
Maycotts La. TN12 .... 135 D1
Mayday Gdns. SE3 .... 5 E5
Mayerne Rd. SE9 .... 5 D2
Mayes Cl. BR8 .... 40 A5
Mayeswood Rd. SE12 .... 22 C4
Mayfair. ME2 .... 47 C8
Mayfair Ave. Bexley DA16 .... 7 D6
Mayfair Ave.
  Maidstone ME15 .... 107 A8
Mayfield Rd. DA1 .... 9 D2
Mayfield. Bexley DA7 .... 7 F4
Mayfield. Swanscombe DA10 11 E1
Mayfield Ave. BR6 .... 37 F2
Mayfield Cl. Chatham ME5 .. 62 A1
Mayfield Cl. Gillingham ME8 49 E2
Mayfield Cl. La. TN5 .... 174 D4
Mayfield Pk. TN5 .... 174 E5
Mayfield Rd. Bromley BR1 ... 36 E4
Mayfield Rd. Erith DA17 .... 4 C2
Mayfield Rd.
  Northfleet DA11 .... 29 F8
Mayfield Rd. Royal Tunbridge Wells
  TN4 .... 148 F4
Mayfield Villas. DA14 .... 24 C2
Mayford Rd. ME5 .... 62 D2
Mayhill Rd. SE7 .... 5 B8
Maylam Ct. TN10 .... 117 C4
Maylands Dr. DA14 .... 24 D5
Maynard Cl. DA8 .... 8 F7
Maynard Pl. ME5 .... 48 D2
Maynard's La. TN12 .... 135 E1
Maynards. TN12 .... 138 C5
Mayor's Pl. **9** TN30 .... 183 A7
Mayors La. DA2 .... 26 C3
Mayplace Ave. DA1 .... 9 A3
Mayplace Cl. DA7 .... 8 B4
Mayplace La. Woolwich SE18 .. 6 B7
Mayplace La. Woolwich SE18 6 B8
Mayplace Prim Sch. DA7 .... 8 D3
Mayplace Rd E. DA7 .... 8 C4
Mayplace Rd W. DA7 .... 8 A3

Maypole Cotts. BR6 .... 53 A4
Maypole Cres. DA8 .... 9 D8
Maypole Cty Prim Sch.
  DA5 .... 25 E6
Maypole La. TN17 .... 167 F8
Maypole Rd.
  Gravesend DA12 .... 30 F7
Maypole Rd. Maypole BR6 ... 52 F4
Maytham Bglws. TN17 ...... 182 A1
Maytham Rd. TN17 .... 182 A1
Mayweed Ave. ME5 .... 61 E4
Mc Call Cres. SE7 .... 1 E1
Mc Dowall Cl. **11** E16 .... 1 A8
Mc Kenzie Rd. ME5 .... 62 A3
McAlpine Cres. ME15 .... 106 F3
McAuley Cl. SE9 .... 6 A2
McCabe Cl. TN12 .... 139 E2
McCudden Rd. DA1 .... 9 F4
McCudden Row. **4** ME4 ..... 48 A6
McDermott Rd. TN15 .... 86 F7
McKenzie Cl. ME20 .... 90 F8
McLeod Rd. SE2 .... 3 B2
Mead Cl. BR8 .... 40 A4
Mead Cres. DA1 .... 26 D7
Mead Rd. Chislehurst BR7 ... 23 C2
Mead Rd. Dartford DA1 ...... 26 D7
Mead Rd. Edenbridge TN8 . 128 D7
Mead Rd. Gravesend DA11 .. 30 B6
Mead Road Inf Sch. BR7 ..... 23 C2
Mead The. Leybourne ME19 . 74 E2
Mead The.
  New Ash Green DA3 .... 56 E8
Mead The. Royal Tunbridge Wells
  TN2 .... 149 C2
Mead Wall. ME3 .... 15 F8
Mead Way. BR2 .... 36 A3
Meades Cl. TN12 .... 138 B6
Meadfield Rd. DA13 .... 58 A8
Meadow Bank. Leigh TN11 . 115 F1
Meadow Bank.
  West Malling ME19 .... 89 C8
Meadow Bank Cl. TN15 ...... 55 F2
Meadow Cl. Bexley DA6 .... 7 F2
Meadow Cl. Chatham ME5 ... 61 F5
Meadow Cl. Chislehurst BR7 23 B3
Meadow Cl. Halstead TN14 .. 68 A3
Meadow Cl.
  Sevenoaks TN13 .... 84 A4
Meadow Cl.
  Upper Halling ME2 .... 59 E4
Meadow Cres. ME2 .... 59 E4
Meadow Croft. BR1 .... 36 F6
Meadow Gdns. TN15 .... 71 F3
Meadow Hill Rd. **6**
  TN1 & TN2 .... 149 B3
Meadow La.
  Marlpit Hill TN8 .... 112 B4
Meadow Rd.
  Gillingham,Rainham ME8 .... 49 A2
Meadow Rd. Royal Tunbridge Wells
  TN1 .... 149 A4
Meadow Rd.
  Royal Tunbridge Wells,
  Southborough TN4 .... 132 F1
Meadow Rd. Rusthall TN4 .. 148 C4
Meadow Rd.
  Tonbridge TN9 .... 133 B8
Meadow The.
  Chislehurst BR7 .... 23 C2
Meadow The.
  Pembury TN2 .... 150 E8
Meadow View. DA15 .... 24 B8
Meadow View Cotts.
  Hurst Green TN19 .... 184 A3
Meadow View Cotts.
  Laddingford ME18 .... 120 E5
Meadow View Rd. ME17 .... 107 B3
Meadow Way. Dartford DA2 27 C8
Meadow Way.
  Marden TN12 .... 138 G6
Meadow Way.
  Orpington BR6 .... 51 A7
Meadow Wlk.
  Maidstone ME15 .... 92 B3
Meadow Wlk. Snodland ME6 74 F7
Meadow Wlk.
  Wilmington DA2 .... 26 D8
Meadowbank Rd. ME4 .... 48 A4
Meadowdown. ME14 .... 92 E4
Meadowlands. ME7 .... 63 A4
Meadowlands. TN15 .... 84 F7
Meadows. TN17 .... 170 D1
Meadows Sch (Barnados).
  TN4 .... 132 F2

Meadows The.
  Biddenden TN27 ....
Meadows The.
  Halstead TN14 ....
Meadows The.
  Maidstone ME15 ....
Meadows The.
  Orpington BR6 ....
Meadowside. Dartford DA1 ..
Meadowside. Eltham SE9 .....
Meadowside Cotts. TN5 ..... C2
Meadowsweet Cl. **3** E16 ...
Meadowview. BR5 ....
Meadowview Rd. DA5 ....
Meads The. TN17 ....
Meadside Wlk. ME5 ....
Meadway. Halstead TN14 ....
Meadway.
  Hildenborough TN11 ....
Meadway The.
  Orpington BR6 ....
Sevenoaks TN13 ....
Meath Cl. BR5 ....
Medbury Rd. DA12 ....
Mede House. BR1 ....
Medebourne Cl. SE3 ....
Medhurst Cres. DA12 ....
Medhurst Gdns. DA12 ....
Medick Ct. RM17 ....
Medina House. **6** DA8 ....
Medina Rd.
  Tonbridge TN10 ....
Medina Rd. Ditton ME20 .....
Medina Rd.
  Tonbridge TN10 ....
Medlar Gr. ME7 ....
Medlar House. **3** DA14 ......
Medlar Rd. RM17 ....
Medlars The.
  Maidstone ME14 ....
Meopham Station DA13 ....
Medway Ave.
  High Halstow ME23 ....
Medway Ave.
  Yalding ME18 ....
Medway Com Coll. ME4 ......
Medway Cotts. TN17 ....
Medway Ct. **20** BR5 ....
Medway Ent Ctr. ME2 ....
Medway Gdns. ME4 ....
Medway Heritage Ctr. ME4 ..
Medway Hospl. ME7 ....
Medway House. **1** ME15 .
Medway Meadows. TN12 .
Medway Rd. Crayford DA1 ...
Medway Rd. Gillingham ME7 ..
Medway Rd.
  Gillingham,Rainham ME8 ...
Medway Rd. Royal Tunbridge
  TN1 ....
Medway Service Area. ME8 ..
Medway St. Chatham ME4 ...
Medway St.
  Maidstone ME14 ....
Medway Trad Est. ME16 .....
Medway View.
  Barnes Street TN11 ....
Medway View.
  Lower Stoke ME3 ....
Medway Wharf Rd. TN9 .....
Medway Wharf Rd. TN9 ......
Meerbrook Rd. SE3 & SE9 ...
Meeson's La. RM17 ....
Meeting House La. ME4 ......
Megby Cl. ME8 ....
Megrims Hill. TN18 ....
Meirs Court Rd. ME8 ....
Melanda Cl. BR7 ....
Melanie Cl. DA7 ....
Melba Gdns. RM18 ....
Melbourne Cl. BR6 ....
Melbourne Ct. **3** DA11 ......
Melbourne Rd.
  Chatham ME4 ....
Melbourne Rd. Tilbury RM18
Melbury Cl. BR7 ....
Meldrum Cl. BR5 ....
Melford Dr. ME16 ....
Melliker La. DA13 ....
Melling St. SE18 ....
Mellish Ind Est. E16 ....
Mells Cres. SE9 ....
Melody Cl. ME8 ....
Melrose Cl. Lewisham SE12 ..
Melrose Cl.
  Maidstone ME15 ....
Melrose Cres. BR6 ....
Melthorpe Gdns. SE3 ....
Melville Ct. ME4 ....
Melville Rd.
  Maidstone ME15 ....

ille Rd. Sidcup DA14 ...... 24 C6
ess Path. **4** SE18 .... 6 A8
dian Rd. A2
dip Rd. DA2 .... 8 E6
dip Wlk. TN2 .... 149 D5
nie House. SE18 .... 5 F6
L Ct. **21** BR5 .... 38 D1
oham Cty Prim Sch.
.... 44 A2
oham Sch. DA13 .... 58 A8
tham Sta. DA13 .... 44 A4
Dr. DA7 .... 8 A3
bury Rd. SE28 .... 2 E4
bury St. SE18 .... 2 B3
Ct. Dr. ME17 .... 110 F6
er St. TN1 .... 149 B5
er Way. ME17 .... 108 B1
ters. Hawkhurst TN18 .. 179 A1
ers.
gton Green TN3 .... 148 A3
igham TN12 .... 135 C6
tant Pl. TN12 .... 138 C5
hland Rd. SE9 .... 23 C7
ury Cl. ME1 .... 47 A3
Cl. BR6 .... 51 B8
esborough Cotts. ME8 .. 63 F1
esborough La.
.8 & ME9 .... 64 B5
esborough Rd. ME8 ...... 64 A7
esbere Rd. 51 A8
wood Cl. **1** BR1 .... 37 A7
wood Rd. DA7 .... 8 C5
worth Cl. ME8 .... 49 A3
worth Cty Prim Sch.
.8 .... 103 C8
worth Ho. **6** ME15 ... 9 F4
worth House. ME2 .... 33 C1
worth Rd.
reworth ME18 .... 103 C7
worth Rd.
yal Tunbridge Wells
.... 149 A6
den Cl. BR1 .... 22 D1
dian Pk. ME2 .... 47 E6
dian Rd. DA7 .... 8 A3
dian Trad Est. SE7 ...... 1 B2
field Rd. SE9 .... 5 C3
ino Pl. DA15 .... 7 A2
vale Gr. ME3 .... 62 B4
ewood. TN13 .... 84 B4
ewood Dr. DA7 .... 36 F8
in Ave. ME20 .... 74 F2
in Cl. TN10 .... 117 E4
in Gdns. BR1 .... 22 A5
in Prim Sch. BR1 .... 22 A5
in Rd. DA16 .... 7 A3
in Rd N. DA16 .... 7 A3
maid Cl. ME5 .... 62 A6
nerus Gdns. DA12 .... 30 F4
rals Wood Rd. ME2 ...... 46 E5
ilees Rd. DA15 .... 23 E8
sey Rd. SE3 .... 5 C6
iments La.
.18 & TN19 .... 184 D5
ion Cl. TN4 .... 149 B7
ion Way. TN4 .... 149 B7
y Boys Rd. ME3 .... 33 B8
ydown Way. BR7 .... 36 F8
yfield. SE3 .... 5 A5
yfield Ct. **2** TN9 ... 133 B8
yfield House. SE12 ...... 22 C5
yfields. ME2 .... 33 A1
yweater Cl. DA1 .... 9 F1
yton Rd. TN10 .... 117 B5
ton Ave. DA3 .... 42 F5
Cl. ME5 .... 62 C5
ton Court Prep Sch.
.14 .... 24 C4
ton Ct. DA16 .... 7 B5
ton Gdns. BR5 .... 37 B4
ton Rd. ME17 .... 108 C1
yn Ave. BR7 & SE9 ...... 23 C6
yn Stockwood House.
.9 .... 23 C6
ne Way. TN14 .... 68 F7
sent Rd. SE9 .... 5 D2
seter Pl. SE9 .... 6 A1
eor Rd. ME19 .... 88 F3
heen Rd. Bexley DA6 .... 7 F3
huen Rd. Erith DA17 .... 4 B2
o Ctr The. BR5 .... 38 B3
us The. Longfield DA3 .. 42 E6
us The. Maidstone ME16 91 E5
us The. Pembury TN2 .. 150 C6
us The. Rochester ME2 47 F7
us The. **5** ....
yal Tunbridge Wells
.... 149 B3
us The. Sevenoaks TN13 84 A3
er Rd. DA8 .... 8 D8
awber Cl. ME5 .... 62 A1

Michael Gdns. DA12 ...... 30 E3
Michael Marshall House.
SE9 .... 23 C6
Michael Tetley Hall (Nursery Trng
Coll, Dr Barnardo's Home).
TN2 .... 149 D6
Michaels La. DA3 .... 56 C8
Michele Cotts. ME3 .... 32 C6
Micklefield Wadhurst Sch.
TN5 .... 174 C4
Micklehain Cl. BR5 .... 38 A7
Micklehain Rd. BR5 ...... 38 A7
Mid Comp Cotts. TN15 ... 87 E6
Mid Kent Coll (City Way Ctr).
ME1 .... 47 E4
Mid Kent Coll of Higher & F Ed.
Chatham ME1 & ME4 .... 61 E6
Mid Kent Coll of H & F Ed.
Maidstone ME16 .... 91 E3
Mid Kent Coll of H & F Ed.
Maidstone,Cherry Orchard
ME16 .... 91 C3
Mid Kent Golf Course.
DA11 .... 30 B5
Mid Kent Sch for Girls.
ME14 .... 92 A5
Middle Field. TN2 .... 149 C4
Middle Garth. TN17 ... 169 D4
Middle La. TN15 .... 84 F6
Middle Mill Rd. ME19 ... 89 F7
Middle Park Ave. SE9 .... 22 F6
Middle Park Inf & Jun Sch.
SE9 .... 22 D8
Middle Pl. TN9 .... 164 A5
Middle Row. **6** ME15 .. 91 F4
Middle St. **5** ME4 .... 48 A6
Middle Wlk. TN2 .... 149 E8
Middlefields. ME8 .... 64 A8
Middleham Cl. **12** DA2 .. 10 B1
Middlesex Rd. ME15 .... 107 D7
Middleton Ave. DA14 .... 24 C3
Middleton Cl. ME8 .... 63 E4
Middleton Ct. BR1 .... 22 B1
Middlings Rise. TN13 .... 83 F1
Middlings The. TN13 .... 83 F2
Middlings Wood. TN13 .. 84 A2
Midfield Ave. Bexley DA7 .. 8 C4
Midfield Ave. Hextable BR8 .. 26 B2
Midfield Prim Sch. BR5 .. 24 A1
Midfield Way. BR5 .... 38 B8
Midhurst Cl. ME15 .... 92 A3
Midhurst Hill. DA6 .... 8 A2
Midley Cl. ME16 .... 91 C7
Midsummer Cl. SE12 ...... 5 A3
Midsummer Rd. ME6 ...... 74 E8
Midway The. TN4 .... 148 D2
Midwinter Cl. **3** DA16 .. 7 A4
Miers Court Cty Prim Sch.
ME8 .... 63 F7
Mierscourt Cl. ME8 .... 64 A8
Mierscourt Rd. ME8 ...... 63 E6
Mike Spring Cl. DA12 .... 30 F4
Milburn Rd. ME7 .... 48 C7
Mildmay Pl. TN4 .... 68 F8
Mildred Cl. DA1 .... 10 A1
Mildred Rd. DA8 .... 4 E1
Mile La. TN17 .... 168 B8
Mile Oak Rd. TN12 ...... 136 C3
Mile Stone Rd. DA2 ...... 10 B1
Milebush La. TN12 ...... 122 E1
Miles Pl. ME1 .... 47 D3
Milestone Sch. DA2 ...... 10 B1
Milford Cl. Erith SE2 ...... 7 E8
Milford Cl. Maidstone ME16 .. 91 D5
Military Rd. ME4 .... 47 F5
Milk House Cotts. TN17 .. 170 A8
Milk St. Newham E16 ...... 2 B5
Mill Bank. TN27 .... 141 C6
Mill Brook Rd. BR5 .... 38 C5
Mill Cl. Lenham ME17 .. 111 C4
Mill Cl. Rochester ME2 .. 33 B1
Mill Cotts. ME15 .... 105 B6
Mill Cres. TN9 .... 117 C2
Mill Ct. Sutton at Hone DA4 .. 41 C7
Mill Ct. **14** Woolwich SE28 .. 3 B6
Mill Hall Bsns Est The.
ME20 .... 75 D2
Mill Hall Rd.
New Hythe ME20 .... 75 C2
Mill Hill. TN8 .... 128 D7
Mill Hill La. DA12 .... 31 D3
Mill House Cl. DA4 .... 40 E1
Mill La. Benover ME18 .. 121 A7
Mill La.
Biddenden Green DA7 .. 143 A2
Mill La.
Chatham,Bluebell Hill ME5 .. 61 D1

Mill La. Chatham,Luton ME5 .. 48 C1
Mill La. Coxheath ME17 .... 106 D4
Mill La. Eynsford DA4 .... 40 E1
Mill La. Farthing Street BR6 .. 51 B1
Mill La.
Frittenden TN12 & TN17 .. 156 D8
Mill La. Hartlip Hill ME9 ... 64 E6
Mill La. Ightham TN15 .... 86 D5
Mill La. Maidstone ME15 .... 91 E4
Mill La.
Sevenoaks TN13 & TN14 .. 84 D6
Mill La. Shoreham TN14 .... 53 F1
Mill La. Sissinghurst TN17 .. 169 F8
Mill La. Snodland ME6 .... 75 B8
Mill La. Tonbridge TN9 .. 117 C2
Mill La.
Wateringbury ME18 .... 104 D7
Mill La. Watt's Cross
TN11 & TN15 .... 100 C2
Mill La.
West Thurrock RM16 ...... 11 D8
Mill La. Westerham TN16 .. 96 C8
Mill La. Woolwich SE18 .... 2 A1
Mill La.
Yewtree Green TN12 .... 137 B1
Mill Pl. Chislehurst BR7 .. 37 B8
Mill Pl. Crayford DA1 ...... 9 A3
Mill Pond Ct. TN13 .... 84 D6
Mill Pond Rd. DA1 .... 9 E1
Mill Rd. Erith DA8 .... 8 C7
Mill Rd. Gillingham ME7 .. 48 C6
Mill Rd. Hawley DA2 ...... 26 F4
Mill Rd. Newham E16 ...... 1 B5
Mill Rd. Northfleet DA11 .. 29 F8
Mill Rd. Purfleet RM16 .. 10 B8
Mill Rd. Rochester ME2 .. 47 B8
Mill Rd. Sevenoaks TN13 .. 83 E6
Mill St.
Iden Green TN17 & TN18 .. 180 C3
Mill St. Loose ME15 ...... 106 F5
Mill St. Maidstone ME15 .. 91 F4
Mill St. Mill Street ME19 .. 89 F7
Mill St. Snodland ME6 .... 75 B8
Mill St. Westerham TN16 .. 96 D8
Mill Stone Cl. DA4 .... 41 C7
Mill Vale. BR2 .... 36 A7
Mill View. TN11 .... 102 D1
Mill Wlk. ME16 .... 91 A3
Mill Wlk. RM18 .... 13 A7
Millais Pl. RM18 .... 13 A7
Millbank Way. SE12 .... 5 A2
Millbro. BR8 .... 40 A8
Millbrook. ME19 .... 74 D1
Millbrook Ave. DA16 ...... 6 D3
Millbrook Cl. TN15 .... 91 F1
Millcroft Rd. ME3 .... 16 B4
Miller Cl. DA7 .... 8 B4
Miller Rd. DA12 .... 31 A6
Miller Way. DA2 .... 33 D2
Millers Cotts. TN11 ...... 134 C6
Millers Wharf. ME16 ...... 91 E2
Millers Wlk. DA13 .... 58 A7
Millfield.
High Halden TN26 .... 173 D7
Millfield.
New Ash Green DA3 .... 56 E8
Millfield Cl. DA11 .... 29 E6
Millfield La. DA3 .... 56 E8
Millfield Rd. TN15 .... 55 D4
Millfields. ME5 .... 62 D2
Millfields Cl. BR5 .... 38 B5
Millfields Cotts. BR5 .... 38 B5
Millfordhope Rd. ME2 .... 46 C7
Millhall. ME20 .... 75 E2
Millhouse La. ME19 ...... 73 D3
Millican St. SE3 .... 5 B7
Millpond Cl. ME2 .... 47 B8
Millpond La. TN27 & TN30 .. 172 D2
Mills Cres. TN15 .... 84 F8
Mills Rd. ME20 .... 90 E8
Mills Terr. ME4 .... 48 A3
Millside Ind Est. DA1 ...... 9 D3
Millstock Terr. ME15 ...... 91 E2
Millstone Mews. DA4 .... 41 C8
Millstream Cl. TN3 .... 146 D2
Millward Wlk. **14** SE18 .. 6 A8
Millwood Rd. BR5 .... 38 C6
Milne Gdns. SE9 .... 5 E2
Milne House. **15** SE18 .. 1 F2
Milner Rd. ME7 .... 48 D7
Milroy Ave. DA11 .... 29 E6
Milstead Cl. ME14 .... 92 C5
Milsted Rd. ME8 .... 49 C3
Milton Ave.
Badgers Mount TN14 .... 53 B1
Milton Ave.
Cliffe Woods ME3 .... 33 B8
Milton Ave. Gravesend DA12 .. 30 C7
Milton Cl. DA12 .... 30 C6
Milton Dr. TN1 & TN2 ... 149 D7
Milton Gdns. Tilbury RM18 .. 13 B6

Milton Gdns.
Tonbridge TN9 .... 132 F7
Milton Hall Rd. DA12 .... 30 D7
Milton House. DA1 .... 8 E2
Milton Lodge. **3** DA14 .. 24 A4
Milton Pl. DA12 .... 13 C1
Milton Rd. Bexley DA16 .. 6 F6
Milton Rd. Erith DA17 .... 4 A2
Milton Rd. Gillingham ME7 .. 48 C3
Milton Rd. Gravesend DA12 .. 30 C8
Milton Rd. Sevenoaks TN13 .. 83 E6
Milton Rd.
Swanscombe DA10 ...... 11 E1
Milton St. Maidstone ME16 .. 91 C2
Milton St.
Swanscombe DA10 ...... 11 D1
Milverton Way. SE9 .... 23 A4
Mimosa Cl. BR6 .... 52 C8
Mincers Cl. ME5 .... 62 C2
Mineral St. SE18 .... 2 E2
Minerva Cl. DA14 .... 23 E4
Minerva Rd. ME2 .... 47 A8
Ministry Way. SE9 .... 22 F6
Minshaw Ct. DA14 .... 23 F4
Minster Rd. Bromley BR1 .. 22 B1
Minster Rd. Gillingham ME8 .. 49 C3
Minters Orch. TN15 .... 87 B7
Miranda House. **5** DA17 .... 4 A1
Mirfield St. SE7 .... 1 D3
Miriam Ct. DA14 .... 24 B4
Miriam Rd. SE18 .... 2 E1
Mirror Path. SE12 .... 22 C5
Miskin Cotts. ME3 .... 16 B6
Miskin Rd. Dartford DA1 .. 26 D8
Miskin Rd.
Hoo St Werburgh ME3 .. 34 E5
Miskin Way. DA12 .... 30 D2
Mitchell Ave. Chatham ME4 .. 47 F2
Mitchell Ave.
Northfleet DA11 .... 29 D6
Mitchell Cl. Dartford DA1 .. 26 E6
Mitchell Cl. Erith DA17 .... 4 C3
Mitchell Cl. Lenham ME17 .. 111 C5
Mitchell Cl. Woolwich SE2 .. 3 C2
Mitchell Rd. Bromley BR1 .. 36 A8
Mitchell Rd. Orpington BR6 .. 51 F6
Mitchell Wlk. Newham E6 .... 1 F8
Mitchell Wlk.
Swanscombe DA10 ...... 28 E8
Mitchem Cl. TN15 .... 55 E3
Mitre Cl. **5** Erith DA17 .. 4 A2
Mitre Ct. Tonbridge TN9 .. 117 C2
Mitre Rd. ME1 .... 47 B4
Moat Cl. BR6 .... 51 F4
Moat Croft. DA16 .... 7 C4
Moat Ct. Eltham SE9 .... 5 F1
Moat Ct. Sidcup DA15 .... 23 F5
Moat Farm Rd. ME4 .... 18 D6
Moat La. Cowden TN8 ..... 145 E7
Moat La. Erith DA8 .... 9 A6
Moat Rd. TN27 .... 141 B5
Moatbridge Sch. SE9 ...... 5 D1
Moatlands Ave.
TN17 & TN12 .... 171 C4
Model Farm Cl. SE9 ...... 22 E5
Modest Cnr. TN4 .... 132 E1
Moira Rd. SE9 .... 5 F3
Molash Rd. BR5 .... 38 D5
Molehill Copse Cty Prim Sch.
ME15 .... 107 D7
Moles Mead. TN8 .... 112 C2
Molescroft. SE9 .... 23 C5
Molescroft Way. TN9 .... 132 F7
Mollison Rise. DA12 ...... 30 E3
Molyneux Almshouses.
TN4 .... 148 B4
Molyneux Ct. TN4 .... 148 F4
Molyneux Park Rd. TN4 .. 148 F4
Monarch Cl. Chatham ME5 .. 62 A6
Monarch Cl. Hayes BR4 ... 50 A6
Monarch Cl. Tilbury RM18 .. 13 B5
Monarch Dr. E16 .... 1 D8
Monarch Rd. **8** DA17 .... 4 A3
Monckton's Ave. ME14 .. 91 F7
Monckton's Dr. ME14 .... 91 F7
Moncktons La. ME14 .... 91 F7
Moncrieff Cl. **4** E6 .... 1 E7
Moncrif Cl. ME14 .... 93 B4
Monds Cotts. TN14 .... 82 E3
Monica James House. **12**
DA14 .... 24 A5
Monk Dr. E16 .... 1 A7
Monk St. SE18 .... 2 A2
Monkdown. ME15 .... 93 A1
Monkleed Villas. DA3 .... 43 D4
Monks Cl. SE2 .... 3 D2
Monks La. TN5 .... 175 B8
Monks Orch. DA1 .... 26 D6
Monks Way. BR5 .... 37 D1
Monks Wlk. Southfleet DA13 .. 29 A2

Mel – Mor **219**

Monks Wlk. **5**
Tonbridge TN9 .... 133 B8
Monkton Rd. Bexley DA16 .. 6 F5
Monkton Rd.
Borough Green TN15 .... 86 F7
Monkwood Cl. ME1 .... 61 B8
Monmouth Cl. Bexley DA16 .. 7 A3
Monmouth Cl.
Gillingham ME8 .... 49 D2
Mons Way. BR2 .... 36 E3
Monson Rd. TN1 .... 149 B4
Montacute Cl. TN2 .... 149 B4
Montacute Gdns. TN2 .. 148 F2
Montacute Rd. TN2 ...... 149 A1
Montague Cl. BR8 .... 39 F5
Montague Terr. **1** BR2 .. 36 A5
Montbelle Prim Sch. SE9 .. 23 B5
Montbelle Rd. SE9 .... 23 B5
Montbretia Cl. BR5 .... 38 C5
Montcalm Cl. BR2 .... 36 A3
Montcalm Rd. SE7 .... 5 D7
Monteith Cl. TN3 .... 148 A3
Monterey Cl. DA5 .... 25 C6
Montfort Rd. Chatham ME5 .. 61 F2
Montfort Rd. Kemsing TN14 .. 69 E2
Montfort Rd.
Rochester ME2 .... 47 A8
Montgomery Ave. ME5 .. 62 A7
Montgomery Cl. DA15 .... 6 F1
Montgomery Rd.
Gillingham ME7 .... 48 C3
Montgomery Rd.
Royal Tunbridge Wells
TN4 .... 149 B7
Montgomery Rd.
South Darenth DA4 ...... 41 D8
Montpelier Ave. DA5 ..... 24 D8
Montpelier Gate. ME16 .. 91 B5
Montreal Rd.
Sevenoaks TN13 .... 84 B4
Montreal Rd. Tilbury RM18 .. 13 A5
Montrose Ave. Bexley DA16 .. 6 F4
Montrose Ave.
Chatham ME5 .... 48 E2
Montrose Ave. Sidcup DA15 .. 24 A8
Montrose Cl. DA16 .... 6 F4
Monypenny. TN17 .... 181 F3
Moon Cl. SE12 .... 5 A3
Moon's La. TN8 .... 128 A1
Moonstone Dr. ME5 ...... 62 B2
Moor Hill. TN18 .... 184 F8
Moor La. TN8 .... 128 A4
Moor Park Cl. ME8 .... 64 A8
Moor Rd The. TN14 .... 84 C7
Moor St. TN8 .... 64 B8
Moor The. TN18 .... 184 F8
Moorcroft Gdns. BR1 .... 36 F4
Moorden La. TN11 .... 115 A1
Moordown. SE18 .... 6 B6
Moore Ave. Grays RM16 .. 11 E8
Moore Ave. Tilbury RM18 .. 13 B5
Moore Rd. DA10 .... 11 E1
Moore St. ME2 .... 47 A8
Moorfield Rd. BR6 .... 38 A2
Moorhead Way. SE3 .... 5 B4
Moorhouse Rd. RH8 ...... 96 A6
Mooring Rd. ME1 .... 47 D1
Moorings The. E16 .... 1 C8
Moorside Rd. BR1 .... 22 A4
Morants Court Cross. TN14 .. 68 C1
Morants Court Rd.
TN13 & TN14 .... 83 C8
Morden Rd. SE3 .... 5 A5
Morden Road Mews. SE3 .. 5 A5
Morden St. ME1 .... 47 C4
More Park RC Prim Sch.
ME19 .... 89 D8
Morel Ct. TN13 .... 84 B5
Morella Wlk. ME17 ...... 111 C5
Morello Cl. BR8 .... 39 D5
Morement Rd. ME3 .... 34 D6
Moreton Almshouses. TN16 .. 81 D1
Moreton Cl. DA1 .... 8 E4
Morewood Cl. TN13 .... 83 F4
Morgan Dr. DA2 .... 27 E8
Morgan Rd. BR1 .... 22 A1
Morgan St. E16 .... 1 A8
Morhen Cl. ME18 .... 74 E7
Morland Ave. DA1 .... 9 B2
Morland Dr.
Lamberhurst TN3 .... 166 B5
Morland Dr. Rochester ME2 .. 33 A1
Morley Cl. BR6 .... 51 B8
Morley Dr. TN12 .... 153 A6
Morley Rd. Chislehurst BR7 .. 37 C8
Morley Rd. Tonbridge TN9 .. 117 D1
Morley's Rd. TN14 .... 99 D2
Morne Cotts. TN14 .... 68 F8

Morning Cross Cotts. ME3 .... 16 B4
Mornington Ave. BR1 .... 36 D6
Mornington Ct. DA5 .... 25 D7
Morris Cl. East Malling ME19 74 F1
Morris Cl. Orpington BR6 ..... 51 E7
Morris Gdns. DA1 .... 10 A2
Morry La. ME17 .... 125 D7
Morstan Gdns. SE9 .... 22 F4
Mortimer Rd. Erith DA8 .... 8 D8
Mortimer Rd.
   Orpington BR6 .... 38 A2
Mortimers Ave. ME4 .... 33 A8
Mortlake Rd. E16 .... 1 B7
Morton Cl. BR7 .... 39 E7
Morvale Cl. DA17 .... 3 F2
Mosquito Rd. ME19 .... 88 F3
Mossbank. ME5 .... 62 A3
Mossdown Cl. DA17 .... 4 A2
Mosslea Rd. Bromley BR2 ..... 36 D4
Mosslea Rd. Orpington BR6 .. 51 C7
Mossy Glade. ME8 .... 63 E6
Mostyn Rd. ME14 .... 92 C4
Mosul Way. BR2 .... 36 E3
Mosyer Dr. BR5 & BR6 .... 52 D8
Mote Ave. ME15 .... 92 B3
Mote Cotts. TN15 .... 101 A7
Mote Pk. ME15 .... 92 D2
Mote Rd.
   Ivy Hatch TN15 & TN11 .... 101 A7
Mote Rd. Maidstone ME15 .... 92 A3
Mote The. DA3 .... 56 F8
Motherwell Way. RM16 ...... 11 A8
Mottingham Ct. SE9 .... 22 F7
Mottingham Gdns. SE9 .... 22 D7
Mottingham La.
   Eltham SE12 .... 22 C8
Mottingham La.
   Lewisham SE12 & SE9 .... 22 C7
Mottingham Prim Sch. SE9 .. 22 F5
Mottingham Rd. SE9 .... 22 F5
Mottingham Sta. SE9 .... 22 F7
Mottisfont Rd. SE2 .... 3 B2
Mouat Ct. ME5 .... 62 A3
Moultain Hill. BR8 .... 40 A5
Mound The. SE9 .... 23 A5
Mount Ave. ME18 .... 105 A1
Mount Cl. Bromley BR1 .... 36 E8
Mount Cl. Sevenoaks TN13 .. 83 F4
Mount Culver Ave. DA14 ...... 24 D2
Mount Dr. Bexley DA6 .... 7 E2
Mount Dr. Maidstone ME14 .. 93 B4
Mount Edgcumbe Rd.
   TN4 .... 149 A3
Mount Ephraim.
   TN1 & TN4 .... 149 A2
Mount Ephraim Ct. TN4 ..... 148 F4
Mount Ephraim Rd. TN1 ... 149 A4
Mount Harry Rd. TN13 .... 84 B4
Mount La. Hartlip ME9 .... 64 D4
Mount La. Maidstone ME14 .. 93 B4
Mount Lodge. ME1 .... 47 B2
Mount Pleasant.
   Aylesford ME20 .... 76 A3
Mount Pleasant.
   Gillingham ME4 .... 48 B3
Mount Pleasant.
   Hildenborough TN11 ...... 116 D6
Mount Pleasant.
   Hook Green TN3 .... 165 E6
Mount Pleasant.
   The Hill TN14 .... 97 F4
Mount Pleasant.
   Paddock Wood TN12 ...... 135 F6
Mount Pleasant.
   Sparrow's Green TN5 ...... 174 E5
Mount Pleasant.
   Tenterden TN30 .... 183 C8
Mount Pleasant.
   The Moor TN18 .... 184 F8
Mount Pleasant Ave. 2
   TN2 .... 149 B3
Mount Pleasant Ct. TN11 . 116 D6
Mount Pleasant Dr. ME14 .. 93 A5
Mount Pleasant La. TN3 ... 166 A6
Mount Pleasant Rd.
   Dartford DA1 .... 9 F1
Mount Pleasant Rd.
   Royal Tunbridge Wells
   TN1 & TN2 .... 149 A3
Mount Pleasant Rd.
   Sevenoaks Weald TN14 ..... 99 B2
Mount Pleasant Terr.
   ME17 .... 110 E2
Mount Pleasant Wlk. DA5 ... 8 C2
Mount Rd. Bexley DA6 .... 8 A2
Mount Rd. Chatham ME4 ..... 47 F3
Mount Rd. Crayford DA1 ...... 8 F1
Mount Rd. Rochester ME2 ... 47 B2

Mount Sion. TN1 .... 149 A2
Mount The. DA6 .... 8 B2
Mountain Cl. TN15 .... 71 F3
Mountbatten Ave.
   Chatham ME5 .... 62 A7
Mountbatten Ave.
   Higham ME3 .... 32 C4
Mountbatten Cl. SE18 .... 6 E8
Mountfield. TN15 .... 87 A7
Mountfield Cl. DA13 .... 57 F2
Mountfield Ct. 4 TN1 .... 149 B3
Mountfield Gdns. TN2 .... 149 B3
Mountfield Pk. TN9 .... 133 C8
Mountfield Rd. TN2 .... 149 B3
Mountfield Way. 1 BR5 ...... 38 C5
Mounthurst Rd. BR2 .... 36 A2
Mountjoy Cl. SE2 .... 3 B4
Mounts Hill. TN17 .... 180 B7
Mounts La. TN17 .... 182 A3
Mountsfield Cl. ME16 .... 91 D5
Mountview Rd. BR6 .... 38 A2
Moyle Cl. ME8 .... 63 D4
Mozart Ct. ME4 .... 47 E3
Muir Rd. ME15 .... 92 A2
Muir St. E16 .... 1 E5
Mulbarton Ct. BR7 .... 23 D2
Mulberry Cl.
   Gillingham ME7 .... 63 A4
Mulberry Cl. Greenwich SE7 5 D8
Mulberry Cl.
   Meopham Station DA13 .... 44 B3
Mulberry Rd. Royal Tunbridge Wells
   TN2 .... 133 D1
Mulberry Rd. DA11 .... 29 E4
Mulberry Way. DA17 .... 4 C4
Mulgrave House. 20 SE18 .... 1 F2
Mulgrave Prim Sch. SE18 .... 2 A2
Mullein Ct. 6 RM17 .... 12 D8
Mullender Ct. DA12 .... 31 A7
Muller House. SE18 .... 2 A1
Multon Rd. TN15 .... 55 E4
Munday Bois Cotts. TN27 . 143 F8
Munday Bois Rd. TN27 ...... 127 E1
Munday Rd. E16 .... 1 A6
Munday Works Est. TN9 ... 117 C1
Munford Dr. DA10 .... 28 E8
Mungeam House. ME1 .... 47 C4
Mungo Park Rd. DA12 .... 30 D3
Mungo Park Way. BR5 .... 38 D2
Munn's La. ME9 .... 64 E6
Munnery Way. BR6 .... 51 B8
Munro Dr. Bexley DA6 .... 24 E7
Murrain Dr. ME15 .... 93 A1
Murray Ave. BR1 .... 36 B7
Murray Bsns Ctr. BR5 .... 38 B6
Murray Rd. ME15 .... 92 A1
Murray Rd. Rochester ME2 .. 47 C8
Murray Rd.
   St Paul's Cray BR5 .... 38 B6
Murray Sq. E16 .... 1 B6
Murton-Neale Cl. 3
   TN18 .... 179 A2
Muscovy House. DA18 .... 3 E4
Museum of Kent Rural Life.
   ME14 .... 76 D1
Museum St. ME14 .... 91 F7
Musket La.
   Eyhorne Street ME17 .... 94 B2
Musket La. Silver Hill ME17 .. 94 A2
Mussenden La. DA3 & DA4 .. 41 E3
Mustang Rd. ME19 .... 88 F3
Mycenae Rd. SE3 .... 5 A8
Mynn Cres. ME14 .... 93 A4
Myra St. SE2 .... 3 A2
Myrtle Alley. SE18 .... 2 A3
Myrtle Cl. DA8 .... 9 A5
Myrtle Cres. ME5 .... 61 F5
Myrtle Pl. DA2 .... 27 D8
Myrtle Rd. DA1 .... 26 D6
Myrtledene Rd. SE2 .... 3 C1

Nadine St. SE7 .... 1 C1
Nag's Head La. Bexley DA16 .. 7 B4
Nag's Head La.
   Chatham ME1 .... 47 D4
Nagpur House. 4 ME15 ... 107 E5
Nairn Ct. RM18 .... 12 F5
Nansen Rd. DA12 .... 30 D4
Napier Cl. Lewisham SE12 ... 22 B5
Napier Ct. Maidstone ME14 .. 91 F7
Napier Cty Prim Sch. ME7 .. 48 D4
Napier Rd. Bromley BR2 ...... 36 B5
Napier Rd. Erith DA17 .... 3 F2
Napier Rd. Gillingham ME7 .. 48 D4
Napier Rd. Northfleet DA11 .. 29 F7
Napier Rd. Royal Tunbridge Wells
   TN2 .... 149 D2
Napoleon Dr. TN12 .... 138 D5
Napoleon Wlk. ME17 .... 111 C5
Napwood Cl. ME8 .... 63 D6

Nares Rd. ME8 .... 63 D4
Narrow Way. BR2 .... 36 E3
Naseby Ct. DA4 .... 23 F4
Nash Bank. DA13 .... 43 F7
Nash Cl. ME5 .... 62 C2
Nash Croft. DA11 .... 29 E4
Nash Gn. BR1 .... 22 A2
Nash La. BR2 .... 50 A4
Nash St. DA13 .... 44 A7
Nashenden Farm La. ME1 ... 61 A8
Nashenden La. ME1 .... 46 F1
Nassau Path. 8 SE28 .... 3 C5
Natal Rd. ME4 .... 48 A3
Nathan Way. SE28 & SE18 ... 2 E3
National Sea Trng Coll.
   DA12 .... 14 A1
Naylor's Cotts. ME7 .... 63 B1
Neal Rd. TN15 .... 55 E5
Neale St. ME4 .... 47 F2
Neath Ct. 2 ME15 .... 107 E8
Neatscourt Rd. E16 .... 1 D8
Neills Rd. TN3 .... 165 D2
Nellington Ct. TN4 .... 148 B4
Nellington Rd. TN3 & TN4 . 148 B4
Nelson Ave. TN9 .... 117 A1
Nelson House. 5
   Park Wood ME15 .... 107 F5
Nelson House.
   Swanscombe DA9 .... 11 D2
Nelson Mandela Rd. SE3 ...... 5 C4
Nelson Pl. DA14 .... 24 A4
Nelson Rd. Bromley BR2 ..... 36 C5
Nelson Rd. Dartford DA1 ...... 9 C1
Nelson Rd. Erith DA17 .... 3 F1
Nelson Rd. Gillingham ME7 .. 48 D4
Nelson Rd. Northfleet DA11 . 29 F6
Nelson Rd. Royal Tunbridge Wells
   TN2 .... 149 D2
Nelson Rd. Sidcup DA14 ...... 24 A4
Nelson Rd. Wouldham ME1 .. 60 C5
Nelson Terr. ME5 .... 48 C1
Nepicar La. TN15 .... 72 D3
Neptune Bsns Pk. ME2 .... 47 F7
Neptune Cl. ME2 .... 47 E7
Neptune Wlk. DA8 .... 4 D2
Nesbit Rd. SE9 .... 5 D3
Nesbitt House. DA6 .... 8 B2
Ness Rd. DA8 .... 9 D8
Nestor Ct. ME18 .... 105 A8
Nethercombe House. 4
   SE3 .... 5 A8
Nethewode Ct. DA17 .... 4 B3
Netley Cl. ME14 .... 92 D6
Nettlestead La. ME18 .... 104 A6
Nevill Ct. ME19 .... 74 C1
Nevill Gate. TN2 .... 149 B1
Nevill Golf Course.
   TN2 & TN3 .... 163 D7
Nevill Lodge. TN2 .... 149 C4
Nevill Pk. TN4 .... 148 E3
Nevill Pl. ME6 .... 75 A7
Nevill Rd. ME6 .... 75 A7
Nevill Ridge. TN4 .... 148 D3
Nevill St. TN1 & TN2 .... 149 A2
Nevill Terr. TN2 .... 148 F2
Neville Cl. Maidstone ME14 . 92 B8
Neville Cl. Sidcup DA15 .... 23 F5
Neville Rd. ME4 .... 47 E2
New Ash Green Cty Prim Sch.
   DA3 .... 56 F8
New Ash Jun & Inf Sch.
   DA3 .... 42 F1
New Barn Pk. BR8 .... 39 E8
New Barn Rd.
   Hawkenbury ME17 .... 124 E2
New Barn Rd.
   Northfleet Green DA13 .... 39 F3
New Barn Rd. Swanley BR8 . 39 F7
New Barn St. E13 .... 1 B8
New Barns Rd. ME14 .... 92 A8
New Bassetts Cotts. TN12 153 B5
New Beacon Sch The.
   TN13 .... 99 A8
New Cotts. Bean DA2 .... 28 B5
New Cotts.
   Shipbourne TN11 .... 101 D5
New Cotts. Shorne DA12 .... 31 A6
New Covenant Pl. ME1 .... 47 D4
New Cut. 2 TN9 .... 117 C2
New Cut. Chatham ME4 ...... 47 F4
New Cut.
   Dean Street ME15 .... 106 D7
New Cut Rd. ME14 .... 92 D5
New Delhi House. 5
   ME15 .... 107 E5
New Eltham Sta. SE9 .... 23 C7
New England Rd. TN4 .... 149 A7
New Farm Ave. BR2 .... 36 A5
New Hall Farm La. ME1 ...... 19 B6
New House La. DA11 .... 30 A6
New Hythe La. ME20 .... 75 B3

New Hythe Sta. ME20 .... 75 C4
New Inn Cotts. ME15 .... 106 C7
New Lydenbury Commercial Est.
   E16 .... 1 C3
New Lydenbury St. SE7 .... 1 C3
New Mill Rd. BR5 .... 38 C8
New Pond Rd. TN17 .... 180 D6
New Pound La. ME18 .... 88 C1
New Rd. Bexley DA16 .... 7 B5
New Rd. Burham ME1 .... 60 F1
New Rd. Chatham ME1 .... 47 D4
New Rd. Chatham ME4 .... 47 F4
New Rd. Cliffe ME3 .... 16 B6
New Rd. Cranbrook TN17 .. 169 B4
New Rd.
   Ditton ME19 & ME20 .... 75 C1
New Rd. East Malling ME19 .. 90 A8
New Rd. Egerton TN27 ...... 127 F3
New Rd. Erith SE2 .... 3 D1
New Rd. Gravesend DA11 .. 13 B1
New Rd. Grays RM17 .... 12 A8
New Rd. Grays RM17 .... 12 D8
New Rd. Headcorn TN27 ... 141 D5
New Rd. Hextable BR8 .... 25 F1
New Rd. Langley ME17 ...... 108 C5
New Rd.
   Meopham Station DA13 .... 43 F4
New Rd. Orpington BR6 .... 52 D8
New Rd.
   Paddock Wood TN12 ...... 136 A6
New Rd. Saint's Hill TN11 .. 131 A1
New Rd. South Darenth DA4 41 D7
New Rd. Sundridge TN14 .... 82 E2
New Rd. Swanley BR8 .... 39 F6
New Road Ave. ME4 .... 47 E4
New Road Cty Prim Sch.
   ME4 .... 47 E4
New Road Hill. BR2 & BR6 .. 50 F2
New St. Chatham ME4 .... 47 E3
New St. New Street TN15 .... 57 D4
New St. Westerham TN16 .... 96 C8
New Street Hill. BR1 .... 22 C3
New Street Rd.
   DA13 & TN15 .... 57 C6
New Strs. ME4 .... 47 F6
New Swan Yd. 7 DA11 .... 13 B1
New Villas. ME15 .... 106 C7
New Wharf Rd. TN9 .... 117 B1
New Wlk. TN15 .... 71 F3
New Years La. BR6 & TN14 .. 67 A5
Newark Ct. 1 ME2 .... 47 B7
Newark Knok. E6 .... 2 A8
Newark Way. ME2 .... 47 B7
Newbarn La. TN14 & TN16 .. 66 C2
Newbery Rd. DA8 .... 8 F6
Newborough Ct. TN10 ...... 117 C6
Newbury Ave. ME16 .... 91 C6
Newbury Cl. ME3 .... 33 B8
Newbury Cotts. TN5 .... 175 B8
Newbury Ct. DA14 .... 23 F4
Newbury La. TN15 .... 175 C8
Newbury Rd. BR2 .... 36 A6
Newchurch Rd. ME15 .... 92 A1
Newcomen Rd. TN4 .... 149 A5
Newenden Cl. ME14 .... 92 D6
Newenden Rd. ME2 .... 33 C2
Newham Coll of FE
   (Royal Docks Campus). E16 2 C5
Newham St. ME4 .... 48 B3
Newham Way. E13 .... 1 A8
Newhaven Gdns. SE9 .... 5 D3
Newhaven La. 4 E16 .... 1 A8
Newhouse Terr. TN8 .... 112 C3
Newick Cl. DA5 .... 8 B1
Newing Gn. BR1 .... 22 D1
Newington CE Prim Sch.
   ME9 .... 65 B7
Newington Ct. TN5 .... 176 E1
Newington Ent Ctr. ME9 .... 65 C8
Newington House. 9 BR5 .. 38 D1
Newington Ind Est. ME9 ..... 64 F6
Newington Sta. ME9 .... 65 B6
Newington Wlk. ME14 .... 92 C6
Newitt Rd. ME3 .... 34 E5
Newland Green La. TN27 . 143 D8
Newland St. E16 .... 1 F5
Newlands. TN3 .... 148 A3
Newlands Ct. 8 SE9 .... 6 A1
Newlands La. DA13 .... 57 F1
Newlands Rd. TN4 .... 149 B7
Newlands Rise. TN4 .... 149 A6
Newlands Way. TN4 .... 149 B7
Newling Cl. E6 .... 1 F7
Newlyn Cl. 1 ME14 .... 92 A4
Newlyn Dr. TN12 .... 139 F5
Newlyn Rd. DA16 .... 6 F5
Newman Rd. BR1 .... 36 A8
Newman's Rd. DA11 .... 29 F6
Newmarket Gn. SE9 .... 22 D8
Newnham Cl. ME8 .... 49 C2

Newnhams Cl. BR1 .... 3 .
Newports. BR8 .... 3 .
Newstead Ave. BR6 .... 5 .
Newstead Woods Sch for Girl
   BR6 .... 5 .
Newton Abbot Rd. DA11 ..... 3 .
Newton Ave. TN10 .... 11 .
Newton Cl. Chatham ME5 ... 6 .
Newton Cl. 1
   Maidstone ME16 9
Newton Gdns. TN12 .... 13 .
Newton Rd. Bexley DA16 ....
Newton Rd. Royal Tunbridge W
   TN1 .... 14 .
Newton Rd. Tilbury RM18 ... 3 .
Newton Terr. BR2 .... 5 .
Newton Willows. TN12 .... 16 .
Newton's Ct. DA9 .... 3 .
Newtown Cotts. TN12 .... 1 .
Nichol La. BR1 2
Nicholas Cl. ME16 9
Nicholas Ct. SE12 2
Nicholas Stacey House. 3
   SE7 ....
Nicholson House. SE18 ....
Nickelby Cl. SE28 ....
Nickleby Cl. ME1 ....
Nickleby Rd. DA12 ....
Nicola Terr. DA7 ....
Nicolson Rd. BR5 3
Nicolson Way. TN13 8
Nigeria Rd. SE7 ....
Nightingale Cl.
   Gillingham ME8 ....
Nightingale Cl.
   Larkfield ME20 ....
Nightingale Cl.
   Northfleet DA11 2
Nightingale Cnr. BR5 3
Nightingale Gr. 4 DA1 1
Nightingale House. SE18 ......
Nightingale La.
   Bromley BR1 ....
Nightingale La.
   Goathurst Common TN14 .. 9
Nightingale Pl. Sch. SE18 ....
Nightingale Rd.
   Kemsing TN14 ....
Nightingale Rd.
   Orpington BR5 ....
Nightingale Vale. SE18 ....
Nightingale Way.
   Newham E6 ....
Nightingale Way.
   Swanley BR8 ....
Nightingales The.
   Royal Tunbridge Wells
   TN4 .... 14 .
Nightingales The.
   Sissinghurst TN17 .... 17 .
Nile Path. 6 SE18 ....
Nile Rd. ME7 ....
Nine Acres Rd. ME2 ....
Nine Acres Sch. SE18 ....
Nine Elms Gr. DA11 ....
Nineveh La. TN17 & TN18 .. 17
Ninhams Wood. BR6 ....
Nita Ct. SE12 ....
Nithdale Rd. SE18 ....
Nizels La. TN11 11
No 1 St. SE18 ....
No 2 St. SE18 ....
Noah's Ark. TN15 ....
Noble Tree Cross. TN11 ... 11 .
Noble Tree Rd. TN11 .... 11 .
Nook The. ME18 .... 10 .
Norah La. ME3 3
Nordenfeldt Rd. DA8 ....
Nore Cl. ME7 ....
Norfield Rd. DA2 & DA5 2
Norfolk Cl. Chatham ME5 ... 6
Norfolk Cl. Dartford DA1 1
Norfolk Cl. Gillingham ME8 .. 4
Norfolk Cres. DA15 2
Norfolk Gdns. DA7 ....
Norfolk Pl. DA16 ....
Norfolk Rd.
   Gravesend DA12 3
Norfolk Rd.
   Maidstone ME15 10
Norfolk Rd. Royal Tunbridge We
   TN1 14
Norfolk Rd. Tonbridge TN9 11 .
Norham Ct. 11 DA2 1
Norlands Cres. BR7 ....
Norman Cl. Gillingham ME8 .. 4
Norman Cl. Kemsing TN14 .. 6
Norman Cl. Maidstone ME14 9 .
Norman Cl. Orpington BR6 .. 5 .

an Ct. TN8 .... 112 B2
an Rd. Dartford DA1 ..... 26 E7
an Rd. Erith DA17 .... 4 B3
an Rd. Erith DA17 .... 4 B5
n Rd.
  Town ME19 .... 89 B8
in Rd. Royal Tunbridge Wells
  .... 149 B5
an Rd. Snodland ME6 .. 75 A6
an Rise. TN17 ...... 169 D4
an St. TN14 .... 97 F5
an Villas. **4** TN18 ... 178 F2
andy Prim Sch. DA7 ... 8 D6
andy Terr. E16 .... 1 B7
andy Way. DA7 & DA8 .. 8 E6
anhurst Ave. DA16 ..... 7 D6
anhurst Rd.
ugh Green TN15 ..... 87 A7
anhurst Rd.
aul's Cray BR5 .... 38 B7
ans Cl. DA11 .... 30 A8
ys Rd. ME8 .... 63 E7
agton Rd. ME15 ... 107 B6
Way. DA1 .... 8 F4
ead Gdns. TN4 ...... 149 B7
ed La. BR6 .... 67 B8
Ash Rd. DA3 .... 56 F7
Bank Cl. ME2 .... 46 F5
Basin One Rd. ME4 .... 34 A1
Beckton Prim Sch.
  .... 1 F8
Borough Cty Jun Sch.
  .... 92 A6
Cl. DA6 .... 7 D3
Cray Prim Schs.
  .... 24 E2
Cray Rd.
h Cray DA5 & DA14 .... 25 A6
Cray. Sidcup DA14 ..24 E4
Cres. ME17 .... 106 D4
Dane Way. ME5 ...... 62 C4
Down. TN12 .... 139 E4
Downs Bsns Pk.
  .... 68 C3
Downs Terr. ME19 .... 73 A5
Dr. BR6 .... 51 E6
End La. BR6 .... 51 B2
End Trad Est. DA8 ..... 8 E6
Farm La.
al Tunbridge Wells
  .... 133 E2
Farm La.
al TN2 .... 149 D8
Farm Rd.
h TN4 .... 149 C8
Folly Rd. ME15 ...... 105 F3
Glade. DA5 .... 24 F7
Hill Rd. TN18 .... 178 C1
Kent Ave. DA11 ...... 12 C1
Lockside Rd. ME4 .... 48 D8
Meadow. ME19 .... 88 D7
Pasley Rd. ME4 .... 48 B7
Pk. SE9 .... 6 A1
Pole La. BR2 .... 50 A4
Pole Rd.
S & ME18 & ME19 ..... 90 C2
Pondside Rd. ME4 .... 48 A8
Rd. Bromley BR1 ..... 36 B8
Rd. Cliffe ME3 .... 16 B6
Rd. Dartford DA1 ..... 9 A1
Rd. Erith DA17 .... 4 B4
Rd.
ngham ME4 & ME7 .... 48 A7
Rd. Goudhurst TN17 ..153 E1
Rd. Woolwich SE18 .... 2 E2
Riding. DA3 .... 43 D6
Side Three Rd. ME4 .. 48 C8
St. Bexley DA7 .... 8 A3
St. Biddenden TN27 ..158 A2
St. Bromley BR1 ...... 36 A8
St. Cowden TN8 ...... 145 A6
St. Dartford DA1 ..... 26 D8
St. Gravesend DA11 .. 30 B8
St. Headcorn TN27 .. 141 C5
St. Maidstone ME16 .. 90 F2
St. Rochester ME2 .... 47 B7
St. Royal Tunbridge Wells
  .... 149 C3
St.
n Valence ME17 .... 124 E8
Terr. ME3 .... 33 F6
View. TN15 .... 92 B1
View Ave. RM18 .... 13 A6
View Cotts. ME15 .... 106 C7
View Rd. TN13 .... 84 C6
Way. ME4 .... 92 B7
West Kent Coll of Tech.
  .... 30 F7
Woolwich Rd. E16 ...... 1 B5
Woolwich Rdbt. E16 ... 1 D5

North Woolwich Sta. E16 ... 2 A4
Northall Rd. DA7 .... 8 C5
Northbourne. BR2 .... 36 A2
Northbourne Rd. ME8 .... 49 B4
Northcote Rd.
Gravesend DA11 .... 29 F7
Northcote Rd.
Rochester ME2 .... 47 A7
Northcote Rd.
Sidcup DA14 .... 23 E4
Northcote Rd. **2**
Northcourt Cty Prim Sch.
  .... 30 E7
Northdown. ME9 .... 79 D8
Northdown Cl.
Maidstone ME14 .... 92 B7
Northdown Cl.
Paddock Wood TN12 .. 135 F6
Northdown Rd. Bexley DA16 . 7 C5
Northdown Rd.
Kemsing TN15 .... 69 E2
Northdown Rd.
Longfield DA3 .... 42 E7
Northdown View. ME17 ... 110 F6
Northend Prim Sch. DA8 ... 8 F6
Northend Rd. DA8 .... 8 F6
Northfield. DA3 .... 42 F6
Northfield Ave. BR5 .... 38 C3
Northfield Cl. BR1 & BR7 .. 36 E8
Northfields.
Maidstone ME16 ...... 90 F2
Northfields.
Speldhurst TN3 ...... 148 A8
Northfleet Cl. ME14 .... 92 C5
Northfleet Ind Est. DA11 .. 11 F3
Northfleet Sch for Boys.
  .... 29 D7
Northfleet Sch for Girls.
  .... 29 C6
Northgate. ME1 .... 47 C6
Northgrove Rd. **9** TN18 .. 178 F2
Northiam Sta. TN31 ... 187 C2
Northlands Ave. BR6 .... 51 E6
Northlands Cotts. TN32 .. 185 C1
Northleigh Cl. ME15 .... 107 A6
Northolme Rise. BR6 ... 51 E8
Northover. ME1 .... 22 A4
Northpoint Bsns Est. ME2 .. 47 D8
Northridge Rd. DA11 ... 30 A6
Northside Rd. BR1 ...... 36 A8
Northumberland Ave.
Bexley DA16 .... 6 E4
Northumberland Ave.
Gillingham ME8 ...... 49 E1
Northumberland Cl. DA8 .. 8 C7
Northumberland Ct.
ME15 .... 107 D7
Northumberland Gdns.
BR1 .... 37 A5
Northumberland Heath Inf Sch.
  .... 8 B7
Northumberland Heath Jun Sch.
  .... 8 B7
Northumberland Pk. DA8 .. 8 C7
Northumberland Rd.
Istead Rise DA13 ..... 29 F1
Northumberland Rd.
Maidstone ME15 ..... 107 D8
Northumberland Rd.
Newham E6 .... 1 E7
Northumberland Way.
DA7 & DA8 .... 8 D6
Northview. BR8 .... 39 E7
Northward Hill Nature Reserve.
ME23 .... 17 E5
Northwood Ave. ME23 ... 17 E4
Northwood Pl. DA18 .... 3 F3
Northwood Prim Sch. DA18 .. 3 F3
Northwood Rd. TN10 ... 117 C6
Norton Cres. TN10 ..... 117 B7
Norton Rd. ME15 .... 61 E3
Norton House. **8** SE18 ... 2 A2
Norton Rd.
Five Wents ME17 ..... 108 D1
Norton Rd. Royal Tunbridge Wells
TN4 .... 133 A1
Nortons La. TN27 & TN30 .. 172 E5
Nortons Way. TN12 ... 135 B7
Norvic House. DA8 ...... 8 F7
Norway Terr. **4** ME4 .... 92 A7
Norwich Ave. TN10 ... 117 D5
Norwich Cl. ME2 .... 46 D6
Norwich Pl. **7** DA6 ...... 8 A3
Norwood Cl. ME3 .... 16 B4
Norwood Cl. **6** DA1 .... 10 A3
Norwood La. DA13 .... 44 B3
Notre Dame RC Prim Sch.
SE18 .... 6 B8
Nottidge Rd. TN4 ..... 148 D1

Nottingham Ave.
Maidstone ME15 ..... 107 D7
Nottingham Ave.
Newham E16 .... 1 C7
Nottingham Wlk. ME2 ... 46 D6
Novar Cl. BR6 .... 37 F2
Novar Rd. SE9 .... 23 C7
Nower The. TN14 ...... 81 F8
Nuffield Hospl. TN2 ... 149 C3
Nuffield Rd. BR8 ...... 26 A2
Nugent Ind Pk. BR5 ... 38 C5
Nunnery La. TN11 .... 146 F8
Nunnington Sq. TN19 ... 22 E5
Nursery Ave. Bexley DA7 .. 7 F4
Nursery Ave.
Maidstone ME16 ...... 91 B6
Nursery Ave.
Maidstone,Bearsted ME14 .. 93 B3
Nursery Cl. Dartford DA2 .. 27 C8
Nursery Cl. Orpington BR6 .. 38 A2
Nursery Cl. Sevenoaks TN13 .. 84 C5
Nursery Cl. Swanley BR8 .. 39 C7
Nursery Cl.
Tonbridge TN10 ..... 117 E4
Nursery Cl.
Union Street TN5 .... 177 B3
Nursery Gdns. BR7 .... 23 B2
Nursery Pl. TN13 ...... 83 D4
Nursery Rd. Ditton ME20 .. 75 C1
Nursery Rd. Gillingham ME8 . 63 D8
Nursery Rd.
Meopham Station DA13 .. 44 A4
Nursery Rd.
Paddock Wood TN12 ... 135 F8
Nursery Rd. Royal Tunbridge Wells
TN4 .... 149 B8
Nursery The.
Westerham TN16 ...... 96 C8
Nurstead Ave. DA3 .... 43 D6
Nurstead Church La. DA13 .. 44 A5
Nurstead La. DA3 ..... 43 D5
Nurstead Rd. DA8 ...... 8 A7
Nut Tree Cl. BR6 .... 52 D7
Nutfield Cl. ME5 .... 62 B8
Nutfield Way. BR6 ..... 51 B8
Nutfields. TN15 .... 86 B4
Nuthatch. DA3 .... 43 B7
Nuthatch Gdns. SE28 .. 2 D4
Nutley Cl. BR8 .... 39 F8
Nutmead Cl. DA5 .... 25 C7
Nuttall Ct. BR5 .... 38 B6
Nutwood Cl. ME14 ..... 92 E4
Nuxley Rd. DA17 .... 4 A1
NW Kent Coll of Tech. DA1 .. 26 D8
Nyanza St. SE18 .... 6 D8

O'Neill Path. **11** SE18 .... 6 A8
Oak Ave. Gillingham ME7 .. 48 E6
Oak Ave. Sevenoaks TN13 .. 99 B7
Oak Cl. Crayford DA1 .... 8 F3
Oak Cl.
Hoo St Werburgh ME3 .. 34 E3
Oak Cl. Swanley BR8 .... 39 E6
Oak Cotts. TN8 .... 113 B6
Oak Ct. BR1 .... 36 F7
Oak Dr. Higham ME3 ... 32 B4
Oak Dr. Larkfield ME20 .. 75 B2
Oak End Cl. TN4 .... 133 A2
Oak Farm Gdns. TN27 .. 141 D6
Oak Farm La. TN15 .... 57 E1
Oak Hill Rd. TN13 ..... 84 A2
Oak House. **6**
Chatham ME5 .... 61 F4
Oak House. Sidcup DA15 .. 24 A5
Oak La. Headcorn TN27 .. 141 D5
Oak La.
Moor Street ME8 & ME9 .. 64 D8
Oak La. Sevenoaks TN13 .. 99 A8
Oak Lodge La. TN16 .... 81 D2
Oak Rd.
Hoo St Werburgh ME3 .. 34 E3
Oak Rd. Orpington BR6 .. 52 A3
Oak Rd. Rochester ME2 .. 46 E6
Oak Rd. Royal Tunbridge Wells
TN1 .... 149 D7
Oak Rd. Stone DA9 ..... 10 E1
Oak Rd. Westerham TN16 .. 81 D2
Oak Terr. **3** TN18 ..... 178 F2
Oak Tree Ave. ME15 ... 107 C7
Oak Tree Cl. Marden TN12 ... 138 D5
Oak Tree Cl. Royal Tunbridge Wells
TN1 .... 149 A1

Oak Tree Gdns. BR1 .... 22 B3
Oak Trees Cty Prim Sch.
ME15 .... 107 C7
Oak View. TN8 .... 112 B2
Oakapple La. ME16 ..... 91 A3
Oakbrook Cl. BR1 & SE12 ... 22 B4
Oakcroft. SE12 .... 22 B7
Oakdale La. TN8 .... 96 C2
Oakdale Rd. TN4 ...... 148 F4
Oakdene Ave.
Chislehurst BR7 ...... 23 A3
Oakdene Ave. Erith DA8 .. 8 C8
Oakdene Rd. Orpington BR5 38 A3
Oakdene Rd.
Sevenoaks TN13 ...... 84 A5
Oakenden Rd. DA13 .... 44 E1
Oakenholt House. **1** SE2 .. 3 D4
Oakes Cl. E6 .... 1 F7
Oakfield. Hawkhurst TN18 .. 178 F2
Oakfield.
Rolvenden Layne TN17 .. 182 A1
Oakfield Cotts. TN17 ... 180 D4
Oakfield Court Rd. TN2 .. 149 C3
Oakfield Cty Prim Sch.
DA1 .... 26 E6
Oakfield La. Dartford DA1 .. 26 C6
Oakfield La. Keston BR2 .. 50 D6
Oakfield Park Rd. DA1 .. 26 D6
Oakfield Pl. DA1 .... 26 D6
Oakfield Rd.
Marlpit Hill TN8 ...... 112 B5
Oakfield Rd. Matfield TN12 151 D8
Oakfields. TN13 .... 84 B1
Oakham Dr. BR2 .... 36 A5
Oakhill House. BR5 .... 38 A8
Oakhill Rd. BR6 .... 51 F8
Oakhouse Rd. DA6 ...... 8 A2
Oakhurst Ave. DA7 ..... 7 E7
Oakhurst Cl. ME5 ...... 61 F3
Oakhurst Gdns. DA7 .... 7 E7
Oakland Cl. ME5 .... 61 F3
Oakland Villas. TN3 .... 161 B7
Oaklands. TN17 ...... 169 D4
Oaklands Ave. DA15 .... 23 F8
Oaklands Cl. Bexley DA6 .. 7 F2
Oaklands Cl. Orpington BR5 . 37 E3
Oaklands Cl.
West Kingsdown TN15 .. 55 E4
Oaklands Cty Prim Sch.
ME5 .... 61 F4
Oaklands Rd. Bexley DA6 .. 7 F2
Oaklands Rd. Dartford DA1 .. 27 C7
Oaklands Rd.
Groombridge TN3 ..... 161 B6
Oaklands Rd.
Hawkhurst TN18 ..... 179 A1
Oaklands Rd.
Northfleet DA11 ...... 29 F4
Oaklands Way. TN11 ... 116 F4
Oaklea Rd. TN12 ..... 135 F6
Oakleigh Cl. Chatham ME5 .. 61 E2
Oakleigh Cl. Swanley BR8 .. 39 E6
Oakleigh Gdns. BR6 .... 51 E6
Oakleigh Park Ave. BR7 .. 37 A8
Oakley Cl. **7** Newham E6 .. 1 E7
Oakley Cl.
West Thurrock RM16 .. 11 C8
Oakley Dr. Dartford DA1 .. 27 B7
Oakley Dr. Keston Mark BR2 50 E7
Oakley Dr. Sidcup SE9 ... 23 D7
Oakley Pk. DA5 & DA15 ... 24 C8
Oakley Rd. BR2 .... 50 F8
Oakmead. Meopham DA13 .. 58 A8
Oakmead. Tonbridge TN10 . 117 C6
Oakmead Ave. BR2 ..... 36 A3
Oakmere Rd. SE2 .... 7 A8
Oakmont Pl. BR6 ...... 37 D1
Oaks Bsns Village The.
ME5 .... 62 C1
Oaks Dene. ME5 .... 61 F1
Oaks Forstal. TN18 ... 186 C5
Oaks Rd. TN30 .... 183 B8
Oaks The. Aylesford ME20 .. 75 E1
Oaks The.
Smarden Bell TN27 ... 142 F2
Oaks The. Swanley BR8 .. 39 E7
Oaks The. Woolwich SE18 .. 2 C1
Oakum Ct. ME4 .... 48 B2
Oakway Cl. DA5 .... 7 E1
Oakways. SE9 .... 6 B1
Oakwood Cl.
Chislehurst BR7 ...... 23 A2
Oakwood Cl. Dartford DA1 .. 27 B7
Oakwood Cl.
Maidstone ME16 ...... 91 D3
Oakwood Ct. Swanley BR8 .. 39 C7
Oakwood Dr. Bexley DA7 .. 8 D4
Oakwood Dr.
Sevenoaks TN13 ...... 84 B4

Oakwood Hospl. ME16 ... 91 B3
Oakwood Park Gram Sch.
ME16 .... 91 C3
Oakwood Rd.
Maidstone ME16 ...... 91 D3
Oakwood Rd.
Orpington BR6 .... 51 C8
Oakwood Rise.
Longfield DA3 .... 42 E6
Oakwood Rise.
Royal Tunbridge Wells
TN2 .... 149 E7
Oast Cl. DA11 .... 30 B6
Oast Cl. TN1 .... 149 D7
Oast Ct. ME18 .... 104 F1
Oast House Way. BR5 .. 38 B5
Oast La. TN11 .... 117 A4
Oast View. TN12 ...... 153 A6
Oast Way. DA3 .... 42 E3
Oastfield Ct. TN15 .... 84 C2
Oasts The. ME14 .... 93 C4
Oastview. ME8 .... 64 A8
Oatfield Cl. TN17 ..... 169 C5
Oatfield Dr. TN17 ..... 169 C5
Oatfield Rd. BR6 .... 37 F1
Occupation La. SE18 .... 6 B6
Ockham Dr. BR5 .... 24 A1
Ockley La. TN18 ...... 179 A3
Ockley Rd. TN18 ...... 179 A2
Octavia Cl. ME5 .... 62 B3
Octavia Way. **12** SE28 .. 3 B6
Odeon Ct. **8** E16 .... 1 A8
Odeon Par. SE9 .... 5 E3
Offen's Dr. TN12 ..... 139 E3
Offenham Rd. BR7 & SE9 .. 22 F4
Offham Cty Prim Sch.
ME19 .... 88 D8
Offham Rd. ME19 ...... 89 A7
Officers' Rd. ME4 ..... 48 B8
Ogilby St. SE18 .... 1 F2
Okehampton Cres. DA16 .. 7 C6
Okemore Gdns. BR5 .... 38 C5
Old Ashford Rd. ME17 .. 111 E5
Old Barn Cl. Gillingham ME7 62 F6
Old Barn Cl. Kemsing TN15 .. 70 A2
Old Barn Cl. Tonbridge TN9 132 F8
Old Barn Rd. ME19 ..... 74 E2
Old Barn Way. DA7 ..... 8 D4
Old Bexley CE Prim Sch.
DA5 .... 25 A7
Old Bexley CE Sch. DA5 .. 24 F7
Old Bexley La. Dartford DA1 25 F7
Old Bexley La. Maypole DA5 25 E6
Old Carriageway The.
Gillingham ME7 ...... 62 F4
Old Carriageway The.
Sevenoaks TN13 ...... 83 C5
Old Castle Wlk. ME8 ... 63 B8
Old Chapel Rd. BR8 .... 39 C2
Old Chatham Rd.
Kit's Coty ME20 ...... 76 D6
Old Chatham Rd.
Maidstone ME14 ...... 76 F1
Old Church La. ME18 .. 103 E4
Old Church Rd.
Burham ME1 .... 60 C1
Old Church Rd.
Matfield TN12 ...... 134 D2
Old Church Rd.
Mereworth ME18 .... 103 D5
Old Church Rd.
Penbury TN2 .... 150 D8
Old Clem Sq. **12** SE18 ... 6 A8
Old Coach Rd. TN15 .... 71 E5
Old Ctyd The. BR1 ..... 36 B8
Old Dartford Rd. DA4 .. 40 F3
Old Dover Rd. SE3 & SE7 .. 5 B7
Old Downs. DA3 .... 42 E4
Old Dr. ME15 .... 106 F6
Old Farm Ave. DA15 .... 23 E6
Old Farm Gdns. BR8 ... 39 F6
Old Farm Rd E. DA15 .. 24 A6
Old Farm Rd W. DA15 .. 23 F6
Old Forge La. ME9 ..... 79 F3
Old Forge Way. DA14 ... 24 B5
Old Garden The. TN13 .. 83 D4
Old Gardens Cl. TN2 ... 163 B8
Old Hadlow Rd. TN10 .. 117 F4
Old Ham La. ME17 .... 111 A4
Old Hill. Chislehurst BR7 .. 37 A8
Old Hill. Orpington BR6 .. 51 E4
Old Homestead Rd. BR2 .. 36 C5
Old House La. TN3 .... 147 D4
Old House Rd. ME9 ..... 64 E4
Old Kent Rd. TN12 .... 136 A6
Old La. TN15 .... 86 C4
Old Lain. ME17 .... 110 F6

222 Old – Par

Old London Rd. Badgers Mount TN14 53 A1
Old London Rd. Tonbridge TN10 117 C3
Old London Rd. Wrotham TN15 71 F4
Old Loose Hill. ME15 106 F4
Old Maidstone Rd. BR8 & DA14 24 F1
Old Manor Dr. DA12 30 C7
Old Manor Way. Bexley DA7 8 D5
Old Manor Way. Chislehurst BR7 & SE9 22 F3
Old Mill Cl. DA4 40 E1
Old Mill La. ME20 76 C3
Old Mill Rd. Silver Hill ME17 93 F1
Old Mill Rd. Woolwich SE18 6 D8
Old Oast Bsns Ctr The. ME20 76 A1
Old Orch. TN11 115 A3
Old Orch The. ME8 64 A8
Old Orchard La. ME19 74 D1
Old Otford Rd. TN14 69 B1
Old Park Rd. SE2 3 A1
Old Parsonage Ct. ME19 89 C7
Old Pattens La. ME1 47 D2
Old Perry St. Chislehurst BR7 23 E1
Old Perry St. Northfleet DA11 29 E6
Old Polhill. TN14 68 D4
Old Rd. Chatham ME4 47 F4
Old Rd. Crayford DA1 & DA7 8 D3
Old Rd. East Peckham TN12 120 A6
Old Rd. Wateringbury ME18 104 C7
Old Rd E. DA12 30 D7
Old Rd W. DA11 & DA12 30 B7
Old Regent Dr. TN17 181 E4
Old Riding School The. TN3 161 B2
Old School Cl. ME17 111 D4
Old School Ct. Chattenden ME3 33 F4
Old School Ct. Egerton TN27 127 F3
Old School House The. TN8 112 C1
Old School La. ME19 73 F4
Old Soar Rd. TN15 87 C1
Old Station Rd. TN5 174 E6
Old Tannery Cl. TN30 182 F7
Old Terry's Lodge Rd. TN15 71 A4
Old Timber Top Cotts The. TN13 84 C4
Old Tovil Rd. ME15 92 A2
Old Trafford Cl. ME16 91 B6
Old Tramyard. SE18 2 E2
Old Tree La. ME17 107 D3
Old Wardsdown. TN5 177 B3
Old Watling St. Cuxton ME2 46 B8
Old Watling St. Gravesend DA13 30 A3
Old Wlk The. TN14 69 C2
Old Yews The. DA3 43 B6
Oldborough Manor Com Coll. ME15 107 B6
Oldbury Cl. Oldbury TN15 86 B5
Oldbury Cl. Orpington BR5 38 D5
Oldbury Cotts. TN15 86 B6
Oldbury La. TN15 86 B6
Oldchurch Ct. 3 ME16 91 E3
Oldfield Cl. Bromley BR1 36 F5
Oldfield Cl. Gillingham ME8 63 D8
Oldfield Cl. Maidstone ME15 92 E1
Oldfield Rd. Bexley DA7 7 E5
Oldfield Rd. Bromley BR1 36 F5
Oleander Cl. BR6 51 D5
Olive Rd. DA1 26 D7
Oliver Cl. Chatham ME4 48 B2
Oliver Cl. West Thurrock RM16 10 F7
Oliver Cres. DA4 40 F2
Oliver Ct. SE18 2 C2
Oliver Gdns. E6 1 E8
Oliver Rd. Staplehurst TN12 139 E4
Oliver Rd. Swanley BR8 39 D6
Oliver Rd. West Thurrock RM16 11 A7
Oliver Twist Cl. ME1 47 B4
Olivers Cotts. ME14 93 C4
Olivers Mill. DA3 56 E8
Olivine Cl. ME5 77 A8
Olliffe Cl. ME5 61 F2
Olron Cres. DA6 7 E2
Olven Rd. SE18 6 C8
Olyffe Ave. DA16 7 A5
Onslow Cres. BR7 37 B8
Onslow Dr. DA14 24 D6
Onslow Rd. ME1 47 D3
Opal Cl. E16 1 D7
Opal Gn. ME5 62 B2
Openshaw Rd. SE2 3 B2
Orache Dr. ME14 92 E5
Orange Court La. BR6 51 A2
Orange Terr. ME1 47 D5
Orangery La. SE9 5 F2
Orbit Cl. ME5 77 A8
Orbital One. DA1 27 B6
Orchard Ave. Aylesford ME20 75 E1
Orchard Ave. Dartford DA1 26 B7
Orchard Ave. Erith DA17 7 F8
Orchard Ave. Gravesend DA11 30 B3
Orchard Ave. Rochester ME2 32 F1
Orchard Bank. ME17 108 B1
Orchard Bsns Ctr. Maidstone ME16 91 C8
Orchard Bsns Ctr. Paddock Wood TN12 136 A8
Orchard Bsns Ctr. Royal Tunbridge Wells TN4 149 D8
Orchard Bsns Ctr. Tonbridge TN9 117 E1
Orchard Cl. Bexley DA7 7 E6
Orchard Cl. Coxheath ME17 106 C3
Orchard Cl. Edenbridge TN8 112 B2
Orchard Cl. Horsmonden TN12 152 F6
Orchard Cl. Langley Heath ME17 108 E4
Orchard Cl. New Barn DA3 43 B7
Orchard Cl. Royal Tunbridge Wells TN1 149 D6
Orchard Cl. Sevenoaks TN14 84 C7
Orchard Cotts. ME16 106 A8
Orchard Cres. TN12 153 A6
Orchard Ct. TN17 180 D6
Orchard Dr. Edenbridge TN8 112 B2
Orchard Dr. Meopham Station DA13 43 F4
Orchard Dr. Newington ME9 65 A5
Orchard Dr. Tonbridge TN10 117 E5
Orchard Glade. TN27 141 E5
Orchard Gn. BR6 51 E8
Orchard Gr. Larkfield ME20 75 B2
Orchard Gr. Orpington BR6 37 F1
Orchard Gr. Royal Tunbridge Wells TN1 149 B5
Orchard Hill. DA1 8 E2
Orchard House. DA8 8 F6
Orchard Ind Est. ME15 107 F3
Orchard Pl. 2 Maidstone ME16 91 E3
Orchard Pl. St Paul's Cray BR5 38 C6
Orchard Pl. Sundridge TN14 82 D3
Orchard Rd. Bexley DA16 7 B4
Orchard Rd. Bromley BR1 36 C8
Orchard Rd. East Peckham TN12 120 A6
Orchard Rd. Erith DA17 4 A2
Orchard Rd. Maidstone ME14 92 E4
Orchard Rd. Northfleet DA11 29 C6
Orchard Rd. Orpington BR6 51 B5
Orchard Rd. Otford TN14 68 F3
Orchard Rd. Pratt's Bottom BR6 52 C1
Orchard Rd. Sevenoaks TN13 83 E5
Orchard Rd. Sidcup DA14 23 E4
Orchard Rd. St Michaels TN30 173 A3
Orchard Rd. Swanscombe DA10 11 E2
Orchard Rise. TN3 161 B7
Orchard Rise E. DA15 6 F2
Orchard Rise W. DA15 6 E2
Orchard St. Dartford DA1 9 E1
Orchard St. Gillingham ME8 63 E8
Orchard St. Maidstone ME15 92 A3
Orchard Terr. DA9 10 E2
Orchard The. Maidstone ME14 93 B4
Orchard The. Sevenoaks TN13 83 E6
Orchard The. Swanley BR8 39 D7
Orchard View. TN30 183 C8
Orchard Villas. TN12 122 A4
Orchard Way. Horsmonden TN12 153 A6
Orchard Way. Kemsing TN15 70 A2
Orchard Way. Snodland ME6 74 F7
Orchard Way. Turnden TN17 169 B4
Orchard Way. Wilmington DA2 26 D5
Orchardlea. DA13 28 F3
Orchards Sh Ctr The. DA1 9 E1
Orchid Cl. 1 Newham E16 1 E8
Orchid Cl. Rochester ME2 46 C6
Orchidhurst. TN2 149 D7
Ordnance Rd. Gravesend DA12 13 C1
Ordnance Rd. Woolwich SE18 6 A8
Ordnance St. ME4 47 E3
Ordnance Terr. ME4 47 E4
Oregon Sq. BR6 37 D1
Oriental Rd. E16 1 D5
Oriole Way. Larkfield ME20 74 F2
Oriole Way. Woolwich SE28 3 B6
Orion Rd. ME1 61 C7
Orissa Rd. SE18 2 E1
Orlestone Gdns. BR6 52 E5
Orlick Rd. DA12 31 B7
Ormesby Cl. SE28 3 D6
Ormiston Rd. SE10 1 A1
Ormond Ave. BR6 51 C8
Ormsby Gn. ME8 63 E3
Ormsby Point. 6 SE18 2 B2
Orpines The. ME18 104 F7
Orpington By-Pass Rd. TN14 53 A2
Orpington Coll. BR6 38 A1
Orpington Hospl. BR6 51 F6
Orpington Rd. BR7 37 E6
Orpington Sta. BR6 51 E8
Orpington Trad Est. BR5 38 C5
Orwell Cl. Lunsford ME20 74 F3
Orwell Cl. Rainham RM9 4 D8
Orwell House. 6 ME15 107 E8
Osberton Rd. SE12 5 A2
Osborne Rd. Erith DA17 7 F8
Osborne Rd. Gillingham ME7 48 C5
Osbourne Rd. DA2 10 B1
Osgood Ave. BR6 51 F5
Osgood Gdns. 1 BR6 51 F5
Osmers Hill. TN5 174 F7
Osmunda Ct. TN2 149 C4
Osney House. 4 SE2 3 D4
Osney Way. DA12 30 F6
Osprey Ave. ME5 & ME7 48 E2
Osprey Cl. E6 1 E8
Osprey Wlk. ME20 74 F1
Ospringe Ct. SE9 6 D1
Osterberg Rd. DA1 9 F3
Osterley Cl. BR5 38 A8
Ostlers Ct. 2 ME6 75 A8
Otford Cl. Bromley BR1 37 A6
Otford Cl. Sidcup DA5 8 B1
Otford Court (St Michael's Sch). TN14 69 E4
Otford Cty Prim Sch. TN14 69 B3
Otford La. TN14 68 B6
Otford Rd. TN14 84 B7
Otford Sta. TN14 69 C3
Otham La. ME15 93 C2
Otham St. Maidstone ME15 93 C2
Otham St. Otham ME15 108 B7
Otley Rd. E16 1 C7
Otlinge Cl. BR5 38 D5
Ottawa Rd. RM18 13 A5
Otterbourne Pl. ME15 92 E1
Otterden Cl. BR6 51 E6
Otterham Quay La. ME8 64 B8
Otteridge Rd. ME14 93 A3
Ottershaw House. BR5 38 B8
Otway St. ME4 48 A3
Otway Terr. 1 ME4 48 A3
Our Lady of Grace RC Jun Mix Sch. SE7 5 B8
Our Lady of Hartley RC Prim Sch. DA3 42 F4
Our Lady of the Rosary RC Prim Sch. DA15 6 E1
Our Lady's RC Prim Sch. DA1 9 D1
Oval The. New Barn DA3 43 C6
Oval The. Sidcup DA15 24 A8
Ovenden Rd. Chevening TN14 82 F6
Ovenden Rd. Sundridge TN14 82 D6
Over Minnis. DA3 56 F7
Overcliffe. DA11 13 A1
Overcourt Cl. DA15 7 B1
Overdale. TN14 99 B2
Overmead. Eltham SE9 23 D8
Overmead. Swanley BR8 39 E4
Overton Rd. SE2 3 D3
Overy Liberty. DA1 26 E8
Overy St. DA1 9 E1
Owen Cl. East Malling ME19 89 F8
Owen Cl. Woolwich SE28 3 C5
Owenite St. SE2 3 B2
Owens Way. ME7 49 A6
Owletts. DA12 44 F6
Ox La. TN30 173 B2
Ox Lea. TN3 148 A3
Oxenden Wood Rd. BR6 52 E1
Oxenhill Rd. TN14 69 E2
Oxenhoath Rd. TN11 102 D4
Oxfield. TN8 112 D3
Oxford Cl. DA12 30 F6
Oxford Mews. DA5 25 A7
Oxford Rd. Gillingham ME7 48 D3
Oxford Rd. Maidstone ME15 107 D8
Oxford Rd. Sidcup DA14 24 B3
Oxford St. ME6 75 A8
Oxhawth Cres. BR2 37 B3
Oxleas. E6 2 B7
Oxleas Cl. DA16 6 D5
Oxley Shaw La. ME19 & ME20 74 E2
Oyster Catchers Cl. E16 1 B7
Ozolins Way. E16 1 A7

Pacific Rd. E16 1 A7
Packer Pl. ME5 62 A8
Packham Rd. DA11 29 F5
Packhorse Rd. TN13 83 C4
Packmores Rd. SE9 6 E2
Pad's Hill. ME15 92 A4
Paddlesworth Rd. ME6 59 D1
Paddock Cl. Fordcombe TN3 147 B5
Paddock Cl. Greenwich SE3 5 A5
Paddock Cl. Orpington BR6 51 B6
Paddock Cl. Platt TN15 87 C6
Paddock Cl. South Darenth DA4 41 C8
Paddock Rd. DA6 7 E3
Paddock The. Chatham ME4 47 F4
Paddock The. Hadlow TN11 102 E1
Paddock The. Pembury TN2 150 C6
Paddock The. Vigo Village DA13 72 F7
Paddock The. Westerham TN16 81 C1
Paddock Way. BR7 23 D1
Paddock Wood Cty Prim Sch. TN12 136 A6
Paddock Wood Sta. TN12 136 A7
Paddocks Cl. BR5 52 D8
Paddocks The. Cowden TN8 145 B7
Paddocks The. East Peckham TN12 119 E6
Paddocks The. Gillingham ME7 63 A5
Paddocks The. Sevenoaks TN13 84 D3
Padsole La. ME15 92 A4
Padstow Manor. ME7 48 C6
Page Cl. DA2 28 C5
Page Cres. DA8 8 F7
Page Heath La. BR1 36 D6
Page Heath Villas. BR1 36 D6
Pageant Cl. RM18 13 C6
Pagehurst Rd. TN12 139 B3
Paget Gdns. BR7 37 B8
Paget Rise. SE18 6 A7
Paget Row. ME7 48 C5
Paget St. ME7 48 C5
Paget Terr. SE18 6 B8
Pagitt St. ME4 47 E3
Paiges Farm Cl. TN14 99 C2
Painters Ash La. DA11 29 D5
Palace Ave. ME15 92 A4
Palace Ct. Chatham ME5 48 D2
Palace Ct. Eltham SE9 5 F1
Palace Gr. BR1 36 B8
Palace Ind Est. ME15 107 F4
Palace Rd. Bromley BR1 36 B8
Palace Rd. Hill Park TN16 81 A6
Palace View. Bromley BR1 36 B6
Palace View. Lewisham SE12 22 A6
Palace Wood Cty Inf Sch. ME16 91 C6
Palace Wood Cty Jun Sch. ME16 91 C6
Palewell Cl. BR5 38 B7
Pallant Way. BR6 51 A7
Pallet Way. SE18 5 E6
Palm Ave. DA14
Palmar Cres. DA7
Palmar Rd. Bexley DA7
Palmar Rd. Maidstone ME16
Palmarsh Cl. BR5
Palmeira Rd. DA16
Palmer Ave. DA12
Palmers Brook. TN11 1
Palmers Green La. TN12 1
Palmers Orch. TN14
Palmerston Cres. SE18
Palmerston Rd. Chatham ME4
Palmerston Rd. Grays RM16
Palmerston Rd. Orpington BR6
Panbro House. SE18
Panfield Rd. SE28
Pankhurst Rd. ME3
Pannell Rd. ME3
Panter's. BR8
Pantiles The. Bromley BR1
Pantiles The. Erith DA7
Pantiles The. 17 Royal Tunbridge Wells TN2 1
Panton Cl. ME5
Pantyles The. TN14
Papillons Wlk. SE3
Papion Gr. ME5
Parade The. Crayford DA1
Parade The. Gravesend DA12
Parade The. Kemsing TN14
Parade The. Meopham Station DA13
Parade The. Staplehurst TN12 1
Parade The. Swanscombe DA10
Paradise Cotts. ME9
Paradise Pl. 15 SE7
Paragon Cl. E16
Paragon The. SE3
Parham Rd. ME4
Parish CE Prim Sch. BR1
Parish Gate Dr. DA15
Parish Wharf. 6 SE18 & SE7
Park App. DA16
Park Ave. Bromley BR1
Park Ave. Edenbridge TN8 1
Park Ave. Gillingham ME7
Park Ave. Gravesend DA12
Park Ave. Hildenborough TN11 1
Park Ave. Loose ME17 1
Park Ave. Maidstone ME14
Park Ave. Northfleet DA11
Park Ave. Orpington,Goddington BR6
Park Ave. Orpington,Locksbottom BR6
Park Ave. West Thurrock RM16
Park Barn Rd. ME17 1
Park Corner Rd. DA13
Park Cotts. 8 TN18 1
Park Cres. Chatham ME4
Park Cres. Erith DA8
Park Crescent Rd. DA8
Park Dr. Longfield DA3
Park Dr. Woolwich SE7
Park Farm Houses. ME19
Park Farm Rd. Bromley BR1
Park Farm Rd. Ryarsh ME19
Park Gdns. DA8
Park Gr. Bexley DA7
Park Gr. Bromley BR1
Park Hill. Bromley BR1
Park Hill. Meopham Station DA13
Park Hill Rd. TN14
Park House. Maidstone ME14
Park House. Sevenoaks TN13
Park House. Sidcup DA14
Park House Gdns. TN4 1
Park La. Cock Street ME17 1
Park La. Gill's Green TN18 1
Park La. Godden Green TN15
Park La. Kemsing TN15
Park La. Maidstone ME14
Park La. Sevenoaks TN13
Park La. Swanley Village BR8
Park Manor. ME7
Park Mead. DA15
Park Mews. BR7
Park Pl. Gravesend DA12
Park Pl. Sevenoaks TN13
Park Rd. Addington ME19

Rd. Bromley BR1 .... 36 B8
Rd. Chislehurst BR7 ...... 23 B2
Rd. Dartford DA1 .... 27 A8
Rd.
k's Green TN11 .... 102 C5
Rd. Gravesend DA11 ...... 30 B7
Rd. Leybourne ME19 ..... 74 D3
Rd.
den Thorn TN12 .... 139 A4
Rd. Mereworth ME18 ... 103 F5
Rd. Orpington BR5 .... 38 C4
Rd.
al Tunbridge Wells,
hborough TN4 .... 133 A2
al
al Tunbridge Wells,St John's
.... 149 B5
Rd. Swanley BR8 .... 39 F5
Rd. Swanscombe DA10 .. 11 E1
Road Ind Est. BR8 .... 39 F6
St. TN2 .... 149 C3
Terr. Sundridge TN14 ... 82 D3
Terr.
anscombe DA9 .... 11 B2
The. DA14 .... 24 A3
View. TN15 .... 57 C2
View Cl. TN8 .... 112 B2
View Ct. ME15 .... 92 E1
View Rd. Bexley DA16 .... 7 C4
View Rd. Eltham SE9 ..... 23 B6
Villas. TN11 .... 102 F1
Wallis. DA11 .... 12 B2
Way. Coxheath ME17 ... 106 D3
Way.
en's Wood DA5 .... 25 E5
Way. Maidstone ME15 .. 92 B1
Way Cty Prim Sch.
S 92 B1
Wood Cty Prim Schs.
.... 63 E5
Wood Gn. ME8 .... 63 D5
Wood La. TN12 .... 140 C1
Wood Par. ME15 .... 107 F5
Wood Trad Est.
.... 107 F4
dale Rd. SE18 .... 2 E1
er Ave. RM18 .... 13 C6
er Cl. Gillingham ME8 .. 63 E5
er Cl. Newham E16 .... 1 E5
er House. 4 SE18 .... 2 B1
er Rd. RM17 .... 11 F8
er St. E16 .... 1 E5
er's Cnr. ME3 .... 19 C8
field. Hartley DA3 .... 42 E5
field. Wilderness TN15 .. 84 F4
field Rd. ME8 .... 49 F1
field Way. BR2 .... 36 F4
fields. ME2 .... 46 C7
gate Cotts. BR6 .... 53 C6
gate Rd. BR6 .... 53 C6
hill Rd. Sidcup DA15 ... 23 E5
hill Rd. Sidcup DA5 ..... 24 F8
hurst Gdns. 2 DA5 ...... 25 A8
hurst Rd. DA5 .... 25 A8
and Cl. TN13 .... 99 D6
ands. TN4 .... 148 E8
side. Cliffe Woods ME3 .. 33 B7
side. Halstead TN14 ..... 67 F6
side. Sidcup DA14 .... 24 B6
side Ave. Bromley BR1 .. 36 E5
side Ave.
yford DA1 & DA7 .... 8 E5
side Ave. Tilbury RM18 . 13 B5
side Cross. DA7 .... 8 E5
side Ct. TN30 .... 182 F7
side Lodge. DA17 .... 4 C1
side Rd. DA17 .... 4 C2
view Ct. DA11 .... 30 A6
way. Erith DA18 .... 3 E3
way. Tonbridge TN10 .. 117 D5
way Prim Sch. DA18 .... 3 E3
wood Cl. TN1 .... 149 C6
wood Hall Sch. BR8 ..... 40 B6
wood Rd. DA5 .... 24 F8
wood Rd. DA17 .... 4 A3
Ave. ME7 .... 48 D6
ock Ave. DA12 .... 30 C7
ock Rd. DA12 .... 30 C7
ock St. DA11 .... 30 B8
ock The. DA12 .... 30 C7
s Head Mews. ME1 ...... 47 C6
ly PI. SE18 .... 2 B2
onage Cl. TN4 .... 148 B5
onage La.
al Harbour ME9 .... 65 F8
onage La.
nberhurst TN3 .... 166 B6
onage La.
chester ME2 .... 47 C8
onage La. Sidcup DA14 . 24 F4

Parsonage La.
Sutton at Hone DA4 ...... 27 B2
Parsonage Manorway.
DA8 & DA17 .... 8 A8
Parsonage Rd.
Rusthall TN4 .... 148 B5
Parsonage Rd.
West Thurrock RM16 ...... 11 C8
Parsons La. Heath Side DA2 . 26 B5
Parsons La. Stansted TN15 .. 56 E1
Partridge Cl. 1 E16 .... 1 D8
Partridge Dr. BR6 .... 51 C7
Partridge Grn. SE9 .... 23 A5
Partridge Rd. DA14 .... 23 E4
Partridge Sq. 3 E6 .... 1 E8
Pasley Rd. ME7 .... 48 A7
Pasley Rd E. ME7 .... 48 A7
Pasley Rd W. ME4 .... 48 A7
Passey PI. SE9 .... 5 F1
Passfield House. SE18 ...... 2 D2
Passfield Path. 13 SE28 .... 3 B6
Paston Cres. SE12 .... 22 B8
Patch The. TN13 .... 83 E5
Patience Cotts. TN14 ...... 99 B2
Patricia Ct. Bexley SE2 .... 7 B7
Patricia Ct. Chislehurst BR7 . 37 D8
Patrixbourne Ave. ME8 .... 49 C2
Pattenden Gdns. TN12 ... 120 A7
Pattenden La. TN12 ...... 138 C7
Pattens Gdns. ME4 .... 47 E2
Pattens La. ME4 .... 47 E1
Pattens PI. ME1 .... 47 D2
Patterdale Rd. DA2 .... 27 D7
Patterson Ct. DA1 .... 10 A2
Pattinson Point. 14 E16 .... 1 A8
Pattison Wlk. SE18 .... 2 C1
Paulinus Cl. BR5 .... 38 C6
Pavement The. TN30 ..... 173 B3
Pavilion Gdns. TN13 .... 84 C3
Pavilion L Ctr The. BR1 .... 36 A7
Pavilion La. ME18 .... 104 A8
Pavilion The. 5 TN9 ...... 117 B1
Paxton Rd. BR1 .... 22 A1
Payne's La. ME15 .... 107 B7
Paynes Cotts. TN13 .... 68 D1
Peace Cotts. ME15 .... 121 D7
Peace St. SE18 .... 6 A8
Peach Croft. DA11 .... 29 E4
Peacock Mews. 7 ME6 .... 91 E4
Peacock St. DA12 .... 30 C8
Pear Tree Ave. ME20 ...... 75 D1
Pear Tree Cl. Bexley DA7 .. 26 B6
Pear Tree Cl.
Cranbrook TN17 .... 169 D3
Pear Tree Cl. Swanley BR8 . 39 D7
Pear Tree La.
Gillingham ME7 .... 62 E7
Pear Tree La.
Maidstone ME15 .... 107 B6
Pear Tree PI. ME3 .... 32 B3
Pear Tree Row. ME7 ..... 108 B5
Pear Tree Wlk. ME9 .... 65 A5
Pearesewood Rd. DA8 ..... 8 F6
Pearl Cl. E6 .... 2 A7
Pearse PI. TN3 .... 166 B5
Pearson Way. DA1 .... 26 F6
Pearson's Green Rd.
TN12 .... 136 F3
Pearson's Green Rd. TN12 . 136 D5
Peartree Cotts. ME8 .... 64 B8
Peartree La. ME2 .... 32 A2
Pease Hill. TN15 .... 56 F4
Peasley La. TN17 .... 167 D6
Peat Way. ME3 .... 20 E6
Peatfield Cl. DA15 .... 23 E5
Peckham Cl. ME2 .... 47 C8
Peckham Ct. TN12 .... 119 F6
Peckham House. 6 BR5 .. 38 D1
Peel Rd. BR6 .... 51 C5
Peel St. ME1 .... 47 C4
Peel Yates House. 13 SE7 ... 1 E2
Peens La. ME17 .... 123 C7
Pegasus Ct. DA12 .... 30 C5
Peggoty Cl. ME3 .... 32 B3
Pegley Gdns. SE12 .... 22 A6
Pegwell St. SE18 .... 6 E7
Pelham Cotts. DA5 .... 25 B7
Pelham Prim Sch. DA7 ..... 8 A4
Pelham Rd. Bexley DA7 .... 8 A4
Pelham Rd.
Gravesend DA11 .... 30 A8
Pelham Rd S. DA11 .... 29 F7
Pelham Terr. DA11 .... 29 F8
Pelican Cl. ME2 .... 46 C6
Pelican Ct. ME18 .... 104 E7
Pell Cl. TN5 .... 175 A6
Pellipar Gdns. SE18 .... 1 F1
Pellipar Rd. SE18 .... 1 F1
Pells La. TN15 .... 71 A7
Pemberton Gdns. BR8 .... 39 E7

Pemberton Sq. ME2 .... 47 C8
Pemble Cl. TN12 .... 135 A7
Pembroke. ME4 .... 48 B8
Pembroke Cl. DA8 .... 4 D2
Pembroke Ct. ME4 .... 48 A4
Pembroke Gdns. ME8 ..... 63 E4
Pembroke PI. DA4 .... 41 B8
Pembroke Rd. Bromley BR1 . 36 D7
Pembroke Rd.
Coxheath ME17 .... 106 C3
Pembroke Rd. Erith DA8 .... 4 D2
Pembroke Rd. Newham E6 .. 1 F8
Pembroke Rd.
Sevenoaks TN13 .... 84 B2
Pembroke Rd.
Tonbridge TN9 .... 117 A1
Pembury Cl. TN2 .... 150 D7
Pembury Cres. DA14 ...... 24 E6
Pembury Cty Prim Sch.
TN2 .... 150 D8
Pembury Gdns. ME16 ..... 91 D3
Pembury Gr. TN9 .... 133 C8
Pembury Grange. TN2 .... 150 A6
Pembury Hall Rd.
TN11 & TN2 .... 134 C3
Pembury Hospl. TN2 ..... 150 B7
Pembury Rd. Erith DA7 .... 7 E8
Pembury Rd.
Pembury TN11 .... 134 A2
Pembury Rd.
Royal Tunbridge Wells TN2 149 E4
Pembury Rd.
Tonbridge TN11 & TN9 . 133 D7
Pembury Walks.
TN11 & TN2 .... 134 C2
Pembury Way. ME8 .... 49 C2
Pen Way. TN10 .... 117 E5
Pencroft Dr. DA1 .... 26 C8
Penda Rd. DA8 .... 8 B7
Pendennis Rd.
Orpington BR6 .... 52 C8
Pendennis Rd.
Sevenoaks TN13 .... 84 B4
Penderel Mews. TN30 .... 183 B8
Pendlebury House. SE18 .. 5 A6
Pendragon Rd. BR1 & SE12 . 22 A5
Pendragon Sec Sch. BR1 .. 22 A5
Pendrell St. SE18 .... 6 D8
Pendrill PI. TN5 .... 174 F5
Penenden. DA3 .... 56 F8
Penenden Ct. ME14 .... 92 B7
Penenden Heath Rd. ME14 . 92 C7
Penenden St. ME14 .... 92 A6
Penfold Cl. Chatham ME5 . 62 B7
Penfold Cl.
Park Wood ME15 .... 107 E5
Penfold Hill. ME17 .... 109 B8
Penfold House. 14 SE18 .. 6 B8
Penfold La. DA5 .... 24 D7
Penfold Way. ME15 ...... 106 F6
Penfolds Cl. TN10 .... 117 C5
Penford Gdns. SE9 .... 5 D4
Pengarth Rd. DA5 .... 7 D1
Penguin Cl. ME2 .... 46 D6
Penhall Rd. SE7 .... 1 D2
Penhill Rd. DA5 .... 24 C8
Penhurst Cl. ME14 .... 92 F5
Penlee Cl. TN8 .... 112 C2
Penmon Rd. SE2 .... 3 A3
Penn Gdns. BR7 .... 37 B7
Penn La. DA5 .... 7 E1
Penn Yd. TN2 .... 150 C6
Pennant Rd. ME1 .... 61 C7
Penney Cl. DA1 .... 26 D8
Pennine Way. Erith DA7 ... 8 E6
Pennine Way.
Maidstone ME15 .... 93 A1
Pennine Way.
Northfleet DA11 .... 29 E5
Pennine Wlk. TN2 .... 149 D5
Pennington Manor. 1
TN4 .... 132 F2
Pennington PI. TN4 .... 133 B1
Pennington Rd. TN4 ...... 133 A2
Pennington Way. SE12 ... 22 B6
Pennyfields. TN17 .... 169 D4
Pennyroyal Ave. E6 .... 2 A7
Penpool La. DA16 .... 7 B4
Penryn Manor. ME7 ...... 48 C6
Penshurst Ave. DA15 ...... 7 A1
Penshurst CE Prim Sch.
TN11 .... 131 A4
Penshurst Cl.
Gillingham ME8 .... 49 E2
Penshurst Cl.
New Barn DA3 .... 43 D7
Penshurst Enterprise Ctr.
TN11 .... 131 C4
Penshurst Place. TN11 ... 131 B4

Penshurst Rd. Bexley DA7 ... 7 F6
Penshurst Rd.
Penshurst TN11 .... 131 C8
Penshurst Rd.
Poundsbridge
TN11 & TN3 .... 147 E8
Penshurst Rd. Printstile
TN11 & TN3 & TN4 ..... 131 E3
Penshurst Sta. TN11 .... 114 F1
Penshurst Vinyard. TN11 . 130 F2
Penshurst Way. BR5 ...... 38 C5
Penstocks The. ME16 ..... 91 D2
Penton House. 3 SE2 ...... 3 D4
Penventon Ct. 3 RM18 .. 13 A5
Pepingstraw Cl. ME19 .... 88 D7
Pepper Cl. E6 .... 1 F8
Pepper Hill. DA11 .... 29 C5
Pepy's Way. ME2 .... 46 F8
Pepys Cl. 5 Dartford DA1 . 10 A3
Pepys Cl. Northfleet DA11 . 29 D5
Pepys Ct. Tilbury RM18 .. 13 C6
Pepys Cres. E16 .... 1 A5
Pepys Rise. BR6 .... 37 F1
Perch La. TN3 .... 151 D1
Percival Rd. BR6 .... 51 B8
Percy Rd. DA7 .... 7 E5
Percy St. 8 RM17 .... 12 C8
Peregrine Ct. DA16 .... 6 F6
Peregrine Dr. ME18 .... 89 A2
Peridot St. E6 .... 1 E8
Perimeter Rd. ME20 ...... 75 C3
Periton Rd. SE9 .... 5 D9
Perkins Cl. DA9 .... 10 F2
Perpins Rd. SE9 .... 6 C3
Perran Cl. DA3 .... 42 F5
Perry Gr. DA1 .... 10 A3
Perry Hall Cl. BR6 .... 38 A2
Perry Hall Prim Sch. BR6 . 37 F3
Perry Hall Rd. BR6 .... 38 A2
Perry Hill. ME3 .... 16 C1
Perry St. Chatham ME4 ... 47 E3
Perry St. Chislehurst BR7 . 23 E2
Perry St. Crayford DA1 ..... 8 E4
Perry St. Maidstone ME14 . 91 F6
Perry St. Northfleet DA11 . 29 F7
Perry Street Gdns. BR7 .. 23 E2
Perryfield St. ME14 .... 91 F6
Perrys La. BR6 & TN14 ... 67 C6
Perth House. 4 RM18 .... 13 A5
Pescot Ave. DA3 .... 43 B6
Pested Bars Rd. ME17 ... 107 D5
Peter St. 5 DA11 .... 30 B8
Peterborough Gdns. ME2 . 46 C6
Peterhouse Gdns. BR6 .... 52 A1
Petersfield. TN2 .... 150 E7
Petersfield Dr. DA13 ...... 57 F1
Petersham Dr. BR5 .... 38 A6
Petersham Gdns. BR5 .... 37 F7
Peterstone Rd. SE2 .... 3 B4
Petham Court Cotts. BR8 . 39 F4
Petham Gn. ME8 .... 49 C2
Petrie House. 3 SE18 ...... 6 A8
Pett St. SE7 .... 1 E2
Petten Cl. BR5 .... 38 D1
Petten Gr. BR5 .... 38 D1
Pettings La. TN12 .... 151 F7
Pettits Row. TN12 .... 137 D8
Pettman Cres. SE18 & SE28 . 2 D3
Petts Wood Rd. BR5 ...... 37 D4
Petts Wood Sta. BR5 ..... 37 C4
Petworth Rd. DA6 .... 8 A2
Peverel. E6 .... 2 A7
Peverel Dr. ME14 .... 93 A5
Peverell Gn. ME8 .... 63 D4
Peverill Ct. 3 DA2 .... 10 B1
Pheasant Cl. E16 .... 1 A7
Pheasant La. ME15 .... 107 B8
Pheasant Rd. ME4 .... 48 C2
Phelps Cl. TN15 .... 55 E4
Philpot Almshouse. 5 SE9 . 5 F1
Philpot Path. SE9 .... 5 F1
Philippa Gdns. SE9 .... 5 D2
Phillip Ave. BR8 .... 39 D5
Phillips Cl. DA1 .... 9 B1
Phillips Ct. ME8 .... 49 B2
Philpots Cl. TN11 .... 115 E6
Philpott's Cross. TN18 .. 178 E2
Phineas Pett Road Rd. SE9 . 5 E4
Phipps House. 1 SE7 ...... 1 B1
Phoenix Cotts. ME18 .... 104 D6
Phoenix Dr.
Keston Mark BR2 .... 50 D7
Phoenix Dr.
Wateringbury ME18 ..... 104 E7
Phoenix Ind Est. ME2 ..... 47 D7
Phoenix Pk. ME15 .... 107 F4
Phoenix PI. DA1 .... 26 D8
Phoenix Rd. ME5 .... 62 B2
Phoenix Yard Cotts. ME18 . 89 F1
Picardy Manorway. DA17 . 4 B3
Picardy Rd. DA17 .... 4 A2

Picardy Sch (Beeches Site).
DA17 .... 4 B2
Picardy St. DA17 .... 4 A3
Piccadilly The. 4 ME4 .... 48 B3
Pickering Ct. 8 DA2 ...... 10 B1
Pickering House. 4 SE28 . 2 A2
Pickering St. ME15 ...... 107 B6
Pickford Cl. DA7 .... 7 E5
Pickford La. DA7 .... 7 E5
Pickford Rd. DA7 .... 7 E4
Pickforde La. TN5 .... 176 D1
Pickhill Oast. TN30 ...... 183 B4
Pickhurst La. BR2 .... 36 A1
Pickle's Way. ME3 .... 16 A6
Pickmoss La. TN14 .... 69 A3
Pickwick Cres. ME1 .... 47 C3
Pickwick Ct. SE9 .... 22 F7
Pickwick Gdns. DA11 ..... 29 D5
Pickwick House. DA11 .... 29 D5
Pickwick Way. BR7 .... 23 C2
Piedmont Rd. SE18 .... 2 D1
Pier Approach Rd. ME7 ... 48 D7
Pier Par. 3 E16 .... 2 A3
Pier PI. ME2 .... 34 A3
Pier Rd. Erith DA8 .... 8 F8
Pier Rd. Gillingham ME7 ... 48 E7
Pier Rd. Newham E16 ...... 2 A4
Pier Rd. Northfleet DA11 .. 12 F1
Pier Rd. Swanscombe DA9 . 11 B3
Pier Rd East Est. ME7 ..... 48 D7
Pier Way. SE18 .... 2 D3
Pierce Mill La. TN11 ..... 119 C6
Piermont PI. BR1 .... 36 E7
Pigdown La. TN8 .... 129 D4
Piggott's Cross. TN8 ..... 113 D7
Pigsdean Rd. DA13 .... 45 B2
Pike Cl. BR1 .... 22 B3
Pikefields. ME8 .... 49 C2
Pikefish La. TN12 .... 120 F7
Pikey La. ME19 .... 89 E5
Pilgrim's Way Cotts. TN15 . 70 A2
Pilgrims Ct. Dartford DA1 . 10 A2
Pilgrims Ct. Greenwich SE3 . 5 A6
Pilgrims Lakes. ME17 .... 110 E6
Pilgrims' Rd. DA10 .... 11 E3
Pilgrims View.
Sandling ME14 .... 76 E3
Pilgrims View.
Swanscombe DA9 .... 11 C1
Pilgrims Way. Boxley ME14 . 77 E3
Pilgrims Way.
Broad Street ME14 & ME17 . 94 C6
Pilgrims Way. Cuxton ME2 .. 46 C3
Pilgrims Way. Dartford DA1 . 27 B8
Pilgrims Way. Detling ME14 . 78 B1
Pilgrims Way. Eccles ME20 . 76 B6
Pilgrims Way.
Hollingbourne ME17 ..... 94 F3
Pilgrims' Way.
Kemsing TN15 & TN14 .. 70 C3
Pilgrims Way.
Lenham ME17 .... 111 B7
Pilgrims Way.
Wrotham TN15 .... 72 A3
Pilgrims Way.
Wrotham TN15 .... 72 C4
Pilgrims Way E. TN14 .... 69 D3
Pilgrims Way W.
Otford TN14 .... 68 F3
Pilgrims Way W.
Twitton TN13 .... 68 D3
Pilkington Rd. BR6 .... 51 C8
Pillar Box La. TN11 ...... 102 D5
Pillar Box Rd. TN15 .... 85 E5
Pilot Rd. ME1 .... 61 C8
Pilots PI. DA11 .... 13 C1
Pimp's Court Cotts. ME15 . 106 E6
Pimp's Court Farm Ctr.
ME15 .... 106 E6
Pimpernel Cl. ME14 .... 93 B4
Pimpernel Way. ME5 ...... 61 E4
Pinchbeck Rd. BR6 .... 51 F4
Pincott Rd. DA6 .... 8 A3
Pincroft Wood. DA3 .... 43 C6
Pine Ave. DA12 .... 30 D7
Pine Cl. Larkfield ME20 .. 75 A2
Pine Cl. Swanley BR8 ..... 39 F5
Pine Cotts. ME14 .... 91 E8

Pine Glade. BR6 .... 50 F6
Pine Gr. Edenbridge TN8 ... 112 B2
Pine Gr. Gillingham ME7 ...... 63 A5
Pine Gr. Maidstone ME14 ..... 92 B6
Pine House. 3 ME5 .... 61 F5
Pine Lodge. ME16 .... 91 C3
Pine Rd. ME2 .... 46 F6
Pine Ridge. TN10 .... 117 B6
Pine Rise. DA13 .... 44 A3
Pine Tree La. TN15 .... 86 A2
Pine View. TN15 .... 87 C7
Pinecrest Gdns. BR6 .... 51 B6
Pinecroft. DA16 .... 7 A7
Pinecroft Wood. DA3 .... 43 C6
Pinehurst. Chislehurst BR7 ... 23 B2
Pinehurst.
  Sevenoaks TN14 & TN15 .... 84 E6
Pinehurst Wlk. 4 BR6 .... 37 D1
Pineneedle La. TN13 .... 84 B4
Pines Rd. BR1 .... 36 E7
Pinesfield La. ME19 .... 73 B6
Pinewood. BR7 .... 23 A2
Pinewood Ave.
  Sevenoaks TN13 .... 84 D6
Pinewood Ave.
  Sidcup DA15 .... 23 E7
Pinewood Cl. Orpington BR6 37 D1
Pinewood Cl.
  Paddock Wood TN12 .... 135 F6
Pinewood Cl. TN4 .... 133 A1
Pinewood Dr.
  Chatham ME14 .... 77 D8
Pinewood Dr.
  Orpington BR6 .... 51 E5
Pinewood Gdns. TN4 .... 133 A1
Pinewood Rd. Bromley BR2 . 36 A5
Pinewood Rd. Erith SE2 .... 7 A8
Pinewood Rd.
  Royal Tunbridge Wells
  TN2 .... 149 D5
Pinkham. TN12 .... 120 A5
Pinkham Gdns. TN12 .... 120 A6
Pinks Hill. BR8 .... 39 E4
Pinnacle Hill. DA7 .... 8 B3
Pinnacle Hill N. DA7 .... 8 B3
Pinnell Rd. SE9 .... 5 D3
Pinnock La. TN12 .... 139 E1
Pinnock's Ave. DA11 .... 30 B7
Pintail Cl. Grain ME3 .... 21 B6
Pintail Cl. Newham E6 .... 1 E8
Pintails The. ME4 .... 34 B1
Pinto Way. SE3 .... 5 B3
Pinton Hill. TN5 .... 176 B3
Pioneer Way. BR8 .... 39 E6
Piper's Green Rd. TN16 .... 97 B7
Pipers Cl. TN5 .... 175 A4
Pipers La. TN16 .... 97 A8
Pippenhall. SE9 .... 6 E1
Pippin Cl. ME17 .... 106 B2
Pippin Croft. ME7 .... 63 A6
Pippin Rd. TN12 .... 119 F6
Pippin Way. ME18 .... 89 A2
Pippins The. DA13 .... 44 A3
Pirbright Cl. ME5 .... 62 D2
Pirie St. E16 .... 1 B5
Pirrip Cl. DA12 .... 30 F6
Pit La. TN8 .... 112 C4
Pitfield. DA3 .... 42 F5
Pitfield Cres. SE28 .... 3 A5
Pitfield Dr. DA13 .... 57 F7
Pitfold Rd. SE12 .... 5 A1
Pitt Rd.
  Langley Heath ME17 .... 109 A2
Pitt Rd. Maidstone ME16 ..... 91 B1
Pitt Rd. Orpington BR6 .... 51 C6
Pittlesden. TN30 .... 183 A7
Pittlesden Pl. 1 TN30 .... 183 A7
Pittsmead Ave. BR2 .... 36 A2
Pittswood Cotts. TN11 .... 118 A8
Pix's La. TN11 .... 182 A3
Pixot Hill. TN12 .... 136 B2
Pizien Well Rd. ME18 .... 104 B7
Place Farm Ave.
  BR5 & BR6 .... 37 D1
Place La. ME9 .... 64 D4
Plain Rd. TN12 .... 138 C4
Plain The. TN17 .... 167 E8
Plains Ave. ME15 .... 92 C1
Plaistow Dr. BR1 .... 22 B1
Plaistow La. BR1 .... 36 C8
Plaistow Sq. ME14 .... 92 C6
Plane Ave. DA11 .... 29 D8
Plane Tree House. SE7 .... 1 D1
Plane Wlk. TN10 .... 117 C7
Plantagenet House. SE18 ..... 1 F3
Plantation Dr. BR5 .... 38 D1
Plantation La. ME14 .... 93 A3
Plantation Rd. Erith DA8 .... 9 A6

Plantation Rd.
  Gillingham ME7 .... 49 A6
Plantation Rd. Hextable BR8 26 A2
Plantation The. SE3 .... 5 A5
Plat The. TN8 .... 112 D1
Platt CE Prim Sch. TN15 ...... 87 C7
Platt Comm. TN15 .... 87 D7
Platt House La. TN15 .... 72 C6
Platt Ind Est. TN15 .... 87 C8
Platt The. Frant TN3 .... 163 B1
Platt The.
  Sutton Valence ME17 ...... 124 E7
Platt's Heath Cty Prim Sch.
  ME17 .... 110 F2
Platters The. ME8 .... 63 C7
Plaxdale Green Rd. TN15 ... 71 D7
Plaxtol Cl. BR1 .... 36 C4
Plaxtol Cty Prim Sch.
  TN15 .... 101 E7
Plaxtol La. TN15 .... 101 D8
Plaxtol Rd. DA8 .... 8 A7
Playstool Cl. ME9 .... 65 B6
Playstool Rd. ME9 .... 65 A6
Pleasance Rd. BR5 .... 38 B6
Pleasant Row. 2 ME4 .... 48 A6
Pleasant View. DA8 .... 4 E1
Pleasant View Pl. BR6 .... 51 C5
Pleasaunce Ct. SE9 .... 5 F3
Pleasure House Rd. ME17 . 125 A8
Plewis House. ME7 .... 48 E7
Plomley Cl. ME8 .... 63 D4
Plough Cotts. ME17 .... 108 E2
Plough Hill. TN15 .... 86 F4
Plough Wents Rd. ME17 ... 108 B2
Plough Wlk. TN8 .... 112 C3
Ploughmans Way.
  Chatham ME5 .... 62 A1
Ploughmans Way.
  Gillingham ME8 .... 63 E6
Plover Cl. Chatham ME5 ...... 62 D1
Plover Cl. Marlpit Hill TN8 .. 112 C8
Plover Rd. ME20 .... 74 F2
Plowenders Cl. ME19 .... 73 D2
Pluckley Cl. ME8 .... 49 C3
Pluckley Rd. TN27 .... 143 D2
Plug La. DA13 .... 58 D5
Plum La. SE18 .... 6 C7
Plum Tree Cotts. TN18 ...... 184 E8
Plum Tree Rd. ME9 .... 79 B8
Plumcroft Prim Sch. SE18 ..... 6 C8
Plumey Feather Cotts.
  TN3 .... 160 E3
Plummer La. TN30 .... 182 F6
Plummers Croft. TN13 .... 83 E6
Plumpton Wlk. 6 ME15 .... 107 F6
Plumstead Common Rd.
  SE18 .... 6 C8
Plumstead High St.
  SE18 & SE2 .... 2 E2
Plumstead Manor Sch. SE18 6 D8
Plumstead Rd. SE18 & SE28 . 2 C2
Plumstead Sta. SE18 .... 2 D2
Plumtree Gr. ME7 .... 63 A4
Plumtree Rd.
  Plumtree Green ME27 .... 125 A1
Plumtree Rd.
  Plumtree Green TN27 ..... 140 F7
Plumtrees. ME16 .... 91 A2
Plymouth Dr. TN13 & TN15 .. 84 C3
Plymouth Pk. TN15 .... 84 C3
Plymouth Rd. Bromley BR1 .. 36 B8
Plymouth Rd. Newham E16 .. 1 A8
Plympton Cl. 3 DA17 .... 3 E3
Plymstock Rd. DA16 .... 7 C7
Poachers Cl. ME5 .... 62 A2
Pococks Bank. TN8 .... 113 C3
Podkin Wood. ME5 .... 76 F8
Pointer Cl. SE28 .... 3 D7
Pointer Sch The. SE3 .... 5 A7
Pointers Ash Cty Prim Sch.
  DA11 .... 29 D5
Pokes Cott. TN17 .... 166 F2
Polebrook Rd. SE3 .... 5 C4
Polesden Rd. TN2 .... 149 D2
Polhill. TN14 .... 68 C4
Polhill Dr. ME5 .... 61 F2
Police Station Rd. ME19 ..... 89 C8
Pollard Cl. E16 .... 1 A6
Pollard Ct. ME7 .... 48 C5
Pollard Wlk. DA14 .... 24 C2
Polley Cl. TN2 .... 150 D7
Pollyhaugh. DA4 .... 54 E7
Pollyhough. DA4 .... 54 E8
Polperro Cl. BR6 .... 37 F3
Polthorne Gr. SE18 .... 2 D2
Polytechnic St. SE18 .... 2 A2
Pond Cl. SE3 .... 5 A5
Pond Farm Rd.
  Hucking ME17 .... 79 D1
Pond Farm Rd.
  Oad Street ME9 .... 65 F1

Pond La. TN15 .... 85 E2
Pond Path. BR7 .... 23 B2
Pondfield La. DA12 .... 31 E1
Pondfield Rd. BR6 .... 51 B7
Pondwood Rise. BR6 .... 37 E2
Pontefract Rd. BR1 .... 22 A3
Pontoise Cl. TN13 .... 83 F5
Pook La. TN27 .... 158 D3
Poona Rd. TN1 & TN2 .... 149 B2
Pootings Rd. TN8 .... 112 E7
Pope Dr. TN12 .... 139 E4
Pope House La. TN30 .... 173 B4
Pope Rd. BR2 .... 36 D4
Pope St. ME16 .... 91 C2
Pope Street Ct. SE9 .... 22 F7
Poplar Ave. Gravesend DA12 30 C4
Poplar Ave. Orpington BR6 .. 51 B8
Poplar Cl. ME3 .... 34 E3
Poplar Field. TN30 .... 189 D4
Poplar Gr. ME16 .... 91 C5
Poplar Mount. DA17 .... 4 A1
Poplar Pl. SE28 .... 3 C6
Poplar Rd. Rochester ME2 ... 46 E5
Poplar Rd.
  Wittersham TN30 .... 189 D4
Poplar Wlk. DA13 .... 44 B3
Poplars Cl. DA3 .... 43 C6
Poplicans Rd. ME2 .... 46 B3
Poppy Cl. ME7 .... 48 E5
Popular Cl. ME2 .... 46 F5
Porchester Cl. Hartley DA3 .. 42 F5
Porchester Cl.
  Maidstone ME15 .... 107 A6
Porchfield Cl. DA12 .... 30 C6
Porcupine Cl. SE9 .... 22 E6
Porrington Cl. BR7 .... 37 A8
Port Ave. DA9 .... 11 B1
Port Cl. Chatham ME5 .... 62 B3
Port Cl. Maidstone ME14 ..... 93 A5
Port Hill. BR6 .... 67 B7
Port Rise. ME4 .... 47 F4
Port Victoria Rd. ME3 .... 21 C4
Porter Cl. RM16 .... 11 C8
Porter Rd. E6 .... 1 F7
Porters Cl. TN12 .... 151 F6
Porters Wlk. ME17 .... 108 E4
Porters Wood. TN12 .... 151 E6
Porteus Ct. DA1 .... 26 D6
Porthkerry Ave. DA16 .... 7 A3
Portland Ave.
  Gravesend DA12 .... 30 B6
Portland Ave. Sidcup DA15 .. 7 A1
Portland Cres. SE9 .... 22 E2
Portland Pl. 1 ME6 .... 75 A8
Portland Rd. Bromley BR1 ... 22 C3
Portland Rd.
  Chislehurst SE9 .... 22 E6
Portland Rd. Gillingham ME7 48 E6
Portland Rd.
  Gravesend DA11 .... 30 B7
Portland Rd.
  Northfleet DA11 .... 12 D1
Portland St. ME4 .... 48 B2
Portman Cl. Bexley DA7 .... 7 E4
Portman Cl. Maypole DA5 .... 25 E7
Portman Pk. TN10 & TN9 .. 117 C3
Portobello Par. TN15 .... 56 A2
Portsdown Cl. ME16 .... 91 B2
Portsea Rd. RM18 .... 13 C6
Portsmans Cotts. ME19 .... 89 B5
Portsmouth Cl. ME2 .... 46 D6
Portway Gdns. SE18 .... 5 D7
Portway Rd. ME3 .... 33 B7
Post Barn Rd. ME4 .... 47 F2
Post Office Rd. 7 TN18 ... 178 F2
Postern La. TN9 .... 117 E1
Postley Commercial Ctr.
  ME15 .... 92 A2
Postley Rd. ME15 .... 92 A1
Postmill Dr. ME15 .... 91 F1
Potash La. TN15 .... 87 C6
Potter's La. TN18 .... 179 A6
Pottery Cl. Coldblow DA5 ... 25 C6
Pottery Rd.
  Hoo St Werburgh ME3 ...... 34 D5
Potyn House. ME1 .... 47 C4
Poulters Wood. BR2 .... 50 D5
Pound Bank Cl. TN15 .... 55 F2
Pound Cl. BR6 .... 51 D8
Pound Court Dr. BR6 .... 51 D8
Pound Green Ct. 4 DA5 ...... 25 A8
Pound House. TN11 .... 118 E8
Pound La.
  Knockholt Pound TN14 ...... 67 D4
Pound La. Sevenoaks TN13 . 84 C3
Pound Park Rd. SE7 .... 1 D2
Pound Pl. SE9 .... 6 A1
Pound Rd. TN12 .... 119 F6
Poundfield Rd. TN18 .... 186 B5

Poundsbridge Hill.
  TN11 & TN3 .... 147 D7
Pounsley Rd. TN13 .... 83 E6
Pout Rd. ME6 .... 74 F7
Poverest Prim Sch. BR5 ...... 38 A4
Poverest Rd. BR5 .... 38 A4
Povey Ave. ME2 .... 33 C2
Powder Mill La.
  Dartford DA1 .... 26 F6
Powder Mill La.
  Leigh TN11 .... 116 B1
Powder Mill La.
  Powder Mills TN11 .... 116 C2
Powder Mill La.
  Royal Tunbridge Wells
  TN4 .... 149 B8
Powdermill Cl. TN4 .... 149 C8
Powell Cl. ME20 .... 76 A3
Power Ind Est Dartford 9 A6
Powerscroft Rd. DA14 .... 24 C2
Powis St. SE18 .... 2 A2
Powlett Rd. ME2 .... 33 C1
Powster Rd. BR1 .... 22 B3
Powys Cl. DA7 .... 7 D8
Poynder Rd. RM18 .... 13 B6
Poynings Cl. BR6 .... 52 C8
Poyntell Cres. BR7 .... 37 D8
Poyntell Rd. TN12 .... 139 F4
Pragnell Rd. SE12 .... 22 B6
Prall's La. TN12 .... 135 E2
Pratling St. ME20 .... 76 C4
Pratt's Bottom Prim Sch.
  TN14 .... 67 C8
Prebend Pear. ME20 .... 75 E1
Prentis Ct. SE7 .... 1 D2
Prescott Ave. BR5 .... 37 B3
Presentation House. 9
  DA11 .... 30 B8
Prestbury Sq. SE9 .... 22 F4
Prestley Dr. TN10 .... 117 E7
Preston Ave. ME7 .... 48 E1
Preston Ct. DA14 .... 23 F4
Preston Dr. DA7 .... 7 D6
Preston Hall Hospl. ME20 .. 75 F1
Preston House. 1 SE18 .... 2 A2
Preston Rd. Northfleet DA11 29 E7
Preston Rd. Tonbridge TN9 117 A1
Prestons Rd. BR2 .... 50 A8
Prestwood Cl. SE18 .... 2 F2
Pretoria House. 4 Erith DA8 8 E7
Pretoria House. 8
  Park Wood ME15 .... 107 E5
Pretoria Rd. Chatham ME4 .. 47 F2
Pretoria Rd. Gillingham ME7 48 D3
Prettymans La. TN8 .... 112 F4
Pridmore Rd. ME4 .... 48 B5
Priest's Wlk. DA12 .... 31 A6
Priestfield Rd. ME7 .... 48 E5
Priestfield Stad (Gillingham FC).
  ME7 .... 48 E5
Priestfields. ME1 .... 47 B3
Priestlands Park Rd. DA15 .. 23 F5
Priestley Dr. Lunsford ME20 74 F4
Priestley Dr.
  Tonbridge TN10 .... 117 E7
Priestwood Rd. DA13 .... 58 D5
Primrose Ave. ME8 .... 63 B5
Primrose Cl. ME1 .... 61 E7
Primrose Dr. ME20 .... 75 D1
Primrose Rd. ME2 .... 59 E5
Primrose Terr. DA12 .... 30 C7
Prince Arthur Rd. ME7 .... 48 B6
Prince Charles Ave.
  Chatham ME5 .... 62 B4
Prince Charles Ave.
  South Darenth DA4 .... 41 D7
Prince Charles House. DA4 . 41 D7
Prince Consort Dr. BR7 .... 37 D8
Prince Henry Rd. SE7 .... 5 D7
Prince Imperial Rd.
  Chislehurst BR7 .... 23 B1
Prince Imperial Rd.
  Woolwich SE18 .... 5 F6
Prince John Rd. SE9 .... 5 E2
Prince Of Wales Rd.
  Greenwich SE3 .... 5 A6
Prince Of Wales Rd.
  Newham E16 .... 1 C7
Prince Regent La. E16 .... 1 C7
Prince Regent Sta. E16 .... 1 C6
Prince Rupert Rd. SE9 .... 5 F3
Prince's Plain. BR2 .... 36 E1
Prince's Plain Prim Sch.
  BR2 .... 36 E2
Prince's St. Rochester ME1 .. 47 C4
Prince's St. Royal Tunbridge Wells
  TN2 .... 149 C3
Princes Ave. Chatham ME5 .. 62 B5
Princes Ave. Dartford DA2 .. 27 B7
Princes Ave. Orpington BR5 . 37 E4
Princes Cl. DA14 .... 24 D5

Princes Rd. Dartford DA1 2
Princes Rd. Dartford DA1 2
Princes Rd.
  Dartford,Fleet-Down
  DA1 & DA2 2
Princes Rd. Gravesend DA12 3
Princes Rd. Hextable BR8 2
Princes St. Bexley DA7 ....
Princes St. Gravesend DA11 .
Princes St. Maidstone ME14 .
Princes View. DA1 ....
Princes Way. ME14 ....
Princess Christian's Hospl.
  TN11 1
Princess Margaret Rd.
  RM18 ....
Princess Mary Ave. ME7 ......
Princess Par. BR6 ....
Prinys Dr. ME8 ....
Priolo Rd. SE7 ....
Prior's Way. TN8 1
Priorsdean Cl. ME16 ....
Priorsford Ave. BR5 ....
Priory Ave. BR5 ....
Priory Cl.
  Bromley BR1 & BR7 ....
Priory Cl. Dartford DA1 ....
Priory Cl.
  East Farleigh ME15 1
Priory Ct. 3 Dartford DA1 ...
Priory Ct. Gillingham ME8 ....
Priory Ctr The. DA1 ....
Priory Dr. SE2 ....
Priory Fields. DA4 ....
Priory Gate. 4 ME14 ....
Priory Gdns. DA1 ....
Priory Gr. Aylesford ME20 ...
Priory Gr. Tonbridge TN9 ... 1
Priory Hill. DA1 ....
Priory House. 3 SE7 ....
Priory La. DA4 ....
Priory Leas. SE9 ....
Priory Mews. DA2 ....
Priory Pl. DA1 ....
Priory Rd. Dartford DA1 ....
Priory Rd. Dartford DA1 ....
Priory Rd. Gillingham ME8 ...
Priory Rd. Maidstone ME15 ..
Priory Rd. Rochester ME2 ....
Priory Rd. Tonbridge TN9 ... 1
Priory Sch The. BR5 ....
Priory St. TN9 1
Priory Way. TN30 1
Priory Wlk. TN9 ....
Prospect Ave. ME2 ....
Prospect Cl. DA17 ....
Prospect Cotts.
  Pratt's Bottom BR6 ....
Prospect Cotts.
  The Down TN11 1
Prospect Gr. DA12 ....
Prospect Pk. TN4 1
Prospect Pl. Bromley BR2 ....
Prospect Pl.
  Collier Street TN12 1
Prospect Pl. Dartford DA1 ...
Prospect Pl.
  Gravesend DA12 ....
Prospect Pl. Grays RM17 ....
Prospect Pl.
  Maidstone ME16 ....
Prospect Rd. Royal Tunbridge
  TN1 & TN2 1
Prospect Rd.
  Royal Tunbridge Wells,
  Southborough TN4 1
Prospect Rd.
  Sevenoaks TN13 ....
Prospect Row.
  Chatham ME4 ....
Prospect Row.
  Gillingham ME4 ....
Prospect Vale. SE18 & SE7 ...
Prospero House. 6 DA17 ...
Provender Way. ME14 ....
Providence Chapel. TN12 .. 1
Providence Cotts.
  Groombridge TN3 1
Providence Cotts.
  Higham ME3 ....
Providence La. ME1 ....
Providence Pl. TN27 ....
Providence Sq. 9 DA9 ....
Prudhoe Ct. 13 DA2 ....
Pudding La.
  Maidstone ME14 ....
Pudding La. Seal TN15 ....
Pudding Rd. ME8 ....
Puddingcake La. TN17 1

edock La.
able BR8 & DA2 .... 25 F2
s Hill TN16 & TN8 .... 97 A3
Rd. ME3 .... 21 B5
gton Cotts. TN17 ..... 180 E6
an Pl. SE9 .... 5 E2
Cl. ME19 .... 74 D1
La. Gillingham ME8 ..... 49 D2
Cl.
gham ME7 & ME8 ...... 49 D3
Croft. DA3 .... 56 E7
ck Rd. ME4 .... 47 E2
Ave. TN10 .... 117 F6
eet By-Pass. RM16 ...... 10 D8
ys Rd. SE9 .... 5 D3
Rd. SE18 .... 2 F1
Way. ME7 .... 48 C7
nden Rd. TN11 .... 101 F3
Orch. TN16 .... 82 C3
Cl. SE2 .... 3 B3
m Cl. ME5 .... 77 A8

ant The. DA7 .... 7 D7
gy Wlk. SE3 .... 5 A3
ar Cl. TN13 .... 84 D4
ar Dr. TN17 .... 169 D6
ar La. TN17 .... 169 D6
ar's Hall La. TN13 ...... 84 C5
ars Cl. DA3 .... 42 E6
ock Rd. DA1 .... 8 E5
ies The. ME17 .... 107 C4
gy Cotts. TN5 .... 174 D7
gy Hill. TN15 .... 84 D4
gy Hill Par. **1** TN9 .... 133 B8
gy Hill Rd.
  ough Green TN15 .... 86 F6
gy Hill Rd.
  bridge TN9 .... 133 B8
gy Rd. ME15 .... 92 A2
gy Rise. TN9 .... 133 A7
gy Sq. ME14 .... 92 A5
gy Way. RM16 .... 10 F8
gy Wood Ind Est.
  .... 90 E8
La. DA9 .... 11 B3
Rd. TN1 .... 149 B5
side. ME4 .... 48 B8
ec Ave. TN16 .... 81 D1
ec Cotts. **6** TN16 ...... 81 D1
ec Rd. RM18 .... 13 A5
ec Sq. **5** TN16 .... 81 D1
n Anne Ave. BR2 .... 36 A6
n Anne Gdns. DA7 ...... 7 D4
n Anne Rd. ME14 ...... 92 B4
n Borough Gdns. BR7 .. 23 D2
n Elizabeth
  tary Hospl The. SE7 ... 5 E7
n Elizabeth Pl. RM18 ... 13 A3
n Elizabeth Sq.
  .5 .... 107 D6
n Mary's Hospl. DA14 .. 24 A2
n Mother Ct The.

n St. Bexley DA7 .... 7 F4
n St. Chatham ME4 ...... 48 A4
n St. Erith DA8 .... 8 E8
n St. Gravesend DA11 ... 13 B1
n St. Queen St TN12 .. 136 D7
n St. Rochester ME1 ... 47 C4
n St. Sandhurst TN18 186 B5
n's Ave.
dstone ME16 .... 91 D5
n's Ave. Snodland ME6 75 A8
n's Dr. TN14 .... 84 C7
n's Farm Rd. DA12 ...... 31 E7
n's Gdns. TN4 .... 149 B6
n's Mews. **12** TN18 ... 179 A2
n's Pas. BR7 .... 23 B2
n's Rd. Bexley DA6 ..... 7 B5
n's Rd. Bromley BR1 ... 36 A7
n's Rd. Chatham ME5 .. 48 D1
n's Rd. Chislehurst BR7 23 B2
n's Rd. Gillingham ME7 48 C4
n's Rd.
xkhurst TN18 .... 179 A2
n's Rd.
dstone ME16 .... 91 C4
n's Rd. Royal Tunbridge Wells
  .... 149 B6
ns Cotts. TN5 .... 174 E6
ns Ctn.
enbridge TN8 .... 112 D1
ns Ct. **11**
xkhurst TN18 .... 179 A2
n's Rd.
ns Gate Gdns. BR7 .... 37 D8
ens Gdns. DA1 & DA2 ... 27 B7

Queens Rd. Erith DA8 ...... 8 E8
Queens Rd. Gravesend DA12 30 C5
Queens Way. ME14 .... 78 A1
Queenscroft Rd. SE9 ...... 5 D1
Queensland House. **2** E16 .. 2 A5
Queensway.
  Allhallows-on-Sea ME3 .... 19 D9
Queensway.
  Hayes BR2 & BR4 ...... 50 A6
Queensway. Orpington BR5 . 37 C3
Queenswood Rd.
  Kit's Coty ME20 .... 76 D7
Queenswood Rd.
  Sidcup DA15 .... 6 F1
Quern The. ME15 .... 91 E1
Quernmore Cl. BR1 ...... 22 A2
Quernmore Rd. BR1 ...... 22 A2
Quested Way. ME17 ...... 110 C6
Quickrells Ave. ME3 ...... 16 B5
Quickthorn Cres. ME5 .... 61 E5
Quiet Nook. BR2 .... 50 D7
Quilter Gdns. BR5 ...... 38 C1
Quilter Rd. BR5 .... 38 D1
Quilter St. SE18 .... 2 F1
Quincewood Gdns. TN10 .. 117 B7
Quinion Cl. ME5 .... 77 A8
Quinnell St. ME8 .... 49 E1
Quixote Cres. ME2 ...... 33 B1

Rabbits Rd. DA4 .... 41 E7
Rablus Pl. DA4 .... 40 F3
Racefield Cl. DA12 ...... 31 E1
Radfield Way. SE9 ...... 23 D8
Radland Rd. E16 .... 1 A7
Radleigh Gdns. ME4 ...... 47 E1
Radley House. **13** SE2 .... 3 D4
Radnor Ave. DA16 .... 7 B2
Radnor Cl. BR7 .... 23 E2
Radnor Cres. SE18 ...... 2 A7
Raeburn Ave. DA1 ...... 9 B2
Raeburn Cl. TN10 ...... 117 E6
Raeburn Pl. DA10 .... 11 E2
Raeburn Rd. DA15 ...... 6 E1
Rafford Way. BR1 ...... 36 B6
Raggatt Pl. ME15 ...... 92 B2
Ragge Way. TN15 .... 84 F7
Ragglesowod. BR7 ...... 37 A8
Raglan Cl. SE12 .... 5 A2
Raglan Prim Sch. BR2 .... 36 D5
Raglan Rd. Bromley BR2 .. 36 C5
Raglan Rd. Erith DA17 .... 3 F2
Raglan Rd. Woolwich SE18 .. 2 C1
Ragstone Ct. ME19 ...... 90 C8
Ragstone Rd. ME15 ...... 93 A2
Railway App. TN9 ...... 133 B8
Railway Cotts.
  Cowden TN8 .... 145 D8
Railway Cotts.
  Hartley TN15 .... 168 E2
Railway Pl. Erith DA17 .... 4 A3
Railway Pl. **18**
Gravesend DA11 .... 13 B1
Railway Sidings The. DA13 . 44 B4
Railway St. Chatham ME4 .. 47 F4
Railway St. Gillingham ME7 .. 48 D6
Railway St. Northfleet DA11 . 12 A2
Railway Terr. TN16 ...... 81 D1
Rainham Ct. Ethan SE9 .... 6 E1
Rainham Cl.
  Maidstone ME15 .... 92 A1
Rainham Mark Gram Sch.
  ME8 .... 49 D2
Rainham Rd. ME5 & ME7 ... 48 C3
Rainham Sch for Girls.
  ME8 .... 63 C8
Rainham Sta. ME8 ...... 49 F1
Rainton Rd. SE7 .... 1 A1
Raleigh Cl. Chatham ME5 .. 62 A6
Raleigh Cl. Erith DA8 ...... 8 F8
Raleigh Mews. **6** BR6 .... 51 F5
Ramac Ind Est. SE7 ...... 1 B1
Ramac Way. SE7 .... 1 B1
Ramillies Cl. ME5 ...... 62 A6
Ramillies Rd. DA15 ...... 7 B1
Rammell Mews. TN17 .... 169 D4
Rampion Cl. ME14 ...... 92 E5
Ramsden La. TN17 ...... 180 F4
Ramsden Prim Sch. BR5 ... 38 C2
Ramsden Rd. Erith DA8 .... 8 D7
Ramsden Rd.
  Orpington BR5 & BR6 .... 38 B1
Ramslye Rd. TN2 & TN4 .. 162 E8
Ramus Wood Ave. BR6 .... 51 E5
Rance House. **12** SE2 .... 3 C1
Rancliffe Gdns. SE9 ...... 5 E3
Randall Cl. DA8 .... 8 C8
Randall Hill Rd. TN15 .... 71 F3
Randall Rd. ME4 .... 47 E1

Randall St. ME14 .... 91 F6
Randalls Row. ME15 ...... 106 F5
Randle's La. BR6 & TN14 ... 67 D5
Randolph App. E16 ...... 1 C7
Randolph Cl. DA7 ...... 8 C4
Randolph Cotts. ME2 .... 33 B1
Randolph Rd.
  Gillingham ME7 .... 48 C5
Randolph Rd.
  Keston Mark BR2 ...... 36 F1
Ranelagh Gdns. DA11 .... 29 F8
Range Rd. DA12 .... 30 E8
Rangefield Rd. BR1 ...... 22 A3
Rangeworth Pl. DA15 .... 23 F5
Rankine Rd. TN1 .... 149 D7
Ranleigh Gdns. DA7 ...... 7 F7
Ranmore Path. BR5 ...... 38 A5
Ranscombe Cl. ME2 ...... 46 D5
Ranscombe Farm Cotts.
  ME2 .... 46 C4
Ransom Rd. **1** SE7 ...... 1 C1
Ranters La. TN17 ...... 167 C7
Ranters Oak. TN17 ...... 181 B4
Ranworth Cl. DA7 & DA8 ... 8 E5
Raphael Ave. RM18 ...... 13 B7
Raphael Ct. TN11 ...... 116 E7
Raphael Rd. DA12 ...... 30 D8
Rare Farm Animals Pk.
  TN11 .... 100 C2
Rashleigh Way. DA4 ...... 41 C5
Ratcliff Cl. SE12 .... 22 A8
Ratcliffe Highway.
  Hoo St Werburgh ME3 .... 34 C7
Ratcliffe Highway.
  St Mary Hoo ME3 ...... 18 D5
Rathmore Rd.
  Gravesend DA11 .... 30 B8
Rathmore Rd. Greenwich SE7 1 B1
Raven Cl. ME20 .... 75 A1
Ravens Dane Cl. ME15 .... 93 A1
Ravens Knowle. ME1 ..... 60 D4
Ravens Way. SE12 & SE3 ... 5 A3
Ravens Wood Sch for Boys.
  BR2 .... 50 D7
Ravensbourne Coll of Design
  & Communication. BR7 .... 22 F3
Ravensbourne Ct. **23**
  .... 38 D1
Ravensbourne Rd.
  Bromley BR1 & BR2 ...... 36 A6
Ravensbourne Rd.
  Crayford DA1 .... 9 A4
Ravensbourne Sch. BR2 ... 36 B4
Ravensbury Rd. BR5 ...... 38 A5
Ravenscourt Rd. BR5 .... 38 B7
Ravenscroft Pl. **5** E16 .... 1 A8
Ravenscroft Cres. SE9 .... 22 F5
Ravenscroft Rd. E16 ...... 1 A8
Ravenshill. BR7 .... 37 B8
Ravensquay Bsns Ctr. BR5 . 38 B4
Ravenswood. DA5 ...... 24 E7
Ravenswood Ave.
  Rochester ME2 .... 33 B1
Ravenswood Ave.
  Royal Tunbridge Wells
  TN1 & TN2 .... 149 D6
Ravenswood Rd. SE9 .... 22 F4
Ravine Gr. SE18 .... 6 E8
Rawdon Rd. ME15 ...... 92 A3
Rawlings Cl. **3** BR6 .... 51 F5
Rawsthorne Cl. E16 ...... 1 F5
Rayfield Cl. BR2 .... 36 E3
Rayford Cl. DA1 .... 9 C2
Rayleas Cl. SE18 .... 6 B6
Raymer Rd. ME14 ...... 92 B8
Raymere Gdns. SE18 .... 6 E7
Raymond Postgate Ct. **5**
  .... 3 B6
Raynehurst Cty Prim Sch.
  DA12 .... 30 F5
Rayners Ct. DA11 ...... 12 B1
Raynham Villas. TN12 .... 122 A4
Rays Hill. DA4 .... 41 C4
Read Way. DA12 .... 30 E3
Reader's Bridge Rd.
  TN27 & TN30 .... 172 E4
Reading Rd. ME8 ...... 63 D5
Rebecca Ct. DA14 ...... 24 B4
Recreation Ave. ME6 ..... 75 A8
Recreation Cl. ME14 .... 92 B6
Recreation Ground Rd.
  TN30 .... 183 B7
Rectory Bsns Ctr. ME14 ... 24 B4
Rectory Cl. Crayford DA1 ... 8 E3
Rectory Cl. Sidcup DA14 .. 24 B4
Rectory Cl. Snodland ME6 ... 75 A8
Rectory Cl. Wouldham ME1 . 60 C5
Rectory Dr. TN4 .... 132 D3
Rectory Field Cres. SE7 ... 5 C7
Rectory Fields. TN17 .... 169 D5
Rectory Grange. ME1 .... 47 C2

Rectory La. Brasted TN16 .. 82 C3
Rectory La.
  Harrietsham ME17 ...... 110 E5
Rectory La. Ightham TN15 .. 86 C5
Rectory La. Maidstone ME16 91 A1
Rectory La. Sevenoaks TN13 84 C1
Rectory La. Sidcup DA14 ... 24 C4
Rectory La.
  Sutton Valence ME17 .... 124 C6
Rectory La.
  Sutton Valence ME17 .... 124 F7
Rectory La N. ME19 ...... 74 E2
Rectory La S. ME19 ...... 74 E1
Rectory Meadow. DA13 ... 29 A2
Rectory Paddock Sch
  & Research Unit. BR5 .... 38 C7
Rectory Park Rd. TN12 .. 153 A2
Rectory Pl. SE18 .... 2 A2
Rectory Rd. Cliffe ME3 ... 16 A3
Rectory Rd. **3** Grays RM17 12 D8
Rectory Rd. Keston BR2 .. 50 D3
Rectory Rd.
  Low Street ME18 ...... 13 D8
Rectory Rd. Ridley TN15 .. 57 C5
Rectory Rd.
  Swanscombe DA10 ...... 28 E8
Reculver Wlk.
  Maidstone ME15 .... 107 F6
Reculver Wlk.
  Maidstone ME15 .... 107 F6
Red Barracks Rd. **4** SE18 ... 1 F2
Red Cedars Rd. BR6 ...... 37 E2
Red Hill. Chislehurst BR7 .. 23 B3
Red Hill. Red Hill ME18 .... 89 F1
Red Hill Prim Sch. BR7 .... 23 B3
Red House Gdns. ME18 ... 104 C7
Red House La. DA6 ...... 7 E3
Red Lion Cl. BR5 .... 38 C3
Red Lion La. SE18 ...... 6 A6
Red Lion Pl. SE18 ...... 6 A6
Red Lodge Cres. DA5 .... 25 E5
Red Lodge Rd. DA5 ...... 25 D5
Red Oak. TN18 .... 184 E8
Red Oak Cl. BR6 .... 51 B8
Red Oast Cotts. TN5 ...... 177 C3
Red Robin Cotts. ME9 .... 65 B6
Red St. DA13 .... 29 B2
Redbank. ME19 .... 74 E2
Redbridge Cl. ME5 ...... 62 C4
Redcliffe La. ME14 ...... 92 B7
Reddy Rd. DA8 .... 8 F8
Rede Court Rd. ME2 ...... 46 E8
Rede Wood Rd. ME16 .... 90 F3
Redfern Ave. ME7 ...... 48 E5
Redgate Dr. BR2 .... 50 B8
Redhill Rd. TN15 ...... 56 F6
Redhill Wood. DA3 ...... 57 A7
Redland Shaw. ME4 ...... 47 E1
Redlands Rd. TN13 ...... 83 F3
Redleaf Cl. Erith DA17 .... 8 A8
Redleaf Cl. Royal Tunbridge Wells
  TN2 .... 149 D6
Redmans La. BR6 & TN14 .. 53 E4
Redpoll Way. SE2 ...... 3 D3
Redpoll Wlk. TN12 ...... 136 A5
Redruth Manor. ME7 ...... 48 C6
Redsells Cl. ME15 ...... 93 A1
Redstart Cl. E6 .... 1 E8
Redvers Rd. ME4 ...... 48 A2
Redwall La. ME5 & ME17 . 122 C6
Redwell La. TN15 ...... 86 B4
Redwing Cl. ME20 ...... 75 A2
Redwing Path. SE28 ...... 2 D4
Redwing Rd. ME5 ...... 62 B7
Redwings La. TN2 ...... 134 E2
Redwood Cl. Chatham ME5 . 62 B2
Redwood Cl. Sidcup DA15 . 24 A7
Redwood Cl. DA1 .... 10 A1
Redwood Pk.
  TN11 & TN12 .... 135 A5
Reed Ave. BR6 .... 51 E7
Reed Cl. Eltham SE12 .... 5 A2
Reed Cl. Newham E16 ... 1 A8
Reed Ct. ME3 .... 16 B6
Reedham Cres. ME3 ...... 33 B7
Reeds Cotts. TN17 ...... 170 A8
Reeds La. TN11 .... 101 E5
Reeves Cl. TN12 .... 139 E4
Reeves Cres. BR8 ...... 39 D6
Reeves Ct. TN15 .... 147 B5
Reeves Rd. SE18 .... 6 B8
Reeves Terr. TN15 ...... 176 E1
Reform Rd. ME4 .... 48 B2
Regency Cl. Gillingham ME8 63 C3
Regency Cl.
  West Kingsdown TN15 ... 55 E4
Regency Hall. **19** TN2 .... 149 A2
Regency Way. DA7 ...... 7 D8
Regent Dr. ME15 ...... 107 A8
Regent Pl. TN2 .... 149 D3

Regent Rd. ME7 .... 48 C4
Regent Sq. DA17 .... 4 B2
Regent St. TN17 .... 181 E4
Regent's Pl. SE3 .... 5 A5
Regents Ct. **2** DA11 .... 13 B1
Regents Dr. BR2 .... 50 D5
Regina Ct. TN4 .... 148 F4
Reginald Ave. ME2 ...... 46 C3
Reginald Rd. ME16 ...... 91 E3
Reidhaven Rd. SE18 ...... 2 E2
Reigate Rd. BR1 & SE12 .. 22 A5
Reinden Gr. ME15 ...... 92 F1
Rembrandt Cl. TN10 .... 117 C6
Rembrandt Dr. DA11 .... 29 E5
Remington Rd. E6 .... 1 E7
Rendlebury House. **17**
  SE18 .... 1 F2
Renfrew Cl. E6 .... 2 A6
Rennets Cl. SE9 .... 6 E2
Rennets Wood Rd. SE9 ... 6 D2
Renown Rd. ME5 ...... 62 C2
Renshaw Cl. **7** DA17 ...... 7 F8
Renton Dr. BR5 .... 38 D2
Repository Rd. SE18 & SE17 . 1 F1
Repton Rd. BR6 .... 52 A6
Repton Way. ME5 ...... 61 F4
Resolution Cl. ME5 ...... 62 A6
Resolution Wlk. SE18 .... 1 F3
Restharrow Rd. ME14 .... 92 E4
Restons Cres. SE9 ...... 6 E1
Retreat The. Grays RM17 .. 12 B8
Retreat The. Orpington BR6 . 52 B4
Revell Rise. SE18 .... 6 F8
Revenge Rd. ME5 ...... 77 C8
Reventlow Rd. SE9 ...... 23 C7
Reynard Cl. BR1 .... 37 A6
Reynolds Cl. TN10 ...... 117 E6
Reynolds Fields. ME3 .... 32 C6
Reynolds La. TN4 ...... 148 F6
Reynolds Pl. SE3 .... 5 B7
Rhode St. ME4 .... 48 A4
Rhodes House. ME5 ...... 62 C2
Rhodewood Cl. ME15 .... 93 A1
Rhododendron Ave. DA13 . 58 A2
Ribblesdale Rd. DA2 .... 27 C7
Ribston Cl. BR2 .... 36 F1
Ribston Gdns. TN12 .... 135 F7
Ricardo Path. **5** SE28 .... 3 C5
Rich Ind Est. DA7 ...... 8 F2
Richard Cl. SE18 .... 1 E2
Richard St. Chatham ME4 .. 47 F4
Richard St. Rochester ME1 . 47 C3
Richard's Cl. TN11 ...... 114 F2
Richardson Cl. DA9 ...... 11 A2
Richardson Rd. TN4 .... 149 A5
Richborough Cl. BR5 ..... 38 D5
Richborough Drive. ME1 .. 33 A1
Richings House. BR5 .... 38 A8
Richmer Rd. DA8 ...... 9 A7
Richmond Cl. Chatham ME5 62 B4
Richmond Cl.
  Upper Upton ME2 ...... 33 F1
Richmond Cty Inf Sch.
  ME7 .... 48 C6
Richmond Pl. SE18 ...... 2 C2
Richmond Rd.
  Gillingham ME7 .... 48 C7
Richmond Rd. **1**
  Grays RM17 .... 12 C8
Richmond Way. ME15 .... 107 A8
Richmount Gdns. SE3 ... 5 A4
Rickyard Path. SE9 ...... 5 E3
Riddlesdale Ave. TN4 ... 149 A6
Riddons Rd. SE12 ...... 22 C4
Rideout St. SE18 .... 1 F2
Rider Cl. DA15 .... 6 E1
Ridge Ave. DA1 .... 8 F1
Ridge La. DA13 .... 58 A2
Ridge Meadow Cty Prim Sch.
  ME5 .... 61 F6
Ridge The.
  Groombridge TN3 ...... 161 A6
Ridge The. Orpington BR6 . 51 D8
Ridge The. Sidcup DA5 .... 24 F8
Ridge Way. Crayford DA1 .. 8 F1
Ridge Way.
  Marlpit Hill TN8 .... 112 D4
Ridgebrook Rd. SE3 & SE9 .. 5 D4
Ridgecroft Cl. DA5 ...... 25 C7
Ridgelands. TN3 ...... 132 C4
Ridgeway. Hayes BR2 .... 50 A8
Ridgeway.
  Hurst Green TN19 ...... 184 A3
Ridgeway. Lane End DA2 .. 27 E3
Ridgeway. Pembury TN2 .. 150 D7
Ridgeway. The Moor TN18 . 184 E8
Ridgeway Ave. DA12 .... 30 B5
Ridgeway Bglws. DA12 ... 31 F1

Ridgeway Cres.
Orpington BR6 .... 51 E7
Ridgeway Cres.
Tonbridge TN10 .... 117 D4
Ridgeway Crescent Gdns.
BR6 .... 51 E7
Ridgeway Dr. BR1 .... 22 E4
Ridgeway E. DA15 .... 6 F2
Ridgeway The.
Chatham ME4 .... 61 E7
Ridgeway The.
Gillingham ME7 .... 48 C2
Ridgeway The.
Shorne Ridgeway DA12 ... 31 E1
Ridgeway The.
Tonbridge TN10 .... 117 D4
Ridgeway W. DA15 .... 6 E2
Ridgewaye The. TN4 .... 133 B1
Ridgewood. DA3 .... 43 C7
Ridgway. ME16 .... 91 B2
Ridgwell Rd. E16 .... 1 C8
Riding La. TN11 .... 100 D2
Riding Pk. TN11 .... 116 D7
Ridings The.
Paddock Wood TN12 ...... 136 A7
Ridings The. Royal Tunbridge Wells
TN2 .... 149 F6
Ridley Rd. Bexley DA16 ...... 7 B6
Ridley Rd. Bromley BR2 .... 36 A6
Ridley Rd. Rochester ME1 .. 47 C4
Riefield Rd. SE9 .... 6 C2
Riggs Way. TN15 .... 71 F3
Ring Cl. BR1 .... 22 B1
Ringden Ave. TN12 .... 135 F5
Ringer's Rd. BR1 .... 36 A6
Ringle Gn. TN18 .... 186 C5
Ringlestone Cres. ME14 .... 91 F8
Ringlestone Rd. ME17 ...... 95 D4
Ringmer Way. BR1 .... 36 F4
Rings Hill. TN11 .... 116 B4
Ringshall Rd. BR5 & BR7 .. 38 A6
Ringwood Ave. ME6 .... 52 C1
Ringwood Cl. ME8 .... 63 D8
Ringwood Rd. ME15 .... 107 C8
Ripley Cl. BR1 .... 36 F4
Ripley Rd. Erith DA17 .... 4 A2
Ripley Rd. Newham E16 ...... 1 C7
Ripon Cl. ME8 .... 49 D3
Ripon Rd. SE18 .... 6 B8
Rippersley Rd. DA16 .... 7 A6
Rippolson Rd. SE18 .... 2 F1
Risden La. TN18 .... 185 D7
Rise The. Crayford DA1 ...... 8 F3
Rise The. Gillingham ME7 .. 63 A3
Rise The. Gravesend DA12 .. 30 E4
Rise The. Rochester ME1 .... 47 D3
Rise The. Sevenoaks TN13 .. 99 C7
Rise The. Sidcup DA5 .... 24 C8
Risedale Rd. DA7 .... 8 C4
Riseden Rd. TN5 .... 174 C1
Ritch Rd. ME2 .... 46 B8
Ritter St. SE18 .... 6 A8
River Cl. ME15 .... 106 A7
River Cotts. BR5 .... 38 C7
River Ct. TN13 .... 83 E5
River Dr. ME2 .... 46 E7
River Lawn Rd. TN9 .... 117 B1
River Park View. BR6 .... 38 E7
River Rd. IG11 .... 3 A8
River St. ME4 .... 48 A6
River View. **7** Dartford DA1 10 A3
River View. Gillingham ME8 . 49 D3
River View. Maidstone ME15 91 F2
River Way. ME20 .... 75 B4
River Wlk. TN9 .... 117 B1
Riverdale Est. TN9 .... 133 D8
Riverdale Rd. Erith DA8 ...... 4 C1
Riverdale Rd. Sidcup DA5 .... 7 F1
Riverdale Rd. Woolwich SE18 2 F1
Riverhead Cl. ME16 .... 91 D6
Riverhead Cty Inf Sch.
TN13 .... 83 F5
Riverhill. TN13 & TN15 ...... 99 F5
Riverhill Cotts. TN15 .... 99 E5
Riverhill House Gdns.
TN15 .... 99 E5
Rivers Wlk. ME17 .... 111 C5
Riversdale. DA11 .... 29 F5
Riverside. Edenbridge TN8 . 112 C1
Riverside. Eynsford DA4 .... 54 D8
Riverside. Greenwich SE7 .... 1 B3
Riverside Cl. BR5 .... 38 C7
Riverside Ct. **2** BR5 .... 38 C4
Riverside Ctry Pk. ME7 .... 49 D5
Riverside East Rd. ME4 .... 34 C1
Riverside Ind Est. DA1 ...... 9 F7
Riverside North Rd. ME4 .. 34 B2

Riverside Rd. DA14 .... 24 E6
Riverside Sch. DA18 .... 3 E4
Riverside Way. DA1 .... 9 E2
Riverside West Rd. ME4 .... 34 A2
Riverston Sch. SE12 .... 5 A2
Riverview Cty Inf Sch.
DA12 .... 30 E4
Riverview Cty Jun Sch.
DA12 .... 30 E4
Riverview Hts. SE18 .... 6 F8
Riverview Rd. DA9 .... 11 A2
Riverwood La. BR7 .... 37 D8
Rixon House. SE18 .... 6 B8
Roach St. ME2 .... 47 A7
Roan Ct. ME2 .... 46 F8
Robert Napier Sch The.
ME7 .... 48 E3
Robert St. Newham E16 ...... 2 B5
Robert St. Woolwich SE18 .... 2 D2
Roberton Dr. BR1 .... 36 C8
Roberts Cl. Eltham SE9 ...... 23 D7
Roberts Cl. **8**
Orpington BR5 .... 38 C4
Roberts House. SE18 .... 5 E6
Roberts Orchard Rd. ME16 . 90 F3
Roberts Rd. Erith DA17 ...... 4 A1
Roberts Rd. Gillingham ME8 63 E8
Roberts Rd. Snodland ME6 .. 74 F8
Robertson House. SE18 .... 5 F6
Robin Cres. E6 .... 1 D8
Robin Hill Dr. BR7 .... 22 E2
Robin Hood Gn. BR5 .... 38 A4
Robin Hood La. Bexley DA6 .. 7 E2
Robin Hood La.
Chatham ME5 .... 61 D1
Robin Hood Lane (Lower).
ME5 .... 61 F2
Robin Hood Lane (Upper).
ME5 .... 61 E1
Robin House. **5** ME16 ...... 91 E4
Robin Way. BR5 .... 38 B6
Robina Cl. DA6 .... 7 F3
Robina Cl. BR8 .... 40 A5
Robins Ave. DA11 .... 29 D8
Robins Ave. ME17 .... 111 C5
Robins Cl. ME17 .... 111 C4
Robins Ct. Lewisham SE12 .. 22 C5
Robins Ct. Maidstone ME14 .. 92 B7
Robins Gr. BR4 .... 50 A7
Robinwood Dr. TN15 .... 84 F8
Robson Dr. TN15 .... 1 E7
Robson Dr. Aylesford ME20 . 75 D2
Robson Dr.
Hoo St Werburgh ME3 .... 34 D6
Robyns Croft. **6** DA11 .... 29 E5
Robyns Way.
Edenbridge TN8 .... 128 D8
Robyns Way.
Sevenoaks TN13 .... 83 F5
Rocfort Rd. ME6 .... 75 A8
Rochdale Rd.
Royal Tunbridge Wells TN1 149 C6
Rochdale Rd. Woolwich SE2 .. 3 B2
Rochester Airport.
ME1 & ME5 .... 61 C6
Rochester Ave.
Bromley BR1 .... 36 B7
Rochester Ave.
Rochester ME1 .... 47 C4
Rochester Cath. ME1 .... 47 C6
Rochester Cl. **1** DA16 ...... 7 B1
Rochester Cres. ME3 .... 34 D6
Rochester Ct. ME2 .... 47 E8
Rochester Dr. DA5 .... 8 A1
Rochester Gram Sch
for Girls The. ME1 .... 47 C5
Rochester House. **1**
ME15 .... 107 D7
Rochester Rd. Burham ME1 . 60 E2
Rochester Rd. Chalk DA12 .. 31 B6
Rochester Rd.
Chatham ME5 .... 61 C4
Rochester Rd. Dartford DA1 27 A8
Rochester Rd.
Pratling Street ME20 ...... 76 B4
Rochester Rd.
Rochester ME2 .... 46 D4
Rochester Rd.
Tonbridge TN10 .... 117 D4
Rochester Rd.
Wouldham ME1 .... 60 C7
Rochester St. ME4 .... 47 E3
Rochester Sta. ME1 .... 47 D5
Rochester Way.
Dartford DA1 .... 25 F8
Rochester Way. Eltham SE9 . 6 B4
Rochester Way.
Eltham,Kidbrooke SE3 & SE9 5 D4
Rock Ave. ME7 .... 48 C3
Rock Cotts. TN15 .... 163 B1
Rock Farm Cotts. ME18 .. 104 C6

Rock Hill. BR6 .... 53 B4
Rock Hill Rd. TN27 .... 127 E2
Rock Rd.
Borough Green TN15 .... 86 F7
Rock Rd. Maidstone ME14 .. 92 A6
Rock Villa Rd. TN1 .... 149 A4
Rockdale. TN13 .... 84 B2
Rockdale Rd. TN13 .... 84 C2
Rockliffe Manor Prim Sch.
SE18 .... 6 F8
Rockmount Rd. SE18 & SE2 .. 2 F1
Rocks Cl. ME19 .... 90 A6
Rocks Hill. TN17 .... 156 A4
Rocks Rd The. ME19 .... 90 A6
Rocky Hill. ME16 .... 91 E4
Rocky Hill Terr. **2** ME16 .. 91 E4
Roding Rd. E6 .... 2 B8
Rodmell Rd. TN1 .... 149 A2
Rodney Ave. TN10 .... 117 E4
Rodney Gdns. BR4 .... 50 A6
Rodway Rd. BR1 .... 36 B8
Roebourne Way. E16 .... 2 A4
Roebuck Rd. ME1 .... 47 C5
Roedean Cl. BR6 .... 52 B6
Roedean Rd. TN1 & TN2 .. 149 A1
Roehampton Cl. DA12 ...... 30 E8
Roehampton Dr. BR7 .... 23 C2
Roethorne Gdns. TN30 .. 183 B8
Roffen Rd. ME1 .... 47 C2
Rogers Ct. BR8 .... 40 A5
Rogers Rough Rd. TN17 .. 167 B2
Rogers Wood La. TN15 ...... 56 B6
Rogersmead. TN30 .... 183 A7
Rogley Hill. TN27 .... 171 B6
Rogues Hill. TN11 .... 131 C3
Rokesby Cl. DA16 .... 6 D5
Rolinsden Way. BR2 .... 50 D6
Rollesby Way. SE28 .... 3 C7
Rolleston Ave. BR5 .... 37 B3
Rolleston Cl. BR5 .... 37 B2
Rollo Rd. BR8 .... 25 F1
Rolvenden Ave. ME8 .... 49 C3
Rolvenden Cty Prim Sch.
TN17 .... 181 E3
Rolvenden Gdns. BR1 ...... 22 D1
Rolvenden Hill.
TN17 & TN30 .... 182 C5
Rolvenden Rd.
Rochester ME2 .... 33 C2
Rolvenden Rd.
Tenterden TN30 .... 182 E7
Rolvenden Sta. TN30 ...... 182 D6
Roman Cl. ME5 .... 62 A8
Roman Hts. ME14 .... 92 C6
Roman Rd.
Edenbridge TN8 .... 128 D5
Roman Rd. Northfleet DA11 . 29 C5
Roman Rd. Snodland ME6 .. 74 F8
Roman Sq. SE28 .... 3 A5
Roman Villa Rd.
DA2 & DA4 .... 41 E2
Roman Way. Crayford DA1 .. 8 E2
Roman Way. Rochester ME2 46 F4
Romany Cl. ME15 .... 48 D1
Romany Rd. ME8 .... 49 C2
Romany Rise. BR5 .... 37 C1
Romden Rd.
Haffenden Quarter TN27 . 159 B8
Romden Rd. Romden TN27 143 D1
Romero Sq. SE9 .... 5 C2
Romford Rd. TN2 & TN12 .. 150 F7
Romney Cl. ME14 .... 93 A3
Romney Dr. BR1 .... 22 D1
Romney Gdns. DA7 .... 7 F6
Romney Pl. ME15 .... 92 A4
Romney Rd. Chatham ME5 .. 62 B5
Romney Rd.
Northfleet DA11 .... 29 E5
Romney Rd. Woolwich SE18 .. 2 C3
Romney Way. TN10 .... 117 E5
Romsey Cl. Orpington BR6 .. 51 C6
Romsey Cl. Rochester ME2 . 46 E8
Ronald House. SE7 .... 5 C3
Ronalds Rd. BR1 .... 36 A8
Ronaldstone Rd. DA15 ...... 6 E1
Ronfearn Ave. BR5 .... 38 D4
Ronver Rd. SE12 .... 22 A7
Rook La. ME9 .... 65 F6
Rookdean. TN13 .... 83 C5
Rookery Cres. ME3 .... 16 B6
Rookery Ct. RM16 .... 11 A8
Rookery Dr. BR7 .... 37 A8
Rookery Gdns. BR5 .... 38 D4
Rookery Hill. ME6 .... 74 F8
Rookery La. BR2 .... 36 D3
Rookery Rd. BR6 .... 51 A1
Rookery The. TN16 .... 11 A8
Rookery View. **4** RM17 .. 11 C8
Rookesley Rd. BR5 .... 38 C8
Rookley Cl. TN2 .... 149 D2
Rooks Hill. TN15 .... 100 D6

Roopers. TN3 .... 148 A7
Roosevelt Ave. ME5 .... 62 A8
Rope Wlk. ME4 .... 47 F5
Rope Wlk The. TN18 .... 186 B5
Rope Yard Rails. SE18 .... 2 B3
Ropemakers Ct. ME4 .... 48 A1
Roper Cl. **1** SE9 .... 6 A1
Roper St. **1** SE9 .... 6 A1
Roper's Gate. TN2 .... 148 E1
Roper's Green La. ME3 .... 18 B2
Roper's La. ME3 .... 34 F8
Ropery Bsns Est. SE7 .... 1 C2
Ropewalk. TN17 .... 169 C5
Rose Ave. DA12 .... 30 E7
Rose Bruford Coll The.
DA15 .... 24 B7
Rose Ct. ME17 .... 106 D1
Rose Dale. BR6 .... 51 B8
Rose Hill Sch. TN4 .... 148 E5
Rose St. Northfleet DA11 .. 12 B1
Rose St. Rochester ME1 .... 47 D2
Rose St. Tonbridge TN9 .. 133 C8
Rose Terr. ME17 .... 88 D7
Rose Villas. BR6 .... 52 C2
Rose Way. SE12 .... 5 A2
Rose Yd. ME14 .... 92 A4
Roseacre Gdns. ME14 ...... 93 A4
Roseacre Jun Sch. ME14 .. 93 A4
Roseacre La. ME14 .... 93 A4
Roseacre Rd. ME16 .... 7 B4
Rosebank Wlk. **14** SE7 .... 1 E2
Roseberry Gdns.
Dartford DA1 .... 26 C8
Roseberry Gdns.
Orpington BR6 .... 51 F7
Roseberry Ave. DA15 .... 23 E8
Rosebery Rd. Chatham ME4 47 E2
Rosebery Rd.
Gillingham ME7 .... 48 D7
Rosebery Rd. Grays RM17 .. 11 E8
Rosecroft Cl. BR5 .... 38 C3
Rosedale Cl. Dartford DA2 .. 27 B8
Rosedale Cl. Woolwich SE2 .. 3 B3
Rosedene Cl. DA1 .... 26 C8
Rosefield. TN13 .... 84 A3
Rosegarth. DA13 .... 43 E8
Rosehill Wlk. TN1 .... 149 A3
Roseholme. ME16 .... 91 D2
Roselare Cl. TN16 .... 81 D1
Roseleigh Ave. ME16 .... 91 C5
Rosemary Cl. **4** ME5 ...... 61 F4
Rosemary La.
Hodsoll Street TN15 .... 57 D3
Rosemary La.
Stonecrouch TN5 .... 177 A5
Rosemary La.
Swift's Green TN27 .... 142 F5
Rosemary Rd. Bexley DA16 .. 6 F6
Rosemary Rd.
East Malling ME19 .... 74 F1
Rosemary Rd.
Maidstone ME15 .... 93 A3
Rosemount Cl. ME15 ...... 106 F4
Rosemount Dr. BR1 .... 36 F5
Rosenheath Cl. BR6 .... 52 C3
Rosetta Prim Sch. E16 ...... 1 B8
Roseveare Rd. SE12 .... 22 C4
Rosewood. DA14 .... 24 C5
Rosewood. DA14 .... 24 C5
Rosewood Ct. BR1 .... 36 D8
Rosherville CE Prim Sch.
DA11 .... 12 E1
Rosherville Way. DA11 .... 12 E1
Roslin Way. BR1 .... 22 A3
Ross Ct. BR7 .... 22 F1
Ross House. SE18 .... 5 E6
Ross Rd. DA1 .... 9 A1
Ross St. ME1 .... 47 D4
Ross Way. SE9 .... 5 E4
Rossdale. TN2 .... 149 D5
Rosse Mews. SE3 .... 5 B6
Rossell Rd. RM18 .... 12 F5
Rossland Cl. DA6 .... 8 A2
Rosslyn Gn. ME16 .... 91 B5
Rother Ct. **24** BR5 .... 38 D1
Rother House. **5** ME15 .. 107 D8
Rother Rd. TN10 .... 117 C5
Rother Vale. ME5 .... 62 C3
Rothermere Cl. TN17 ...... 180 E6
Rothesay Ct. SE12 .... 22 B5
Rothley Cl. TN30 .... 183 B8
Rouge La. DA11 .... 30 B7
Roughetts Rd. ME19 .... 73 F3
Roughway La. TN11 .... 102 C7
Round Ash Way. DA2 .... 43 D1
Round Green Cotts. TN17 .. 154 F4
Round St. DA12 & DA13 .... 44 D5
Roundel Way. TN12 .... 138 D5
Roundhay. ME19 .... 74 E1
Roundhill Rd. TN2 .... 149 D1
Roundlyn Gdns. BR5 .... 38 B5

Roundtable Rd. BR1 ....
Roundwell. ME14 ....
Roundwood. BR7 ....
Routh St. E6 ....
Rover Rd. ME5 ....
Row The. DA3 ....
Rowan Cl. Aylesford ME20 ..
Rowan Cl. Longfield DA3 ....
Rowan Cl.
Meopham Station DA13 ....
Rowan Cl. Putlands TN12 ..
Rowan Cres. DA1 ....
Rowan House. **4**
Chatham ME5 ....
Rowan House. Sidcup DA14 .
Rowan Lea. ME5 ....
Rowan Rd. Bexley DA7 ......
Rowan Rd. Swanley BR8 ....
Rowan Shaw. TN10 ....
Rowan Tree Rd. TN2 ....
Rowan Wlk. Chatham ME4 ..
Rowan Wlk.
Keston Mark BR2 ....
Rowanwood Ave. DA15 ....
Rowbrocke Cl. ME8 ....
Rowdow La. TN14 ....
Rowhill Cotts. DA2 ....
Rowhill Rd. DA2 ....
Rowhill Sch. DA2 ....
Rowland Ave. ME7 ....
Rowland Cl. ME5 ....
Rowlatt Cl. DA2 ....
Rowlatt Rd. DA2 ....
Rowley Ave. DA15 ....
Rowley Hill. TN2 ....
Rowntree Path. **1** SE28 ..
Rowton Rd. SE18 ....
Rowzill Rd. BR8 ....
Royal Albert Sta. E16 ....
Royal Albert Way.
Newham,Custom House E16
Royal Albert Way.
Newham,Cyprus E6 ....
Royal Ave. TN9 ....
Royal Blackheath Golf Cours
SE9 ....
Royal Chase. TN4 & TN1 ..
Royal Ct. SE9 ....
Royal Docks Rd. E6 ....
Royal Eagle Cl. ME2 ....
Royal Engineers' Rd. ME14 .
Royal Oak Rd. DA6 ....
Royal Par. BR7 ....
Royal Parade Mews. BR7 ..
Royal Park Prim Sch. DA14 ..
Royal Pier Rd. DA11 ....
Royal Rd. Hawley DA2 ......
Royal Rd. Newham E16 ......
Royal Rd. Sidcup DA14 ......
Royal Sovereign Ave. ME7 ..
Royal Star Arc. **5** ME14 ..
Royal Tunbridge Wells Bsns
TN1 ....
Royal Victoria Place Sh Ctr.
TN2 ....
Royal Victoria Sta. E16 ......
Royal West Kent Ave.
TN10 ....
Roydene Rd. SE18 ....
Roydon Hall. TN12 ....
Roydon Hall Rd. TN12 ......
Royston Rd. Crayford DA1 ..
Royston Rd.
Maidstone ME15 ....
Roystons Cl. ME8 ....
Royton Ave. ME17 ....
Ruck La. TN12 ....
Ruckinge Way. ME8 ....
Ruddstreet Cl. SE18 ....
Rudge Cl. ME5 ....
Rudland Rd. DA7 ....
Ruegg House. **5** SE18 ....
Ruffet Ct. TN2 ....
Ruffets Wood. DA12 ....
Rugby Cl. ME5 ....
Rumania Wlk. DA12 ....
Rumstead La. ME7 & ME9 ..
Rumstead Rd. ME9 ....
Runmwood Ct. ME17 ....
Runciman Cl. BR6 ....
Runham La. ME17 ....
Running Horse Rndbt The.
ME20 ....
Runnymede Ct. DA2 ....
Rural Vale. DA11 ....
Ruscombe Cl. TN4 ....
Rush Cl. ME5 ....
Rushbrook Rd. SE9 ....
Rushdean Rd. ME2 ....

ene. SE2 .... 3 D3
el Rd. BR5 .... 38 A7
ts Rd. TN15 .... 55 E3
ord Cl. TN27 .... 141 D5
rove Ct. SE18 .... 1 F2
ey Cl. BR2 .... 50 E6
ey Cl. TN3 .... 163 F5
nead Dr. ME15 .... 107 A7
nore Ct. TN15 .... 86 D7
hore Rd. BR1 .... 36 E6
hore Hill. BR6 & TN14 .. 67 D6
mead. TN15 .... 70 A1
n Ave. DA16 .... 7 A5
n Cl. ME19 .... 89 F8
Cl. SE9 .... 5 F1
n Dr. Bexley DA16 .... 7 A4
n Dr. Orpington BR6 ..... 51 E7
n Gr. Bexley DA16 .... 7 A5
n Gr. Dartford DA1 ...... 10 A2
n Rd. DA17 .... 4 A2
n Wlk. BR2 .... 36 F3
nse Rd. ME8 .... 51 D7
ll Cl. Bexley DA7 .... 8 A3
ll Cl. Crayford DA1 .... 9 A3
ll Cl. Greenwich SE7 ..... 5 C7
ll Ct. ME4 .... 48 B3
ll House Sch. TN14 ...... 69 C3
ll Pl. DA4 .... 41 A8
ll Rd.
esend DA12 .... 13 D1
ll Rd. Kit's Coty ME20 .. 76 D7
ll Rd. Newham E16 .... 1 B7
ll Rd. Tilbury RM18 ..... 12 F6
ll Sq. DA3 .... 42 D6
ll Terr. DA4 .... 41 C5
lls Ave. ME8 .... 64 A8
e Cl. ME2 .... 46 E8
e Cl. ME17 .... 106 C3
st House. RM17 .... 12 C7
st Way. ME18 .... 88 F2
ts The.
stone ME16 .... 91 B5
ts The.
tham Station DA13 ...... 44 A3
tt Cl. Ditton ME20 .... 90 E8
tt Cl. Orpington BR6 ... 52 B5
tt Rd. TN12 .... 119 F6
tt Way. BR8 .... 39 D8
all Grange. TN4 .... 148 D4
all High St. TN4 .... 148 C4
all Pk. TN4 .... 148 D4
all Rd. TN4 .... 148 D4
House. ME16 .... 91 E5
rford Way. TN10 .... 117 D7
rglen Rd. SE2 .... 7 A8
n Rd. SE3 .... 5 A8
nd Ave. DA15 .... 24 A8
nd Cl. Dartford DA1 .. 26 D8
nd Cl. Sidcup DA5 .... 24 D7
nd Ct. Chislehurst BR7 . 37 A8
nd Ct. Sidcup BR7 .... 23 C6
nd Gate. DA17 .... 4 B1
nd House. ME18 SE18 .. 63 C3
nd Way.
stone ME15 .... 107 E8
nd Way.
ington BR5 .... 38 C3
n Cl. DA14 .... 24 E2
n Cnr. DA14 .... 24 E2
Corner Ind Est.
.... 24 D2
n Golf Course. BR5 .... 38 D8
n Manor Prim Sch.
.... 23 A4
n Cl. BR8 .... 39 E6
n Cl. BR8 .... 39 E6
Cl. SE9 .... 5 C3
Dr. ME15 .... 93 A2
n Cres. BR6 .... 51 E6
n Cty Prim Sch.
.... 74 A4
n La. ME19 .... 74 B1
n Rd. ME19 .... 74 B5
Cl. DA18 .... 63 D3
ft La. TN14 .... 98 E5
Cl. TN4 .... 148 E5
Dr. Bexley DA7 .... 8 A6
Dr. Royal Tunbridge Wells
.... 148 E5
Cl. ME15 .... 62 B8
ns House. SE9 .... 22 C5
r Cl. BR1 .... 22 B3
s. TN3 .... 148 A3
ns Cl. SE9 .... 5 E4
l. DA5 .... 8 B1
r BR5 .... 38 D1
eld. EZ BR5 .... 38 D1
a. Otford TN14 .... 69 A2

Rye La.
Sevenoaks TN13 & TN14 .... 83 F7
Rye Rd. TN18 .... 179 B1
Rye Wood Cotts. TN13 .. 83 F7
Ryecourt Cl. ⁴ ME16 ..... 91 E3
Ryecroft. DA12 .... 30 E3
Ryecroft Rd. Orpington BR5 . 37 D3
Ryecroft Rd. Otford TN14 .. 69 A3
Ryedale Ct. TN13 .... 83 E6
Ryegrass Cl. ME5 .... 62 C6
Ryelands Cres. SE12 .... 5 C1
Rymers Cl. TN1 .... 149 D7
Rymill St. E16 .... 2 A5
Rysted La. TN16 .... 81 D1

Sabre Ct. ME7 .... 49 A1
Sackville Ave. BR2 .... 36 A1
Sackville Cl. TN13 .... 84 B5
Sackville Rd. DA1 .... 26 C6
Sackville Rd. TN11 ...... 116 C6
Sacred Heart Sch. TN5 . 174 D5
Saddington St. DA12 ..... 30 C8
Saddler's Pk. DA4 .... 54 D7
Saddlers Cl. ME4 .... 92 E5
Sadlers Cl. ME5 .... 61 D2
Saffron Way. ❶ ME5 ...... 61 F5
Sage Cl. ❼ E6 .... 1 F8
Saigasso Cl. E16 .... 1 D7
Sailfield Cl. ME4 .... 47 F7
Sailmakers Ct. ME4 .... 48 B2
SS Peter & Paul RC Prim Sch.
BR5 .... 37 E7
St Aidan's Way. DA12 .... 30 E5
St Alban's Cl. DA12 .... 30 D5
St Alban's Gdns. DA12 .. 30 D5
St Alban's Rd.
St Albans Rd Cty Sch. DA1 .. 9 F1
St Albans Cl. ME7 .... 48 E7
St Albans Rd. ME4 .... 46 C6
St Alfege Rd. SE7 .... 5 D8
St Andrew Rd. ME7 .... 48 D7
St Andrew's Cl. ME16 .... 91 A2
St Andrew's Cl. ⁴ BR8 .... 39 E6
St Andrew's Rd. ❿
Gravesend DA11 .... 30 B8
St Andrew's Rd.
Tilbury RM18 .... 12 E5
St Andrews Wlk. ME3 .... 19 D8
St Andrews Cl. TN12 .. 136 A6
St Andrews Ct. ㉓
Gravesend DA11 .... 13 B1
St Andrews Ct.
Royal Tunbridge Wells
TN4 .... 133 A1
St Andrews Dr. BR5 & BR6 .. 38 B2
St Andrews Mews. SE3 .... 5 A7
St Andrews Park Rd. TN4 .. 133 A1
St Andrews Rd.
Paddock Wood TN12 ... 136 A6
St Andrews Rd.
Sidcup DA14 .... 24 D5
St Ann's Green La. TN12 .. 138 F8
St Anne Ct. ME16 .... 91 E4
St Anselm's RC Prim Sch.
DA1 .... 10 A2
St Anthony's Ct. BR6 .... 51 B8
St Aubyns Cl. BR6 .... 51 F7
St Aubyns Gdns. BR6 .... 51 F8
St Audrey Ave. DA7 .... 8 A5
St Augustine of Canterbury RC
Prim Sch. ME8 .... 63 D3
St Augustine's Ave.
BR1 & BR2 .... 36 E4
St Augustine's Jun Sch.
DA17 .... 3 F2
St Augustine's RC Prim Sch.
TN4 .... 149 A7
St Augustine's Rd. DA17 . 3 F2
St Barnabas CE Prim Sch.
TN1 .... 149 B5
St Barnabas Cl.
Gillingham ME7 .... 48 D3
St Barnabas Cl.
Maidstone ME16 .... 91 C6
St Barnabas' Cl.
Royal Tunbridge Wells
TN1 .... 149 B5
St Bartholomew's Hospl.
ME1 .... 47 E4
St Bartholomew's La. ME1 .. 47 E4
St Bartholomew's Terr.
ME1 .... 47 E4
St Bartholomews RC Prim Sch.
BR8 .... 39 E6
St Benedict Rd. ME6 ...... 74 E8
St Benedict's Ave. DA12 .. 30 E6
St Benedicts RC Prim Sch.
ME5 .... 62 C2
St Benets Cl. TN30 ...... 183 B8

St Benets Way. TN30 .... 183 B8
St Benjamins Dr. BR6 .... 52 C2
St Bernards Rd. TN10 .. 117 C6
St Blaise Ave. BR1 .... 36 B7
St Botolph Rd. DA11 ..... 29 D5
St Botolph's Ave. TN13 .. 84 A3
St Botolph's CE Prim Sch.
DA11 .... 29 D8
St Botolph's Rd. TN13 .. 84 B3
St Brelade's Ct. TN8 .... 112 A3
St Brides Cl. DA18 .... 3 A4
St Catherine's Hospl. ME1 .. 47 D4
St Catherine's Sch for Girls.
DA6 .... 8 B2
St Chad's Dr. DA12 .... 30 E5
St Chad's Rd. RM18 ...... 13 A7
St Chad's Sch. RM18 .... 13 A6
St Christopher's (Trng Coll,
Dr Barnardo's Home).
.... 149 D4
St Clement's Ave. RM16 .. 11 B8
St Clement's House. ME1 .. 47 D5
St Clement's Rd. RM16 .. 11 C7
St Clements Cl. DA11 .... 29 F5
St Clements Ct. RM17 ... 11 F8
St Clere Hill Rd. TN15 .. 70 F7
St Columba's Cl. DA12 .. 30 E5
St Columba's RC Boys Sch.
DA6 .... 8 B2
St David's Bridge. TN17 . 169 D4
St David's Cres. DA12 .... 30 D4
St David's Rd.
Allhallows ME3 .... 19 D8
St David's Rd. Hextable BR8 . 25 F1
St David's Rd.
Royal Tunbridge Wells
TN4 .... 149 B6
St Domingo House. SE18 .... 1 F3
St Dunstan's Dr. DA12 .. 30 E5
St Edith's Rd. TN15 .... 70 A2
St Edmund's Cotts. TN15 . 56 A2
St Edmund's Cl. TN15 .. 56 A2
St Edmunds Cl. DA18 ..... 3 D4
St Edmunds Rd. DA1 .... 10 A3
St Faith's La. ME14 .... 93 B4
St Faith's St. ME14 .... 91 F4
St Fidelis RC Sch. DA8 ... 8 C8
St Fidelis' Rd. DA8 .... 4 D1
St Francis Ave. DA12 ..... 30 E4
St Francis Cl. BR6 .... 37 E3
St Francis RC Prim Sch.
ME14 .... 92 B7
St Francis' Rd. Erith DA8 ...... 4 D2
St Francis Rd. Harvel DA13 .. 58 B3
St Francis Sch. ME14 ..... 92 B7
St George's Bickley CE Prim Sch.
BR1 .... 36 D7
St George's CE Prim Sch.
TN15 .... 71 F3
St George's CE Sch. DA11 .. 30 A6
St George's Cres. DA12 .. 30 D4
St George's Ctr. TN15 .... 71 F3
St George's Ctr. DA11 ... 13 B1
St George's Pk. TN2 .... 162 F8
St George's Rd.
Gillingham ME7 .... 48 C6
St George's Rd.
Sevenoaks TN13 .... 84 B5
St George's Rd.
Sidcup DA14 .... 24 D2
St George's Sch. TN2 ... 150 A5
St George's Sq. ME16 .... 91 E3
St George's Wlk. ME3 .... 19 D8
St Georges Mews. ❽ TN9 . 133 B8
St Georges Rd. Bromley BR1 . 36 F6
St Georges Rd.
Orpington BR5 .... 37 D3
St Georges Rd.
Swanley BR8 .... 39 F5
St Georges Rd W. BR1 ... 36 E7
St Georges Sq. DA3 .... 42 E6
St German's Pl. SE3 .... 5 A6
St Giles Cl. BR6 .... 51 D5
St Gregory's Catholic Comp Sch.
TN4 .... 149 A7
St Gregory's Cres. DA12 . 30 E6
St Gregory's Ct. DA12 .... 30 E6
St Helens CE Prim Sch.
ME3 .... 16 B5
St Helens La. ME15 ...... 105 E8
St Helens Rd. ❼ DA18 .... 3 D4
St Helier's Cl. ME16 .... 91 B2
St Hilary's Sch. TN13 .... 84 B5
St Hilda's Way. DA12 .... 30 E5
St Hildas. TN15 .... 101 F8
St James' CE Aided Inf Sch.
TN2 .... 149 C4
St James' CE Jun Sch.
TN2 .... 149 C4
St James' CE (VA) Sch.
ME3 .... 21 B6

St James Cl.
East Malling ME19 .... 89 E8
St James Cl. Grain ME3 .. 21 B6
St James Ct. SE3 .... 5 B6
St James' Cty Inf Sch.
ME19 .... 89 F8
St James' La. DA2 & DA4 . 27 E8
St James Oaks. DA11 ..... 30 A8
St James' Pk. TN1 & TN2 .. 149 C5
St James' Pl. DA1 .... 9 D1
St James RC Prim Sch.
BR5 .... 37 B4
St James Rd. Grain ME3 .. 21 B5
St James' Rd.
Royal Tunbridge Wells
TN1 & TN2 .... 149 C5
St James Sq. DA3 .... 42 E6
St James Way. DA14 ...... 24 E3
St James's Cl. SE18 .... 2 C1
St James's Ct. TN1 .... 149 B4
St James's Rd.
Sevenoaks TN13 .... 84 B5
St James's St. DA11 .... 13 A1
St Joachim's RC Sch. E16 . 1 C7
St John Fisher Catholic
Comp Sch. ME4 .... 47 E3
St John Fisher Catholic Sch
(Lower Sch). ME4 .... 47 F2
St John Fisher RC Prim Sch.
DA18 .... 3 E3
St John's CE Prim Sch.
Royal Tunbridge Wells
TN4 .... 149 A5
St John's CE Prim Sch.
Sevenoaks TN13 .... 84 D4
St John's CE (VA) Prim Sch.
ME14 .... 92 E3
St John's Cl. ME3 .... 32 C4
St John's Cl. TN13 .... 84 D5
St John's Hill. TN13 & TN14 . 84 C5
St John's La. DA3 .... 42 F3
St John's Par. DA14 .... 24 B4
St John's Pk.
Royal Tunbridge Wells
TN4 .... 149 A8
St John's RC Prim Sch.
DA12 .... 30 E7
St John's RC Sch. DA2 ... 30 D7
St John's Rd. Bexley DA16 . 7 B4
St John's Rd. Dartford DA2 . 27 C8
St John's Rd. Erith DA8 ... 4 D1
St John's Rd.
Gillingham ME7 .... 48 C3
St John's Rd.
Gravesend DA12 .... 30 D8
St John's Rd. Higham ME3 . 32 C4
St John's Rd. Newham E16 . 1 A7
St John's Rd.
Orpington BR5 & BR6 .. 37 E3
St John's Rd.
Royal Tunbridge Wells
TN1 & TN4 .... 149 A6
St John's Rd.
Sevenoaks TN13 .... 84 C5
St John's Rd. Sidcup DA14 . 24 B4
St John's Terr. SE18 .... 6 D8
St Johns CE Prim Sch.
TN4 .... 149 B7
St Johns Rd. ME3 .... 34 D6
St Johns Way. ME1 .... 47 A2
St Joseph's RC Prim Sch.
Bromley BR1 .... 22 B1
St Joseph's RC Prim Sch.
Crayford DA1 .... 8 E3
St Joseph's RC Prim Sch.
Northfleet DA11 .... 29 D8
St Josephs Cl. BR6 .... 51 F6
St Justin Cl. BR5 .... 38 D6
St Katherine's Cty Prim Sch.
ME6 .... 74 F7
St Katherine's La. ME6 .. 74 F7
St Katherines Rd. DA18 .. 3 D3
St Keverne Rd. BR7 & SE9 .. 22 E4
St Kilda Rd. BR6 .... 37 F1
St Laurence Ave. ME16 .. 91 C8
St Laurence Cl. BR5 .... 38 D6
St Lawrence Ave. TN4 .. 132 D3
St Leonard's St. ME19 ... 89 B7
St Leonards Ave. ME4 .... 47 F2
St Leonards Cl. ❹ DA16 . 7 A4
St Leonards Rd. ME4 ..... 91 C8
St Leonards Rise. BR6 ... 51 E6
St Luke's Ave. ME14 ...... 92 B5
St Luke's CE Inf Sch. TN4 . 149 C7
St Luke's Rd.
Maidstone ME14 .... 92 B5

St Luke's Rd.
Royal Tunbridge Wells
TN4 .... 149 B6
St Luke's Way. ME3 .... 19 D8
St Lukes Cl. Lane End DA2 . 27 E3
St Lukes Cl. Swanley BR8 .. 39 D7
St Margaret Clitherow RC
Prim Sch. Tonbridge TN10 . 117 B6
St Margaret Clitherow RC
Prim Sch. Woolwich SE28 .. 3 B5
St Margaret's at Troy Town CE
Prim Sch. ME1 .... 47 C4
St Margaret's Banks. ME1 .. 47 D5
St Margaret's CE Inf Sch.
ME8 .... 63 E8
St Margaret's CE Jun Sch.
ME8 .... 63 E8
St Margaret's CE Prim Sch.
SE18 .... 2 C1
St Margaret's Cres. DA12 . 30 E5
St Margaret's St. ME23 .. 17 E3
St Margaret's Gr. SE18 .... 6 C8
St Margaret's Mews. ME1 . 47 C5
St Margaret's Rd.
Northfleet DA11 .... 29 E7
St Margarets DA2 & DA4 . 27 E2
St Margaret's Terr. SE18 .. 2 C1
St Margarets Ave. DA15 .. 23 D5
St Margarets Cl.
Maidstone ME16 .... 91 B2
St Margarets Cl.
Orpington BR6 .... 52 B6
St Margarets Dr. ME8 .... 63 C5
St Margarets Villas. TN12 . 137 D8
St Mark's Ave. DA11 ...... 29 F8
St Mark's CE Prim Sch.
Bromley BR2 .... 36 A6
St Mark's CE Prim Sch.
Royal Tunbridge Wells
TN4 .... 148 D1
St Mark's Rd. Bromley BR2 . 36 B6
St Mark's Rd.
Royal Tunbridge Wells
TN2 .... 162 F7
St Marks CE Inf Sch. ME20 . 75 F6
St Marks Cl. ME20 .... 75 F6
St Marks House. ME7 .... 48 C5
St Marks Ind Est. E16 ..... 1 D5
St Martin's Cl. ME14 ..... 78 A1
St Martin's Dr. DA4 .... 54 D7
St Martin's Rd. DA1 .... 9 F1
St Martins Cl.
Newington ME9 .... 65 C7
St Martins Meadow. TN16 . 82 C4
St Mary Cray Prim Sch.
BR5 .... 38 C3
St Mary Cray Sta. BR5 ... 38 B5
St Mary St. SE18 .... 2 A2
St Mary & St Joseph's Sch.
DA14 .... 24 A3
St Mary's. ME3 .... 18 D5
St Mary's Abbey. ME1 ... 89 C8
St Mary's CE (VA) Prim Sch.
BR8 .... 39 D8
St Mary's Church Rd. TN14 . 82 F2
St Mary's Cl.
Gravesend DA12 .... 30 C6
St Mary's Cl. Grays RM17 . 12 D8
St Mary's Cl.
Laddingford ME18 ..... 120 E4
St Mary's Cl. Platt TN15 . 87 C7
St Mary's Cl.
St Paul's Cray BR5 ...... 38 C7
St Mary's Cl.
Ticehurst TN5 .... 176 D1
St Mary's Cty Prim Sch.
ME2 .... 47 B7
St Mary's Gdns. ME7 ..... 48 B7
St Mary's La.
Speldhurst TN3 .... 148 A8
St Mary's RC Prim Sch.
Newington ME9 .... 65 C7
St Mary's Pl.
Eltham SE9 .... 6 A2
St Mary's RC Prim Sch.
Gillingham ME7 .... 48 D6
St Mary's RC Prim Sch.
Tilbury RM18 .... 12 F5
St Mary's RC Prim Sch. Coldblow DA5 . 25 C7
St Mary's Rd.
Gillingham ME7 .... 48 C6

Rus – St M 227

St Mary's Rd.
Rochester ME2 .... 47 B7
St Mary's Rd.
St Mary's Island ME4 .... 34 A2
St Mary's Rd. Stone DA9 ...... 10 E2
St Mary's Rd. Swanley BR8 .. 39 E5
St Mary's Rd.
Tonbridge TN9 .... 133 B7
St Mary's View. ME9 .... 65 C7
St Mary's Wlk. ME1 .... 60 F1
St Marys Ct. SE7 .... 5 D7
St Marys Rd. TN15 .... 72 A2
St Marys Way. DA3 .... 42 E6
St Matthew's CE (VC) Inf Sch.
ME1 .... 47 A2
St Matthew's Cl. ME4 .... 65 C7
St Matthew's High Brooms CE
(VC) Prim Sch. TN4 .... 149 B8
St Matthew's Way. ME3 .... 19 D8
St Matthews Dr.
Bromley BR1 .... 36 F6
St Matthews Dr.
Rochester ME1 .... 47 A2
St Merryn Cl. SE18 .... 6 D7
St Michael's CE Inf Sch.
ME16 .... 91 E3
St Michael's CE Jun Sch.
ME16 .... 91 E3
St Michael's CE Prim Sch.
TN30 .... 173 A3
St Michael's Cl.
Chatham ME4 .... 47 F3
St Michael's Cl. Erith DA18 .. 3 D4
St Michael's Cl. ME2 .... 47 A8
St Michael's Cty Prim Sch.
TN7 .... 160 B5
St Michael's East Wickham CE
GM Prim Sch. DA16 .... 7 C6
St Michael's RC Prim Sch.
ME4 .... 47 F3
St Michael's Rd. Bexley DA16 7 B4
St Michael's Rd.
Maidstone ME16 .... 91 D3
St Michael's Rd.
Royal Tunbridge Wells
TN4 .... 149 B7
St Michael's Rise. DA16 .... 7 B6
St Michael's Terr. TN30 ..... 173 B3
St Michaels Cl. 4
Newham E16 .... 1 D8
St Michaels Cl. Pratling Street
ME14 & ME20 .... 76 C3
St Michaels Dr. TN14 .... 69 E3
St Mildred's Cl. 2 TN30 .. 183 A7
St Mildreds Rd. 2 SE12 ..... 22 A8
St Nicholas CE Inf Sch.
ME2 .... 47 A7
St Nicholas Dr. TN13 .... 84 C1
St Nicholas Gdns. ME2 .... 46 F8
St Nicholas La. SE18 .... 2 F1
St Nicolas La. BR7 .... 36 E8
St Olave's Sch. ME9 .... 52 B7
St Olaves Prep Sch. SE9 ...... 23 B6
St Patrick's Gdns. DA12 ...... 30 D5
St Patrick's RC Prim Sch.
SE18 .... 2 D2
St Paul's CE Prim Sch. BR8 . 40 B8
St Paul's Cl. Greenwich SE7 .. 1 D1
St Paul's Cl. Rochester ME2 . 46 D5
St Paul's Cl.
Swanscombe DA10 .... 28 E8
St Paul's Cray Rd. BR7 .... 37 D8
St Paul's Ct. TN4 .... 148 C4
St Paul's Rd. DA8 .... 8 C7
St Paul's Sq. BR2 .... 36 A7
St Paul's St. TN4 .... 148 C4
St Paul's Wood Hill.
BR5 & BR7 .... 37 F7
St Paulinus' CE Prim Sch.
DA1 .... 8 E3
St Paulinus Ct. DA1 .... 8 E3
St Pauls CE Inf Sch. TN4 .. 148 B4
St Pauls CE Jun Sch. TN4 .. 148 B4
St Pauls Cl. TN10 .... 117 D5
St Pauls Cray CE Prim Sch.
BR5 .... 38 D6
St Pauls Cty Inf Sch. ME14 . 92 A7
St Peter Chanel RC Prim Sch.
DA14 .... 24 C3
St Peter St. ME1 .... 47 D4
St Peter's Bridge. ME16 ...... 91 F4
St Peter's CE Prim Sch.
Aylesford ME20 .... 76 A3
St Peter's CE Prim Sch.
Royal Tunbridge Wells TN2 149 C3

St Peter's Cl. DA10 .... 28 F8
St Peter's Ct. ME19 .... 75 C1
St Peter's Cty Inf Sch.
ME1 .... 47 C3
St Peter's Path. ME1 .... 47 C3
St Peter's RC Prim Sch.
SE18 .... 2 B2
St Peter's St. TN2 .... 149 C3
St Peters Cl.
Chislehurst BR7 .... 23 D1
St Peters Cl. Ditton ME19 ... 75 B1
St Peters Pl. ME20 .... 75 F6
St Peters Rd. ME19 .... 75 B1
St Peters Row. TN3 .... 147 A5
St Peters St. ME16 .... 91 F4
St Philip's Ave. ME15 .... 92 B2
St Philip's CE Prim Sch.
ME15 .... 92 A3
St Philips Ct. TN1 .... 149 D6
St Philomena's Prim Sch.
BR5 .... 38 C2
St Quentin Rd. DA16 .... 6 F4
St Ronan's Cl. ME15 .... 107 C7
St Ronan's Sch. TN18 .... 179 D2
St. Saviours Rd. ME15 .... 107 D6
St Simon Stock RC Sch.
ME16 .... 91 C3
St Stephen's CE Inf Sch.
ME15 .... 91 E2
St Stephen's Cl. ME9 .... 65 C7
St Stephen's Cty Prim Sch.
TN9 .... 133 D8
St Stephen's RC Prim Sch.
DA16 .... 7 A5
St Stephen's Sq. ME15 .... 91 E2
St Stephen's St. TN9 .... 133 B8
St Stephens Dr. TN1 .... 149 B5
St Thomas Cl. DA6 .... 25 A8
St Thomas' Dr. BR5 .... 37 C1
St Thomas More RC Prim Sch.
Bexley DA7 .... 25 F7
St Thomas More RC Prim Sch.
Eltham SE9 .... 5 E4
St Thomas More RC Sec Sch.
SE9 .... 6 A1
St Thomas More Roman Catholic
Prim Sch. ME5 .... 62 A5
St Thomas of Canterbury Cath
Prim Sch. ME8 .... 49 B2
St Thomas RC Prim Sch.
TN13 .... 84 B2
St Thomas Rd. Erith DA17 .... 4 C4
St Thomas Rd. Newham E16 . 1 A7
St Thomas Rd.
Northfleet DA11 .... 29 E6
St Thomas's Almshouses.
DA11 .... 30 B7
St Thomas's Ave. DA11 .... 30 B7
St Thomas's CE Prim Sch.
TN3 .... 161 C6
St Thomas's Pl. 17 RM17 ... 12 C8
St Thomas-a-Becket RC
Prim Sch. SE2 .... 3 A3
St Timothy's Mews. 3
BR1 .... 36 A8
St Vincents Ave. DA1 .... 10 A2
St Vincents La. TN15 .... 73 A2
St Vincents RC Prim Sch.
SE9 .... 22 E4
St Vincents Rd. DA1 .... 10 A1
St Welcume's Way. ME17 . 110 E6
St Werburgh Cres. ME3 ...... 34 D5
St Werburgh St. ME3 .... 34 D5
St William of Perth RC Prim Sch.
ME1 .... 47 B2
St William's Way. ME1 .... 47 D2
St Williams Hospl. ME1 .... 47 D2
Saints Hill. TN11 .... 147 A8
Sala House. SE3 .... 5 B3
Salamons Way. RM13 .... 4 E7
Salcote Rd. DA12 .... 30 E3
Salem Pl. DA11 .... 29 D6
Salem St. ME15 .... 92 A3
Salisbury Ave.
Gillingham ME8 .... 63 D8
Salisbury Ave. Swanley BR8 40 A5
Salisbury Cl. TN10 .... 117 D5
Salisbury House. 5
ME15 .... 107 D7
Salisbury Mews. BR1 .... 36 A8
Salisbury Rd. Bromley BR2 .. 36 D6
Salisbury Rd. Chatham ME4 . 48 A3
Salisbury Rd. Dartford DA2 . 27 C7
Salisbury Rd.
Gravesend DA11 .... 29 F7
Salisbury Rd. 2
Grays RM17 .... 12 C8
Salisbury Rd.
Kit's Coty ME20 .... 76 D7
Salisbury Rd.
Langton Green TN3 .... 147 F3

Salisbury Rd.
Maidstone ME14 .... 92 A6
Salisbury Rd.
Royal Tunbridge Wells
TN4 .... 149 C8
Salisbury Rd. Sidcup DA5 ... 25 A7
Salisbury Rd.
Tonbridge TN10 .... 117 D4
Salix Rd. RM17 .... 12 D8
Sallows Shaw. DA13 .... 44 C4
Sally Port. ME7 .... 48 A6
Sally Port Gdns. ME7 .... 48 B6
Salmon Rd. DA17 .... 4 A1
Salomons Rd. Newham E13 ... 1 C8
Salomons Rd.
Rusthall TN4 .... 148 C4
Salt La. ME3 .... 15 F4
Salt's Ave. ME15 .... 106 F3
Salter's Cross. ME18 .... 105 A1
Saltford Cl. DA8 .... 4 E1
Saltings Rd. ME6 .... 75 A7
Saltley Cl. E6 .... 1 E7
Salts La. ME15 .... 107 A4
Saltwood Cl. BR6 .... 52 C6
Saltwood Rd. ME15 .... 91 F1
Sam Bartram Cl. SE7 .... 1 C1
Samara Cl. ME5 .... 62 A1
Samphire Cl. ME14 .... 92 E4
Samphire Ct. RM17 .... 12 E8
Sampson Cl. DA17 .... 3 D3
Samson House. SE18 .... 2 C2
Samuel Cl. SE18 .... 1 E2
Samuel Palmer Ct. BR6 .... 38 A2
Samuel St. SE18 .... 1 F2
Sanctuary Cl. DA1 .... 9 D1
Sanctuary Rd. ME8 .... 49 A3
Sanctuary The. DA5 .... 7 D1
Sand La. TN17 .... 156 F4
Sand Rd. TN15 .... 166 A4
Sandalwood House. DA15 ... 23 F5
Sandbach Pl. SE18 .... 2 C1
Sandbanks Hill. DA2 .... 28 B2
Sandbourne Dr. ME14 .... 76 F1
Sandby Gn. SE9 .... 5 E4
Sandcliff Rd. DA8 .... 4 D1
Sanderling Ct. SE28 .... 3 C6
Sanderson Way. TN9 .... 117 E1
Sanderson Ave. TN14 .... 53 B1
Sanderstead Rd. BR5 .... 38 B3
Sandfield Rd. TN11 .... 147 A7
Sandford Rd.
Bexley DA7 & DA6 .... 7 E3
Sandford Rd. Bromley BR2 .. 36 A5
Sandgate Ct. ME8 .... 63 F4
Sandgate Rd. DA16 .... 7 C7
Sandham Point. 10 SE18 ...... 2 B2
Sandhill La. ME3 .... 32 D6
Sandhurst Ave. TN30 .... 150 E6
Sandhurst Cl.
Gillingham ME8 .... 49 C3
Sandhurst Cl.
Royal Tunbridge Wells
TN1 .... 149 C6
Sandhurst Cl.
Sandhurst Cross TN18 ..... 186 A4
Sandhurst Cross. TN12 .... 140 F1
Sandhurst Cty Prim Sch.
TN18 .... 186 C5
Sandhurst House. TN2 .... 149 D5
Sandhurst La. TN17 .... 181 B2
Sandhurst Pk. TN1 .... 149 C6
Sandhurst Rd. Bexley DA5 ... 7 D2
Sandhurst Rd.
Orpington BR6 .... 52 A6
Sandhurst Rd.
Royal Tunbridge Wells
TN1 & TN2 & TN4 .... 149 D6
Sandhurst Rd. Sidcup DA15 . 24 A5
Sandhurst Rd. Tilbury RM18 13 C5
Sandilands. TN13 .... 83 D5
Sandling Cty Prim Sch.
ME14 .... 92 B8
Sandling La. ME14 .... 92 A8
Sandling Rd.
Maidstone ME14 .... 92 A6
Sandling Rd. Maidstone,
Ringlestone ME14 .... 91 F7
Sandling Rise. SE9 .... 23 A5
Sandown Cl. TN2 .... 149 D5
Sandown Court Com Coll.
TN2 .... 149 F5
Sandown Dr. ME8 .... 63 D7
Sandown Gr. TN2 .... 149 C6
Sandown Pk. TN2 .... 149 F6
Sandown Rd.
Gravesend DA12 .... 30 C2
Sandown Rd.
New Town ME19 .... 89 B8
Sandpiper Rd. ME5 .... 62 D2
Sandpiper Way. BR5 .... 38 D6

Sandpipers The. DA12 .... 30 D6
Sandpit Pl. SE7 .... 1 E1
Sandpit Rd. DA1 .... 9 C3
Sandringham Dr. DA16 .... 6 E5
Sandringham House. ME1 .. 47 B4
Sandringham Rd.
Bromley BR1 .... 22 A3
Sandringham Rd.
Gillingham ME8 .... 63 C6
Sandrock House. TN2 .... 149 D4
Sandrock Rd. TN2 .... 149 C4
Sandrock Villas. TN18 .... 178 F3
Sandstone Rd. SE12 .... 22 B6
Sandstone Rise. ME14 .... 77 C8
Sandtoft Rd. SE7 .... 5 B8
Sandway Path. 6 BR5 .... 38 C5
Sandway Rd. Orpington BR5 38 C5
Sandway Rd.
Sandway ME17 .... 110 F4
Sandy Bank Rd. DA12 .... 30 D7
Sandy Bury. BR6 .... 51 D7
Sandy Dell. ME7 .... 63 A3
Sandy Hill Ave. SE18 .... 2 B1
Sandy Hill La. SE18 .... 2 B2
Sandy Hill Rd. SE18 .... 2 B1
Sandy La. Bean DA13 & DA2 28 D5
Sandy La.
Ightham Common TN15 ..... 86 B3
Sandy La. Maidstone,
Harburland ME14 .... 92 C8
Sandy La. Maidstone,
Penenden Heath ME14 ...... 92 C7
Sandy La. Maidstone,Ware Street
ME14 .... 93 B5
Sandy La. New Town ME19 .. 74 A1
Sandy La. Orpington BR6 .... 38 A2
Sandy La. Sevenoaks TN13 . 84 C4
Sandy La. Snodland ME6 ..... 74 E6
Sandy La.
St Paul's Cray BR5 .... 38 D8
Sandy La. Tenterden TN30 183 B7
Sandy La. Tilbury RM17 ..... 13 B8
Sandy La.
West Thurrock RM16 .... 11 B8
Sandy La. Westerham TN16 . 81 D2
Sandy La.
Wrotham Heath TN15 .... 72 F1
Sandy Mount. ME14 .... 92 B8
Sandy Ridge.
Chislehurst BR7 .... 23 A2
Sandy Ridge.
Borough Green TN15 .... 87 A7
Sandy Ridge.
Chislehurst BR7 .... 23 A2
Sandycroft. SE2 .... 7 A8
Sandycroft Rd. ME2 .... 32 F1
Santer House. TN18 .... 184 E8
Sapho Pk. DA12 .... 30 E4
Saphora Cl. BR6 .... 51 D5
Sapphire Cl. E6 .... 2 A7
Sara House. 1 DA8 .... 8 F1
Sara Pk. DA12 .... 30 E4
Sara Turnbull House. 2
SE18 .... 1 F2
Saracen Cl. ME7 .... 49 A1
Saracen Fields.
ME5 & ME14 .... 77 C8
Sark Wlk. E16 .... 1 B8
Sarsen Hts. ME5 .... 61 F1
Sarsens Cl. DA12 .... 44 F6
Sassoon Cl. ME20 .... 75 A4
Satanita Cl. E16 .... 1 D7
Saunder's Cross. TN14 .... 53 B2
Saunders Cl. DA11 .... 29 E6
Saunders Rd.
Royal Tunbridge Wells
TN4 .... 148 E1
Saunders Rd. Woolwich SE18 2 F1
Saunders St. ME7 .... 48 C6
Saunders Way.
Dartford DA1 .... 26 F6
Saunders Way.
Woolwich SE28 .... 3 B6
Savage Gdns. E6 .... 2 A2
Savage Rd. ME5 .... 62 B3
Savill House. E16 .... 2 A8
Saville Rd. E16 .... 1 E5
Savoy Rd. DA1 .... 9 F4
Sawyers Cl. ME4 .... 48 B2
Saxby Wood. TN11 .... 115 F1
Saxbys Rd. TN15 .... 85 D5
Saxon Cl. Kings Hill ME18 .. 88 F2
Saxon Cl. Northfleet DA11 .. 29 C5
Saxon Cl. Otford TN14 .... 69 E1
Saxon Cl. Rochester ME2 .... 32 F1
Saxon Pl. DA4 .... 41 C4
Saxon Rd. Bromley BR2 ...... 22 A1
Saxon Rd. Hawley DA2 .... 26 E4
Saxon Wlk. DA14 .... 24 C2
Saxons Dr. ME14 .... 92 B7
Saxton St. ME7 .... 48 C5
Saxville Rd. BR5 .... 38 B6

Sayer Cl. DA9 ....
Sayers La. 4 TN30 ....
Sayes Court Rd. BR5 ....
Scabharbour Rd.
TN11 & TN14 ....
Scadbury Park Nature Rese
BR7 ....
Scads Hill Cl. BR5 & BR6 .....
Scarborough La. ME1 ....
Scarlet Cl. BR5 ....
Scarlett Cl. ME5 ....
Scarsbrook Rd. SE3 ....
Schofield Wlk. SE3 ....
Scholars Rise. ME2 ....
Scholey Cl. ME2 ....
School App. TN15 ....
School Ave. ME7 ....
School Cl. DA13 ....
School Cotts.
Crockenhill BR8 ....
School Cotts. Sidcup DA14 .
School Cres. DA1 ....
School Field. TN8 ....
School House La. TN12 ....
School La. Bean DA2 ....
School La. Bexley DA16 ....
School La. Borden ME9 ....
School La. Hadlow TN11 .....
School La. Hextable BR8 ......
School La. Higham ME3 ....
School La.
Horton Kirby DA3 & DA4 ...
School La. Knockmill TN15 ...
School La. Maidstone ME15 .
School La. Newington ME9 ...
School La.
Platt's Heath ME17 ....
School La.
Plaxtol TN11 & TN15 ....
School La. Seal TN15 ....
School La.
Sutton Valence ME17 ....
School La. Trottiscliffe ME19
School La. Vigo Village DA13
School La. Wouldham ME1 ...
School Rd. Chislehurst BR7 .
School Rd. Gravesend DA12
School Rise. TN2 ....
School Terr. 8 TN18 ....
School Villas. ME18 ....
Schoolfield Rd. RM16 ....
Schooner Ct. DA9 ....
Scilla Ct. 10 RM17 ....
Scimitar Cl. ME7 ....
Scords La. TN16 ....
Scotby Ave. ME5 ....
Scotland La. Cobham DA12 ..
Scotland La. Cobham DA12 ..
Scotney Castle. TN3 ....
Scotney House. ME2 ....
Scotsdale Cl. BR5 & BR7 .....
Scotsdale Rd. SE12 ....
Scott Ave. ME8 ....
Scott Cl. ME19 & ME20 ....
Scott Cres. DA8 ....
Scott House. 4 DA12 ....
Scott Rd. Gravesend DA12 ..
Scott Rd. Tonbridge TN9 .....
Scott St. ME14 ....
Scott Wilkie Prim Sch. E16 ..
Scott's Terr. ME4 ....
Scotteswood Ave. ME4 ....
Scotts Park Prim Sch. BR1 ..
Scotts Rd. BR1 ....
Scotts Way. Royal Tunbridge
TN2 ....
Scotts Way.
Sevenoaks TN13 ....
Scoulding Rd. E16 ....
Scragged Oak Rd.
Detling ME14 ....
Scragged Oak Rd.
Hucking ME14 ....
Scratchers La. TN15 ....
Scratton Fields. DA12 ....
Scrubbs La. ME16 ....
Scudders Hill. DA3 ....
Seabrook Rd. TN11 1
Seabrooke Rise. RM17 ....
Seaford Cl. ME5 ....
Seaford Ct. ME1 ....
Seagull Rd. ME2 ....
Seal CE Prim Sch. TN15 ......
Seal Dr. TN15 ....
Seal Hollow Rd.
TN13 & TN15 ....
Seal Rd.
TN13 & TN14 & TN15 ....
Seal St Lawrence CE Prim Sc
TN15 ....

...and Ct. ME1 .... 47 B5
...mew Ct. ME2 .... 46 C7
...ton Rd. Dartford DA1 .. 26 A8
...ton Rd. Gillingham ME7 .. 48 B3
...view. ME3 .... 21 B5
...germere ME4 .... 48 C4
...ond Ave.
...atham ME4 & ME5 .... 48 C1
...ham Ave. Gillingham ME7 48 E3
...ond Ave.
...est Thurrock RM16 ...... 11 A8
...etan Rd. ME1 .... 47 B1
...combe Cl. DA14 .... 24 C4
...ge Cres. ME5 .... 61 E4
...gebrook Rd. SE3 .... 5 D4
...germere Rd. SE2 .... 3 C3
...ury DA13 .... 29 A2
...ey Cl. Aylesford ME20 ... 75 F2
...ey Cl. Cliffe Woods ME3 33 C7
...ey Cl. Gillingham ME8 ... 63 C3
...ey's Cle Fst Sch. DA13 .. 29 A3
...n Cl. BR5 .... 37 F5
...on Rd. BR5 .... 37 F5
...ont House. 4 RM17 ...... 12 B8
...ne Rd. BR8 .... 39 C8
...orne Ave. DA5 .... 24 E7
...ourne Rd. DA14 .... 24 B4
...ourne Cl. DA3 .... 43 D6
...ourne Rd. ME7 .... 48 D7
...ourne Wlk. ME15 .... 107 F6
...ey Cl. Chislehurst BR7 ... 23 A2
...y Cl. Newham E6 .... 1 E8
...y Rd. Newham E13 .... 1 B8
...y Rd. Park Wood ME15 107 F4
...irk Dr. DA8 .... 8 E6
...ourne Pk. TN3 .... 163 C4
...nge Gn. ME9 .... 49 C3
...wood Cl. DA1 .... 27 B7
...ey Cres. DA16 .... 7 D6
...ane Rd. ME8 .... 49 C2
...eyan Cres. DA16 .... 7 B3
...ryn Pl. 1 BR5 .... 38 B6
...y Rd. RM18 .... 12 F5
...ple Gdns. ME4 .... 47 E3
...acre La. ME15 .... 107 E6
...acre Sq. ME5 .... 61 B4
...acre Tech Coll. ME15 . 107 D6
...acre Wood Cty Prim Sch.
   ME15 .... 107 F7
...stor Wlk. SE28 .... 2 D3
...cler House. SE2 .... 7 D8
...ac Pl. TN3 .... 161 C7
...cac Rd. SE12 .... 22 B7
...en Wlk. SE9 .... 22 E5
...ocke Ct. TN13 .... 84 B2
...ola Gdns. BR6 .... 37 F2
...non Dr. BR8 .... 39 C6
...entine Cl. TN13 .... 84 D5
...entine Rd.
   3 & TN15 .... 84 D4
...den Dr. BR1 .... 36 D8
...ord Rd. ME5 .... 62 C6
...ington Ave. ME5 .... 48 C1
...n Acres.
   ckenhill BR8 .... 39 D3
...n Acres.
   by Ash Green DA3 ...... 56 E7
...n Mile La.
   ne Pound ME11 .... 88 A3
...n Mile La.
   eworth TN11 & TN12 ... 103 E3
...n Mile La.
   otham Heath TN15 ...... 87 F7
...n Wents. TN15 .... 86 A4
...noaks By-Pass.
   3 & TN14 .... 98 F7
...noaks Cty Prim Sch.
   3 .... 84 B5
...noaks Hospl.
   enoaks TN13 .... 84 B2
...noaks Hospl.
   enoaks,St John's TN13 . 84 C6
...noaks Prep Sch. TN15 . 85 A1
...noaks Rd.
   ough Green TN15 .... 86 F7
...atham Common TN15 ... 86 B4
...noaks Rd.
   ington BR6 .... 51 F6
...noaks Rd. Otford TN14 . 69 B3
...noaks Rd.
   tt's Bottom BR6 & TN14 52 C2
...noaks Sta. TN13 .... 84 C1
...noaks Sta. TN13 .... 84 A3
...noaks Way. ME5 .... 38 C7
...noaks Wildfowl Reserve.
   .... 84 A7
...rn Cl. TN10 .... 117 C5
...rn Rd. ME5 .... 62 C5

Sevington Pk. ME15 ...... 106 F6
Sewell Rd. SE28 .... 3 B4
Sextant Pk. ME2 .... 47 E6
Sexton Rd. RM18 .... 12 F6
Seymour Dr. BR2 .... 36 F1
Seymour Rd. 1
   Chatham ME4 .... 48 B3
Seymour Rd.
   Moor Street ME8 .... 64 C8
Seymour Rd.
   Northfleet DA11 .... 29 F6
Seymour St. SE18 .... 2 C3
Seymour Wlk. DA10 ...... 28 E8
Shacklands Rd. TN14 .... 53 D1
Shackleton Cl. ME5 ...... 62 B6
Shades The. ME2 .... 46 C7
Shaftesbury Cl. ME19 .... 74 F1
Shaftesbury Ct. 3 SE28 .. 3 C5
Shaftesbury Dr. ME16 .... 91 C6
Shaftesbury La. DA1 ..... 10 B3
Shaftesbury Rd. TN4 .... 149 A5
Shaftesbury Ct. E6 .... 2 A7
Shakespeare Ave. RM18 .. 13 B6
Shakespeare Farm Rd.
   ME3 .... 18 F7
Shakespeare House. 1
   DA17 .... 4 A1
Shakespeare Rd. Bexley DA7 . 7 E6
Shakespeare Rd.
   Dartford DA1 .... 10 B3
Shakespeare Rd.
   Gillingham ME7 .... 48 C3
Shakespeare Rd.
   Tonbridge TN9 .... 132 F8
Shalder House. ME7 ..... 48 D7
Shalford Cl. BR6 .... 51 C6
Shallons Rd. SE9 .... 23 B4
Shambles The. ME13 .... 84 C2
Shamel Bsns Ctr. ME2 ... 47 C7
Shamley Rd. ME5 .... 62 D2
Shamrock Rd. DA12 ..... 30 F8
Shandon Cl. TN2 .... 149 C4
Shanklin Cl. ME5 .... 62 C8
Shannon Ct. BR6 .... 38 A2
Sharfleet Dr. ME2 .... 46 B7
Sharland Rd. DA12 ...... 30 C6
Sharman Cl. DA14 .... 24 A4
Sharnal La. ME6 .... 75 A7
Sharnal St. ME3 .... 18 A2
Sharnbrooke Cl. DA16 ... 7 C4
Sharon Cres. ME5 .... 61 F4
Sharp Way. DA1 .... 9 F4
Sharp's Field. TN27 ..... 141 E5
Sharsted Way.
   Gillingham ME7 .... 63 A3
Sharsted Way.
   Maidstone ME14 .... 93 B5
Shaw Cl. Cliffe Woods ME3 .. 33 B8
Shaw Cl. Woolwich SE28 ... 3 B5
Shaw Cres. RM18 .... 13 B6
Shaw House. 6 Erith DA17 . 3 F1
Shaw House. 6
   Newham E16 .... 2 A5
Shaw The. TN2 .... 149 C2
Shawbrooke Rd. SE9 .... 5 D3
Shawcroft Sch. BR5 ..... 38 E4
Shawfield Pk. BR1 .... 36 D7
Shaws Way. ME1 .... 47 C3
Shawstead Rd. ME7 & ME7 . 62 D8
Sheafe Dr. TN17 .... 169 C5
Sheal's Cres. ME15 ..... 92 A2
Sheals Ct. ME15 .... 92 A2
Shearers Cl. ME14 ...... 92 E4
Shears Green Cl. DA11 .. 30 A6
Shears Green Cty Inf Sch.
   DA11 .... 29 F5
Shears Green Cty Jun Sch.
   DA11 .... 29 F5
Shearwater.
   Maidstone ME16 .... 91 B5
Shearwater. New Barn DA3 . 43 B6
Shearwater Cl. ME2 ..... 46 C7
Sheerwood Cres. DA1 ... 9 A4
Sheen Rd. BR5 .... 37 F5
Sheepcote La. BR5 & BR8 . 38 F4
Sheephurst La. TN12 ... 137 E5
Sheerness Harbour Est.
   ME12 .... 21 F3
Sheerwater Rd. E16 ..... 1 D8
Sheet Hill. TN15 .... 86 D2
Sheffield Rd. 4 TN4 .... 132 F2
Sheilings The. TN15 .... 84 F7
Shelbury Cl. DA14 ...... 24 A5
Shelden Rd. ME8 .... 63 F8
Shelden Bsns Ctr. ME2 .. 47 D8
Sheldon Cl. SE12 .... 5 B2
Sheldon Rd. DA7 .... 7 F6
Sheldon Way. ME20 .... 75 B3
Sheldrake Cl. E16 .... 1 F5
Shell Cl. BR2 .... 36 E3

Shellbank La. DA2 .... 28 B4
Shelldrake Cl. ME3 ...... 21 B5
Shelley Cl. BR6 .... 51 E7
Shelley Dr. DA16 .... 6 E6
Shelley Pl. RM18 .... 13 B6
Shelleys La. TN14 .... 67 A3
Shelton Cl. TN10 .... 117 C5
Shenden Cl. TN13 .... 99 C7
Shenden Way.
   TN13 & TN15 .... 99 C7
Shenfield House. SE18 ... 5 D7
Shenley Gr. ME14 .... 76 F2
Shenley Rd. DA1 .... 27 A8
Shenstone Sch. DA1 ..... 8 D2
Shepherd St. DA11 ...... 29 D8
Shepherds Cl. BR6 ...... 51 F7
Shepherds Gate. ME7 ... 62 F5
Shepherds Gate Dr. ME14 . 92 E6
Shepherds Gn. BR7 ..... 23 D1
Shepherds La. DA1 ...... 26 B8
Shepherds Leas. SE9 .... 6 D3
Shepherds Way.
   Langley Heath ME17 ... 108 E4
Shepherds Way.
   Lower Stoke ME3 ...... 19 C4
Shepherds Wlk. TN2 .... 149 D4
Shepherdsgrove La.
   RH19 .... 144 A4
Shepperton Cl. ME5 .... 62 C4
Shepperton Rd. BR5 .... 37 C3
Sheppey Cl. DA8 .... 9 B7
Sheppey Rd. ME15 ...... 107 A7
Sheppey Cty Jun Sch.
   ME15 .... 107 E8
Shepway Cty Inf Sch.
   ME15 .... 107 E8
Shepway Cty Jun Sch.
   ME15 .... 107 E8
Sherard Rd. SE9 .... 5 E2
Sheraton Ct. ME5 .... 61 F1
Sherborne Rd. BR5 ..... 37 F4
Sherbourne Cl.
   Royal Tunbridge Wells
   TN2 .... 149 D2
Sherbourne Cl.
   West Kingsdown TN15 .. 55 E4
Sherbourne Dr. ME16 ... 91 B2
Sherbrooke Cl. DA7 ..... 8 A3
Sherenden Cl. TN12 .... 154 D8
Sherenden Pk. TN11 .... 119 A5
Sherenden Rd. TN11 ... 134 D7
Sherfield Rd. RM17 ..... 12 B8
Sheridan Cl. Chatham ME5 . 62 C7
Sheridan Cl.
   Maidstone ME14 .... 91 E8
Sheridan Cl. Swanley BR8 .. 39 F6
Sheridan Cres. BR7 ..... 37 B7
Sheridan Ct. DA1 .... 10 A3
Sheridan Rd. Bexley DA7 . 7 E4
Sheridan Rd. Erith DA17 . 4 A2
Sheriff Dr. ME5 .... 62 A2
Sherington Prim Sch. SE7 . 5 B8
Sherington Rd. SE7 ..... 5 B8
Sherlies Ave. BR6 ...... 51 E8
Sherman Cl. ME7 .... 49 B1
Sherman Rd. BR1 .... 36 A8
Shernden La. TN8 ...... 128 C4
Shernold Sch. ME16 .... 91 D5
Shernolds. ME15 .... 107 B7
Sherway Cl. TN27 ...... 141 E5
Sherway Rd. TN27 ..... 142 D6
Sherwin Knight Cty Prim Sch.
   ME2 .... 46 E5
Sherwood Ave. ME5 .... 62 A2
Sherwood Cl. DA5 ...... 7 C1
Sherwood House.
   Chatham ME5 .... 62 A2
Sherwood House. Erith DA8 . 8 E8
Sherwood Park Ave. DA15 . 7 B1
Sherwood Rd. Bexley DA16 . 6 E4
Sherwood Rd.
   Royal Tunbridge Wells
   TN2 .... 149 E5
Sherwood Way. TN2 ... 149 D6
Shieldhall St. SE2 .... 3 C2
Shillingheld Cl. ME14 ... 92 F5
Shinecroft. TN14 .... 69 A3
Shingle Barn La. ME15 . 105 C3
Shinglewell Rd. DA8 .... 8 A7
Ship La. Chatham ME1 .... 47 B4
Ship La. Sutton at Hone BR8 . 40 E8
Shipbourne Cty Prim Sch.
   TN11 .... 101 C4
Shipbourne Rd.
   Shipbourne TN11 & TN10 . 101 D2
Shipbourne Rd.
   Tonbridge TN10 .... 117 C5
Shipley Ct. SE14 .... 92 A4

Shipley Hills Rd.
   Meopham DA13 .... 43 E1
Shipman Rd. E16 .... 1 C7
Shipwrights Ave. ME4 .. 48 B2
Shire Ct. SE2 .... 3 D3
Shire La.
   Farthing Street BR6 & BR2 . 51 C3
Shire La. Orpington BR6 . 51 E5
Shirebrook Rd. SE3 ..... 5 D4
Shirehall Rd. DA2 .... 26 E4
Shires The. TN12 .... 136 A7
Shirley Ave. Chatham ME5 . 61 D5
Shirley Ave. Sidcup DA5 . 24 D7
Shirley Cl. Chalk DA12 .. 31 B6
Shirley Cl. Dartford DA1 . 9 C3
Shirley Gdns. TN4 ...... 148 C5
Shirley Gr. TN4 .... 148 C5
Shirley House Dr. SE7 .. 5 C7
Shirley Rd. DA15 .... 23 E5
Shirley Way. ME15 ..... 93 A3
Sholden Gdns. BR5 ..... 38 C4
Sholden Rd. ME2 .... 33 C1
Shooters Hill. SE18 ..... 6 A6
Shooters Hill Golf Course.
   SE18 .... 6 C6
Shooters Hill Rd.
   SE18 & SE3 & SE7 ..... 5 D6
Shore The. Northfleet DA11 . 12 C2
Shore The. Northfleet DA11 . 12 F1
Shoreham Cl. DA5 ...... 7 B1
Shoreham Cty Prim Sch.
   TN14 .... 68 F8
Shoreham House. TN14 . 69 A8
Shoreham La.
   Badgers Mount TN14 ... 68 A7
Shoreham La. Maypole BR6 . 53 A3
Shoreham La.
   Sevenoaks TN13 .... 83 F4
Shoreham La.
   St Michaels TN30 ...... 173 A3
Shoreham Pl. TN14 ..... 69 A7
Shoreham Rd. Otford TN14 . 69 B5
Shoreham Rd.
   St Paul's Cray BR5 ..... 38 B7
Shoreham Sta. TN14 ... 69 B8
Shoreham Way. BR2 .... 36 A3
Shoreham Wlk. ME15 .. 107 F7
Shorehill La. TN15 ...... 69 F4
Shoreland Ct. ME1 ...... 47 B5
Shorne CE Prim Sch. DA12 . 31 E3
Shorne Cl. Orpington BR5 . 38 D5
Shorne Cl. 3 Sidcup DA15 . 7 B1
Shorne Ifield Rd. DA12 . 31 C2
Shorne Wood (Ctry Pk).
   DA12 .... 31 C1
Shornefield Cl. BR1 ..... 37 A6
Short La. Brenchley TN12 . 152 A6
Short La. Gillingham ME7 . 49 A6
Short St. 3 ME4 .... 48 B3
Shortlands Cl. DA17 .... 3 F3
Shortlands Gn. ME15 .. 107 F5
Shorts Way. ME1 .... 47 A3
Shortway. SE9 .... 5 E4
Shottenden Rd. ME7 ... 48 D7
Shottery Cl. SE9 .... 22 E5
Showfields Rd. TN2 .... 148 F1
Shrapnel Cl. SE18 ...... 5 F4
Shrapnel Rd. SE9 .... 5 F4
Shrewsbury La. SE18 ... 6 B6
Shroffold Rd. BR1 ...... 22 A5
Shropshire Terr. 3
   ME15 .... 107 E7
Shrubbery Rd.
   Gravesend DA12 .... 30 C7
Shrubbery Rd.
   South Darenth DA4 ..... 41 D8
Shrubcote. TN30 .... 183 C7
Shrublands Ct.
   Royal Tunbridge Wells
   TN2 .... 149 C4
Shrublands Cl. 1
   Tonbridge TN9 .... 117 C2
Shrubsall Cl. SE9 .... 22 E7
Shrubsole Dr. ME14 .... 76 F3
Shurlock Ave. BR8 ..... 39 D7
Shurlock Dr. BR6 .... 51 C6
Shuttle Cl.
   Biddenden TN27 .... 158 A2
Shuttle Cl. Sidcup DA15 . 23 F8
Shuttle Rd. DA1 .... 9 A4
Shuttlemead. DA5 ...... 24 E8
Sibley Cl. DA6 .... 7 E2
Sibthorpe Rd. SE12 ..... 22 C8
Sidcup By Pass Rd.
   Sidcup DA14 .... 23 F3
Sidcup By Pass Rd.
   St Paul's Cray BR5 & BR7 . 24 B1
Sidcup Hill. DA14 ...... 24 B3
Sidcup Hill Gdns. DA14 . 24 C3
Sidcup Hill Prim Sch. DA14 . 24 B3
Sidcup Pl. DA14 .... 24 A3

Sidcup Rd.
   Eltham SE12 & SE9 .... 22 D7
Sidcup Rd. Eltham SE9 ... 22 E7
Sidcup Rd.
   Eltham BR7 & SE9 ..... 23 B6
Sidcup Sta. DA14 & DA15 . 24 A4
Sidewood Rd. SE9 ..... 23 D7
Sidmouth Ct. DA1 ..... 27 B7
Sidmouth Rd. Bexley DA16 . 7 C7
Sidmouth Rd.
   Orpington BR5 .... 38 B5
Sidney Cl. TN2 .... 162 F8
Sidney Gdns. TN14 .... 69 C2
Sidney House. SE18 ..... 5 F6
Sidney Rd. Gillingham ME7 . 48 C7
Sidney Rd. Rochester ME1 . 47 A2
Sidney St. ME16 .... 91 C2
Siebert Rd. SE3 & SE7 .. 5 A8
Siedle House. 9 SE18 ... 6 A8
Siemens Rd. SE18 ...... 1 D3
Sigers The. ME14 ...... 92 C7
Silecroft Rd. DA7 ...... 8 A6
Silk Cl. SE12 .... 5 A1
Silver Bank. ME5 ...... 62 A6
Silver Birch Ave. DA13 . 57 F1
Silver Birch Cl. DA2 .... 25 E4
Silver Birches. ME5 .... 62 A3
Silver Cl. TN9 .... 133 B6
Silver Hill. Chatham ME4 . 47 F3
Silver Hill. Rochester ME1 . 46 F2
Silver Hill. Silver Hill TN19 . 184 B1
Silver Hill. Tenterden TN30 . 173 B1
Silver Hill Gdns. ME4 .. 47 F3
Silver Rd. DA12 .... 30 E6
Silver Spring Cl. DA8 ... 8 B8
Silver St. ME9 .... 80 F5
Silver Tree. ME5 .... 62 B1
Silverdale. Hartley DA3 . 42 F5
Silverdale. Maidstone ME15 . 91 A2
Silverdale Dr.
   Chislehurst SE9 .... 22 E6
Silverdale Dr.
   Gillingham ME8 .... 63 F7
Silverdale La. TN4 ..... 149 B6
Silverdale Rd. Bexley DA7 . 8 B5
Silverdale Rd.
   Orpington BR5 .... 37 C5
Silverdale Rd.
   Royal Tunbridge Wells
   TN4 .... 149 B6
   St Paul's Cray BR5 ..... 38 A6
Silverden Cotts. TN18 . 185 F4
Silverhurst Dr. TN10 ... 117 C7
Silverland St. E16 ...... 1 F5
Silverlocke Rd. RM17 .. 12 D8
Silverspot Cl. ME8 ..... 63 F7
Silversted La. TN16 .... 81 D6
Silverstone Cl. 6 BR1 .. 22 A3
Silvertown By-Pass. E16 . 1 D5
Silvertown Sta. E16 .... 1 E5
Silvertown Way. E16 ... 1 A5
Silverweed Rd. ME5 ... 61 F4
Silwood Cl. TN2 .... 149 E7
Simmonds Cl. TN4 .... 148 B4
Simmonds Dr. DA3 .... 43 A4
Simmonds La. ME15 ... 108 B6
Simmons Rd. SE18 ..... 2 B1
Simnel Rd. SE12 .... 22 B8
Simon Cl. 5 SE28 ...... 3 B5
Simone Cl. BR1 .... 36 D8
Simpson Rd. ME6 ...... 75 A6
Simpson's Cotts. BR2 .. 50 C7
Simpson's Rd. BR2 .... 36 A6
Sinclair Cl. ME8 .... 63 E5
Sinclair Way. DA2 ..... 27 D4
Singapore Dr. ME7 .... 48 B5
Single St. BR6 & TN16 . 66 B4
Single's Cross. TN14 ... 66 D4
Single's Cross La. TN14 . 67 C5
Singlewell Cty Prim Sch.
   DA12 .... 30 D2
Singlewell Rd. DA11 ... 30 B4
Sinkertweazel. TN17 ... 169 E2
Sir David's Pk. TN4 .... 132 E1
Sir Evelyn Rd. ME1 .... 47 B1
Sir John Hawkins Way.
   ME4 .... 47 F4
Sir Joseph Williamson's
   Mathematical Sch. ME1 . 47 C1
Sir Martin Bowes House. 15
   SE18 .... 6 A8
Sir Thomas Longley Rd.
   ME2 .... 47 E6
Sirdar Strand. DA12 .... 30 F3
Siskin Gdns. TN12 ..... 136 A5
Siskin Wlk. ME20 ...... 74 F2
Sissinghurst Castle. TN17 . 156 D1

Sissinghurst Cty Prim Sch.
TN17 .... 170 B8
Sissinghurst Dr. ME16 ...... 91 B4
Sissinghurst Rd.
Biddenden TN27 & TN17 ... 157 C2
Sissinghurst Rd.
Sissinghurst TN17 .... 170 D8
Sittingbourne Rd.
Maidstone,Detling ME14 ... 92 E8
Sittingbourne Rd.
Penenden Heath ME14 ..... 92 B6
Siward Rd. BR2 .... 36 C6
Six Bells La. TN13 .... 84 C1
Six Fields Path. TN30 ...... 183 A7
Skeet Hill La. BR5 & BR6 ... 52 E8
Skeffington St. SE18 .... 2 C3
Skeynes Rd. TN8 .... 112 B1
Skibbs La. BR5 & BR6 ...... 52 E7
Skinner Gdns. TN17 .... 170 A8
Skinner La. TN8 .... 112 D2
Skinner St. Chatham ME4 ... 47 F3
Skinner St. Gillingham ME7 .. 48 C5
Skinner St. Gillingham ME7 .. 48 C6
Skinner Street Cty Prim Sch.
ME7 .... 48 C6
Skinner's Way. ME17 ..... 108 E4
Skinners La. ME20 .... 76 A6
Skinners La. TN8 .... 112 D2
Skinners' Sch The. TN4 ... 149 A6
Skippers Cl. DA9 .... 11 B2
Skua Cl. ME2 .... 46 C7
Skye Cl. ME15 .... 107 A7
Slade Cl. ME5 .... 62 B2
Slade Cty Prim Sch. TN9 .. 117 B2
Slade Gdns. DA8 .... 8 F6
Slade Green Inf Sch. DA8 ... 9 A7
Slade Green Jun Sch. DA8 ... 9 A7
Slade Green Rd. DA8 .... 9 A6
Slade Green Sta. SE28 ...... 9 A6
Slade The. The Down TN3 .. 166 A3
Slade The. Tonbridge TN9 .. 117 B2
Slade The. Woolwich SE18 ... 6 A8
Sladebrook Rd. SE3 .... 5 D4
Sladedale Rd. SE18 .... 2 E1
Slades Dr. BR7 .... 23 C4
Slaney Rd. TN12 .... 139 F4
Slaters. TN8 .... 113 F2
Slatin Rd. ME2 .... 47 B8
Sleeches Cross. TN3 ...... 163 B2
Sleepers Stile Rd. TN5 .... 165 B1
Slicketts Hill. ME4 .... 48 A4
Slip Mill Rd. TN18 .... 178 E2
Slip Rd. ME4 .... 48 A8
Slip The. TN16 .... 81 C1
Slipway Rd. ME2 .... 21 F3
Sloane Gdns. BR6 .... 51 C7
Sloane Sq. DA3 .... 42 E6
Slocum Cl. SE28 .... 3 C6
Small Bridge Cotts. TN17 . 153 B2
Small Bridge Rd.
TN12 & TN17 .... 153 B2
Small Grains. DA3 .... 56 B7
Small Hythe Rd. TN30 .... 183 C3
Small Profits. ME18 ...... 105 A4
Smallhythe Rd. TN30 ..... 183 A6
Smarden Bsns Est. TN27 .. 158 D7
Smarden Cl. 7 DA17 .... 4 A1
Smarden Cty Prim Sch.
TN27 .... 143 A1
Smarden Gr. SE9 .... 22 F4
Smarden Rd.
East End TN27 .... 142 B4
Smarden Rd.
Standen TN27 .... 158 B6
Smarts Cotts. ME14 .... 93 C4
Smarts Hill. TN11 .... 131 A1
Smarts Rd. DA12 .... 30 C6
Smith Rd. ME5 .... 62 B3
Smith St. ME7 .... 47 A6
Smith's Hill. ME15 .... 105 C5
Smithers Cl. TN11 .... 102 E1
Smithers Cl. TN12 .... 120 A7
Smithers La. TN12 .... 120 A7
Smithfield Rd. ME3 .... 21 C5
Smithies Rd. SE2 .... 3 B2
Smiths La. TN8 .... 96 C2
Smithy Field. 7 TN8 ...... 112 D3
Smugglers Mews. TN18 ... 179 A1
Smugglers Wharf. DA9 .... 11 B2
Smythe Cl. TN4 .... 132 E3
Smythe Rd. DA4 .... 41 A8
Snag La. TN14 .... 66 D7
Snape View. TN5 .... 174 F4
Snelling Ave. DA11 .... 29 F6
Snipe Cl. Erith DA8 .... 9 B7
Snipe Cl. Pembury TN2 ... 150 E8
Snipe Cl. ME2 .... 46 C7
Snoad La. TN12 .... 155 A8
Snodhurst Ave. ME5 ...... 61 E5

Snodland CE Prim Sch. ME6 74 F8
Snodland Rd. ME19 .... 74 D7
Snodland Sta. ME6 .... 75 B8
Snodlands Cl. BR6 .... 51 A1
Snoll Hatch Rd. TN12 .... 119 F5
Snow House. ME7 .... 48 E7
Snowdon Ave. ME14 .... 92 B5
Snowdon Cl. ME5 .... 62 B7
Snughorne La. TN27 ..... 158 D8
Sole Fields. TN13 .... 99 C8
Sole St. DA12 & DA13 ..... 44 A8
Sole Street Sta. DA13 ..... 44 D4
Solefield Prep Sch. TN13 ... 99 C8
Solefields Rd. TN13 .... 99 C8
Solent Gdns. ME5 .... 62 B8
Soleoak Dr. TN13 .... 99 C8
Solomon Rd.
Gillingham ME8 .... 49 F1
Solomon Rd.
Gillingham ME8 .... 64 A8
Solomons Rd. ME4 .... 47 F4
Somerden Rd. BR5 .... 38 C2
Somerfield Cl. ME16 ...... 91 D5
Somerfield Hospl The.
ME16 .... 91 E5
Somerfield La. ME16 ...... 91 D4
Somerfield Rd. ME16 ...... 91 D4
Somerhill Ave. DA15 ...... 24 B8
Somerhill Rd. Bexley DA16 .. 7 B5
Somerhill Rd.
Tonbridge TN9 .... 133 D8
Somerset Ave. DA16 .... 6 F3
Somerset Cl. ME5 .... 62 C8
Somerset Rd. Dartford DA1 . 26 B8
Somerset Rd.
Maidstone ME15 .... 91 E1
Somerset Rd.
Orpington BR6 .... 38 A2
Somerset Rd.
Royal Tunbridge Wells TN4 149 A6
Somerset Villas. TN3 ..... 161 C7
Somersham Rd. DA7 .... 7 E5
Somertrees Ave. SE12 .... 22 B6
Somerville Gdns. TN4 .... 148 F4
Somerville Rd. DA1 .... 9 F1
Somner Wlk. ME15 .... 107 F4
Soper's La. TN12 .... 151 C5
Sophia Rd. E13 .... 1 B7
Sophurst La. TN12 .... 151 C5
Sopurst Wood. TN12 ..... 151 D5
Sorrel Cl. SE28 .... 3 A5
Sorrel Cl. 7 RM17 .... 12 D8
Sorrel Gdns. E6 .... 1 E8
Sorrell Cl. 4 TN8 .... 112 D3
Sorrell Rd. ME5 .... 61 F4
Sorrell Way. DA11 .... 29 E4
Sounds Lodge. BR8 .... 39 C3
South Ash Rd. TN15 .... 56 E4
South Ave. ME8 .... 49 B2
South Aylesford Ret Pk.
ME20 .... 90 E8
South Bank.
Cliffe Woods ME3 .... 16 B2
South Bank.
Staplehurst TN12 .... 139 E2
South Bank.
Sutton Valence ME17 .... 124 E7
South Bank.
Westerham TN16 .... 81 D1
South Borough Cty Prim Sch.
ME15 .... 92 A2
South Bush La. ME8 .... 64 B6
South Cl. DA6 .... 7 D5
South Cres. ME17 .... 106 C4
South Dr. BR6 .... 51 C5
South Eastern Rd. ME2 .... 47 C7
South Frith. TN4 .... 133 A6
South Glade. DA5 .... 24 F7
South Gr. TN1 .... 149 A2
South Green La. ME9 ...... 79 F6
South Hall Cl. DA4 .... 40 F2
South Hill. BR7 .... 22 F2
South Hill Rd. DA12 .... 30 C7
South Kent Ave. DA11 .... 12 C1
South La. ME17 .... 124 E6
South Molton Rd. E16 ...... 1 A7
South Park Bsns Village.
ME15 .... 92 A1
South Park Rd. ME15 ..... 92 C1
South Pk. TN13 .... 84 B2
South Pondside Rd. ME4 ... 48 A8
South Rd. Erith DA8 .... 8 F7
South Rd. Gillingham ME7 .. 48 A7
South Rd. Gillingham ME4 .. 48 A8
South Rd. Marden TN12 .. 138 E5
South Rise Jun & Inf Sch.
SE18 .... 2 D1
South Row. Greenwich SE3 .. 5 A5
South Row.
Weller's Town TN8 ...... 130 D5

South Side Three Rd. ME4 .. 48 C8
South St. Bromley BR1 .... 36 A7
South St. Gravesend DA11 .. 30 B8
South St. Maidstone ME16 .. 90 E1
South St.
Meopham Green DA13 .... 57 F7
South Terr. Deal ME9 ..... 79 C7
South Terr. DA4 .... 40 F2
South View. BR1 .... 36 C7
South View Ave. RM18 .... 13 A6
South View Cl. DA5 .... 7 F1
South View Rd.
Royal Tunbridge Wells
TN4 .... 149 B8
South View Rd.
Turner's Green TN5 ..... 174 F6
South View Rd.
West Thurrock RM16 ..... 11 C8
South View Rd.
Wilmington DA2 .... 26 D5
South Wharf Rd. RM17 .... 11 F8
Southborough CE Prim Sch.
TN4 .... 148 F8
Southborough Ct. TN4 ... 133 A2
Southborough La.
BR1 & BR2 .... 36 F4
Southborough Prim Sch.
BR2 .... 37 A4
Southborough Rd.
BR1 & BR2 .... 36 E5
Southbourne. BR2 .... 36 A2
Southbourne Gdns. SE12 .. 5 B2
Southbourne Gr. ME5 .... 62 A4
Southcroft Ave. DA16 ...... 6 E4
Southcroft Rd. BR6 .... 51 E7
Southcote. TN14 .... 67 F6
Southend Cl. SE9 .... 6 B1
Southend Cres. SE9 .... 6 B1
Southern Pl. BR8 .... 39 D5
Southern Rd. TN27 ...... 126 E1
Southey Way. 1 ME20 .... 74 F4
Southey Wlk. RM18 ...... 13 B6
Southfield Rd.
Royal Tunbridge Wells
TN4 .... 149 A6
Southfield Rd.
Speldhurst TN3 .... 148 A7
Southfield Rd.
St Paul's Cray BR7 .... 38 A6
Southfield Shaw. DA13 ... 58 B1
Southfields. Rochester ME1 . 47 C3
Southfields.
Turner's Green TN5 ..... 174 F6
Southfields Rd. TN15 ..... 55 F2
Southfields Sch. DA12 ..... 30 C3
Southlands Way. TN4 .... 149 B8
Southfleet Ave. DA3 ...... 43 B7
Southfleet Rd. Bean DA2 .. 28 C4
Southfleet Rd. 7
Northfleet DA11 .... 29 F7
Southfleet Rd.
Orpington BR6 .... 51 E6
Southfleet Rd.
Swanscombe DA10 ...... 29 A7
Southgate. TN4 .... 148 F3
Southgate Rd. TN30 ..... 183 C7
Southill Rd. Chatham ME4 .. 47 F3
Southill Rd. Chislehurst BR7 22 F1
Southlake Prim Sch. SE2 ... 3 D4
Southland Rd. SE18 .... 6 F7
Southlands Ave. BR6 ..... 51 E5
Southlands Gr. BR1 .... 36 E6
Southlands Rd. BR1 & BR2 .. 36 D5
Southlees La. ME9 .... 79 F3
Southold Rise. SE9 .... 22 F5
Southover. BR1 .... 22 A3
Southport Rd. SE18 .... 2 D2
Southspring. SE9 .... 23 D8
Southview Cl. BR8 .... 40 A5
Southwark Pl. BR1 .... 36 F6
Southwark Rd. ME2 ...... 46 D6
Southway. BR2 .... 36 A2
Southways. ME17 .... 124 E7
Southwell Rd. ME2 .... 46 D6
Southwold Rd. DA5 .... 8 B1
Southwood. Ave. TN4 ... 149 A6
Southwood Cl. BR1 .... 36 F5
Southwood House. SE9 ... 23 B6
Southwood Rd. Eltham SE9 . 23 B6
Southwood Rd.
Rusthall TN4 .... 148 B5
Southwood Rd.
Woolwich SE28 .... 3 B5
Sovereign Bvd.
Gillingham ME7 .... 48 F2
Sovereign Bvd.
Gillingham,Twydall ME8 .. 49 A2
Sovereign Cl. Bromley BR2 .. 36 F4
Sovereign Cl.
Sutton at Hone DA4 ...... 41 B8

Sovereign House. SE18 .... 1 F3
Sovereign Way. TN9 ..... 117 C1
Sovereigns The. ME16 .... 91 D4
Sovereigns Way. TN12 .. 138 C6
Sowerby Cl. SE9 .... 5 F2
Spa Golf Course. TN4 ... 148 E3
Spa Ind Est. TN2 .... 149 E8
Spade La. ME8 & ME9 .... 64 C6
Sparepenny La. DA4 ...... 40 E1
Sparkeswood Ave. TN17 . 181 F3
Sparkeswood Cl. TN17 .. 181 F3
Sparrow Dr. BR5 .... 37 D1
Sparrow's Farm L Ctr. SE9 . 23 C8
Sparrows Green Rd. TN5 . 174 F5
Sparrows La. SE9 .... 23 C7
Spearhead Rd. ME14 ...... 91 F7
Spearman St. 8 SE18 ...... 6 A8
Spectrum Bsns Ctr. ME2 .. 47 E8
Spectrum Bsns Est. ME15 . 107 F4
Speedgate Hill. DA3 ...... 56 A8
Speedwell Ave. ME5 ...... 61 F4
Speedwell Cl.
Gillingham ME7 .... 48 E5
Speedwell Cl.
Maidstone ME14 .... 92 E5
Speedwell Cl. 5
Marlpit Hill TN8 .... 112 D3
Speedwell Ct. RM17 ...... 12 E7
Spekehill. SE9 .... 22 F5
Spekes Rd. ME7 .... 63 B6
Speldhurst CE Prim Sch.
TN3 .... 148 A7
Speldhurst Cl. ME16 ...... 91 D4
Speldhurst Hill. TN3 ..... 148 B8
Speldhurst Rd.
Langton Green TN3 ..... 147 F4
Speldhurst Rd.
Royal Tunbridge Wells
TN3 & TN4 .... 148 E8
Spelmonden Rd.
TN12 & TN17 .... 152 F2
Spencer Cl. Chatham ME5 .. 62 A5
Spencer Cl. Orpington BR6 .. 51 F8
Spencer Cl. 5 BR6 .... 51 C5
Spencer Flats. ME5 .... 62 B8
Spencer Mews. 6 TN1 ... 149 A2
Spencer St. DA11 .... 30 A8
Spencer Way. ME15 ..... 107 E7
Spencer Wlk. RM18 ...... 13 B5
Spencer's Mews. 4 TN1 .. 149 B4
Spenlow Dr. ME5 .... 77 A8
Spenny La. TN12 .... 137 B7
Speranza St. SE18 .... 2 F1
Speyside. TN10 .... 117 B5
Spielman Rd. DA1 .... 9 F3
Spiers The. ME7 .... 49 C5
Spillway The. ME15 ...... 91 D2
Spindle Glade. ME14 ..... 92 C5
Spindle House. 8 DA15 ... 24 A5
Spindles. RM18 .... 13 A7
Spindlewood Cl. ME5 .... 62 B3
Spinel Cl. SE18 .... 2 F1
Spinnaker Ct. 3 ME1 ..... 47 C1
Spinnens Acre Cty Jun Sch.
ME5 .... 62 C1
Spinners Cl. TN27 .... 158 A2
Spinners Wents. TN15 ... 102 D8
Spinney Oak. BR1 .... 36 E1
Spinney The. Chatham ME5 . 62 B1
Spinney The.
Maidstone ME15 .... 92 B2
Spinney The. Sidcup DA14 . 24 E3
Spinney The. Swanley BR8 . 39 E7
Spinney The.
Tonbridge TN9 .... 133 A7
Spinney Way. TN14 .... 66 D8
Spinneys The. BR1 .... 36 F7
Spire Cl. DA12 .... 30 B7
Spires The. Dartford DA1 .. 26 D6
Spires The. Maidstone ME16 91 D4
Spires The. Rochester ME2 .. 46 D5
Spital St. DA1 .... 9 D1
Spitfire Cl. ME5 .... 62 B6
Spitfire Rd. ME19 .... 88 F3
Spode La. TN8 .... 145 A7
Sponden La.
Field Green TN18 .... 185 F8
Sponden La.
Sandhurst TN18 .... 186 A7
Spongs La. TN17 .... 156 A1
Sportsfield. ME14 .... 92 B5
Sportsmans Cotts. ME19 .. 89 A5
Spot La. ME15 .... 93 A2
Spout La. Brenchley TN12 . 152 C5
Spout La. Crockham Hill TN8 96 C1
Spray Hill. TN3 .... 166 B4
Spray St. SE18 .... 2 B2
Sprig The. ME14 .... 93 A4
Spring Cross. DA3 .... 57 A7
Spring Gdns. Orpington BR6 52 A3
Spring Gdns. Rusthall TN4 148 B4

Spring Gr. DA12 3
Spring Head Rd. TN15 6
Spring Hill. TN11 & TN3 ... 14
Spring La. Bidborough TN4 13
Spring La. Oldbury TN15 ... 8
Spring Lodge. 3 BR5 3
Spring Shaw Rd. BR5 3
Spring Vale. Bexley DA7 .....
Spring Vale. Dartford DA1 .. 2
Spring Vale.
Maidstone ME16 6
Spring Vale.
Swanscombe DA9 ....
Spring Vale Cl. BR8 3
Spring Vale N. DA1 ....
Spring Vale S. DA1 ....
Springcroft. DA3 4
Springdale Cotts. ME3 3
Springett Almshouses.
TN18 18
Springett Cl. ME20 7
Springett Way. ME17 ..... 1(
Springfield Ave.
Maidstone ME14 9
Springfield Ave.
St Michaels TN30 17
Springfield Ave.
Swanley BR8 ....
Springfield Cotts. TN12 ... 1
Springfield Gdns. BR1 3
Springfield Gr. SE7 ....
Springfield Ind Est. TN18 . 17
Springfield Rd.
Bexley,Bexleyheath DA7 ...
Springfield Rd.
Bexley,Welling DA16 ......
Springfield Rd. Bromley BR1 3
Springfield Rd.
Edenbridge TN8 11
Springfield Rd.
Gillingham ME7 4
Springfield Rd.
Groombridge TN3 16
Springfield Rd.
Lunsford ME20 7
Springfield Rd.
Royal Tunbridge Wells
TN4 14
Springfield Way. BR5 3
Springfield Wlk. 3 BR6 3
Springfields. TN5 1
Springhead. TN2 14
Springhead Ent Pk. DA11 .. 2
Springhead Rd. Erith DA8 ...
Springhead Rd.
Northfleet DA11 3
Springrove Cotts. TN12 ... 13
Springshaw Cl. TN13 8
Springvale. ME8 4
Springvale Ct. Eltham SE12 ..
Springvale Ct.
Northfleet DA11 3
Springview Apartments.
TN1 14
Springwater Cl. SE18 ....
Springwell Rd. TN9 13
Springwood Cl. ME16 9
Springwood Rd. ME16 .....
Spruce Cl. ME20 ....
Sprucedale Cl. BR8 ....
Spur Rd. BR6 ....
Spurgeons Cotts. ME14 ... 1(
Spurrell Ave. DA2 & DA5 .. 2
Spurway. ME14 ....
Square Hill. ME15 ....
Square Hill Rd.
ME14 & ME15 ....
Square The. Cowden TN8 .. 1
Square The. Hadlow TN11 . 13
Square The. Newham ME15 13
Square The. Leigh TN11 .. 13
Square The. Lenham ME17 13
Square The. Swanley BR8 .. 3
Square The. Wadhurst TN5 . 1
Squerryes Court. TN16 ....
Squerryes Mede. TN16 .....
Squires Cl. ME2 ....
Squires Field. BR8 ....
Squires House. 3 SE18 .....
Squires Way. DA2 ....
Squires Wood Dr. BR7 .....
Squirrel Way. TN2 ....
Stable Cl. ME5 ....
Stabledene Way. TN9 1
Stables End. BR6 ....
Stace Cl. TN30 ....
Stacey Cl. DA12 ....
Stacey Rd. TN11 ....
Staceys St. ME14 ....
Stack La. DA3 ....
Stack Rd. DA4 ....

ands Cl. TN15 .... 55 E4
m Rd. SE18 & SE7 ...... 5 F8
m Way. DA1 .... 8 E2
Rd. ME15 .... 107 A7
rd Cl. DA9 .... 10 F2
rd Rd.
ll Tunbridge Wells
.... 149 E4
rd Rd.
rd Rd. Sidcup DA14 ..... 23 E4
rd Rd.
ridge TN9 .... 117 B2
rd St. ME7 .... 48 C5
rd Way. TN13 .... 99 C8
ld. Chatham ME5 .... 62 B5
ltd. Royal Tunbridge Wells
.... 149 D8
er House. SE9 .... 5 C3
m Rd. TN10 .... 117 F6
es Wlk. DA14 .... 24 C2
nore Cl. BR7 .... 37 D8
Rd. TN10 .... 117 F4
oot La. TN13 .... 83 C5
La. ME2 .... 60 A6
s Rd. TN15 .... 86 F7
am Ct. ME7 .... 63 B4
Ave. ME5 .... 62 B8
ield Pl. BR6 .... 51 A1
pers The. ME15 .... 91 D2
a. ME18 .... 103 A7
m Rd. TN2 .... 150 E6
ridge Rd. TN8 .... 112 B2
rook Rd.
hfleet DA11 .... 29 F8
rook Rd. Woolwich SE2 3 B4
ard Ind Est. E16 .... 1 F4
ard Rd. Bexley DA6 ..... 7 E3
ard Rd. Erith DA17 ...... 4 A1
ard Rd.
aning Street BR6 .... 51 A1
en Cl. ME8 .... 63 E4
en St.
s Green TN17 & TN18 180 D2
en St. Royal Tunbridge Wells
.... 149 A5
ings Cross. TN12 .... 135 E1
ish House. SE3 .... 5 B3
 Way. SE18 .... 5 E7
ord Dr. ME16 .... 91 C3
ord La. TN11 & TN12 .. 103 C2
ord Way. ME2 .... 46 C2
ard Rd. Birling ME19 ... 74 B8
ate Rd.
hester ME2 .... 46 C7
rove Rd. TN8 .... 112 C1
am Pl. DA1 .... 9 A3
am Rd. DA1 .... 9 C2
ill Cotts. DA2 .... 25 D2
ope Ave. BR2 .... 36 A1
ope Cl. ME14 .... 91 E7
ope Rd. Bexley DA7 ...... 7 E5
ope Rd.
hester 47 A7
ope Rd.
al Tunbridge Wells
.... 149 C5
ope Rd.
ope Rd. Sidcup DA15 ... 24 A4
ope Rd.
anscombe DA10 .... 11 F1
ope Way. TN13 .... 83 D5
ey Cl.
lehurst TN12 .... 139 E4
ey Cl. Stone DA9 .... 10 E2
ey Cotts. DA2 .... 27 E3
ey Cres. DA12 .... 30 D3
ey Rd. Bromley BR2 .... 36 C5
ey Rd. Chatham ME5 .. 62 C6
ey Rd. Gillingham ME7 48 C6
ey Rd. Grays RM17 ..... 12 B8
ey Rd. Marden TN12   138 D5
ey Rd. Orpington BR6 .. 37 F1
ey Rd. Royal Tunbridge Wells
.... 149 B5
ey Rd. Sidcup DA14 ... 24 A5
ey Rd.
anscombe DA10 .... 11 F1
ey Way. BR5 .... 38 B4
nore Rd. DA17 .... 4 C2
sfield Rd. E6 .... 1 D7
sted CE Prim Sch.
.5 .... 56 F1
sted Cl. ME16 .... 91 D7
sted Cres. DA5 .... 24 D7
sted Hill. TN15 .... 57 A1
La. TN15 .... 56 C1
on Cl. BR5 .... 38 C2
on Cl. **5** DA15 .... 24 A5
e Cl. DA5 .... 25 D5
le Dr. TN12 .... 139 F4
leford Ct. TN13 .... 83 F4
ehurst Cty Prim Sch.
.... 139 E3

Staplehurst House. BR5 .. 38 C4
Staplehurst Rd.
Bogden TN12 .... 123 C2
Staplehurst Rd.
Gillingham ME8 .... 49 B3
Staplehurst Sta. TN12 .. 139 E5
Staplers Ct. ME14 .... 92 B8
Stapleton Rd. Erith DA7 .. 7 F8
Stapleton Rd.
Orpington BR6 .... 51 F7
Stapley Rd. DA17 .... 4 A1
Star Bsns Ctr. RM9 .... 4 D8
Star Hill. Crayford DA1 ... 8 E2
Star Hill. Rochester ME1 .. 47 D5
Star La. Gillingham ME7 . 63 A7
Star La. St Paul's Cray BR5 . 38 E5
Star Mill Cl. ME5 .... 48 D2
Star Mill La. ME5 .... 48 D2
Starboard Ave. DA9 ..... 11 B1
Starling Cl. DA3 .... 43 B6
Starnes Ct. **5** ME14 ...... 92 A5
Starr Cotts. TN12 .... 121 C2
Starts Cl. BR6 .... 51 A7
Starts Hill Ave. BR6 ..... 51 B6
Starts Hill Ave. BR6 ..... 51 B6
Starts Hill Rd. BR6 ...... 51 B6
Starvecrow Cl. TN11 .... 117 D8
State Farm Ave. BR6 .... 51 C6
Station App.
Bexley,Barnehurst DA7 . 8 C5
Station App.
Bexley,Bexleyheath DA7 . 7 E5
Station App.
Bexley,Welling DA16 ..... 7 A5
Station App.
Chislehurst BR7 .... 37 A7
Station App.
Chislehurst,Elmstead BR7 . 22 E2
Station App. Dartford DA1 . 9 E1
Station App.
Edenbridge TN8 .... 112 C2
Station App. Grays RM17 12 A8
Station App. Greenwich SE3 . 5 B4
Station App. Halling ME2 . 60 A5
Station App. Hayes BR2 . 36 A1
Station App.
Maidstone ME16 .... 91 F3
Station App. Orpington BR6 . 51 F8
Station App.
Orpington,Chelsfield BR6 . 52 B5
Station App.
Paddock Wood TN12 ... 136 A7
Station App.
St Paul's Cray BR5 .... 38 B5
Station App.
Staplehurst TN12 .... 139 E5
Station App. Swanley BR8 . 39 E5
Station Approach Rd.
RM18 .... 13 A3
Station Cotts.
Gill's Green TN18 .... 178 F5
Station Cotts.
Horsmonden TN12 ...... 153 B5
Station Cres. SE3 .... 1 A1
Station Ct. TN15 .... 86 F7
Station Hill.
Chiddingstone Causeway
TN11 .... 114 F1
Station Hill.
Chiddingstone Causeway
TN11 .... 131 A8
Station Hill. Hayes BR2 .. 50 A8
Station Rd. Aylesford ME20 . 75 E2
Station Rd. Betsham DA13 . 29 A4
Station Rd. Bexley DA7 .... 7 E4
Station Rd.
Borough Green TN15 ..... 86 F7
Station Rd. Brasted TN16 . 82 B4
Station Rd. Bromley BR1 .. 36 A8
Station Rd. Cliffe ME3 ..... 16 B3
Station Rd. Crayford DA1 . 8 F1
Station Rd. Cuxton ME2 .. 46 C2
Station Rd.
Groombridge TN3 .... 161 C7
Station Rd. Halstead TN14 . 67 F8
Station Rd.
Harrietsham ME17 .... 110 D6
Station Rd.
Headcorn TN27 .... 141 D5

Station Rd.
Hurst Green TN19 .... 184 A3
Station Rd. Longfield DA3 . 42 E6
Station Rd. Maidstone ME14 . 91 F5
Station Rd.
Meopham Station DA13 . 44 A4
Station Rd.
Nettlestead Green ME18 . 104 C1
Station Rd. Newington ME9 . 65 B6
Station Rd. Northfleet DA11 . 12 B1
Station Rd. Northiam TN31 . 187 C1
Station Rd. Orpington BR6 . 51 F8
Station Rd. Otford TN14 .... 69 C3
Station Rd.
Paddock Wood TN12 ... 135 F7
Station Rd. Rochester ME2 . 47 C7
Station Rd. Rockrobin TN5 . 174 C6
Station Rd. Sevenoaks TN13 . 83 E7
Station Rd. Shoreham TN14 . 69 A7
Station Rd.
Sidcup DA14 & DA15 ... 24 A5
Station Rd.
St Paul's Cray BR5 .... 38 C5
Station Rd.
Staplehurst TN12 .... 139 F5
Station Rd.
Sutton at Hone DA4 ...... 41 B7
Station Rd. Swanley BR8 .. 39 E5
Station Rd.
Swanscombe DA9 .... 11 A2
Station Rd.
Tenterden TN30 .... 183 A7
Station Rd. Withyham TN7 . 160 B5
Station Rd N. DA17 .... 4 B3
Station Sq. BR5 .... 37 C4
Station St. E16 .... 2 B5
Steadman Cl. ME3 .... 32 C6
Stede Hill. ME17 .... 95 F3
Stedman Cl. DA5 .... 25 E5
Steele Ave. DA9 .... 11 A2
Steele St. ME7 .... 47 A8
Steele's La. DA13 .... 58 A6
Steep Cl. BR6 .... 51 F4
Steerforth Cl. ME1 .... 47 C2
Steers Pl. TN11 .... 102 E2
Stella Cl. TN12 .... 138 D5
Stelling Rd. DA8 .... 8 D7
Stephen Cl. BR6 .... 51 F7
Stephen Rd. DA7 .... 8 C4
Stephen's Rd. TN4 ...... 149 B6
Stephenson Ave. ME18 . 13 A6
Stephenson House. SE2 .. 3 D1
Stepneyford La. TN17 ... 181 C7
Steps Hill Rd. ME9 .... 79 D6
Sterling Ave. ME6 .... 91 C5
Sterling House. SE3 .... 5 B3
Sterndale Rd. DA1 .... 26 F8
Stevanne Ct. **1** DA17 .... 4 A1
Stevedale Rd. DA16 .... 7 C5
Stevens Cl.
Joyden's Wood DA5 ..... 25 D4
Stevens Cl. Lane End DA2 . 27 E5
Stevens Cl. Maidstone ME15 . 91 F3
Stevens Cl. Snodland ME6 . 75 A8
Stevens Rd. ME20 .... 75 F6
Stevenson Cl. DA8 .... 9 B7
Stevenson Way. ME20 ... 74 F4
Stewart Cl. BR7 .... 23 B4
Stewart House. ME3 ...... 33 F6
Stewart Rd. TN4 .... 149 C7
Steyning Gr. SE9 .... 22 F4
Steynton Ave. DA5 .... 24 D6
Stickens La. ME19 .... 89 E7
Stickfast La. TN27 .... 125 D3
Stickland Rd. **2** DA17 ... 4 A2
Stilebridge La.
Underling Green TN12 .. 122 E3
Stilebridge La.
Underling Green ME17 ... 123 A5
Stiles Cl. Bromley BR2 .... 36 F3
Stiles Cl. Erith DA8 .... 4 B1
Still La. TN4 .... 132 F2
Stirling Cl. Gillingham ME8 . 63 E4
Stirling Cl. Rochester ME1 . 47 A3
Stirling Dr. BR6 .... 52 B5
Stirling House. **5** SE18 ... 2 B1
Stisted Way. TN27 .... 127 F3
Stock La. DA2 .... 26 C4
Stockbury Dr. ME16 ...... 91 D7
Stockbury House. **7** BR5 . 38 D1
Stockenbury. TN12 ...... 119 F6
Stockett La. ME15 .... 106 D6
Stockfield. **1** TN8 .... 112 D3
Stockland Green Rd. TN3 . 148 B8
Stocks Green Cty Prim Sch.
TN11 .... 116 E5
Stocks Green Rd. TN11 . 116 C5
Stocks Rd. TN30 .... 189 F3
Stockton Cl. ME14 .... 92 B8
Stockwell Cl. BR1 .... 36 B7
Stofield Gdns. SE9 .... 22 D5

Stoke Cty Prim Sch. ME3 . 19 C5
Stoke Rd. Allhallows ME3 . 19 C7
Stoke Rd.
Hoo St Werburgh ME3 ... 34 F6
Stoke Rd. Kingsnorth ME3 . 35 C8
Stoke Rd. Stoke ME3 ..... 19 C5
Stone CE Prim Sch. DA2 . 27 E8
Stone Cotts. TN3 .... 165 F4
Stone Court La. TN2 ..... 150 E8
Stone Cross Rd. TN5 ... 175 A4
Stone Crossing Halt. DA9 . 10 E2
Stone Ct. DA8 .... 4 F1
Stone Hill Rd. TN27 ..... 127 F2
Stone House Hospl. DA2 . 10 C1
Stone Lodge Farm Park.
DA2 .... 10 D1
Stone Pit La. TN18 ...... 186 E5
Stone Place Rd. DA9 ..... 10 E2
Stone Rd. BR2 .... 36 A5
Stone Row. TN5 .... 147 B5
Stone Row Cotts. TN3 .. 147 D1
Stone St. Cranbrook TN17 . 169 D5
Stone St. Gravesend DA11 . 13 B1
Stone St. Royal Tunbridge Wells
TN1 .... 149 B4
Stone Street Rd. TN15 .. 85 E2
Stone Wood. DA2 .... 28 C5
Stoneacre Cl. ME8 .... 63 D5
Stoneacre La. ME15 .... 108 B7
Stoneacre (NT). ME15 .. 108 B7
Stonebridge Green Rd.
TN27 .... 127 F4
Stonebridge Rd. DA11 .. 12 B2
Stonechat Sq. **6** E6 .... 1 E8
Stonecroft Rd. DA8 .... 8 E7
Stonecroft Rd. DA8 .... 8 C7
Stonecross La. ME8 ..... 48 C1
Stonefield Cl. DA7 .... 8 A4
Stonefield Way. SE7 ...... 5 D7
Stonegate Cl. BR5 .... 38 C6
Stonegate Rd. TN5 ...... 175 C1
Stonehorse La. ME3 ...... 33 A2
Stonehouse Cnr. RM16 .. 10 E8
Stonehouse La.
Pratt's Bottom BR6 & TN14 . 52 E1
Stonehouse La.
Purfleet RM16 .... 10 D8
Stonehouse Rd. BR6 ..... 52 D1
Stoneings La. TN14 .... 81 F8
Stoneness Rd. RM16 ..... 11 C7
Stones Cross Rd. BR9 ... 39 C4
Stonestile Rd. TN27 .... 141 A7
Stonewall. E6 .... 2 A8
Stonewall Park Rd. TN3 . 147 E3
Stonewood Rd. DA8 .... 4 E1
Stoney Alley. SE18 .... 6 A5
Stoney Bank. ME7 .... 48 F1
Stony Cnr. DA3 .... 43 E6
Stony La. ME5 .... 61 C5
Stonyfield. TN8 .... 112 D3
Stopford Rd. ME7 .... 48 D4
Storehouse Wharf. ME12 . 21 F3
Storey Prim Sch. E16 ..... 2 B5
Storey St. E16 .... 2 A4
Stornaway Strand. DA12 . 30 F4
Stour Cl. Keston BR2 .... 50 C6
Stour Cl. Rochester ME2 . 46 F7
Stour Cl. Tonbridge TN10 . 117 B5
Stour Ct. **22** BR5 .... 38 D1
Stour House. **4** ME15 ... 107 D8
Stour Rd. DA1 .... 9 A4
Stowe Rd. BR6 .... 52 B6
Stowting Rd. BR6 .... 51 E6
Strait Rd. E6 .... 1 F6
Strand Approach Rd. ME7 . 48 F7
Strand Cl. DA13 .... 44 A3
Strandfield Cl. SE18 ...... 2 E1
Stratfield House. SE12 ... 22 A6
Stratford Ave. ME8 .... 63 D8
Stratford House Ave. BR1 . 36 E6
Stratford La. ME8 .... 63 F8
Stratford Rd. ME19 .... 89 A8
Strathford St. TN1 .... 149 C5
Strathaven Rd. SE12 ..... 5 B1
Stratheden Par. SE3 .... 5 A7
Stratheden Rd. SE3 .... 5 A7
Stratton Cl. DA7 .... 7 E4
Stratton Rd. DA7 .... 7 E4
Stratton Terr. TN16 ...... 96 C8
Straw Mill Hill. ME15 .... 91 E1
Strawberry Cl. TN2 ...... 162 E7
Strawberry Fields. BR8 ... 39 E7
Strawberry Vale. TN9 ... 117 C1
Stream La. TN18 .... 185 A7
Stream Lane Cotts. TN18 . 185 A7
Stream Pit La. TN18 ..... 186 B6
Stream Side. TN10 .... 117 D6
Stream The. ME19 .... 75 C1
Stream Way. DA17 .... 8 A8
Streamdale. SE2 .... 7 B8

Streamside. ME19 .... 75 B1
Streamside Cl. BR2 .... 36 A5
Streatfield. TN8 .... 112 D1
Street End Rd. ME5 ...... 48 B1
Street Farm Cotts. ME3 . 34 F6
Street The. Ash TN15 .... 56 E5
Street The.
Benenden TN17 .... 180 D6
Street The. Boxley ME14 . 77 C3
Street The. Bredhurst ME7 . 62 B3
Street The. Cobham DA12 . 44 F6
Street The. Detling ME14 . 78 A1
Street The. Egerton TN27 . 127 F3
Street The. Fenn Street ME3 . 18 A3
Street The. Hartlip ME9 .. 64 D5
Street The.
High Halstow ME23 .... 17 E3
Street The.
Horton Kirby DA4 .... 41 C5
Street The. Ightham TN15 . 86 D6
Street The. Maidstone ME14 . 93 C4
Street The. Meopham DA13 . 44 A1
Street The.
Mereworth ME18 .... 103 D8
Street The. Plaxtol TN15 . 101 F7
Street The. Ryarsh ME19 . 73 F4
Street The. Shorne ME3 .. 31 E3
Street The.
Silver Street ME9 .... 80 F5
Street The.
Sissinghurst TN17 .... 170 B8
Street The. Teston ME18 . 105 A7
Street The.
Trottiscliffe ME19 .... 73 A5
Street The. Ulcombe ME17 . 125 F7
Street The.
Upper Halling ME2 .... 59 E5
Street The.
Wittersham TN30 .... 189 D3
Street The. Wormshill ME9 . 95 F7
Streetfield. ME17 .... 125 F7
Streetfield Mews. SE3 ..... 5 A4
Streetfield Rd. ME8 .... 49 F1
Strettitt Gdns. TN12 .... 119 F5
Strickland Ave. DA1 .... 9 F4
Strickland Way. **4** BR6 .. 51 F6
Strongbow Cres. SE9 ..... 5 F2
Strongbow Rd. SE9 .... 5 F2
Strood Sta. ME2 .... 47 C7
Strover St. ME7 .... 48 C7
Strumer Ct. ME18 .... 99 B2
Struttons Ave. DA11 ...... 29 F6
Stuart Ave. BR2 .... 36 A1
Stuart Cl. Hextable BR8 .. 26 A1
Stuart Cl. Maidstone ME14 . 92 C6
Stuart Cl. Royal Tunbridge Wells
TN2 .... 162 F8
Stuart Evans Cl. DA16 ..... 7 C4
Stuart Mantle Way. DA8 .. 8 E7
Stuart Rd. Bexley DA16 ... 7 B6
Stuart Rd. Gillingham ME7 . 48 D3
Stuart Rd. Gravesend DA11 . 13 A1
Stuart Rd. Royal Tunbridge Wells
TN2 .... 149 D5
Stubbs Cl. ME8 & TN14 .. 67 C6
Stubbygrove Cotts. TN3 . 163 E4
Stubblefield. Cl. DA15 .... 23 F5
Studley Cres. DA3 .... 43 C7
Studley Cl. DA14 .... 24 B3
Stumble Hill. TN11 ...... 101 C5
Sturdee Ave. ME7 .... 48 E4
Sturdee Cotts. ME3 .... 35 A6
Sturges Field. BR7 .... 23 D2
Sturla Rd. ME4 .... 48 A3
Sturry Way. ME8 .... 49 C2
Styants Bottom Rd. TN15 . 85 F5
Style Cl. ME8 .... 63 E4
Styles Cl. TN8 .... 113 B5
Styles Cotts. TN8 .... 113 B5
Sudbury. E6 .... 2 A7
Sudbury Cres. BR1 .... 22 A3
Suffolk Ave. ME8 .... 49 F1
Suffolk Rd. Dartford DA1 . 9 E1
Suffolk Rd. Gravesend DA12 . 13 D1
Suffolk Rd.
Maidstone ME15 .... 107 D8
Suffolk Rd. Sidcup DA14 . 24 C2
Suffolk Way. TN13 & TN15 . 84 C2
Sullivan Ave. E16 .... 1 D8
Sullivan Cl. DA1 .... 26 C8
Sullivan Rd. Tilbury RM18 . 13 A6
Sullivan Rd.
Tonbridge TN10 .... 117 E5
Sultan Rd. ME5 .... 62 C2
Summer Cl. TN30 .... 173 C1
Summer Hill. BR7 .... 37 A7
Summerfield. **6**
Bromley BR1 .... 36 B8
Summerfield.
Winchet Hill TN17 .... 154 B6

Summerfield St. SE12 .... 22 A8
Summerhill. TN27 .... 141 A6
Summerhill Ave. TN4 .... 132 F1
Summerhill Cl. BR6 .... 51 E7
Summerhill Rd.
Bogden TN12 .... 123 C1
Summerhill Rd.
Dartford DA1 .... 26 D8
Summerhouse Dr.
DA2 & DA5 .... 25 D4
Summerlands Lodge. BR6 .. 51 A6
Summerton Way. SE28 ...... 3 D7
Summervale Rd.
TN2 & TN4 .... 148 E1
Sumner Cl. Orpington BR6 ... 51 C6
Sumner Cl.
Rolvenden TN17 .... 181 F3
Sun Ct. DA8 .... 8 F5
Sun Hill. DA3 .... 56 A8
Sun La. Gravesend DA12 .... 30 C6
Sun La. Greenwich SE3 ...... 5 B7
Sun Rd. DA10 .... 11 F1
Sun Terr. ME5 .... 62 B4
Sunburst Cl. TN12 .... 138 D5
Sunbury St. SE18 .... 1 F3
Sunderland Cl. ME1 .... 47 A3
Sunderland Dr. ME8 .... 62 A4
Sunderland House. 2
ME7 .... 48 C7
Sundew Ct. 6 RM17 ...... 12 D8
Sundorne Rd. SE7 .... 1 C1
Sundridge Ave. Bexley DA6 6 D4
Sundridge Ave.
Bromley BR1 & BR7 ...... 22 E1
Sundridge & Brasted
CE Prim Sch. TN14 ...... 82 E2
Sundridge Cl. DA1 .... 10 A1
Sundridge Dr. ME5 .... 62 A4
Sundridge Hill. Cuxton ME2 . 46 C3
Sundridge Hill.
Knockholt TN14 .... 67 C1
Sundridge Hospl. TN14 ...... 97 E8
Sundridge La. TN14 .... 67 C2
Sundridge Park Golf Course.
BR1 .... 22 C2
Sundridge Park Sta. BR1 .... 22 B1
Sundridge Rd. TN14 ...... 83 B8
Sunfields Pl. SE3 .... 5 B7
Sunhill Ct. TN2 .... 150 C6
Sunland Ave. DA6 .... 7 E3
Sunningdale Cl. ME8 ...... 63 D6
Sunningdale Cl. ME15 .... 92 B4
Sunningdale Dr. ME8 ...... 63 D6
Sunningdale Rd.
BR1 & BR2 .... 36 E4
Sunninghill. DA11 .... 29 E6
Sunnybank. TN5 & TN19 ... 177 E3
Sunnydale. BR6 .... 51 A8
Sunnydale Rd. ME15 ...... 93 A2
Sunnyfield Rd. BR5 & BR7 .. 38 A6
Sunnyfields Cl. ME8 ...... 63 A8
Sunnymead Ave. ME7 ...... 48 E5
Sunnyside. TN8 .... 112 B3
Sunnyside Rd. TN4 ...... 148 C4
Sunray Ave. BR2 .... 36 F3
Sunrise Ind Pre-Prep Sch.
ME17 .... 108 D4
Sunset Cl. DA8 .... 9 B7
Sunset Rd. SE28 .... 3 A5
Superabbey Ent ME20 ...... 76 B2
Superior Dr. 4 BR6 ...... 51 F4
Surgeon's Gn. SE28 ...... 3 D6
Surrenden Rd. TN12 ...... 139 C3
Surrey Cl. TN2 .... 162 F8
Surrey Rd. ME15 .... 107 D8
Susan Rd. SE3 .... 5 B5
Susan Wood. ME7 ...... 37 A8
Sussex Cl. TN2 .... 149 C1
Sussex Dr. ME5 .... 62 A4
Sussex Mews. 16 TN2 ..... 149 A2
Sussex Rd. Dartford DA1 .... 27 A8
Sussex Rd. Erith DA8 ...... 4 E7
Sussex Rd.
Maidstone ME15 .... 107 D8
Sussex Rd. Orpington BR5 ... 38 C3
Sussex Rd. Sidcup DA14 .... 24 B3
Sussex Rd. Tonbridge TN9 . 133 A8
Sussex Road Cty Prim Sch.
TN9 .... 133 A8
Sutcliffe Rd. Bexley DA16 .... 7 C5
Sutcliffe Rd. Woolwich SE18 .. 6 E8
Sutherland Ave. Bexley DA16 6 E3
Sutherland Ave.
Orpington BR5 .... 37 F4
Sutherland Cl. DA12 ...... 30 B6
Sutherland Gdns. ME8 .... 63 E6
Sutherland House. SE18 .... 5 F6
Sutherland Rd. Erith DA17 .. 4 A3
Sutherland Rd.
Royal Tunbridge Wells
TN1 & TN2 .... 149 B3
Sutlej Rd. SE7 .... 5 C7
Sutton at Hone CE Prim Sch.
DA4 .... 27 A1
Sutton Cl. ME8 .... 64 A8
Sutton Cl. TN12 .... 138 C5
Sutton Forge. TN12 ...... 138 C5
Sutton Rd. Langley ME17 .. 108 C5
Sutton Rd.
Maidstone ME15 .... 107 D6
Sutton St. ME14 .... 93 D4
Sutton Valence Cty Prim Sch.
ME17 .... 124 E7
Sutton Valence Sch.
ME17 .... 124 E7
Swadelands Cl. ME17 .... 111 C5
Swadelands Sch. ME17 .... 111 C5
Swaffield Rd. TN13 ...... 84 C5
Swain Cl. ME2 .... 46 F8
Swain Rd. Gillingham ME8 .. 63 B6
Swain Rd.
St Michaels TN30 .... 173 D3
Swaisland Rd. DA1 .... 9 B1
Swaislands Dr. DA1 ...... 8 F2
Swale House. 1 ME15 ... 107 E7
Swale Rd. Crayford DA1 ...... 9 A3
Swale Rd. Rochester ME2 .. 46 C7
Swaledale Rd. DA2 ...... 27 C7
Swallow Cl. Erith DA7 ...... 8 A6
Swallow Cl. Stone DA9 .... 10 F2
Swallow Cl. 3 SE12 ...... 22 A8
Swallow Dr. TN2 .... 149 F6
Swallow House. 4 ME16 .. 91 E4
Swallow Rd. ME20 ...... 74 F2
Swallow Rise. ME5 ...... 62 A5
Swallow St. E6 .... 1 E8
Swallowfield Rd. SE7 ...... 1 B1
Swallowfields. 2 DA11 .... 29 E5
Swan Apartments. 10
ME15 .... 107 E5
Swan App. E6 .... 1 E8
Swan Bsns Pk. DA1 ...... 9 C3
Swan Cl. BR5 .... 38 A6
Swan Cotts. TN30 .... 189 D4
Swan La. Brandfold TN17 .. 153 F3
Swan La. Dartford DA1 .... 25 F8
Swan La. Marlpit Hill TN8 .. 112 C4
Swan Rd. SE18 .... 2 C2
Swan Ridge. TN8 .... 112 D4
Swan St. West Malling ME19 89 C8
Swan St. Wittersham TN30 . 189 C3
Swanbridge Rd. DA7 ...... 8 B6
Swanland Dr. TN2 ...... 132 F7
Swanley Ctr. BR8 ...... 39 F6
Swanley La. BR8 .... 39 F6
Swanley Rd. DA16 ...... 7 C6
Swanley Sch. BR8 ...... 39 E6
Swanley Sta. BR8 .... 39 F5
Swanley Village Rd. BR8 .... 40 B8
Swanmead Way. TN9 .... 117 D2
Swanscombe Bsns Ctr.
DA10 .... 11 E2
Swanscombe Cty Inf Sch.
DA10 .... 11 F1
Swanscombe House. 1
BR5 .... 38 B7
Swanscombe Sta. DA10 .. 11 F1
Swanscombe Sta. DA10 ... 11 B7
Swanton Rd. Erith DA8 .... 8 B7
Swanton Rd.
Swanton ME18 .... 103 A8
Swanzy Rd. TN14 ...... 84 C7
Sward Rd. BR5 .... 38 A3
Swattenden La. TN17 .... 169 B1
Swaylands Rd. DA17 ...... 8 A8
Sweeps Hill Cl. TN2 ...... 150 D7
Sweeps La. BR5 .... 38 B5
Sweetings La. TN3 & TN5 . 165 D1
Sweets La. ME19 .... 90 A4
Swetenham Wlk. SE18 ...... 2 C1
Sweyn Pl. SE3 .... 5 A5
Sweyne Cty Prim Jun Sch The.
DA10 .... 28 F8
Sweyne Rd. DA10 .... 11 E1
Swift Cl. ME20 .... 75 A2
Swift Cres. ME5 .... 62 C6
Swift House. 6 ME14 .... 91 E4
Swift's Cl. TN15 .... 85 A6
Swifts View. TN17 ...... 169 D6
Swiller's La. DA12 .... 31 E3
Swinburne Gdns. RM18 .... 13 B5
Swingate Ave. ME3 ...... 16 B6
Swingate Cl. ME5 .... 62 B2
Swingate Cty Inf Sch. ME5 . 62 C1
Swingate La. SE18 .... 6 E7
Swinton Ave. ME3 ...... 33 F5
Swires Shaw. BR2 .... 50 D6
Swithland Gdns. SE9 ...... 23 A4
Sycamor Ct. DA8 .... 4 D1
Sycamore Ave. DA15 ...... 6 F1
Sycamore Cl. Eltham SE9 .... 22 E6
Sycamore Cl.
Gravesend DA12 .... 30 D8
Sycamore Cl. Tilbury RM18 .. 13 A5
Sycamore Cotts. TN12 .... 150 C6
Sycamore Cres. ME16 ...... 91 C5
Sycamore Ct. DA2 ...... 27 E8
Sycamore Dr.
Aylesford ME20 .... 75 E1
Sycamore Dr. Swanley BR8 . 39 E7
Sycamore Gdns. TN12 .... 135 F5
Sycamore Lodge. BR6 .... 52 A8
Sycamore Rd. Dartford DA1 26 D7
Sycamore Rd.
Rochester ME2 .... 46 E5
Sychem La. TN11 & TN12 .. 135 A6
Sychem Pl. TN12 .... 135 A7
Sydney Rd. Bexley DA6 ...... 7 D3
Sydney Rd. Chatham ME4 .. 48 A3
Sydney Rd. Erith SE2 ...... 3 D3
Sydney Rd. Sidcup DA14 .... 23 D4
Sydney Rd. Tilbury RM18 .. 13 A5
Sydney St. SE18 .... 2 C3
Sydney Terr. TN18 .... 178 F3
Sylewood Cl. ME1 ...... 61 B8
Sylvan Glade. ME5 ...... 77 A8
Sylvan Rd. ME8 .... 63 C8
Sylvan Wlk. BR1 .... 36 F6
Sylvester Ave. BR7 ...... 22 F2
Sylvestre Cl. ME2 ...... 60 A4
Sylvestres. TN13 .... 83 E6
Symonds Cl. TN15 ...... 55 E5
Symonds Rd. ME8 ...... 120 F6
Symonds Rd. ME3 ...... 34 A4
Syon Ave. ME4 .... 48 A2
Syon Lodge. 9 SE12 ...... 22 A8
Syringa Ct. 9 RM17 ...... 12 D8
Tabor Ct. TN12 .... 153 A6
Tadburn Gn. ME5 .... 62 A4
Taddington Wood La. ME5 . 61 E2
Tadley Ct. ME7 .... 48 F6
Tail Race The. ME15 ...... 91 E2
Tainter Rd. TN11 .... 102 E1
Talbot Pk. TN2 .... 149 D5
Talbot Rd. Maidstone ME16 . 91 C6
Talbot Rd. The Moor TN18 . 184 F8
Tall Trees Cl. ME17 ...... 109 D2
Tallents Cl. DA4 .... 27 B1
Tallis Cl. E16 .... 1 B7
Tallis Gr. SE7 .... 5 B8
Tamar House. 4 ME15 .... 107 E8
Tamar Rd. TN10 .... 117 B5
Tamar St. SE7 .... 1 D2
Tamarind Cl. ME7 ...... 63 A4
Tamesis Strand. DA12 .... 30 E3
Tan Yard La. DA5 .... 25 A8
Tandridge Dr. BR5 & BR6 .. 37 D1
Tandridge Pl. 2 BR6 ...... 37 D1
Tangier La. TN3 .... 163 B6
Tangleberry Cl. BR1 ...... 36 F5
Tanglewood Cl. ME8 ...... 63 C6
Tanglewood Ct. BR5 ...... 38 C6
Tangmere Cl. ME7 ...... 48 F5
Tanker Hill. ME8 .... 63 D6
Tanners Mead. TN8 ...... 112 C1
Tannery Rd. TN9 .... 117 C1
Tansy Cl. E6 .... 2 A7
Tanyard. Rolvenden TN17 .. 181 E4
Tanyard. Sandhurst TN18 .. 186 B5
Tanyard Cotts. DA12 ...... 31 E1
Tanyard Hill. DA12 ...... 31 E2
Tanyard La. TN4 .... 132 F1
Tanyard The. TN7 .... 169 D4
Tapsell's La. TN5 ...... 174 D5
Tarbutts. TN17 .... 169 D4
Target Bsns Ctr. ME15 .... 107 F4
Tarling Cl. DA14 .... 24 B5
Tarnwood Pk. SE9 .... 22 F7
Tasker Cl. ME15 .... 93 B3
Tasman Wlk. E16 .... 1 D7
Tasmania House. RM18 .... 13 A6
Tate Rd. E16 .... 1 F5
Tates Orch. DA3 .... 42 F3
Tatler Cl. ME5 .... 62 D2
Tatsfield Cl. ME8 ...... 49 A2
Tatsfield La. TN16 ...... 81 A6
Tattersall Cl. SE9 ...... 5 E2
Tattlebury La. TN17 ...... 153 F1
Tattlebury Rd. TN27 ...... 141 C8
Taunton Cl. Bexley DA7 .... 8 D5
Taunton Cl.
Maidstone ME15 .... 107 F6
Taunton Rd. DA11 ...... 12 A2
Taunton Vale. DA12 ...... 30 D5
Tavern Cl. TN15 .... 86 F7
Tavern Cotts. TN15 ...... 85 A3
Taverners Rd. ME8 ...... 63 E7
Tavistock Cl. Chatham ME5 . 61 F1
Tavistock Cl.
Gillingham ME8 .... 63 E7
Tavistock Rd. Bexley DA16 .. 7 C5
Tavistock Rd. 2
Bromley BR2 .... 36 A5
Tavy Bridge. SE2 .... 3 C4
Tawney Rd. SE28 .... 3 B6
Tay Cl. ME5 .... 62 B5
Taylor Cl. 3 BR6 ...... 51 F6
Taylor Rd. ME6 .... 74 F8
Taylor St. TN1 .... 149 A8
Taylor's Bldgs. SE18 ...... 2 B2
Taylor's La.
Lower Higham ME3 ...... 32 B5
Taylor's La. Rochester ME2 . 47 B7
Taylors Cl. DA14 .... 23 F4
Taylors La. ME19 ...... 72 F6
Tea Garden La.
TN4 .... 148 C2
Teal Cl. Grain ME3 ...... 21 B5
Teal Cl. Newham E16 ...... 1 D8
Teapot La. ME20 .... 75 E1
Teasaucer Hill. ME15 ...... 106 F8
Teasel Cl. ME14 .... 92 F4
Teasel Rd. ME5 .... 61 F4
Teasels. TN27 .... 158 A1
Tebbs Way. TN15 ...... 86 C3
Ted Williams Ct. 6 SE18 .... 1 F2
Tedder Ave. ME5 .... 62 A7
Tedder Rd. TN4 .... 149 B7
Tedham La. TN27 ...... 155 C7
Tees House. 9 ME5 ..... 107 E7
Teesdale Rd. DA2 ...... 27 C7
Teeswater Ct. SE2 .... 3 D3
Teignmouth Rd. DA16 ...... 7 C5
Telegraph Hill. ME4 ...... 48 A2
Telemann Sq. SE3 ...... 5 B4
Telford House. 2 Erith DA17 4 A3
Telford House. 1
Maidstone ME14 .... 92 A6
Telford Rd. BR7 .... 23 D6
Tellson Ave. SE18 ...... 5 E6
Telscombe Cl. BR6 ...... 51 E8
Telston La. TN13 & TN14 .. 68 F2
Tempest Rd. ME19 ...... 88 F3
Templar Dr. Erith SE28 ...... 3 D7
Templar Dr.
Gravesend DA11 .... 30 A3
Templars St. 11 TN8 ..... 112 D3
Temple Cl. SE18 .... 6 A7
Temple Gdns. ME2 ...... 47 A6
Temple Hill. DA1 .... 9 F2
Temple Hill Cty Prim Inf Sch.
DA1 .... 10 A2
Temple Hill Cty Prim Jun Sch.
DA1 .... 9 F2
Temple Hill Sq. DA1 ...... 9 F2
Temple Sch. ME2 ...... 33 B2
Temple Way. ME19 ...... 74 F1
Templemore. DA14 ...... 24 B3
Tenby Rd. DA16 .... 7 D6
Tenney House. RM17 ...... 12 B7
Tennyson Ave. ME3 ...... 33 B7
Tennyson Cl. DA16 ...... 6 F6
Tennyson House. 2 DA17 .. 3 F1
Tennyson Rd. Dartford DA1 . 10 A2
Tennyson Rd.
Gillingham ME7 .... 48 C3
Tennyson Wlk.
Northfleet DA11 .... 29 D5
Tennyson Wlk.
Tilbury RM18 .... 13 B5
Tensing Ave. DA11 ...... 29 E5
Tenterden CE Jun Sch.
TN30 .... 183 B7
Tenterden Cl. SE9 ...... 22 F4
Tenterden Cty Inf Sch.
TN30 .... 183 B7
Tenterden Rd.
Biddenden TN27 .... 172 B7
Tenterden Rd.
Chatham ME5 .... 62 B5
Tenterden Rd.
Parkgate TN27 .... 171 F4
Tenterden Rd.
Strood TN17 .... 182 A5
Tenterden Town Sta.
TN30 .... 183 A8
Tenzing Ct. SE9 .... 22 E6
Terence Cl. Chatham ME4 .. 48 A2
Terence Cl. Gravesend DA12 30 F6
Terence Ct. 6 DA17 ...... 7 F8
Terminus Rd. ME16 ...... 91 A2
Tern Cres. ME2 .... 46 C6
Terrace Rd. ME16 ...... 91 E3
Terrace St. DA11 .... 13 B1
Terrace The. Chatham ME4 .. 47 F7
Terrace The. 22
Gravesend DA11 .... 13 B1
Terrace The.
Gravesend DA11 .... 13 C1
Terrace The. Rochester ME1 4
Terrace The.
Sevenoaks TN13 8
Terraces The. DA2 2
Terry Wlk. ME20 7
Terry's Lodge Rd. TN15 7
Teston House. ME18 10
Teston La. ME15 & ME18 .. 10
Teston Rd. Kings Hill ME19 .. 8
Teston Rd.
Offham TN15 & ME19 8
Teston Rd. Red Hill ME19 8
Teston Rd.
St Leonard's Street ME19 .. 8
Tetty Way. BR1 & BR2 3
Teviot Cl. DA16 ....
Tewson Rd. SE18 ....
Teynham Gn.
Gillingham ME8 ....
Teynham Gn. Hayes BR2 3
Teynham House. SE9 ....
Thackeray Ave. RM18 ....
Thackeray Rd. ME20 ....
Thames Ave.
Gillingham ME8 6
Thames Ave.
High Halstow ME23 1
Thames Barrier Visitor Ctr.
SE18 ....
Thames Gate. DA1 ....
Thames House. 3 ME15 . 10
Thames Rd. Crayford DA1 ....
Thames Rd. Grays RM17 1
Thames Rd. Newham E16 .. 1
Thames Rd.
Tonbridge TN10 11
Thames Road Ind Est. E16 .. 1
Thames Terr. ME3 ....
Thames View. ME3 3
Thames View Cotts. ME3 3
Thames View Cty Inf Sch.
ME8 ....
Thames View Cty Prim Sch (...
ME8 4
Thames Way.
Gravesend DA11 ....
Thames Way.
Northfleet DA11 2
Thamesbank Pl. SE28 ....
Thameside Cty Jun Sch.
RM17 ....
Thameside Ind Est. E16 ....
Thamesmere Dr. SE28 ....
Thamesview Sch. DA12 3
Thanet Dr. BR2 5
Thanet House. 6 DA11 2
Thanet Rd. Erith DA8 ....
Thanet Rd. Sidcup DA5 2
Thanington Ct. SE7 ....
Thatch Barn Rd. TN27 14
Thatcher Cl. DA1 ....
Thatcher Rd. TN12 13
Thatchers La. ME3 1
Thatchers The. ME19 ....
Thaxted Rd. SE9 ....
Theatre Sq. 5 TN30 18
Thelma Cl. DA12 ....
Thelma Gdns. SE18 ....
Theobalds. TN18 17
Theobalds Cl. TN15 ....
Theodore Cl. TN2 14
Theodore Pl. ME7 ....
Thicketts. TN13 8
Third Ave.
Chatham ME4 & ME5 4
Third Ave. Gillingham ME7 .. 4
Third Ave.
West Thurrock RM16 1
Third St. TN3 14
Thirlmere Cl.
Gillingham ME7 ....
Thirlmere Cl.
Rochester ME2 3
Thirlmere Rd. Bexley DA7 ....
Thirlmere Rd.
Royal Tunbridge Wells
TN4 14
Thirza Rd. DA1 ....
Thistle Cl. DA1 ....
Thistle Rd. DA12 3
Thistlebank. ME5 6
Thistlebrook. SE2 ....
Thistledown.
Gravesend DA12 3
Thistledown.
Maidstone ME14 9
Thistlemead. ME7 6
Thistlemead. BR7 3
Thomas Aveling Sch The.
ME1 ....
Thomas Cotts. DA13 2

...nas Dinwiddy Rd.
... . 22 B6
...nas Dr. DA12 .... 30 D6
...nas St. Rochester ME1 ... 47 C3
...nas St. Royal Tunbridge Wells
... . 149 A5
...nas St. Woolwich SE18 ... 2 B2
...nas Tallis Sch. SE3 .... 5 B4
...nas Wyatt Way. TN15 ... 71 F3
...mpson Cl. ME8 .... 64 A8
...nson Cl. ME6 .... 60 A1
...g La. Basted TN15 .... 86 F5
...g La. Tonbridge DA12 .... 31 A2
...n Cl. Bromley BR2 .... 37 A3
...n Cl. Chatham ME5 .... 61 D1
...n Rd. TN12 .... 138 E4
...n's Meadow. TN16 .... 82 C4
...ndale Cl. ME5 .... 61 D4
...nden Ct. TN17 .... 188 A8
...nden La. TN17 .... 182 A1
...ndike Cl. ME4 .... 61 F8
...ndon Cl. BR5 .... 37 F7
...ndon Rd. BR5 .... 37 F7
...ndyke Way. TN15 .... 71 F3
...ne Cl. Erith DA8 .... 8 B8
...ne Cl. Newham E16 .... 1 A7
...net Wood Rd. RE1 .... 37 A6
...ney Croft Cl. ME17 .... 109 D2
...mfield Gdns. TN2 .... 149 F5
...nham Rd. ME8 .... 49 C3
...nhall Ave. SE18 .... 6 E7
...nhill Pl. ME14 .... 92 A6
...nton Rd. Bromley BR1 .. 22 A3
...nton Rd. Erith DA17 .... 4 B2
...ntree Inf Sch. SE7 .... 1 B1
...ntree Rd. SE7 .... 1 D1
...old Rd. ME4 .... 48 B3
...pe Ave. TN10 .... 117 C5
...pe Cl. BR6 .... 51 E8
...pe Wlk. ME8 .... 63 D3
...pe Works. TN4 .... 148 F8
...e Way. ME8 .... 63 E4
...e Corners. DA7 .... 8 B5
...e Elm La.
... 0 & TN11 .... 118 D5
...e Gates Rd. DA3 .... 42 A2
...e Oaks La. TN5 .... 174 D7
...sher Field. TN8 .... 130 A6
...shers Dr. ME14 .... 92 E5
...e The. DA2 .... 28 C5
...ckmorten Rd. E16 .... 1 B7
...wley Cl. SE2 .... 3 C3
...ush Cl. ME5 .... 62 B7
...stone CR. ME14 .... 91 F6
...arte Cl. DA8 .... 8 C8
...ort Cl. BR6 .... 51 C6
...s Court La. TN12 .... 152 A7
...hurst Cl. BR5 .... 24 A1
...borne Cl. ME16 .... 91 C6
...ord Cl. SE2 .... 3 C4
...Basin Rd. E16 .... 1 A6
...brook Cl. BR5 .... 38 C5
...way The. ME1 .... 61 C8
...ord Rd. DA16 .... 6 F5
...e La. BR2 .... 36 B5
...ook Rd. SE3 & SE9 .... 5 D4
...ry Gdns. RM18 .... 13 A3
...ary Manor Cty Jun Sch.
...8 .... 13 B7
...ary Town Sta. RM18 ..... 12 F5
...rt Cl. TN26 .... 173 D7
...n Gill Rd. TN30 .... 183 C7
...en La. TN12 .... 122 C3
...n Rd. TN27 .... 125 E2
...Farm Rd. BR6 .... 51 D7
...Fields. ME17 .... 94 D2
...Kiln La. Coldblow DA5 .. 25 C6
...Kiln La. Joyden's Wood
...3 & DA5 .... 25 F5
...arn Cnr. TN10 .... 117 E4
...hurst Point. 2 SE2 .... 3 C4
...man Way. ME14 .... 60 B1
...Ave. DA4 .... 40 F2
...gbourne Gn. BR5 .... 38 A5
...ans Mead. DA4 .... 41 A2
...en La. TN17 .... 169 E3
...Vard App. SE9 .... 5 F1
...Rd. TN15 .... 86 F7
...er Bank. DA13 .... 72 F8

Timber Cl. BR7 .... 37 A7
Timber Tops. ME14 .... 77 D8
Timberbank. ME5 .... 62 A6
Timbercroft Jun Sch. SE18 .. 6 E7
Timbercroft La. SE18 .... 6 E7
Timothy Cl. DA6 .... 7 E3
Timothy House. DA18 .... 3 E4
Tinker Pot La. TN15 .... 70 D6
Tinkerpot Rise. TN15 .... 70 C5
Tinkers La. TN5 .... 176 E3
Tintagel Gdns. ME2 .... 46 F7
Tintagel Manor. ME7 .... 48 C6
Tintagel Rd. BR5 .... 38 C1
Tintern Rd. ME16 .... 91 D7
Tippens Cl. TN17 .... 169 D4
Titan Rd. RM17 .... 12 B8
Titchfield Cl. 5 ME15 ...... 107 F6
Titchfield Rd. ME15 .... 107 F6
Tithe Yd. ME17 .... 111 D5
Titmuss Ave. SE28 .... 3 B6
Tiverton Dr. SE9 .... 23 C7
Tivoli Gdns.
...Gravesend DA11 .... 30 B7
Tivoli Gdns. 3 .... 1 E2
Woolwich SE7 .... 1 E2
Tobruk Way. ME5 .... 61 F6
Toby Gdns. TN11 .... 118 E8
Toddington Cres. ME5 .... 61 D1
Tolcairn Ct. 2 DA7 .... 4 A1
Tolgate La. ME2 .... 47 B7
Tolgate Way. ME14 .... 76 E4
Tolhurst Rd. TN12 .... 135 A7
Tollgate Pl. TN27 .... 141 E5
Tollgate Rd. Dartford DA2 .. 27 D8
Tollgate Rd. Newham E6 ..... 1 E8
Tolsey Mead. TN15 .... 87 A8
Tom Coombs Cl. SE9 .... 5 E3
Tom Cribb Rd. SE18 & SE28 .. 2 D3
Tom Joyce Cl. ME6 .... 74 F7
Tomlin Cl. Snodland ME6 .... 75 A8
Tomlin Cl.
...Staplehurst TN12 .... 139 E4
Tonbridge By-Pass. Stocks Green
...TN11 & TN9 & TN4 .... 116 B5
...TN4 & TN15 .... 116 B5
Tonbridge By-Pass.
...Tonbridge TN11 & TN4 .. 133 C6
Tonbridge Chambers. 3
...TN9 .... 133 B8
Tonbridge Cottage Hospl.
...TN11 .... 133 C6
Tonbridge Ct. ME16 .... 91 D3
Tonbridge Gram Sch for Girls.
...TN9 .... 133 C7
Tonbridge House. ME2 .... 33 C1
Tonbridge Rd.
...Hadlow TN11 & TN11 ..... 118 C7
Tonbridge Rd.
...Hildenborough TN11 ...... 116 E5
Tonbridge Rd.
...Ightham Common TN15 .. 86 C3
Tonbridge Rd.
...Little Mill TN11 & TN12 .. 119 D4
Tonbridge Rd.
...Maidstone ME16 .... 90 E1
Tonbridge Rd.
...Royal Tunbridge Wells
...TN2 & TN4 .... 150 A7
Tonbridge Rd.
...Sevenoaks TN13 & TN15 .. 99 D7
Tonbridge Rd.
...Wateringbury ME18 ...... 104 C8
Tonbridge Sch. TN10 .... 117 B3
Tonbridge Sta. TN9 .... 117 B1
Tong La. TN12 .... 152 B2
Tong Rd. TN12 .... 152 A4
Tongswood Dr. TN18 .... 179 C1
Tooley St. DA11 .... 29 D8
Top Dartford Rd. BR8 .... 26 A2
Topcliffe Dr. BR6 .... 51 D6
Topley St. SE9 .... 5 D3
Tor Rd. DA16 .... 7 C7
Torbay Rd. TN12 .... 120 B5
Tormount Rd. SE18 .... 6 E8
Toronto Rd. Gillingham ME7 .. 48 E4
Toronto Rd. Tilbury RM18 .. 13 A5
Torrens Wlk. DA12 .... 30 E3
Torrington Ct. ME18 .... 103 D8
Torver Way. BR6 .... 51 D7
Totnes Rd. DA16 .... 7 C7
Tovil Gn. ME15 .... 91 F1
Tovil Green Bsns Pk. ME15 .. 91 E1
Tovil Hill. ME15 .... 91 E2
Tovil Rd. ME15 .... 91 F2
Tower Cl. Gravesend DA12 .. 30 E3
Tower Cl. Orpington BR6 ... 51 F7
Tower Croft. DA4 .... 54 E8
Tower Gdns. ME14 .... 93 B4
Tower Hill. ME4 .... 88 D7
Tower Ind Est. TN15 .... 71 D5
Tower La. ME14 .... 93 B4

Tower Rd. Bexley DA7 .... 8 A3
Tower Rd. Dartford DA1 ...... 9 C1
Tower Rd. Erith DA17 .... 4 C2
Tower Rd. Orpington BR6 ... 51 F7
Tower View. ME1 .... 89 B5
Towers Wood. ME4 .... 41 D8
Town Acres. TN10 & TN9 .. 117 C4
Town Hill.
...Lamberhurst TN3 .... 166 A4
Town Hill.
...West Malling ME19 .... 74 C1
Town Hill ME19 .... 74 C1
Town Lock House. 3
...TN9 .... 117 C2
Town Meadow. TN17 .... 169 D4
Town Pier. 4 DA11 .... 13 B1
Town Rd. ME3 .... 33 A6
Town Sq. DA8 .... 8 E8
Town Station Cotts. TN8 .. 112 D1
Towncourt Cres. BR5 .... 37 D5
Towncourt La. BR5 .... 37 D2
Townfield Cnr. DA12 .... 30 D7
Townland Cl. TN27 .... 158 A2
Townlands Rd. TN5 .... 174 F4
Towning Gram Sch for Girls.
...DA5 .... 7 F1
Townley Rd. DA6 .... 7 F2
Townsend.
...Snodland ME6 .... 74 F8
Townsend.
...Woolwich SE18 .... 2 B3
Townshead Cl. DA14 .... 24 C2
Townshend House. 19
...SE18 .... 1 F2
Townshend Rd. BR7 .... 23 B3
Toy's Hill. TN16 & TN8 .... 97 C3
Toynbec Cl. BR7 .... 23 B4
Tracies The. ME9 .... 65 C6
Trader Rd. E6 .... 2 B7
Tradescant Dr. DA13 .... 44 B3
Trafalgar Rd. Dartford DA1 .. 26 E6
Trafalgar Rd.
...Gravesend DA11 .... 30 A8
Trafalgar Rd.
...Wouldham ME1 .... 60 C4
Trafalgar St. ME7 .... 48 C5
Tranquil Rise. DA8 .... 4 E1
Transfesa Rd. TN12 .... 136 A7
Transmere Cl. BR5 .... 37 C3
Transmere Rd. BR5 .... 37 C3
Transom House. 2 ME1 ..... 47 C1
Trapfield Cl. ME14 .... 93 C4
Trapfield La. ME14 .... 93 C4
Trapham Rd. ME16 .... 91 D5
Travers Gdns. ME9 .... 80 F5
Travertine Rd. ME5 .... 62 B1
Trebble Rd. DA10 .... 11 E1
Trebilco Cl. TN1 .... 149 D7
Tredegar Rd. DA2 .... 26 A5
Tredwell Cl. BR2 .... 36 E5
Tree La. TN15 .... 101 E8
Tree Rd. E16 .... 1 C7
Treetops. Gravesend DA12 .. 30 B4
Treetops. Tonbridge TN9 .. 133 B7
Treetops Cl. SE2 .... 3 E1
Treewall Gdns. BR1 .... 22 A4
Trefoil House. Erith DA18 .... 3 E4
Trefoil House. Grays RM17 .. 12 B7
Trelawn Cres. ME8 .... 62 B2
Trellyn Cl. ME16 .... 90 F2
Trench Rd. TN10 .... 117 C6
Trent House. 2 ME15 ...... 107 E7
Trenton Cl. ME16 .... 91 B7
Trevale Rd. ME1 .... 47 B1
Trevelyan Cl. DA1 .... 9 F3
Trevereux Hill. RH8 .... 96 A3
Trevino Dr. ME5 .... 61 F2
Trevithick Dr. DA1 .... 9 F3
Trevor Cl. BR2 .... 36 A2
Trevor Dr. ME16 .... 91 C5
Trewin Cl. ME20 .... 75 D2
Trewsbury House. 2 SE2 .... 3 D4
Triangle Ct. E16 .... 1 C8
Trident Cl. ME2 .... 47 D7
Trinity Cl. Keston Mark BR2 .. 36 E1
Trinity Ct. Aylesford ME20 .. 76 A3
Trinity Ct. Dartford DA1 ...... 27 B7
Trinity Ct. Eltham SE9 .... 6 B1
Trinity Pl. DA6 .... 7 F3
Trinity Rd. Gillingham ME7 .. 48 C6
Trinity Rd. Gravesend DA12 .. 30 C8
Trinity Sch, Belvedere.
...DA17 .... 4 C2
Trinity St. 12 E16 .... 1 A8
Tristan Gdns. TN4 .... 148 D4
Triumph Rd. E6 .... 1 F7
Trivett Cl. DA9 .... 11 A2

Trolling Down Hill. DA2 ...... 27 C6
Troodos Hill. ME4 .... 91 F8
Trosley Ave. DA11 .... 30 B6
Trosley Ctry Pk. ME19 .... 73 A7
Trosley Rd. DA17 .... 8 A8
Trottiscliffe CE Prim Sch.
...ME19 .... 73 A5
Trottiscliffe Rd. ME19 .... 73 D3
Trotts La. TN16 .... 96 C8
Trotwood Cl. ME5 .... 77 A8
Troughton Rd. SE7 .... 1 B1
Troutbeck House. ME19 ..... 75 C1
Troy Cl. 5 SE18 .... 2 B2
Troys Mead. ME17 .... 94 D2
Trubridge Rd. ME3 .... 34 E5
Truro Cl. ME8 .... 49 D3
Truro Rd. DA12 .... 30 D5
Truro Wlk. TN10 .... 117 D5
Trusedale Rd. E6 .... 1 F7
Trycewell La. TN15 .... 86 D6
Tuam Rd. SE18 .... 6 C8
Tubbenden Cl. BR6 .... 51 E7
Tubbenden Dr. BR6 .... 51 D6
Tubbenden Inf & Jun Sch.
...BR6 .... 51 D6
Tubbenden La. BR6 .... 51 E7
Tubbenden La S. BR6 .... 51 D5
Tubs Hill. TN13 .... 84 B3
Tubs Hill Par. TN13 .... 84 A3
Tudeley La. Tonbridge TN9 .. 133 D7
Tudeley La.
...Tudeley TN11 & TN9 .... 134 B8
Tudor Ave. ME14 .... 92 B6
Tudor Cl. Dartford DA1 .... 9 B1
Tudor Cl. Northfleet DA11 .. 29 E7
Tudor Cres. TN14 .... 69 D3
Tudor Ct. Crockenhill BR8 .. 39 C2
Tudor Ct. Royal Tunbridge Wells
...TN2 .... 148 E1
Tudor Ct. Sidcup DA14 .... 24 A5
Tudor Dr. Gravesend DA12 .. 30 E3
Tudor Dr.
...Maidstone ME14 .... 69 C3
Tudor Gr. Chattenden ME3 .. 33 F4
Tudor Gr. Gillingham ME8 .. 63 F8
Tudor Par. SE9 .... 5 E2
Tudor Way. BR5 .... 37 D3
Tudor Wlk. DA5 .... 7 E1
Tudway Rd. SE3 & SE9 .... 5 C3
Tufa Cl. ME5 .... 62 B1
Tuff Cotts. ME3 .... 19 C3
Tuffield House. 9 SE18 .... 2 A2
Tufnail Rd. DA1 .... 9 F1
Tufton Rd. ME8 .... 49 F1
Tufton St. ME14 .... 92 A4
Tugboat St. SE28 .... 2 E4
Tugmutton Cl. BR6 .... 51 B6
Tulip Cl. 5 E6 .... 1 F8
Tulip Tree Cl. TN9 .... 133 B8
Tumblefield Est. TN15 .... 71 F8
Tumblefield Rd. TN15 .... 71 E7
Tumblers Hill. ME17 .... 124 F7
Tunbridge Wells Golf Club.
...TN4 .... 148 E3
Tunbridge Wells Gram
...Sch for Boys. TN4 .... 149 A7
Tunbridge Wells Gram
...Sch for Girls. TN4 .... 149 A6
Tunbridge Wells Ind Hospl The.
...TN3 .... 147 B3
Tunbury Ave. Chatham ME5 .. 61 F1
Tunbury Ave. Chatham ME5 .. 61 F2
Tunbury Ave S. ME5 .... 61 F1
Tunbury Cty Prim Sch.
...ME5 .... 61 F1
Tunman Leys. E6 .... 2 A7
Tunnel Ave. SE10 .... 1 A1
Tunnel Est. RM16 .... 10 F8
Tunnel Rd. TN1 .... 149 B4
Tunstall Cl. BR6 .... 51 E6
Tunstock Way. DA17 .... 3 E3
Tupman Cl. ME1 .... 47 B4
Turkey Ct. ME17 .... 108 E4
Turks Hall Pl. ME2 .... 59 E5
Turley Cotts. TN3 .... 148 A8
Turley Way. BR6 .... 37 D1
Turnbull Cl. DA2 .... 27 E8
Turnden Rd. TN17 .... 169 A3
Turner Ave. TN17 .... 169 D3
Turner Ct. DA1 .... 9 C2
Turner House. DA12 .... 30 C6
Turner Rd. Bean DA2 .... 28 B5
Turner Rd. Tonbridge TN10 .. 117 C5
Turner St. ME3 .... 16 B5
Turners Ave. TN30 .... 183 B8
Turners Gdns. TN13 .... 99 C7
Turners Green La. TN5 ...... 174 F6
Turners Green Rd. TN5 ..... 174 F6
Turnpike Ct. DA6 .... 7 D3
Turnpike Dr. BR6 .... 52 D2
Turnpike La. RM18 .... 13 D8
Turnstone. DA13 .... 43 A7

Turnstone Rd. ME5 .... 62 C1
Turnstones The. DA12 .... 30 C6
Turpin La. DA8 .... 9 A8
Turpington Cl. BR2 .... 36 E2
Turpington La. BR2 .... 36 E3
Turton House. 5 SE18 .... 6 B8
Turton Rd. ME5 .... 62 C1
Tuscan Rd. SE18 .... 2 D1
Tutsham Way. TN12 .... 135 F6
Tuxford Rd. TN4 .... 148 B5
Tweed Rd. TN10 .... 117 C5
Tweedy Rd. BR1 .... 36 A8
Twigg Cl. DA8 .... 8 E7
Twisden Rd. ME19 .... 89 F8
Twiss House. 6 SE18 .... 2 B1
Twistleton Ct. DA1 .... 9 D1
Twitton La. TN14 .... 68 E3
Twitton Meadows. TN14 .... 68 E3
Two Gates Hill. ME3 .... 32 F5
Twydall Cty Inf Sch. ME8 ... 49 B2
Twydall Cty Prim Jun Sch.
...ME8 .... 49 B2
Twydall Gn. ME8 .... 49 B3
Twydall La. ME8 .... 49 B2
Twyford Ct. ME14 .... 92 D6
Twyford Rd. TN11 .... 102 E1
Twysden Cotts. TN18 .... 186 A4
Tydeman Rd. ME15 .... 92 F2
Tye La. BR6 .... 51 C5
Tyeshurst Cl. SE2 .... 3 E1
Tyland La. ME14 .... 76 F3
Tyler Cl. ME19 .... 89 F8
Tyler Dr. ME8 .... 63 E4
Tyler Gr. DA1 .... 9 F3
Tylers Green Rd. BR8 .... 39 C2
Tylney Rd. BR1 .... 36 D7
Tyndall Rd. DA16 .... 6 F4
Tyne Cl. ME5 .... 62 C5
Tyne House. 10 ME15 .... 107 E7
Tyne Rd. TN10 .... 117 B5
Tynedale Cl. DA2 .... 27 D7
Tynemouth Cl. E6 .... 2 B7
Typhoon Rd. ME19 .... 88 F3
Tyron Way. DA14 .... 23 F3
Tyrrell Ave. DA16 .... 7 B2
Tyrrells Hall Cl. RM17 .... 12 D8

Uckfield La. TN8 .... 129 D4
Ufton Cl. ME15 .... 92 E1
Ulcombe CE Prim Sch.
...ME17 .... 125 F6
Ulcombe Hill. ME17 .... 109 F1
Ulcombe Rd.
...Headcorn TN27 .... 141 C6
Ulcombe Rd.
...Langley Heath ME17 ...... 108 E3
Underdown Ave. ME4 .... 47 F1
Underhill Jun Sch. ME17 .. 124 C7
Underlyn Ind Est. TN12 .... 122 F2
Underlyn La. TN12 .... 122 D1
Underriver House Rd.
...TN11 & TN15 .... 100 D5
Underwood. ME19 .... 88 D7
Underwood Cl. ME15 .... 91 F2
Underwood The. SE9 .... 22 F6
Unicorn Wlk. DA9 .... 10 F2
Unicumes La. ME16 .... 91 C2
Union Pk. ME15 .... 107 F4
Union Rd. ME2 .... 36 D4
Union Sq. 18 TN2 .... 149 A2
Union St. Chatham ME4 ...... 48 A3
Union St. Maidstone ME14 .. 92 A5
Union St. Rochester ME1 .... 47 C5
Union St. Union Street TN5 .. 177 B3
Unity Way. SE18 .... 1 D3
Univ of Greenwich. SE18 .... 2 A2
Univ of Greenwich
...Avery Hill Campus. SE9 ..... 6 C1
Univ of Greenwich
...Avery Hill Campus
...Southwood Site. SE9 ...... 23 D8
Univ of Greenwich
...(Dartford Campus). DA1 .. 26 C6
Univ of Greenwich
...(Riverside House Annexe).
...SE18 .... 2 A3
Univ of Greenwich
...(Southwold Site). SE9 .... 6 C2
University Gdns. DA5 .... 24 F8
University Pl. DA8 .... 8 C7
University Way. DA1 .... 9 E4
Unwin Cl. ME20 .... 76 A3
Upbury Manor High Sch.
...ME7 .... 48 B4
Upbury Way. ME4 .... 48 A4
Upchat Rd. ME2 & ME3 .... 33 F3
Updale Rd. DA14 .... 23 F4
Upland Inf Sch. DA7 .... 7 F4

Upland Jun Sch. DA7 .... 7 F4
Upland Rd. DA7 .... 7 F4
Uplands Cl. Rochester ME2 .. 46 D6
Uplands Cl. Sevenoaks TN13 83 E4
Uplands Com Coll. TN5 .... 175 A4
Uplands Rd. BR6 .... 38 B1
Uplands Way. TN13 .... 83 F4
Upnor Castle. ME2 .... 33 F2
Upnor Rd. Rochester ME2 .... 47 D8
Upnor Rd. Upper Upton ME2 33 E2
Upper Abbey Rd. DA17 .... 4 A2
Upper Austin Lodge Rd.
DA4 .... 54 D4
Upper Ave. DA13 .... 43 E8
Upper Barn Hill. ME15 ...... 105 E3
Upper Britton Pl. ME7 .... 48 B5
Upper Bush Rd. ME2 .... 45 F2
Upper Church Hill. DA9 .... 10 E2
Upper Cumberland Wlk.
TN1 .... 149 B1
Upper Dunstan Rd. TN4 .. 149 B6
Upper East Rd. ME4 .... 48 B8
Upper Fant Rd. ME16 .... 91 D2
Upper Green La. TN11 ...... 101 D5
Upper Green Rd. TN11 ...... 101 D5
Upper Grosvenor Rd.
TN1 & TN4 .... 149 B6
Upper Grove Rd. DA17 .... 7 F8
Upper Haysden La.
TN4 & TN9 .... 132 E6
Upper Holly Hill Rd. DA17 ... 4 B1
Upper Hunton Hill. ME15 . 106 A3
Upper Luton Rd.
ME4 & ME5 .... 48 C2
Upper Mill. ME18 .... 104 D8
Upper Nellington. TN3 ...... 148 B4
Upper Park Rd.
Bromley BR1 .... 36 C8
Upper Park Rd. Erith DA17 ... 4 B2
Upper Platts. TN5 .... 176 F1
Upper Profit. TN3 .... 148 A3
Upper Rd. ME15 .... 92 B2
Upper Sheridan Rd. DA17 ... 4 A2
Upper Spring La. TN15 ...... 86 B5
Upper St.
Hollingbourne ME17 .... 94 E3
Upper St. Leeds ME17 ...... 108 F5
Upper St. Rusthall TN4 .... 148 D4
Upper Stephens. TN3 .... 148 A3
Upper Stone St. ME15 .... 92 A3
Upper Street N. DA3 .... 56 F8
Upper Street S. DA3 .... 56 F8
Upper Wickham La. DA16 .... 7 B4
Upperton Rd. DA14 .... 23 F3
Upton Cl. DA5 .... 7 F1
Upton Day Hospl. DA6 .... 7 E3
Upton Prim Sch. DA6 .... 7 E2
Upton Quarry. TN3 .... 147 F3
Upton Rd. Bexley DA6 .... 7 E2
Upton Rd. Woolwich SE18 .... 6 C8
Upton Rd S. DA5 .... 7 F1
Upton Villas. 4 DA6 .... 7 E3
Uptons. TN27 .... 141 C6
Upwood Rd. SE12 .... 5 A1
Uridge Cres. TN10 .... 117 C4
Uridge Rd. TN10 .... 117 C4
Urquhart Cl. ME5 .... 62 A5
Ursula Lodge. DA14 .... 24 B3
Usborne Cl. TN12 .... 139 E3

Vale. Royal Tunbridge Wells,
Mount Sion TN1 .... 149 A3
Vale Ave. Royal Tunbridge Wells,
Southborough.TN4 .... 132 F1
Vale Cl. BR6 .... 51 A6
Vale Cotts. ME9 .... 80 A8
Vale Ct. TN4 .... 133 A2
Vale Dr. ME5 .... 61 E6
Vale Rd. Bromley BR1 & BR7 37 A7
Vale Rd. Dartford DA1 .... 26 B7
Vale Rd. Hawkhurst TN18 .. 178 F3
Vale Rd. Loose ME15 .... 106 C4
Vale Rd. Northfleet DA11 ... 29 E7
Vale Rd. Royal Tunbridge Wells,
Mount Sion TN1 .... 149 A3
Vale Rd. Royal Tunbridge Wells,
Southborough.TN4 .... 132 F1
Vale Rd. Tonbridge TN9 .... 117 D1
Vale Rd. Tonbridge TN9 .... 133 C8
Vale Rise. TN9 .... 133 C8
Valence House. ME15 ...... 107 C7
Valence Rd. DA8 .... 8 D7
Valence Sch. TN16 .... 81 F1
Valence View. TN17 .... 156 E7
Valentine Ave. DA5 .... 24 E7
Valentine Cl. ME7 .... 49 A1
Valentine Rd. ME15 .... 107 E7
Valerian Cl. ME5 .... 61 E4

Valiant House. 5 SE7 .... 1 C1
Valiant Rd. ME5 .... 62 C2
Valiant Way. E6 .... 1 F8
Valley (Charlton Athletic FC) The.
SE7 .... 1 C1
Valley Cl. DA1 .... 8 F1
Valley Dr. Gravesend,
Riverview Park DA12 ...... 30 D4
Valley Dr.
Gravesend,Singlewell DA12 30 E1
Valley Dr. Maidstone ME15 106 F6
Valley Dr. Sevenoaks TN13 .. 84 B1
Valley Forge Cl. TN10 ...... 117 F4
Valley Gdns. DA9 .... 11 B1
Valley Gr. SE7 .... 1 C1
Valley L Ctr. SE9 .... 23 C8
Valley La. DA13 .... 58 B2
Valley Rd. Crayford DA1 .... 8 F1
Valley Rd. Erith DA8 .... 4 D2
Valley Rd.
Fawkham Green DA3 .... 42 C2
Valley Rd. Gillingham ME7 .. 48 E4
Valley Rd. Rusthall TN4 .... 148 D4
Valley Rd.
St Paul's Cray BR5 .... 38 B8
Valley Rise. ME5 .... 61 F1
Valley The. ME17 .... 106 D3
Valley View. Royal Tunbridge Wells
TN4 .... 133 A2
Valley View.
Swanscombe DA9 .... 11 B1
Valley View Rd. ME1 .... 47 B1
Valley View Terr. DA4 .... 40 F1
Valleyside. SE7 .... 1 D1
Valliers Wood Rd. DA15 .... 23 E7
Vambery Rd. SE18 .... 6 C8
Vanbrugh Pk. SE3 .... 5 A7
Vanbrugh Cl. 2
Newham E16 .... 1 D8
Vanburgh Cl. Orpington BR6 37 E1
Vancouver Dr. ME8 .... 49 C1
Vandome Cl. E16 .... 1 B7
Vandyke Cross. SE9 .... 5 E2
Vanessa Cl. DA17 .... 4 A1
Vanessa Way. DA5 .... 25 D5
Vanessa Wlk. DA12 .... 30 F3
Vange Cottage Mews. ME1 .. 47 B4
Vanity La. ME17 .... 106 D1
Vanoc Gdns. BR1 .... 22 A4
Vanquisher Wlk. DA12 ...... 30 F5
Varley Rd. E16 .... 1 B7
Varnes St. ME20 .... 75 F6
Vaughan Ave. TN10 .... 117 E6
Vaughan Rd. DA16 .... 6 F5
Vauxhall Cl. DA11 .... 29 F8
Vauxhall Cres. ME6 .... 75 A6
Vauxhall Gdns. TN9 .... 133 C7
Vauxhall La.
Bidborough TN11 & TN4 .. 133 B4
Vauxhall La.
Tonbridge TN11 & TN9 ... 133 D6
Vauxhall Pl. DA1 .... 26 E8
Veitchil Barn. BR8 .... 39 F8
Veles Rd. ME6 .... 74 F8
Venture Cl. 4 DA17 .... 4 A2
Venners Cl. DA7 .... 8 E5
Ventnor Cl. ME5 .... 62 C8
Venture Cl. DA5 .... 24 A1
Venture Ct. 5 SE12 .... 22 A8
Venus Rd. SE18 .... 1 F3
Verdun Rd. SE18 & SE2 .... 7 A8
Vermont Rd. TN4 .... 148 C4
Vernham Rd. SE18 .... 6 C8
Vernon Ct.
St Paul's Cray BR5 .... 38 B6
Vernon Cl.
West Kingsdown TN15 ...... 55 F2
Vernon Rd. Royal Tunbridge Wells
TN1 .... 149 C6
Vernon Rd.
Swanscombe DA10 .... 11 F1
Veroan Rd. DA7 .... 7 E5
Verona Gdns. DA12 .... 30 E4
Verona House. DA8 .... 8 F7
Vert House. RM17 .... 12 C7
Vesper Ct. TN27 .... 143 A1
Vestry Cotts. DA3 .... 43 C5
Vestry Rd. TN14 .... 84 C8
Via Romana. DA12 .... 30 D4
Viaduct Terr. DA4 .... 41 C7
Vicarage Ave. SE3 .... 5 A7
Vicarage Cl. Aylesford ME20 75 F3
Vicarage Cl. Erith DA8 .... 4 C8
Vicarage Cl. Halling ME2 ... 60 A5
Vicarage Cl. Stoke ME3 ...... 19 A3
Vicarage Cl. Chalk DA12 .... 31 A7
Vicarage Ct.
Newington ME9 .... 65 B7
Vicarage Dr. DA11 .... 12 C1
Vicarage Hill. TN16 .... 81 D1
Vicarage La.
East Farleigh ME15 .... 106 B6
Vicarage La.
Hoo St Werburgh ME3 ...... 34 E4
Vicarage La.
Sevenoaks TN13 .... 83 D8
Vicarage Pk. SE18 .... 2 C2
Vicarage Rd. Coldblow DA5 25 B7
Vicarage Rd.
Gillingham ME7 .... 48 C5
Vicarage Rd. Halling ME2 ... 59 F5
Vicarage Rd. Rochester ME2 47 B8
Vicarage Rd. Royal Tunbridge Wells
TN4 .... 132 F2
Vicarage Rd. Woolwich SE18 2 B3
Vicarage Rd. Yalding ME18 105 A1
Vicarage Row. ME3 .... 32 C4
Vicarage Sq. RM17 .... 12 A8
Vicarage Way. TN19 .... 184 A3
Vicary Way. ME16 .... 91 D5
Vickers Rd. DA8 .... 4 F7
Victor Mills Cotts. BR8 ...... 25 A1
Victoria Ave. 3 DA11 .... 30 B8
Victoria Bsns Ctr. DA16 .... 7 B5
Victoria Cl. Chatham ME5 .. 61 D2
Victoria Cl.
Edenbridge TN8 .... 128 C8
Victoria Cotts.
Cranbrook TN17 .... 169 D5
Victoria Cotts.
Edenbridge TN8 .... 128 C8
Victoria Ct. 6 ME16 .... 91 E3
Victoria Dock Rd. E16 .... 1 B6
Victoria Dr. Kings Hill ME18 88 F1
Victoria Dr.
South Darenth DA4 .... 41 D7
Victoria Hill Rd. BR8 .... 40 A8
Victoria Ind Pk. DA1 .... 9 E2
Victoria Rd. Bexley DA6 .... 8 A3
Victoria Rd. Bromley BR2 .. 36 D4
Victoria Rd.
Chatham,Luton ME4 .... 48 A2
Victoria Rd.
Chatham,Walderslade ME5 61 E3
Victoria Rd. Chislehurst BR7 23 A3
Victoria Rd. Dartford DA1 .... 9 F2
Victoria Rd.
Edenbridge TN8 .... 128 C8
Victoria Rd. Erith DA8 .... 8 E8
Victoria Rd.
Golden Green TN11 .... 118 F6
Victoria Rd.
Gravesend DA11 .... 29 F7
Victoria Rd. Royal Tunbridge Wells
TN1 .... 149 B4
Victoria Rd. Royal Tunbridge Wells,
Modest Corner TN4 .... 132 E1
Victoria Rd.
Sevenoaks TN13 .... 84 B2
Victoria Rd. Sidcup DA15 ... 24 A5
Victoria Rd. St. Eccles ME20 75 F6
Victoria Rd. St. Erith DA17 .... 3 F1
Victoria Rd. St. Gillingham ME7 48 D6
Victoria Rd. St. Maidstone ME16 91 E3
Victoria Rd. St. Rochester ME2 47 B7
Victoria Rd. St.
Rochester,Troy Town ME1 47 D5
Victoria Terr. ME1 .... 47 A2
Victoria Way. SE7 .... 1 B1
Victoria Wharf. DA1 .... 9 F2
Victory Cotts. TN12 .... 99 C2
Victory Pk. ME2 .... 47 E7
Vidal Manor. ME7 .... 48 C5
Vidgeon Ave. ME3 .... 34 D6
View Rd. ME3 .... 33 B7
View The. SE2 .... 3 A1
Viewfield Rd. DA5 .... 24 C7
Viewland Rd. SE18 .... 2 F1
Viewlands Ave. TN16 .... 81 F7
Viewpoint Ct. DA3 .... 42 F5
Vigilant Way. DA12 .... 30 F3
Vigo Cty Prim Sch. DA13 ... 73 A8
Vigo Rd. TN15 .... 72 C7
Viking Gdns. E6 .... 1 E8
Viking Rd. DA11 .... 29 F5
Viking House. 3 SE7 .... 1 C2
Viking Way.
Erith DA8 & DA17 .... 4 C3
Viking Way.
West Kingsdown TN15 ...... 55 E5
Villa Cl. DA12 .... 31 B6
Villa Ct. DA1 .... 26 E6
Villa Rd. ME3 .... 32 B3
Villacourt Rd. SE18 & SE2 ... 7 A8
Village Green Rd. DA1 .... 9 A3
Village The. SE7 .... 5 D8
Villas Rd. SE18 .... 2 C2
Vincent Cl. Bromley BR2 ... 36 B5
Vincent Cl. Sidcup DA15 ... 23 E7
Vincent Rd. Kit's Coty ME20 76 C7
Vincent Rd. Woolwich SE18 .. 2 B2

Vincent St. 13 E16 .... 1 A8
Vine Ave. TN3 .... 148 B3
Vine Court Rd. TN13 .... 84 C4
Vine Ct. ME18 .... 104 D8
Vine Lodge Ct. TN13 .... 84 C3
Vine Rd. BR6 .... 51 F4
Vine The. TN13 .... 84 C3
Vine Wlk. TN12 .... 139 E3
Vineries The. ME7 .... 48 A5
Vines La. Rochester ME1 .... 47 C5
Vines La.
Watt's Cross TN11 .... 100 C1
Viney's Gdns. TN30 .... 173 C1
Vineyard La. TN5 .... 176 C2
Vinson Cl. BR6 .... 38 A1
Vinters Rd. ME14 .... 92 B4
Vinters Sch for Boys. ME14 92 C4
Vintners Way. ME14 .... 92 E4
Viola Ave. SE2 .... 3 B1
Violet Cl. ME5 .... 77 A8
VIP Trad Est. SE7 .... 1 C2
Virginia Rd. ME7 .... 48 C7
Virginia Wlk. DA12 .... 30 E2
Viscount Dr. E6 .... 1 F8
Vista The. SE9 .... 22 E8
Vixen Cl. ME5 .... 62 C6
Voce Rd. SE18 .... 6 D7
Volante Way. DA12 .... 30 E4
Vulcan Cl. ME5 .... 62 B7
Vyne The. DA7 .... 8 B4
Vyvyan Cotts. TN17 .... 180 C3
Vyvyon House. SE18 .... 6 A6

Wadard Terr. BR8 .... 40 C4
Wade Ave. BR5 .... 38 D2
Wade Rd. E16 .... 1 C7
Wadeville Cl. DA17 .... 4 A1
Wadhurst Bsns Pk. TN5 ... 174 B7
Wadhurst CE Prim Sch.
TN5 .... 174 F5
Wadhurst Par. TN5 .... 174 F4
Wadhurst Sta. TN5 .... 174 C6
Wadlands Rd. ME3 .... 16 B5
Waghorn Rd. ME6 .... 75 A8
Waghorn St. ME4 .... 48 B3
Wagon La. ME12 .... 120 C1
Wagoners Cl. ME14 .... 92 E4
Waid Cl. DA1 .... 9 F1
Wainscott Cty Prim Sch.
ME2 .... 33 D2
Wainscott Rd. ME2 .... 33 D2
Wainscott Wlk. ME2 .... 33 D3
Waite Davies Rd. 6 SE12 ... 22 A8
Wake Rd. ME1 .... 61 C8
Wakefield Cl. ME2 .... 46 D6
Wakefield Rd. DA9 .... 11 C2
Wakehurst Cl. ME17 .... 106 B3
Wakeleys Cotts. ME8 .... 64 B8
Wakerly Cl. 6 E6 .... 1 F7
Waldair Ct. E16 .... 2 B4
Waldeck Rd. DA1 .... 10 A1
Waldegrave Rd. BR1 .... 36 F5
Walden Ave. BR7 .... 22 F4
Walden Cl. DA17 .... 3 F1
Walden Rd. BR7 .... 23 A3
Waldenhurst Rd. BR5 .... 38 D2
Waldens Cl. BR5 .... 38 D2
Waldens Rd. BR5 .... 38 E3
Waldens The. ME17 .... 109 E2
Walderslade Cty Prim Sch.
ME5 .... 62 A3
Walderslade Girls Sch.
ME5 .... 61 F5
Walderslade Rd. ME5 .... 61 F6
Walderslade Woods.
Chatham ME5 .... 61 E2
Walderslade Woods.
Chatham ME5 & ME14 .... 77 B8
Waldo Ind Est. BR1 .... 36 D6
Waldo Rd. BR1 .... 36 D6
Waldrist Way. DA18 .... 3 F4
Waldron Dr. ME15 .... 106 F6
Walk The. ME17 .... 109 E2
Walkden Rd. BR7 .... 22 A3
Walker Cl. Crayford DA1 ..... 8 F4
Walker Cl. Woolwich SE18 ... 2 C2
Walkhurst Cotts. TN17 .... 180 F7
Walkhurst Rd. TN17 .... 180 F7
Walkley Rd. DA1 .... 9 B2
Walks The. TN3 .... 161 C8
Wall Cl. ME3 .... 34 D7
Wallace Cl. Erith SE28 .... 3 D6
Wallace Cl. Royal Tunbridge Wells
TN2 .... 163 A8
Wallace Gdns. DA10 .... 11 E1
Wallace Rd. ME1 .... 61 E8
Wallace Terr. TN15 .... 56 E4
Waller Hill. TN17 .... 156 B5
Wallers. TN3 .... 148 A8
Wallhouse Rd. DA8 .... 9 C7
Wallis Ave. ME15 .... 107 E5

Wallis Cl. DA2 .... 2 ?
Wallis Field. TN3 .... 16 ?
Walmer Cl. BR6 .... 5 ?
Walmer Cl. 3 ME14 .... 9 ?
Walmer House. ME2 .... ?
Walmer Terr. SE18 .... ?
Walmers Ave. ME3 .... ?
Walnut Cl. Chatham ME5 .. 6 ?
Walnut Cl.
Paddock Wood TN12 ...... 13 ?
Walnut Cl. Yalding ME18 .. 10 ?
Walnut Hill Rd.
DA3 & DA13 .... 4 ?
Walnut Tree Ave.
Dartford DA1 .... ?
Walnut Tree Ave.
Loose Hill ME15 .... 10 ?
Walnut Tree Cl. BR7 .... ?
Walnut Tree Ct. ME20 .... ?
Walnut Tree La. ME15 ...... 10 ?
Walnut Tree Rd. DA8 .... ?
Walnut Tree Way. DA13 .... 4 ?
Walnut Way.
Royal Tunbridge Wells
TN2 & TN4 .... 11 ?
Walnut Way. Swanley BR8 .. 3 ?
Walnuts Rd. BR6 .... 3 ?
Walnuts The. BR6 .... 3 ?
Walpole Cl. ME19 .... 7 ?
Walpole Pl. 3 SE18 .... ?
Walpole Rd. BR2 .... 3 ?
Walsham Cl. SE28 .... ?
Walsham Rd. ME5 .... 6 ?
Walshaw House. 2 ME14 .. 6 ?
Walsingham Cl. ME8 .... ?
Walsingham House. 3
ME14 .... ?
Walsingham Pk. BR7 .... ?
Walsingham Rd. BR5 .... ?
Walsingham Wlk. DA17 ...... ?
Walter Burke Ave. ME1 ..... 6 ?
Walter's Farm Rd. TN9 .... 13 ?
Walters Green Rd.
TN11 & TN3 .... 14 ?
Walters Rd. ME3 .... ?
Walters Yd. BR1 .... ?
Waltham Cl. Dartford DA1 .. ?
Waltham Cl. Orpington BR5 .. ?
Waltham Rd. ME8 .... ?
Walthamstow Hall. TN13 ... 8 ?
Walthamstow Hall Jun Sch.
TN13 .... 8 ?
Walton Rd. Sidcup DA14 ... 2 ?
Walton Rd.
Tonbridge TN10 .... 11 ?
Walwyn Ave. BR1 .... ?
Wanden La. TN27 .... 14 ?
Wansbury Way. BR8 .... ?
Wanstead Cl. BR1 .... ?
Wanstead Rd. BR1 .... ?
Wansunt Rd. DA5 .... ?
Warblers Cl. ME2 .... ?
Ward Cl. Durgates TN5 ..... 17 ?
Ward Cl. Erith DA8 .... ?
Warde's. TN5 .... 13 ?
Warde's. ME18 .... ?
Warden Cl. ME16 .... ?
Warden Mill Cl. ME18 .... 10 ?
Warden Rd. ME1 .... ?
Wardens Field Cl. 2 BR6 ... ?
Wardona Cl. DA10 .... ?
Wardwell La. ME9 .... ?
Ware St. ME14 .... ?
Warepoint Dr. SE28 .... ?
Warham Rd. TN14 .... 6 ?
Waring Cl. BR6 .... ?
Waring Dr. BR6 .... ?
Waring Rd. DA14 .... 2 ?
Warland Rd.
West Kingsdown TN15 ...... ?
Warland Rd. Woolwich SE18 .. ?
Warmlake. ME17 .... 10 ?
Warmlake Est. ME17 .... 10 ?
Warmlake Rd. ME17 .... 10 ?
Warne Pl. 4 DA15 .... ?
Warner St. ME4 .... ?
Warnett Cl. ME6 .... ?
Warnford Gdns. ME15 ...... 10 ?
Warnford Rd. BR6 .... ?
Warren Ave. BR6 .... ?
Warren Cl. DA6 .... ?
Warren Cotts. TN11 .... 13 ?
Warren Ct. TN15 .... 8 ?
Warren Dr. BR6 .... ?
Warren Farm La. TN3 .... 16 ?
Warren Gdns. BR6 .... ?
Warren La. Hartlip ME9 ..... ?
Warren La. Woolwich SE18 .. ?
Warren Rd. Bexley DA6 ...... ?
Warren Rd. Dartford DA1 ... ?
Warren Rd. Hayes BR2 .... 5 ?

...en Rd.
...er Coty ME5 & ME20 ...... 76 D7
...er Bush DA12 & DA13 .... 45 D3
...en Rd. Orpington BR6 ..... 52 C5
...en Rd. Sidcup DA14 ...... 24 C5
...en Rd. Southfleet DA13 .. 29 B3
...en Ridge. TN3 .... 163 C3
...en Road Prim Sch. 51 F6
...en Rd.
..avesend DA12 .... 30 D4
...en The.
..hurst TN11 .... 131 A4
...en The. Ticehurst TN5 .. 176 E1
...en View. DA12 .... 31 E2
...en Wlk. **1** SE7 .... 5 C8
...en Wood Cl. BR2 .... 50 A8
...en Wood Cty Prim Sch. ... 61 C8
...er Mead ME1 .... 61 C7
...ens The. DA3 .... 42 F3
...rington Rd. TN12 .... 136 A6
...er Ave. DA12 .... 30 C4
...opite Rd. SE18 & SE7 ..... 1 E3
..wall. E6 .... 2 B7
...wick Cl. Orpington BR6 .. 52 A7
...wick Cl. Sidcup DA5 ...... 24 F8
...wick Cres. ME1 .... 46 F2
...wick Gdns. DA13 .... 58 A8
...wick Pk. TN1 & TN2 ...... 149 B1
...wick Pl.
..dstone ME16 .... 91 E3
...wick Pl. Northfleet DA11 . 12 B2
...wick Rd. Bexley DA16 ..... 7 C4
...wick Rd. **4**
..al Tunbridge Wells 149 A2
...wick Rd. Sidcup DA14 ..... 24 B3
...wick Terr. SE18 .... 6 A2
..hneys Rd. BR6 & TN14 .... 67 B6
..nwell La. TN5 .... 174 F3
..sall La. TN17 .... 187 C7
..Tyler Way. ME15 .... 92 A4
..ngate. DA2 .... 27 E3
...er La.
..ar Wents TN18 .... 179 B4
...er La.
..rietsham ME17 .... 110 B5
...er La.
..adcorn TN12 & TN27 ...... 141 A4
...er La. Kingswood ME17 .. 109 F3
...er La. **4**
..dstone ME15 .... 92 A4
...er La.
..dstone,Bearsted ME14 .... 93 E6
...er La. Shoreham TN14 .... 68 F6
...er La. Sidcup DA14 .... 24 F6
..arden Bell TN27 .... 142 F2
...er La.
..st Malling ME19 .... 89 C8
...er Mill Way. DA4 .... 41 B7
...er Slippe. TN11 .... 102 D1
..rcress Cl. TN4 .... 84 C7
..rcress Dr. TN4 .... 84 C7
..rcroft Rd. TN14 .... 52 F1
..erdale Rd. SE2 .... 7 A8
..erdales. DA11 .... 29 D7
..erdown Rd. TN4 .... 148 E1
..erfield. TN2 .... 163 A7
..erfield Cl. Erith DA17 .... 4 A3
..erfield Cl.
..olwich SE28 .... 3 B5
..erfield Sch. SE28 .... 3 A5
..erfrets Cotts. TN3 .... 147 F5
..ergate House. **5** SE18 .. 2 A2
..erglade Ind Pk. 10 F8
..erhead Cl. DA8 .... 8 E7
..erhouse Cl. E16 .... 1 D8
..eringbury CE Prim Sch.
..18 .... 104 E6
..eringbury Pl. BR5 .... 38 B7
..eringbury Rd. ME19 .... 89 F3
..eringbury Sta. ME18 ..... 104 E6
..erlakes. TN8 .... 128 C8
..erloo Pl.
..anbrook TN17 .... 169 D5
..erloo Pl.
..bridge TN9 .... 133 B8
..erloo Rd.
..anbrook TN17 .... 169 D6
..erloo Rd.
..ingham ME7 .... 48 C4
..erloo St. **1**
..avesend DA12 .... 30 C8
..erlow St.
..dstone ME15 .... 92 A3
..erlow Rd.
..dstone ME14 .... 92 A6

Waterlow Rd.
  Vigo Village DA13 .... 72 F7
Waterman's La. TN12 ...... 136 B3
Watermeadow Cl. ME7 ..... 62 F6
Watermill Cl.
  Maidstone ME16 .... 91 B5
Watermill Cl.
  Rochester ME2 .... 47 C8
Waters Cotts. TN5 .... 175 A4
Waters Edge. ME15 .... 91 F2
Waters Pl. ME7 .... 63 A6
Waterside. DA1 .... 8 F2
Waterside Cl. ME20 .... 74 E2
Waterside La. ME7 .... 48 F7
Waterside Mews. ME18 ... 104 D6
Watersmeet Way. SE28 .... 3 D7
Waterton Ave. DA12 ...... 30 E8
Watery La.
  Heaverham TN15 .... 85 D7
Watery La. Sidcup DA14 ... 24 B2
Watford Rd. E16 .... 1 A8
Watkins Cl. TN12 .... 139 E5
Watling Ave ME5 .... 48 D2
Watling House. **10** SE18 . 6 A8
Watling St.
  Bexley DA6 & DA7 .... 8 C3
Watling St.
  Chatham ME5 & ME7 ...... 48 D2
Watling St.
  Dartford DA1 & DA2 .... 27 C8
Watling St.
  Gillingham ME5 & ME7 .... 48 D2
Watling St. Gravesend DA11 . 30 B3
Watling St. Gravesend DA11 . 30 C2
Watling St.
  Northfleet DA11 & DA13 .. 29 C5
Watling St. Rochester ME2 . 46 D7
Watson Ave. ME5 .... 61 D5
Watson Cl. RM16 .... 11 A6
Watt's Cross Rd. TN11 .... 116 B6
Watt's La. BR7 .... 37 C8
Watts' Ave. ME1 .... 47 C4
Watts Cl. Snodland ME6 ... 75 B8
Watts Cl. Wadhurst TN5 .. 174 F4
Watts' St. ME4 .... 47 E3
Wavell Dr. DA15 .... 6 E1
Waveney House. **7** ME15 107 E8
Waveney Rd. TN10 .... 117 B5
Waverley Cl. Bromley BR2 . 36 D4
Waverley Cl. Chatham ME5 . 62 D2
Waverley Cl.
  Coxheath ME17 .... 106 C3
Waverley Cres. SE18 .... 2 D1
Waverley Dr. TN2 .... 149 F6
Waverley Gdns. E6 .... 1 E8
Waverley Rd. SE18 .... 2 D1
Wayfield Cty Prim Sch.
  ME5 .... 62 A7
Wayfield Link. SE9 .... 6 D1
Wayfield Rd. ME5 .... 62 A7
Waylands. BR8 .... 39 F5
Waylands Cl. TN14 .... 67 E4
Wayne Cl. BR6 .... 51 F7
Wayne Ct. ME2 .... 33 D2
Wayside. TN30 .... 173 B2
Wayside Ave. TN30 .... 173 B3
Wayside Dr. TN8 .... 112 D3
Wayside Flats. TN30 ...... 173 B2
Wayside Gr. BR7 & SE9 ... 22 F4
Wayville Rd. DA1 .... 27 B8
Weald Cl. Istead Rise DA13 . 29 E1
Weald Cl. Keston Mark BR2 . 50 E8
Weald Cl. Maidstone ME15 107 C6
Weald Cl.
  Sevenoaks Weald TN14 ... 99 C2
Weald Cl. TN11 .... 116 D6
Weald Cty Prim Sch. TN14 . 99 B2
Weald of Kent Gram
  Sch for Girls The. TN9 ... 133 C7
Weald Rd. TN13 .... 99 B7
Weald The. BR7 .... 22 F2
Weald View.
  Castle Hill TN12 .... 136 E1
Weald View.
  Frittenden TN17 .... 156 E6
Weald View.
  Turner's Green TN5 ...... 174 F6
Weald View Rd. TN9 .... 133 B7
Wealden Ave. TN30 .... 173 B1
Wealden Cl. TN11 .... 116 C5
Wealden Cl. **5** ME4 ...... 48 B3
Wealden Pl. TN13 .... 84 D6
Wealden Way. ME20 .... 90 E7
Wealdon View. TN17 ...... 167 E8
Weardale Ave. DA2 .... 27 C7
Weare Rd. TN4 .... 149 C8
Weatherly Cl. ME1 .... 47 C4
Weathersfield Ct. SE9 .... 5 F1
Weaver Cl. E16 .... 2 B6
Weaver's Orch. DA13 ...... 29 A2
Weavering St. ME2 .... 33 B2

Weavering Cotts. ME14 ... 92 E3
Weavering St. ME14 .... 92 F4
Weavers Cl.
  Gravesend DA11 .... 30 A7
Weavers Cl.
  Staplehurst TN12 .... 139 F4
Weavers Cotts. TN17 ..... 167 E8
Weavers La. TN14 .... 84 C6
Weavers The.
  Biddenden TN27 .... 158 A1
Weavers The.
  Maidstone ME16 .... 91 B5
Webb Cl. ME3 .... 34 D6
Webb Ct. **6** SE28 .... 3 B6
Webb's Meadow. TN15 .... 84 C2
Webber Cl. DA8 .... 9 B7
Webster Rd. ME8 .... 49 F1
Wedgewood Cl. ME16 ..... 91 B5
Wedgewood Cl. DA5 ...... 24 F8
Wedgewood Dr. ME5 ...... 62 A7
Weeds Wood Rd. ME5 .... 61 F4
Week St. ME14 .... 92 A4
Weeks La. TN27 .... 158 A5
Weigall Rd. SE12 & SE3 .... 5 A3
Weinhouse Cl. TN8 .... 112 D3
Weir Rd. DA5 .... 25 B8
Weird Wood. DA3 .... 43 C6
Welbeck Ave. Bromley BR1 22 B4
Welbeck Ave.
  Royal Tunbridge Wells TN4 149 C8
Welbeck Ave. Sidcup DA15 . 24 A7
Welcombe St. ME8 .... 63 D8
Weld Cl. TN12 .... 139 F4
Well Cl. TN11 .... 115 F1
Well Field. DA3 .... 42 F5
Well Hall Par. SE9 .... 5 F2
Well Hall Rd. Eltham SE9 ... 5 F2
Well Hall Rd.
  Eltham SE18 & SE9 .... 5 F5
Well Hill. BR6 .... 53 B5
Well Hill La. BR6 .... 53 B4
Well Penn Rd. ME3 .... 16 C3
Well Rd. Maidstone ME14 . 92 A5
Well Rd. Otford TN14 ...... 69 C3
Well St.
  Loose ME15 & ME17 ..... 106 E4
Well St. Well Street ME19 . 89 E6
Wellan Cl. DA16 .... 7 B2
Welland House. **8** ME15 107 E8
Welland Rd. DA16 .... 7 B2
Welland Rd. TN10 .... 117 B4
Wellands Cl. BR1 .... 36 F7
Wellbrook Rd. BR6 .... 51 A6
Wellcome Ave. DA1 .... 9 E3
Weller Ave. ME1 .... 47 D2
Weller Pl. BR6 .... 66 A8
Weller Rd. TN4 .... 148 C4
Wellers Cl. TN16 .... 96 C8
Wellesley Cl. **8** SE7 ...... 1 C1
Welling High Sch. DA16 .... 7 B4
Welling Sch. DA16 .... 7 B6
Welling Sta. DA16 .... 7 A5
Welling Way. DA16 .... 6 D4
Wellingfield Cl. **7**
  Welling Ave. Sidcup DA15 . 7 A1
Wellington Ave.
  Woolwich SE18 .... 2 C3
Wellington Cotts.
  Gill's Green TN18 .... 178 E4
Wellington Cotts.
  Meopham Green DA13 ..... 58 A7
Wellington Gdns. SE7 .... 1 C1
Wellington House. **6**
  ME15 .... 107 E5
Wellington Par. DA15 .... 7 A2
Wellington Pl.
  Maidstone ME14 .... 91 F6
Wellington Pl.
  Sparrow's Green TN5 .... 174 F5
Wellington Rd. Bexley DA5 . 7 D2
Wellington Rd.
  Bromley BR2 .... 36 C5
Wellington Rd. Dartford DA1 . 9 F1
Wellington Rd. Erith DA17 .. 3 F7
Wellington Rd.
  Gillingham ME7 .... 48 C4
Wellington Rd.
  Orpington BR5 .... 38 C3
Wellington Rd.
  Tilbury RM18 .... 13 A5
Wellington St.
  Gravesend DA11 .... 30 C8
Wellington St.
  Woolwich SE18 .... 2 A2
Wellington Way. ME19 ..... 88 F3
Wellingtonia Way. TN8 ... 112 C2
Wellmeade Dr. TN13 ...... 99 B8
Wells Cl. Royal Tunbridge Wells
  TN1 .... 149 A3
Wells Cl.
  Tonbridge TN10 & TN9 .. 117 D4

Wells Cotts. ME18 .... 104 C2
Wells House. BR1 .... 22 B3
Wells Rd. Bromley BR1 .... 36 F7
Wells Rd. Maidstone ME20 46 D5
Wellsmoor Gdns. BR1 ..... 37 A6
Welton Cl. TN9 .... 132 F7
Welton Rd. SE18 .... 6 E7
Wemmick Cl. ME1 .... 61 D7
Wendover Cl. ME2 .... 60 B5
Wendover Ct. BR2 .... 36 B6
Wendover Rd.
  Bromley BR1 & BR2 ...... 36 B6
Wendover Rd. Eltham SE9 .. 5 D4
Wendover Way.
  Bexley DA16 .... 7 A3
Wendover Way.
  Orpington BR6 .... 38 A3
Wensley Cl. SE9 .... 5 F1
Wents Wood. ME14 .... 92 F5
Wentworth Cl.
  Gravesend DA11 .... 30 A3
Wentworth Cl. Hayes BR2 . 50 A8
Wentworth Cl.
  Orpington BR6 .... 51 E5
Wentworth Cty Prim Sch.
  DA1 .... 26 A8
Wentworth Dr.
  Cliffe Woods ME3 .... 33 B8
Wentworth Dr. Dartford DA1 . 9 A1
Wentworth Dr.
  Gillingham ME8 .... 63 E7
Wenvoe Ave. DA7 .... 8 B5
Wernbrook St. SE18 .... 6 C8
Wesley Ave. E16 .... 1 A5
Wesley Cl. Maidstone ME15 . 90 F3
Wesley Cl.
  St Paul's Cray BR5 .... 38 C6
Wessex Dr. DA8 .... 8 E6
West App. BR5 .... 37 C4
West Borough Cty Prim Sch.
  ME16 .... 91 B3
West Brow. BR7 .... 23 B3
West Common Rd. BR2 .... 50 B7
West Crescent Rd. DA11 .. 13 C1
West Cross. TN30 .... 182 F7
West Cross Gdns. TN30 .. 182 F7
West Dr.
  Chartway Street ME17 ... 125 B7
West Dr. Chatham ME5 .... 61 D5
West End. Brasted TN16 .. 82 B2
West End. Kemsing TN15 .. 70 A2
West End. Marden TN12 .. 138 C5
West Hallowes. SE9 .... 22 E7
West Heath Cl. DA1 .... 8 F1
West Heath La. TN13 ...... 99 B7
West Heath Rd. Crayford DA1 8 F1
West Heath Rd. Erith SE2 .. 7 D8
West Heath Sch. TN13 .... 99 B6
West High Sch for Boys.
  DA1 .... 26 D8
West High Sch for Girls.
  DA1 .... 26 D8
West Hill. DA1 .... 9 D1
West Hill Cty Prim Inf Sch.
  DA1 .... 9 C1
West Hill Cty Prim Jun Sch.
  DA1 .... 9 C1
West Hill Dr. DA1 .... 9 C1
West Hill Hospl. DA1 .... 9 D1
West Hill Rise. DA1 .... 9 D1
West Holme. DA8 .... 8 C6
West Kent Ave. DA11 ...... 12 C1
West Kent Coll. TN9 ...... 133 A7
West Kent Coll of FE.
  TN4 .... 149 A7
West Kingsdown CE Jun Sch.
  TN15 .... 56 A2
West Kingsdown Cty Inf Sch.
  TN15 .... 56 A2
West Kingsdown Ind Est.
  TN15 .... 55 F2
West La. ME3 .... 21 A6
West Lodge Sch. DA14 .... 24 A5
West Malling CE Prim Sch.
  ME19 .... 89 B8
West Malling Ind Pk. ME19 73 E2
West Malling Sta. ME19 ... 89 D8
West Mill. DA11 .... 12 F1
West Mill Rd. ME20 .... 75 C4
West Park Ave. TN4 ...... 132 F1
West Park Rd. ME15 ...... 92 B2
West Pk. SE9 .... 22 E7
West Rd. Goudhurst TN17 . 167 E8
West Shaw. DA3 .... 42 D7
West St. Bexley DA7 .... 7 F4
West St. Bromley BR1 ..... 36 A7
West St. Erith DA8 .... 4 E1
West St. Gillingham ME7 .. 48 D6
West St. Gravesend DA11 . 13 B1
West St. Grays RM17 ...... 12 A8

West St.
  Harrietsham ME17 .... 110 C6
West St. Hunton ME15 .... 121 D7
West St. Rochester ME2 .... 33 B1
West St. West Malling ME19 89 B8
West St.
  Woodside Green ME17 ... 111 E8
West St. Wrotham TN15 ... 71 F3
West Terr. 23 E7
West Thurrock Cty Prim Sch.
  RM16 .... 11 A8
West Thurrock Way. RM16 . 11 B8
West View Hospl. TN30 ... 182 E6
West View Rd.
  Crockenhill BR8 .... 39 D3
West View Rd. Dartford DA1 . 9 F1
West View Rd. Swanley BR8 40 A5
West Way. BR5 .... 37 D4
West Wlk. ME16 .... 91 B3
West Wood Rd. ME9 .... 79 B8
West Woodside. DA5 ...... 24 E7
Westbere House. BR5 .... 38 C4
Westbourne Rd. DA7 .... 7 E7
Westbrook Cl. SE3 .... 5 B6
Westbrook Dr. BR5 .... 38 D1
Westbrook Rd. SE3 .... 5 B6
Westbrook Terr. TN2 ..... 149 D1
Westbrooke Cl. ME4 ...... 48 A2
Westbrooke Cres. DA16 .... 7 C4
Westbrooke Rd.
  Bexley DA16 .... 7 B4
Westbrooke Rd.
  Sidcup DA15 .... 23 D6
Westbrooke Sch. DA16 .... 7 D4
Westbury Rd. BR1 .... 36 D8
Westbury Terr. TN16 ...... 96 C8
Westcombe Hill. SE3 & SE10 5 A8
Westcombe Park Rd. SE3 .. 5 A7
Westcombe Park Sta. SE3 .. 1 A1
Westcott Ave. DA11 .... 30 A5
Westcott Cl. BR1 .... 36 F4
Westcourt Cty Prim Sch.
  DA12 .... 30 E6
Westcourt Rd. ME4 .... 48 A6
Westdale Rd. SE18 .... 6 B8
Westdean Ave. SE12 ...... 22 C7
Wested Farm Cotts. BR8 .. 39 F2
Wested La. Swanley BR8 .. 40 A3
Wested La. Swanley BR8 .. 40 A4
Westerdale Rd. **3** SE10 .. 1 A1
Westergate Rd. Erith SE2 .. 7 E8
Westergate.
  Rochester ME2 .... 32 F1
Westerham Cl. ME8 .... 49 B3
Westerham Dr. DA15 .... 7 B1
Westerham Hill. TN16 ..... 81 B5
Westerham Rd.
  Brasted TN16 .... 82 A2
Westerham Rd. Keston BR2 50 D4
Westerham Rd.
  Sevenoaks TN13 & TN14 .. 83 C4
Westerham Rd.
  Westerham TN16 .... 96 A8
Westerhill Rd. ME17 ..... 106 C1
Westerland. BR2 .... 23 C2
Western Ave. **7** TN18 ... 178 F2
Western Cross Cl. DA9 .... 11 C1
Western Gateway. E16 ..... 1 B6
Western Rd.
  Borough Green TN15 ..... 86 F7
Western Rd.
  Hawkhurst TN18 .... 178 F2
Western Rd.
  Maidstone ME16 .... 91 C2
Western Rd. Royal Tunbridge Wells
  TN1 .... 149 C5
Western Rd.
  Royal Tunbridge Wells,
  Southborough TN4 ...... 133 A1
Western Rd.
  Turner's Green TN5 ...... 174 F6
Western Way. SE28 .... 2 E4
Westfield.
  New Ash Green DA3 ...... 56 F6
Westfield. **1** Orpington BR6 51 C5
Westfield. Sevenoaks TN13 . 84 C5
Westfield Bsns Ctr. ME2 .. 47 C7
Westfield Cl. DA12 .... 30 C2
Westfield Cotts.
  Cudham TN14 .... 66 D3
Westfield Cotts.
  West Kingsdown TN15 .... 55 F4
Westfield House. TN30 ... 182 F1
Westfield Rd. DA7 .... 8 C4
Westfield Sole Rd. ME14 .. 77 D8
Westfield St. SE18 .... 1 D3
Westfield Terr. TN17 ..... 168 F1
Westgate Ct. SE12 .... 22 A7

Westgate Cty Prim Sch.
DA1 .... 26 D8
Westgate Rd. DA1 .... 9 D1
Westharold. BR8 .... 39 D6
Westhill Cl. DA11 .... 30 B7
Westholme. BR6 .... 37 F2
Westhorne Ave. SE12 & SE9 .. 5 C2
Westhurst Dr. BR7 .... 23 B3
Westland House. **1** E16 .... 2 A5
Westland Lodge. **1** BR1 ... 36 C7
Westleigh Dr. BR1 .... 36 E8
Westmarsh Cl. ME15 .... 107 F7
Westmead. ME20 .... 75 C4
Westminster Ind Est. E16 ... 1 D3
Westmoor St. SE7 .... 1 D3
Westmoreland Ave. DA16 .. 6 E3
Westmoreland Pl. **5** BR1 .. 36 A6
Westmoreland Rd. BR2 .... 36 A5
Westmorland Cl. ME15 .... 107 E7
Westmorland Gn. ME15 ... 107 E7
Westmorland Rd.
Bromley BR2 .... 36 A5
Westmorland Rd.
Maidstone ME15 .... 107 E7
Westmount Ave. ME4 ...... 47 F3
Westmount Rd. SE9 .... 6 A3
Weston Ave. RM16 .... 10 F8
Weston Rd. ME2 .... 47 A8
Westport Rd. E13 .... 1 B8
Westree Rd. ME16 .... 91 E3
Westrise. TN9 .... 133 A7
Westway. Coxheath ME17 .. 106 C3
Westway. Pembury TN2 ... 150 D7
Westways. Marlpit Hill TN8 112 C2
Westways.
Westerham TN16 .... 81 C1
Westwell Cl. BR5 .... 38 D1
Westwell Ct. TN30 .... 182 F7
Westwell House. TN30 ..... 182 F7
Westwood Cl. BR1 .... 36 D6
Westwood Inf Sch. DA16 .... 6 E3
Westwood Jun Sch. DA16 ... 6 E3
Westwood La. DA16 .... 6 F4
Westwood Rd.
East Peckham TN12 ...... 119 E6
Westwood Rd.
Maidstone ME15 .... 107 A7
Westwood Rd. Newham E16 . 1 B5
Westwood Rd.
Rusthall TN4 .... 148 C5
Westwood Rd.
Westwood DA13 .... 28 E2
Westwood Tech Coll. DA16 .. 6 E3
Westwood Way. TN13 ...... 83 F5
Wetheral Dr. ME5 .... 62 B4
Wey Cl. ME5 .... 62 C5
Weybridge Cl. ME5 .... 62 C4
Weyhill Cl. ME14 .... 92 C6
Weyman Rd. SE3 & SE7 .... 5 C6
Weymouth Cl. E6 .... 2 B7
Wharf La. ME3 .... 16 B6
Wharf Rd. Gillingham ME7 .. 48 C7
Wharf Rd. Gravesend DA12 . 13 E1
Wharf Rd. Grays RM17 ..... 11 F8
Wharf Rd. Maidstone ME15 . 91 E2
Wharfedale Rd. DA2 .... 27 C7
Wharncliffe. DA9 .... 11 B1
Wharton Rd. BR1 .... 36 B8
Whatman Cl. ME14 .... 92 C6
Wheatcroft Gr. ME8 .... 63 F7
Wheatear Way. ME5 .... 62 B7
Wheatfield. ME19 .... 74 E1
Wheatfield Cl. TN17 ...... 169 C5
Wheatfield Dr. TN17 ...... 169 C5
Wheatfield Lea. TN17 ..... 169 C5
Wheatfield Way. TN17 .... 169 C5
Wheatfields. Chatham ME5 .. 62 D2
Wheatfields.
Maidstone ME14 .... 92 D4
Wheatfields. Newham E6 .... 2 B7
Wheatley Cl. DA9 .... 11 A2
Wheatley Terrace Rd. DA8 .. 8 F8
Wheatsheaf Cl. ME15 ..... 107 B8
Wheatsheaf Hill.
Ide Hill TN14 .... 97 F4
Wheatsheaf Hill.
Maypole TN14 .... 52 F2
Wheatsheaf Way. TN10 ... 117 D6
Wheelbarrow Park Est.
TN12 .... 138 B7
Wheeler St.
Headcorn TN27 .... 141 E5
Wheeler St.
Maidstone ME14 .... 92 A5
Wheeler's La. ME17 ...... 122 E7
Wheelers The. ME8 .... 63 B6
Whenman Ave. DA5 .... 25 C5
Whernside Cl. SE28 .... 3 C6

Whetsted Rd.
Five Oak Green TN12 .... 135 C8
Whetsted Rd.
Whetsted TN12 .... 119 F1
Whetstone Rd. SE3 .... 5 D6
Whiffen's Ave. ME4 .... 47 F5
Whiffen's Ave W. ME4 .... 47 F5
Whimbrel Cl. SE28 .... 3 C6
Whimbrel Gn. ME20 .... 74 F2
Whimbrel Wlk. ME5 .... 62 C1
Whinchat Rd. SE18 & SE28 .. 2 D3
Whinfell Way. DA12 .... 30 F4
Whinyates Rd. SE9 .... 5 E4
Whippendell Cl. BR5 ...... 38 B8
Whippendell Way. BR5 .... 38 B7
Whistler Rd. TN10 .... 117 D6
Whitby Cl. DA9 .... 11 A2
Whitby Rd. SE18 .... 1 F2
Whitchurch Cl. ME16 ..... 91 E4
Whitcombe Cl. ME5 .... 62 C3
White Ave. DA11 .... 29 F5
White Bear Pas. **3**
TN1 & TN4 .... 149 A2
White Cottage Rd. TN10 .. 117 D6
White Hart Cl. TN13 .... 99 C7
White Hart Par. TN13 ..... 83 E5
White Hart Rd.
Orpington BR6 .... 38 A2
White Hart Rd.
Woolwich SE18 .... 2 E2
White Hart Wood. TN13 ... 99 C6
White Hill Rd. ME14 ...... 63 D1
White Horse Hill.
BR7 & SE9 .... 23 A4
White Horse La.
Harvel DA13 .... 58 C2
White Horse La.
Otham Hole ME15 .... 108 A6
White Horse Rd. DA13 .... 58 E1
White House La. TN14 .... 98 F5
White House Rd. TN14 .... 98 F5
White Lodge. TN1 .... 149 C4
White Lodge Cl. TN13 .... 84 B4
White Oak Cl. **10** TN9 .... 133 B8
White Oak Cty Prim Sch.
BR8 .... 39 E7
White Oak Cty Prim Sch.
BR8 .... 39 E7
White Oak Gdns. DA15 .... 23 F8
White Oak Sq. **3** BR8 .... 39 E6
White Post. Four Elms TN8 113 A6
White Post.
Hollingbourne ME17 ..... 95 B5
White Post Cnr. TN11 .... 101 F5
White Post Hill. DA4 ...... 41 A2
White Post La. DA13 ...... 44 B5
White Rd. ME4 .... 48 A2
White Rock Cl. ME16 ..... 91 E3
White Rock Pl. **5** ME16 .. 91 E3
White's La. TN18 .... 179 B2
White's Meadow. BR1 .... 37 A5
Whitebeam Ave. BR2 ..... 37 A3
Whitebeam Dr. ME17 .... 106 B3
Whitebine Gdns. TN12 ... 120 A6
Whitebread La. TN31 .... 187 D1
Whitecroft. BR8 .... 39 E7
Whitefield Cl. BR5 .... 38 C6
Whitefield Rd. TN4 ...... 149 A6
Whitefriars. TN13 .... 99 A8
Whitegate Cl. TN4 .... 149 A8
Whitegates Ave. TN15 .... 55 E4
Whitegates La. TN5 ...... 174 D8
Whitehall Dr. ME17 ..... 109 D3
Whitehall La. Erith DA8 .... 8 F5
Whitehall La. Grays RM17 .. 12 C8
Whitehall Rd.
Broad Street ME14 ...... 94 A6
Whitehall Rd. Bromley BR2 . 36 D5
Whitehaven Cl. BR2 ...... 36 A5
Whitehead Cl. DA2 .... 26 C5
Whiteheads La. ME14 ..... 93 B4
Whitehill. TN15 .... 72 B3
Whitehill Cty Inf Sch.
.... 30 C5
Whitehill Cty Jun Sch.
DA12 .... 30 C5
Whitehill La. DA12 .... 30 D5
Whitehill Par. DA12 ...... 30 C5
Whitehill Rd. Crayford DA1 . 9 A2
Whitehill Rd.
Gravesend DA12 .... 30 C6
Whitehill Rd.
Longfield,Whitehill DA13 .. 42 D8
Whitehill Rd.
Meopham DA13 .... 58 B7
Whitehorse Hill. ME4 .... 48 B3
Whitehouse Cl. ME13 ..... 34 E4
Whitehouse Cres. ME1 ... 76 A8
Whitelake Rd. TN10 ..... 117 C5
Whiteleaves Rise. ME2 ... 46 B3
Whitelimes. TN18 .... 178 D8

Whiteoak Ct. **1** BR8 ..... 39 E6
Whitepost La.
Culverstone Green DA13 .. 57 F2
Whitepost La.
Vigo Village DA13 .... 73 A8
Whites Cl. DA9 .... 11 C1
Whitewall Ctr. ME2 .... 47 D8
Whitewall Rd. ME2 .... 47 D7
Whitewall Way. ME2 ..... 47 D7
Whitewebbs Way. BR5 ..... 37 F8
Whitfield Rd. DA7 .... 7 F7
Whitings Way. E6 .... 2 A8
Whitmore St. ME16 .... 91 D2
Whittaker St. ME4 .... 48 A4
Whitworth Rd. SE18 .... 6 A7
Whybourne Crest. TN2 .. 149 D1
Whyman Ave. ME4 .... 48 A1
Wichling Cl. BR5 .... 38 D1
Wicken House. ME16 ..... 91 E4
Wickenden Rd. TN13 ..... 84 C5
Wickens Pl. ME19 .... 89 C8
Wickets The. TN14 .... 99 C2
Wickham Ave. DA11 ...... 30 A4
Wickham Cl. ME19 .... 65 B6
Wickham Common Prim Sch.
BR4 .... 50 A6
Wickham Ct. DA16 .... 6 E5
Wickham Field. TN14 .... 68 F3
Wickham Gdns. TN4 .... 148 D5
Wickham La. SE2 & SE18 .... 7 A8
Wickham Pl. ME17 ...... 111 D5
Wickham St. Bexley DA16 ... 7 A6
Wickham St.
Rochester ME1 .... 47 D3
Wickhams Way. DA3 ...... 42 F4
Wickhurst Rd. TN14 ...... 98 F3
Wicks Cl. SE12 .... 22 D4
Wicksteed Cl. DA5 .... 25 D5
Widbury Cl. TN3 .... 147 F2
Widecombe Rd. SE9 ...... 22 E5
Widgeon Cl. E16 .... 1 B7
Widgeon Path. SE28 .... 2 D3
Widgeon Rd. ME2 .... 46 D6
Widmore Lodge Rd. BR1 .. 36 D7
Widmore Rd. BR1 .... 36 C7
Wierton Hill. ME17 ...... 123 D7
Wierton La. ME17 .... 107 E1
Wierton Rd. ME17 ...... 123 E8
Wigmore Rd.
Gillingham ME8 .... 63 B4
Wigmore Rd.
Gillingham ME8 .... 63 B5
Wilberforce Ct. **2** SE28 ... 3 C5
Wilberforce Rd. ME17 ... 106 D3
Wilberforce Way. DA12 ... 30 D3
Wilde Cl. RM18 .... 13 C5
Wilde Rd. DA8 .... 8 A7
Wilderness Rd. BR7 ...... 23 B1
Wilderness Sch for Boys The.
TN15 .... 84 E6
Wilderness Ave. TN15 .... 84 E5
Wildernesse Golf Course.
TN15 .... 85 A4
Wildernesse Mount. TN13 . 84 D5
Wildfell Cl. ME14 .... 77 C8
Wildfell Rd. TN13 .... 83 D2
Wildwood Cl.
Kingswood ME17 .... 109 E2
Wildwood Cl. **1**
Lewisham SE12 .... 22 A8
Wildwood Glade. ME7 .... 63 B4
Wilford House. **3** SE18 ... 2 B1
Wilfred St. **20** DA11 .... 13 B1
Wilkinson Cl. Dartford DA1 .. 9 F3
Wilkinson Cl. **1**
Dartford DA1 .... 10 A3
Wilkinson Rd. E16 .... 1 C7
Wilks Ave. DA1 .... 26 F6
Will Adams Ct. ME7 ...... 48 C6
Will Adams Way. ME7 .... 48 F1
Will Crooks Gdns. SE9 ..... 5 D3
Will Thorne Pav The. E16 ... 1 E7
Willard Rd. SE18 .... 2 B1
Willersley Ave.
Orpington BR6 .... 51 D7
Willersley Ave. Sidcup DA15 23 F7
Willersley Cl. DA15 .... 23 F7
Willesley Gdns. TN17 .... 169 D6
Willett Cl. BR5 .... 37 E3
Willett Way. BR5 & BR6 ... 37 E3
Willetts Cotts. TN3 ...... 146 C4
Willetts La. TN3 .... 146 C4
William Baker House.
ME20 .... 90 F8
William Barefoot Dr. SE9 .. 23 A5
William House. **4** DA11 .. 30 B8
William Judge Cl. TN30 .. 183 D7
William Luck Cl. TN12 ... 119 E6
William Rd. ME2 .... 46 C2
William Smith House. **10**
DA17 .... 4 A3
William St. Gravesend DA11 30 B8

Winchester Rd.
Hawkhurst TN18 .... 178 ...
Winchester Rd.
Orpington BR6 ....
Winchester Rd.
Tonbridge TN10 ....
Winchester Way. ME8 ....
Wincliff Rd. TN9 ....
Wincrofts Dr. SE9 ....
Windermere Cl.
Dartford DA1 ....
Windermere Cl.
Orpington BR6 ....
Windermere Dr. ME8 ....
Windermere Rd. DA7 ....
Windhover Way. DA12 ....
Windmill Cl. ME2 ....
Windmill Cotts.
Lower Stoke ME3 ....
Windmill Cotts.
Wilsley Green TN17 ...... 1 ...
Windmill Ct. Boughton Monch
TN2 ....
Windmill Ct. Royal Tunbridge
TN2 ....
Windmill Dr. BR2 ....
Windmill Hill.
Hill Top TN12 ....
Windmill Hill. Platt TN15 ....
Windmill La.
Pye Corner ME17 ....
Windmill La. Durgates TN5 . ...
Windmill Hts. ME14 ....
Windmill La.
Cousley Wood TN5 ....
Windmill La.
Wrotham Heath TN15 ....
Windmill La E. ME19 ....
Windmill La W. ME19 ....
Windmill Pk. TN15 ....
Windmill Rd.
Gillingham ME7 ....
Windmill Rd.
Sevenoaks TN13 ....
Windmill Rd.
Wrotham Heath TN14 ....
Windmill St.
Gravesend DA11 ....
Windmill St. Rochester ME2 ...
Windmill St. Royal Tunbridge
TN2 ....
Windrush Prim Sch. SE28 ... ...
Windsor Ave. ME4 ....
Windsor Cl. Chislehurst BR7 ...
Windsor Cl.
Maidstone ME14 ....
Windsor Cl. BR1 ....
Windsor Dr. Dartford DA1 ... ...
Windsor Dr. Orpington BR6 . ...
Windsor Rd. Bexley DA6 ....
Windsor Rd.
Gillingham ME7 ....
Windsor Rd.
Gravesend DA12 ....
Windsor Rd.
Maidstone ME14 ....
Windy Ridge. BR1 ....
Windyridge. ME7 ....
Winfield La. TN15 ....
Wingate Rd. DA14 ....
Wingfield Prim Sch. SE3 ....
Wingfield Rd. DA11 ....
Wingham Cl.
Gillingham ME8 ....
Wingham Cl.
Maidstone ME15 .... 1 ...
Wingrove Dr.
Maidstone ME14 ....
Wingrove Dr.
Rochester ME2 ....
Winifred Rd. Dartford DA1 .. ...
Winifred Rd. Erith DA8 ....
Winifred Rd.
Maidstone ME15 ....
Winifred St. E16 ....
Winn Common Rd. SE18 ....
Winn Rd. SE12 & SE9 ....
Winnipeg Dr. **3** BR6 ....
Winser Rd. TN17 ....
Winsor Prim Sch. E6 ....
Winsor Terr. E6 ....
Winston Cl. DA9 ....
Winston Ct. **7** BR1 ....
Winston Dr. ME2 ....
Winston Rd. ME2 ....
Winstone Scott Ave. TN3 .. 1 ...
Winterborne Ave. BR6 ....
Winterfield La. ME3 ....
Wintergreen Cl. **7** E6 ....
Winters Croft. DA12 ....
Winton Ct. BR8 ....

Winchester Rd.
Hawkhurst TN18 ....

Whiteoak Ct. ... section continues

Whiteleaves Rise. ME2 ... 46 B3

William St. Gravesend DA11 30 B8

Winchester Gn. ME15 ..... 107 E7
Willington St. ME15 .... 92 F2
Willis House. ME1 .... 47 C4
Willis Rd. DA8 .... 4 D2
Willoughby Way. SE7 .... 1 B2
Willow Ave.
Hoo St Werburgh ME3 .... 34 E3
Willow Ave. Sidcup DA15 .. 7 A1
Willow Ave. Swanley BR8 .. 39 F5
Willow Cl. Bromley BR2 ... 36 F4
Willow Cl. Orpington BR5 .. 38 B2
Willow Cl. Sidcup DA5 ...... 7 F1
Willow Cres.
Five Oak Green TN12 .... 135 B7
Willow Cres.
Staplehurst TN12 .... 139 F5
Willow Gr. BR7 .... 23 B2
Willow House. **2** ME5 .... 61 F5
Willow La. TN12 .... 136 E6
Willow Lea. TN10 .... 117 C7
Willow Pk. TN14 .... 68 F2
Willow Rd. Dartford DA1 .. 26 D7
Willow Rd. Erith DA8 ...... 9 A6
Willow Rd. Larkfield ME20 . 74 F3
Willow Rd. Rochester ME2 . 46 E6
Willow Rise. ME15 .... 92 F1
Willow Terr. DA4 .... 54 E8
Willow Tree Cl. DA14 ..... 23 F3
Willow Tree Rd. TN2 ..... 148 F1
Willow Tree Wlk. BR1 ..... 36 B8
Willow Vale. BR7 .... 23 B2
Willow Way. ME15 .... 92 B3
Willow Wents. ME18 ...... 88 D1
Willow Wlk.
Culverstone Green DA13 .. 57 F3
Willow Wlk. Orpington BR6 . 51 B7
Willow Wlk. Royal Tunbridge Wells
TN2 .... 149 E8
Willow Wood Rd. DA13 ... 57 F2
Willowbank Dr. ME23 ..... 17 E4
Willowby Gdns. ME8 ...... 63 E4
Willowmead. ME20 .... 74 E2
Willows The.
Gillingham ME8 .... 49 E2
Willows The. Grays RM17 .. 12 D8
Willows The.
Newington ME9 .... 65 B6
Willowside. ME6 .... 60 A1
Willrose Cres. SE2 .... 3 B1
Willys Cotts. TN8 .... 96 C2
Wilman Rd. TN4 .... 149 B7
Wilmar Way. TN15 .... 84 F7
Wilmecote Ct. ME8 .... 63 D8
Wilmington Ave. BR6 ..... 52 C8
Wilmington Court Rd. DA2 . 26 A6
Wilmington Gram Sch for Boys.
DA2 .... 26 B5
Wilmington Hall Sch. DA2 . 26 B5
Wilmington Prim Sch. DA2 . 26 B5
Wilmington Way. ME8 .... 49 B2
Wilmot Rd. DA1 .... 9 B2
Wilmount St. SE18 .... 2 B2
Wilson Ave. ME1 .... 61 E7
Wilson Cl.
Hildenborough TN11 .... 116 E5
Wilson Cl. Maidstone ME15 107 E7
Wilson House. **2** SE7 ..... 5 C8
Wilson Rd. TN10 .... 117 E5
Wilson La. ME15 .... 106 A5
Wilsons Way. DA13 .... 57 F3
Wilton Dr. ME19 .... 90 B8
Wilton Rd. SE2 .... 3 C2
Wiltshire Cl. Chatham ME5 . 62 C8
Wiltshire Cl. Dartford DA2 . 27 D8
Wiltshire Rd. BR6 .... 38 A2
Wiltshire Way.
Maidstone ME15 .... 107 E8
Wiltshire Way.
Royal Tunbridge Wells TN1 149 D7
Wimborne. DA14 .... 24 B4
Wimborne Ave. BR5 & BR7 . 37 F6
Wimbourne Dr. ME8 ...... 63 D6
Wimpole Rd. ME15 .... 91 F1
Winch Cl. TN17 .... 169 D3
Winch's Garth. TN12 .... 139 F5
Winchcomb Gdns. SE9 ..... 5 D4
Winchelsea Ave. DA7 .... 7 F8
Winchelsea Rd. ME5 ...... 62 B5
Winchester Ave. ME5 ..... 61 F4
Winchester Cl. **11** E6 ...... 1 F7
Winchester Cres. DA12 ... 30 D5
Winchester Gr. TN13 ..... 84 B4
Winchester House.
Greenwich SE18 .... 5 F1
Winchester House. **4**
Maidstone ME15 .... 107 D7
Winchester Pl. **7** ME14 .. 92 A5
Winchester Rd. Bexley DA16 . 7 D5

l Rd. BR6 .... 51 B6
l Wood Cl. BR7 .... 23 A2
ls The. ME5 .... 62 A4
l La. TN15 .... 56 E2
acre. TN3 .... 166 A3
art Rd. SE3 .... 5 D5
ry Rd. BR5 .... 24 B1
aria Cl. BR6 .... 51 B8
aria Gdns. BR8 .... 39 D7
nes La. TN13 .... 83 D4
am Way. ME2 .... 46 F7
ens Cl. BR5 .... 38 C5
erston Way. SE9 ...... 23 A5
rham Rd. TN3 .... 161 A6
rsham CE (VA) Prim Sch.
.... 189 D2
orsham TN15 .... 62 B5
ersham House. 2 BR5 38 D1
ersham Rd. Potman's Heath
7 & TN30 .... 188 D4
ersham Rd.
tersham TN30 .... 189 C5
orsham Road Sta.
.7 .... 188 D6
m House. SE9 .... 5 C3
orn Cl. 1 DA6 .... 7 E3
ehouse Cl. TN4 .... 74 F4
rham Pl. BR2 .... 36 C5
rham Rd. BR2 .... 36 C5
s Dr. BR6 .... 51 A6
Cl. BR2 .... 36 A3
Cres. SE7 .... 1 D1
Rd. ME16 .... 91 B2
aston Cl. ME4 .... 48 B8
eley Rd. TN4 .... 149 C7
ley Cl. SE9 .... 5 F1
ney Mews. BR6 .... 51 F5
ney Cl. DA1 .... 8 E2
ercote Rd. SE2 .... 3 D4
abwell Gdns. DA11 .. 29 E6
l. Ditton ME20 .... 90 E8
d Cl.
den's Wood DA5 .... 25 E5
d Dr. Chislehurst BR7 22 E2
d Dr. Sevenoaks TN13 83 F1
d La. East End TN17 .. 171 C3
d La. Lane End DA2 .. 27 F4
d Lodge Gdns. BR1 .. 22 E1
d Lodge Grange. TN13 84 C5
d Point. 10 E16 .... 1 A8
d Ride. BR5 .... 37 E5
d St. Cuxton ME2 ..... 46 B2
d St. Gillingham ME7 48 A6
d St. 6 Grays RM17 . 12 C8
d St. Newham E16 ...... 1 B6
d St. Royal Tunbridge Wells
.... 149 B4
d St.
anley Village BR8 ... 40 D8
d View. TN15 .... 55 E3
d Way. BR6 .... 51 A8
dberry Gr. DA5 .... 25 D5
dbine Rd. DA15 .... 23 E7
dbridge Dr. ME15 ..... 91 F1
dbrook Rd. SE2 .... 7 B8
dbury Cl. TN4 .... 149 A5
dbury Rd. TN30 .... 183 A7
dbury Park Gdns. TN4 149 B5
dbury Park Rd. TN4 .. 149 B5
dbury Rd.
dbury Rd.
wkhurst TN18 .... 179 A2
dchurch Cl.
dchurch ME5 .... 62 B5
dchurch Cl. Sidcup DA15 23 D5
dchurch Cres. ME8 .. 49 C2
dchurch Ct. 1 BR5 .. 38 C4
dchurch Dr. DA11 .... 22 D1
dcroft. SE9 .... 22 F5
dcroft La. ME4 .... 48 A8
dfall Dr. DA1 .... 8 F3
dfalls Ind Est. ME18 . 120 D6
dfield Ave.
avesend DA11 .... 30 B6
dfield Ave.
dfield Way. ME3 .... 33 E4
dfields. TN13 .... 83 D4
dford House. 13 SE18 6 B8

Woodford Rd. ME16 ... 91 B2
Woodgate La. ME9 .... 65 C2
Woodgate Rd. ME19 . 73 D4
Woodgate Way. TN9 . 133 E7
Woodgers Gr. BR8 ..... 39 F7
Woodget Cl. E6 .... 1 E7
Woodhatch Cl. E6 .... 1 E8
Woodhayes. BR7 ...... 23 B2
Woodhead Dr. BR6 .... 51 E8
Woodhill. SE18 & SE7 . 1 E2
Woodhill Pk. TN2 ..... 150 C6
Woodhill Prim Sch. SE18 1 E2
Woodhurst. ME5 .... 61 D4
Woodhurst Ave. BR5 . 37 C3
Woodhurst Cl. ME2 ... 46 B2
Woodhurst Rd. SE2 ... 3 A2
Woodington Cl. SE9 .... 6 A1
Woodknoll Dr. BR7 .... 36 F8
Woodland Ave. DA3 .. 42 F5
Woodland Cl.
New Barn DA3 .... 43 C6
Woodland Cl.
New Town ME19 .... 89 A8
Woodland Cl.
Royal Tunbridge Wells TN4 149 C7
Woodland Dr. TN8 .... 112 D3
Woodland Rd. TN4 ... 149 C7
Woodland Rise. TN15 84 E4
Woodland Terr. SE7 .... 1 E2
Woodland View. TN30 189 E4
Woodland Way.
Bidborough TN4 ...... 132 D3
Woodland Way. Erith SE2 3 D2
Woodland Way.
Maidstone ME14 ...... 92 B7
Woodland Way.
Orpington BR5 .... 37 C4
Woodland Way.
Swanscombe DA9 .... 11 A3
Woodlands. Chatham ME5 62 A2
Woodlands.
Coxheath ME17 .... 106 B3
Woodlands.
Paddock Wood TN12 135 F7
Woodlands. Romford TN2 150 F7
Woodlands. Royal Tunbridge Wells
TN4 .... 133 A2
Woodlands. Swanley BR8 39 E6
Woodlands.
Wilsley Green TN17 . 169 D6
Woodlands Ave. Sidcup DA15 23 E7
Woodlands Ave.
Snodland ME6 .... 74 F8
Woodlands Cl. Bromley BR1 36 F7
Woodlands Cl.
Maidstone ME14 ...... 92 B7
Woodlands Cl. Swanley BR8 39 F7
Woodlands Cl.
Teston ME18 .... 105 B8
Woodlands Cty Jun Sch.
TN10 .... 117 E6
Woodlands Cty Prim Sch.
ME7 .... 48 F4
Woodlands High Sch. ME7 48 F4
Woodlands La. DA12 . 31 E1
Woodlands Manor Golf Course.
TN15 .... 70 D6
Woodlands Pk. DA5 .. 25 D4
Woodlands Rd. Bexley DA7 7 E4
Woodlands Rd. Bromley BR1 36 F7
Woodlands Rd. Ditton ME20 90 D8
Woodlands Rd.
Gillingham ME7 .... 48 F4
Woodlands Rd.
Orpington BR6 .... 52 A4
Woodlands Rd.
Tonbridge TN9 .... 133 A7
Woodlands Rise. BR8 39 F7
Woodlands Terr. BR8 . 39 B3
Woodlands The. BR6 . 52 B4
Woodlands View. TN14 53 A1
Woodlea. ME20 .... 74 F2
Woodleas. ME16 .... 90 F2
Woodley Rd. BR6 ...... 52 C8
Woodman Pk. 4 E16 .... 2 A5
Woodman St. E16 .... 2 A5
Woodmere. SE9 .... 22 F7
Woodmount. SE9 .... 39 D2
Woodpecker Cl. 2 TN8 112 D3
Woodpecker Glade. ME8 63 D6
Woodpecker Rd.
Larkfield ME20 .... 74 F1
Woodpecker Rd.
Woolwich SE28 .... 3 C6
Woodside. SE18 .... 1 F2
Woods Green Cotts. TN5 174 F7
Woodsgate Way. TN2 150 B6
Woodside. Gillingham ME8 63 E4
Woodside. Orpington BR6 52 B5
Woodside.
Vigo Village DA13 .... 72 F8

Woodside Ave. BR7 ... 23 C3
Woodside Cl.
Crayford DA1 & DA7 ... 8 D3
Woodside Cl.
Pembury TN2 .... 150 E6
Woodside Cres. DA15 23 E5
Woodside Dr. DA2 .... 25 E4
Woodside Gn. ME3 ... 33 B7
Woodside La. DA5 .... 7 E8
Woodside Rd. Bromley BR1 36 E4
Woodside Rd. Crayford DA7 8 D3
Woodside Rd.
Maidstone ME15 ...... 107 C7
Woodside Rd.
Pembury TN2 .... 150 E6
Woodside Rd.
Rusthall TN4 .... 148 D4
Woodside Rd.
Sevenoaks TN13 ...... 84 B4
Woodside Rd. Sidcup DA15 23 E5
Woodside Rd.
Sundridge TN14 ...... 82 E3
Woodside Rd.
Tonbridge TN9 .... 133 B7
Woodside Sch. DA7 .... 8 D3
Woodstock Cl. DA5 ... 24 F7
Woodstock Ct. SE12 .... 5 A1
Woodstock Rd. ME2 .. 47 A7
Woodvale Ct. BR1 ...... 36 B7
Woodview Cl. BR6 ..... 51 C8
Woodview Cres. TN11 116 F5
Woodview Cty Prim Sch.
DA3 .... 43 A6
Woodview Rd. BR8 ... 39 D7
Woodview Rise. ME2 . 32 F1
Woodville. SE3 .... 5 B6
Woodville Cl. SE12 ...... 5 A2
Woodville Pl. DA11 ... 30 B8
Woodville Rd. ME15 .. 92 A2
Woodville St. 16 SE7 .... 1 E2
Woodward Terr. DA9 . 10 E1
Woodyates Rd.
Lewisham SE12 .... 5 A1
Woodyates Rd.
Lewisham SE12 .... 22 B8
Woolacombe Rd. SE3 .. 5 C5
Woolaston Cl. ME15 .. 91 F1
Wooldeys Rd. ME8 .... 49 F2
Woolf Cl. SE28 .... 3 B5
Woolf Wlk. RM18 ...... 13 C5
Woollett Cl. DA1 .... 9 A3
Woolley St. ME14 ...... 92 A5
Woolley Cl. TN4 .... 132 F1
Woolley Rd.
Maidstone ME15 ...... 107 F7
Woolley Rd. Royal Tunbridge Wells
TN4 .... 132 F1
Woolpack Cnr. TN27 . 172 A7
Woolwich Arsenal Sta. SE18 2 B2
Woolwich Church St.
SE18 & SE7 .... 1 E3
Woolwich Cl. ME5 ..... 62 A7
Woolwich Coll. SE18 .... 2 C2
Woolwich Coll (Charlton).
SE7 .... 1 D2
Woolwich Comm.
Woolwich SE18 .... 2 A7
Woolwich Comm.
Woolwich SE18 .... 6 A8
Woolwich Dockyard Ind Est.
SE18 .... 1 E3
Woolwich Dockyard Sta.
SE18 .... 1 F2
Woolwich High St. SE18 2 A3
Woolwich Manor Way.
Newham,Beckton E6 .. 2 A7
Woolwich Manor Way.
Newham,North Woolwich E16 2 B5
Woolwich Manorway. E16 2 B4
Woolwich Poly Sch.
Woolwich SE18 .... 2 B1
Woolwich Poly Sch .
Woolwich SE18 .... 2 B3
Woolwich Rd. Bexley DA7 8 A4
Woolwich Rd. Erith SE2 3 E1
Woolwich Rd.
Greenwich SE10 & SE7 1 C2
Wootton Gn. ME8 ..... 49 D3
Wootton House. SE9 ... 6 D1
Wopsle Cl. ME1 .... 61 D7
Worcester Ave.
ME18 & ME19 .... 89 A2
Worcester Cl.
Istead Rise DA13 ..... 29 F1
Worcester Cl. Rochester ME2 46 E8
Worcester Cl.
Swanscombe DA9 .... 11 B3
Worcester Rd. ME15 . 107 D7
Wordsworth Cl.
Chatham ME5 .... 62 C7

Wordsworth Cl.
Tilbury RM18 .... 13 C5
Wordsworth House. 15
SE18 .... 6 A8
Wordsworth Rd. Bexley DA16 6 E6
Wordsworth Rd.
Maidstone ME14 ...... 92 B7
Wordsworth Way.
Dartford DA1 .... 10 A3
Wordsworth Way.
Lunsford ME20 .... 75 A4
Workhouse La. ME15 106 C4
Workhouse Rd.
Charlway Street ME17 125 A8
Workhouse Rd.
Ryarsh ME19 .... 73 F4
Worlds End La. BR6 .. 52 B3
Wormdale Hill. ME9 .. 65 B3
Wormdale Rd. ME9 ... 65 B4
Worsenden. TN27 .... 157 E1
Worships Hill. TN13 .. 83 E4
Worth Cl. BR6 .... 51 E6
Wotton Cl. ME15 ...... 107 E5
Wotton Gn. BR5 .... 38 C5
Wouldham CE Prim Sch.
ME1 .... 60 C5
Wouldham Rd. Grays RM16 11 E8
Wouldham Rd.
Rochester ME1 .... 46 E1
Wouldham Terr. 3 BR5 38 B6
Wrangleden Cl. ME15 107 E5
Wrangleden Rd. ME15 107 E5
Wrangling La. DA13 .. 58 F3
Wratham Road Cty Prim Sch.
DA11 .... 30 B8
Wrekin Rd. SE18 .... 6 C7
Wren Cl. Larkfield ME20 74 F1
Wren Cl. St Paul's Cray BR5 38 D6
Wren Ind Est. ME15 . 107 F4
Wren Path. SE28 .... 2 D4
Wren Rd. DA14 .... 24 C5
Wren Way. ME5 .... 62 B6
Wren Wlk. RM18 .... 13 B7
Wrens Croft. DA11 .... 29 E4
Wrens Rd. ME9 .... 80 F6
Wrickelmarsh Rd.
Greenwich SE3 .... 5 A6
Wrickelmarsh Rd.
Greenwich SE3 .... 5 D6
Wright Cl. Gillingham ME8 49 C2
Wright Cl.
Swanscombe DA10 .. 11 D1
Wright's Cl. TN30 ..... 183 A8
Wrot & Hill Cl. DA4 ... 41 B8
Wrotham Hill Rd. TN15 72 A6
Wrotham Rd.
Borough Green TN15 87 A8
Wrotham Rd.
Culverstone Green DA13 57 E2
Wrotham Rd.
Gravesend DA11 & DA13 30 A4
Wrotham Rd.
Meopham Station DA13 44 A3
Wrotham Rd. TN15 ... 72 A1
Wrotham Water La. ME19 72 E5
Wrotham Water Rd. TN15 72 E4
Wrottesley Rd. SE18 .. 6 C8
Wroxham Rd. SE28 ..... 3 D6
Wulfred Way. TN15 ... 70 B1
Wyatt Cl. TN15 .... 86 E1
Wyatt House. 2 ME2 . 47 A7
Wyatt Pl. ME2 .... 47 A7
Wyatt St. ME14 .... 92 A4
Wyborne Prim Sch. SE9 23 B7
Wybourne Rise. TN2 . 163 B8
Wybournes La. ME23 17 C3
Wycliffe Cl. DA16 .... 6 F6
Wycliffe House. 5 DA11 29 F7
Wycliffe Row. DA11 .. 29 F7
Wycombe Cl. SE3 .... 5 A7
Wydeville Manor Rd. SE12 22 B4
Wye Cl. BR6 .... 37 F2
Wye Rd.
Borough Green TN15 87 A8
Wye Rd. Gravesend DA12 30 D6
Wye Rd. Tonbridge TN10 117 C5
Wyfold House. 10 SE2 .. 3 D4
Wyke Manor Rd. ME14 92 A4
Wykeham Cl. DA12 .... 30 E2
Wykeham Cotts. ME17 106 F2
Wykeham Gr. ME17 .. 109 A7
Wykeham St. ME2 ..... 47 B8
Wyles Rd. ME4 .... 47 E2
Wyles St. ME7 .... 48 C7
Wylie House. ME3 ..... 33 B6
Wylie Rd. ME9 .... 34 D6
Wyncham Ave. DA15 . 23 E7
Wyncroft Cl. BR1 ...... 36 F6
Wyndam Rd. ME4 ..... 47 E2

Wyndcliff Rd. SE3 & SE7 .... 5 B8
Wyndham Cl. TN11 ... 115 F1
Wyndham Cl. Leigh TN11 115 F1
Wyndham Cl. Orpington BR6 37 C1
Wynford Gr. BR5 ...... 38 B6
Wynford Pl. DA17 .... 8 A8
Wynford Way. SE9 ... 22 F5
Wyn's Ave. DA15 .... 7 A2
Wytchlings The. ME17 109 D2
Wythens Wlk. SE9 ...... 6 B1
Wytherling Cl. ME14 . 92 F5
Wythes Cl. BR1 .... 36 F7
Wythes Rd. E16 .... 1 E5
Wythfield Rd. SE9 .... 5 F1
Wyvern Cl. Dartford DA1 .. 26 C8
Wyvern Cl. Orpington BR6 52 B7
Wyvern House. 3 RM17 12 B8
Wyville Cl. ME4 .... 63 E5

Yalding Cl. Orpington BR5 .. 38 D5
Yalding Cl. Rochester ME2 33 B1
Yalding Hill. ME18 .... 105 A3
Yalding Prim Sch. ME18 105 A1
Yalding Sta. ME18 .... 104 D1
Yantlet Dr. ME2 .... 46 C7
Yardley Cl. TN9 .... 117 D3
Yardley Park Rd. TN9 117 D3
Yarnton Way. DA17 & DA18 3 E4
Yarrow Cres. E6 .... 1 E8
Yarrow Ct. ME14 .... 92 F5
Yarrow Rd. ME5 .... 61 F4
Yateley St. SE18 & SE7 .... 1 D3
Yaugher La. ME9 .... 64 C3
Yelsted La. Chatham ME14 77 D7
Yelsted La. Yelsted ME9 .... 64 A1
Yelsted Rd. ME9 .... 79 A7
Yeoman Ct. ME14 ..... 93 B3
Yeoman Dr. ME7 .... 48 F1
Yeoman Gdns. TN12 . 135 F6
Yeoman La. ME14 ..... 93 B4
Yeoman Way. ME15 .. 93 B3
Yeoman's Meadows. TN13 .. 84 A1
Yeovil Ct. BR6 .... 51 E8
Yester Dr. BR7 .... 22 E1
Yester Pk. BR7 .... 22 F2
Yester Rd. BR7 .... 22 F1
Yew Rd. ME3 .... 34 E3
Yew Tree Cl.
Aylesford ME20 .... 75 E1
Yew Tree Cl. Bexley DA16 .. 7 A5
Yew Tree Cl. Chatham ME5 62 D1
Yew Tree Cl. New Barn DA3 43 D7
Yew Tree Cl.
Sevenoaks TN13 ...... 83 D4
Yew Tree Cotts.
Groombridge TN3 .... 161 F8
Yew Tree Cotts.
Halstead TN14 .... 67 F7
Yew Tree Cotts.
Sandling ME14 .... 76 F1
Yew Tree Green Rd. TN12 137 A1
Yew Tree Pl. ME7 ...... 63 B3
Yew Tree Rd. TN4 ..... 149 B8
Yews The. DA12 .... 30 D7
Yewtree Ind Est. ME20 75 D2
Yolande Gdns. SE9 ...... 5 E2
Yopps Gn. TN15 .... 86 E1
York Ave. Chatham ME5 61 F3
York Ave. ME7 .... 48 C4
York Ave. Sidcup DA15 23 F6
York Cl. E6 .... 1 F7
York Hill. ME4 .... 48 C2
York Par. TN10 .... 117 C6
York Pl. RM17 .... 12 A8
York Rd. Dartford DA1 26 F8
York Rd. Gravesend DA12 30 C5
York Rd. Maidstone ME15 92 C2
York Rd. Northfleet DA11 29 D8
York Rd. Rochester ME1 47 C3
York Rd. Royal Tunbridge Wells
TN1 .... 149 A4
York Rd. Tonbridge TN10 117 D5
York Rise. BR6 .... 51 E8
York Road Cty Jun Sch.
DA1 .... 26 F8
York Terr. DA8 .... 8 C6
Yorkland Ave. DA16 .... 6 F3
Youens Rd. ME3 .... 32 B3
Young Rd. E16 .... 1 C7

Zambra Way. TN15 .... 84 F7
Zangwill Rd. SE18 & SE3 .... 5 D6
Zealand House. 4 SE18 .... 1 E2
Zelah Rd. BR5 .... 38 C2
Zetland Ave. ME7 ..... 48 E2
Zion Pl. DA11 .... 30 B8
Zion St. TN15 .... 84 F6

Town and village index

Addington 73 C3
Allhallows 19 D7
Allhallows-on-Sea 19 D1
Ash 56 E5
Aylesford 75 F2
Badgers Mount 53 B1
Barnes Street 119 A5
Basted 86 F4
Bean 28 C5
Beltring 120 A4
Benenden 180 E6
Benover 121 A6
Berner's Hill 177 A2
Betsham 28 F4
Bewlbridge 166 D1
Bexley 7 C3
Bidborough 132 D3
Biddenden 157 E2
Biddenden Green 143 B2
Birling 74 C6
Bitchet Green 85 D1
Blackham 146 A4
Bogden 123 C2
Borough Green 86 F8
Bough Beech 113 F2
Boughton Malherbe ... 127 A8
Boughton Monchelsea .. 107 B3
Boxley 77 D2
Brandfold 153 F3
Brasted 82 C3
Bredhurst 63 B1
Brenchley 152 B8
Broad Ford 153 C4
Broad Street 94 B6
Broadstone 126 D4
Bromley 36 B6
Broomfield 109 D5
Burham 60 E1
Capel 134 F5
Castle Hill 136 E1
Chainhurst 122 A4
Chalk 31 A7
Chart Sutton 108 B1
Chartway Street 109 C1
Chatham 48 A1
Chattenden 33 F4
Chelsfield 52 E5
Chestnut Street 65 E4
Chevening 82 F8
Chiddingstone 130 C7
Chiddingstone
  Causeway 114 F2
Chislehurst 23 E1
Cliffe 16 B5
Cliffe Woods 33 B7
Cobbarn 161 F3
Cobham 44 F6
Cock Street 107 D2
Cold Harbour 65 F6
Coldblow 25 D7
Collier Street 137 D8
Colt's Hill 135 B4
Cooling 16 E4
Cousley Wood 175 C7
Cowden 145 A6
Coxheath 106 C2
Cranbrook 169 C6
Cranbrook Common ... 156 A2
Crayford 8 E2
Crockenhill 39 D3
Crockham Hill 96 C2
Crouch 87 B4
Cudham 66 D4
Culverstone Green 57 E2
Cuxton 46 B2
Darenth 27 B4
Dartford 9 B2
Dean Street 106 D7
Detling 78 B1
Devil's Den 124 B3
Ditton 75 C1

Downe 66 A8
Dunk's Green 102 A6
Durgates 174 E5
Durrant Green 173 B6
East End (Nr Headcorn) 142 B4
East End (Nr Tenterden) 171 C5
East Farleigh 106 B7
East Malling 90 A7
East Peckham 119 F6
East Tilbury 14 C7
Eccles 75 F6
Edenbridge 112 D1
Egerton 127 F4
Egerton Forstal 127 D1
Eltham 5 F2
Erith 8 F8
Eyhorne Street 94 C2
Eynsford 54 D7
Fairbourne Heath 110 B1
Fairseat 72 C7
Farningham 40 F2
Farthing Street 50 F2
Fawkham Green 56 B8
Fenn Street 18 B4
Field Green 185 E8
Five Oak Green 135 B7
Five Wents 108 D2
Flimwell 177 C3
Fordcombe 147 B5
Forstal 76 B2
Fosten Green 171 D5
Four Elms 113 B5
Four Throws 185 D8
Four Wents 179 B6
Frant 163 C3
Frittenden 156 F7
Gadshill 32 C2
Gill's Green 178 F5
Gillingham 48 D3
Goathurst Common ... 98 B5
Goddard's Green 170 F2
Godden Green 85 B3
Golden Green 118 F5
Goose Green 103 B2
Goudhurst 167 F8
Grafty Green 126 F7
Grain 21 B6
Gravesend 13 B2
Grays 12 A7
Green Street Green 28 A2
Greenwich 1 A1
Groombridge 161 C7
Hadlow 102 E1
Haffenden Quarter 159 A7
Hall's Green 115 A7
Halling 60 B5
Halstead 67 F6
Harrietsham 110 D5
Hartley (Longfield) 42 F3
Hartley (Nr Cranbrook) 168 F1
Hartlip 64 E5
Hartlip Hill 64 E7
Harvel 58 C3
Hawkenbury 140 D7
Hawkhurst 179 A2
Hawley 26 F3
Hayes 36 A2
Headcorn 141 D4
Hearnden Green 125 B1
Heath Side 25 F5
Heaverham 70 E2
Henhurst 44 E8
Herne Pound 88 D2
Hever 129 D6
Hextable 25 E1
High Halden 173 D7
High Halstow 17 E4
High Street 178 D2
Higham 32 B4
Hilden Park 116 F4
Hildenborough 116 E6

Hill Park 81 B4
Hill Top 136 B1
Hodsoll Street 57 D2
Hollingbourne 94 E2
Hoo St Werburgh 34 F5
Hook Green 165 C4
Horsmonden 153 A5
Horton Kirby 41 D5
Hucking 79 E1
Hunton 121 D8
Hurst Green 184 B3
Ide Hill 97 F4
Iden Green 180 D4
Ightham 86 D6
Ightham Common 86 B3
Isle of Grain 20 D5
Istead Rise 43 E8
Ivy Hatch 86 B1
Joyden's Wood 25 F4
Kemsing 69 F2
Kent Street 88 F2
Keston 50 D6
Keston Mark 50 D8
Key's Green 151 C4
Kings Hill 89 A3
Kingsnorth 35 D5
Kingswood 109 E3
Kipping's Cross 151 B5
Kit's Coty 76 C7
Knockholt 67 B2
Knockholt Pound 67 D4
Knockmill 70 E7
Knox Bridge 155 F6
Laddingford 120 E5
Lamberhurst 166 B5
Lamberhurst Quarter .. 151 D1
Lane End 27 D3
Langley 108 C4
Langley Heath 108 F4
Langton Green 147 E3
Larkfield 75 A2
Lashenden 157 F6
Leeds 109 A7
Leigh 115 E2
Lenham 111 D5
Lewisham 22 B6
Leybourne 74 D2
Lidsing 62 F1
Linkhill 186 E4
Linton 106 F1
Little Mill 119 D5
London Beach 173 B5
Longfield 42 E7
Longfield Hill 43 D5
Loose 106 F4
Low Street 13 F8
Lower Bush 45 F3
Lower Cousley Wood .. 175 E8
Lower Higham 32 D6
Lower Stoke 19 C5
Luddesdown 44 F1
Lunsford 74 E4
Maidstone 92 C3
Marden 138 C5
Marden Thorn 138 F3
Marlpit 107 E2
Marlpit Hill 112 C4
Matfield 151 D8
Maypole (Nr Orpington) .. 52 F4
Maypole (Nr Sidcup) .. 25 E7
Meopham 58 B8
Meopham Green 58 A7
Meopham Station 44 B4
Mereworth 103 D8
Mill Street 89 E7
Moor Street 64 E7
Nettlestead 104 D6
Nettlestead Green 104 B2
New Ash Green 56 F8
New Barn 43 A7
New Hythe 75 B4

New Street 57 D5
New Town 89 A8
Newenden 187 D3
Newington 65 A6
Noah's Ark 85 A8
North Cray 24 F5
Northfleet 12 D1
Northfleet Green 29 C3
Oad Street 65 E1
Offham 88 D6
Oldbury 86 B6
Orpington 51 F8
Otford 69 A3
Otham 108 B7
Otham Hole 108 B6
Paddock Wood 135 F7
Park Wood 107 E4
Parkgate 172 B2
Pembury 150 C6
Penshurst 131 B4
Platt 87 C7
Platt's Heath 110 E1
Plaxtol 101 E8
Plaxtol Spoute 102 A8
Plumtree Green 141 A8
Potman's Heath 188 E4
Potter's Forstal 127 B2
Poundsbridge 147 D8
Powder Mills 116 E2
Pratling Street 76 C3
Pratt's Bottom 52 D1
Printstile 132 A3
Purfleet 10 A8
Putlands 135 F5
Pye Corner 126 A6
Queen St 136 D7
Rabbit's Cross 123 E3
Red Hill 89 F1
Ridley 57 B4
Rochester 47 E5
Rockrobin 174 D6
Rolvenden 181 F4
Rolvenden Layne 182 B1
Romden 143 C1
Royal Tunbridge Wells 149 D3
Rusthall 148 C4
Ryarsh 73 F4
St Leonard's Street 89 B6
St Margarets 27 D1
St Mary Hoo 18 D6
St Mary's Island 34 B2
St Michaels 173 B4
Sandhurst 186 C6
Sandhurst Cross 185 F4
Sandling 76 F1
Sandway 111 A3
Seal 85 A6
Sepham Heath 68 B6
Sevenoaks 84 D2
Sevenoaks Weald 99 C5
Sheerness 21 F3
Shipbourne 101 C5
Shoreham 68 F8
Shorne 31 E3
Shorne Ridgeway 31 E2
Sidcup 24 A3
Silver Hill 93 E2
Silver Street 80 B6
Sinkhurst Green 140 E1
Sissinghurst 170 B7
Smarden 143 B1
Smarden Bell 142 D2
Snodland 75 B7
Sole Street 44 C4
South Darenth 41 D8
South Green 80 A5
South Street 81 A8
Southborough 133 B1
Southfleet 29 A3
Sparrow's Green 174 F5
Speldhurst 148 B7

Standen ....
Stansted ....
Staplehurst ....
Stick Hill ....
Stockbury ....
Stocks Green ....
Stoke ....
Stone ....
Stone Cross ....
Stone Street ....
Stonecrouch ....
Strood ....
Styants Bottom ....
Sundridge ....
Sutton at Hone ....
Sutton Valence ....
Swanley ....
Swanley Village ....
Swanscombe ....
Swanton ....
Swift's Green ....
Tenterden ....
Teston ....
The Down ....
The Harbour ....
The Moor ....
The Quarries ....
Thong ....
Thurnham ....
Ticehurst ....
Tilbury ....
Tonbridge ....
Toy's Hill ....
Trottiscliffe ....
Tudeley ....
Turnden ....
Turner's Green ....
Twitton ....
Tylden ....
Ulcombe ....
Underling Green ....
Union Street ....
Upper Halling ....
Upper Haysden ....
Upper Upnor ....
Vigo Village ....
Wadhurst ....
Wateringbury ....
Watt's Cross ....
Well Street ....
Weller's Town ....
West Farleigh ....
West Kingsdown ....
West Malling ....
West Peckham ....
West Thurrock ....
Westerham ....
Westfield Sole ....
Westwood ....
Whetsted ....
White Post ....
Wilderness ....
Wilmington ....
Wilsley Green ....
Wilsley Pound ....
Winchet Hill ....
Withyham ....
Wittersham ....
Woodside Green ....
Woolwich ....
Wormshill ....
Wouldham ....
Wrotham ....
Wrotham Heath ....
Yalding ....
Yewtree Green ....
Yopps Green ....

Ordnance Survey

Updated annually

MOTORING ATLAS

Britain

The best-selling *OS Motoring Atlas Britain* uses unrivalled and up-to-date mapping from the Ordnance Survey digital database. The exceptionally clear mapping is at a large scale 3 miles to 1 inch (Orkney/Shetland Islands at 5 miles to 1 inch).

special feature of the atlas is its wealth of tourist and leisure information. It contains comprehensive directories, including descriptions and location details, of the properties of the National Trust in England and Wales, the National Trust for Scotland, English Heritage and

Historic Scotland. There is also a useful diary of British Tourist Authority Events listing more than 300 days out around Britain during the year.

Available from all good bookshops or direct from the publisher:
Tel: 01933 443863

The atlas includes:

◆ **112 pages of fully updated mapping**
◆ **45 city and town plans**
◆ **8 extra-detailed city approach maps**
◆ **route-planning maps**
◆ **restricted motorway junctions**
◆ **local radio information**
◆ **distances chart**
◆ **county boundaries map**
◆ **multi-language legend**

STREET ATLASES ORDER FORM

The Street Atlases are available from all good bookshops or by mail order direct from the publisher. Orders can be made in the following ways. **By phone** R our special Credit Card Hotline on **01933 443863** during office hours (9am to 5pm) leave a message on the answering machine, quoting your full credit card number plus date and your full name and address. **By post or fax** Fill out the order form below (may photocopy it) and post it to: **Philip's Direct, 27 Sanders Road, Wellingboro Northants NN8 4NL** or fax it to: **01933 443849.** Before placing an order by pos fax or on the answering machine, please telephone to check availability and prices.

COLOUR LOCAL ATLASES	PAPERBACK	Quantity @ £3.50 each	£ Total
CANNOCK, LICHFIELD, RUGELEY		☐ 0 540 07625 2 ➤	☐
DERBY AND BELPER		☐ 0 540 07608 2 ➤	☐
NORTHWICH, WINSFORD, MIDDLEWICH		☐ 0 540 07589 2 ➤	☐
PEAK DISTRICT TOWNS		☐ 0 540 07609 0 ➤	☐
STAFFORD, STONE, UTTOXETER		☐ 0 540 07626 0 ➤	☐
WARRINGTON, WIDNES, RUNCORN		☐ 0 540 07588 4 ➤	☐

COLOUR REGIONAL ATLASES				
	HARDBACK	SPIRAL	POCKET	
	Quantity @ £10.99 each	Quantity @ £8.99 each	Quantity @ £4.99 each	£ Total
MERSEYSIDE	☐ 0 540 06480 7	☐ 0 540 06481 5	☐ 0 540 06482 3	➤ ☐
	Quantity @ £12.99 each	Quantity @ £8.99 each	Quantity @ £5.99 each	£ Total
BERKSHIRE	☐ 0 540 06170 0	☐ 0 540 06172 7	☐ 0 540 06173 5	➤ ☐
	Quantity @ £12.99 each	Quantity @ £9.99 each	Quantity @ £4.99 each	£ Total
DURHAM	☐ 0 540 06365 7	☐ 0 540 06366 5	☐ 0 540 06367 3	➤ ☐
	Quantity @ £12.99 each	Quantity @ £9.99 each	Quantity @ £5.50 each	£ Total
GREATER MANCHESTER	☐ 0 540 06485 8	☐ 0 540 06486 6	☐ 0 540 06487 4	➤ ☐
TYNE AND WEAR	☐ 0 540 06370 3	☐ 0 540 06371 1	☐ 0 540 06372 X	➤ ☐
	Quantity @ £12.99 each	Quantity @ £9.99 each	Quantity @ £5.99 each	£ Total
BEDFORDSHIRE	☐ 0 540 07801 8	☐ 0 540 07802 6	☐ 0 540 07803 4	➤ ☐
BIRMINGHAM & WEST MIDLANDS	☐ 0 540 07603 1	☐ 0 540 07604 X	☐ 0 540 07605 8	➤ ☐
BUCKINGHAMSHIRE	☐ 0 540 07466 7	☐ 0 540 07467 5	☐ 0 540 07468 3	➤ ☐
CHESHIRE	☐ 0 540 07507 8	☐ 0 540 07508 6	☐ 0 540 07509 4	➤ ☐
DERBYSHIRE	☐ 0 540 07531 0	☐ 0 540 07532 9	☐ 0 540 07533 7	➤ ☐
EDINBURGH & East Central Scotland	☐ 0 540 07653 8	☐ 0 540 07654 6	☐ 0 540 07656 2	➤ ☐
NORTH ESSEX	☐ 0 540 07289 3	☐ 0 540 07290 7	☐ 0 540 07292 3	➤ ☐
SOUTH ESSEX	☐ 0 540 07294 X	☐ 0 540 07295 8	☐ 0 540 07297 4	➤ ☐
GLASGOW & West Central Scotland	☐ 0 540 07648 1	☐ 0 540 07649 X	☐ 0 540 07651 1	➤ ☐
NORTH HAMPSHIRE	☐ 0 540 07471 3	☐ 0 540 07472 1	☐ 0 540 07473 X	➤ ☐